Street by Street

BUCKINGHAMSHIRE

Enlarged areas AYLESBURY, HIGH WYCOMBE, MILTON KEYNES

Plus Amersham, Beaconsfield, Berkhamsted, Brackley, Buckingham, Henley-on-Thames, Leighton Buzzard, Maidenhead, Marlow, Slough, Uxbridge, Windsor

2nd edition June 2005
© Automobile Association Developments Limited
2005

Original edition printed May 2001

Published by AA Publishing (a trading name of Automobile Association Developments Limited, whose registered office (from 1st October 2005) will be Fanum House, Basing View, Basingstoke, Hampshire RG21 4EA.
Registered number 1878835).

Mapping produced by the Cartography Department of The Automobile Association. (A02382)

A CIP Catalogue record for this book is available from the British Library.

Printed by Oriental Press in Dubai

The contents of this atlas are believed to be correct at the time of the latest revision. However, the publishers cannot be held responsible or liable for any loss or damage occasioned to any person acting or refraining from action as a result of any use or reliance on any material in this atlas, nor for any errors, omissions or changes in such material. This does not affect your statutory rights. The publishers would welcome information to correct any errors or omissions and to keep this atlas up to date. Please write to Publishing, The Automobile Association, Fanum House (FH17), Basing View, Basingstoke, Hampshire, RG21 4EA.

Ref: ML092z

Key to map symbols	ii
Key to map pages	1
Enlarged map pages	2-7
Main map pages	8-197
Index – towns & villages	198-199
Index – streets	200-231
Index – featured places	231-236
Acknowledgements	236

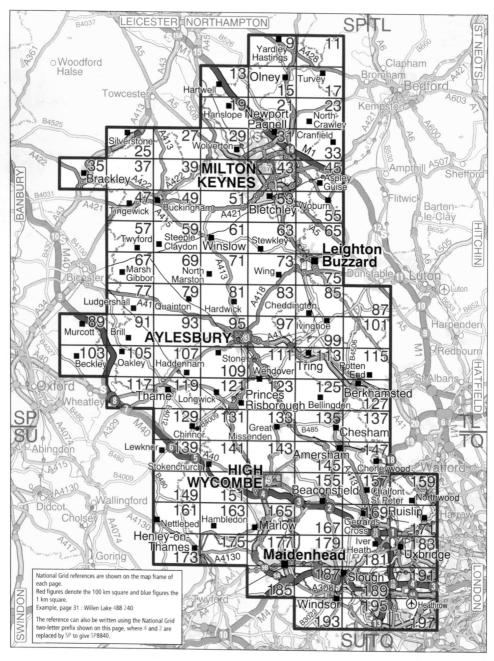

National Grid references are shown on the map frame of each page.
Red figures denote the 100 km square and blue figures the 1 km square.
Example, page 31 : Willen Lake 488 240

The reference can also be written using the National Grid two-letter prefix shown on this page, where 4 and 2 are replaced by SP to give SP8840.

Scale of enlarged map pages 1:10,000

6.3 inches to 1 mile

0   miles   1/4

0   kilometres   1/4   1/2

Scale of main map pages 1:25,000

2.5 inches to 1 mile

0   miles   1/2

0   1/2   kilometres   1

Junction 9	Motorway & junction	*(Mounds)*	Mounds	*(flag)*	Golf course
Services	Motorway service area	47	Page continuation 1:25,000	▲	Camping AA inspected
	Primary road single/ dual carriageway	3	Page continuation to enlarged scale 1:10,000	⊕	Caravan site AA inspected
Services	Primary road service area		River/canal, lake	▲⊕	Camping & caravan site AA inspected
	A road single/dual carriageway		Aqueduct, lock, weir		Theme park
	B road single/dual carriageway	465 ▲ Winter Hill	Peak (with height in metres)		Abbey, cathedral or priory
	Other road single/ dual carriageway		Beach		Castle
	Minor/private road, access may be restricted		Woodland		Historic house or building
← ←	One-way street		Park	Wakehurst Place NT	National Trust property
	Pedestrian area		Cemetery	Ⓜ	Museum or art gallery
	Track or footpath		Built-up area		Roman antiquity
	Road under construction		Featured building		Ancient site, battlefield or monument
	Road tunnel	⊓⊔⊓⊔	City wall		Industrial interest
P	Parking	A&E	Hospital with 24-hour A&E department	❋	Garden
P+🚌	Park & Ride	PO	Post Office	◉	Garden Centre Garden Centre Association Member
🚌	Bus/coach station	📖	Public library		Garden Centre Wyevale Garden Centre
	Railway & main railway station	𝒾	Tourist Information Centre		Arboretum
	Railway & minor railway station	𝒾	Seasonal Tourist Information Centre		Farm or animal centre
⊖	Underground station	🚩🚩	Petrol station, 24-hour Major suppliers only		Zoological or wildlife collection
⊖	Light railway & station	✝	Church/chapel		Bird collection
	Preserved private railway	🚻	Public toilets		Nature reserve
LC	Level crossing	♿	Toilet with disabled facilities		Aquarium
	Tramway	PH	Public house AA recommended	V	Visitor or heritage centre
	Ferry route	🍴	Restaurant AA inspected		Country park
Madeira Hotel		Hotel AA inspected		Cave
	Airport runway	🎭	Theatre or performing arts centre	✗	Windmill
	County, administrative boundary	🎦	Cinema		Distillery, brewery or vineyard

I grid square represents 250 metres

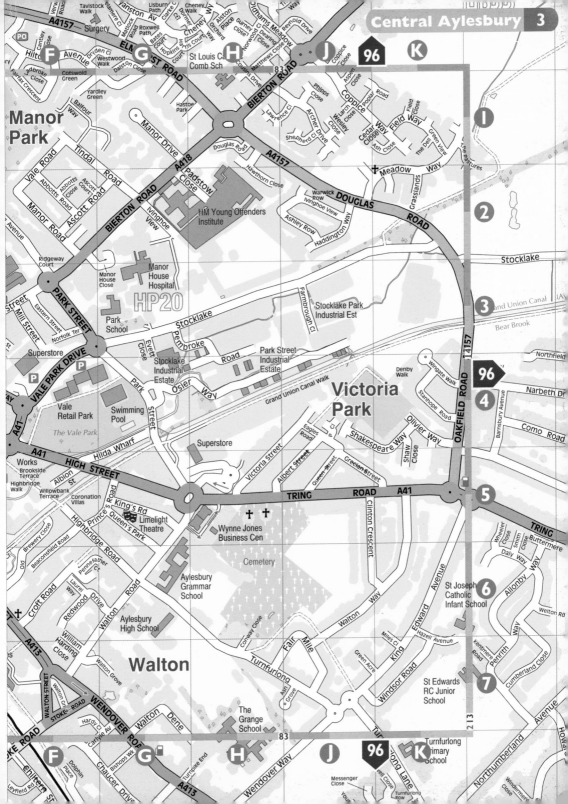

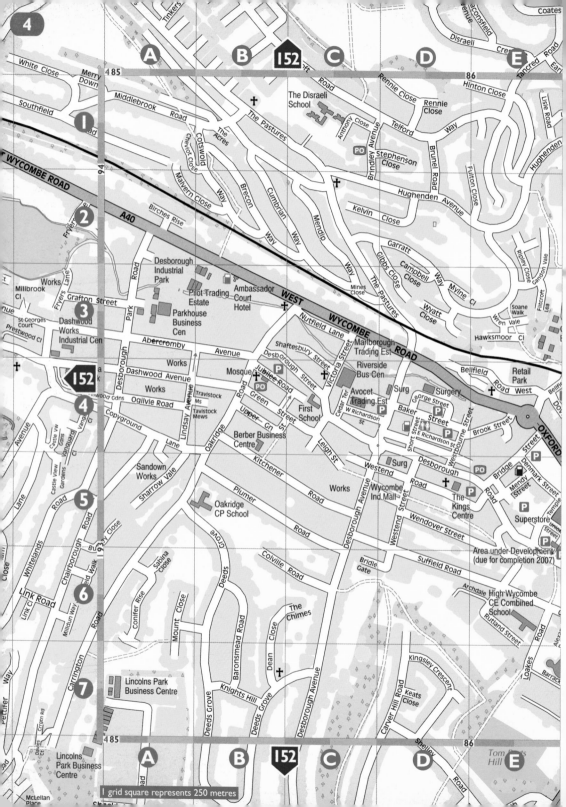

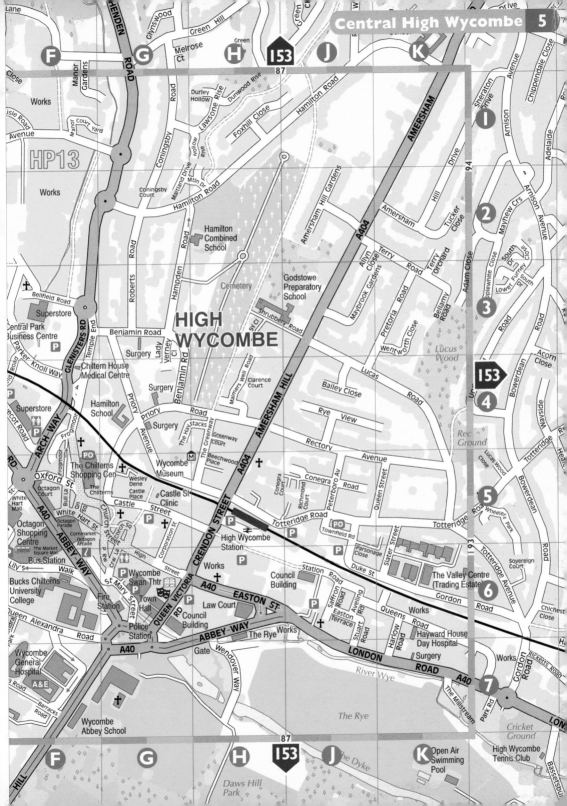

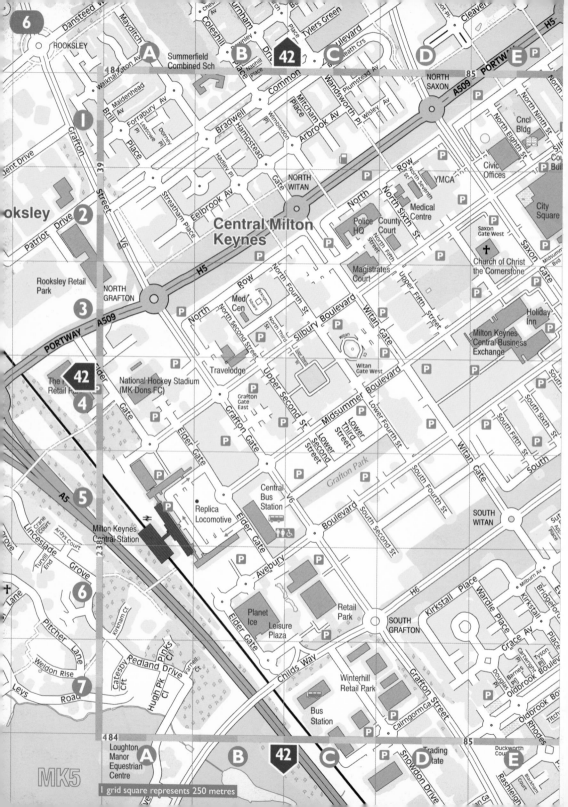

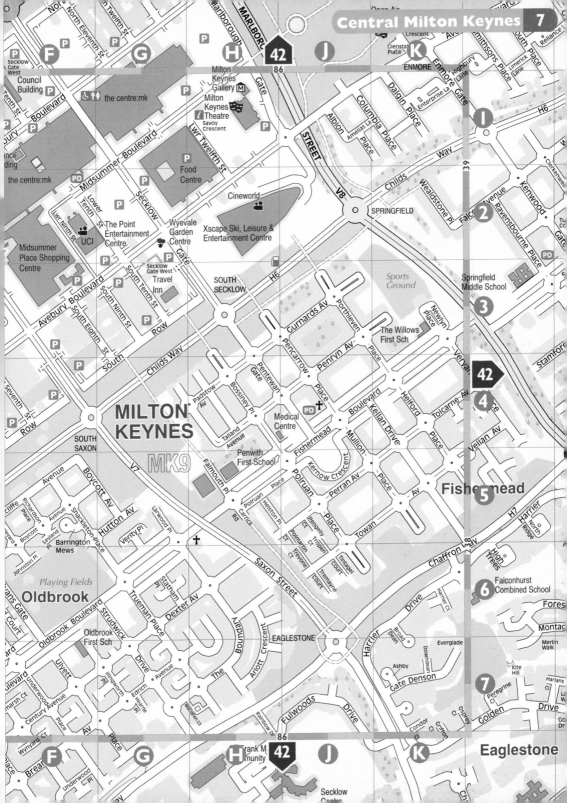

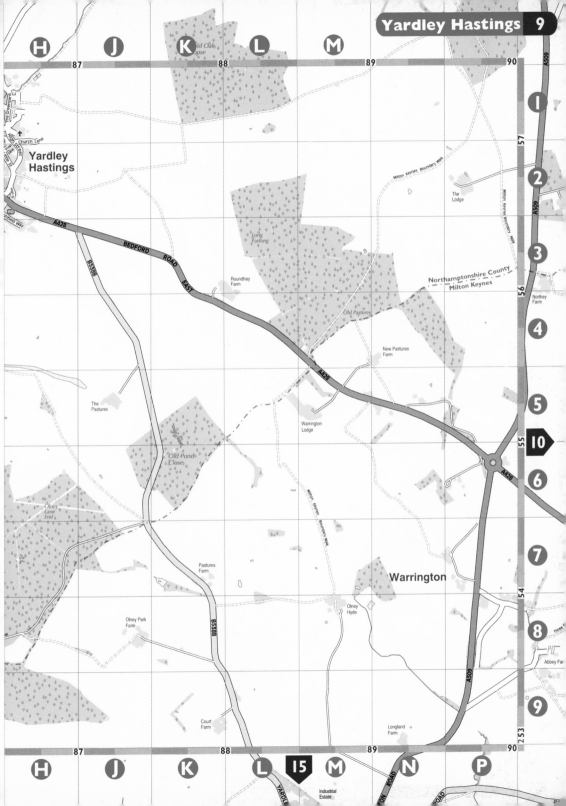

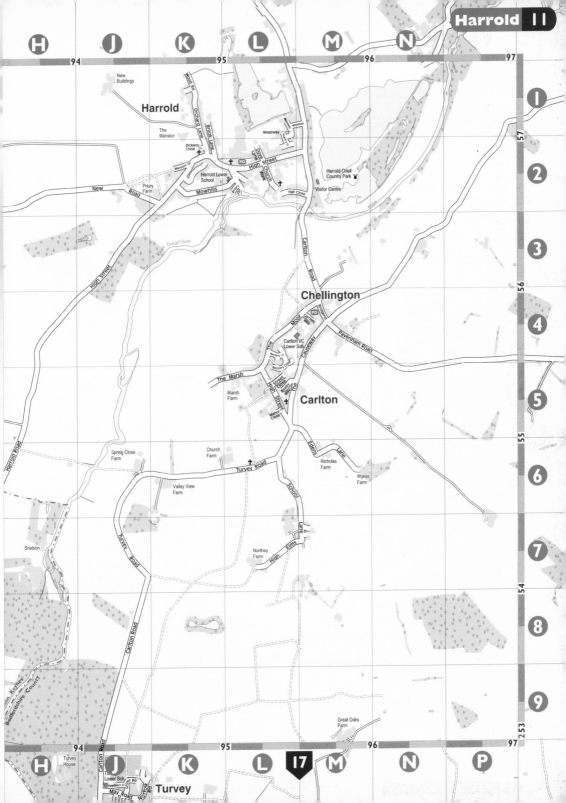

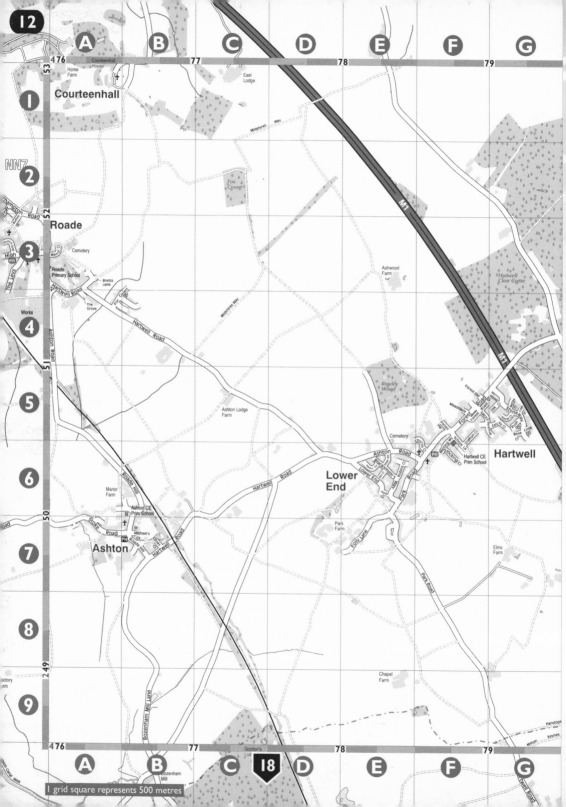

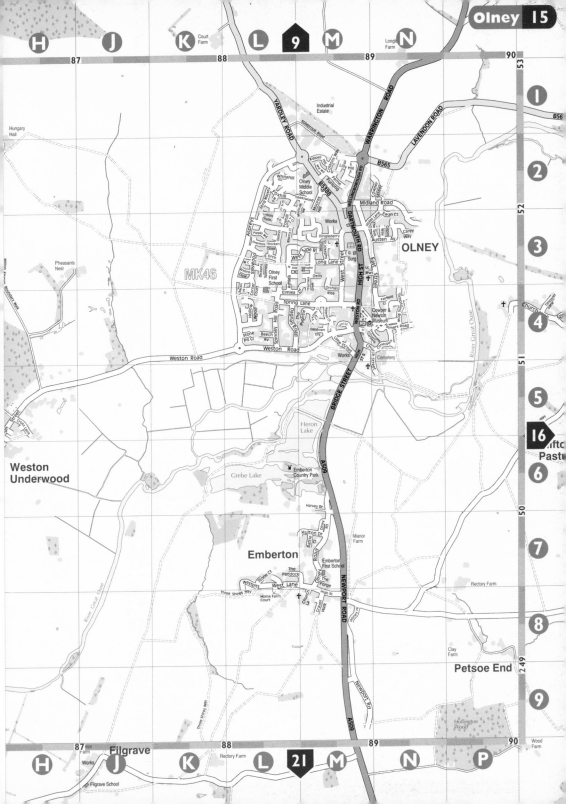

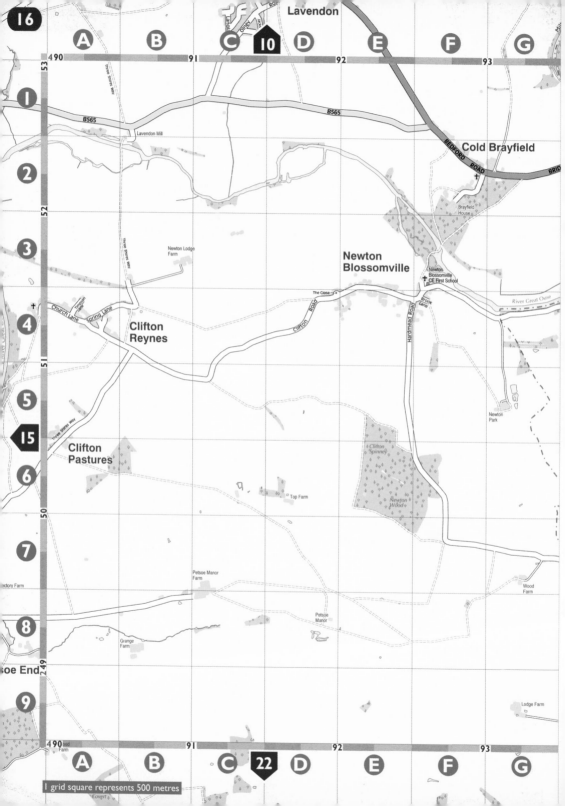

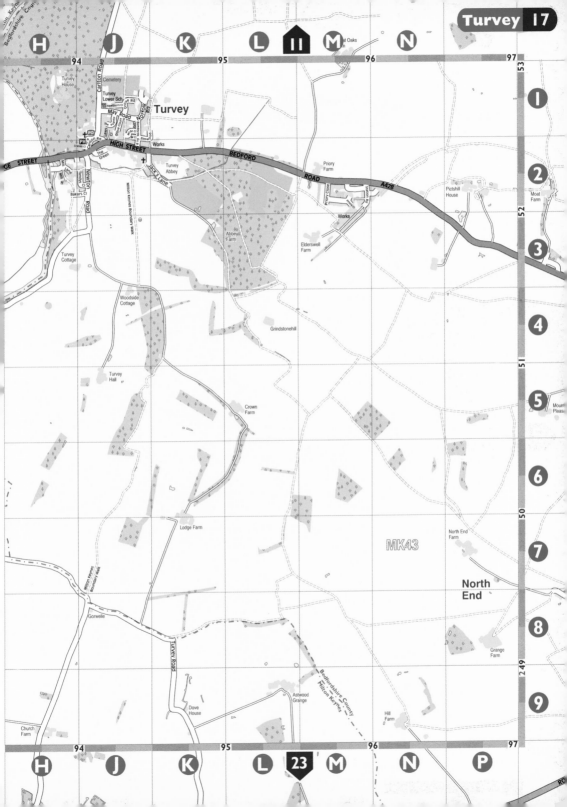

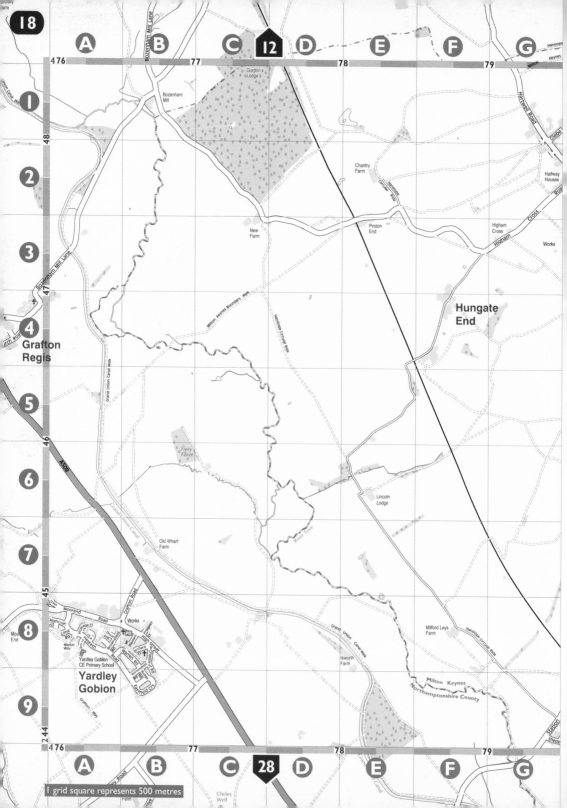

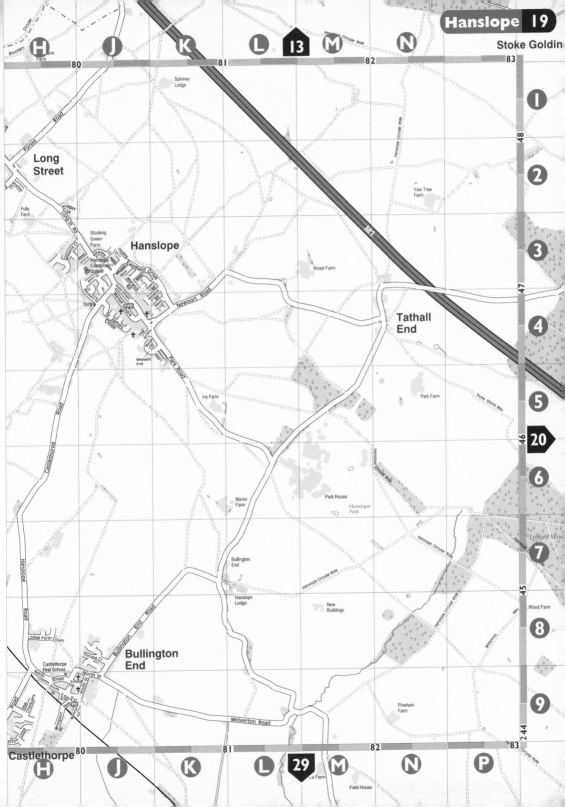

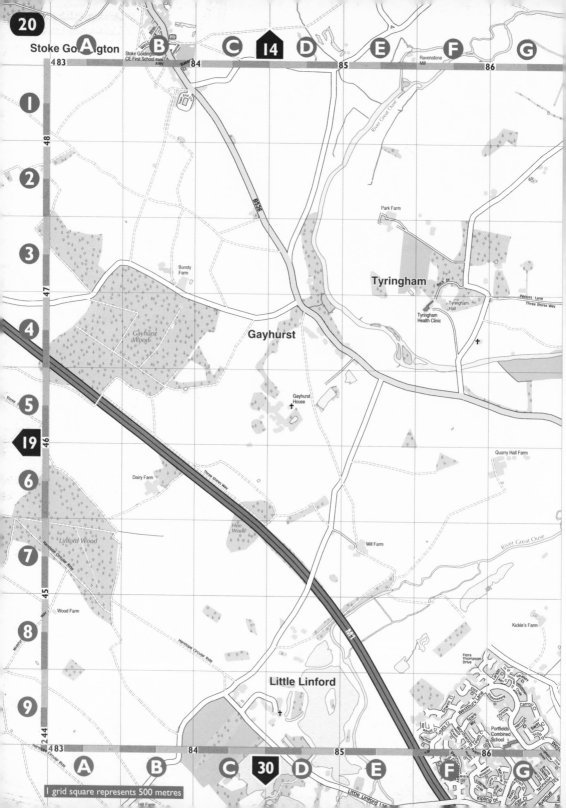

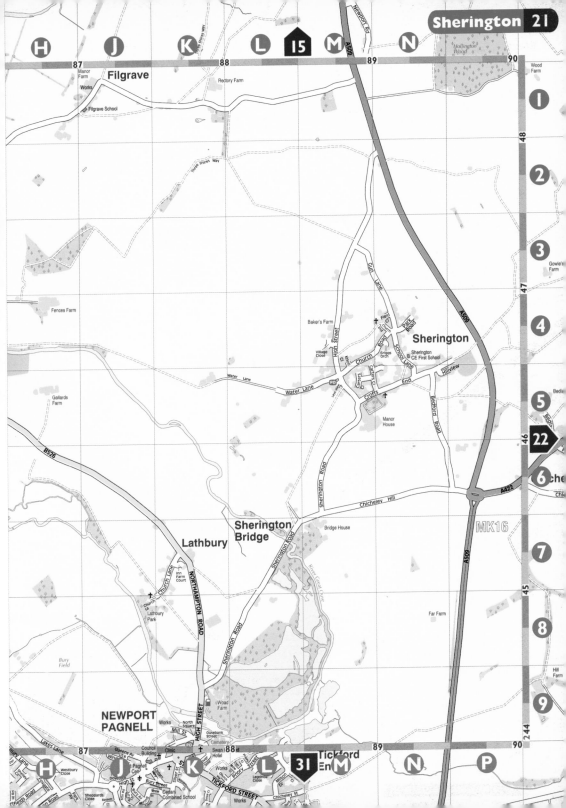

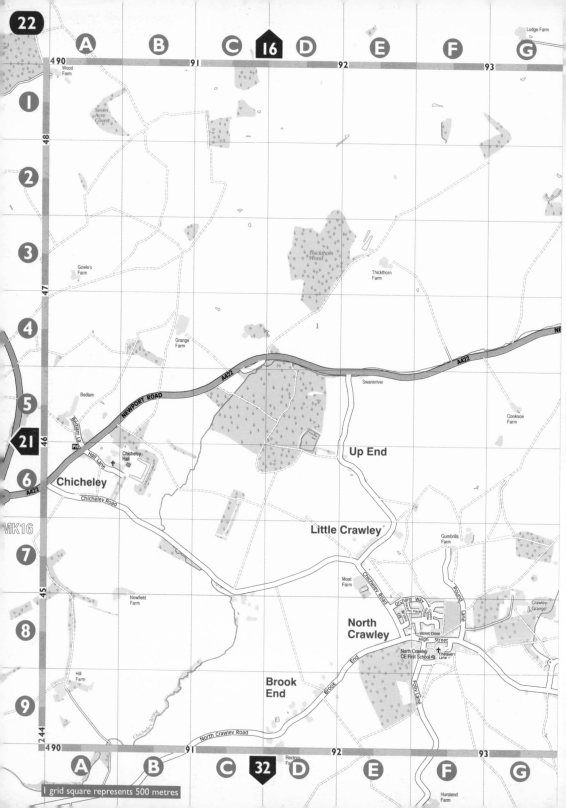

H   J   K   L   **17**   M

Church Farm

Dove House

Astwood Grange

Yardshire County Milton Keynes

Hill Farm

94   95   96   97

1

NEWPORT PAGNELL RO

48

Dovecot Farm

Turvey Road

2

Ducksworth

Hardmead

A422

Home Farm

College Farm

Main   Road

Astwood

3

West End Farm

47

Manor Farm

WPORT ROAD

Canfield Road

4

Beacon Hill Barn

Green Valley Farm

5

Chicheley Brook

Milton Keynes Boundary Walk

Jacob's Wood

Eyreswood Farm

46

6

Dollars Grove Farm

7

Boxhedge Farm

Astwood Road

Milton Keynes Boundary Walk

8

45

East End

Horse Shoe Farm

Hill Green Farm

Lodge Farm

Bourne End

Brook Farm

9

Longcro Spinney

Milton Keynes Bedfordshire County

Ringtail Farm

244

94   95   96   97

H   J   K   L   **33**   M   N   P

Murtland's Farm

Rings Wharley Farm

Perry Hill Farm

Bourne End Road

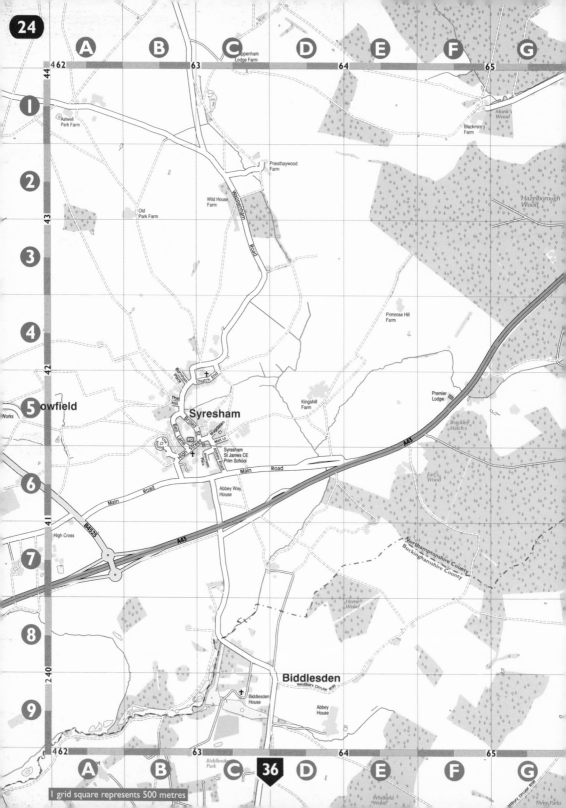

H Blackmires Lane
Church Street
Puddledock
The Willows
Little Surgery
Works
Whittlebury Road
A43

J **Silverstone**
K
L
M
N

66
67
68
69
44

Monkswood
Hazelwood
Silverstone Infant Sch
Silverstone CE Junior Sch
High Street
Towcester Road
Murswell La

West End
Graham Hill
Jim Clark
Ayrton Senna

Cattle End

Brackley Road
Dadford Rd
A43
Works

I
Whittlebury CE Prim
Whittlebury

Golf Course
Kennel Road

West Park Farm
2

43
Whittlebury Hall Hotel
3

Foxhole Copse

Wild Wood

Cheese Copse

Chapel Copse

Silverstone Motor Racing Circuit

Whittlebury Park Golf & Country Club
Golf Course

The Straights

Lodge Copse

Northamptonshire County
Buckinghamshire County
42

Becketts Corner

4

5

26

6

Pentimore Wood

Buttockspire Wood

Welley's Wood

Stowe Corner

41

Hatch-hill Farm

7

Golf Course

Silverstone Golf Club

Red Ditches Farm

Point Copse
Sawpit Wood

Home Wood
8

Westbury Circular Ride

Thatcham Ponds Farm
Dadford Road

Blackpit Farm

240

Tilehouse Wood

Parkfields
Woodlands Farm
Stowe Woods

9

66
67
37
68
69

H
J
K
L
M
N
P

A B C D E F G

455   56   57   58

1

Globe
Farm

A43 9

Steane

Manor
House

Steane
Park

A422

2

Hill
Farm

Brackley
Grange

Brackley Fields
Farm

NN13

3

Steane Gro
Farm

38

Bracken Leas
Primary Sch
Recreation
Centre
Surg

Brackley
RFC

Pavilions Way

4

Hinton Grounds
Farm

Johnson
Av

Brackley
Swimming Poo
Winchest
House P
Prep Sch

5

Manor
Farm

37

Waynflete
Infant Sch

Waynflete Avenue

Magdalen
College
School

Beaumont Crs

New
Rd

Charterhouse

Hales
La

6

Hinton-in-
the-Hedges

Norris
Acre

Duck
End

Southfield
Primary
School

Hinton Road

A422

Castle Mt
Superstore

Oxford

7

36

8

A43

Elm Tree
Farm

9

235

Plomers Firs
Farm

Church
Leys

Broad

455   56   57   58

A B C D E F G

1 grid square represents 500 metres

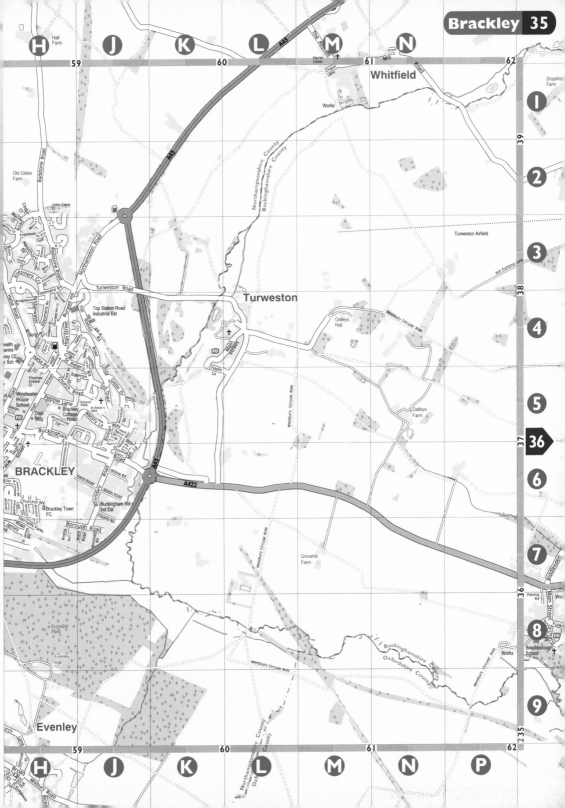

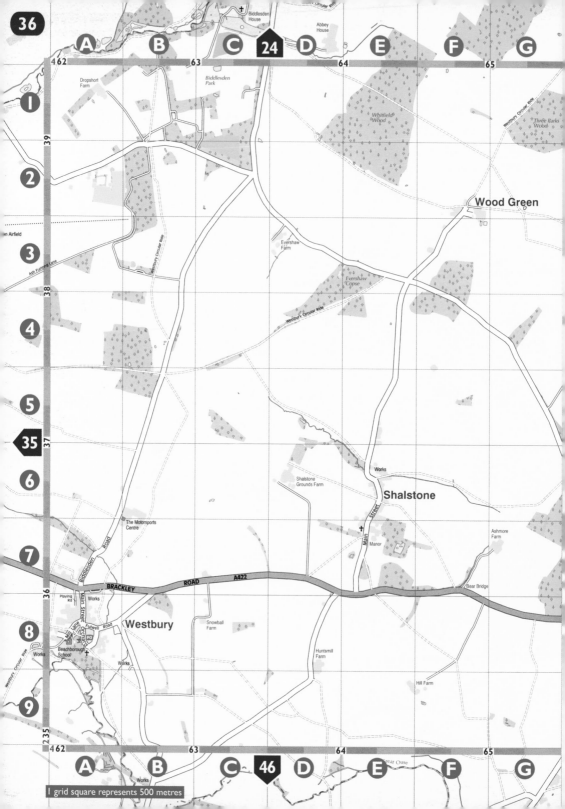

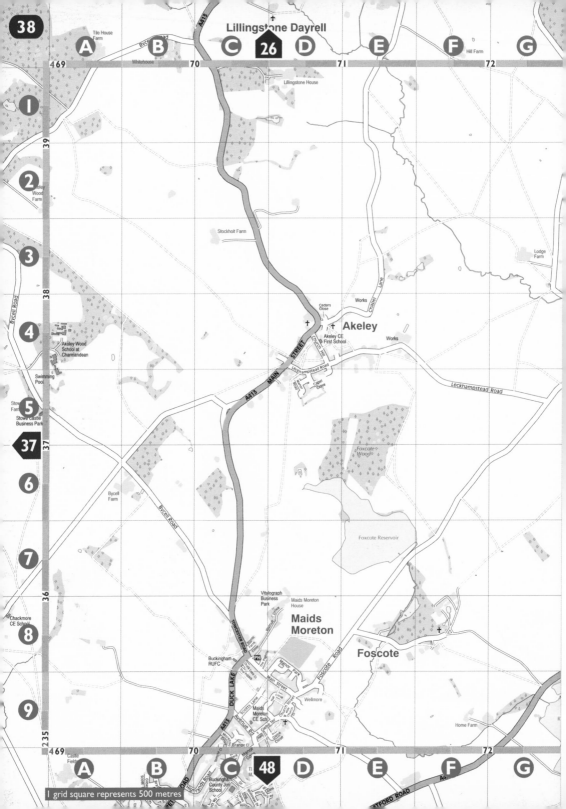

38

A **B** **C** **26** **D** **E** **F** **G**

Lillingstone Dayrell

Tile House Farm

Bycell Road

Whitehouse

469 70 71 72

1

Lillingstone House

2

keley Wood Farm

Stockholt Farm

39

3

Lodge Farm

38

Bycell Road

4

Akeley Wood School at Charmandean

Cedars Close

Works

Crabtr Lane

Akeley

Akeley CE First School

Works

Swimming Pool

5

Stow Farm

Stowe Castle Business Park

STREET

MAIN

A413

Leckhampstead Road

Capel Close

37

37

37

6

Bycell Farm

Foxcote Woods

Bycell Road

7

Foxcote Reservoir

36

8

Chackmore CE School

Vitalograph Business Park

Maids Moreton House

Maids Moreton

Foscote

DUCK LAKE

Buckingham RUFC

PH

Manor Park

Foscote Road

Home Farm

9

Maids Moreton CE Sch

Avenue Rd

Wellmore

235

469 70 71 72

A **B** **C** **48** **D** **E** **F** **G**

Buckingham County Jun School

STRATFORD ROAD

I grid square represents 500 metres

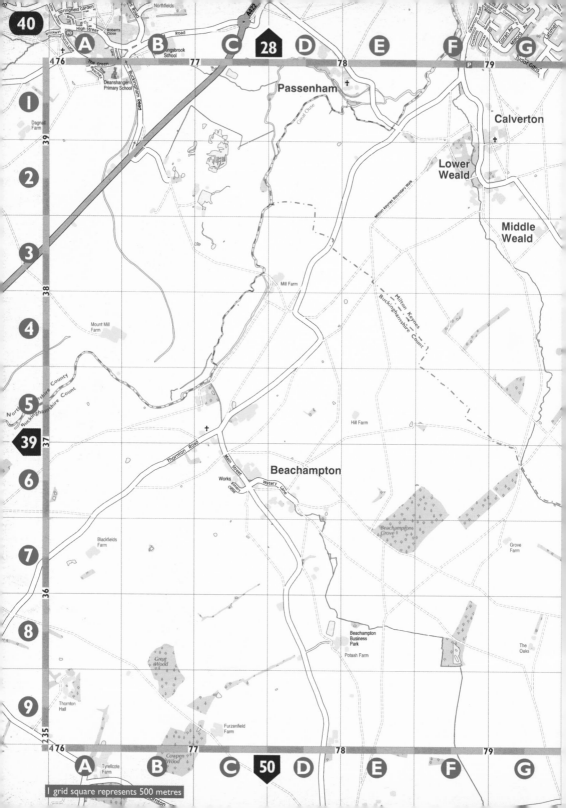

A · B · C · **36** · D · E · F · G

462 · 63 · 64 · 65

I

Water Stratf

Works
Fulwell
House

River Great Ouse

Bacon's
House

2

Stonepit
Spinney

Oxfordshire County
Buckinghamshire County

Sandpit Hill
Farm

3

Finmere
Grounds

Warren
Farm

4

Finmere

Fullwell Road

Cemetery

Sandpit

Hill

33

A421

Mere

Road

Finmere
CE Primary
School

Chinalls
Close

Mere Lane

Back Lane

5

Widmore
Farm

A421

A421

Ti
In S

6

32

7

Tingewick
Wood

8

Round Wood

Newton
Purcell

Surgery

Barley
Fields

Barton
Hartshorn

Manor
House

9

Soulsmere

Courtfield
Farm

462 · 63 · 64 · 65

A · B · C · **56** · D · E · F · G

A421

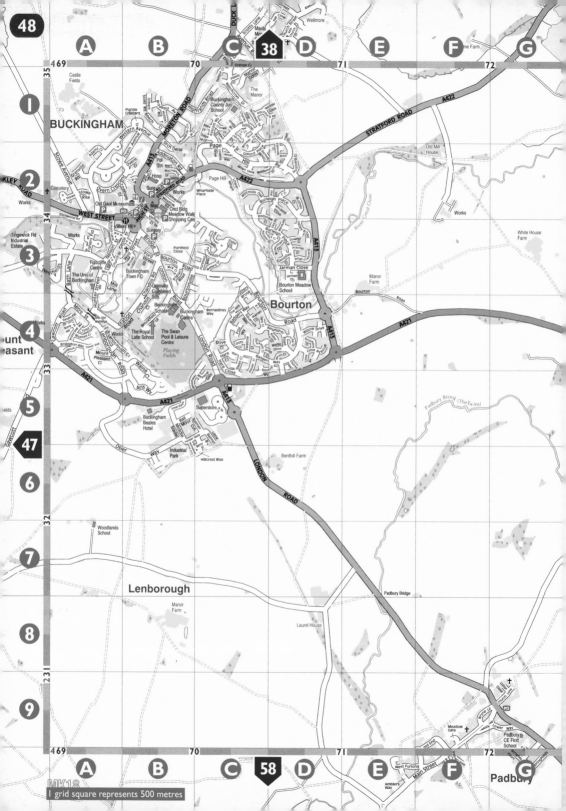

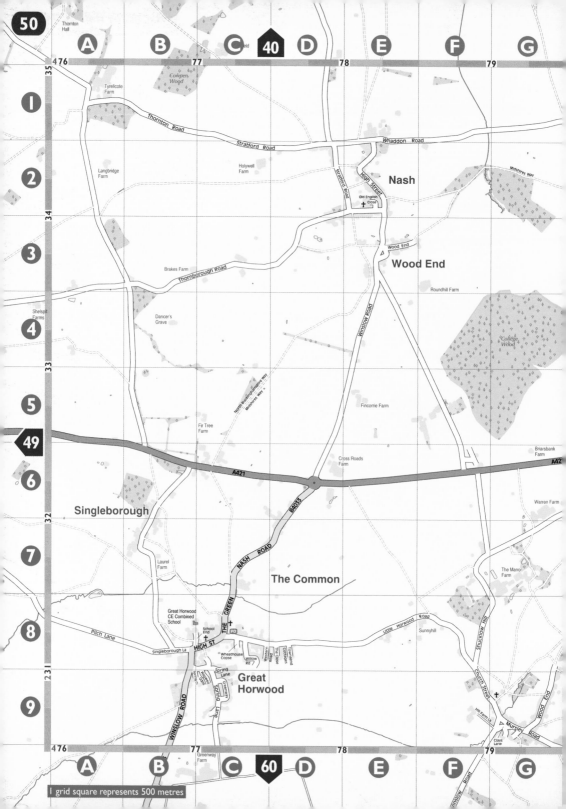

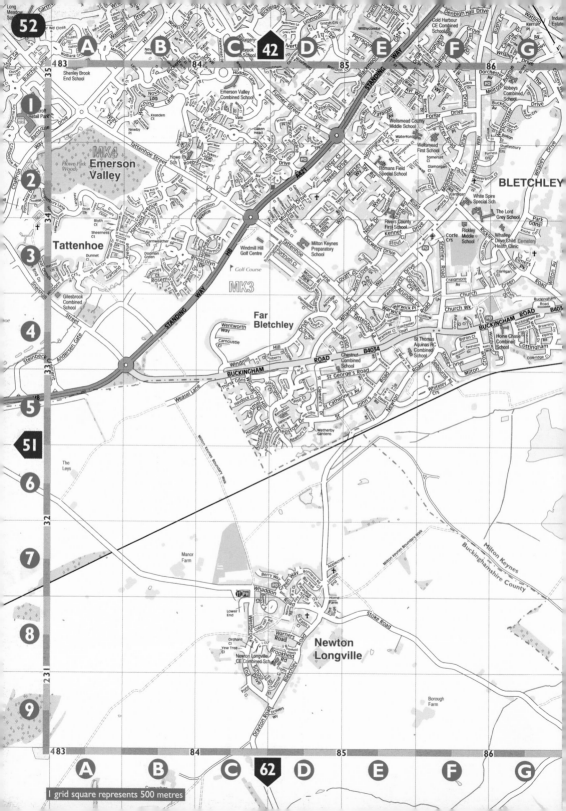

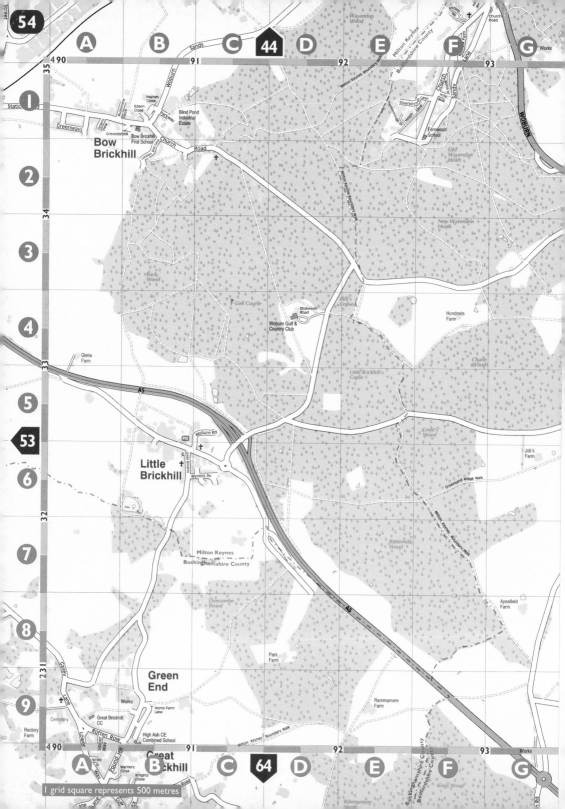

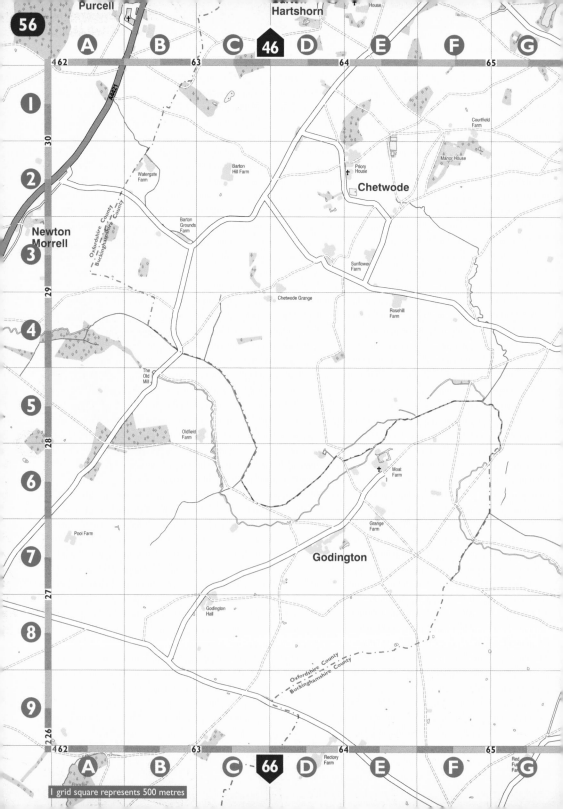

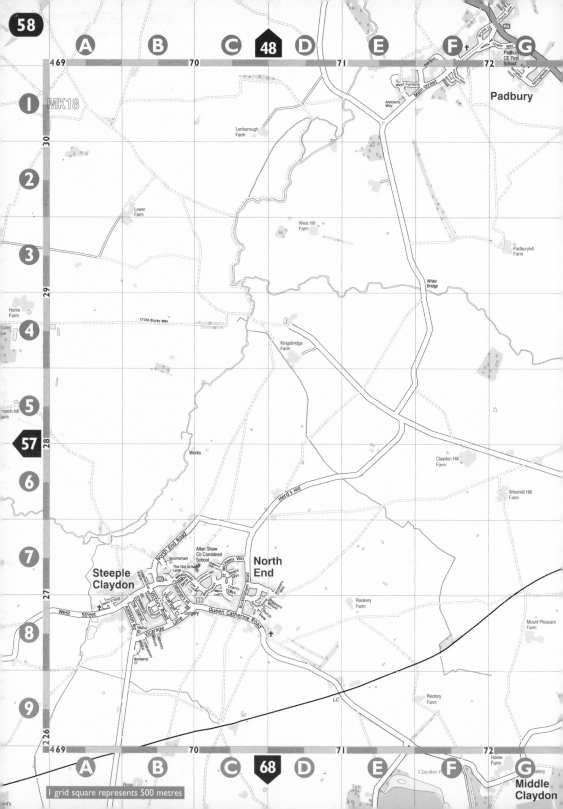

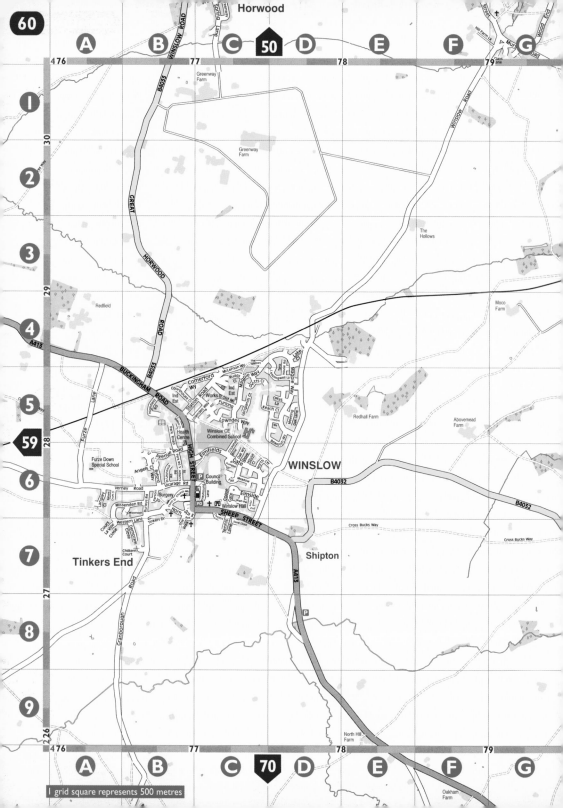

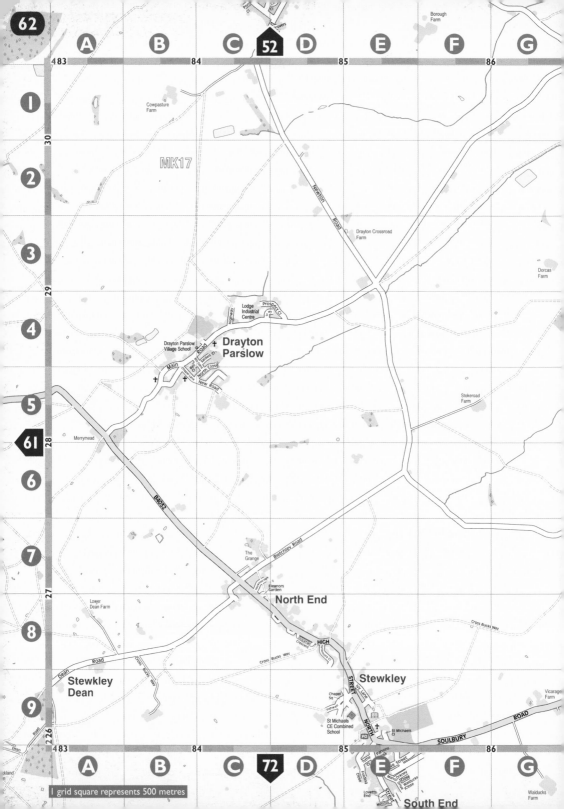

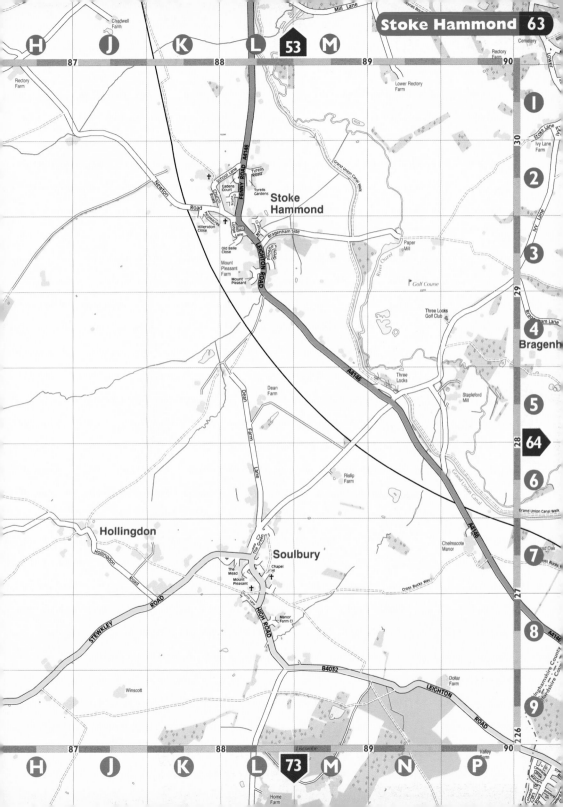

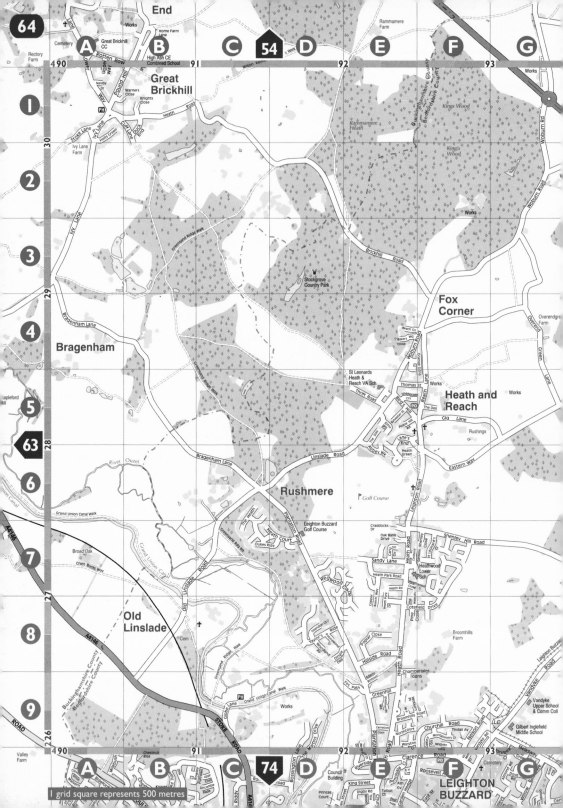

Sheeplane

H J K L **55** M

94 **95** **96** **97**

Bushycommon Wood

Milton Lodge

Milton Bry **1**

Maggs Lane

Hill Farm

Mead's Close

Le Fa

Manor Farm

2

Potsgrove

Battlesden Avenue

Hungerhill Wood

A5

Battlesden Avenue

3

Home Wood

Hockliffe Rd

29

Battlesden Park

Battlesden **4**

Works

Eastern Way

Hill Farm

5

Kingsway Farm

Fourne Hill Farm

28 **66**

Miletree Road

Miletree Farm

6

Stonehenge Works Station

Lane End Farm

Hockliffe Grange

Church Lane

A5

7

LC

Church End

Hockliffe Lower School

Cemetery

Gospel Green

27

Grange Farm

Manor Farm

8

Clipstone

Field Farm

A4012

9

Leighton Road

226

Clipstone Brook

94 **95** **96** **97**

H J K L **75** M N P

Appenine Saturn Cl

Beaudesert Lower School

Leighton Road A4012

Leighton Road

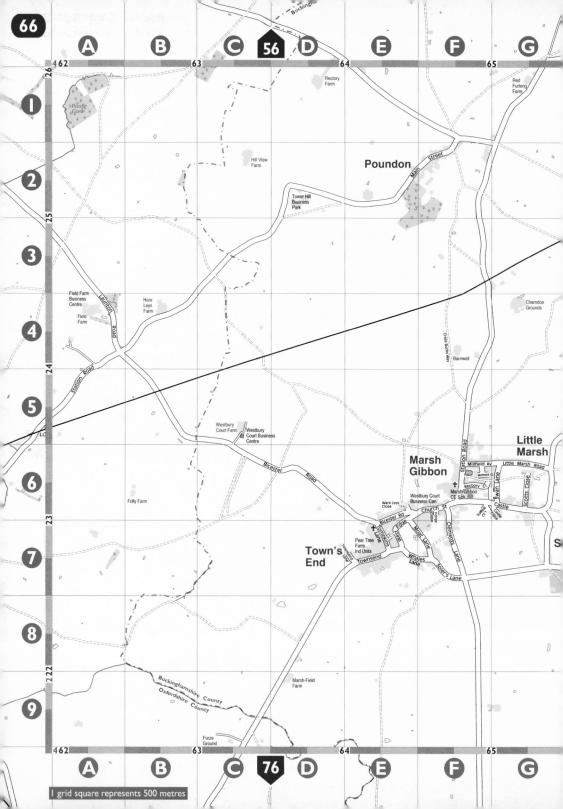

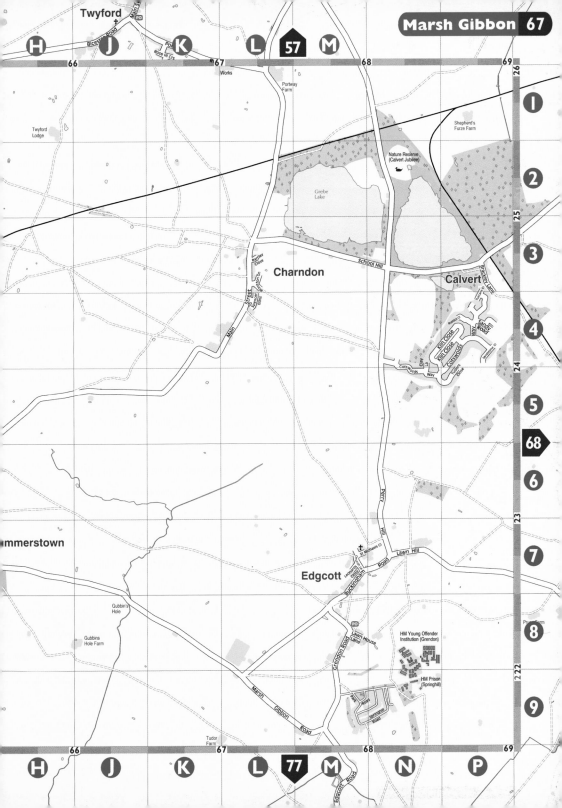

Twyford

H J K L 57 M

66 67 68 69

26

1

Twyford
Lodge

Shepherd's
Furze Farm

2

Nature Reserve
(Calvert Jubilee)

25

Grebe
Lake

3

School Hill

Charndon

Calvert

Barclay Close

Street

Spencer
Gdns

Main

Kiln Close
Kiln Close
Kiln Close

Grange
Road

Way

Cotswold

4

24

Cotswolds
Way

Tudor
Close

CMW

5

68

6

Perry

Hill

23

mmerstown

7

St Michaels Cl

Lawn Hill

Edgcott

Buckingham

Road

PO

222

HM Young Offender
Institution (Grendon)

Prune Farm

8

Gubbin's
Hole

Lawn House

Lawn
Lane

Grendon Road

HM Prison
(Springhill)

Gubbins
Hole Farm

Park

Road

Springhill
Road

9

Marsh

Gibbon

Road

Tudor
Farm

66 67 68 69

H J K L 77 M N P

Edgcott
Road

A B C **58** D E F G

469 70 71 72

1

2

3

4

5

67

6

7

8

9

469 70 71 72

A B C **78** D E F G

Rose
Hill Farm

Middle
Claydon

Claydon Park

Rectory
Farm

Home
Farm

Cemetery

Claydon
House (NT)

Catherine
Farm

Blackmoorhill
Farm

Great
Pond Farm

Shrubs
Wood

Decoypond
Wood

Home
Wood

Muxwell
Farm

Three Points Lane

Knowlhill
Farm

Sheephouse
Wood

Romer
Wood

Balmore
Wood

Prune Farm

Greatmoor

Finemerehill
House

Finemere
Wood

Woodlands
Farm

Brackley Lane

Lawn Hill

erd's
Farm

ert

1 grid square represents 500 metres

East Claydon

Botolph Claydon

Sion Hill Farm

Church Way

East Claydon School

Orchard Way

Bernwood Farm

Lower Farm

Claydon Lawn

Middle Farm

Runt's Woods

Hogshaw Farm

Fulbrook Farm

Stonehill Farm

Hogshaw Hill Farm

Dry Leys Farm

Ship Lee

Lee House

Hill Farm

186 Quainton Hill

Denham Farm

St Mary's Road

Sandhill Road

McInnes Way

Hogshaw Road

Weir Lane

H J K L 59 M

H J K L 79 M N P

1 2 3 4 5 70 6 7 8 9

73 74 75 76

26 25 24 23 22

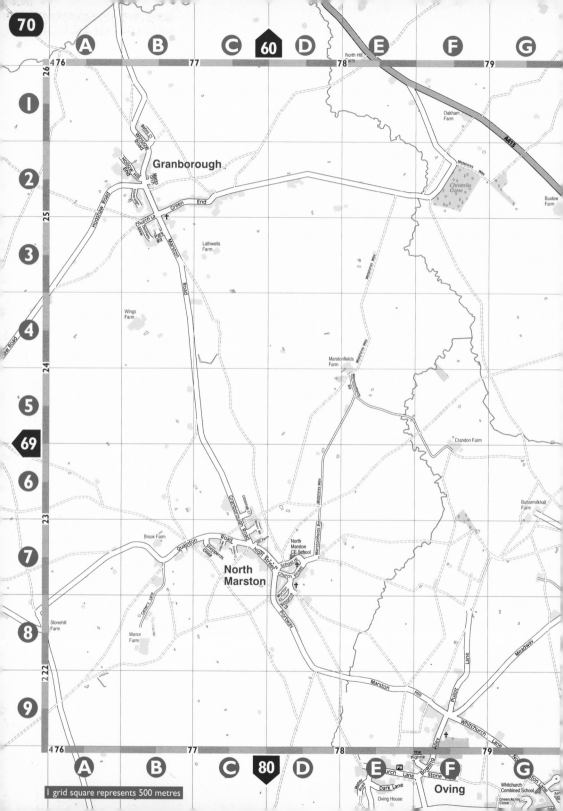

H J K L 61 M

80 81 82 83

26

Blackland
Farm

1

Hoggeston

2

25

3

Dunton
Manor

4

Manor
Farm

Dunton

24

5

72

6

23

Hartwell
Hill Farm

7

Maynes
Hill

Hurdlesgrove

8

222

Creslow

9

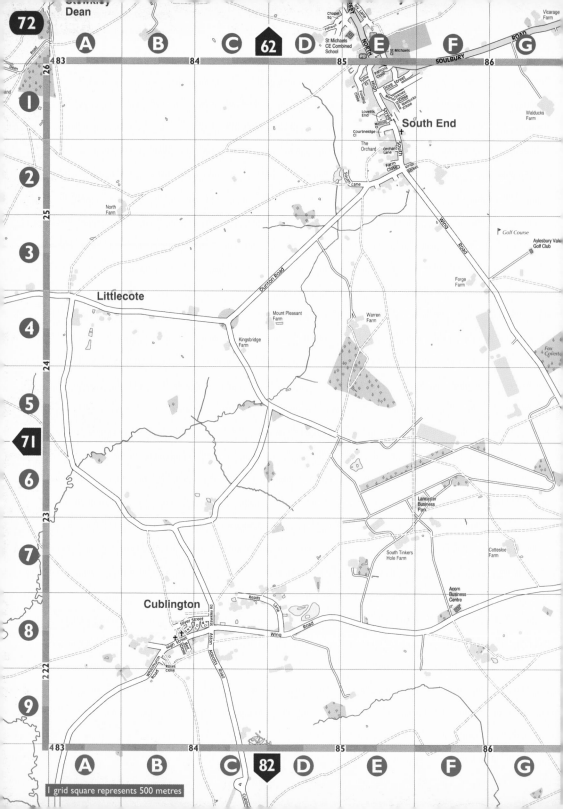

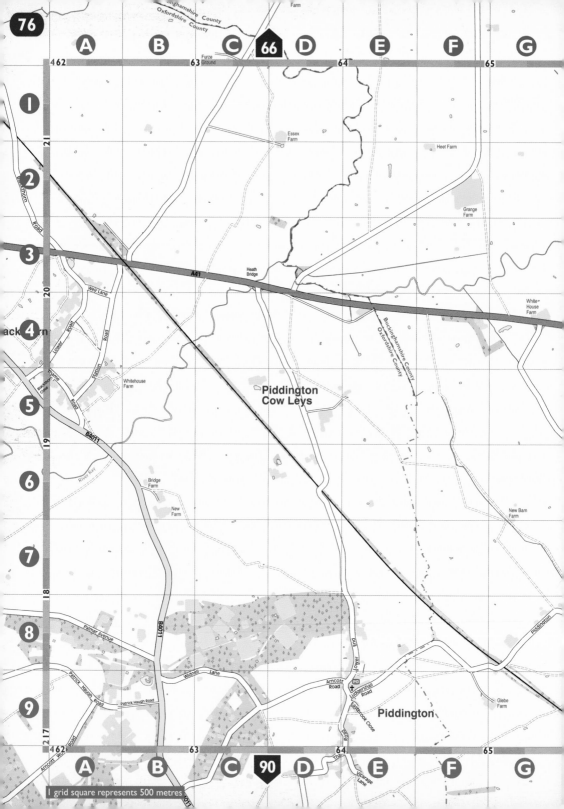

Grendon Underwood

Tetchwick

Ludgershall

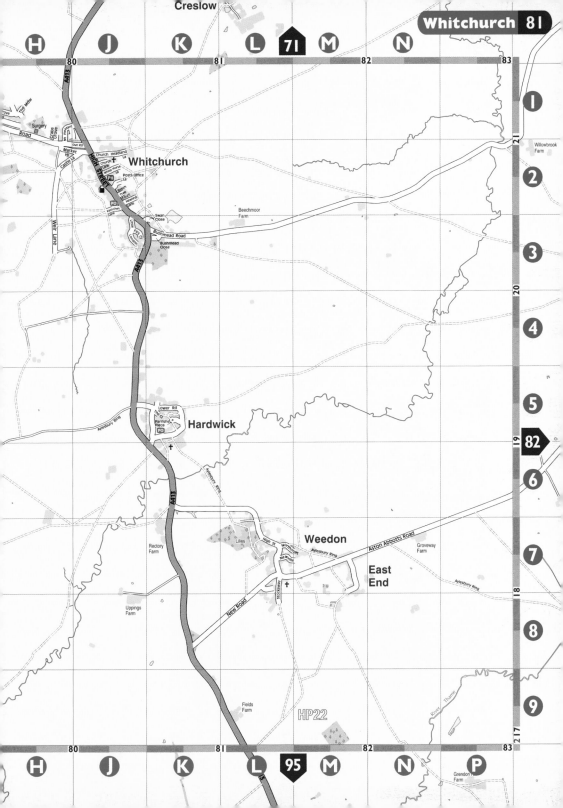

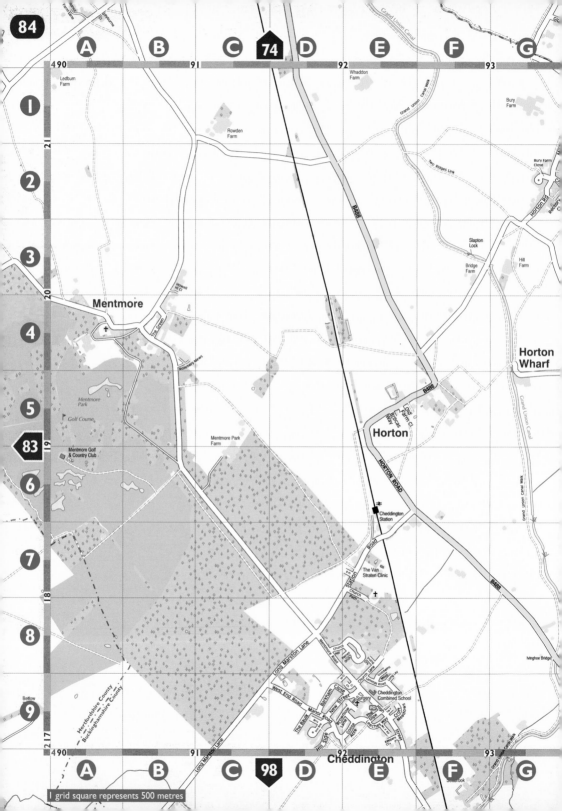

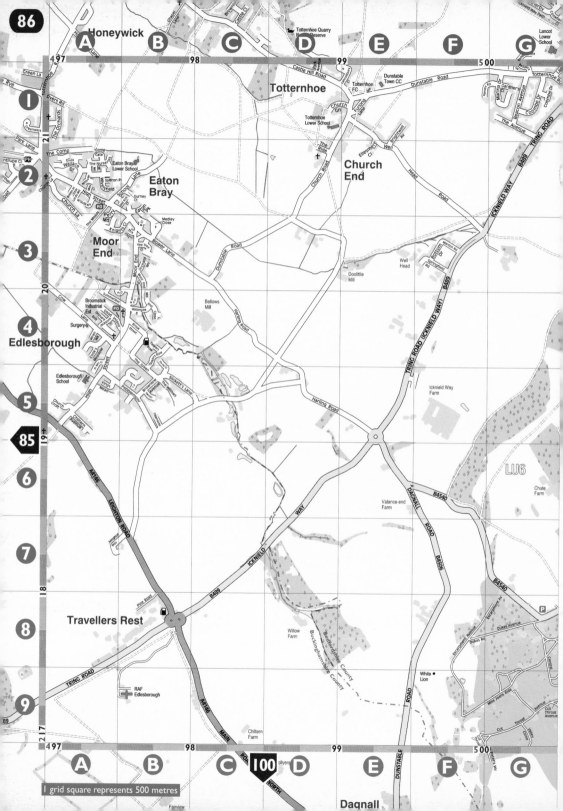

A B C D E F G

Honeywick

497 98 99 500

Totternhoe Quarry Nature Reserve

Lancot Lower School

1

Totternhoe

Rye

Green La

Overs Rd

The Orchards

Castle Hill Road

Dunstable Town CC

Dunstable Road

TRING ROAD

Martins Dr

Gardner's La

Combe Dr

Beacon Avenue

Totternhoe FC

The Avenue

2

The Comp

Comp Gate

The Nurse

Eaton Bray's Lower School

Wallace Dr

Saffron R

High Street

PO

Eaton Bray

Gurney Ct

Eaton Pk

Church Gn

Totternhoe Lower School

The Ride

Church End

Ellesmere Ci

Well Head

Church Road

ICKNIELD WAY

B489

3

Moor End

Knight's

Medley Close

Bower Lane

Dunstable Road

Well Head

Doolittle Mill

Merdon Rd

Springfield

B489

4

Edlesborough

Broomstick Industrial Est

PO

Surgery

Bellows Mill

Harling Road

5

Edlesborough School

High Street

Chiltern Avenue

Church Cres

Slicketts Lane

The Green

Harling Road

Icknield Way Farm

85

19

6

A4146

LEIGHTON ROAD

ICKNIELD WAY

TRING ROAD (ICKNIELD WAY)

LU6

Chute Farm

7

DAGNALL ROAD

B4540

B456

8

Travellers Rest

Pine Road

B489

Willow Farm

Valance-end Farm

Bedfordshire County

Buckinghamshire County

White Lion

P

Dukes Avenue

9

TRING ROAD

A4146

RAF Edlesborough

MAIN ROAD

Chiltern Farm

DUNSTABLE ROAD

Cut Throat Avenue

217

497 98 99 500

A B C D E F G

100

DAGNALL

I grid square represents 500 metres

A   B   C   **82**   D   E   F   G

483   84   85   86

17

1

16

2

3

15

4

Hulcott

Hale Farm

Works

Aylesbury Golf Centre

Golf Course

Barnett House

Moat End

AYLESBURY ROAD

Bierton

Bierton CE Combined School

Old Orchards

Bishops Meadow

Burcott La

Marshalls Lea

Burcott

Broughton Lane

5

95

Douglas Road

Stocklake

DOUGLAS ROAD

HM Young Offenders Institute

6

Stocklake

Stocklake Park Industrial Est

Bear Brook

Grand Union Canal Walk

Grand Union Canal Walk

Grand Union Canal

Rare Breeds Park

Ivy La

Broughton Lane

Park Street Industrial Estate

Victoria Park

OAKFIELD ROAD

Surgery

Northfield Rd

Narbeth Drive

Como Road

Broughton Infant School

Broughton Junior School

Broughton

Old Manor Farm

3

7

Victoria St

TRING ROAD   A41

Broughton

Avenue

Bramcote

Heron

8

Clinton Crs

Walton Way

St Josephs Catholic Infant School

St Edwards RC Junior School

TRING

ROAD

Queens Mead

Tring Road

Weston Mead Farm

Wynne Jones Business Centre

Aylesbury Grammar School

Cemetery

The Grange School

alton

A413

Turnfurlong Primary School

Northumberland Avenue

Limes Av

Bedgrove

Weedon Ditch

New Road

Holiday Inn

ASTON CLINTON ROAD

9

WENDOVER ROAD

Aylesbury & District Sports Club

Messenger Cl

Health Centre

Surgery

Bedgrove Junior School

Stratton Grn

Normill Terrace

483   84   85   86

A   B   C   **110**   D   E   F   G

Bedgrove

1 grid square represents 500 metres

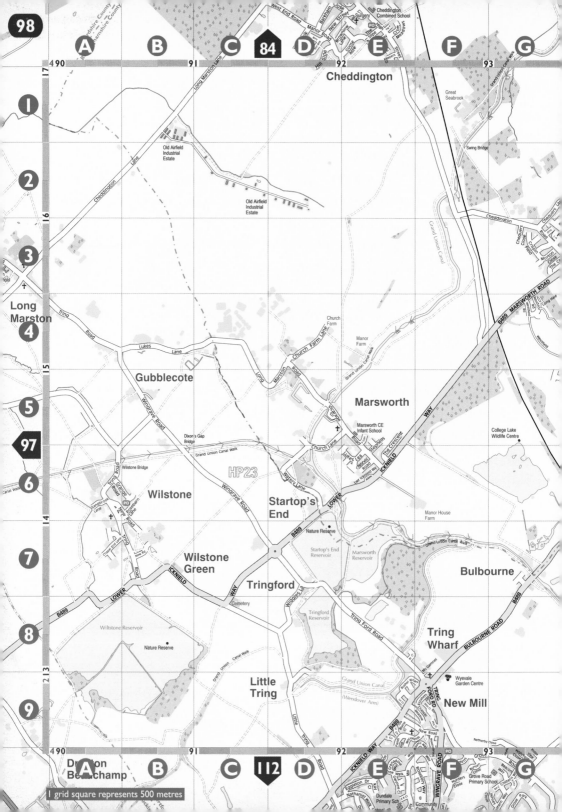

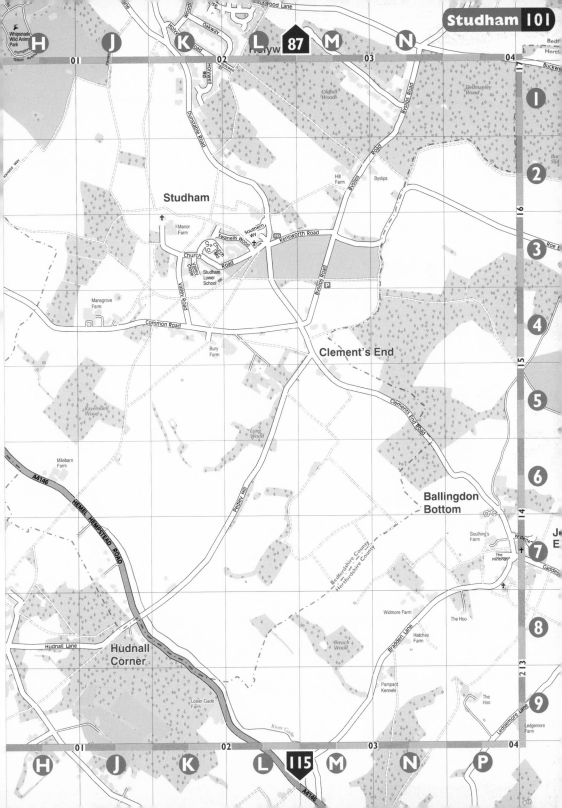

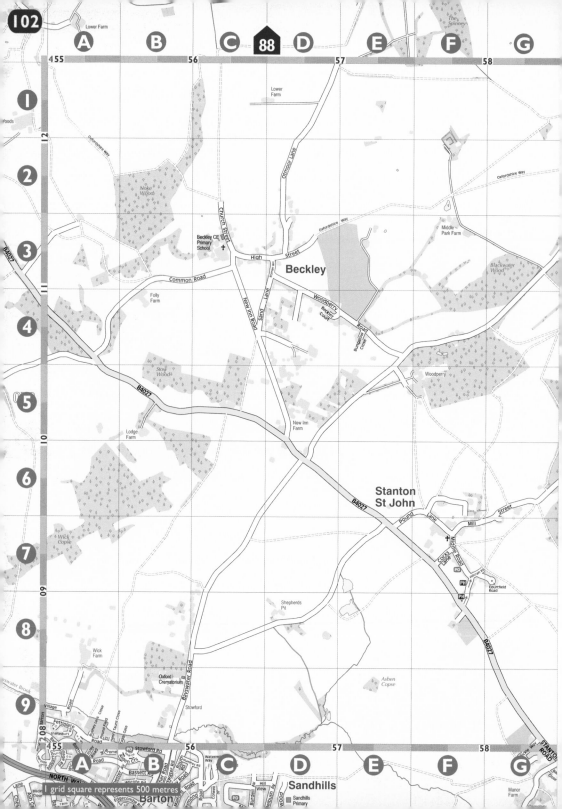

I 12

2

3

11

4

5

10 106

6

7

09

8

208

9

Parkpale Farm

Buttermilk Hall

B4011

THAME ROAD

Addingrove Farm

Hornage Farm

B4011

Dorton Hill

Camp Farm

Chilton

Brill Road

Dorton Road

Thame Road

Chapel Lane

Princes Close

Poppyfields Park

Easington

Easington Lane

Woodway Fm Industrial Est

Westfield Farm

Lower End

Long Crendon School

Carters Lane

Frances Road

Chearsley Road

B4011

PH

Long Crendon

BICESTER ROAD

Bigmarsh Farm

Sandy Lane

Peppershill

Sycamore Close

Frogmore

Redding's Farm

Long Crendon Road

Thame Valley Walk

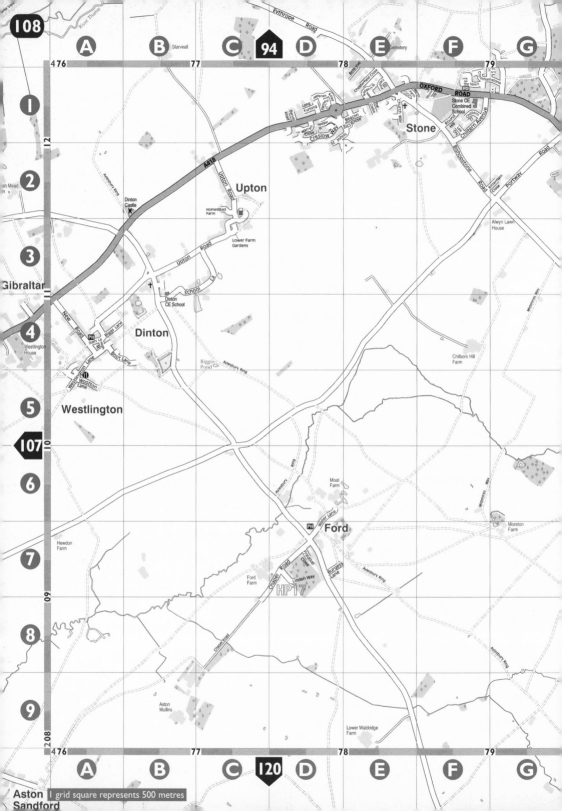

A483 WENDOVER ROAD

A

B

C

D

E

F

G

84

85

86

I

Bedgrove

Stoke Mandeville Sports Stadium

Stoke Mandeville Hospital

William Harding Combined School

Weston Turville Golf & Squash Club

Rectory Farm

2

Aylesbury College

Aylesbury RFC

LOWER ROAD

3

B

WENDOVER ROAD

A413

Weston Turville CE School

BROOK END

Weston Turville

Weston Way Industrial Estate

Moat Farm

STATION ROAD

Stoke Mandeville Combined School

A4010

Stoke Mandeville Station

MAIN STREET

Innkeeper's Lodge

Manor Farm Cl

MARROWAY

B4544

4

Stoke Mandeville

Meadow Park

5

Whitehorn Farm

A4010

Triangle Business Park

A413 WENDOVER ROAD

Weston Turville Reservoir

6

Goat Centre

RISBOROUGH ROAD

World's End

WENDOVER ROAD B4009

Wyevale Garden Centre

AYLESBURY RD

AYLESBURY

7

Northlee Lane

World's End

A413

Nash Lee End

8

North Lee

LEE ROAD

B4009

Nash Lee Lane

9

B208

Nash Lee

Chiltern Brewery

Grove Farm

Thornton Crescent

83

84

85

86

A

B

C

D

E

Wellwick Farm

F

G

Terrick

The Three Hundreds of Aylesbury

1 grid square represents 500 metres

Chalkshire

Wendover Sta

A   B   C   98   D   E   F   G

490   91   92   93

Little Tring

New Mill

Garden Centre

Union Canal (Wendover Arm)

Drayton
Beauchamp

TRING

Upper
Dunsley

Travel
Inn

Chivery

A   B   C   124   D   E   F   G

Hastoe

Spencersgreen

I grid square represents 500 metres

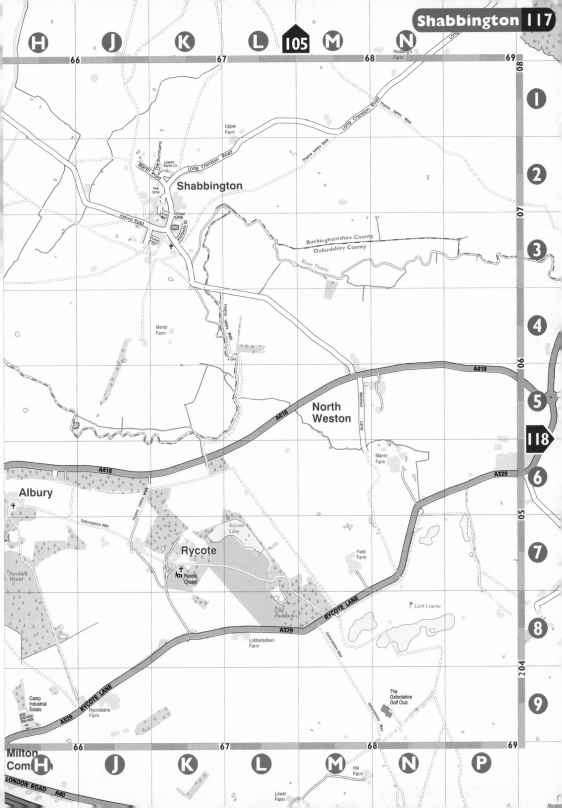

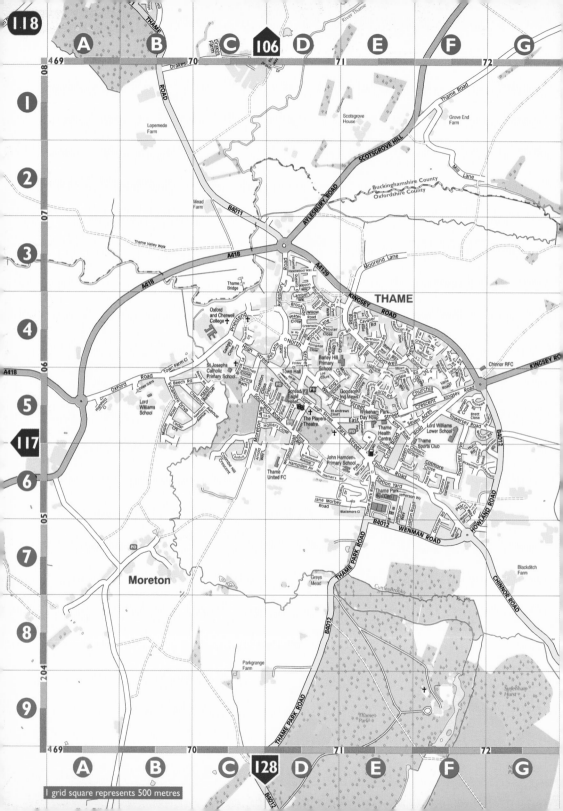

H   J   K   L **107** M   N

73   74   75   76   08

I

Aston
Sandford

2

07

Decoy Pond

Tythrop
House

3
A4129

Kingsey

A4129

Silvove
Furlong
Farm

4

06

A4129

5

Grange
Farm

120

Thame Road

Windmill
Close

Windmill Road

Court La

6

Towersey

05

Church La

Chinnor Road

Manor Road

Manor Road

7

Grovehill
Farm

Penn
Farm

8

204

New Close
Farm

Westbrook
Farm

9

Watt
Farm

Home

120

A   B   C   **108**   D   E   F   G

476   77   78   79

Aston
Mullins

Lower Waldr
Farm

1   08

Aston
Sandford

Waldridge
Village

2   07

Waldridge
Manor

Black Barn
Farm

Whirlbush
Farm

3   A4129

Pasture
Farm

Stockwell Lane
Farm

4   06

A4129

Manor
Farm

Owlswick

Bumpers

Ray
Farm

5   05

Ilmer

Midshires Way

119

Bar Lane

Weavers
Road
Blacksmiths
C Road
Wheelwright
Road

6

Orchard
Close

Toll Bar
A4129

Longwick

7

Longwick CE
Combined
School

THAME ROAD

Bell Crescent

Barn
Road

CHESTNUT WAY

Williams
Way

IVY CL

8   204

Cuttle Brook

Midshires Way

North Mill Road

B4444

SUMMER

9

The Ford

Sandpit Lane

**Forty
Green**

ICKNIELD WAY

LOWER

476   77   78   79

A   B   C   **130**   D   E   F   G

Hol
Gre

B4009

Chapel
Lane

Holly Lane

Green Lane

Princes Risborough Railway
Icknield Line

Pitch

B4444

1 grid square represents 500 metres

Home

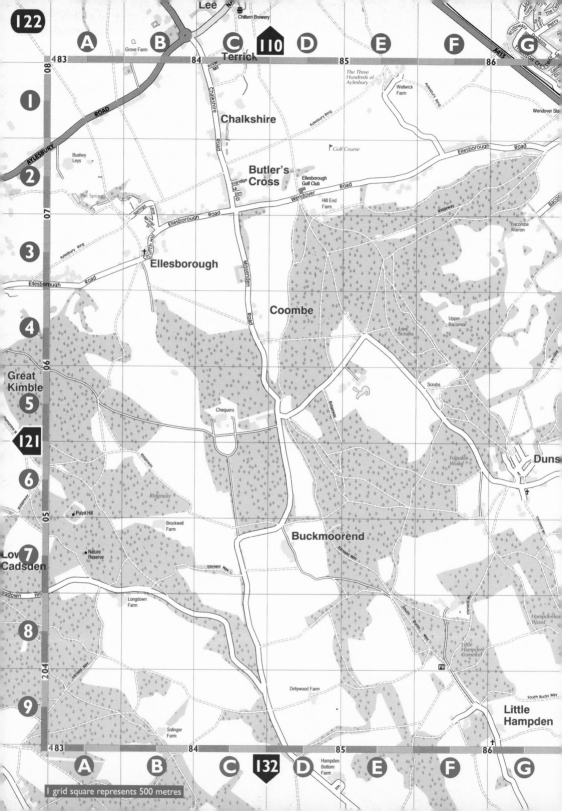

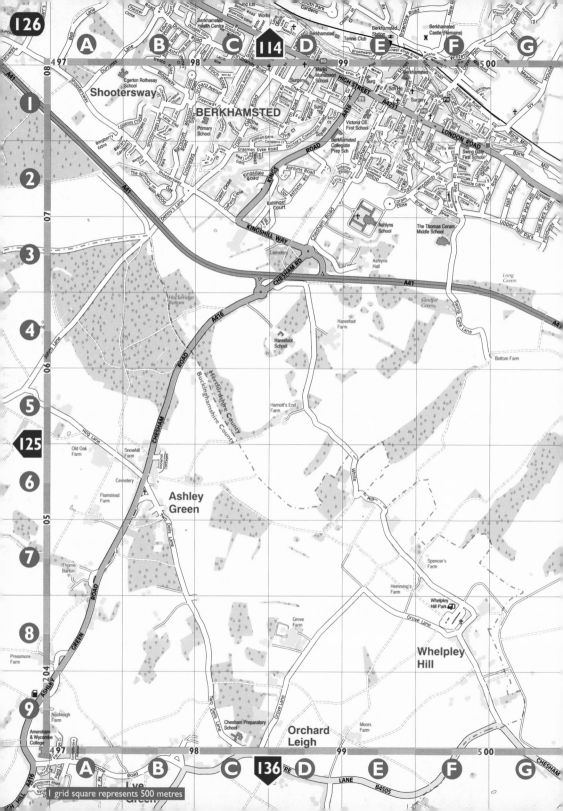

121

132

141

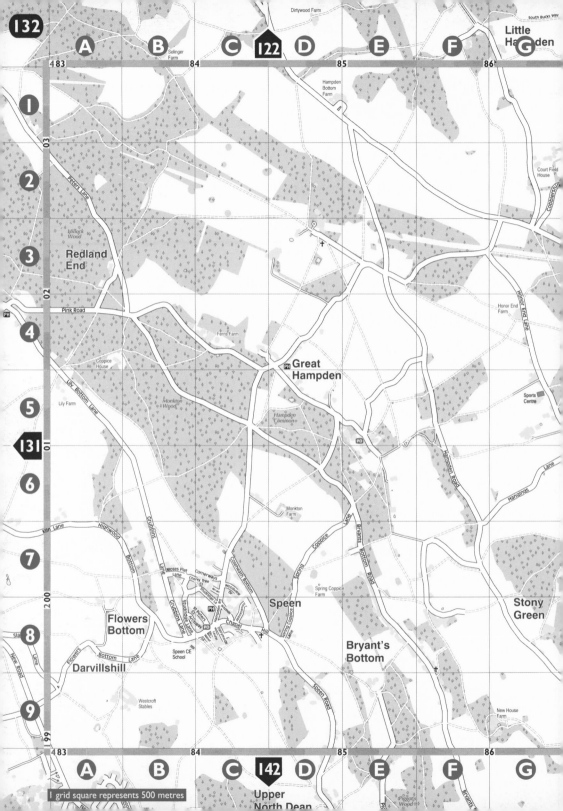

H J K L 129 M N

73 74 75 76 99

I

Crowell Hill

2

98

3

4

97

5

140

6

7

195

8

9

H J K L 149 M N P

73 74 75 76

Aston Rowant CE Primary School

School Lane

Aston Rowant CC

B4009

Park Lane

Kingston House

Church Lane

CHINNOR ROAD

Woodway Farm

Swan's Way

Kingston

Kingston Grove

Grove Wood

Aston Wood

ASTON HILL

A40

Hill Farm

Crowellhill Wood

Crowell Hill

Crowellhill Farm

Kingston Wood

High Wood

Gurdon's Farm

Hallbottom Farm

Court

Nature Reserve

Kiln Farm

OXFORD ROAD

M40

M40

The Kings Arms Hotel

Little Wd

CR Bates Industrial Estate

Slade

Court

Junction 5

Independent Business Park

Green Lane

Wallace Hill

Mill La

Chalford Ridge

Mill

Ibstone Road

Upper Vicar's Farm

Lower Vicar's Farm

Little Studdridge

Cowleaze Wood

Lydall's Wood

Wellground Farm

Bowley's Wood

Commonhill Wood

Studdridge Farm

Wormsley Park

Buckinghamshire Co

Oxfordshire Co

Hartmoor Wood

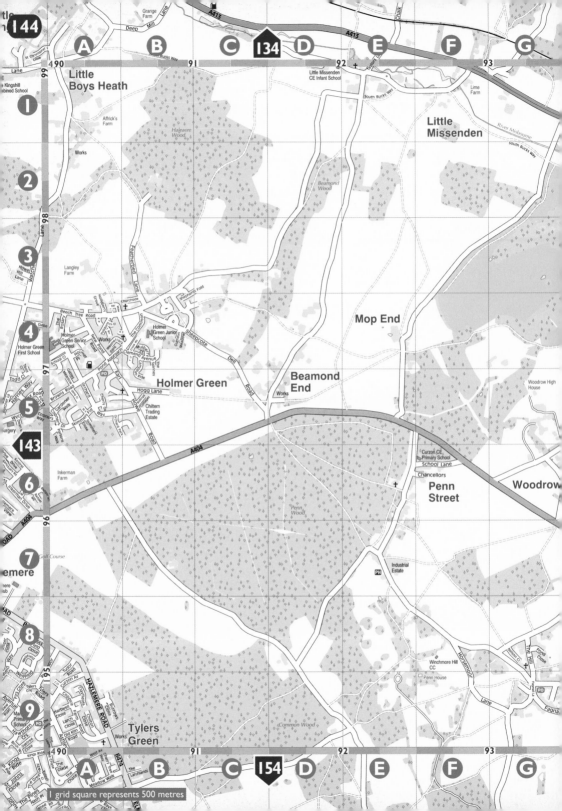

A B **134** C D E F G

490 99 91 92 93

1

Little
Boys Heath

Little Missenden
CE Infant School

Lime
Farm

St. Christopher's
Close

Kingshill
Combined School

Deep Mill Lane

Grange
Farm

A413

A413

Chalk

Taylors Lane

South Bucks Way

River Misbourne

Little
Missenden

south Bucks Way

2

Affrick's
Farm

Works

98

Haleacre
Wood

Beamond
Wood

3

Watchet
Hill
Lane

Newell

Langley
Farm

97

Churchside

Shepherds Fold

Mop End

4

Holmer Green
First School

Holmer
Green Junior
School

Holmer
Green Senior
School

Beech Tree Road

Works

Sheepcote

Dell Road

Beamond
End

Woodrow High
House

Holmer Green

Clements Avenue

Mill

5

Todd Cl

Harris's Way

Hogg Lane

Chiltern
Trading Estate

Works

Curzon C.E.
Primary School

School Lane

Woodrow

WYCO

Surgery

143

A404

Chancellors

Penn
Street

6

Inkerman Drive View

Inkerman
Farm

96

A404

Penn
Wood

✝

7

emere

Goff Course

Industrial
Estate

PH

8

95

Horsemoor Lane

Nash Pk

The Hill

Dene Cl

PO

9

Primary
School

PO

Tylers
Green

Common Wood

Winchmore Hill
CC

Penn House

Fagna

Kings Ride

B474

HAZLEMERE ROAD

West Av

The
Larchlands

490 91 92 93

A B **154** C D E F G

ELM

1 grid square represents 500 metres

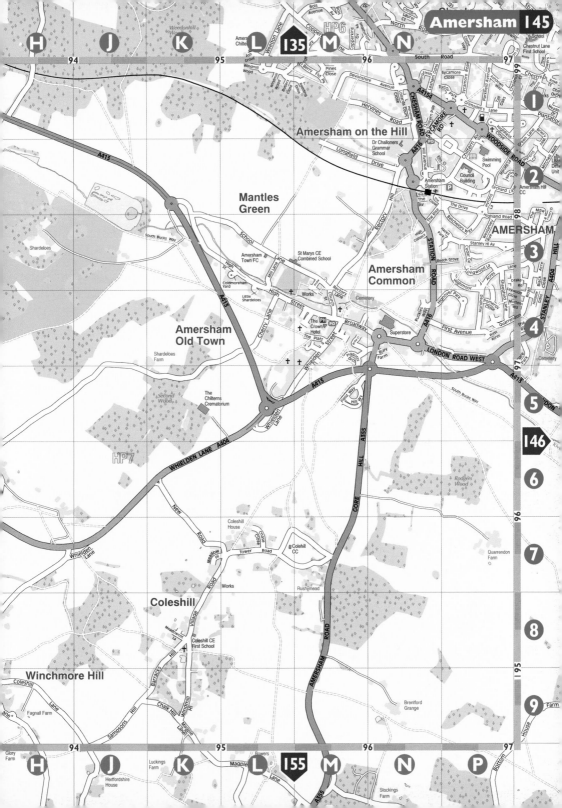

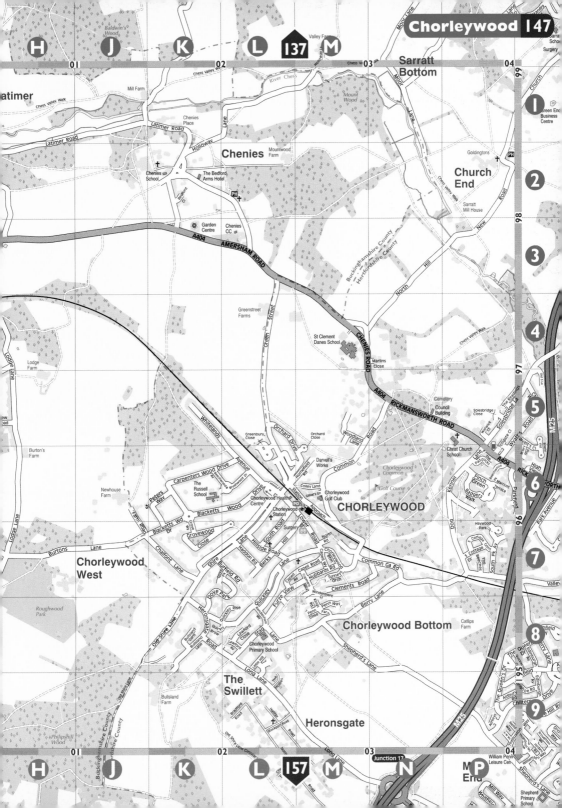

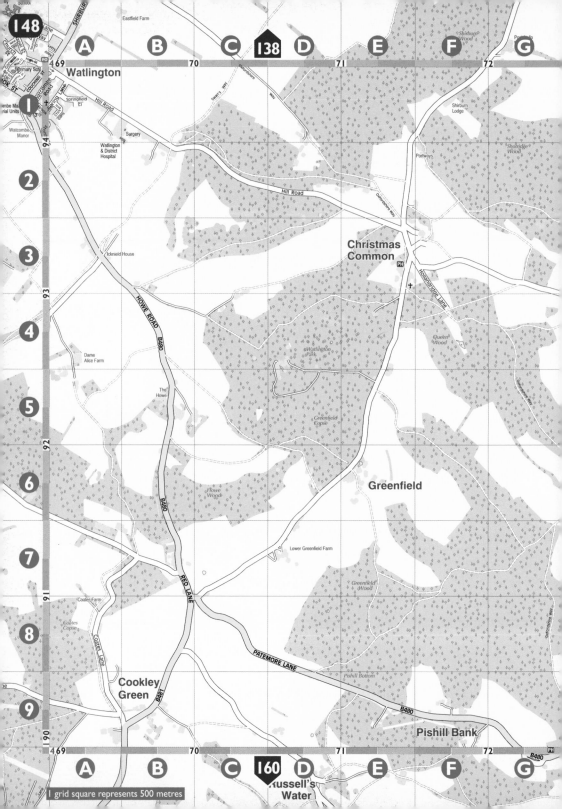

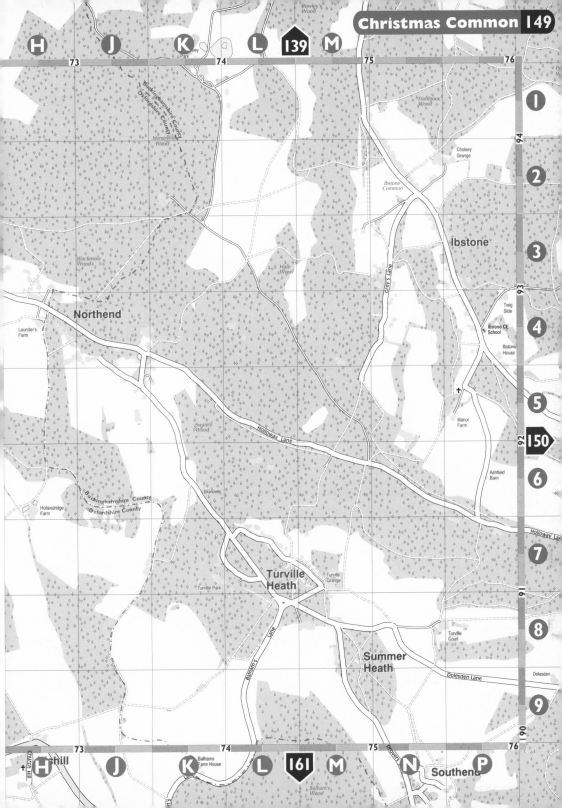

H   J   K   L   139   M

73   74   75   76

I

94   2

Bowley's Wood

Hartmoor Wood

3

Cholsey Grange

Ibstone Common

Ibstone

93   4

Twig Side

Ibstone CE School

Ibstone House

Buckinghamshire County
Oxfordshire County

Hungerhill Wood

Blackmoor Wood

Hale Wood

Northend

Launder's Farm

Grey's Lane

5

92   150

Manor Farm

Ashfield Barn

6

Holloway Lane

Swain's Wood

Holloway Lan

7

Buckinghamshire County
Oxfordshire County

Hollandridge Farm

Blundells

Turville Park

Turville Heath

Turville Grange

91   Turville Court

8

Summer Heath

Dolesden Lane

Dolesden

9

Church Hill

Balham's Lane

Drovers Lane

90

73   74   75   76

Hill   J   K   L   161   N   P   Southend   M

Balhams Farm House

Balham's Wood

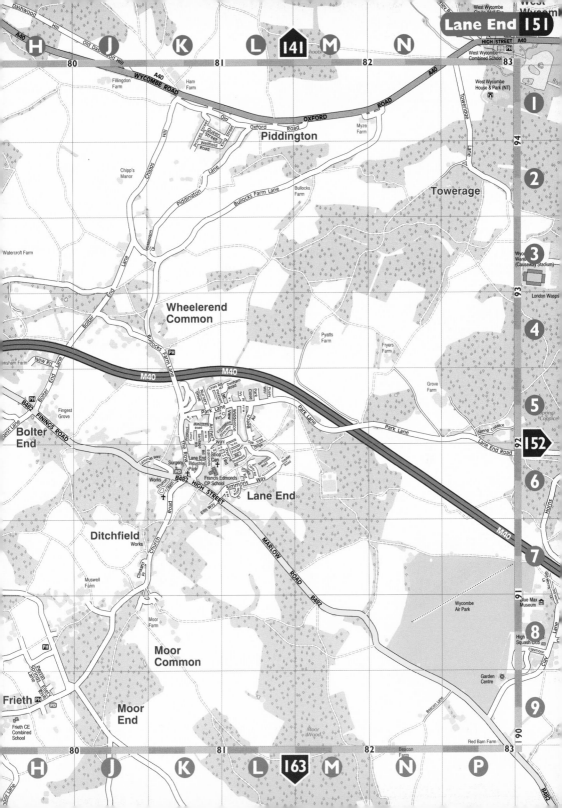

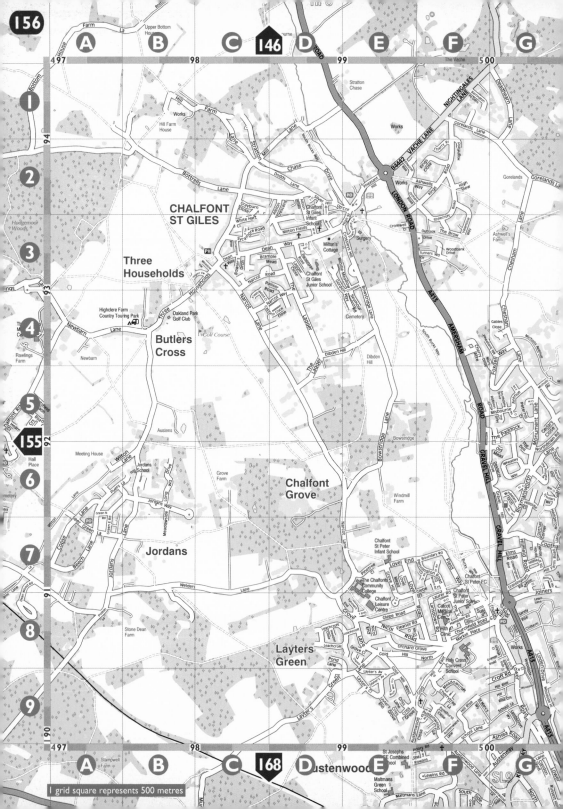

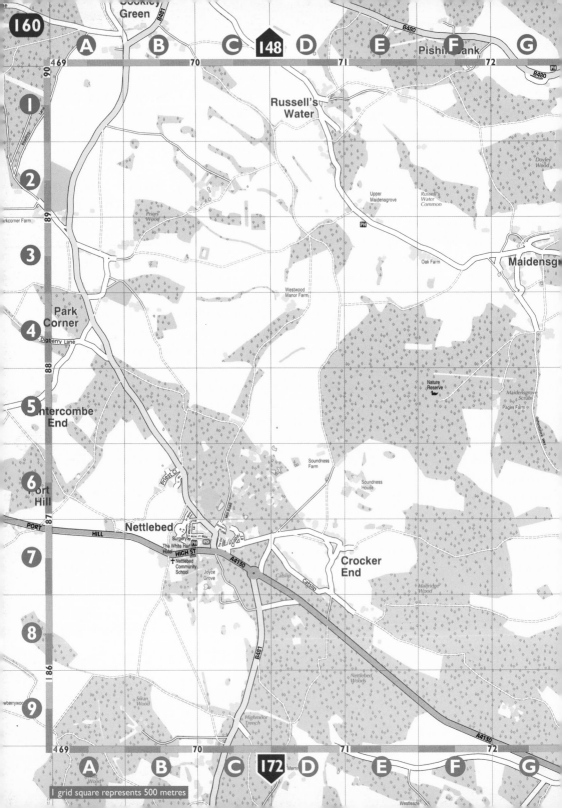

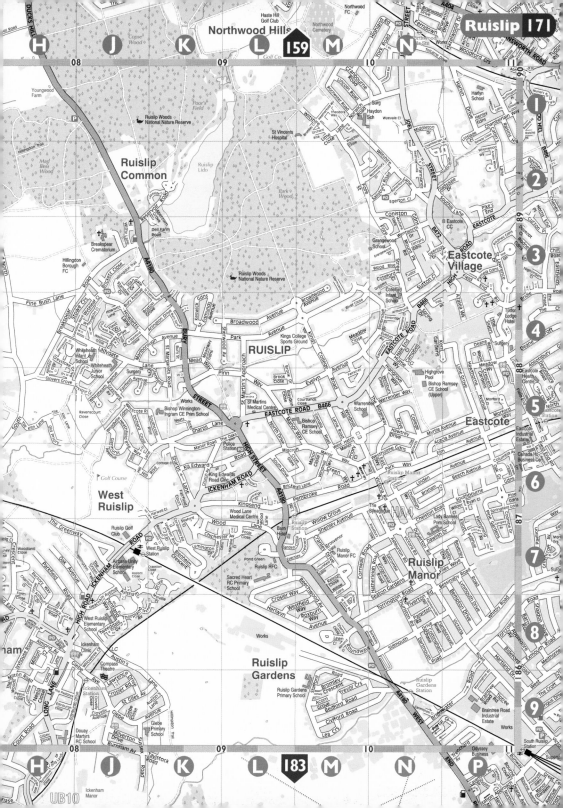

H   J   K   L   163   M

80   81   82   83

85

1

2

3

84

4

5

83   176

6

7

82

8

9

81

H   J   K   L   M   N   P

Widefield Wood

A4155

Rassler Wood

Kings Barn Farm

Danesfield School

Buckingham Gate

Thames Reach

Golf Course

Home Copse

Danesfield

Harleyford Golf Club

School Lane

Bockmer Lane

A4155

Harleyford Manor

Buckinghamshire County

Windsor and Maidenhead

Harleyford Manor

Westfield Farm

A4155

Danesfield House Hotel

River Thames

Thames Path

Medmenham

Ferry Lane

Lowbrook

Mill Lane

Hurley Riverside Park

Spinney

Hurley

Frogmill

Thames Path

Hurley Lane

Works

Shepherds Lane

Lower Culham Farm

Frogmill

Frogmill Farm

Black Boy Lane

Shepherds Cl

High Street

Temple Pk

New Road

Hurley Bottom

HENLEY ROAD   A4130

Prospect

Wokingham

Windsor and Maidenhead

Rosehill

HENLEY ROAD   A4130

Honey Lane

Rose Lane

Hall Place

Top Farm

Honey Lane

Juddmonte House

Dean Place Farm

Rose Lane

Juddmonte Farm North

Warren Rw Rd

Warren Rw Rd

Ashley Hills Forest

Crazies Hill CE School

Rose Lane

Warren Row Road

Larren Row

Pudding Hill

Crazies Hill

Holly

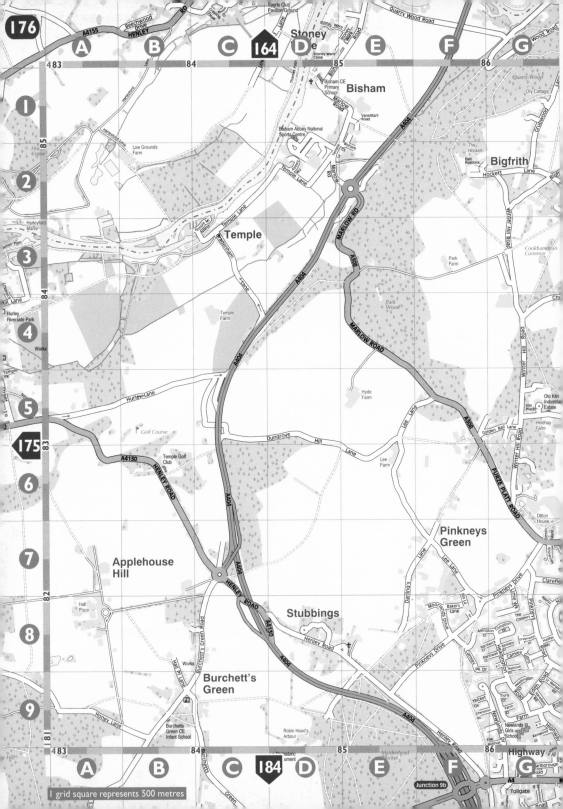

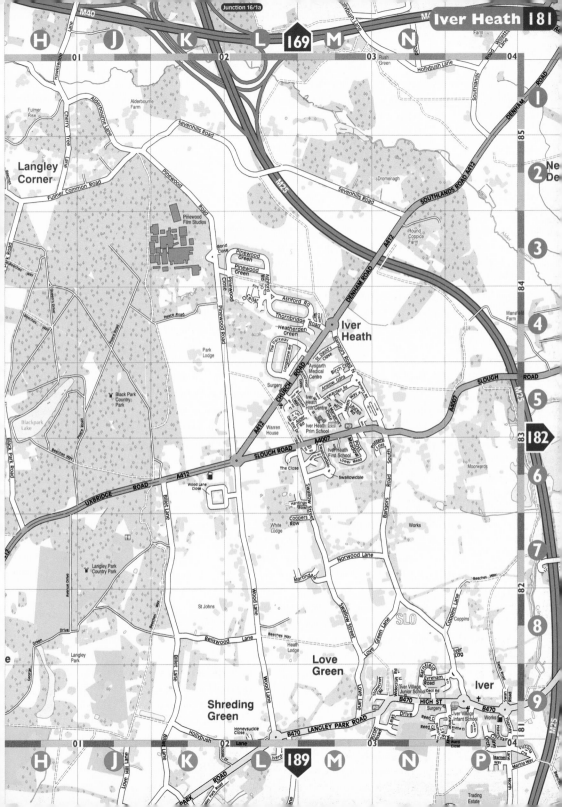

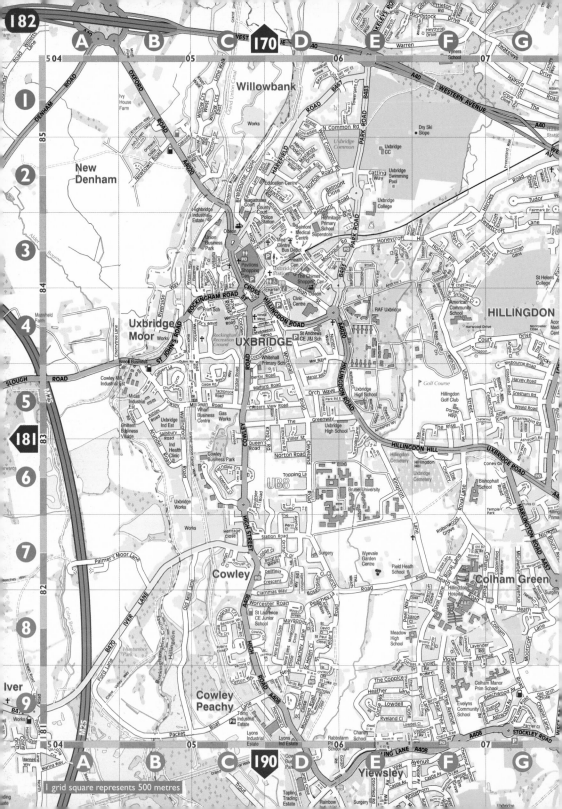

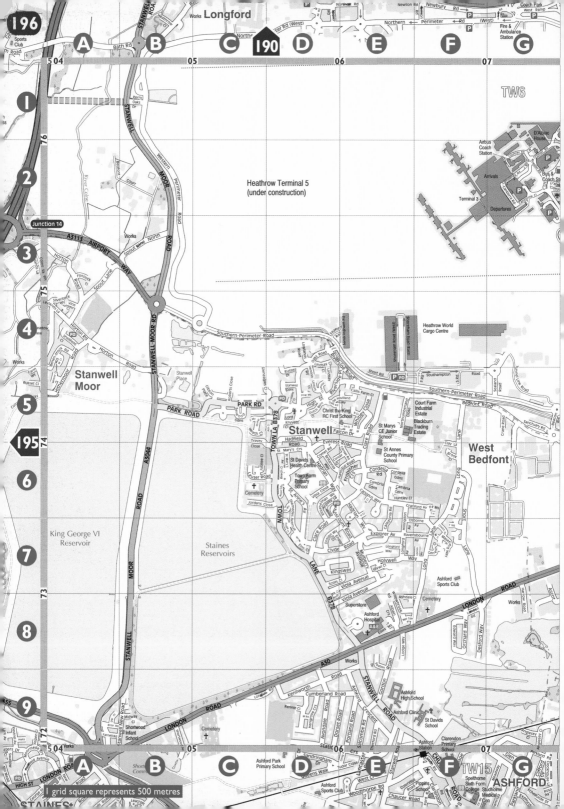

Addington	59	L4
Adstock	59	K1
Adwell	128	B8
Akeley	38	E4
Albury	117	H6
Aldbury	99	N9
Alscot	121	J8
Altmore	184	E3
Amersham	145	P5
Amersham Common	145	P5
Amersham Old Town	145	K4
Amersham on the Hill	145	M1
Applehouse Hill	176	A7
Ashendon	92	D6
Asheridge	125	H8
Ashley Green	126	B6
Ashton	12	A7
Askett	121	L6
Aspley Guise	45	A3
Aspley Heath	44	E8
Aston	174	E3
Aston Abbotts	82	D3
Aston Clinton	111	J1
Aston Rowant	138	G1
Aston Sandford	119	P1
Astrope	97	P4
Astwood	23	L3
Atterbury	31	M9
Austenwood	168	D1
Aylesbury	2	A4
Baker's Wood	169	N6
Ballindon Bottom	101	N6
Ballinger Bottom	124	C9
Ballinger Bottom South	134	D3
Ballinger Common	134	C1
Bancroft	29	P8
Bancroft Park	29	P8
Barley End	99	N7
Barton Hartshorn	46	D9
Batchworth	158	F2
Batchworth Heath	158	G4
Battlesden	65	P4
Beachampton	40	D6
Beacon Hill	154	B5
Beacon's Bottom	140	D7
Beaconsfield	154	C9
Beamond End	144	D5
Beanhill	42	G7
Beaumont	194	D7
Beckley	102	D3
Bedgrove	110	C1
Bellingdon	125	J6
Belsize	137	N5
Bennett End	140	D4
Berghers Hill	168	E5
Berkhamsted	126	C1
Biddlesden	24	D9
Bierton	96	B4
Bigfrith	176	G2
Billington	75	J7
Billington Park	75	H1
Birchmoor Green	55	K5
Bisham	176	E1
Bishopstone	109	K4
Bix	173	H1
Blakelands	31	H4
Bleak Hall	42	F7
Bledlow	130	D3
Bledlow Ridge	140	C5
Bletchley	52	G2
Blue Bridge	29	N7
Boarstall	90	B6
Bockmer End	163	L8
Bolter End	151	H5
Booker	152	B6
Botley	136	C4
Botolph Claydon	69	K3
Bourne End	23	N9
Bourne End	127	L4
Bourne End	165	M5
Bourton	39	K5
Boveney	186	G7
Bovingdon	127	K9
Bovingdon Green	137	H2
Bovingdon Green	164	A6
Bow Brickhill	54	A2
Boyn Hill	185	K2
Brackley	35	H6
Bradenham	141	N4
Bradville	30	A6
Bradwell	30	A9
Bradwell Common	42	B1
Bragenham	64	A4
Brands Hill	189	K8
Bray	186	B4
Bray Wick	185	N3
Brill	91	H6
Brinklow	44	A4
Britwell	179	K7
Broad Green	33	M2
Broadplat	173	J4
Brogborough	45	P3
Brook End	22	D9
Broughton	31	N8
Broughton	96	D7
Browns Wood	44	A8
Bryant's Bottom	132	E8
Buckingham	48	A1
Buckland	97	M9
Buckland Common	124	E2
Bucklandwharf	111	N2
Buckmoorend	122	D7
Buffler's Holt	37	J9
Bulbourne	98	F7
Bullington End	19	J8
Bulstrode	137	N1
Burchett's Green	176	C9
Burcott	73	K5
Burcott	96	C4
Burnham	178	G5
Burroughs Grove	164	F2
Butler's Cross	122	C2
Butlers Cross	156	B4
Bye Green	110	C3
Cadmore End	150	E5
Caldecote	31	K4
Caldecote	43	M9
California	2	B6
Calvert	67	P3
Calverton	41	K9
Camp Corner	116	F8
Carlton	11	M5
Castlethorpe	29	H1
Cattle End	25	J1
Central Milton Keynes	6	B2
Chackmore	37	P8
Chalfont Common	157	H4
Chalfont Grove	156	D6
Chalfont St Giles	156	B2
Chalfont St Peter	157	J7
Chalford	127	H2
Chalkshire	122	C1
Charlton	36	E1
Charlton-on-Otmoor	88	B3
Charndon	67	L5
Chartridge	134	C1
Chaulden	127	M5
Chearsley	106	E4
Cheddington	98	D1
Chellington	11	M4
Chenies	147	L2
Chesham	135	N4
Chesham Bois	135	N9
Chessmount	136	A5
Chetwode	56	E2
Chicheley	22	A6
Chilton	105	N2
Chinnor	129	P5
Chisbridge Cross	163	L3
Chivery	124	A1
Cholesbury	124	C3
Chorleywood	147	M6
Chorleywood Bottom	147	M8
Chorleywood West	147	J7
Christmas Common	148	E3
Church End	45	L7
Church End	67	P6
Church End	86	E2
Church End	87	M5
Church End	99	J5
Church End	107	L9
Church End	187	J4
Cippenham	187	H2
The City	140	F5
Clanking	121	M2
Clement's End	101	M4
Clewer Green	193	L2
Clewer New Town	193	L1
Clewer Village	193	L1
Clifton Pastures	16	A6
Clifton Reynes	16	B4
Clipstone	65	J9
Codmore	136	A3
Coffee Hall	42	F6
Cold Brayfield	16	F2
Cold Harbour	16	F3
Coleshill	145	K8
Colham Green	182	F7
Colnbrook	189	L9
Colstrope	162	E4
The Common	50	D7
Conniburrow	30	C9
Cookham	177	P1
Cookham Dean	177	H1
Cookham Rise	177	M2
Cookley Green	148	A3
Coombe	122	D4
Cooper's Hill	194	F9
Cores End	166	A5
Cosgrove	28	F4
Courteenhall	12	A1
Court Garden	164	D8
Cowley	182	C7
Cowley Peachy	182	C9
Cow Roast	113	C5
Cox Green	185	J4
Crafton	83	M4
Cranbourne	192	F8
Cranfield	33	M4
Cranford	191	N8
Creslow	71	K9
Cressex	152	D6
Crocker End	160	D7
Cross End	44	D5
Crowell	129	N5
Crowell Hill	139	P2
Crownfield	131	K8
Crownhill	41	N5
Cryers Hill	143	K5
Cublington	72	D8
Cuddington	107	L4
Dadford	37	K5
Dagnall	100	E1
Danesfield	175	M2
Darvillshill	132	A1
Datchet	188	D9
Datchet Common	194	E1
Deanshanger	27	P9
Dedworth	187	H9
Denbigh West	41	N8
Denham	79	P5
Denham	170	A7
Denham Green	169	N4
Dinton	108	B4
Ditchfield	151	J7
Dorney	186	F6
Dorney Reach	186	D6
Dorton	91	M6
Downhead Park	30	C7
Downley	142	D8
Down's Barn	30	C8
Downside	87	N2
Draycot	116	G5
Drayton Beauchamp	112	A1
Drayton Parslow	62	C4
Duck End	61	P6
Dudswell	113	P6
Dunsmore	122	G6
Dunton	71	N4
Eaglestone	43	H5
Easington	105	N5
East Bedfont	197	H6
East Burnham	179	K4
Eastbury	159	M4
East Claydon	69	K1
Eastcote	171	P5
Eastcote Village	171	P3
East End	23	K8
East End	33	M3
East End	81	N7
Eaton Bray	86	B2
Eaton Green	85	N3
Edgcott	67	M7
Edlesborough	85	P4
Eggington	75	L2
Egypt	167	M9
Eilesborough	122	B3
Elmhurst	95	M5
Emberton	15	L7
Emerson Valley	52	A2
Emmington	129	L3
Eton	187	N7
Eton Wick	187	K5
Evenley	35	H9
Eythorne Bletchley	52	C4
Farnham Common	179	P2
Farnham Park	179	N4
Farnham Royal	179	N5
Fawley	161	N7
Fawley Bottom	161	L7
Feltham	197	P8
Fencott	88	E2
Fenny Stratford	53	K1
Fern	165	K4
Fields End	127	M1
Fifield	186	B5
Filgrave	21	J1
Fingest	150	C7
Finmere	46	D4
Fishermead	7	K5
Fishery	185	N1
Flackwell Heath	165	N2
Flaunden	137	J2
Flowers Bottom	132	A8
Ford	108	D7
Forty Green	120	A9
Forty Green	154	E6
Foscote	38	E8
Four Ashes	143	J7
Fox Corner	64	F4
Frieth	151	H9
Frith-hill	134	B5
Frithsden	115	J6
Frithsden Gardens	114	G5
Fullers Slade	29	K9
Fulmer	168	F9
Furze Platt	177	K6
Furzton	42	D8
Gadebridge	115	P9
Gawcott	47	M7
George Green	180	G8
Gerrards Cross	168	E5
Gibraltar	107	P3
Giffard Park	30	E3
Goddards	150	E9
Godington	56	D7
Gossard's Green	33	N1
Granborough	70	D2
Gravel Hill	157	H6
Great Brickhill	64	B1
Great Gaddesden	115	M3
Greatgap	99	H1
Great Hampden	132	D4
Great Hivings	135	L1
Great Holm	41	M4
Great Horwood	50	C9
Great Kimble	121	P5
Great Kingshill	143	L3
Great Linford	30	F4
Great Missenden	133	M5
Greatmoor	68	C8
Green End	54	B9
Green End	127	P3
Green End	141	J8
Greenend	148	E6
Green Hailey	131	P1
Greenlands	162	C9
Greenleys	29	K8
The Green	28	G3
The Green	31	J2
The Green	157	H8
Grendon Underwood	87	M3
Greys Green	173	H6
Grove	74	D7
Gubblecote	98	B5
Haddenham	107	L9
Haddington Hill	111	K5
Halton	111	K5
Hambleden	162	D8
Ham Green	78	B6
Hanslope	19	J3
Hardmead	23	H2
Hardwick	83	M1
Harefield	158	C9
Harefield Grove	158	D7
Harlington	191	J7
Harmondsworth	190	C7
Harrold	11	J1
Hartwell	12	G6
Hatton	197	L3
Haversham	29	M3
Hawks Hill	166	A3
Hayes	183	J8
Hayes End	183	H7
Hazlemere	143	P7
Heath and Reach	64	F5
Heath End	25	J2
Heath End	143	K2
Hedgerley	167	P6
Hedgerley Green	168	B5
Hedgerley Hill	168	A6
Hedsor	166	D6
Heelands	30	B9
Hempton Wainhill	130	C5
Henley-on-Thames	173	M7
Henton	130	A2
Heronsgate	147	M9
Higher Denham	169	L5
Highmoor	172	C2
Highmoor Cross	172	B5
Highway	184	G1
High Wycombe	5	G3
Hill End	158	B6
Hillesden	57	N4
Hillesden Hamlet	57	M1
Hillingdon	182	C4
Hillingdon Heath	183	H8
Hilltop	135	P2
Hinton-in-the-Hedges	34	A6
Hoggeston	71	J2
Hogpits Bottom	137	K5
Hollingdon	63	J7
Holloway	184	C2
Hollybush Hill	180	D3
Holly Green	130	C1
Holmer Green	144	B5
Holtspur	154	P9
Holyport	185	N8
Holywell	87	L9
Horn Hill	157	K4
Horsenden	131	H2
Horsleys Green	140	E8
Horton	81	A1
Horton	195	J2
Horton-cum-Studley	103	H1
Horton Wharf	84	G4
Hotley Bottom	133	J4
Hudnall	100	G8
Hudnall Corner	101	J8
Hughenden Valley	142	C4
Hulcote	45	J2
Hulcott	96	D1
Hungate End	18	F4
Hunt's Green	125	N9
Hunt's Hill	142	D6
Hurley	175	H4
Hurley Bottom	175	H1
Hurst End	32	F2
Husborne Crawley	45	M7
Hyde Heath	134	G7
Hythe End	195	K9
Ibstone	149	P3
Ickenham	170	G8
Ickford	116	G2
Ilmer	120	B5
Iver	181	P9
Iver Heath	181	M4
Ivinghoe	99	K2
Ivinghoe Aston	85	P1
Jordans	156	B7
Kensworth Common	87	N7
Kents Hill	43	N4
Kimble Wick	121	K1
Kingsash	123	M5
Kingsey	119	L3
Kingston	44	A2
Kingston Blount	129	J9
Kingston Stert	128	C5
Knotty Green	154	C4
Lacey Green	131	N7
Lake End	186	F3
Lane End	151	L6
Lanes End	124	A2
Langley	189	H4
Langley Corner	181	H2
Lathbury	21	K7
Latimer	146	D3
Lavendon	10	D9
Layters Green	156	D8
Leckhampstead	39	H5
Ledburn	74	A8
Lee Clump	124	A8
Lee Common	124	C1
Leedon	74	G1
Lee Gate	123	P5
The Lee	123	P7
Leighton Buzzard	74	F1
Lenborough	48	B7
Lent	178	E7
Lent Rise	178	E6
Lewknor	138	E3
Ley Hill	136	D5
Lillingstone Dayrell	26	C9
Lillingstone Lovell	26	D7
Linslade	74	A2
Little Billington	74	G8
Little Boys Heath	144	A1
Little Brickhill	54	B6
Little Chalfont	146	D4
Littlecote	72	A4
Little Crawley	22	D7
Littlefield Green	185	H2
Little Gaddesden	100	F8
Little Hampden	122	G9
Little Heath	115	J9
Little Horwood	51	H9
Little Kimble	121	P3
Little Kingshill	133	L9
Little Linford	20	D9
Little London	104	F1
Little London	123	J6
Little Marsh	165	J4
Little Missenden	144	F1
Little Tring	98	D6
Littlewick Green	184	C2
Little Wood Corner	134	D4
Littleworth Common	167	N6
Long Crendon	105	N9
Longford	190	C9
Long Marston	97	P4
Long Street	19	H2
Longwick	120	F6
Loosley Row	131	L6
Loudwater	154	B8
Loughton	42	B5
Love Green	181	M8
Lower Assendon	173	K2
Lower Bois	135	N7
Lower Cadsden	121	P7
Lower End	12	D6
Lower End	44	F3
Lower End	49	K2
Lower End	105	P7
Lower Feltham	197	L9
Lower Hartwell	95	H8
Lower Highmoor	172	C2
Lower North Dean	142	D7
Lower Pollicott	92	C9
Lower Wainhill	130	B5
Lower Weald	40	F2
Lower Winchendon or Nether Winchendon	107	J1
Lower Woodend	163	N6
Ludgershall	77	K8
Lye Green	136	B1
Maidenhead	177	N8
Maidenhead Court	178	A4
Maidensgrove	160	G3
Maids Moreton	38	D8
Manor Park	3	F1
Manor Park	185	L2
Mantles Green	145	L2
Maple Cross	157	M4
Marlow	164	C6
Marlow Bottom	164	C3
Marsh	109	M3
Marsh Gibbon	67	J2
Marsworth	98	E5
Meadle	121	K5
Medmenham	175	K3
Mentmore	84	A4
Mickelfield	153	L5
Middle Assendon	161	G3
Middle Claydon	68	G3
Middle Green	188	G1
Middle Weald	40	G3
Mill End	157	P1
Mill End	174	L1
Milton Bryan	65	P1
Milton Keynes	7	J4
Milton Keynes Village	43	M1
Mobwell	133	N4
Moneyhill	158	B1
Moneyrow Green	185	N8
Monks Risborough	121	J7
Monkston	32	J2
Monkston Park	43	L3
Moor Common	151	K8
Moor End	86	A3
Moor End	151	J9
Moor Park	158	E2
Mop End	144	E4
Moreton	118	B7
Moulsoe	32	B5
Mount Pleasant	47	P4
Mount Pleasant	158	B8
Murcott	88	C2
Nashway	61	M4
Naphill	142	C4
Nash	50	E2
Nash Lee	110	C9
Nearton End	61	K8
Neath Hill	30	E7
Netherfield	43	H6
Nettlebed	160	B7
Nettleden	115	K4
New Bradwell	29	P5
New Denham	182	A2
New Ground	113	A4
Newlands	23	L4
New Mill	98	F9
Newport Pagnell	21	J9
Newton Blossomville	16	B3
Newton Longville	52	D8
Newton Purcell	56	A9
Newtown	135	N2
Newtown	174	A8
Newyears Green	170	G5
Northall	85	L3
Northchurch	113	P8
North Crawley	22	B8
North End	17	P7
North End	62	D8
North End	143	P4
North Feltham	197	H4
Northfield	31	M8
North Hillingdon	183	H3
North Lee	110	A8
North Marston	70	D2
North Town	177	N7
North Weston	117	M5
Northwood	159	H3
Northwood Hills	159	K4
Nup End	82	G5
Oakgrove	43	K2
Oakley	104	D1
Oakley	129	M7
Oakley Green	192	E1
Oldbrook	7	F6
Old Farm Park	44	A8
Old Linslade	64	A8
Old Stratford	28	G6
Old Windsor	194	B5
Olney	15	N3
Orchard Leigh	126	D9
Oving	80	F1
Owlswick	120	G4
Padbury	58	C1
Park Corner	160	A2
Parmoor	162	G2
Parslow's Hillock	131	P4
Passenham	40	D1
Pednor Bottom	134	G2
Pednormead End	135	K2
Penn	154	C2
Penn Bottom	144	E2
Penn Street	144	D6
Pennyland	30	D6
Petsoe End	15	P9
Pheasants	162	G4

Pheasant's Hill 162 E6
Piddington 76 E9
Piddington 151 L1
Piddington Cow Leys 76 C5
Pineham 31 L6
Pinfoldpond 55 J5
Pinkneys Green 176 F7
Pishill 161 H1
Pishill Bank 148 F9
Pitchcott 80 D2
Pitch Green 130 E1
Pitstone 99 H4
Pitstone Green 99 J3
Pond Park 135 M2
Postcombe 128 D8
Potsgrove 65 K2
Potten End 115 J8
Potterspury 28 A3
Pouchen End 127 M5
Poundon 66 E2
Poyle 189 N9
Preston Bissett 57 J2
Prestwood 133 K6
Princes Risborough 131 L2
Pudds Cross 136 C1
Puttenham 97 M5
Puxley 27 P6
Quainton 79 L3
Quarrendon 95 K5
Radclive 47 M2
Radnage 140 F2
Ravenstone 14 D5
Redland End 132 A3
Remenham 174 C3
Remenham Hill 174 E6
Richings Park 189 N4
Ringshall 100 D6
Rockwell End 163 H4
Rooksley 42 A2
Rose Hill 178 E3
Rotherfield Greys 172 G7
Rotherfield Peppard 172 D9
Rout's Green 140 F2
Rowsham 82 E7
Ruislip 171 L4
Ruislip Common 171 J2
Ruislip Gardens 171 L8
Ruislip Manor 171 N7
Rushmere 64 D6
Russell's Water 160 D1
St Leonards 124 C2
St Margaret's 115 L2
Salcey Green 13 J8
Salden 61 N2
Salford 44 C1
Salt Hill 187 P2
Sandhill 59 J8
Sands 152 B3

Sarratt Bottom 137 N9
Satwell 172 D4
Saunderton 130 C5
Saunderton Lee 131 J8
Sedrup 108 G2
Seer Green 155 M6
Shabbington 117 K2
Shalstone 36 E6
Sheeplane 55 H9
Sheepridge 165 M2
Shenley Brook End 41 N9
Shenley Church End 41 L6
Shenley Lodge 42 B8
Shenley Wood 41 N8
Shepherd's Green 172 E5
Sherington 21 N4
Sherington Bridge 21 L7
Shipton 60 D7
Shipton Lee 79 H1
Shirburn 138 A7
Shootersway 126 A1
Shreding Green 181 K9
Simpson 43 L8
Singleborough 50 A6
Sipson 190 F6
Skirmett 150 D9
Skittle Green 130 B1
Slapton 85 H2
Slough 188 D2
Smoky Row 121 N4
Soulbury 54 L7
Southcourt 95 L9
South End 72 E1
Southend 161 N1
South Field 187 M6
South Harefield 170 D2
South Heath 134 C4
South Oxhey 159 P5
South Weston 138 C2
Speen 132 D8
Spinfield 164 A8
Spital 193 M3
Sprig's Alley 140 A1
Springfield 43 H2
Spurlands End 143 N5
Stacey Bushes 29 N9
Stanbridge 75 N4
Stanbridgeford 75 P6
Stantonbury 30 C6
Stanton St John 102 E6
Stanwell 196 D5
Stanwell Moor 196 A5
Startop's End 98 D6
Steeple Claydon 58 A7
Stewkley 62 E9
Stewkley Dean 62 A9
Stoke Goldington 13 P9
Stoke Green 180 C7

Stoke Hammond 63 L2
Stoke Mandeville 110 B5
Stokenchurch 140 B6
Stoke Poges 180 A3
Stone 108 E1
Stonebridge 29 N6
Stoney Ware 164 D9
Stonor 161 J3
Stony Green 132 G8
Stony Stratford 28 G8
Stubbings 176 D8
Stud Green 185 L7
Studham 101 K2
Studley Green 140 G8
Summer Heath 149 M8
Summerstown 66 C7
Sunnymeads 194 G3
Sutton 189 L6
Swan Bottom 124 B7
Swanbourne 61 J7
The Swillett 147 L9
Sydenham 129 H4
Syresham 24 B5
Taplow 178 C7
Tathall End 31 N4
Tatling End 169 K6
Tattenhoe 52 A3
Temple 176 C3
Terrick 110 C9
Terriers 143 K9
Tetchwick 77 M6
Thame 118 E4
Thornborough 49 M3
Thorney 190 B3
Thornton 39 N7
Three Households 156 B3
Tickford End 31 M1
Tiddington 116 C6
Tingewick 47 H4
Tinkers End 60 A7
Tittle Row 185 H1
Tongwell 31 J5
Totteridge 153 K1
Tottenhoe 86 D1
Touchen-end 185 K9
Towerage 151 N2
Tower Hill 137 P2
Towersey 119 K6
Town End 140 E2
Town's End 21 M5
Townsend 107 K7
Travellers Rest 86 A8
Tring 112 F3
Tringford 98 C7
Tring Wharf 98 F8
Turvey 17 K1
Turville 150 D7
Turville Heath 149 L7

Turweston 35 L4
Two Mile Ash 41 M2
Twyford 57 J9
Tylers Green 144 B9
Tyler's Hill 136 C4
Tyringham 20 E5
Up End 22 E6
Upper Dunsley 112 G5
Upper North Dean 142 C1
Upper Pollicott 92 C7
Upper Weald 41 J4
Upper Winchendon 93 M6
Upton 102 A9
Upton 188 C4
Upton Lea 180 C9
Uxbridge 182 C4
Uxbridge Moor 182 B4
Venus Hill 137 K4
Verney Junction 59 K7
Victoria Park 3 J4
The Village 193 M9
Waddesdon 79 M9
Walnut Tree 43 P8
Walter's Ash 142 C2
Walton 3 C7
Walton 43 M7
Walton Court 109 L1
Wardrobes 131 L4
Warners End 127 N1
Warrington 9 N7
Water Eaton 53 H5
Water End 115 P5
Watermead 95 P3
Waterperry 116 A4
Waterside 135 P6
Waterstock 116 D5
Water Stratford 46 C1
Watlington 148 A1
Wavendon 44 C6
Wavendon Gate 44 B5
Weedon 81 M7
Well End 165 M4
Wendover 123 J1
Wendover Dean 123 K7
West Bedfont 196 F6
Westbrook Hay 127 L6
Westbury 36 B8
Westcott 78 F9
West Drayton 190 D4
West Hyde 157 N7
Westlington 108 A5
Weston Turville 110 C4
Weston Underwood 15 H6
West Ruislip 171 J6
West Wycombe 142 A9
Wexham Street 180 E4
Whaddon 51 K2

Wharley End 32 G3
Wheelerend Common 151 K4
Whelpley Hill 126 F8
Whipsnade 87 J8
Whitchurch 81 J2
Whiteleaf 121 M8
White Waltham 184 E8
Whitfield 35 N1
Whittlebury 25 P1
Wicken 39 M1
Widmer End 143 L5
Widmoor 166 C6
Wigginton 113 H4
Wigginton Bottom 113 H6
Willen 31 K6
Willen Park 31 J7
Willowbank 182 C1
Wilstone 98 B6
Wilstone Green 98 B7
Wilton Park 155 M8
Winchmore Hill 145 H9
Windsor 188 A9
Wing 73 L7
Wingrave 83 J5
Winkfield 192 B9
Winkfield Place 192 E6
Winslow 60 D6
Witheridge Hill 172 A3
Woburn 55 J4
Woburn Sands 44 E8
Wolverton 29 J7
Wolverton Mill 29 J7
Wooburn 166 A5
Wooburn Common 166 D2
Wooburn Green 166 D2
Woodcock Hill 158 E4
Wood End 50 E3
Wood End 51 H9
Wood End 183 L9
Wood End Green 183 L8
Wood Green 36 F2
Woodham 78 C7
Woodlands 31 J4
Woodlands Park 184 F5
Woodrow 144 G6
Woolley Green 184 E2
Woolstone 43 J1
World's End 110 F7
Worminghall 104 E8
Wotton Underwood 92 A3
Woughton on the Green 43 K4
Wraysbury 194 G6
Wycombe Marsh 153 L6
Wymbush 41 P2
Yardley Gobion 18 A3
Yardley Hastings 9 H2
Yiewsley 190 E1

USING THE STREET INDEX

Street names are listed alphabetically. Each street name is followed by its postal town or area locality, the Postcode District, the page number, and the reference to the square in which the name is found.

Standard index entries are shown as follows:

Abbey Barn La *WYM* HP11 ....**153**   L7

Street names and selected addresses not shown on the map due to scale restrictions are shown in the index with an asterisk:

Abbey Sq *RBEDW* MK43 * **17**   J2

GENERAL ABBREVIATIONS

ACC....ACCESS	CTYD....COURTYARD	HLS....HILLS	MWY....MOTORWAY	SE....SOUTH EAST
ALY....ALLEY	CUTT....CUTTINGS	HO....HOUSE	N....NORTH	SER....SERVICE AREA
AP....APPROACH	CV....COVE	HOL....HOLLOW	NE....NORTH EAST	SH....SHORE
AR....ARCADE	CYN....CANYON	HOSP....HOSPITAL	NW....NORTH WEST	SHOP....SHOPPING
ASS....ASSOCIATION	DEPT....DEPARTMENT	HRB....HARBOUR	O/P....OVERPASS	SKWY....SKYWAY
AV....AVENUE	DL....DALE	HTH....HEATH	OFF....OFFICE	SMT....SUMMIT
BCH....BEACH	DM....DAM	HVN....HAVEN	ORCH....ORCHARD	SOC....SOCIETY
BLDS....BUILDINGS	DR....DRIVE	HWY....HIGHWAY	OV....OVAL	SP....SPUR
BND....BEND	DRO....DROVE	IMP....IMPERIAL	PAL....PALACE	SPR....SPRING
BNK....BANK	DRY....DRIVEWAY	IN....INLET	PAS....PASSAGE	SQ....SQUARE
BR....BRIDGE	DWGS....DWELLINGS	IND EST....INDUSTRIAL ESTATE	PAV....PAVILION	ST....STREET
BRK....BROOK	E....EAST	INF....INFIRMARY	PDE....PARADE	STN....STATION
BTM....BOTTOM	EMB....EMBANKMENT	INFO....INFORMATION	PH....PUBLIC HOUSE	STR....STREAM
BUS....BUSINESS	EMBY....EMBASSY	INT....INTERCHANGE	PK....PARK	STRD....STRAND
BVD....BOULEVARD	ESP....ESPLANADE	IS....ISLAND	PKWY....PARKWAY	SW....SOUTH WEST
BY....BYPASS	EST....ESTATE	JCT....JUNCTION	PL....PLACE	TDG....TRADING
CATH....CATHEDRAL	EX....EXCHANGE	JTY....JETTY	PLN....PLAIN	TER....TERRACE
CEM....CEMETERY	EXPY....EXPRESSWAY	KG....KING	PLNS....PLAINS	THWY....THROUGHWAY
CEN....CENTRE	EXT....EXTENSION	KNL....KNOLL	POL....POLICE STATION	TNL....TUNNEL
CFT....CROFT	F/O....FLYOVER	L....LAKE	PR....PRINCE	TOLL....TOLLWAY
CH....CHURCH	FC....FOOTBALL CLUB	LA....LANE	PREC....PRECINCT	TPK....TURNPIKE
CHA....CHASE	FK....FORK	LDG....LODGE	PREP....PREPARATORY	TR....TRACK
CHYD....CHURCHYARD	FLD....FIELD	LGT....LIGHT	PRIM....PRIMARY	TRL....TRAIL
CIR....CIRCLE	FLDS....FIELDS	LK....LOCK	PROM....PROMENADE	TWR....TOWER
CIRC....CIRCUS	FLS....FALLS	LKS....LAKES	PRS....PRINCESS	U/P....UNDERPASS
CL....CLOSE	FM....FARM	LNDG....LANDING	PT....PORT	UNI....UNIVERSITY
CLFS....CLIFFS	FT....FORT	LTL....LITTLE	PT....POINT	UPR....UPPER
CMP....CAMP	FWY....FREEWAY	LWR....LOWER	PTH....PATH	V....VALE
CNR....CORNER	FY....FERRY	MAG....MAGISTRATE	PZ....PIAZZA	VA....VALLEY
CO....COUNTY	GA....GATE	MAN....MANSIONS	QD....QUADRANT	VIAD....VIADUCT
COLL....COLLEGE	GAL....GALLERY	MD....MEAD	QU....QUEEN	VIL....VILLA
COM....COMMON	GDN....GARDEN	MDW....MEADOWS	QY....QUAY	VIS....VISTA
COMM....COMMISSION	GDNS....GARDENS	MEM....MEMORIAL	R....RIVER	VLG....VILLAGE
CON....CONVENT	GLD....GLADE	MKT....MARKET	RBT....ROUNDABOUT	VLS....VILLAS
COT....COTTAGE	GLN....GLEN	MKTS....MARKETS	RD....ROAD	VW....VIEW
COTS....COTTAGES	GN....GREEN	ML....MALL	RDG....RIDGE	W....WEST
CP....CAPE	GND....GROUND	MNR....MANOR	REP....REPUBLIC	WD....WOOD
CPS....COPSE	GRA....GRANGE	MS....MEWS	RES....RESERVOIR	WHF....WHARF
CR....CREEK	GRG....GARAGE	MSN....MISSION	RFC....RUGBY FOOTBALL CLUB	WK....WALK
CREM....CREMATORIUM	GT....GREAT	MT....MOUNT	RI....RISE	WKS....WALKS
CRS....CRESCENT	GTWY....GATEWAY	MTN....MOUNTAIN	RP....RAMP	WLS....WELLS
CSWY....CAUSEWAY	GV....GROVE	MTS....MOUNTAINS	RW....ROW	WY....WAY
CT....COURT	HGR....HIGHER	MUS....MUSEUM	S....SOUTH	YD....YARD
CTRL....CENTRAL	HL....HILL		SCH....SCHOOL	YHA....YOUTH HOSTEL
CTS....COURTS				

POSTCODE TOWNS AND AREA ABBREVIATIONS

AMS ....Amersham
AMSS ....Amersham south
ASHF ....Ashford (Surrey)
AYL ....Aylesbury
AYLS ....Aylesbury south
AYLW ....Aylesbury west
BDWL ....Bradwell
BEAC ....Beaconsfield
BERK ....Berkhamsted
BIC ....Bicester
BNEND ....Bourne End
BNFD ....Binfield
BOZ/IR/WOL ....Bozeat/Irchester/
Wollaston
BRACKY ....Brackley
BTCHLY ....Bletchley
BUCK/WIN ....Buckingham/Winslow
CAV/SC ....Caversham/
Sonning Common
CFSP/GDCR ....Chalfont St Peter/
Gerrards Cross
CHNR ....Chinnor
CMK ....Central Milton Keynes
CNH/GTH/TMA ....Crownhill/
Great Holm/
Two Mile Ash

CSHM ....Chesham
CSTG ....Chalfont St Giles
DBGH ....Denbigh
DEN/HRF ....Denham/Harefield
DTCH/LGLY ....Datchet/Langley
DUN/HR/TOD ....Dunstable/
Houghton Regis/
Toddington
DUN/WHIP ....Dunstable/
Whipsnade
EAG/OLD/WTN ....Eaglestone/
Oldbrook/
Woughton
EBED/NFELT ....East Bedfont/
North Feltham
EGH ....Egham
EMV/FZ.......Emerson Valley/Furzton
FELT ....Feltham
FLKWH ....Flackwell Heath
GTLIN ....Great Linford
GTMIS/PWD ....Great Missenden/
Prestwood
HADM ....Haddenham
HAZ/HG.......Hazlemere/Holmer Green
HEAD ....Headington
HEN ....Henley-on-Thames

HEST ....Heston
HGDN/ICK ....Hillingdon/Ickenham
HHNE ....Hemel Hempstead
northeast
HHS/BOV ....Hemel Hempstead
south/Bovingdon
HHW ....Hemel Hempstead west
HSLWW ....Hounslow west
HTHAIR ....Heathrow Airport
HWYN ....High Wycombe north
HWYW ....High Wycombe west
HYS/HAR ....Hayes/Harlington
IVER ....Iver
KCLGY ....Kings Langley
KID ....Kidlington
LBUZ ....Leighton Buzzard
LTN ....Luton
MDHD ....Maidenhead
MLW ....Marlow
MKV ....Milton Keynes Village
NPAG ....Newport Pagnell
NTHLT ....Northolt
NTHWD ....Northwood
NWDGN ....Norwood Green
OLN ....Olney
OXHEY ....Oxhey

PIN ....Pinner
PRRI ....Princes Risborough
RAYLNE/WEN ....Rural Aylesbury
north & east/
Wendover
RAYLW ....Rural Aylesbury west
RBEDW ....Rural Bedford west
RBICN ....Rural Bicester north
RBICS/W ....Rural Bicester
south & west
RKW/CH/CXG ....Rickmansworth/
Chorleywood/
Croxley Green
RMKN ....Rural Milton Keynes north
RMKS/WB ....Rural Milton Keynes
south/Woburn
RNHPTN ....Rural Northampton
RSLP ....Ruislip
SHEN ....Shenley
SKCH ....Stokenchurch
SL ....Slough
SLN ....Slough north
STA ....Staines
STAD ....Stadmapton
STALW/RED ....St Albans west/
Redbourn

STKPK ....Stockley Park
STSTR ....Stoney Stratford
STWL/WRAY ....Stanwell/
Wraysbury
THAME ....Thame
TOW ....Towcester
TRING ....Tring
UX/CGN ....Uxbridge/
Colham Green
WAR/TWY ....Wargrave/Twyford
WATW ....Watford west
WDR/YW ....West Drayton/
Yiewsley
WDSR ....Windsor
WEAT ....Water Eaton
WHLY ....Wheatley
WLLN ....Willen
WOLV ....Wolverton
WTLGN ....Watlington
WTR/OFPK ....Walnut Tree/
Old Farm Park
WYM ....Wycombe Marsh
YEAD ....Yeading

A

Abbey Barn La *WYM* HP11 ...**153** L7
Abbey Barn Rd *WYM* HP11 ...**153** M6
Abbey Cl *HYS/HAR* UB3 ....**191** P7
  PIN HA5...............................**171** P1
  SL SL1 ....**187** J1
Abbeydore Gv *MKV* MK10.......**43** M5
Abbey Ms *DUN/WHIP* LU6......**87** L2
Abbey Rd *AYLW* HP19 ....**95** K5
  BDWL MK13 ....**30** A9
  BNEND SL8 ....**165** M4
  BRACKY NN13 ....**24** C6
  EAG/OLD/WT MK6 ....**43** L7
Abbey Sq *RBEDW* MK43 * ...**17** J2
The Abbey *BNEND* SL8 * ...**165** M5
Abbey Wk
  GTMIS/PWD HP16 * **133** P5
  LBUZ LU7 ....**64** E6
Abbey Wy *BDWL* MK13 ....**30** A7
  MLW SL7.............................**176** D2
  OLN MK46 ....**14** E5
  WYM HP11...........................**153** J6
Abbot Rdg *RAYLW* HP18 ...**106** B9
Abbots Cl *BDWL* MK13 * ...**30** A9
Abbotsfield
  EAG/OLD/WT MK6 ....**43** H4
Abbot's Wk *WDSR* SL4...........**193** J1
Abbots Wy *HWYW* HP12 ...**152** D7
  PIN HA5...............................**121** K8
Abbotswood *PRRI* HP27 ...**132** C8
Abbotswood Wy
  HYS/HAR UB5.......................**191** P7
Abbotts Cl *AYL* HP20 ....**3** F2
  UX/CGN UB8.......................**182** D8
Abbotts Rd *AYL* HP20 ....**3** F2
Abbotts V *CSHM* HP5 ....**135** N1
Abbotts Wy
  RAYLNE/WEN HP22 ....**82** G4
  SL SL1.................................**187** P2
Abell Gdns *MDHD* SL6...........**176** C7
Abercorn Gv *RSLP* HA4...........**171** K2
Abercromby Av *HWYW* HP12......**4** A5
Aberdeen Av *SL* SL1...............**187** L1
Aberdeen Cl *BTCHLY* MK3.......**52** F1
Abingdon Cl *HGDN/ICK* UB10...**182** F4
  THAME OX9 ....**118** D4
Abney Court Dr *BNEND* SL8......**165** M7
Abraham Cl *WLLN* MK15.......**32** D4
Abrahams Rd *HEN* RG9 ....**173** N5
Abstacle Hl *TRING* HP23 ...**112** D5
Acacia Av *RSLP* HA4...............**171** N6
  STWL/WRAY TW19 ....**194** G3
  WDR/YW UB7.......................**190** F1
  YEAD UB4.............................**183** M9
Acacia Cl *BRACKY* NN13 ......**35** H5
  CSHM HP5...........................**135** L3
  LBUZ LU7.............................**75** H3
Acacia Gv *BERK* HP4...............**126** D2
Acacia Ms *WDR/YW* UB7...........**190** D7
Accommodation La
  WDR/YW UB7.......................**190** C7
Ackerman Cl *BUCK/WIN* MK18...**48** B9
Acol Crs *RSLP* HA4...............**183** P1
Acorn Cl *HWYN* HP15 ....**153** K3
Acorn Gv *HYS/HAR* UB3.........**191** M8
Acorn Rd *HYS/HAR* UB3 ...**191** M8
Acorn Wk *CMK* MK9 * **7** F2
Acrefield Rd *CFSP/GDCR* SL9 ...**168** F2
Acre Pas *WDSR* SL4...............**187** P9
Acres End *AMS* HP7...............**146** A3
The Acres *HWYN* HP13.............**4** B1
The Acre *MLW* SL7.................**164** F7
Acre Wy *NTHWD* HA6.............**158** D8
Adam Cl *HWYN* HP13...............**5** K3
  SL SL1.................................**187** L2
Adam Ct *HEN* RG9.................**173** N2
Adams Bottom *LBUZ* LU7.......**64** E9
Adams Cl *BUCK/WIN* MK18......**48** A8
Adams Ct *EAG/OLD/WT* MK6...**43** J2
Adams Wy *TRING* HP23.........**112** F1
Adastral Av *LBUZ* LU7...........**75** H4
Addington Cl *WDSR* SL4.......**193** L2

Addington Rd *BUCK/WIN* MK18...**48** B2
Addison Cl *IVER* SL0...............**189** N1
  NTHWD HA6.......................**159** N8
Addison Rd *BUCK/WIN* MK18...**58** B8
  CSHM HP5...........................**135** N2
Addison Wy *NTHWD* HA6.......**159** N8
  YEAD UB4.............................**183** N9
Adelaide Cl *SL* SL1...............**187** L3
Adelaide Rd *HWYN* HP15.......**153** K2
  SL SL1.................................**188** B9
Adelaide Sq *WDSR* SL4.........**193** P1
Adelphi Crs *YEAD* UB4...........**183** L6
Adelphi Gdns *SL* SL1...........**188** A3
Adelphi St *CMK* MK9...............**7** F5
Adelphi Wy *YEAD* UB4...........**183** M6
Adhara Rd *NTHWD* HA6.........**159** N5
Adkins Cl *AYLW* HP19.............**95** H4
Admiral Wy *BERK* HP4...........**114** B8
Adrian Cl *DEN/HRF* UB9 ...**182** D3
Adrians Wk *SLN* SL2...............**188** B2
Adstock Ms *CFSP/GDCR* SL9 * ...**156** F8
Adwell Sq *HEN* RG9...............**173** P6
Agars Pl *DTCH/LGLY* SL3.......**188** C7
Aidan Cl *AYLS* HP21...............**110** A2
Ailward Rd *AYLW* HP19.............**95** J5
Aikwyns Acre *RBEDW* MK43...**13** K8
Ainsdale Cl *BTCHLY* MK3.......**52** D2
Aintree Cl *DTCH/LGLY* SL3......**189** N9
  SL SL1.................................**188** F5
  UX/CGN UB8.......................**183** H9
Airport Wy *STWL/WRAY* TW19...**196** A3
Ajax Av *SL* SL1...............**187** M1
Akeman St *TRING* HP23.........**112** E3
Akerman Cl *WOLV* MK12.........**29** K8
Akister Cl *BUCK/WIN* MK18......**48** C3
Alabama Cir *WYM* HP11.........**153** H6
Alabama Dr *WYM* HP11.........**153** H6
Alandale Dr *PIN* HA5.............**159** P6
Alan Wy *DTCH/LGLY* SL3.......**180** C9
Alaska St *WYM* HP11.............**153** H6
Albain Crs *ASHF* TW15.........**196** E8
Albany Cl *HGDN/ICK* UB10...**182** D5
Albany Ga *CSHM* HP5...........**135** M3
Albany Pk *DTCH/LGLY* SL3......**189** M8
Albany Pl *AYLW* HP19.............**95** J5
Albany Rd *LBUZ* LU7...............**74** F3
  WDSR SL4...........................**193** N1
Albany Ter *TRING* HP23 * ...**98** F9
Albert Cl *DTCH/LGLY* SL3.......**194** D2
Albert Ct *DUN/WHIP* LU6.......**87** L1
Albert Pl *WDSR* SL4...............**187** L6
Albert Rd *CSHM* HP5...........**135** N4
  HEN RG9.............................**174** A7
  HYS/HAR UB3.......................**191** L4
  WDR/YW UB7.......................**190** D7
  WDSR SL4...........................**194** A3
Albert St *AYL* HP20...................**3** H5
  MDHD SL6...........................**177** M9
  SL SL1.................................**188** B4
  TRING HP23.......................**112** E3
  WDSR SL4...........................**193** N1
  WEAT MK2.............................**53** J5
Albion Cl *SLN* SL2...............**188** C2
Albion Crs *CSTG* HP8.............**156** D3
Albion Rd *SL* SL1...................**193** L1
Albion Rd *CSTG* HP8...........**156** H7
  HWYW HP12 ....**152** C5
  HYS/HAR UB3.......................**183** J9
  LBUZ LU7.............................**99** H2
Albion St *AYLS* HP21...............**3** F5
Aldborough La
  DTCH/LGLY SL3 ....**168** G9

Alderbury Rd
  DTCH/LGLY SL3 ....**189** H3
Alderbury Rd West
  DTCH/LGLY SL3 ....**189** H3
Alder Cl *SL* SL1...................**187** K2
Aldergill *BDWL* MK13.............**30** C8
Alderley Ct *BERK* HP4...........**126** D2
Aldermead *WOLV* MK12.........**29** M9
Alderney Pl *SHEN* MK5...........**41** P8
Alder Rd *DEN/HRF* UB9.........**182** B2
  IVER SL0.............................**181** L5
Alderson Cl *AYLW* HP19 ....**95** J5
The Alders *DEN/HRF* UB9 * ...**182** C2
Alderton Dr *BERK* HP4...........**100** C7
Aldin Av North *SL* SL1...........**188** C3
Aldin Av South *SL* SL1...........**188** C3
Aldrich Dr *WLLN* MK15...........**31** L6
Aldridge Rd *SLN* SL2...............**179** L7
Aldwick Dr *MDHD* SL6...........**185** K1
Aldwycks Cl *SHEN* MK5...........**41** P6
Alexander Rd *AYL* HP20 ....**2** D3
Alexander St *CSHM* HP5.......**135** N3
Alexandra Dr *NPAG* MK16.......**31** J1
Alexandra Rd *HWYN* HP13...**153** L5
  MDHD SL6...........................**177** K8
  SL SL1.................................**188** B4
  UX/CGN UB8.......................**182** D6
  WDSR SL4...........................**193** P1
Alford Rd *HWYW* HP12...........**152** C7
Alham Rd *AYLS* HP21...............**95** L9
Alice Cl *HAZ/HG* HP15...........**144** A4
Alice La *SL* SL1...................**187** L8
Alladale Pl *WOLV* MK12...........**29** M9
Allanson Rd *MLW* SL7...........**164** A3
Allcot Cl *EBED/NFELT* TW14 ...**197** M7
Allenby Rd *MDHD* SL6...........**177** H9
Allen Dr *SKCH* HP14...............**149** J4
Alleyns La *BRACKY* NN13.......**34** F5
Allerds Rd *SLN* SL2...............**179** J5
Allerford Ct *EMV/FZ* MK4.......**42** C8
Alleyns La *MDHD* SL6...........**165** K9
Allington Av *WLLN* MK15.......**31** N2
Allison Ct *WLLN* MK15...........**31** J5
Allonby Dr *RSLP* HA4...........**171** H5
Allonby Wy *AYLS* HP21...........**96** B8
All Saints Av *MDHD* SL6.......**176** B2
All Saints Vw *SHEN* MK5.......**42** B4
Allyn Cl *HWYN* HP13...............**5** K5
Alma Rd *BERK* HP4...............**114** A8
  CSHM HP5...........................**135** N2
  WDSR SL4...........................**193** J1
Almond Av *HGDN/ICK* UB10...**171** H8
  WDR/YW UB7.......................**190** C4
Almond Cl *FELT* TW13...........**197** N7
  HYS/HAR UB3.......................**191** L1
  RSLP HA4.............................**171** M8
  WDSR SL4...........................**193** M1
Almond Rd *LBUZ* LU7...........**74** C1
  SL SL1.................................**178** F6
Almond Wk *HAZ/HG* HP15 ...**143** P8
Almons Wy *SLN* SL2...............**180** D8
Alnwick Dr *TRING* HP23.........**85** M9
Alpha Est *HYS/HAR* UB3 * ...**191** L3
Alpha Rd *HGDN/ICK* UB10...**183** H7
Alpha St North *SL* SL1.........**188** B4
Alpha St South *SL* SL1.........**188** B4
Alpine Cl *MDHD* SL6...........**185** N1
Alpine Cft *SHEN* MK5...............**42** A8
Alscot La *PRRI* HP27...............**121** J8
Alston Dr *BDWL* MK13.............**41** N1
Alstonefield *MDHD* SL6 * ...**185** H2
Alston Gdns *MDHD* SL6.......**177** L8
Altair Wy *NTHWD* HA6...........**159** L5
Althorne Crs *BDWL* MK13.......**30** A7
Altmore *MDHD* SL6...............**184** E3
Altona Rd *FLKWH* HP10.......**154** A7
Altona Wy *SL* SL1...................**179** N9
Alton Ga *EMV/FZ* MK4.............**42** B8
Altwood Bailey *MDHD* SL6...**185** H1
Altwood Cl *MDHD* SL6...........**185** H2
  SL SL1.................................**187** N1
Altwood Dr *MDHD* SL6.........**185** H2
Altwood Rd *MDHD* SL6.........**184** G2
Alverton *GTLIN* MK14.............**30** F5
Alvista Av *MDHD* SL6...........**178** D9

Alwin Cl *AYLS* HP21...............**109** L2
Alwins Fld *LBUZ* LU7...............**74** B1
Alwyn Rd *MDHD* SL6.............**177** H8
Alyngton *BERK* HP4...............**114** A7
Alyson Ct *MDHD* SL6 * **177** J9
Amanda Ct *DTCH/LGLY* SL3...**188** F4
Ambergate *MKV* MK10...........**31** N9
Ambergate Wy *MDHD* SL6...**185** H3
Amberley Cl *MDHD* SL6.........**176** A5
Amberley Pl *WDSR* SL4...........**187** P9
Amberley Rd *RNHPTN* NN7 ...**12** C1
  SLN SL2...............................**179** J8
Amberley Wk
  EMV/FZ MK4.........................**51** N2
Amberley Wy
  HGDN/ICK UB10...............**182** G6
Ambers Wy *BUCK/WIN* MK18...**58** E1
Ambleside *AYLS* HP21...........**110** B1
Ambleside Dr
  EBED/NFELT TW14 ....**197** M7
Ambridge Gv
  EAG/OLD/WT MK6...............**43** J5
Ambrose Cl *WLLN* MK15.........**43** J2
Amelias La *CMK* MK9...............**7** J1
Amerden Cl *MDHD* SL6.........**178** B9
Amerden La *MDHD* SL6.........**186** B5
Amerden Wy *SL* SL1...............**187** L3
Amersham Hl *HWYN* HP13.......**5** J1
Amersham Hill Dr *HWYN* HP13...**5** K2
Amersham Hill Gdns
  HWYN HP13.........................**5** J2
Amersham Pl *AMS* HP7...........**147** J6
Amersham Rd *AMS* HP6.........**135** M8
  BEAC HP9...........................**145** P8
  BEAC HP9...........................**155** L5
  CFSP/GDCR SL9 ....**169** J2
  CSTG HP8...........................**146** D8
  HAZ/HG HP15.......................**143** L9
  HWYN HP13.........................**5** K1
Amersham Wy *AMS* HP6.......**146** G3
Amos Ct *BDWL* MK13.............**30** B9
Ampleforth *MKV* MK10...........**43** M5
Amy La *CSHM* HP5...............**135** M5
Ancastle Gn *HEN* RG9...........**173** N7
Ancell Rd *STSTR* MK11.........**43** J5
Anchor La *AYL* HP20...............**2** C4
Ancona Gdns *SHEN* MK5.........**41** P9
Andermans *WDSR* SL4...........**187** H9
Andersen Ga *EMV/FZ* MK4.......**52** A4
Anderson Cl *DEN/HRF* UB9...**158** A8
  SKCH HP14.........................**140** B7
Anding Cl *WLLN* MK15...........**15** L3
Andover Cl
  EBED/NFELT TW14 ....**197** M7
  UX/CGN UB8.......................**182** B5
Andrewes Cft *GTLIN* MK14.......**30** F5
Andrew Hill La *SLN* SL2.........**167** N6
Andrews Wy *MLW* SL7...........**164** C1
  RAYLW HP18.......................**95** J8
Anershall *RAYLNE/WEN* HP22...**83** H5
Angel Cl *WLLN* MK15...............**30** G6
Angelica Cl *WDR/YW* UB7.......**190** A2
Angelica Ct *WTR/OFPK* MK7...**43** N7
Angel La *DTCH/LGLY* SL3.......**188** C4
Angle Cl *HGDN/ICK* UB10...**182** G4
Anglefield Rd *BERK* HP4.......**126** C1
Anglesey Cl *ASHF* TW15.......**196** D5
Anglesey Ct
  CNH/GTH/TM MK8...............**41** P4
Angood Ct *PRRI* HP27...........**131** J1
Angora Cl *SHEN* MK5.............**42** A3
Angstrom Cl *EAG/OLD/WT* MK6...**43** J2
Angus Dr *BTCHLY* MK3...........**52** F1
Angus Rd *AYLW* HP19.............**95** J4
Annandale Gv
  HGDN/ICK UB10.................**171** J8
Anne Cl *MDHD* SL6...............**177** L6
Annes Gv *GTLIN* MK14.............**30** F4
Annesley Rd *NPAG* MK16.......**31** N4
Annie Brookes Cl *STA* TW18...**195** M9
Anns Cl *AYLS* HP21...............**110** A2
Anscutf Rd *SLN* SL2...............**179** L6
Anslow Gdns *IVER* SL0.........**181** M5
Anson Cl *AYLS* HP21...........**109** N2
  HHW HP1.............................**127** H6
Anson Rd *WOLV* MK12...........**29** L7

Anson Wk *NTHWD* HA6.........**159** J4
Anstey Brook
  RAYLNE/WEN HP22...........**110** G3
Anstey Cl *RAYLW* HP18...........**79** M9
Anthony St *SL* SL1.................**187** H1
Anthony Wy *SL* SL1...............**187** H1
Anthus Ms *NTHWD* HA6.......**159** K7
Anton Wy *AYLS* HP21...........**109** L3
Anvil Cl *HHS/BOV* HP3...........**137** K1
Anxey Wy *HADM* HP17...........**107** K8
Aplin Rd *AYLS* HP21...............**96** C9
Apollo Av *NTHWD* HA6.........**159** M5
Apollo Cl *DUN/HR/TOD* LU5...**87** M1
Appenine Wy *LBUZ* LU7...........**75** H1
Appleacres *RMKS/WB* MK17...**63** K2
Appleby Gdns *DUN/WHIP* LU6...**87** K1
  EBED/NFELT TW14 * **197** M2
Appleby Heath *WEAT* MK2.......**53** K4
Apple Cottages
  HHS/BOV HP3.......................**127** J9
Applecroft *BERK* HP4...........**114** A8
  MDHD SL6...........................**185** J4
  RMKS/WB MK17.................**52** D7
Appledore Av *RSLP* HA4.......**171** P8
Applefield *AMSS* HP7.............**146** E5
Appleton Cl *AMSS* HP7.........**146** D4
Appleton Ms *EMV/FZ* MK4.......**42** B9
Apple Tree Av *WDR/YW* UB7...**182** F9
Apple Tree Cl *LBUZ* LU7...........**74** B5
Appletree Dell
  RKW/CH/CXG WD3 * **147** P6
Appletree La *DTCH/LGLY* SL3...**188** C4
Appletree Wk *CSHM* HP5.......**135** P7
Applewick La *HWYW* HP12.......**152** C2
Applewood Cl
  HGDN/ICK UB10.................**170** E9
Appleyard Pl
  EAG/OLD/WT MK6...............**6** E5
Approach Rd *MDHD* SL6.......**178** C9
The Approach
  CNH/GTH/TM MK8...............**41** M1
April Cl *FELT* TW13...............**197** N9
Aquarius Wy *NTHWD* HA6.......**159** N5
Aquila Rd *LBUZ* LU7...............**75** H1
Arborfield Cl *SL* SL1...............**188** A4
Arbour Vw *AMSS* HP7...........**146** D3
Arbroath Cl *BTCHLY* MK3.......**42** F9
Arbroath Gn *OXHEY* WD19 ...**159** N3
Arbrook Av *BDWL* MK13...........**6** C1
The Arcade *BEAC* HP9 * **5** J4
  MDHD SL6 * **177** P1
Archdale *WYM* HP11...............**4** D6
Archer Cl *MDHD* SL6.............**177** K8
Archer Dr *AYL* HP20...............**3** J1
Archers Wy *SKCH* HP14.........**151** K5
Archery Cl *MDHD* SL6...........**187** N9
The Arches *WDSR* SL4 * ...**187** N9
Archford Cft *EMV/FZ* MK4.......**42** C9
Archive Cl
  RAYLNE/WEN HP22...........**111** K1
Archive Rd
  RAYLNE/WEN HP22...........**111** K1
Arch Wy *HWYN* HP13...............**5** P5
Archwary *PRRI* HP27...........**132** B8
Arden Cl *HHS/BOV* HP3.........**137** J1
Ardenham La *AYLW* HP19.........**2** B5
Ardenham St *AYLW* HP19.........**2** B5
Arden Mhor *PIN* HA5...............**171** G2
Ardley Cl *DUN/WHIP* LU6...........**87** L3
Ardrossan Cl *SLN* SL2...........**179** N7
Ardross Av *NTHWD* HA6.......**159** L5
Ardwell La *WOLV* MK12...........**29** M8
Ardys Ct *SHEN* MK5.............**42** B5
The Arena *STKPK* UB11 * ...**191** J2
Argosy La *STWL/WRAY* TW19...**196** D6
Argyle Av *AYLW* HP19.............**95** J5
Argyll Av *SL* SL1...................**187** L1
Ariel Wy *HSLWW* TW4...........**197** L2
Aries Ct *LBUZ* LU7.................**74** C1
Aris Wy *BUCK/WIN* MK18...**48** B5
Arizona St *WYM* HP11...........**153** H6
Arkley Ct *MDHD* SL6.............**185** H3
Arkwright Rd
  DTCH/LGLY SL3 ....**195** N1
Arlington Cl *MDHD* SL6.........**176** F8
Arlington Ct *EMV/FZ* MK4.......**42** B9
  HYS/HAR UB3.......................**191** K6

Arlington Dr *RSLP* HA4 ....171 K4
Arlott Crs *EAG/OLD/WT* MK6 ....7 H7
Armadale Rd
 EBED/NFELT TW14 ....197 N4
Armourer Dr *GTLIN* MK14 ....30 F7
Armstrong Cl
 CNH/GTH/TM MK8 ....41 N6
 RSLP HA4 ....171 N4
Arncliffe Dr *BDWL* MK13 ....30 C8
Arncott Rd *RBICS/W* OX25 ....76 D9
Arncott Wy *HWYW* HP19 ....95 H7
Arncott Wood Rd
 RBICS/W OX25 ....89 P1
Arne La *WTR/OFPK* MK7 ....44 B7
Arnison Av *HWYW* HP13 ....153 K2
Arnold Cl *RAYLNE/WEN* HP22 .....110 C3
Arnold Ct *AYLS* HP21 ....95 P9
Arnold Wy *THAME* OX9 ....118 C6
Arnott's Yd *RAYLW* HP18 ....106 B8
Arrewig La *TRING* HP23 ....124 A4
Arrow Pl *WEAT* MK2 ....53 K7
Arthur Rd *SL* SL1 ....187 P3
 WDSR SL4 ....187 N9
Artichoke Dell
 RKW/CH/CXG WD3 * 147 N9
Arundel Cl *MDHD* SL6 ....176 G8
Arundel Ct *DTCH/LGLY* SL3 ....188 F5
Arundel Gn *AYL* HP20 ....95 P4
Arundel Gv *BTCHLY* MK3 ....52 B5
Arundel Rd *HWYW* HP12 ....152 B5
 UX/CGN UB8 ....182 A5
Ascot Cl *BDWL* MK13 ....42 A1
Ascot Pl *BTCHLY* MK3 ....52 D5
 MDHD SL6 ....185 M8
Ascott Ct *AYL* HP20 ....3 F2
 PIN HA5 * 171 N2
Ashbourne Sq *NTHWD* HA6 ....159 L6
Ashbourne End *AYLS* HP21 ....109 L2
Ashbrook Rd *MDHD* SL6 ....185 J4
Ashburn Ham Cl *EMV/FZ* MK4 ......52 C2
Ashburnham Cl *LBUZ* LU7 ....74 C3
 OXHEY WD19 * 159 N3
Ashburnham Crs *LBUZ* LU7 ....74 C3
Ashburnham Dr
 OXHEY WD19 ....159 N5
Ashburton Rd *RSLP* HA4 ....171 N7
Ashby Dr *HGDN/ICK* UB10 ....171 H7
Ashby *EAG/OLD/WT* MK6 ....7 H9
Ashby Rd *BDWL* MK13 ....113 P7
Ashby Wy *WDR/YW* UB7 ....190 C8
Ash Cl *AYL* HP20 ....3 J1
 DEN/HRF UB9 ....158 D9
 DTCH/LGLY SL3 ....188 D2
 SKCH HP14 ....142 B3
Ashcroft Ct *SL* SL1 ....178 F5
Ashcroft Dr *DEN/HRF* UB9 ....169 P4
Ashcroft Rd *MDHD* SL6 ....177 J3
Ashdale Cl
 STWL/WRAY TW19 ....196 E8
Ashdown *MDHD* SL6 ....177 N5
Ashdown Ct *GTLIN* MK14 ....30 C9
Ashdown Rd
 HGDN/ICK UB10 ....182 G6
 HWYW HP13 ....153 N2
Ashdown Wy *AMS* HP6 ....145 P1
Ashenden Wk *SL* SL2 ....167 P9
Ashendon Rd *RAYLW* HP18 ....142 B3
Asheridge Rd *CSHM* HP5 ....135 K1
Ashfield Av *FELT* TW13 ....197 N7
Ashfield Cl *GTLIN* MK14 ....30 D5
Ashfield La *HAZ/HG* HP15 ....143 P9
Ashfield Rd *WEAT* MK2 ....53 J4
Ashfield Rd *HAZ/HG* HP15 ....143 N9
Ashford Ms *RAYLW* HP18 ....104 D1
Ashford Rd *CSHM* HP5 ....135 P2
Ashford Wy *HAZ/HG* HP15 ....143 P9
Ashford Crs *ASHF* TW15 ....196 A4
 CNH/GTH/TM MK8 ....41 M6
Ashford La *MDHD* SL6 ....186 F5
 IVER SLO 181 L4
Ash Furlong La *BRACKY* NN13 .....35 P3
Ash Gn *DEN/HRF* UB9 ....182 B2
Ash Gv *AMS* HP6 ....135 J5
 AYLS HP21 ....95 H7
 DBGH MK1 ....43 K9
 DEN/HRF UB9 ....158 C8
 EBED/NFELT TW14 ....197 L7
 HYS/HAR UB3 ....191 K1
 LBUZ LU7 ....74 E1
 SLN SL2 ....167 L6
 WDR/YW UB7 ....190 F1
Ashgrove *BUCK/WIN* MK18 ....58 B8
Ashgrove Gdns
 RAYLNE/WEN HP22 ....80 G1
Ash Hill Rd *NPAG* MK16 ....30 C1
Ash La *WDSR* SL4 ....15 L4
Ashlea Cl *CFSP/GDCR* SL9 ....156 C9
Ashley Cl *PUR* SL5 ....159 P9
Ashley Dr *FLKWH* HP10 ....144 K9
Ashley Green Rd *CSHM* HP5 ....125 P9
Ashley Hill Pl
 WAR/TWY RC10 ....175 H9
Ashley Pk *MDHD* SL6 ....177 P6
Ashley Rd *UX/CGN* UB8 ....182 B5
Ashley Rw *AYL* HP20 ....3 J2
Ashleys *RKW/CH/CXG* WD3 ....147 P9
Ashling Cl *LBUZ* LU7 ....74 C2
Ashlyns Ct *BERK* HP4 ....126 D2
Ashlyns Rd *BERK* HP4 ....126 D2
Ash Mead *DEN/HRF* UB9 ....170 A7
Ashmead La *DEN/HRF* UB9 ....170 A7
Ashmead Rd
 EBED/NFELT TW14 ....197 N7
Ashotts La *CHNR* OX39 ....129 M6
Ashpole Furlong *SHEN* MK5 ....42 B5
Ashridge *CHNR* OX39 ....129 N6
Ashridge Cl *BTCHLY* MK3 ....52 D4
 HHS/BOV HP3 ....136 J1
Ashridge La *CSHM* HP5 ....136 F4
Ashridge Ri *BERK* HP4 ....114 B9

Ash Rd *HWYW* HP12 ....152 C6
 PRRI HP27 ....131 K1
 TRING HP23 ....112 D2
Ashton Pl *MDHD* SL6 ....177 M9
Ashton Rd *RNHPTN* NN7 ....12 E6
Ashton Sq *HEAD* OX3 ....159 L7
Ash V *RKW/CH/CXG* WD3 ....157 M5
Ashwells Manor Dr
 FLKWH HP10 ....153 P2
Ashwells St *LBUZ* LU7 ....74 E1
Ashwells Wy *CSTG* HP8 ....156 C2
Ashwin Cl *BRACKY* NN13 ....34 G3
Ashwood *BDWL* MK13 ....30 A6
Ashwood Av *UX/CGN* UB8 ....182 C9
Ashwood Dr *CSHM* HP5 ....135 M3
Ashwood Gdns
 HYS/HAR UB3 ....191 M5
Askett La *PRRI* HP27 ....121 M6
Askew Rd *NTHWD* HA6 ....159 K2
Aspen Cl *AYL* HP21 ....3 J1
 SLN SL2 ....179 M8
 STA TW18 ....195 P9
 WDR/YW UB7 ....190 F2
Aspen Wy *FELT* TW13 ....197 P8
Asplands Ct *RMKS/WB* MK17 ....44 F8
Aspley Hl *RMKS/WB* MK17 ....44 G8
Aspley La *RMKS/WB* MK17 ....15 L3
Aspreys *OLN* MK46 ....15 L3
Assheton Rd *BEAC* HP9 ....155 H6
Astletthorpe
 CNH/GTH/TM MK8 ....41 L7
Astley Rd *THAME* OX9 ....118 F4
Aston Abbotts Rd *LBUZ* LU7 ....72 C8
 RAYLNE/WEN HP22 ....81 N7
Aston Clinton Rd
 RAYLNE/WEN HP22 ....96 E9
Aston Ct *AYLW* HP19 ....95 J4
 SHEN MK5 ....42 B7
Aston Ferry La *HEN* RC9 ....174 E3
Aston Gdns *WTLGN* OX49 ....129 H9
Aston Hl *WTLGN* OX49 ....139 K4
Aston La *HEN* RC9 ....174 E5
Aston Md *WDSR* SL4 ....187 J3
Aston Rd *HADM* HP17 ....107 L9
Astons Rd *NTHWD* HA6 ....159 J3
Astor Cl *MDHD* SL6 ....185 P1
Astronomy Wy *AYLW* HP19 ....95 J7
Astrope La *TRING* HP23 ....97 N7
Astwood Rd *RBEDW* MK43 ....23 N7
Athena Pl *NTHWD* HA6 ....159 M8
Atherstone Ct
 CNH/GTH/TM MK8 ....41 L7
Atherton Cl
 STWL/WRAY TW19 ....196 D5
Athlone Cl *MDHD* SL6 ....177 L7
Athol Cl *PIN* HA5 ....171 H4
Athol Gdns *PIN* HA5 ....159 P8
Athol Wy *HGDN/ICK* UB10 ....182 G6
Atkins Cl *BDWL* MK13 ....42 B1
Atkinson Cl *HEAD* OX3 ....102 A9
Atria Rd *NTHWD* HA6 ....159 N5
Atterbrook *BDWL* MK13 ....41 N9
Atterbury Av *LBUZ* LU7 ....74 F1
Attingham Hl
 CNH/GTH/TM MK8 ....41 P4
Attle Cl *HGDN/ICK* UB10 ....182 H1
Attlee Cl *NTHLT* UB5 * 183 P2
Attlee Rd *YEAD* UB4 ....183 N1
Atwell Cl *CNH/GTH/TM* MK8 ....41 N5
Aubreys Rd *HHW* HP1 ....127 L7
Auckland Cl *MDHD* SL6 ....177 P8
Auckland Pk *DBGH* MK1 ....43 K9
Auckland Rd *HAZ/HG* HP15 ....153 L9
Audience La *NPAG* MK16 ....20 G9
Audley Dr *MDHD* SL6 ....185 H1
Audley Md *BDWL* MK13 ....42 H1
Audley Rd *BDWL* MK13 ....42 H1
August End *DTCH/LGLY* SL3 ....180 C9
Augustine La *DTCH/LGLY* SL3 ......195 M2
Augustus Rd *STSTR* MK11 ....28 F9
Auriol Dr *HGDN/ICK* UB10 ....183 H2
Austen Av *OLN* MK46 ....15 M6
Austen Pl *AYLW* HP19 ....95 J5
Austenway *CFSP/GDCR* SL9 ....168 G1
Austenwood Cl
 CFSP/GDCR SL9 ....156 E9
Austenwood La
 CFSP/GDCR SL9 ....156 F9
Austin Rd *HYS/HAR* UB3 ....191 M3
Austinsgate *MDHD* SL6 ....176 F8
Austin's La *HGDN/ICK* UB10 ....171 K9
Austins Pl *HOW* NN12 ....25 L9
Australia Av *MDHD* SL6 ....177 M8
Australia Rd *SL* SL1 ....188 D3
Austwick La *EMV/FZ* MK4 ....52 B1
Auton Pl *HEN* RC9 ....173 P9
Autumn Cl *AYLW* HP19 ....95 J4
 SL SL1 ....187 N1
Autumn Wk *MDHD* SL6 ....184 C1
Auxiliaries Wy *DEN/HRF* UB9 ....84 P4
Avalon Rd *BNEND* SL8 ....165 P4
Avebury Cl *SL* SL1 ....177 M8
Avebury Bvd *CMK* MK9 ....6 C2
Aveling Rd *HWYW* HP13 ....5 J4
Avenue Bernard
 BRACKY NN13 ....34 G4
 WDR/YW UB7 ....190 D4
Avenue Crs *HEST* TW5 ....190 A1
Avenue Dr *DTCH/LGLY* SL3 ....181 H8
Avenue Gdns *HEST* TW5 ....191 N8
Avenue Rd *BUCK/WIN* MK18 ....38 E7
 BUCK/WIN MK18 ....60 B6
 FELT TW13 ....197 M9
 MDHD SL6 ....185 M9
The Avenue *AMSS* HP7 ....145 N2
 BNEND SL8 ....165 M5
 CHNR OX39 ....129 N6
 DTCH/LGLY SL3 ....188 D3
 DUN/WHIP LU6 ....86 G1
 HEST TW5 ....191 N9
 HGDN/ICK UB10 ....170 D9
 HHW HP1 ....127 N1

MDHD SL6 ....177 P6
NTHWD HA6 ....159 J6
PRRI HP27 ....121 L9
RAYLW HP18 ....104 E9
SLN SL2 ....167 M9
STWL/WRAY TW19 ....194 D3
UX/CGN UB8 ....182 D7
WDSR SL4 ....187 J5
SL SL1 ....178 C6
Averil Ct SL SL1 ....178 C6
Avery Av HWYW HP13 ....142 D9
Avington CNH/GTH/TM MK8 ....41 N3
Avior Dr NTHWD HA6 ....159 N4
Avocet Wy AYL HP20 ....95 N4
Avon Gv NPAG MK16 ....31 N3
 SL SL1 ....187 J1
Avondale MDHD SL6 ....185 H1
Avondale Av HYS/HAR UB3 ....191 N2
Avondale Rd ASHF TW15 ....196 D9
Avon Gv BTCHLY MK3 ....52 E5
Avro Wy AYL HP20 ....95 N4
Axtell Gn NPAG MK16 ....31 J6
Aycliffe Crs SL SL1 ....179 M9
Aylards Ri HADM HP17 ....107 M6
Aylesbury Crs SL SL1 ....179 P9
Aylesbury Rd BEAC HP9 ....155 J9
Aylesbury Ring HADM HP17 ....107 M8
 RAYLNE/WEN HP22 ....81 J5
 RAYLW HP18 ....79 N8
Aylesbury Rd
 GTMIS/PWD HP16 ....133 N3
 HADM HP17 ....107 H7
 HADM HP17 ....121 P2
 LBUZ LU7 ....73 L8
 PRRI HP27 ....121 L8
 RAYLNE/WEN HP22 ....96 B4
 RAYLNE/WEN HP22 ....106 C4
 RAYLW HP18 ....106 A5
 THAME OX9 ....118 D4
 TRING HP23 ....112 C3
Aylesbury St WEAT MK2 ....53 L3
 WOLV MK12 ....29 L7
Aylesbury St West
 WOLV MK12 ....29 K7
Aylesford Gv MKV MK10 ....43 N3
Ayles Rd YEAD UB4 ....183 P6
Ayleswater AYLW HP19 ....95 N5
Aylesworth Av SLN SL2 ....179 N1
Aylesworth Sp WDSR SL4 ....194 C6
Aylsham Dr HGDN/ICK UB10 ....171 J7
Aylward Gdns CSHM HP5 ....135 L3
Aynho Ct CNH/GTH/TM MK8 ....41 P4
Ayres Cl AYLS HP21 ....95 K9
Ayrshire Cl AYLW HP19 ....95 J4
Ayr Wy BTCHLY MK3 ....52 E1
Aysgarth Pk MDHD SL6 ....185 H6
Azalea Cl HAZ/HG HP15 ....143 N8
Azalea Wk PIN HA5 ....171 H4
Azalea Wy DTCH/LGLY SL3 ....180 G9

B

Babington Cl MKV MK10 ....43 N1
Babington Rd
 RAYLNE/WEN HP22 ....111 K8
Baccara Gv WEAT MK2 ....53 J4
Bachelors Acre WDSR SL4 ....187 P9
Back Dr NPAG MK16 ....20 F3
Back La BUCK/WIN MK18 ....46 C5
 GTMIS/PWD HP16 ....133 P5
 WTR/OFPK MK7 ....53 N1
The Backs CSHM HP5 ....135 N4
Back St BUCK/WIN MK18 ....38 M7
 BUCK/WIN MK18 ....49 L3
 RAYLNE/WEN HP22 ....123 H1
 SKCH HP14 ....139 P6
The Back BERK HP4 ....115 K7
Bacombe La
 RAYLNE/WEN HP22 ....122 G2
Bacon Hl OLN MK46 ....15 L4
Baconsmead DEN/HRF UB9 ....170 A7
Bader Gdns SL SL1 ....187 L5
Badger Cl FELT TW13 ....197 P9
Badgemore Ct
 CNH/GTH/TM MK8 ....41 L2
Badgemore La HEN RC9 ....173 P5
Badger Dr FELT TW13 ....197 P9
Badgers Cl HYS/HAR UB3 ....191 C2
Badgers Meadow
 RAYLNE/WEN HP22 ....123 H1
Badgers Oak WTR/OFPK MK7 ....43 P5
Badgers Ri HADM HP17 ....108 E1
Badgers Wk
 BUCK/WIN MK18 ....48 C4
 MLW SL7 ....164 C2
Badgers Wy BUCK/WIN MK18 ....48 C4
Badgers Wd SLN SL2 ....179 N1
Badger Wy HAZ/HG HP15 ....143 P6
Bad Godesberg Wy
 MDHD SL6 ....177 M9
Badminton Rd MDHD SL6 ....185 H1
Badminton Wy
 CNH/GTH/TM MK8 ....41 P3
Badrick Rd AYLW HP19 ....95 H5
Bagley Cl WDR/YW UB7 ....190 E3
Bailey Cl HWYN HP13 ....5 J4
 MDHD SL6 ....185 H8
 WDSR SL4 ....198 J1
Baily Ct SHEN MK5 ....42 A7
Baird Cl SL SL1 ....187 M3
Baker's Cl NPAG MK16 ....14 M9
 RBEDW MK43 ....17 H2
Baker's La DUN/WHIP LU6 ....87 N8
 MDHD SL6 ....176 F8
Bakers Orch FLKWH HP10 ....166 C4
Baker's Piece CHNR OX39 ....129 K8
Baker's Rd UX/CGN UB8 ....182 D3
Baker's Rw MDHD SL6 * 176 F8
Baker St LBUZ LU7 ....74 E2
 RAYLW HP18 ....106 B8
 WAR/TWY RC10 ....11 M4
Bakers Wk
 RAYLNE/WEN HP22 ....110 F4
Bakers Wd DEN/HRF UB9 ....169 M6
Bakers Wood Cl LBUZ LU7 ....64 E4

Bakery Cl RAYLW HP18 ....77 N2
 RBEDW MK43 ....33 M3
Bala Wy WEAT MK2 ....53 J5
Balcary Gdns BERK HP4 ....126 A2
Baldways Cl
 RAYLNE/WEN HP22 ....83 H5
Baldwin Pl MDHD SL6 ....177 J9
Baldwin Rd BEAC HP9 ....155 M9
Baldwin's Shore WDSR SL4 ....187 P9
Balfe Ms WTR/OFPK MK7 ....44 B8
Balfour Pl MLW SL7 ....164 C5
Balfour Wy AYL HP20 ....3 F1
Balham's La HEN RC9 ....161 K1
Ballard Cl AYLS HP21 ....110 B1
Ballard Gn WDSR SL4 ....187 J8
Ballards Rw
 RAYLNE/WEN HP22 * 97 K9
Ballinger Ct BERK HP4 ....126 C2
Ballinger Rd
 GTMIS/PWD HP16 ....134 C3
Balloon Wd HADM HP17 ....107 L5
Balmer Cut BUCK/WIN MK18 ....48 B5
Balmer Cut BUCK/WIN MK18 ....48 B5
Balmerino Cl MKV MK10 ....43 P2
Balmoral CNH/GTH/TM MK8 ....41 N4
Balmoral Cl SL SL1 ....179 J9
Balmoral Dr BRACKY NN13 ....34 G5
 HWYW HP12 ....152 A4
Balmoral Gdns WDSR SL4 ....193 J2
Balsam Cl WTR/OFPK MK7 ....43 P6
Bamfords La HADM HP17 ....17 J1
Bamfords Yd RBEDW MK43 ....17 J2
Bampton Cl EMV/FZ MK4 ....52 E1
Banburies Cl BTCHLY MK3 ....52 C1
Banbury Av SL SL1 ....179 K8
Banbury Rd BRACKY NN13 ....34 F5
 THAME OX9 ....118 F7
Bangors Cl IVER SLO 181 P9
Bangors Pk IVER SLO * 181 P9
Bangors Rd North IVER SLO 181 M5
Bangors Rd South IVER SLO 181 N7
Bank Gn CNH/GTH/TM MK8 ....41 N5
Bank Mi BERK HP4 ....126 C1
Bankmill Br BERK HP4 ....96 B3
Bank Mill La BERK HP4 ....126 C2
Bankside FLKWH HP10 ....154 B2
Bankside RAYLNE/WEN HP22 ....111 H9
Bankside Av NTHLT UB5 ....183 N5
Banks Ct
 RKW/CH/CXG WD3 ....158 A6
Banks Rd HADM HP17 ....107 L8
Banks Sp SL SL1 ....187 M3
Bank St HWYN HP13 ....153 M5
Bannard Rd MDHD SL6 ....184 C2
Bannerman Dr BRACKY NN13 ....34 F5
Bannister Cl DTCH/LGLY SL3 ....195 K3
Bannister Rd THAME OX9 ....118 D6
Bantock Cl WTR/OFPK MK7 ....44 A7
Bannister Cl GTLIN MK14 ....30 F7
Bapchild Crs TRING HP23 ....112 D3
Barbers Wood Cl
 HWYW HP12 ....152 B6
Barbury Ct GTLIN MK14 ....30 C5
Barchester Rd
 DTCH/LGLY SL3 ....189 H3
Barclay Cl RBICN OX27 ....67 L3
Barden Cl DEN/HRF UB9 ....158 B5
Bardney Cl MDHD SL6 ....185 L4
Bardolphs Cl PRRI HP27 ....121 L9
Bardon Gn AYL HP20 ....95 N5
Bardsey Ct MKV MK10 ....43 N2
Bargeman Rd MDHD SL6 ....184 C7
Baring Rd BEAC HP9 ....154 C7
 HWYW HP13 ....153 M5
Barker Cl NTHWD HA6 ....159 M7
Barkestone Cl EMV/FZ MK4 ....52 C1
Barkham Cl LBUZ LU7 ....84 D9
Barkus Wy SKCH HP14 ....140 B4
Bar La PRRI HP27 ....120 F6
Barlee Crs UX/CGN UB8 ....182 B9
Barley Cl HAZ/HG HP15 ....143 N8
 RNHPTN NN7 ....12 G5
Barley Wd MLW SL7 ....164 D8
Barlow Rd
 RAYLNE/WEN HP22 ....111 J9
Barnabas Rd LBUZ LU7 ....74 B3
Barnacre Ct UX/CGN UB8 ....182 D9
Barnard Crs AYLS HP21 ....109 P1
Barnard Gdns YEAD UB4 ....183 P7
Barnards Hl MLW SL7 ....164 C6
Barn Cl HWYW HP12 ....152 C5
Barncroft Ct UX/CGN UB8 ....182 B9
Barncroft Rd BERK HP4 ....126 D3
Barn Dr MDHD SL6 ....185 N9
Barnes Pl EAG/OLD/WT MK6 ....43 K5
Barnes Rd CSHM HP5 ....135 N6
Barnett La EAG/OLD/WT MK6 ....7 E9
Barnett Wy
 RAYLNE/WEN HP22 ....110 F4
Barnfield IVER SLO 181 N9
Barnfield Cl MLW SL7 ....164 C6
Barnfield Dr
 EAG/OLD/WT MK6 ....7 F5
Barnhill Cl MLW SL7 ....164 D5
Barnhill Gdns MLW SL7 ....164 D5
Barnhill La YEAD UB4 ....183 P5
Barnhill Rd MLW SL7 ....164 D5
 YEAD UB4 ....183 P5
Barn La HEN RC9 ....173 N4
Barn Lea RKW/CH/CXG WD3 ....158 A1
Barn Rd PRRI HP27 ....120 F7
Barnsbury Av AYL HP20 ....96 B7

Barnsbury Gdns NPAG MK16 ....31 J2
Barnsdale Rd EMV/FZ MK4 ....51 J3
Barnsfield Pl UX/CGN UB8 ....182 C4
Barnwood Cl RSLP HA4 ....171 K7
Barons Ct WEAT MK2 ....53 J3
Baronsmead Rd HEN RC9 ....173 P5
Baronsmead Rd HWYW HP12 ....4 B7
Barrack Hl RAYLW HP18 ....93 H9
Barrack La WDSR SL4 ....187 P9
Barracks Hl AMSS HP7 ....135 K9
Barracks Rd HWYW HP11 ....4 E7
The Barracks
 BUCK/WIN MK18 * 47 M7
Barra Hall Rd HYS/HAR UB5 ....191 L1
Barrards Wy BEAC HP9 ....155 J6
Barratt Pl HWYW HP11 * 5 N6
Barrett Pl SHEN MK5 ....41 P6
Barrie Cl AYLW HP20 ....95 K9
Barrington Dr DEN/HRF UB9 ....158 A7
Barrington Ms
 EAG/OLD/WT MK6 ....7 F5
Barrington Park Gdns
 CSTG HP8 ....156 F1
Barr's Rd MDHD SL6 ....178 F9
Barry Av BDWL MK13 ....30 C8
 WDSR SL4 ....187 N8
Barry Cl HWYW HP12 ....152 C7
Barry Ter WEAT TW15 * 196 F8
Bartelotts Rd SLN SL2 ....179 L7
Bartholomew Cl
 WTR/OFPK MK8 ....43 N7
Bartholomew Tipping Wy
 SKCH HP14 ....140 B6
Bartlett Ct BRACKY NN13 ....34 B5
Bartlett Pl BUCK/WIN MK18 ....48 C2
Bartletts La MDHD SL6 ....185 N8
Barton Rd DTCH/LGLY SL3 ....189 H3
 WEAT MK2 ....53 J5
Bartons Wy HAZ/HG HP15 ....153 L1
Bartram Cl UX/CGN UB8 ....182 A5
Barwick Dr UX/CGN UB8 ....182 A5
Bascote EAG/OLD/WT MK6 ....43 K7
Base Cl AYL HP20 ....95 N5
Basford Wy WDSR SL4 ....193 H2
Basildon Ct
 CNH/GTH/TM MK8 ....41 P4
 LBUZ LU7 * 74 D1
Basing Rd
 RKW/CH/CXG WD3 ....157 P1
Baskerfield Gv
 EAG/OLD/WT MK6 ....43 J4
Basset Rd SKCH HP14 ....151 J6
Bassetsbury La HWYW HP11 ....153 K5
Bassett Ct NPAG MK16 ....31 J4
Bassett Rd LBUZ LU7 ....74 D2
 UX/CGN UB8 ....182 C3
Bass Md MDHD SL6 ....177 M8
Batchelor Ct AYL HP20 * 3 H3
Batchelors Wy AMSS HP7 ....145 P3
 CSHM HP5 ....135 M2
Batchworth Hl
 RKW/CH/CXG WD3 * 158 E2
Batchworth Hill London Rd
 RKW/CH/CXG WD3 ....158 F2
Batchworth La NTHWD HA6 ....159 J5
Bateman Dr AYLS HP21 ....109 N1
Bates Cl DTCH/LGLY SL3 ....180 C9
 WLLN MK15 ....31 P9
Bates Ct AYL HP20 ....95 P5
Bates Gdns RMKS/WB MK17 ....62 B4
Bates La RAYLNE/WEN HP22 ....110 F4
Bath Ct MDHD SL6 ....185 L4
Bath La BUCK/WIN MK18 ....48 A3
Bath Rd DTCH/LGLY SL3 ....189 N3
 HTHAIR TW6 ....194 D1
 MDHD SL6 ....184 D2
 MDHD SL6 ....185 K1
 SL SL1 ....187 H1
 WDR/YW UB7 ....190 H1
Bathurst Cl IVER SLO 189 P3
Bathurst Wk IVER SLO 181 M8
Battersby Ms AYLS HP21 ....2 A7
Batt Furlong AYLS HP21 ....109 M3
Batting Cl SKCH HP14 ....141 H3
Battings Wood Gdns
 SKCH HP14 ....142 C3
Battle Mead Cl MDHD SL6 ....178 A5
Battlesden Av
 RMKS/WB MK17 ....65 N2
The Baulk LBUZ LU7 ....84 D9
 LBUZ LU7 ....99 K2
Bawtree Rd UX/CGN UB8 ....182 D2
Beacon Cl CNH/GTH/TM MK8 ....41 M9
 HGDN/ICK SLO 183 H6
 SL SL1 ....188 A4
Bayard Av GTLIN MK14 ....30 F8
Bayard Brow BRACKY NN13 ....34 G5
Bayeux Dr NTHWD HA6 ....159 M6
Bayley Crs SL SL1 ....187 L8
Bayley Gdns HEST TW5 ....142 E5
Baylis Pde SL SL1 ....180 A9
Baylis Rd SL SL1 ....187 L5
Bayne Hl BEAC HP9 ....155 P7
Bayly Rd MDHD SL6 ....185 N9
Baynham Ms
 WTR/OFPK MK7 ....43 P4
Baysfarm Ct WDR/YW UB7 ....190 C9
Bayswater Rd HEAD OX3 ....102 B8
Bay Tree Cl HAZ/HG HP15 ....143 N8
Bay Tree Ct SL SL1 ....188 C3
Beacham Rd HWYW HP12 ....152 C8
Beacon Av DUN/WHIP LU6 ....86 F2
Beacon Cl CFSP/GDCR SL9 ....156 C9
 HADM HP17 ....108 E1
 UX/CGN UB8 ....182 D1
Beacon Ct CFSP/GDCR SL9 ....189 L8
 EMV/FZ MK4 ....51 H3
Beacon La MLW SL7 ....151 N9
Beacon Rd BERK HP4 ....100 B5
 HTHAIR TW6 ....196 G5
Beaconsfield Av HWYW HP13 ....152 P1

Beaconsfield Common La
SLN SL2 ....167 N5
Beaconsfield Pl NPAG MK16.....31 J1
Beaconsfield Rd AYLS HP21 ....3 F6
RAYLNE/WEN HP22.............111 L1
SLN SL2 ....179 N2
TRING HP23 ....112 C3
Beacon Vw DUN/WHIP LU6 ....85 M4
HADM HP17 * 122 B2
LBUZ LU7 ....75 P4
Beacon Wy TRING HP23 ....112 G1
Beadlemead
EAG/OLD/WT MK6 ....43 J6
Beales La WTR/OFPK MK7 ....43 N7
Bealings End BEAC HP9 ....155 H5
Beamish Wy BUCK/WIN MK18 ...60 D5
Beanfare EAG/OLD/WT MK6........4 H8
Bearbrook Cl AYLS HP21 ....2 A6
Bearswood End BEAC HP9.......155 J6
Beatrice Cl PIN HA5 ....17 L1
Beauchamp Cl DTCH/LGLY SL3 ...40 E4
Beauchamp Ct GTLIN SL9 ....34 C2
Beauchamp Gdns
RKW/CH/CXG WD3 ....158 A1
Beauclerc Cl FELT TW13 ....197 P7
Beaudesert LBUZ LU7 ....74 E2
Beaufort Cl AYLS HP21 ....96 D8
Beaufort Dr WLLN MK15 ....31 J6
Beaufort Gdns MLW SL7 ....164 E7
Beaufort Rd RSLP HA4 ....171 K7
Beaulah Pl WDSR SL4 * 192 F8
Beaulieu Cl DTCH/LGLY SL3 .....188 D9
Beaumaris Gv SHEN MK5 ....42 A6
Beaumont Cl MDHD SL6 ....184 C4
Beaumont Crs BRACKY NN13.....24 C5
Beaumont Ri MLW SL7 ....164 E7
Beaumont Rd SLN SL2 ....179 P8
WDSR SL4 * 193 N1
Beaumont Wy HAZ/HG HP15 ....43 M7
Beaverbrook Ct BTCHLY MK5 ......52 F7
Beaver Cl BUCK/WIN MK18 ....48 C4
Beckets Sq BERK HP4 * 114 C8
Becketts Cl
EBED/NFELT TW14 ....197 P5
Beckings Wy FLKWH HP10 ....166 A2
Beckinsale Gv
CNH/GTH/TM MK8 ....41 N5
Beckley Ct HEAD OX5 ....102 D4
Beckwell Rd SL SL1 ....187 N3
Bec La WLLN MK15 ....31 H6
Bedder Rd HHYW HP12 ....152 C7
Beddoes Ct SHEN MK5 ....41 N8
Bedfont Cl
EBED/NFELT TW14 ....197 J5
Bedfont Ct
STWL/WRAY TW19 ....196 A2
Bedfont Court Est
STWL/WRAY TW19 * 196 B3
Bedfont Green Cl
EBED/NFELT TW14 ....197 J7
Bedfont La
EBED/NFELT TW14 ....197 L6
Bedfont Rd
EBED/NFELT TW14 ....197 J7
STWL/WRAY TW19 ....196 F5
Bedford Av AMS HP6 ....146 E3
SL SL1 ....179 L9
YEAD UB4 ....183 P9
Bedford Cl MDHD SL6 ....184 C4
RKW/CH/CXG WD3 ....147 K2
Bedford Dr SLN SL2 ....179 M1
NTHWD HA6 ....16 F2
OLN MK46 ....16 E6
RBEDW MK43 ....33 N3
RBEDW MK43 ....45 N4
RSLP HA4 ....171 M9
Bedford Rd East
RNHPTN NN7 ....9 J5
Bedford Rd West
RNHPTN NN7 ....8 F1
Bedford St BERK HP4 ....126 F1
LBUZ LU7 ....74 E2
RMKS/WB MK17 ....55 K4
WEAT MK42 ....53 J3
WOLV MK12 ....29 M7
Bedgebury Ri WTR/OFPK MK7.....43 N4
Bedgrove AYLS HP21 ....95 P1
Bedlam La NPAG MK16 ....22 A5
Bedwell Gdns HYS/HAR UB3 ...191 L4
Bedwins La MDHD SL6 ....177 H2
Beeby Wy RBEDW MK43 ....11 L9
The Beeches
RMKS/WB MK17 ....61 M4
Beech Av OLN MK46 ....15 L3
RSLP HA4 ....171 P6
SKCH HP14 ....151 L5
Beech Cl BUCK/WIN MK18 ....38 B1
DUN/WHIP LU6 ....87 N3
FLKWH HP10 ....153 N8
MDHD SL6 ....177 H8
RAYLNE/WEN HP22 ....96 B4
RMKN MK19 ....29 M3
SKCH HP14 ....151 L2
STWL/WRAY TW19 ....196 D8
WDR/YW UB7 ....190 C4
WYM HP11 ....153 N6
Beech Ct BERK HP4 ....114 F9
MLW SL7 ....164 E7
PRRI HP27 * 121 L8
Beechcroft BERK HP4 ....126 E2
Beechcroft Rd BTCHLY MK3.......52 E1
CSHM HP5 ....135 M3
Beech Dr BERK HP4 ....126 E1
BRACKY NN13 ....34 C3
Beeches Dr SLN SL2 ....167 M9
Beeches Gv HAZ/HG HP15 ....143 N9
Beeches Pk BEAC HP9 ....155 L2
Beeches Rd SLN SL2 ....179 L8
The Beeches AMS HP6 ....135 L2
RAYLNE/WEN HP22 ....111 J9
RKW/CH/CXG WD3 ....147 P7
RMKN MK19 ....40 A1

TRING HP23 * 112 G2
Beeches Wy BNEND SL8 ....165 P9
DTCH/LGLY SL3 ....180 C1
MDHD SL6 ....177 L9
SL SL1 ....178 F6
Beech Fern WTR/OFPK MK7 ....43 N7
Beechfield Pl MDHD SL6 ....185 K5
Beech Gn AYLS HP21 ....95 M9
Beech Gv AMS HP7 ....145 N5
AYLW HP19 ....95 K9
LBUZ LU7 ....74 C2
TRING HP23 ....112 G2
Beech House Dr TOW NN12 ....28 A2
Beechingstoke MLW SL7 ....164 F6
Beechlands HAZ/HG HP15 ....143 L9
Beech La BUCK/WIN MK18 ....58 C7
GTMIS/PWD HP16 ....133 H5
Beech Leys BUCK/WIN HP11 ....95 M8
Beech Pk SKCH HP14 ....142 B2
Beech St WYM HP11 ....153 K5
Beech Tree Av AYLS HP21 ....95 M9
CHNR OX59 ....129 N6
DTCH/LGLY SL3 ....188 C3
DUN/WHIP LU6 ....87 N4
EBED/NFELT TW14 ....197 J4
J5
Beech Tree Cl
RAYLNE/WEN HP22 ....81 J2
Beech Tree Rd HAZ/HG HP15 ....144 A4
Beech Waye CFSP/GDCR SL9.....169 J5
Beechwood Av AMS HP6 ....146 E2
HYS/HAR UB3 ....191 K1
RKW/CH/CXG WD3 ....147 M3
AYLW HP19 * 171 M7
UX/CGN UB8 ....182 F9
Beechwood Cl AMS HP6 ....146 E3
Beechwood Ct
DUN/WHIP LU6 ....87 H1
Beechwood Dr MDHD SL6 ....184 C1
MLW SL7 ....164 G5
TRING HP23 ....113 P1
Beechwood Gdns SL SL1 ....188 A3
Beechwood La
RAYLNE/WEN HP22 ....111 K9
Beechwood Pk
HHS/BOV HP3 ....127 P6
RKW/CH/CXG WD3 ....147 P6
Beechwood Rd BEAC HP9 ....154 G8
HWYN HP13 ....152 C8
SLN SL2 ....179 B9
Beechwood Wy
RAYLNE/WEN HP22 ....111 L1
Beehive Cl HGDN/ICK UB10 ......182 F5
Beel Cl AMSS HP7 ....146 E5
Beethoven Cl WTR/OFPK MK7 ....44 C8
Beeward Cl WOLV MK12 ....29 J8
Beggars La TRING HP23 ....111 J4
Bekonscot Ct GTLIN MK14 ....30 F4
Belfast Av SL SL1 ....179 N9
Belfry Av DEN/HRF UB9 ....158 A4
Belgrave Ms UX/CGN UB8 ....182 D7
Belgrave Pde SL SL1 * 188 A1
Belgrave Rd AYLW HP19 ....95 J4
Bellamy Cl HGDN/ICK UB10 ......170 C9
Bellamy Rd HWYN HP13 ....5 K3
Bell Av WDR/YW UB7 ....190 F4
Bell Cl LBUZ LU7 ....72 B8
PRRI HP27 ....121 H8
RMKS/WB MK17 ....62 B5
SLN SL2 ....180 C1
Bellclose Rd WDR/YW UB7 ....190 E5
Bell Ct MDHD SL6 ....175 P5
Bell Crs PRRI HP27 ....120 G7
Belle Vue RAYLW HP18 ....108 E1
Belle Vue Pl SL SL1 * 188 B4
Belle Vue Rd HEN RG9 ....173 P8
Belle Vue Ter
DEN/HRF UB9 * 158 A4
Bellfield Rd HWYN HP13 ....4 E1
Bellfield Rd West HWYN HP13 ......4 E1
Bell Gn HHS/BOV HP3 * 127 K9
Bellingdon Rd CSHM HP5 ....135 M2
Bellingdon Rd CSHM HP5 * 44 B7
Bellis Gv EAG/OLD/WT MK6 ....43 J9
Bell La DTCH/LGLY SL3 ....195 K2
Bells Meadow WLLN MK15 * 31 H6
Bell St HEN RG9 ....174 A6
MDHD SL6 ....185 M1
PRRI HP27 * 121 H8
Bellswood La IVER SL0 ....193 K4
Bell Vw WDSR SL4 ....193 K2
Bell View Cl WDSR SL4 ....193 K3
Bell Wk BUCK/WIN MK18............60 B5
RAYLNE/WEN HP22 ....85 H5
Bellway RMKS/WB MK17 ....44 C8
Bellweir Cl
STWL/WRAY TW19 ....195 K8
Bellwether Cl HHW HP11 ....29 J9
Bellwood Ri WYM HP11 ....152 C6
Belmers Rd TRING HP23 ....113 H5
Belmont SLN SL2 ....179 L9
Belmont Cl
CNH/GTH/TM MK8 ....41 N5
Belmont Crs MDHD SL6 ....177 H8
Belmont Ms THAME OX9 * 118 D5

Belmont Park Av MDHD SL6 ....177 K7
Belmont Park Rd MDHD SL6 ....177 K8
Belmont Rd CSHM HP5 ....135 M2
MDHD SL6 ....177 L9
UX/CGN UB8 ....182 D3
Belmont V MDHD SL6 ....177 L8
Belmore Av YEAD UB4 ....183 N9
Belsize RKW/CH/CXG WD3 * 137 M6
Belsize Av EAG/OLD/WT MK6 ....43 L8
Belton Rd BERK HP4 ....114 C9
Belvedere GTLIN MK14 ....30 F4
Belvedere La WEAT MK2 ....53 M5
Belvoir Av EMV/FZ MK4 ....43 P9
Bembridge Gdns RSLP HA4 ....171 J7
Bempton Dr RSLP HA4 ....171 P7
Benacre Cft EMV/FZ MK4 ....52 A5
Benbow Ct SHEN MK5 ....42 A5
Benbow Moorings
UX/CGN UB8 ....182 C8
Benbow Wy UX/CGN UB8 ....182 C8
Benchleys Rd HHW HP1 ....127 P5
Bench Manor Crs
CFSP/GDCR SL9 ....156 E9
Bencombe Rd MLW SL7 ....164 D4
Benedict Dr
EBED/NFELT TW14 ....197 K6
Benen-Stock Rd
STWL/WRAY TW19 ....196 A5
Benham Ct CSHM HP5 ....135 M3
Benhams La HEN RG9 ....161 P7
Benjamin Rd HWYN HP13 ....5 G4
Bennet Cl STSTR MK11 ....28 F9
Bennetsfield Rd STKFK UB11 .....191 H2
Bennett Cl NTHWD HA6 ....159 M7
STSTR MK11 ....28 D8
Bennett End SKCH HP14 ....140 E4
Bennetts CSHM HP5 ....135 P5
Bennett Cl BUCK/WIN MK18 ....58 F1
DUN/WHIP LU6 ....87 K1
SL SL1 ....187 J2
Bennetts La
RAYLNE/WEN HP22 ....82 E8
Bennetts Yd UX/CGN UB8 * 182 D5
Benning Cl WDSR SL4 ....193 H2
Benningfield Gdns
BERK HP4 ....114 G8
Bens Cl RMKN MK19 ....35 H9
Benson Cl SLN SL2 ....188 C2
UX/CGN UB8 ....182 E8
Bentall Cl WLLN MK15 ....31 K4
Bentinck Cl CFSP/GDCR SL9 .....168 F3
Bentinck Rd WDR/YW UB7 ....190 D2
Bentley Pk SL SL1 ....179 H5
Bentley Rd SL SL1 ....187 K2
Benton Dr CHNR OX39 ....129 N5
Benwell Cl MDHD SL6 ....184 B3
Benwells CHNR OX39 ....129 N6
Berberis Cl WTR/OFPK MK7 ....43 N7
Berberis Wk WDR/YW UB7 ....190 D5
Bercham CNH/GTH/TM MK8 ....41 N2
Beresford Av AYLW HP19 ....95 J3
SLN SL2 ....188 E1
Beresford Rd EMV/FZ MK4 ....42 B9
Beresford Rd
RKW/CH/CXG WD3 ....157 P1
Beretun CNH/GTH/TM MK8 ....41 N1
Bereville Cl MKV MK10 ....43 L1
Berevilles La MKV MK10 ....43 L1
Bergamot Gdns
WTR/OFPK MK7 ....43 P7
Berkeley Av CSHM HP5 ....135 K2
HEST TW5 ....191 L3
RSLP HA4 ....171 N8
Berkeley Cl CSHM HP5 ....135 L3
RSLP HA4 ....171 N8
Berkeley Dr WDSR SL4 ....192 F7
Berkeley Ms MLW SL7 * 164 F7
Berkeley Ri AYLW HP19 ....95 J5
Berkeley Rd FLKWH HP10 ....154 A5
HGDN/ICK UB10 ....183 J3
THAME OX9 ....118 E4
Berkhampstead Rd
CSHM HP5 ....135 N3
Berkley Cl MDHD SL6 ....177 K8
Berkley Rd BEAC HP9 ....155 H4
Berks HI RKW/CH/CXG WD3 .....147 P4
Berkshire Cl SHEN MK5 ....41 L9
Berkshire Gn SHEN MK5 ....43 M1
Berkshire Rd HEN RG9 ....173 P8
Berling Rd
CNH/GTH/TM MK8 ....41 P2
Bernadines Wy
BUCK/WIN MK18 ....48 C4
Bernard Cl RAYLW HP18 ....107 K4
Bernards Cl
GTMIS/PWD HP16 ....133 N5
RAYLW HP18 ....106 C4
Bernards Wy FLKWH HP10 ....155 H6
Bernay Gdns WLLN MK15 ....31 H6
Berndene Ri PRRI HP27 ....121 K9
Berners Cl SL SL1 ....187 J4
Bernewode Cl RAYLW HP18 ......106 A7
Bernstein Cl WTR/OFPK MK7 ....44 A8
Berries Rd MDHD SL6 ....177 N1
Berryfield LBUZ LU7 ....72 A7
Berry Fld SLN SL2 ....180 C2
Berry Field Pk AMS HP6 ....145 M1
Berryfield Rd AYLW HP19 ....95 K4
Berry HI MDHD SL6 ....177 J1
Berry La RKW/CH/CXG WD3 ....147 M8
Berrymead WTR/OFPK MK7 ....43 P7
Berry Wy RMKS/WB MK17 ....52 C7
Berwald Cl WTR/OFPK MK7 ....44 B7
Berwick Av SL SL1 ....187 M1
Berwick Cl BEAC HP9 ....155 M8
MLW SL7 ....164 C6
Berwick Dr BTCHLY MK3 ....52 A1
Berwick La MLW SL7 ....164 D6
Berwick Rd MLW SL7 ....164 C6
Bessemer Ct GTLIN MK14 ....30 E4
Bessemer Crs RAYLW HP19 ....94 G6
Bessingby Rd RSLP HA4 ....171 N7

Bestobell Rd SL SL1 ....179 N9
Betam Rd HYS/HAR UB3 ....191 K3
Bethany Waye
EBED/NFELT TW14 ....197 L6
Betjeman Ct WDR/YW UB7 * 190 D2
Bettina Gv WEAT MK2 ....53 J4
Bettles Cl UX/CGN UB8 ....182 C5
Betty's Cl RMKS/WB MK17 ....62 C7
Betty's La TRING HP23 ....112 E2
Bevan Hl CSHM HP5 ....135 M4
Bevelwood Gdns
HWYW HP12 ....152 D3
Beverley Cl MLW SL7 ....164 G7
Beverley Gdns MDHD SL6 ....177 H7
Beverley Pl EAG/OLD/WT MK6......43 H6
Beverley Rd RSLP HA4 ....171 P7
Bevin Rd YEAD UB4 ....183 N6
Bewdley Dr LBUZ LU7 ....74 A2
Bexley St WDSR SL4 ....187 M9
Bibshall Crs DUN/WHIP LU6 ....87 C2
Bicester Rd AYLW HP19 ....95 H4
BUCK/WIN MK18 ....57 J9
RAYLW HP18 ....77 J8
RAYLW HP18 ....90 D9
RAYLW HP18 ....106 A8
RBICN OX27 ....95 P9
Bickleigh Crs EMV/FZ MK4 ....42 C9
Biddles Cl SL SL1 ....187 J2
Biddlesden Rd BRACKY NN13 ......36 A7
Bideford Cl LBUZ LU7 ....74 A1
Bideford Rd RSLP HA4 ....171 P8
Bideford Sp SLN SL2 ....179 M9
Bierton Rd AYL HP20 ....3 G2
Bigfrith La MDHD SL6 ....176 C2
Biggs La HADM HP17 ....108 A4
Bigmore La SKCH HP14 ....150 D5
Bignell Cft SHEN MK5 ....42 B3
Bilbrook La EMV/FZ MK4 ....42 C9
Billet La BERK HP4 ....114 C9
IVER SL0 ....181 K6
Billings Cl SKCH HP14 ....140 B6
Billington Cl LBUZ LU7 ....74 C7
Billington Rd LBUZ LU7 ....74 C7
LBUZ LU7 ....75 J7
Billingwell Pl
EAG/OLD/WT MK6 ....43 H1
Billwell RAYLW HP18 ....106 C4
Bilton Rd DBGH MK1 ....53 K2
Bilton Wy HYS/HAR UB3 ....191 L1
Bina Gdns EMV/FZ MK4 ....52 C2
Bingham Rd SL SL1 ....178 E8
The Binghams MDHD SL6 ....185 P4
Birch Av WDR/YW UB7 ....182 F5
Birch Cl AYLS HP21 ....96 D5
Birch Crs HGDN/ICK UB10 ....183 J1
Birchdale CFSP/GDCR SL9 ....168 F3
Birch Dr RKW/CH/CXG WD3 ....157 M5
Birchen Lee EMV/FZ MK4 ....52 C1
The Birches HYS/HAR UB3 ....191 M1
HWYN HP13 ....153 L2
The Birches HHS/BOV HP3 ....127 P5
HWYN HP13 ....153 L2
Birchfield Gv WEAT MK2 ....53 K4
Birch Gdns AMSS HP7 ....146 A3
Birch Gn HHW HP1 ....127 P1
Birch Gv SLN SL2 ....179 H9
WDSR SL4 ....193 N5
Birchington Rd WDSR SL4 ....193 L1
Birch La HHS/BOV HP3 ....137 K6
Birch Rd BERK HP4 ....113 P7
Birch Side DUN/WHIP LU6 ....87 M2
Birchside Cl SHEN MK5 ....41 P1
Birch Tree Cv CSHM HP5 ....136 D5
Birch Wy CSHM HP5 ....135 P2
HAZ/HG HP15 ....143 P9
Birchway HYS/HAR UB3 ....191 N1
Birchwood Cha
HAZ/HG HP15 ....143 J2
Birchwood Dr HHW HP12 ....152 B9
Bircott Rd WTR/OFPK MK7 * 43 N8
Bird's HI LBUZ LU7 ....64 C9
Birds La NPAG MK16 ....15 P9
Birdwood Rd MDHD SL6 ....177 H4
Birinus Ct HWYW HP12 ....152 A8
Birkdale Cl BTCHLY MK3 ....52 C4
Birkett Wy CSTG HP8 ....156 C3
Birley Rd SL SL1 ....179 P9
Birsham Ct MLW SL7 ....176 D3
Birsham Rd MLW SL7 ....176 D3
Bishop Ct MDHD SL6 ....177 L8
Bishop Cl MDHD SL6 ....177 L8
Bishops Av NTHWD HA6 ....159 L4
Bishops Cl BRACKY NN13 ....34 C3
HGDN/ICK UB10 ....182 D5
Bishops Dr
EBED/NFELT TW14 ....197 K5
Bishops Farm Cl WDSR SL4 ......192 F1
Bishops Fld
RAYLNE/WEN HP22 ....111 N2
Bishopsgate Rd WDSR SL4 ....194 C9
Bishops Meadow
RAYLNE/WEN HP22 ....96 A4
Bishops Orch SLN SL2 ....188 C3
Bishop's Rd HYS/HAR UB3 ....183 J9
SL SL1 ....188 C3
Bishopstone BDWL MK13 ....30 A4
HADM HP17 ....117 L8
Bishops Wk AYLS HP21 * 88 A3
FLKWH HP10 ....155 J5
RMKS/WB MK17 ....47 K6
Bissley Dr MDHD SL6 ....176 A1
Bittenham Cl HADM HP17 ....117 J9
Bittern Wy AYLS HP21 * 88 A3
The Bit AMSS HP7 ....145 H3
TRING HP23 ....113 H5
Bix La MDHD SL6 ....176 D9
Bix Rd HEN RG9 ....173 L2
Black Acre Cl AMSS HP7 ....145 N4
Blackamoor La MDHD SL6 ....177 N8
IVER SL0 ....181 P9
NPAG MK16 ....31 N1

Blackbird Cl BRACKY NN13 ....34 G2
Black Boy La WAR/TWY RG10 ...175 L5
Black Butt Cottages
EBED/NFELT TW14 ....197 P1
Blackdown STSTR MK11 ....29 H9
Blacketts Wood Dr
RKW/CH/CXG WD3 ....147 K7
Blackfield La
GTMIS/PWD HP16 ....134 C1
Blackham Ct
EAG/OLD/WT MK6 ....43 D1
Blackheath Crs BDWL MK13 ....42 D1
Blackhill Dr WOLV MK12 ....29 J7
Black Horse Av CSHM HP5 ....135 P6
Black Horse Cl WDSR SL4 ....193 H1
Blackhorse Crs AMS HP6 ....146 A2
Black Horse Pl PIN HA5 * 171 P3
Black Horse Pl EAG/OLD/WT UB8 .182 B4
Blacklands Dr YEAD UB4 ....183 J7
Blackmoor Ga EMV/FZ MK4 ....52 E1
Blackmore Ct THAME OX9 ....118 E6
Blackmore Ga
RAYLNE/WEN HP22 ....111 P2
Blackmore Wy UX/CGN UB8 ....182 D2
Black Park Rd
DTCH/LGLY SL3 ....181 M4
Blackpond La SLN SL2 ....179 M4
Blackpool Gdns YEAD UB4 ....183 L7
Black Rod Cl HYS/HAR UB3 ....191 M4
Blacksmith La
GTMIS/PWD HP16 ....133 J6
Blacksmiths Rw
DTCH/LGLY SL3 ....189 J5
KID 88 C3
Blacksmiths Rd PRRI HP27 ....120 F6
Blacksmith's La
DEN/HRF UB9 ....169 M7
KID 88 C3
Blackthorn Dell
DTCH/LGLY SL3 ....195 N1
Blackthorne Crs
DTCH/LGLY SL3 ....195 N2
Blackthorne La
GTMIS/PWD HP16 ....134 C1
Blackthorne Rd
DTCH/LGLY SL3 ....195 N2
Blackthorn Gv
EAG/OLD/WT MK6 ....44 E8
Blackwater Dr AYLS HP21 ....109 L2
Blackwell End TOW NN12 ....27 N2
Blackwell Hall La CSHM HP5 ......136 E4
Blackwellhall La CSHM HP5 ....136 E4
Blackwell Pl SHEN MK5 ....42 A8
Blackwell Rd SKCH HP14 ....151 K5
Blackwood Crs BDWL MK13 ....42 D1
Blaine Cl TRING HP23 ....98 E9
Blair Cl HYS/HAR UB3 ....191 N5
Blairhead Dr OXHEY WD19 ....159 P3
Blairmont St CMK MK9 ....30 F9
Blair Rd SL SL1 ....188 A2
Blake Cl YEAD UB4 ....183 P6
Blakeney Ct EMV/FZ MK4 ....52 B5
MDHD SL6 ....177 M7
Blake Wy THAME OX9 ....118 E4
Blanchland Cir MKV MK10 ....43 N3
Blandford Cl DTCH/LGLY SL3 ......188 F8
Blandford Rd North
DTCH/LGLY SL3 ....188 F4
Blandford Rd South
DTCH/LGLY SL3 ....188 F4
Blandy Rd HEN RG9 ....173 P6
Blansby Cha EMV/FZ MK4 ....42 C9
Blatherwick Ct SHEN MK5 ....41 P5
Blaydon Cl BTCHLY MK5 ....52 D5
Bleasdale BDWL MK13 * 30 A3
Bledlow Ridge Rd
PRRI HP27 ....130 E3
Bledlow Rd PRRI HP27 ....130 E4
Blegberry Gdns BERK HP4 ....126 A2
Blencowe Dr BRACKY NN13 ....34 F5
Blenheim Av STSTR MK11 ....28 D9
Blenheim Crs RSLP HA4 ....171 K7
Blenheim Pde
HGDN/ICK UB10 * 183 H7
Blenheim Pl AYLS HP21 ....109 N1
BRACKY NN13 ....34 C3
Blenheim Rd DTCH/LGLY SL3 .....188 F5
HWYW HP12 ....152 D6
SL SL1 ....179 L9
UTLW OX49 ....138 C7
Bletcham Wy DBGH MK1 ....53 J1
EAG/OLD/WT MK6 ....43 M9
WTR/OFPK MK7 ....43 M9
Bletchley Rd LBUZ LU7 ....62 D7
RMKS/WB MK17 ....44 D7
Blinco Cl DTCH/LGLY SL3 ....180 C3
Blind La BNEND SL8 ....165 N5
Bliss Av RBEDW MK43 ....33 N5
Bliss Ct WTR/OFPK MK7 ....44 A8
Black Horse Cl WTR/OFPK MK7.....43 N8
Blondell WDR/YW UB7 ....190 D7
Bloomfield Rd MDHD SL6 ....184 G2
Bloomsbury Cl
RMKS/WB MK17 ....55 K5
Blossom Wy HGDN/ICK UB10 ....182 D4
WDR/YW UB7 ....190 C5
Blows Rd DUN/HR/TOD LU5 ....87 M3
Blucher St CMK MK9 ....135 M4
Bluebell Cl BUCK/WIN MK18 ....48 A4
HHW HP1 * 127 N5
Bluebell Cft WTR/OFPK MK7 ....43 P6
Bluemfield Crs SL SL1 ....187 J2
Bluebells Rd BERK MK15 ....30 E7
Blundels Dr DTCH/LGLY SL3 ....189 K5
Blunts Av WDR/YW UB7 ....190 G6
Blyth Cl EMV/FZ MK4 ....52 A3
Blyth Ct AYLS HP21 ....109 M1
NPAG MK16 ....31 N1

Blyth Rd HYS/HAR UB3 ......191 L3
Blyton Cl BEAC HP9 ......155 H6
Boadicea Cl SL SL1 ......187 J2
Boarlands Cl SL SL1 ......187 K1
Bobmore La MLW SL7 ......164 C6
Bockmer La MLW SL7 ......175 K2
Boddington Rd
  RAYLNE/WEN HP22 ......123 J1
Boddington Wy
  BRACKY NN13 ......34 F4
Bodenham Cl
  BUCK/WIN MK18 ......48 D3
Bodiam Cl AYLS HP21 ......110 B1
  SHEN MK5 ......42 A7
Bodle Cl WLLN MK15 ......30 C6
Bodmin Av SLN SL2 ......179 L8
Bodnant Ct EMV/FZ MK4 ......51 J3
Boeing Wy NWDGN UB2 ......191 P4
Bois Av AMS HP6 ......199 N3
Bois Hl CSHM HP5 * 136 C9
Bois La AMS HP6 ......135 P9
Bois Ml CSHM HP5 * 136 C9
Bois Moor Rd CSHM HP5 ......135 N7
Bolan Ct CNH/GTH/TM MK8 ......41 N6
Bolingbroke Wy
  HYS/HAR UB3 ......191 K2
Bolter End La SKCH HP14 ......151 J4
Bolton Av WDSR SL4 ......193 P2
Bolton Cl BTCHLY MK3 ......52 C1
Bolton Crs WDSR SL4 ......193 N2
Bolton Rd WDSR SL4 ......193 N2
Boltons Cl BRACKY NN13 ......34 F3
Bolton's La WDR/YW UB7 ......191 J8
Boltwood Gv SHEN MK5 ......41 N7
Bomer Cl WDR/YW UB7 ......190 C8
Bond Av DBGH MK1 ......43 K9
Bond Cl AYLS HP21 ......95 K9
  IVER SL0 ......181 K3
  WDR/YW UB7 ......190 A8
Bondfield Av YEAD UB4 ......183 N6
Bone Hl BUCK/WIN MK18 ......48 A4
Bonham Carter Rd
  RAYLNE/WEN HP22 ......111 K7
Bonham Ct
  RAYLNE/WEN HP22 ......111 K7
Boniface Rd HGDN/ICK UB10 ...171 H8
Bonnards Rd RMKS/WB MK17...52 B1
Bonnersfield RAYLW HP18 ......106 A7
Booker Av BDWL MK13 ......30 D9
Bookerhill Rd HWYW HP12......152 D5
Booker La HWYW HP12 ......152 D5
Booker Pl HWYW HP12 ......152 B7
Booth Rd DUN/WHIP LU6......86 A2
Boot La HADM HP17 ......108 A4
Borderside SLN SL2 ......180 C9
Borodin Ct WTR/OFPK MK7......44 B7
Borough Rd BRACKY NN13......35 J7
  DUN/WHIP LU6 ......87 M1
Borrowdale Av
  DUN/WHIP LU6 ......87 L2
Bosanquet Cl UX/CGN UB8......182 D8
Bossard Ct LBUZ LU7 ......74 F4
Bossiney Pl EAG/OLD/WT MK6...7 H4
Bossington La LBUZ LU7 ......74 D2
Boss La HAZ/HG HP15 ......161 G3
Bostock Ct BUCK/WIN MK18 * ...48 A3
Boston Dr BNEND SL8 ......165 P6
Boston Gv RSLP HA4 ......171 J4
  SL SL1 ......179 L9
Boston Rd HEN RG9 ......174 A8
Boswell Ct BUCK/WIN MK18......48 C2
Boswell La RMKN MK19 ......28 A9
Boswick La BERK HP4 ......113 P6
Bosworth Cl BTCHLY MK3......52 C1
Botley La CSHM HP5 ......136 C5
Botley Rd CSHM HP5 ......136 A3
Bottesford Cl EMV/FZ MK4......52 D2
Bottom Dr DUN/WHIP LU6......86 F3
Bottom House Farm La
  CSTG HP8 ......155 P1
Bottom House La
  TRING HP23 ......112 C9
Bottom La BEAC HP9 ......155 N6
Bottom Orch RAYLW HP18......106 C5
Bottom Rd SKCH HP14 ......140 G4
  WYM HP11 ......112 B9
Bottrells La CSTG HP8 ......155 M3
Botwell Common Rd
  HYS/HAR UB3 ......191 K1
Botwell Crs HYS/HAR UB3 ......183 L9
Botwell La HYS/HAR UB3 ......183 L9
Boughton Wy AMS HP6 ......199 M6
Boulmer Rd UX/CGN UB8......182 C6
Boulters Cl SL SL1 ......187 L5
Boulters Ct MDHD SL6 ......178 A7
Boulters Gdns MDHD SL6 ......178 A7
Boulters La MDHD SL6 ......178 A6
Boulters Lock CTLIN MK14......30 C7
Boundary Pl FLKWH HP10......166 B3
Boundary Rd BRACKY NN13......35 J6
  CFSP/GDCR SL9 ......156 A7
  FLKWH HP10 ......166 B3
  SL SL1 ......178 C2
The Boundary
  GTMIS/PWD HP16 ......133 J7
Bounty St BDWL MK13 ......29 P6
Bouquet Cl
  GTMIS/PWD HP16 ......133 J7
Bourbon St AYL HP20 ......2 C4
Bourn Av UX/CGN UB8 ......182 C7
Bourne Av NTHLT UB5 * 191 N3
  WDSR SL4 ......193 N3
Bourne Cl BNEND SL8 ......165 P4
Bourne Cl RSLP HA4 ......171 J4
Bourne End La HHNE HP2 ......100 F7
Bourne End Rd FLKWH HP10......166 C4
  NTHWD HA6 ......159 N8
  RBEDW MK43 ......33 M1
Bournemead Av NTHLT UB5 ...183 N6
Bournemead Cl NTHLT UB5 ...183 N6
Bourne Rd BERK HP4 ......114 B9
  SL SL1 ......187 N5

The Bourne HHW HP1 ......127 J9
Bourton Cl HYS/HAR UB3 ......191 J2
Bourton Low WTR/OFPK MK7....43 P7
Bourton Rd BUCK/WIN MK18....48 B3
Bourtonville BUCK/WIN MK18....48 B4
Bouverie Wy DTCH/LGLY SL3 ...188 G6
Boveney Cl SL SL1 ......187 L3
Boveney New Rd WDSR SL4 ...187 J5
Boveney Rd WDSR SL4 ......186 C5
Boveney Wood La SL SL1 ......167 H8
Bovingdon Hts MLW SL7 ......164 B7
Bow Brickhill Rd
  RMKS/WB MK17 ......44 D9
Bow Br WHLY OX33 ......116 C5
Bowden Cl
  EBED/NFELT TW14 ......197 L7
Bowden La WYM HP11 ......153 K5
Bowen Cl WTR/OFPK MK7 ......44 A8
Bowen Ct DUN/WHIP LU6......86 B5
Bowerdean Rd HWYN HP13......153 K3
Bower La DUN/WHIP LU6......86 B3
Bower's La SKCH HP14 ......140 F4
Bower Wy SL SL1 ......187 L1
Bowes La SKCH HP14 ......140 G4
Bowes Lyon Cl WDSR SL4 ......186 C5
Bowland Crs DUN/WHIP LU6......87 J2
Bowland Dr EMV/FZ MK4......52 B2
Bowler Lea HWYN HP13 ......142 D9
Bowler Rd AYLS HP21 ......109 N3
Bowler's Orch CSTG HP8 ......156 C5
Bowling Aly
  RAYLNE/WEN HP22 ......80 F1
Bowling Ct HEN RG9 ......173 L5
Bowling Gn SKCH HP14 ......139 P6
Bowling Green Rd
  RBEDW MK43 ......33 N4
Bowling Leys MKV MK10 ......43 N3
Bowmans La DUN/WHIP LU6......87 L1
Bowmont Dr AYLS HP21 ......109 M3
Bowood Ct WTR/OFPK MK7......44 A7
Bowood La
  GTMIS/PWD HP16 ......123 N8
Bowry Dr STWL/WRAY TW19 ...195 H5
Bowsley Ct FELT TW13 ......197 N8
Bowstridge La CSTG HP8 ......156 E3
Bowyer Crs DEN/HRF UB9 ......169 P4
Bowyer Dr SL SL1 ......187 J1
Bowyers Ms GTLIN MK14 ......30 F1
Boxberry Gdns
  WTR/OFPK MK7 ......44 A6
Boxer Rd PRRI MK27 ......120 C7
Boxgrove Cl MKV MK10 ......43 M3
Box La HHW HP1 ......127 M4
Box Tree Cl HHW HP1 ......135 H6
Box Tree La THAME OX9 ......128 D8
Boxwell Rd BERK HP4 ......114 C4
Boxwood Cl WDR/YW UB7 ......190 D1
Boyce Crs WTR/OFPK MK7......44 B7
Boycott Av EAG/OLD/WT MK6...6 C7
Boydon Rd MDHD SL6 ......177 K9
Boyn Hill Av MDHD SL6 ......185 K1
Boyn Hill Cl MDHD SL6 ......185 K1
Boyn Hill Rd MDHD SL6 ......185 K2
Boyn Valley Rd MDHD SL6 ......185 J2
Brabham Cl TOW NN12 ......25 K1
Bracken Cl SLN SL2 ......167 P9
Brackenfield
  DTCH/LGLY SL3 ......188 E3
Bracken Hl BERK HP4 ......114 C9
Bracken Rd MDHD SL6 ......185 J1
The Brackens WYM HP11 ......153 J5
Brackens Wy AYLW HP19 ......95 K7
Brackley Dr HAZ/HG HP15 ......143 H5
Brackley Gorse
  BRACKY NN13 * 34 D3
Brackley La BUCK/WIN MK18......67 P3
Brackley Rd BRACKY NN13......36 A7
  HAZ/HG HP15 ......143 N5
  TOW NN12 ......25 K3
Bradbury Rd RKW/CH/CXG WD3 ...157 M5
Bradbourne Dr
  WTR/OFPK MK7 ......44 C7
Bradbury Cl BDWL MK13 ......42 A1
Bradcutts La MDHD SL6 ......165 K9
Braddenham Wk AYLS HP21 ...109 N2
Bradden La HHNE HP2 ......101 N4
Braddons Furlong
  RAYLW HP18 ......106 A8
Braden Cl AYLS HP21 ......96 A9
Bradenham Beeches
  SKCH HP14 ......142 A3
Bradenham La MLW SL7 ......142 A3
Bradenham Wd SKCH HP14......141 P6
Bradfield Av BUCK/WIN MK18....48 B1
Bradford Rd
  RKW/CH/CXG WD3 ......147 L9
  SL SL1 ......179 L9
Bradley Cl RAYLW HP18 ......104 C5
Bradley Gv EMV/FZ MK4......52 B1
Bradley Rd SL SL1 ......186 C4
Bradshaw Cl WDSR SL4 ......187 J3
Bradshaw Rd HWYN HP13 ......153 M4
Bradvue Crs BDWL MK13 ......30 A7
Bradwell Common Bvd
  BDWL MK13 ......6 B1
Bradwell Rd BDWL MK13 ......42 A1
  SHEN MK5 ......42 A5
Brae Hl RAYLW HP18 ......90 C7
Brae Hill Cl RAYLW HP18 ......90 C7
Braemar Gdns SL SL1 ......187 L3
Braeside SKCH HP14 ......140 A3
Braford Gdns SHEN MK5 ......42 A7
Bragenham La
  RMKS/WB MK17 ......64 A4
Bragenham Side
  RMKS/WB MK17 ......63 L3
Bragmans La
  RKW/CH/CXG WD3 ......137 M6

Brahms Cl WTR/OFPK MK7......44 A7
The Braid CSHM HP5 ......136 A3
Brainton Av
  EBED/NFELT TW14 ......197 P6
Braintree Rd RSLP HA4 ......171 P9
Brakynbery BERK HP4 ......114 A7
Bralings La CFSP/GDCR SL9 ......157 J4
Bramber Ct BTCHLY MK3 ......52 C1
Bramber Ct SL SL1 ......187 L2
Bramble Av GTLIN MK14 ......30 F4
Bramble Cl CFSP/GDCR SL9 ......156 G6
  LBUZ LU7 ......74 C3
  UX/CGN UB8 ......182 C5
Bramble Dr MDHD SL6 ......184 C3
Bramble La AMSS HP7 ......146 A5
Bramble Md CSTG HP8 ......156 C3
Brambles Farm Dr
  HGDN/ICK UB10 ......182 G6
Brambleside FLKWH HP10 ......153 P6
The Brambles WDR/YW UB7 ......190 D6
Brambling AYLW HP19 ......95 J4
Bramcote Cl AYL HP20 ......96 C7
Bramham Ct HWWH HA6 * 159 L8
Bramley Cha MDHD SL6 ......185 J3
Bramley Ct HYS/HAR UB3 ......191 N1
  MDHD SL6 ......185 J4
  RSLP HA4 ......171 M1
Bramley End
  GTMIS/PWD HP16 ......142 G3
Bramley Mdw NPAG MK16 ......31 H2
Bramley Rd DBGH MK1 ......53 J1
Brampton Ct MDHD SL6 ......177 P8
Brampton Ms MLW SL7 * 164 D8
Brampton Rd
  HGDN/ICK UB10 ......183 H5
  OXHEY WD19 ......159 N3
Branch Rd FLKWH HP10 ......153 P8
Brandon Rd HWYW HP12 ......152 B7
Brands Hill Av HWYN HP13 ......143 J9
Brands Rd DTCH/LGLY SL3 ......189 K7
Brandville Rd WDR/YW UB7 ......190 E3
Bransgill Ct BDWL MK13 ......29 L9
Bransworth Av MKV MK10 ......43 P4
Brantham Cl WTR/OFPK MK7....43 N9
Brasenose Dr BRACKY NN13......34 A7
Brassey Cl
  EBED/NFELT TW14 ......197 N7
Braunston EAG/OLD/WT MK6....43 K6
Braybank MDHD SL6 ......186 A5
Braybourne Cl UX/CGN UB8......182 C2
Braybrooke Dr EMV/FZ MK4......52 C2
Bray Cl MDHD SL6 ......186 A5
Brayfield Rd MDHD SL6 ......186 A3
Bray Rd MDHD SL6 ......185 P5
Brays Cl AMS HP6 ......134 F8
Brays Green La AMS HP6 ......134 G8
Brays Meadow AMS HP6 ......134 F8
Brayton Ct SHEN MK5 ......42 C6
Braziers End CSHM HP5 ......124 G5
Breachwell Pl LBUZ LU7 ......84 C3
Breadcroft La MDHD SL6 ......184 F4
Breadcroft Rd MDHD SL6 ......184 F4
Breakspear Rd North
  DEN/HRF UB9 ......170 D1
Breakspear Rd South
  HGDN/ICK UB10 ......170 D6
Bream Cl MLW SL7 ......164 C9
Breamore Cl
  CNH/GTH/TM MK8 ......41 P4
Brearley Av
  EAG/OLD/WT MK6 ......42 G5
Brearley Cl HGDN/ICK UB10 ......182 E2
Breckland GTLIN MK14 ......30 C5
Brecon Ct MKV MK10 ......43 M3
Brecon Wy HWYN HP13 ......4 ...
Bredward Cl SL SL1 ......178 F6
Bremen Gv SHEN MK5 ......42 A8
Bremer Rd
  STWL/WRAY TW19 ......196 A8
Brenchwood Cl HWYN HP13 ...142 A9
Brendon Cl HYS/HAR UB3 ......191 J8
Brendon Ct EMV/FZ MK4 ......51 P3
Brent EAG/OLD/WT MK6 ......43 H7
Brent Rd BNEND SL8 ......165 N5
Brentwood Wy AYLS HP21 ......96 A9
Bretby Cha EMV/FZ MK4 ......51 P1
Breton STSTR MK11 ......28 C7
Breton Cl THAME OX9 ......118 F5
Bretts La RNHFFN NN12 ......23 J2
Brewery Ct BUCK/WIN MK18 * ...48 B3
Brewhouse La
  RAYLNE/WEN HP22 ......82 C1
Brewin Cl BRACKY NN13 ......34 F5
Briarcliff HHW HP1 ......101 N7
Briar Cl BDWL MK13 ......42 A2
  BRACKY NN13 ......34 F5
  MDHD SL6 ......178 A7
Briar Dene MDHD SL6 ......177 P7
Briars Cl AYL HP20 ......96 C9
Briars Cl AYLW HP19 ......96 A9
The Briars DTCH/LGLY SL3 ......189 H6
  HAZ/HG HP15 ......144 A4
  WYM HP11 ......153 J5
Briarswood SKCH HP14 ......126 E6
Briar Wy BERK HP4 ......114 A7
Briarwood Cl FELT TW13 ......197 M8
Briarwood Dr NTHWD HA6 ......159 N9
Briary Vw RMKS/WB MK17 ......64 A1
Brices Meadow SHEN MK5 ......42 B6
Brick Cl STSTR MK11 ......41 L2
Brickett Cl RSLP HA4 ......159 J2
Brickfield La HYS/HAR UB3 ......191 H1
  SL SL1 ......178 D2
Brickfields Wy WDR/YW UB7......190 E4
Brick Hl RAYLW HP18 ......92 G6

Brickhill Manor Ct
  RMKS/WB MK17 * 54 B5
Brickhill Rd LBUZ LU7 ......64 B3
Brickhill St MK14 ......31 H5
Brick Kiln La
  RAYLNE/WEN HP22 ......96 C3
Bricks La SKCH HP14 ......140 E7
Brickwall La RSLP HA4 ......171 L6
Bricstock RAYLNE/WEN HP22 ...82 C4
Bridens Wy HADM HP17 ......107 K8
Bridge Av MDHD SL6 ......177 L8
Bridge Bank Cl WYM HP11 ......153 N7
Bridge Cl SL SL1 ......187 K1
Bridgeford Ct
  EAG/OLD/WT MK6 ......6 E6
Bridgeman Dr WDSR SL4 ......187 J5
Bridgend RBEDW MK43 ......11 M4
Bridge Pl AMS HP6 ......146 C1
Bridge Rd MDHD SL6 ......177 P9
  RAYLW HP18 ......116 F3
  RMKN MK19 ......28 C3
  UX/CGN UB8 ......182 C5
Bridge St BDWL MK13 ......30 A7
  BERK HP4 ......114 F6
  BUCK/WIN MK18 ......48 B5
  CSHM HP5 ......135 N8
  LBUZ LU7 ......74 D2
  MDHD SL6 ......177 P7
  OLN MK46 ......16 C3
  OLN MK46 ......15 M5
  WYM HP11 ......153 H5
Bridgeturn Av WOLV MK12 ......29 M5
Bridgewater Cl BRACKY NN13 ...35 H4
  DTCH/LGLY SL3 ......189 J8
Bridgewater Crs
  BRACKY NN13 ......35 H4
Bridgewater Hi BERK HP4 ......114 E7
Bridgewater Rd BERK HP4 ......114 C8
  BRACKY NN13 ......35 H4
Bridge Wy HGDN/ICK UB10 ......171 H8
Bridgewater Wy WDSR SL4 ......187 P8
Bridgeway RAYLW HP18 ......107 J3
  RAYLW HP18 ......107 ...
Bridgnorth Dr EMV/FZ MK4 ......51 P3
Bridgwater Rd RSLP HA4 ......171 N9
Bridle Cl MDHD SL6 ......177 K9
  SL SL1 ......187 H4
Bridle Ga WYM HP11 ......153 H6
Bridlepath Wy
  EBED/NFELT TW14 ......197 L6
Bridle Rd MDHD SL6 ......177 L9
Bridle Wy BERK HP4 ......114 C9
Bridleway
  RAYLNE/WEN HP22 ......110 A7
  TRING HP23 ......112 C9
Bridleways
  RAYLNE/WEN HP22 ......110 G9
Bridlington Crs
  HGDN/ICK UB10 ......170 G7
Bridlington Sq SL SL1 ......187 M4
Bridport Wy SLN SL2 ......179 M7
Brierley Cl GTLIN MK14 ......30 E6
Briery Wy AMS HP6 ......146 A1
Brighton Cl HGDN/ICK UB10 ......183 H5
Brighton Sp SLN SL2 ......179 K9
Brightwell Av EMV/FZ MK4 ......86 E2
Brill Cl MDHD SL6 ......177 L6
  MLW SL7 ......164 C7
Brill Pl BDWL MK13 ......42 B1
Brill Rd RAYLW HP18 ......104 F1
  RAYLW HP18 ......105 J3
  WHLY OX33 ......103 J3
Brimmers Hi HAZ/HG HP15 ......143 L5
Brimmers Rd PRRI MK27 ......131 G2
Brimmers Rd AYLW HP19 ......95 H5
Brimmers Wy BERK HP4 ......114 A8
Brindlebrook
  CNH/GTH/TM MK8 ......41 N6
Brindles La BEAC HP9 ......154 E6
Brindley Av HWYN HP13 ......153 M4
Brinkburn Cha MKV MK10 ......43 N3
Brisbane Wy AYLS HP21 ......95 K9
Bristle Hl BUCK/WIN MK18 ......47 N4
Bristol Cl STWL/WRAY TW19 ...196 E5
Bristol Wy SL SL1 ......188 B2
Bristow Ct WEAT MK2 ......53 J3
Britannia Rd CSHM HP5 ......135 N7
Britannia St AYL HP20 ......2 E4
Britannia Wy
  STWL/WRAY TW19 ......196 D6
Britten Gv WTR/OFPK MK7 ......44 B7
Brittons La RMKS/WB MK17 ......44 D3
Britwell Dr BERK HP4 ......114 E5
Britwell Rd SL SL1 ......178 F6
Brive Rd DUN/HR/TOD LU5 ......87 H1
Brixham Crs RSLP HA4 ......171 N6
Broadacre Cl
  HGDN/ICK UB10 ......171 H8
Broad Arrow Cl GTLIN MK14 ......30 E6
Broad Dean EAG/OLD/WT MK6 ...7 K6
Broadfields AYLW HP19 ......95 J2
Broadlands EAG/OLD/WT MK6 ...43 H6
Broadlands Av CSHM HP5 ......135 N3
Broad La BRACKY NN13 ......34 G9
Broadlea Rd PRRI MK27 ......131 ...
Broadmark Rd SLN SL2 ......180 D1
Broadmoor
  WAR/TWY RG10 ......184 B9
Broad Oak CSHM HP5 ......135 N3
Broad Oak SLN SL2 ......179 N7
Broad Piece WLLN MK15 ......30 G6

Broad Platts DTCH/LGLY SL3 ...188 F4
Broad St BRACKY NN13 ......34 B5
  CSHM HP5 ......135 N8
  NPAC MK16 ......31 J2
Broadview Rd CSHM HP5 ......125 M9
The Broad Wk NTHWD HA6 ......159 J4
Broadwater BERK HP4 ......114 E9
  EAG/OLD/WT MK6 ......43 K7
Broadwater Cl
  STWL/WRAY TW19 ......194 C6
Broadwater Gdns
  DEN/HRF UB9 ......170 B2
Broadwater La
  DEN/HRF UB9 ......170 B2
Broadwater Pk
  DEN/HRF UB9 ......170 A4
  MDHD SL6 ......186 A6
Broadwaters Av THAME OX9 ...118 D6
Broadway AMSS HP7 ......145 N4
Broadway AMSS HP7 ......145 M4
  DEN/HRF UB9 ......185 M1
  WDSR SL4 ......192 F7
Broadway Av GTLIN MK14 ......30 F3
Broadway Cl AMSS HP7 ......145 N4
Broadway Pde
  HYS/HAR UB3 * 191 M3
  WDR/YW UB7 * 190 E3
The Broadway BEAC HP9 * 155 J9
  BEAC HP9 ......155 J9
  CFSP/GDCR SL9 ......156 C8
  CSHM HP5 ......135 C5
  KID OX5 ......88 C3
  RAYLW HP18 ......106 A7
Broadwood Av RSLP HA4 ......171 M2
Brocas St WDSR SL4 ......187 P8
Brocas Ter WDSR SL4 ......187 N8
Brocas Wy LBUZ LU7 ......84 A5
Brockhampton WLLN MK15......31 N7
Brockhurst Rd CSHM HP5 ......135 N3
Brock La MDHD SL6 ......185 M1
Brockwell NPAG MK16 ......31 J2
Broken Furlong WDSR SL4 ......187 N6
Broken Gate La
  DEN/HRF UB9 ......158 L6
Bromham Ml GTLIN MK14 ......30 L5
Bromley TRING HP23 ......112 B9
Bromley La AMS HP6 ......134 F2
Brompton Crs AYLW HP19 ......95 K5
Brompton Dr MDHD SL6 ......177 J7
Bromycroft Rd SLN SL2 ......179 L6
Bronte Cl AYLW HP18 ......95 H5
Brookbank FLKWH HP10 ......166 B6
Brook Cl RAYLNE/WEN HP22 ...111 K1
  RSLP HA4 ......171 L5
  STWL/WRAY TW19 ......196 F6
Brook Crs SL SL1 ......179 J4
Brookdene Cl MDHD SL6 ......178 M7
Brookdene Dr NTHWD HA6 ......159 N7
Brooke Dr RSLP HA4 ......171 L4
Brooke Cl BTCHLY MK3 ......52 F1
Brooke Furmston Pl
  MLW SL7 ......164 E6
Brook End NPAC MK16 ......22 D5
Brooke Rd PRRI MK27 ......110 E3
Brookend Cl RSLP HA4 ......121 K9
Brookfield Cl HWYN HP13 ......123 F2
Brookfield La
  BUCK/WIN MK18 ......48 B4
Brookfield Rd FLKWH HP10 ......166 A6
  RMKN MK19 ......29 M3
  RMKS/WB MK17 ......28 D8
Brookhouse Dr FLKWH HP10 ...166 A6
Brooklands Av LBUZ LU7 ......74 F3
Brooklands Rd WEAT MK2 ......53 J3
Brook La BERK HP4 ......114 E9
  RBEDW MK43 ......16 K1
  THAME OX9 ......118 C5
Brooklyn Wy WDR/YW UB7 ......190 D4
Brook Pth SL SL1 ......179 J4
Brooks Ct BUCK/WIN MK18 ......48 B3
Brookside Cl MDHD SL6 ......178 A7
  DTCH/LGLY SL3 ......189 A8
  FLKWH HP10 ......166 A6
  HGDN/ICK UB10 ......170 C1
  RAYLW HP18 ......110 A5
  THAME OX9 ......118 D4
  WOLV MK12 ......29 J2
Brookside
  STWL/WRAY TW19 ......194 F2
  FELT TW13 ......197 N9
  RMKN MK19 ......30 D7
  THAME OX9 ......118 D4
Brookside La HADM HP17 ......121 J5
Brookside Ter HYS/HAR UB3 * ...3 F5
Brookside Wk LBUZ LU7 ......74 C3
Brook St CHNR OX39 ......129 K4
  DUN/WHIP LU6 ......74 C2
  LBUZ LU7 ......74 C2
Brookway RMKN MK19 ......27 P9
Broombarn La
  GTMIS/PWD HP16 ......133 L5
Broom Cl HAZ/HG HP15 * 143 H2
Broomfield WOLV MK12 ......29 M3
Broomfield Cl
  GTMIS/PWD HP16 ......133 L5
Broomfield Ga SLN SL2 ......179 M7
Broom Hl HHW HP1 ......127 N3
  MDHD SL6 ......177 L8
  SLN SL2 ......180 C1
Broomhills Rd LBUZ LU7 ......64 E9
Broomlee BDWL MK13 ......30 A9
Broomstick La CSHM HP5 ......136 C9

Brotheridge Ct *AYLS* HP21 .....95 K9
Brough Cl *SHEN* MK5 .....42 A7
Broughton Av *AYL* HP20 .....96 B7
Broughton Cl
  RAYLNE/WEN HP22 .....96 B4
Broughton La
  RAYLNE/WEN HP22 .....96 C5
Broughton Rd *MKV* MK10 .....43 M2
  RMKS/WB MK17 .....48 A3
Broughton Ter *AYL* HP20 * 96
Browells La *FELT* TW15 .....197 F8
Brownbaker Ct *GTLIN* MK14 .....30 F1
Browells La *FELT* TW15 197
Brownbaker Ct *GTLIN* MK14 .....30 F1
Browne Willis Cl *WEAT* MK2 .....53 K3
Brownfield Gdns *MDHD* SL6 .....185 L2
Browngraves Rd
  WDR/YW UB7 .....191 J8
Browning Cl *NPAG* MK16 .....30 C1
Browning Crs *BTCHLY* MK3 .....52 C4
Brownlow Av *AYL* HP20 .....95 B5
Brownlow La *LBUZ* LU7 .....84 D5
Brownlow Rd *BEAC* HP4 .....114 E9
Brownsfield Rd *TOW* NN12 .....18 A4
Brownslea *LBUZ* LU7 .....74 G3
Brownswood Dr *TOW* NN12 18
Brownswood Rd *BEAC* HP9 .....155 H6
The Brow *CSTG* HP8 .....156 F9
Broxbourne Cl *GTLIN* MK14 .....30 F1
Bruce Cl *SL* SL1 .....187 L2
Bruckner Gdns
  WTR/OFPK MK7 .....44 B7
Brudenell *WDSR* SL4 .....193 K2
Brudenell Dr *MKV* MK10 .....44 A4
  RAYLNE/WEN HP22 .....110 B5
Brunel Cl *HEST* TW5 .....191 P8
  MDHD SL6 .....185 L2
Brunel Rd *AYLW* HP19 .....95 H6
  HWYN HP13 .....153 J5
  MDHD SL6 .....185 K2
Brunel Wy *SL* SL1 .....188 B2
Brunleys *STSTR* MK11 .....41 K1
Brunswick Cl *AYLW* HP19 .....95 J4
Brunswick Dr *EMV/FZ* MK4 .....42 D9
Brushwood Dr
  RKW/CH/CXG WD3 .....147 L6
Brushwood Rd *CSHM* HP5 .....135 P2
Bryans Crs *NPAG* MK16 .....22 E6
Bryanston Av *AYL* HP20 .....95 P5
Bryant Av *SL* SL2 .....179 P8
Bryants Acre
  RAYLNE/WEN HP22 .....111 H9
Bryants Bottom Rd
  GTMIS/PWD HP16 .....132 E7
Bryer Rd *WDSR* SL4 .....193 H2
Bryne La *BUCK/WIN* MK18 .....48 F9
Bryony Cl *UX/CGN* UB8 .....182 F8
Bryony Pl *GTLIN* MK14 .....30 E9
Buccleuch Rd
  DTCH/LGLY SL3 .....188 C8
Buchanan Rd *RBICS/W* OX25 .....89 N1
Buchan Cl *UX/CGN* UB8 .....182 C6
Buckby *EAG/OLD/WT* MK6 .....43 K7
Buckfast Av *BTCHLY* MK3 .....52 C1
Buckingham Av East *SL* SL1 .....179 N9
Buckingham Cl
  HWYN HP13 .....153 N4
Buckingham Dr *HWYN* HP13 .....153 N3
Buckingham Gdns *SL* SL1 .....188 B3
Buckingham Ga
  EAG/OLD/WT MK6 .....43 H3
  MLW SL7 .....175 M1
Buckingham Gv
  HGDN/ICK UB10 .....182 G5
Buckingham Pde
  CFSP/GDCR SL9 .....196 F4
Buckingham Pl *HWYN* HP13 * 4 D4
  BRACKY NN13 .....35 I5
  BTCHLY MK3 .....52 C4
  BUCK/WIN MK18 .....58 C8
  BUCK/WIN MK18 .....60 A5
  RAYLNE/WEN HP22 .....95 M3
  RMKN MK19 .....48 E3
  TRING HP23 .....112 C3
Buckingham Sq *CMK* MK9 .....6 B3
  BUCK/WIN MK18 .....48 C1
  WOLV MK12 .....29 M7
Buckingham Wy
  FLKWH HP10 .....153 N8
Buckland Av *DTCH/LGLY* SL3 .....188 D4
Buckland Crs *WDSR* SL4 .....187 K9
Buckland Dr
  RAYLNE/WEN HP22 .....43 J6
Buckland Ga *DTCH/LGLY* SL3 .....180 D6
Buckland Rd
  RAYLNE/WEN HP22 .....111 N1
Bucklebury Cl *MDHD* SL6 .....186 A9
Buckley Ct *STSTR* MK11 .....29 H9
Buckman Cl *WOLV* MK12 .....29 J8
Buckmaster Rd *HWYW* HP12 .....152 C7
Buckthorn *WOLV* MK12 .....29 K8
Buckwood La *DUN/WHIP* LU6 .....87 D9
Budge Rd *TOW* NN12 .....18 D9
Buffins *MDHD* SL6 .....178 C6
Bulbourne Cl *BERK* HP4 .....114 D8
Bulbourne Ct *TRING* HP23 .....98 E8
Bulbourne Rd *TRING* HP23 .....98 D8
Bulkeley Av *WDSR* SL4 .....193 M2
Bullace Cl *HWW* HP1 .....127 L1
Bullbaiters La *HADM* HP6 .....134 F7
Bullbeggars La *BERK* HP4 .....127 J1
Bullfinch Gdns *AYLW* HP19 .....96 D4
Bullington End Rd
  RMKN MK19 .....19 J8

Bull La *CFSP/GDCR* SL9 .....168 F2
Bullocks Farm La *SKCH* HP14 .....151 J4
Bull Pond La *DUN/WHIP* LU6 .....87 K1
Bulrush Gv *UX/CGN* UB8 .....182 C7
Bull's Br *HYS/HAR* UB3 .....191 N4
Bullsland Gdns
  RKW/CH/CXG WD3 .....147 K8
Bullsland La
  RKW/CH/CXG WD3 .....147 K8
Bulls La *RAYLW* HP18 .....116 G2
Bulmer Cl *MKV* MK10 .....43 P1
Bulstrode Cl *KGLGY* WD4 .....137 L2
Bulstrode La *KGLGY* WD4 .....137 L3
Bulstrode Wy
  CFSP/GDCR SL9 .....168 F3
Bunby Rd *SL* SL2 .....180 B3
Bunces Cl *WDSR* SL4 .....187 M6
Bungalow Cl *HAD* OX5 .....102 E4
Bunkers La *LBUZ* LU7 .....74 B3
Bunstrux *TRING* HP23 .....112 F1
Bunten Meade *SL* SL1 .....187 M2
Burano Cl *TRING* HP23 .....112 F1
Burano Cl *WTR/OFPK* MK7 .....44 A6
Burbage Cl *HYS/HAR* UB3 .....183 K9
Burchard Crs *SHEN* MK5 .....42 A6
Burchetts Green La
  MDHD SL6 .....184 C1
Burchett's Green Rd
  MDHD SL6 .....184 A2
Burcot Gdns *MDHD* SL6 .....177 L5
Burcott Cl *RAYLNE/WEN* HP22 .....96 B4
Burcott La
  RAYLNE/WEN HP22 .....96 C4
Burdeleys La *SHEN* MK5 .....42 A8
Burdett Dr *SKCH* HP14 .....142 B3
Burdock Ct *NPAG* MK16 .....30 F1
Burewelle *CNH/GTH/TM* MK8 .....41 M4
Burfield Rd
  RKW/CH/CXG WD3 .....147 K7
  WDSR SL4 .....194 C6
Burford Cl *HGDN/ICK* UB10 .....170 E9
  MLW SL7 .....164 C4
Burford Gdns *SL* SL1 .....178 G9
Burgage Pl *THAME* OX9 * 118 C5
Burges Cl *DUN/WHIP* LU6 .....87 M5
Burges Gdns *NPAG* MK16 .....30 D7
Burgess La *HADM* HP17 .....108 D7
Burgess Wood Rd *BEAC* HP9 .....154 F9
Burgess Wood Rd South
  BEAC HP9 .....154 F9
Burghley Ct
  CNH/GTH/TM MK8 .....41 H6
Burholme *EMV/FZ* MK4 .....42 C9
Burke Rd *RAYLNE/WEN* HP22 .....111 J9
Burkes Cl *BEAC* HP9 .....155 H6
Burkes Ct *BEAC* HP9 * 155 H7
Burkes Crs *BEAC* HP9 .....155 H6
Burkes Rd *BEAC* HP9 .....155 G6
Burleigh Piece
  BUCK/WIN MK18 .....48 C2
Burleigh Rd *HGDN/ICK* UB10 .....183 H4
Burleys Rd *BUCK/WIN* MK18 .....60 B6
Burlington Cl *SL* SL1 .....188 A3
Burlington Dr
  EBED/NFELT TW14 .....197 K6
Burlington Pl *PIN* HA5 .....171 F1
Burlington Rd *SL* SL1 .....188 A3
Burman Cl *HWYN* HP13 .....153 L4
Burners La *STSTR* MK11 .....29 K9
Burners La South
  STSTR MK11 .....29 K9
Burness Cl *UX/CGN* UB8 .....182 D5
Burnet *GTLIN* MK14 .....30 E8
Burnetts Rd *WDSR* SL4 .....187 L1
Burnham Av *BEAC* HP9 .....167 L1
Burnham Cl *WDSR* SL4 .....187 L1
Burnham Dr *BDWL* MK13 .....42 C1
Burnham Gdns *HEST* TW5 .....191 P6
  HYS/HAR UB3 .....191 K4
Burnham La *SL* SL1 .....179 J9
Burnham Pl *BRACKY* NN13 * 34 B4
Burnham Rd *BEAC* HP9 .....167 J4
  RAYLW HP18 .....78 F9
The Burnhams
  RAYLNE/WEN HP22 .....96 E9
The Burnhams
  RAYLNE/WEN HP22 .....111 J1
  RAYLW HP18 .....117 K2
Burnmoor Cl *WEAT* MK2 .....53 K7
Burns Av *EBED/NFELT* TW14 .....197 N5
Burns Cl *NPAG* MK16 .....31 J2
Burns Rd *BTCHLY* MK3 .....52 C4
Burns Oak Rd *AMSS* HP7 .....155 J8
Burrell Cl *AYLS* HP21 .....95 M9
The Burren *AMS* HP6 * 145 P1
Burroughs Crs *BNEND* SL8 .....145 N5
Burroway Rd
  DTCH/LGLY SL3 .....189 K4
Burrows Cl *FLKWH* HP10 .....153 N6
  RMKS/WB MK17 .....44 A9
Burton La *PRRI* HP27 .....121 L8
Burton's La *CSTG* HP8 .....146 E4
  RKW/CH/CXG WD3 .....146 E4
Burton Wy *WDSR* SL4 .....193 G3
Burtree Cl *WOLV* MK12 .....29 M8
Burt's La *RAYLW* HP18 .....106 B9
Burwell Hill *BRACKY* NN13 .....35 H4
Bury Av *NPAG* MK16 .....31 L1
  RSLP HA4 .....171 J1
  YEAD UB4 .....183 L5
Bury Farm *AMSS* HP7 .....145 N4
Bury Farm La *LBUZ* LU7 .....84 G2

Buryfield La
  GTMIS/PWD HP16 .....133 P5
Bury La *CSHM* HP5 .....135 M4
Bury St *NPAG* MK16 .....31 J1
  RKW/CH/CXG WD3 .....158 D1
Bury Mdw
  RKW/CH/CXG WD3 .....158 D1
Bury Rd *HHS/BOV* HP3 .....127 M7
Bury St *NPAG* MK16 .....31 J1
  RSLP HA4 .....171 K4
The Bury *CSHM* HP5 * 135 M5
Busby Cl *BUCK/WIN* MK18 .....48 D2
Buscot Pt *CNH/GTH/TM* MK8 .....41 H4
Bushel Whf *TRING* 98 E9
Bushes La *BUCK/WIN* MK18 .....57 J1
Bushey Bartrams *SHEN* MK5 .....42 A9
Bushey Cl *BUCK/WIN* MK18 .....48 D2
  HGDN/ICK UB10 .....170 C7
  HWYW HP12 .....152 D4
Bushey Leys Cl *HEAD* OX5 .....102 A4
Bushey Rd *HGDN/ICK* UB10 .....170 C7
  HYS/HAR UB3 .....183 M7
Bushfield Rd *HHS/BOV* HP3 .....127 L7
Bushmead Cl
  RAYLNE/WEN HP22 .....81 K3
The Bush *HADM* HP17 .....107 K9
Bushy Cl *BTCHLY* MK3 .....42 G9
Bushleas La *SHEN* MK5 .....42 A9
Butcher La *EMV/FZ* MK4 .....51 P1
Butchers La *MDHD* SL6 .....184 C6
Bute Brae *BTCHLY* MK3 .....52 E1
Butlers Cl *HWYN* HP13 .....153 N8
Butlers Court Rd *BEAC* HP9 .....155 H5
Butlers Gv *GTLIN* MK14 .....30 D5
Butler St *HGDN/ICK* UB10 .....182 E5
Butler Wk *AYLW* HP19 .....95 J8
Buttercup Cl *DUN/WHIP* LU6 .....87 J1
Buttercup Sq
  GTMIS/PWD TW19 * 196 D7
Butterfield *FLKWH* HP10 .....153 M8
Butterfield Cl *WLLN* MK15 .....43 J2
Butterly Rd *SKCH* HP14 .....142 B3
Butter Market *THAME* OX9 .....118 D5
Buttermere *AYLS* HP21 .....96 B8
Buttermere Av
  DUN/WHIP LU6 .....87 J1
  SL SL1 .....178 D4
Buttermere Cl
  EBED/NFELT TW14 .....197 M2
  WEAT MK2 .....53 K5
Buttinhole
  RKW/CH/CXG WD3 .....157 M5
Button Gv *WDR/OFPK* MK7 * 42 G5
Buttsmead *NTHWD* HA6 .....159 J7
Butts Piece *PRRI* HP27 * 131 K1
Butts Wy *WTR/OFPK* MK7 .....44 A7
Buzzacott La *EMV/FZ* MK4 .....42 C9
Bybend Cl *SLN* SL2 .....179 M4
Bycell Rd *BUCK/WIN* MK18 .....37 N4
By Gn *RAYLNE/WEN* HP22 .....110 G3
Byerly Pl *GTLIN* MK14 .....30 E9
The Byeway
  RKW/CH/CXG WD3 .....158 E2
Byford Pth *SHEN* MK5 .....42 A9
Byford Wy *BUCK/WIN* MK18 .....60 B4
  LBUZ LU7 .....83 K4
Byland Dr *MDHD* SL6 .....185 P6
Byron Av *HSLWW* TW4 .....197 P1
Byron Cl *BTCHLY* MK3 .....52 C4
Byron Ct *WDSR* SL4 .....193 L2
Byron Pde *HGDN/ICK* UB10 * 183 H7
Byron Rd *AYLS* HP21 .....95 P7
Byron Wy *WDR/YW* UB7 .....190 F5
  YEAD UB4 .....183 L1
Byslips Rd *DUN/WHIP* LU6 .....101 M2
Byward Cl *GTLIN* MK14 .....30 C8
Byways *BERK* HP4 .....114 C9
  SL SL1 .....178 E9

C

Cadeby St *MKV* MK10 .....43 P1
Cadman Sq *SHEN* MK5 .....42 C7
Cadogan Cl *MDHD* SL6 .....185 N7
Cadsdean Rd *PRRI* HP27 .....121 N7
Cadwell Dr *MDHD* SL6 .....185 K4
Caenwarron Crs *BTCHLY* MK3 .....52 A5
Caesars Cl *BDWL* MK13 .....30 A8
Caesars Ga *BRACKY* NN13 .....35 H5
Cages Wood Dr *SLN* SL2 .....167 M5
Cain's La *EBED/NFELT* TW14 .....197 K4
Cairngorm Ga
  EAG/OLD/WT MK6 .....43 H3
Cairnside *HWYN* HP13 .....153 J2
Caithness Ct *BTCHLY* MK3 .....52 A4
Calamus Ct *WTR/OFPK* MK7 .....43 P6
Calbroke Rd *SLN* SL2 .....167 L7
Caldecote La *NPAG* MK16 .....31 M3
Caldecote St *NPAG* MK16 .....31 L1
Caldecote Lake Dr
  WTR/OFPK MK7 .....53 L1
Calder Cl *MDHD* SL6 .....177 M7
  DTCH/LGLY SL3 .....188 F4
Calder Gdns *LBUZ* LU7 .....73 P2
Calder Wy *DTCH/LGLY* SL3 .....189 H5
Caldewell *CNH/GTH/TM* MK8 .....41 M1
Caldicot Cl *AYLS* HP21 .....96 D5
Caledonia Rd
  STWL/WRAY TW19 .....196 B2
Caledon Rd *BEAC* HP9 .....155 J7

Calewen *CNH/GTH/TM* MK8 .....41 N3
California Cir *WYM* HP11 .....153 H6
Callis Farm Cl
  STWL/WRAY TW19 .....196 E5
Calluna Dr *BTCHLY* MK3 .....42 G9
Calshot Rd *HTHAIR* TW6 .....197 H5
Calshot Wy *HTHAIR* TW6 .....197 H6
Calumet *BEAC* HP9 .....155 H7
Calverleigh Crs *EMV/FZ* MK4 .....42 D9
Calverley Rd *HWYN* HP13 .....142 F9
Calverton La *KMKN* MK19 .....40 A5
Calverton Rd *STSTR* MK11 .....28 F9
Calves Cl *SHEN* MK5 .....42 A9
Camber Cl *BTCHLY* MK3 .....52 E4
Camberley Av *SL* SL1 .....179 L6
Camberton Rd *LBUZ* LU7 .....74 C4
Camborne Av *AYLS* HP21 .....110 D1
Camborne Cl *HTHAIR* TW6 .....196 G6
Camborne Rd *HTHAIR* TW6 .....196 G6
Cambria Ct *EBED/NFELT* TW14 .....197 J3
Cambria Gdns
  STWL/WRAY TW19 .....196 E6
Cambridge Av *SL* SL1 .....178 F5
  SL SL1 .....179 J9
Cambridge Ct *AYL* HP20 * 2 D3
  WDR/YW UB7 .....190 D7
Cambridge Crs *HWYN* HP13 .....153 L5
Cambridge Pl *AYL* HP20 * 2 C4
Cambridge Rd *BEAC* HP9 .....154 G8
  MLW SL7 .....164 D5
  UX/CGN UB8 .....182 D2
Cambridge St *AYL* HP20 * 2 D3
  WEAT MK2 .....53 J3
  WOLV MK12 .....29 M7
Cambridge Ter *AYL* HP20 * 2 D4
Cambron *CNH/GTH/TM* MK8 .....41 M2
Cam Ct *BTCHLY* MK3 .....52 E1
Camden Rd *BNEND* SL8 .....165 N6
Camden Rd *CSHM* HP5 .....135 N5
Cameron Rd *CSHM* HP5 .....135 N5
Camlet Gv *GTLIN* MK14 .....30 D6
Camley Gdns *MDHD* SL6 .....177 K6
Camley Park Dr *MDHD* SL6 .....176 F8
Camm Av *WDSR* SL4 .....193 J2
Cam Md *AYLS* HP21 .....96 A9
Camomile Ct *WTR/OFPK* MK7 .....43 P7
Camomile Wy *WDR/YW* UB7 .....182 G9
Campania Cl *MKV* MK10 .....43 N2
Campbell Cl *BUCK/WIN* MK18 .....48 C2
  HWYN HP13 .....153 N9
  RSLP HA4 .....171 N4
Campbell Ride *HAZ/HG* HP15 .....144 B3
Campden Rd
  HGDN/ICK UB10 .....170 F9
Camperdown *MDHD* SL6 .....177 P7
Campion Cl *AYL* HP20 .....96 C7
  DEN/HRF UB9 .....170 A8
  UX/CGN UB8 .....182 G9
Campion Rd *HAZ/HG* HP15 .....143 M5
  HWW HP1 .....127 K5
Campions Cl *BERK* HP4 .....126 E2
Campo Rd *CFSP/GDCR* SL9 .....168 F5
Canada Rd *SL* SL1 .....188 D3
Canal Est *DTCH/LGLY* SL3 * 189 J3
Canalside *BERK* HP4 .....114 D8
Canal La *NPAG* MK16 .....22 E6
Canal Wharf *DTCH/LGLY* SL3 .....189 H3
Canal Yd *NWDGN* UB2 * 191 P5
Canberra Rd *HTHAIR* TW6 .....196 G6
Candale Cl *DUN/WHIP* LU6 .....87 L2
Candlemas La *BEAC* HP9 .....155 J8
Candlemas Md *BEAC* HP9 .....155 J8
Candlewicks *WTR/OFPK* MK7 .....44 A6
Candover Cl *WDR/YW* UB7 .....190 D9
Candy La *SHEN* MK5 .....42 C9
Candytuft Gn *HAZ/HG* HP15 .....143 M5
Cane End *PRRI* HP27 .....131 J1
Canesworde Rd
  DUN/WHIP LU6 .....87 J1
Canfield Dr *RSLP* HA4 .....183 M1
Canford Ct *AYLS* HP21 .....109 P1
Cannock Cl *MDHD* SL6 .....185 P6
Cannock Rd *AYLS* HP21 .....95 N4
Cannondown Rd *MDHD* SL6 .....177 L5
Cannon Ga *SLN* SL2 .....188 E1
Cannon Hill Cl *MDHD* SL6 .....186 A5
Cannon La *MDHD* SL6 .....184 G2
Cannon Pl *PRRI* HP27 .....121 K9
Cannon's Wh *FLKWH* HP10 .....153 M8
Cannons Orch
  RAYLNE/WEN HP22 .....79 M3
Canon Hill Cl *MDHD* SL6 .....185 P4
Canon Hill Wy *MDHD* SL6 .....185 P5
Canons Rd *WOLV* MK12 .....29 K6
The Canons *NPAG* MK16 .....31 L2
Canopeners La
  STWL/WRAY TW19 .....196 C6
Cantell Cl *BUCK/WIN* MK18 .....48 D1
Canterbury Av *SLN* SL2 .....179 L9
Canterbury Cl *AMSS* HP7 .....146 A3
Canterbury Rd
  RAYLNE/WEN HP22 .....111 J7
Cantilupe Cl *DUN/WHIP* LU6 .....85 P2
Cantle Av *GTLIN* MK14 .....31 H5
Cantley Cl *AYLW* HP19 .....96 A3
Capel Cl *BUCK/WIN* MK18 .....38 D5
Capel Dr *GTLIN* MK14 .....30 G8
Capella Rd *NTHWD* HA6 .....159 M5
Capel Rd *RKW/CH/CXG* WD3 .....147 N6
Capital Dr *GTLIN* MK14 .....30 G7
Capludi Cook Cl *CSTG* HP8 .....156 D1
Caraway Cl *WTR/OFPK* MK7 .....44 A6
Cardigan Cl *BTCHLY* MK3 .....52 E2
  SL SL1 .....188 C1
Cardinal Rd *FELT* TW13 .....197 P7
Cardinals Wk *MDHD* SL6 .....178 G9

Cardwell Cl *EMV/FZ* MK4 .....52 C1
Carew Rd *NTHWD* HA6 .....159 P8
Carey Cl *AYLS* HP21 .....109 M2
  WDSR SL4 .....193 G2
Careys Ct *BERK* HP4 .....15 E5
Carey Wy *OLN* MK46 .....15 N3
Carfax Rd *HYS/HAR* UB3 .....191 N6
Carhampton Ct *EMV/FZ* MK4 .....42 D9
Carina Dr *LBUZ* LU7 .....74 D1
Carisbrooke Av *HWYW* HP12 .....152 B4
Carisbrooke Cl *MDHD* SL6 .....185 L2
Carisbrooke Ct
  BUCK/WIN MK18 * 48 B1
Carisbrooke Wy *EMV/FZ* MK4 .....51 L6
Carleton Cl *WLLN* MK15 .....31 L6
Carlina Pl *GTLIN* MK14 .....30 E8
Carlisle Cl *DUN/WHIP* LU6 .....87 K2
Carlisle Rd *SL* SL1 .....187 P1
Carlton Av *HYS/HAR* UB3 .....191 L5
Carlton Cl *AYLW* HP19 * 95 J5
  NPAG MK16 .....31 J2
Carlton Gv *LBUZ* LU7 .....64 E7
Carlton Rd *RBEDW* MK43 .....14 A8
  RBEDW MK43 * 17 J2
  SLN SL2 .....188 D1
Carlyle Av *AYLS* HP21 .....95 N9
Carlyle Cl *NPAG* MK16 .....30 C1
Carman Ct *TRING* HP23 .....112 B3
Carmarthen Rd *SL* SL1 .....188 A1
Carnation Cl *HYS/HAR* UB3 .....191 J4
Carnarvon Dr *HYS/HAR* UB3 .....191 J4
Carnation Cl *LBUZ* LU7 .....74 E9
Carnation Wy *AYLS* HP21 .....109 N1
The Carne *STSTR* MK11 .....28 G8
Carnoustie Cl *SHEN* MK5 .....52 C4
Carnweather Ct *EMV/FZ* MK4 .....52 D5
Caroline Cl *WDR/YW* UB7 .....190 F8
Caroline Pl *HYS/HAR* UB3 .....191 L8
Carolus Creek *WLLN* MK15 .....30 G6
Carpenter Ct *GTLIN* MK14 .....30 F7
Carpenters Wood Dr
  RKW/CH/CXG WD3 .....147 K6
Carpenters Yd *TRING* HP23 * 112 F3
Carr Cl *AYLW* HP19 .....95 J5
Carrick Rd *EAG/OLD/WT* MK6 .....7 H5
Carriers Wy *RBEDW* MK43 .....11 N4
Carrington Av *FLKWH* HP10 .....165 N1
Carrington Crs
  RAYLNE/WEN HP22 .....110 G7
Carrington Pl
  HAZ/HG HP15 * 144 A4
  TRING HP23 .....112 F1
Carrington Rd *AYLS* HP21 .....95 M9
  NPAG MK16 .....31 H2
  SL SL1 .....188 A1
Carrington Wy
  GTMIS/PWD HP16 .....133 J7
Carroll Cl *NPAG* MK16 .....31 J2
Carron Cl *WEAT* MK2 .....53 J2
Carron Ct *WEAT* MK2 .....53 J2
Carrs Dr *HWYW* HP12 .....152 C2
Carter Cl *WDSR* SL4 .....194 C6
Carteret Cl *WLLN* MK15 .....31 L5
Carters Cl *NPAG* MK16 .....31 L1
Carter's La *BUCK/WIN* MK18 .....70 B8
  RAYLNE/WEN HP22 .....105 P1
  STSTR MK11 .....41 J1
Carters Meadow
  BUCK/WIN MK18 .....70 C7
Carters Ride
  RAYLNE/WEN HP22 .....110 B4
Carter Wk *FLKWH* HP10 .....154 A2
Cartmel Cl *BTCHLY* MK3 .....52 E4
Cartmel Dr *DUN/WHIP* LU6 .....87 K2
Cartwright Crs *BRACKY* NN13 .....34 F1
Cartwright Pl
  EAG/OLD/WT MK6 .....6 E7
Carver Hill Rd *HWYN* HP13 .....152 F5
Carvers Ms *GTLIN* MK14 * 30 F8
Cascadia Cl *HWYN* HP10 .....153 P8
Cashmere Cl *SHEN* MK5 .....42 A9
Cassiobury Av
  EBED/NFELT TW14 .....197 M6
Casterton Cl *BDWL* MK13 .....30 A3
Castle Acre *MKV* MK10 .....43 M3
  WDR/YW UB7 .....73 T3
Castle Cl *AYL* HP20 .....73 L6
  RBICN OX27 .....66 G6
Castle Dr *MDHD* SL6 .....177 K9
Castlefields
  RAYLNE/WEN HP22 .....110 C3
Castle Gardens Vw
  HWYW HP12 * 152 D3
Castle Gate Wy *BERK* HP4 .....114 C8
Castle Hill *BERK* HP4 .....114 C8
  WDSR SL4 .....187 P9
Castle Hill Av *BERK* HP4 .....114 C8
Castle Hill Cl *BERK* HP4 .....114 C8
Castle Hill Ter *MDHD* SL6 .....177 L8
Castle La *RAYLNE/WEN* HP22 .....81 J2
Castle Meadow Cl
  NPAG MK16 * 31 L1
Castle Ms *BERK* HP4 * 126 L1
  MDHD SL6 .....177 L8
Castle Mt *BRACKY* NN13 .....34 G7
Castle Park Rd
  RAYLNE/WEN HP22 .....110 G8
Castle Pl *HWYN* HP13 .....153 H5
  RAYLNE/WEN HP22 .....83 H6

Castle Rd *DUN/WHIP* LU6 .....87 K2
Castle Rd *OLN* MK46 .....138 B7
  WTLGN OX49 .....138 B7
Castle Rose *EAG/OLD/WT* MK6 .....6 K6
Castlesteads *BDWL* MK13 .....29 N8
Castle St *AYL* HP20 * 2 B3
  BERK HP4 .....114 A5
  BUCK/WIN MK18 .....48 A3
  HWYN HP13 .....5 J3
  RAYLNE/WEN HP22 .....83 H6

RBICN OX27 ....66 G6
SL SL1 ....188 B4
Castlethorpe Rd
  RMKN MK19 ....19 H6
Castle View Gdns
  HWYW HP12 ....152 D3
Castleview Rd
  DTCH/LGLY SL3 ....188 B4
Catalina Rd HTHAIR TW6 ..197 H2
Catchacre DUN/WHIP UL6 ...87 J1
Catchpole Cl WOLV MK12 ...29 K8
Cater Rd SKCH HP14 ......151 L6
Catesby Cft SHEN MK5 ......6 A7
Cathay Cl RMKS/WB MK17 ...53 H4
Catherines Cl
  WDR/YW UB7 * 190 D3
Catherine Ct
  BUCK/WIN MK18 ....48 C1
Catkin Cl RAYLNE/WEN HP22 152 B7
Catlin's La PIN HA5 .....171 P1
Catslip HEN RG9 ....160 D7
Cattleford Br RMKS/WB MK17 39 L1
Causeway
  EBED/NFELT TW14 ......197 P3
The Causeway MDHD SL6 ...186 A3
  MLW SL7 ....164 E8
  RBEDW MK45 ....11 L5
Cautley Cl RAYLNE/WEN HP22 78 E3
Cavalier Gdns HYS/HAR UB3 183 K9
Cavalier Rd WDSR SL4 ....193 M2
Cavandish Wk THAME OX9 ..118 H4
Cavendish Av RSLP HA4 ...183 P1
Cavendish Cl AMS HP6 ..146 D3
  MDHD SL6 ....185 L8
  RAYLNE/WEN HP22 ......111 M8
  YEAD UB4 ....183 L8
Cavendish Ct SHEN MK5 ....42 A4
Cavendish Rd CSHM HP5 ...135 P5
Cavendish The FELT TW13 * 197 N8
Cavenham CNH/GTH/TM MK8 ..41 P7
Caversham Gn AYL HP20 .....2 C3
Cawardon GTLIN MK14 ......30 C6
Cawcott Dr WOLV MK12 ....187 J9
Cawdor Ri EMV/FZ MK4 .....51 N1
Cawkwell Wy WEAT MK2 .....53 J3
Caxton Dr UX/CGN UB8 ....182 C5
Caxton Rd WOLV MK12 .....187 J9
Cecil Rd IVER SL0 ....181 N9
Cecil Wy SLN SL2 ....179 K7
Cecily Ct SHEN MK5 ....42 A7
Cedar Av HAZ/HG HP15 ..143 M9
  HYS/HAR UB3 * 190 F2
Cedar Cha MDHD SL6 ......178 B7
Cedar Cl AYL HP20 ......3 J1
  BRACKY NN13 ....35 H3
  CSHM HP5 ....136 A3
  IVER SL0 ....181 N9
Cedar Crs THAME OX9 .....118 B5
Cedar Dr MDHD SL6 .....177 M2
  MLW SL7 ....164 C2
Cedar Gv AMS HP7 ....145 P3
Cedar Rdg AMS HP6 ....136 G7
Cedar Red BERK HP4 ......126 F2
  EBED/NFELT TW14 ......197 K2
Cedars Av
  RKW/CH/CXG WD3 ....158 G5
Cedars Cl BUCK/WIN MK18 38 D4
  CFSP/GDCR SL9 ....156 G5
Cedars Dr HGDN/ICK UB10 .182 C5
Cedars Rd MDHD SL6 ......177 N9
Ceely Rd AYL HP21 ....95 M9
Celandine Ct WTR/OFPK MK7 43 N6
Celina Cl WEAT MK2 ....53 J4
Cell Farm Av WDSR SL4 ...194 D4
Centauri Cl LBUZ LU7 .....74 C1
Central Av DUN/WHIP UL6 .86 G8
  HYS/HAR UB3 ....191 M3
  RMKS/WB MK17 ....33 J4
Central Dr SL SL1 ....179 L9
Central La WDSR SL4 .....192 F7
Central Wy
  EBED/NFELT TW14 ......197 P4
  NTHWD HA6 ....159 L7
  WDSR SL4 ....192 D7
Centre Pde PRRI HP27 * ..121 L8
Centre Rd WDSR SL4 ......186 G8
The Centre FELT TW13 ....197 N8
Centurion Ct STSTR MK11 ..41 J7
Century Av EAG/OLD/WT MK6 .7 F7
Century Point HWYW HP12 .152 C6
Cervantes Ct NTHWD HA6 ..159 P2
Cestreham Crs CSHM HP5 ..135 P2
Cetus Crs LBUZ LU7 ....74 C1
Chacombe Pl BEAC HP9 ....154 G5
Chadds La EAG/OLD/WT MK6 .43 J4
Chadwick Dr
  EAG/OLD/WT MK6 ....42 G5
Chadwick St HWYN HP13 ...143 J9
Chaffinch Wy BRACKY NN13 .34 D2
Chaffron Wy
  EAG/OLD/WT MK6 ....7 H2
  MKV MK10 ....43 M1
  WLLN MK15 ....43 J1
Chairborough Rd
  HWYW HP12 ....152 D3
Chalcot Pl CNH/GTH/TM MK8 .41 H4
Chalcraft Cl HEN RG9 ....160 D7
Chaldel Cl BERK HP4 .....126 B1
Chalfont Av AMS HP6 .....146 B1
Chalfont Cl BDWL MK13 ....30 A7

Chalfont La
  RKW/CH/CXG WD3 ....147 K7
  RKW/CH/CXG WD3 ....157 L7
Chalfont Rd BEAC HP9 ..147 K5
  CFSP/GDCR SL9 ....157 K5
  HYS/HAR UB3 ....191 N5
Chalfont Station Rd
  AMSS 146 E4
Chalfont Wy WYM WYM11 ...152 D7
Chalford Rd THAME OX9 ...128 E8
Chalgrove Rd AYL HP19 ....95 H7
Chalgrove Cl MDHD SL6 ...185 P1
Chalgrove End
  RAYLNE/WEN HP22 ......110 B4
Chalgrove Rd THAME OX9 ..118 E4
Chalgrove Wk AYLS HP21 ...95 L9
Chalkdell Dr SHEN MK5 ....41 P7
Chalk Farm Br SKCH HP14 .139 P6
Chalk HI ASHV HP7 ....145 K9
Chalklands BNEND SL8 ....165 N5
Chalk La AMSS HP7 ....134 E9
Chalkpit La MLW SL7 .....164 E8
Chalk Pit La SL SL1 .....178 F4
The Chalkpits FLKWH HP10 * 166 C5
Chalkshire Rd HADM HP17 .122 C1
Challacombe EMV/FZ MK4 ...52 D1
Challener Rd HWYN HP13 ..143 J9
Challenge Rd FELT TW13 ..197 J9
Challow Ct MDHD SL6 .....177 L2
Chalmers Wy
  EBED/NFELT TW14 ......197 P4
Chaloner Ct LBUZ LU7 .....74 A4
Chaloner Rd AYLS HP21 ....95 L9
Chaloners HI BUCK/WIN MK18 58 B7
Chalvey Gv SL SL1 ....187 M4
Chalvey Pk SL SL1 ....187 A3
Chalvey Rd East SL SL1 ..188 A3
Chalvey Rd West SL SL1 ..187 P3
Chalwell Rdg SHEN MK5 ....42 B8
Chamberlain La PIN HA5 ..171 N2
Chamberlain Rd AYLW HP19 .95 K6
Chamberlains Gdns LBUZ LU7 64 E9
Chamberlain Wy PIN HA5 ..171 P1
Champflower HWYW HP13 ....42 D9
Champion Ct BRACKY NN13 ..34 C4
Champney Cl DTCH/LGLY SL3 195 J2
Chancellors AMSS HP7 ....144 F6
Chancery Cl BDWL MK13 ....30 A7
Chandlers Cl
  EBED/NFELT TW14 ......197 M6
Chandlers Ct
  EAG/OLD/WT MK6 ....43 L7
  BUCK/WIN MK18 ....48 B4
Chandos Cl AMS HP6 .....146 E2
Chandos Rd BUCK/WIN MK18 .48 B4
Channer Dr FLKWH HP10 ...153 P1
Channory Cl EMV/FZ MK4 ...44 F8
Chantry Cl RMKS/WB MK17 ..44 C1
  WDR/YW UB7 ....190 D1
Chantry Rd AYLW HP19 .....95 L4
The Chantry AYL HP20 * ..2 C3
  UX/CGN UB8 ....182 F6
  TOW NN12 * 25 K1
Chapel Crofts BERK HP4 ..114 M4
Chapel La
  RAYLNE/WEN HP22 ......111 L1
Chapel End CFSP/GDCR SL9 * 156 F9
Chapel End La TRING HP23 .98 A2
Chapel HI LBUZ LU7 .....63 L7
  PRRI HP27 ....132 C2
Chapel La BRACKY NN13 ..35 K5
  BRACKY NN13 ....35 M1
  BUCK/WIN MK18 ....38 E4
  BUCK/WIN MK18 ....48 L5
  DUN/WHIP UL6 ....160 D7
  HEN RG9 ....152 D2
  HWYW HP12 ....110 A5
  RAYLNE/WEN HP22 ......123 N2
  RAYLW HP18 ....105 P5
  RMKS/WB MK17 ....62 B5
  SKCH HP14 ....142 A4
  SLN SL2 ....178 L3
  TRING HP23 ....97 P3
  UX/CGN UB8 ....182 C9
Chapel Rd FLKWH HP10 ..165 N1
  HADM HP17 ....108 D7
Chapel Rw DEN/HRF UB9 ...158 E2
Chapels Cl SL SL1 ....187 J2
Chapel SL SL1 ....187 J2
Chapel St BERK HP4 ....126 E1
  HWYN HP13 ....142 D8
  MLW SL7 ....164 E7
  RMKS/WB MK17 .... F8
  SL SL1 ....188 A1
  TRING HP23 ....112 C9
Chaplin Gv CNH/GTH/TM MK8 .41 M5
Chapman Av CGTLIN MK14 ...30 C8
Chapman Cl WDR/YW UB7 ...190 D1
Chapman La BNEND SL8 ....165 M4
Chapmans Crs CSHM HP5 ...135 L2
Chapmans Dr RMKN MK19 ....28 D6
Chapmans Lea
  RAYLNE/WEN HP22 ....82 D9
Chappel Meadow TRING HP23 98 F9
Chapter EAG/OLD/WT MK6 ...42 F7
Chapter Cl HGDN/ICK UB10 .182 E3
Chapter Ms WDSR SL4 .....187 P5
Chardacre CNH/GTH/TM MK8 .41 K4
Chardins Cl HHW HP1 .....127 P1
Charlotts Pl WDSR SL4 * ..187 P5
Charity Whf LBUZ LU7 * ...74 C1
Charbury Rd
  HGDN/ICK UB10 ....183 H6
Charles Cl AYLS HP21 ....110 B3
Charles Gdns SLN SL2 ....180 C9

Charles St BERK HP4 ...126 D1
  HGDN/ICK UB10 ....183 H7
  TRING HP23 ....112 A9
Charleston Cl FELT TW13 .197 N9
Charles Wy NPAG MK16 .....31 J1
Charlock Ct NPAG MK16 ....30 F1
Charlotte Av SLN SL2 ....188 B1
Charlton WDSR SL4 ....192 C1
Charlton Rd NPAG MK16 ..31 H0
  RMKS/WB MK17 ....61 J7
  SL SL1 ....188 A1
Charmfield Rd AYLS HP21 .110 A1
Charnwood Cl HWYN HP13 ..143 M5
Charnwood Rd
  HGDN/ICK UB10 ....182 C5
Charsley Cl AMS HP6 .....146 E5
Charter Cl SL SL1 ....188 B4
Charterhouse Cl
  BRACKY NN13 ....34 C5
Charter Pl UX/CGN UB8 ...182 D4
Charter Rd SL SL1 ....187 J1
Chartmoor Rd LBUZ LU7 ....74 E4
Chartridge Grange Dr
  CSHM HP5 ....125 H9
Chartridge La CSHM HP5 ..135 H1
Chartwell Rd NPAG MK16 ...31 L2
  NTHWD HA6 ....159 M6
Charville La HGDN/ICK UB10 183 H6
Charville La West
  HGDN/ICK UB10 ....183 H6
Chasden Rd HHW HP1 ......127 L6
Chase Av HTW/OFPK MK7 ....43 N7
Chase Cl AMS HP7 ....145 L9
Chase Park Rd RNHPTN NN7 ..8 F5
Chaseport Cl OLN MK46 ....15 L7
Chaseside Cl LBUZ LU7 ....84 D9
The Chase CSHM HP5 ....135 M2
  FLKWH HP10 ....153 P1
  HGDN/ICK UB10 ....177 K5
  MDHD SL6 ....164 C6
  MLW SL7 ....164 C6
  RMKS/WB MK17 ....52 D8
Chatfield SL SL2 ....179 L8
Chatsworth
  CNH/GTH/TM MK8 ....41 P3
Chatsworth Cl MDHD SL6 ..185 J2
Chatsworth Rd YEAD UB4 ..183 P7
Chaucer Av HSLWW TW4 ..197 P1
  YEAD UB4 ....183 N8
Chaucer Cl BERK HP4 ...126 B9
  NPAG MK16 ....30 C1
Chaucer Dr AYL HP21 ......95 P5
Chaucer Rd BTCHLY MK3 ....52 G4
Chaucer Wy SL SL1 ....188 C2
Chaulden House Gdns
  HHW HP1 ....127 P4
Chaulden La HHW HP1 .....127 P4
Chaulden Ter HHW HP1 ....127 P4
Chauntry Cl MDHD SL6 ....185 P1
Chauntry Ms MDHD SL6 * ..185 P1
Chauntry Rd MDHD SL6 * ..185 P1
Chawridge La WDSR SL4 ...192 D7
Chawton Crs
  CNH/GTH/TM MK8 ....41 P3
Cheapside La DEN/HRF UB9 169 P7
Chearsley Rd RAYLW HP18 .106 C9
Cheddar Waye YEAD UB4 ...183 P9
Cheddington La TRING HP23 .98 A2
Cheddington Rd LBUZ LU7 ..74 A4
Chelsea Gn LBUZ LU7 ......74 A4
Chelston Rd RSLP HA4 ....171 N7
Cheltenham Gdns
  BTCHLY MK3 ....52 D5
Chelwood Cl NTHWD HA6 ...159 J4
Cheney Cl LBUZ LU7 ....84 D9
Cheney Wk BTCHLY MK3 .....52 G9
Cheney Wk AYL HP20 ....95 P5
Chenies Av AMS HP6 ......146 A5
Chenies Pde AMS HP7 * ...146 C6
Chenies Rd
  RKW/CH/CXG WD3 ....147 M4
Cheniston Gv MDHD SL6 ...176 F9
Chequers End
  BUCK/WIN MK18 ....60 C6
Chepping Cl HAZ/HG HP15 .143 N1
Chepstow Dr BTCHLY MK3 ...52 G3
Chequers Ct AYLS HP21 ....98 G3
Chequers Ct AYLS HP21 ....95 M7
Chequers Dr
  GTMIS/PWD HP16 ....133 H5
Chequers La
  CTMIS/PWD HP16 ....133 J5
Chequers Orch IVER SL0 ..181 N9
Chequers Pde MDHD SL6 * .133 J6
The Chequers DUN/WHIP UL6 86 J6
  RMKN MK19 ....19 H9
Cherington Gd MDHD SL6 * 177 N7
Cheriton EMV/FZ MK4 ......42 D9
The Cherries SLN SL2 ....180 C9
Cherry Acre DTCH/LGLY SL3 188 F3
Cherry Cl FLKWH HP10 ..153 N1
  RSLP HA4 ....171 K8
Cherry Cnr FLKWH HP10 ...175 J2
Cherrycourt Wy LBUZ LU7 ..75 J2
Cherry Dr BEAC HP9 ......154 F6
Cherry Garden La MDHD SL6 184 D4
Cherry Gdns TRING HP23 * 144 F5
  HYS/HAR UB3 ....191 P2
  UX/CGN UB8 ....189 D5
Cherry La AMS HP7 .....145 L4
  WDR/YW UB7 ....190 F5
Cherry Leys BUCK/WIN MK18 58 C7

Cherry Orch AMS HP6 ...146 A1
  HHW HP1 ....115 P9
  OLN MK46 .... 15 L1
  SL SL1 ....180 C5
The Cherry Pit HWYN HP13 142 E9
Cherry Ri CSTG HP8 ......156 F2
Cherry Rd NPAG MK16 ......31 H0
Cherry St FLKWH HP10 ....153 N6
Cherry Tree Wy
  WDR/YW UB7 ....190 F5
Cherry Tree HAZ/HG HP15 143 K2
  PRRI HP27 ....132 B7
Cherry Tree Cnr BEAC HP9 * 154 A9
Cherry Tree La
  DTCH/LGLY SL3 ....181 H1
  GTMIS/PWD HP16 ....124 D9
  RKW/CH/CXG WD3 ....157 L1
Cherrytree La
  CFSP/GDCR SL9 ....156 F9
Cherry Tree Rd BEAC HP9 154 A9
  CHNR OX39 ....129 N5
  SLN SL2 ....179 M8
Cherry Tree Wk CSHM HP5 .135 P2
Cherry Wy
  FLKWH HP10 ....154 A1
  DTCH/LGLY SL3 ....195 K4
  HAZ/HG HP15 ....143 K2
Cherrywood Cl BEAC HP9 ..155 P6
Cherrywood Gdns
  FLKWH HP10 ....165 N1
Chertsey Rd FELT TW13 ...197 N9
Chervil EAG/OLD/WT MK6 ...43 H7
Chervil Cl FELT TW13 ....197 N9
Cherwell Cl DTCH/LGLY SL3 189 K7
  MDHD SL6 ....177 H3
Cherwell Rd AYLS HP21 ..95 J3
  BNEND SL8 ....165 P5
Cherwell Wy RSLP HA4 ....171 C4
Chesham Av BDWL MK13 .....43 L4
Chesham La CFSP/GDCR SL9 156 D4
  GTMIS/PWD HP16 ....124 D9
  RAYLNE/WEN HP22 ......123 C5
Chesham Rd AMS HP5 ....145 N1
  BERK HP4 ....125 J9
  CSHM HP5 ....125 J6
  CSHM HP5 ....135 N2
  GTMIS/PWD HP16 ....134 B3
  HHS/BOV HP3 ....136 C1
  TRING HP23 ....113 H6
Cheshire Rd THAME OX9 ...118 F6
Chesil Wy YEAD UB4 ......183 N6
Cheslyn Gdns GTLIN MK14 ..30 G5
Chesney Wold
  EAG/OLD/WT MK6 ....42 F9
Chessbury Rd CSHM HP5 ...135 L6
Chess Cl AYLS HP21 ....197 F9
  CSHM HP5 ....135 L6
Chessfield Rd AMS HP6 ...146 E5
Chessmount Ri CSHM HP5 ..135 N6
Chess Valley Wk CSHM HP5 136 C5
Chesswood Ct
  RKW/CH/CXG WD3 * 158 G7
Chester Cl BTCHLY MK3 ....52 G2
Chesterfield Cl HADM HP17 108 E1
Chesterfield Crs LBUZ LU7 .75 L6
Chesterfield Pl AYLW HP19 .95 K7
Chesterfield Wy
  HYS/HAR UB3 ....191 N3
Chesterholm BDWL MK13 ....29 M8
Chester Pl NTHWD HA6 ....159 J7
Chester Rd HSLWW TW4 ..197 M6
  HTHAIR TW6 ....196 C2
  NTHWD HA6 ....159 J7
  SL SL1 ....179 L9
Chesterton Cl CSHM HP5 ..135 M2
Chesterton Dr
  STWL/WRAY TW19 ....196 F7
Chesterton Gn BEAC HP9 ..154 J8
Chestnut Av DUN/WHIP UL6 135 P2
  DTCH/LGLY SL3 ....188 G3
  HEN RG9 ....161 K9
  RAYLNE/WEN HP22 ......111 J6
  THAME OX9 ....118 B5
  WDR/YW UB7 ....190 F1
  WYM HP11 .... 63 P5
Chestnut Cl AMS HP6 ...145 P7
  BEAC HP9 ....100 E2
  CFSP/GDCR SL9 ....157 H8
  HEN RG9 ....161 K9
  HYS/HAR UB3 ....183 L7
  MDHD SL6 ....185 L8
  PRRI HP27 ....132 A9
  RAYLNE/WEN HP22 ......111 M1
  RAYLW HP18 ....106 E3
  RMKS/WB MK17 ....52 D8
  STSTR MK11 .... 28 F4
  WDR/YW UB7 ....191 H0
Chestnut Crs AYLS HP21 ..95 L9
  WEAT MK2 ....53 K4
Chestnut Dr BERK HP4 ..126 F2
  BRACKY NN13 ....34 C2
  WDSR SL4 ....193 J4
Chestnut End
  RAYLNE/WEN HP22 ......111 J5
Chestnut La LBUZ LU7 ...74 B1
  HAZ/HG HP15 ....143 P7
Chestnut Leys
  BUCK/WIN MK18 ....58 C7
Chestnut Rd BEAC HP9 ..154 F6
  PRRI HP27 ....131 K1
  TOW NN12 .... 25 K1
The Chestnuts
  HHS/BOV HP3 ....127 P6
Chestnut Wk
  CFSP/GDCR SL9 * 156 G7
Chestnut Wy FELT TW13 * .197 P9

PRRI HP27 ....120 G7
RAYLNE/WEN HP22 ....110 A5
Chestwood Gv
  HGDN/ICK UB10 ....182 F3
Chettle Pl TOW NN12 ......28 A3
Chetwode Av WTR/OFPK MK7 .43 H5
Chetwode Cl BUCK/WIN MK18 48 C1
Chevalier Gv
  DUN/WHIP UL6 ....87 L2
Cheveley Gdns SL SL1 ....178 G5
The Cheveralls
  DUN/WHIP UL6 ....87 L2
Cheviot Cl HWYN HP13 ....1 A1
  HYS/HAR UB3 ....191 K8
  MDHD SL6 ....185 P1
Cheviot Rd DTCH/LGLY SL3 189 J8
  CFSP/GDCR SL9 ....168 G6
  LBUZ LU7 .... 99 H3
Chichele Rd
  DUN/WHIP UL6 ....87 L2
Chicheley Ri NPAG MK16 ...21 M6
Chicheley Rd NPAG MK16 ...22 A6
Chicheley St NPAG MK16 ...11 L9
Chichester Av RSLP HA4 ..171 K7
Chichester Cl
  DUN/WHIP UL6 ....87 M1
  MKV MK10 ....31 M9
  SHEN MK5 .... P8
Chillery Leys WLLN MK15 ...43 J4
Chillingham St SHEN MK5 ..42 A8
Chiltern Av AMS HP6 ....145 P2
  DUN/WHIP UL6 ....87 L2
  HADM HP17 ....108 F1
  HWYW HP12 ....108 F1
  HEN RG9 ....160 D7
  HGDN/ICK UB10 ....170 G7
  PRRI HP27 ....131 J1
Chiltern Ct BUCK/WIN MK18 B7
  UX/CGN UB8 ....189 D5
Chiltern Dr
  RKW/CH/CXG WD3 ....147 P9
Chiltern Gdns LBUZ LU7 ..64 E7
  WTLUN OX49 ....148 A1
Chiltern Gn FLKWH HP10 ..165 N1
Chiltern Gv THAME OX9 ...118 E6
Chiltern Hts AMSS HP7 ...146 C5
Chiltern Hills Rd HWYW HP12 156 G6
Chiltern Link CSHM HP5 ..123 L4
Chiltern Manor Pk
  GTMIS/PWD HP16 ....133 N5
Chiltern Pde AMS HP6 ....145 N1
Chiltern Park Av BERK HP4 114 C9
Chiltern Rdg SKCH HP14 ..139 N7
Chiltern Rd AMS HP6 ....135 M7
  HEN RG9 ....172 C9
  MLW SL7 ....164 C7
  RAYLNE/WEN HP22 ....82 G5
  RAYLNE/WEN HP22 ......111 J9
  SL SL1 ....178 F8
Chilterns Cl FLKWH HP10 .165 P2
Chilterns Pk BNEND SL8 ..165 P4
The Chilterns DUN/WHIP UL6 87 P8
Chiltern Vw
  TRING HP23 ....112 G5
Chiltern Vw Rd
  UX/CGN UB8 ....182 C5
Chiltern Wy
  RAYLNE/WEN HP22 ......111 M4
  TRING HP23 ....112 G1
Chilton Cl FLKWH HP10 ...164 A9
Chilton Rd CNH/GTH/TM MK8 135 N2
  RAYLW HP18 ....106 E3
Chilwick Rd SLN SL2 ....1 C6
The Chimes WYM HP11 ....4 C7
Chimney La FLKWH HP10 ...166 C7
Chinalls Cl BUCK/WIN MK18 48 A3
Chingle Cft EMV/FZ MK4 ...52 C1
Chinnor HI CHNR OX39 ....129 L8
Chinnor Rd CHNR OX39 ....129 L8
  PRRI HP27 ....131 J1
  SKCH HP14 ....130 E6
  THAME OX9 ....118 E6
  WTLUN OX49 ....148 G8
Chippendale Cl HWYN HP13 153 K1
Chippendale Waye
  UX/CGN UB8 ....182 D5
Chippenham Cl RSLP HA4 * 171 M2
Chippenham Dr MKV MK10 ...31 A6
Chipperfield Rd BDWL MK13 30 A5
  HHS/BOV HP3 ....137 K1
Chipping V EMV/FZ MK4 ....52 C1
Chipps Hi SKCH HP14 .....150 B6
Chipstead CFSP/GDCR SL9 .156 E8
Chirbury Cl HWYN HP13 ...141 H6
Chisbridge La MLW SL7 * .163 K5
Chislehampton WLLN MK15 ..31 J1
Chiswick Cl EMV/FZ MK4 ...52 C1
  WDR/YW UB7 ....190 G8
Choakes Yd LBUZ LU7 * ...190 G8
Choke La MDHD SL6 ....176 B4
Cholesbury La TRING HP23 124 E3
Cholesbury Rd TRING HP23 113 H9

Chorley Rd SKCH HP14 .....141 N8
Chorleywood Bottom
RKW/CH/CXG WD3 ....147 M7
Chowns Cl THAME OX9 ....118 E6
Chrislaine Cl
STWL/WRAY TW19 .....196 D5
Christchurch Gv WOLV MK6 ...29 K7
Christchurch Rd TRING HP23 ..112 D2
Christian Ct WLLN MK15 .....81 J5
Christie Cl NPAG MK16 .....20 C7
Christmas La SLN SL2 .....167 N8
Christopher Cl SKCH HP14 ...142 E4
Christopher Rd NWDGN UB2 ..191 P5
Chudleigh Wy RSLP HA4 .....171 K8
Church Av LBUZ LU7 .....74 C3
RSLP HA4 * 171 K6
Church Cl BUCK/WIN MK18 ...38 D9
DUN/WHIP LU6 .....101 K3
HEN RG9 .....173 H7
MDHD SL6 .....185 K1
NTHWD HA6 .....159 K3
RAYLW HP18 .....107 K3
RMKN MK19 .....39 M1
RNHPTN NN7 .....12 E1
UX/CGN UB8 .....182 B5
WDR/YW UB7 .....190 E4
WDSR SL4 .....187 D7
YEAD UB4 .....183 L9
Church Cft DUN/WHIP LU6...86 A5
Church Dr MDHD SL6 .....186 A3
Church End BRACKY NN13 ...24 C5
BUCK/WIN MK18 .....59 H4
BUCK/WIN MK18 .....57 P4
BUCK/WIN MK18 .....60 B6
NPAG MK16 .....21 N4
PRRI HP22 .....130 D3
RMKS/WB MK17 .....44 C5
RMKS/WB MK17 .....52 D7
TOW NN12 .....9 J4
Church End Rd SHEN MK5 ...42 A8
Church Farm Cl
RAYLNE/WEN HP22 .....96 A4
Church Farm La TRING HP23 ..98 D4
Churchfield Cl RAYLW HP18...91 M1
Churchfield Ms SLN SL2 .....180 D1
Churchfield Rd
CFSP/GDCR SL9 .....156 F8
Church Ga DUN/WHIP LU6 *..86 A5
Church Gn DUN/WHIP LU6 ...86 B4
HYS/HAR UB3 .....183 M9
Church Green Rd
BTCHLY MK3 .....52 F4
Church Gv HAMS HP6 .....146 C3
DTCH/LGLY SL3 .....180 E8
Church Headland La
RAYLNE/WEN HP22 .....81 J2
Church HI BUCK/WIN MK18 ...38 D4
CNH/GTH/TM MK8 .....41 N1
DEN/HRF UB9 .....170 C2
HADM HP17 .....122 B3
HEN RG9 .....161 H1
LBUZ LU7 .....84 D8
RMKS/WB MK17 .....45 J7
Churchill Av AYLS HP21 .....95 L9
AYLW HP19 .....4 A7
HGDN/ICK UB10 .....183 H1
Churchill Cl
EBED/NFELT TW14 .....197 M7
FLKWH HP10 .....154 A5
Churchill Crs THAME OX9 ....118 F5
Churchill Dr BEAC HP9 .....154 C5
MLW SL7 .....184 D2
Churchill Rd DTCH/LGLY SL3...189 H5
DUN/WHIP LU6 .....86 F3
LBUZ LU7 .....84 F9
Churchill Wy BRACKY NN13 ..35 H6
Church la BERK HP4 .....126 E1
BRACKY NN13 .....34 C3
BUCK/WIN MK18 .....26 E8
BUCK/WIN MK18 .....47 H5
BUCK/WIN MK18 .....48 C3
BUCK/WIN MK18 .....50 B6
BUCK/WIN MK18 .....70 D7
CFSP/GDCR SL9 .....156 F8
CHNR OX39 .....129 P6
DTCH/LGLY SL3 .....180 E8
DUN/WHIP LU6 .....85 P2
GTMIS/PWD HP16 .....133 P5
HAZ/HG HP15 .....143 J7
HEN RG9 .....172 D8
HHS/BOV HP3 .....127 K4
KID OX5 .....88 C3
LBUZ LU7 .....63 L7
LBUZ LU7 .....65 F7
MDHD SL6 .....186 A3
NPAG MK16 .....14 A4
NPAG MK16 .....21 L9
OLN MK46 .....15 M8
OLN MK46 .....16 A4
PRRI HP22 .....121 K9
PRRI HP22 .....131 N8
RAYLNE/WEN HP22 .....80 E1
RAYLNE/WEN HP22 .....83 J6
RAYLNE/WEN HP22 .....110 F5
RAYLNE/WEN HP22 .....111 K2
RAYLNE/WEN HP22 .....123 J2
RAYLW HP18 .....67 M7
RAYLW HP18 .....77 J9
RAYLW HP18 .....80 A1
RAYLW HP18 .....106 F5
RKW/CH/CXG WD3 .....158 A1
RMKN MK19 .....28 A3
RMKS/WB MK17 .....54 B1
RMKS/WB MK17 .....61 L5
RNHPTN NN7 .....9 J4
SHEN MK5 .....42 B4
SKCH HP14 .....140 F2
SKCH HP14 .....141 H3
SKCH HP14 .....142 A4
SLN SL2 .....180 B3
THAME OX9 .....119 K6

TOW NN12 .....28 A2
TRING HP23 .....98 D6
TRING HP25 .....112 D7
WDSR SL4 .....187 P9
WHLY OX33 .....89 H9
WTLGN OX49 .....129 H9
Church Lees GTLIN MK14 ....30 D4
Church Leys BRACKY NN13 ...34 C9
Church Md DUN/WHIP LU6 ..101 K3
Churchmere Wk AYLS HP21 *...95 L9
Church Pth
GTMIS/PWD HP16 .....133 K7
LBUZ LU7 .....84 E7
LBUZ LU7 .....84 E3
Church Piece RAYLW HP18 *..106 F4
Church Rd BEAC HP9 .....155 P6
BERK HP4 .....126 E7
BERK HP4 .....115 K8
BRACKY NN13 .....35 H5
CSHM OX39 .....124 D8
DEN/HRF UB9 .....170 C1
DUN/WHIP LU6 .....86 D2
DUN/WHIP LU6 .....101 K3
FLKWH HP10 .....154 B3
HEST TW5 .....190 F6
HYS/HAR UB3 .....191 M2
IVER SL0 .....181 L5
LBUZ LU7 .....74 C3
LBUZ LU7 .....84 C2
LBUZ LU7 .....99 J2
MDHD SL6 .....177 H2
MDHD SL6 .....185 P2
MLW SL7 .....165 H4
NPAG MK16 .....21 M4
NTHWD HA6 .....159 M7
RMKS/WB MK17 .....44 F9
RMKS/WB MK17 .....54 B1
RMKS/WB MK17 .....52 K3
SKCH HP14 .....139 P6
SLN SL2 .....179 N6
THAME OX9 .....118 C4
UX/CGN UB8 .....182 C7
WDSR SL4 .....192 A9
WDSR SL4 .....194 D4
WTLGN OX49 .....138 F7
Church Rw AYL HP20 * 2
Churchside HAZ/HG HP15 ...144 A4
Church Sq HWYN HP13 * 5 G1
Church St AMSS HP7 .....145 M4
BDWL MK13 .....29 P6
BUCK/WIN MK18 .....38 D9
BUCK/WIN MK18 .....47 M7
BUCK/WIN MK18 .....48 A3
BUCK/WIN MK18 .....58 B8
BUCK/WIN MK18 .....60 B6
BUCK/WIN MK18 .....70 D7
CSHM HP5 .....135 M5
HADM HP17 .....122 B3
HEN RG9 .....173 P7
HHS/BOV HP3 .....127 K9
HWYN HP13 .....5 G3
LBUZ LU7 .....73 L8
LBUZ LU7 .....74 E1
OLN MK46 .....15 M4
PRRI HP22 .....130 A9
RAYLNE/WEN HP22 .....79 M3
RAYLNE/WEN HP22 .....83 H6
RAYLW HP18 .....90 G7
RBICN OX27 .....66 F6
RKW/CH/CXG WD3 .....158 E1
RMKS/WB MK17 .....45 J7
SKCH HP14 .....140 A6
SL SL1 .....178 C7
SL SL1 .....187 P5
SL SL1 .....188 B4
STSTR MK11 .....28 G8
WDSR SL4 .....187 P9
WEAT MK2 .....53 L2
Church Ter RBEDW MK43 *....17 J7
WDSR SL4 .....193 J1
Church Turn LBUZ LU7 .....75 J7
Church Vw BRACKY NN13 ....35 H5
BUCK/WIN MK18 .....58 C8
KID OX5 .....88 C2
MDHD SL6 .....184 E7
NPAG MK16 .....31 K1
RAYLNE/WEN HP22 .....111 J3
TRING HP23 .....97 N9
Church Views MDHD SL6 ....177 H8
BUCK/WIN MK18 .....60 B6
HYS/HAR UB3 .....183 L9
LBUZ LU7 .....75 M2
RAYLNE/WEN HP22 .....11 L2
RBEDW MK43 .....11 G7
RBEDW MK43 .....33 L5
Church Wy BUCK/WIN MK18 ..69 K1
Churchway HADM HP17 .....107 L6
Church Wy HADM HP17 .....108 E1
Church Yd TRING HP23 .....112 E2
The Chure KID OX5 .....88 C3
The Chyne CFSP/GDCR SL9 ..169 H5
Cinnamon Cl WDSR SL4 .....187 M9
Cinnamon Gv WTR/OFPK MK7 ..43 N7
Cippenham Cl SL SL1 .....187 K1
Cippenham La SL SL1 .....187 J1
City Rd SKCH HP14 * 140 F5
The City SKCH HP14 * 141 J4
Clammas Wy UX/CGN UB8 ...182 C8
Clappers Meadow
MDHD SL6 .....177 P7
Clappins La SKCH HP14 .....142 D2
Clapton Ap FLKWH HP10 ....166 F5
Clare Cl NTHWD HA6 .....159 L5
Clare Ct SLN SL2 * 167 M9
Clarefield Cl MDHD SL6 ....176 G7
Clarefield Dr MDHD SL6 ....176 G7

Clarefield Rd MDHD SL6 ....177 H7
Claremont Av STSTR MK11 ...28 G9
Claremont Cl AYLS HP21 ....109 P1
Claremont Gdns MLW SL7 ...164 E7
Claremont Rd MLW SL7 .....164 E7
WDSR SL4 .....193 N1
Clarence Crs WDSR SL4 .....187 N9
Clarence Rd BERK HP4 .....126 B1
HEN RG9 .....173 P6
LBUZ LU7 .....74 E1
WDSR SL4 .....193 L1
Clarendon Ct SLN SL2 .....188 D1
Clarendon Dr
CNH/GTH/TM MK8 .....41 P2
THAME OX9 .....118 E4
Clarendon Rd
GTMIS/PWD HP16 .....133 H6
HWYN HP13 .....153 L4
HYS/HAR UB3 .....191 M3
Clare Pk AMSS HP7 .....146 A4
Clare Rd GTMIS/PWD HP16...133 J6
MDHD SL6 .....178 C9
MDHD SL6 .....185 K1
STWL/WRAY TW19 .....196 A3
Claret Cl SHEN MK5 * 42 C8
Clarke Ct AYL HP20 .....95 P5
Clarke Dr HWYN HP13 .....153 N5
Clarke Rd DBGH MK1 .....43 J8
Clarkes Dr WDR/YW UB7 *...182 E9
Clarkes Field Cl RAYLW HP18 ..91 H7
Clarke's Spring TRING HP23 ..113 K1
Clarkes Wy BRACKY NN13 ...34 C3
Clarkfield RKW/CH/CXG WD3 ..158 A4
Classon Cl WDR/YW UB7 ....190 E3
Clauds Cl HAZ/HG HP15 .....143 N6
Claverton Cl HHS/BOV HP3 ..137 P3
Clay Acre CSHM HP5 .....135 P3
Clay Cl HWYN HP13 .....5 J3
Claycutters BUCK/WIN MK18...60 C6
Claydon Cl AYLS HP21 .....109 M1
Claydon End CFSP/GDCR SL9 ..168 G1
Claydon La CFSP/GDCR SL9 ..168 G1
Clayfield Rd
RAYLNE/WEN HP22 .....111 J6
Clayfields FLKWH HP10 .....166 F7
Clayhall La WDSR SL4 .....194 B4
Clay Hall Rd CNH/GTH/TM MK8 ..41 P9
Clayhill MLW SL7 .....152 A8
Clay La BUCK/WIN MK18 .....47 N4
MLW SL7 .....152 A8
RAYLNE/WEN HP22 .....111 J9
STWL/WRAY TW19 .....196 F5
Claymoor MLW SL7 .....50 G9
Clays La RMKS/WB MK17 .....50 G9
The Clays HADM HP17 .....107 L6
Clayton Ga GTLIN MK14 .....30 G5
Clayton Pde
DTCH/LGLY SL3 * 189 P3
Clayton Rd HYS/HAR UB3 ...191 L3
Claytons Meadow
BNEND SL8 .....165 P7
Clayton Wk AMSS HP7 .....146 B3
Clayton Wy UX/CGN UB8 ...182 B5
Clearbrook Cl FLKWH HP10 ..153 P6
Cleares Pasture SL SL1 .....156 F5
Cleavers CHNR OX39 .....129 N6
Cleavers Av GTLIN MK14 ....42 G1
Cleeve Crs BTCHLY MK3 .....52 C1
Clegg Sq SHEN MK5 .....42 B8
Clement Bois BRACKY NN13 ...34 G4
Clement Gdns HYS/HAR UB3 ..191 L5
Clementi Av HAZ/HG HP15 ..144 B4
Clements Cl SL SL1 .....188 D3
Clements End Rd
DUN/WHIP LU6 .....101 N5
Clements La RBICN OX27 ....66 F7
Clements Rd HEN RG9 .....173 N5
RKW/CH/CXG WD3 .....147 N7
Clerkenwell Pl
EAG/OLD/WT MK6 .....43 H2
Cleve Ct WDSR SL4 .....193 K2
Clevedon Gdns HEST TW5 ...197 N1
Clevehurst Cl SLN SL2 .....180 B2
Cleveland Cl FLKWH HP10 *...154 B5
Cleveland BDWL MK13 .....29 N7
Cleveland Dr LBUZ LU7 .....74 A1
Cleveland Rd AYL HP20 .....95 P5
Cleveland Rd AYL HP20 .....4 A2
UX/CGN UB8 .....182 D6
Clewer Av WDSR SL4 .....193 J1
Clewer Court Rd WDSR SL4 ..187 M8
Clewer Flds WDSR SL4 * 187 N8
Clewer Hill Rd WDSR SL4 ...193 J1
Clewer New Town
WDSR SL4 .....187 L1
Clewer Pk WDSR SL4 .....187 L1
Clifden Rd RAYLW HP18 .....106 E9
Clifford Av WEAT MK2 .....53 J4
Clifford Gdns HGDN/ICK UB10 ..183 M5
Clifford Rd PRRI HP22 .....131 M8
Cliffords Wy BNEND SL8 .....165 N4
Clifton Cl MDHD SL6 .....185 M3
Clifton Gdns HGDN/ICK UB10 ..183 M5
Clifton Gn AYLW HP19 .....5 G1
Clifton Lawns AMS HP6 .....135 N6
Clifton Pl FLKWH HP10 * 154 A5
Clifton Ri WDSR SL4 .....187 J2
Clifton Rd AMS HP6 .....135 N4
HTHAIR TW6 * 197 J1
RBEDW MK43 * 16 D4
Cline Ct CNH/GTH/TM MK8 ...41 N6
Clinkard Pl SKCH HP14 .....151 J7
Clinton Crs AYL HP20 .....95 N4
Clipstone Crs LBUZ LU7 .....74 C2
Clive Ct SL SL1 .....188 B4
Cliveden Md MDHD SL6 .....178 A6
Cliveden Rd MDHD SL6 .....178 B6

MDHD SL6 .....178 C1
Clivemont Rd MDHD SL6 ....177 L7
Clive Rd EBED/NFELT TW14 ..197 N5
Clivesdale Dr HYS/HAR UB3 ..191 N2
Clockhouse La ASHF TW15 ...197 H9
Clockhouse Ms
HYS/HAR UB3 * 147 N5
Cloebury Paddock
WLLN MK15 .....43 J1
Cloister Garth BERK HP4 ....126 E1
The Cloisters AYL HP20 * 2 D5
HWYN HP13 .....143 K9
Clomwel Wy SL SL1 .....178 C9
Closemead Cl NTHWD HA6 ..159 J6
The Close BDWL MK13 .....30 A9
BNEND SL8 .....165 N3
HEN RG9 .....173 P6
HGDN/ICK UB10 .....182 E3
HGDN/ICK UB10 .....183 J3
HHS/BOV HP3 .....137 L1
IVER SL0 .....181 L6
OLN MK46 .....14 C6
RAYLNE/WEN HP22 .....96 A3
RAYLW HP18 .....78 C5
RBEDW MK43 .....33 J5
RKW/CH/CXG WD3 .....158 A6
RMKS/WB MK17 .....53 L7
SL SL1 .....187 K6
Cloudberry WTR/OFPK MK7 ...43 L6
Cloutsham Cl EMV/FZ MK4 ...52 C1
Clovelly Av HGDN/ICK UB10 ..182 A2
Clovelly Cv HGDN/ICK UB10 ..171 J9
PIN HA5 .....171 P1
Clover Cl SHEN MK5 .....42 C8
Clover End BUCK/WIN MK18 ...48 A3
Clover La AYLS HP21 .....109 N1
Clurry Ct WTR/OFPK MK7 ....44 D8
Clyde Rd STWL/WRAY TW19 ..196 D7
Clydesdale Pl GTLIN MK14 ...30 D7
Clyfford Rd RSLP HA4 .....171 M9
Clymping Dene
EBED/NFELT TW14 .....197 P6
Coachmaker Ct GTLIN MK14 ...30 C7
Coach Ride MLW SL7 .....164 D5
Coalmans Wy MDHD SL6 ....178 D9
Coates La HWYN HP13 .....142 F8
HWYN HP13 .....143 G8
Coat Wicks BEAC HP9 .....155 N6
Cobb Cl DTCH/LGLY SL3 .....188 F7
Cobbetts Md BUCK/WIN MK18 ...58 B8
Cobbetts Ride TRING HP23 ..112 D3
Cobb Hall Rd RMKS/WB MK17 ..52 C4
Cobblers Cl SLN SL2 .....179 M5
Cobblershill La
GTMIS/PWD HP16 .....132 C2
Cobbers Wick
RAYLNE/WEN HP22 .....83 H5
Cobbs Ct OLN MK46 * 15 M2
Cobbs Gdn OLN MK46 .....15 M2
Cobden Cl UX/CGN UB8 .....182 C4
Coberley Cl WLLN MK15 .....31 J4
Cobham Cl BUCK/WIN MK18 ...48 A2
SL SL1 .....187 K2
Cochran Cl CNH/GTH/TM MK8 ..42 C7
Cockerell Gv SHEN MK5 .....42 C7
Cockett Rd DTCH/LGLY SL3 ...188 C4
Cock Gv BERK HP4 .....115 N4
Cock la HWYN HP13 .....153 N5
Cockpit Cl HAZ/HG HP15 ....143 L1
Cockpit Rd HAZ/HG HP15 ...145 H1
Cocks La WHLY OX33 .....102 F7
Coddimoor La
RMKS/WB MK17 .....51 K4
Codmore Crs CSHM HP5 ....136 A3
Codmore Wood Rd
CSHM HP5 .....136 E2
Coe Sp SL SL1 .....187 M4
Coftards SL SL1 .....187 L7
Cogan Ct CNH/GTH/TM MK8 ...41 N5
Cogdells Cl CSHM HP5 .....135 N4
Cogdells Cl CSHM HP5 .....124 F9
Coggeshall Gv
WTR/OFPK MK7 .....44 A5
Coin Cl MKV MK10 .....31 N4
Coke's Farm La CSTG HP8 ...146 D5
Coke's La CSTG HP8 .....146 D6
Colbourne Rd HWYN HP13 ..153 K2
Colbrook Av HYS/HAR UB3 ..191 K1
Colbrook Cl HYS/HAR UB3 ..191 K1
Colchester Ct DTCH/LGLY SL3 ..180 B1
Colchester Rd NTHWD HA6 ..159 N9
Coldeaton La EMV/FZ MK4 ...42 B9
Coldharbour Cl HEN RG9 ....173 N6
Coldharbour La
HYS/HAR UB3 .....191 N2
Coldharbour Wy AYLW HP19 ..95 N3
Coldmoorholme La
BNEND SL8 .....165 J3
Coldmorenham Yd AMSS HP7 ..145 J2
Cole Gdns HEST TW5 .....197 P5
Coleheath Bottom
PRRI HP27 .....132 C7
Colenorton Crs WDSR SL4 ...187 J3
Coleridge Cl
DTCH/LGLY SL3 .....189 H3
Coleridge Gv WDR/YW UB7 ..190 F5
YEAD UB4 .....183 L7
Cole Rd AYLS HP21 .....109 L1
Colesbourne Dr WLLN MK15 ..31 J4
Coleshill La AMSS HP7 .....145 J4
Coleshill Pl BDWL MK13 * 30 A5
Coles Ri BRACKY NN13 .....34 A3
Colet Rd RAYLNE/WEN HP22 ..111 J9
Colham Av WDR/YW UB7 ....190 D2
Colham Green Rd
UX/CGN UB8 .....182 D8
Colham Mill Rd
WDR/YW UB7 .....190 D3
Colham UX/CGN UB8 .....182 D7
Colin Wy SL SL1 .....187 M4

College Av MDHD SL6 .....177 L9
SL SL1 .....188 A4
College Crs RAYLW HP18 ....104 E2
College Dr RSLP HA4 .....171 N5
College Gln MDHD SL6 .....177 K8
College Ri MDHD SL6 .....177 K8
College Rd MDHD SL6 .....177 K8
RAYLNE/WEN HP22 .....33 J5
RBEDW MK43 .....33 J5
College Wy HYS/HAR UB3 ...183 N1
NTHWD HA6 .....159 K6
Colley Hi BDWL MK13 .....30 A9
Colley Hill La SLN SL2 .....168 B8
Colley Land
RKW/CH/CXG WD3 .....147 M6
Collier Cl MDHD SL6 .....177 M7
Colliers La HEN RG9 .....172 C8
Collingwood Cl HWYN HP13 ..153 N4
Collingwood Rd
UX/CGN UB8 .....183 H7
Collinswood Rd SLN SL2 ....168 A8
Collum Green Rd SLN SL2 ...168 A8
Collyer Rd SKCH HP14 .....151 J4
Colmore La HEN RG9 .....172 C8
Colnbrook By-Pass
DTCH/LGLY SL3 .....189 L7
WDR/YW UB7 .....190 B8
Coln Ct MDHD SL6 .....177 M8
Colndale Rd UX/CGN UB8 ...182 D1
Colne Av RKW/CH/CXG WD3...158 A2
WDR/YW UB7 .....190 C3
Colne Bank
STWL/WRAY TW19 .....195 L2
Colnedale Rd UX/CGN UB8 ...182 D1
Colne Md WDR/YW UB7 .....190 C3
Colne Orch IVER SL0 .....181 P9
Colne Reach STWL/WRAY TW19 ..195 L1
Colne Valley Trail
HGDN/ICK UB10 .....170 C8
Colne Valley Wy IVER SL0 ...182 A9
Colne Wy STWL/WRAY TW19 ..195 N1
Colonial Rd
EBED/NFELT TW14 .....197 L6
Colons Wy OLN MK46 * 15 M2
Colston Bassett EMV/FZ MK4 ..52 C2
Coltman Av RAYLW HP18 ....106 A8
Coltsfoot Dr WDR/YW UB7 ..182 E9
Coltsfoot Pl GTLIN MK14 ....42 D1
The Coltsfoot HHW MK1 ....127 K7
Coltis Holm Rd WOLV MK12...29 L8
Columbia Dr LBUZ LU7 .....74 C1
Columbia Pl RSLP HA4 .....171 P6
Columbia Pl CMK MK9 .....7 J1
Columbine Rd HAZ/HG HP15 ..143 M5
Columbus Gdns NTHWD HA6 ..159 N8
Colville Ct
GTMIS/PWD HP16 * 133 P5
Colville Rd WYM HP11 .....152 B3
Combe Martin EMV/FZ MK4 ...52 D1
Combe Ri HWYW HP12 .....152 B5
Combermere Ct WDSR SL4 ...193 H1
Comerford Wy
BUCK/WIN MK18 .....60 B6
Comet Rd STWL/WRAY TW19 ..196 F4
Comfrey Cl WTR/OFPK MK7 ...43 N7
The Comfrey FLKWH HP19 *...95 L3
Commercial Sq WYM HP11 *....2 A4
Common FB TRING HP23 ....113 H5
Common Gdns BERK HP4 ....115 K8
Common Gate Rd
RKW/CH/CXG WD3 .....147 M7
SL SL1 .....167 M8
WDSR SL4 .....187 P4
Common Rd DTCH/LGLY SL3 ..189 J5
DUN/WHIP LU6 .....87 L7
DUN/WHIP LU6 .....101 J4
FLKWH HP10 .....154 B3
HAZ/HG HP15 .....143 N9
HEAD OX3 .....147 N6
RKW/CH/CXG WD3 .....147 H7
WDSR SL4 .....187 H5
Common Side HWYN HP13 ...142 D8
Common St OLN MK46 .....14 C5
The Common BERK HP4 .....115 K8
FLKWH HP10 .....165 J1
HAZ/HG HP15 .....143 K7
HAZ/HG HP15 .....144 B4
RKW/CH/CXG WD3 * 147 N7
Commonwealth Av
HYS/HAR UB3 .....183 K9
Common Wd SLN SL2 .....179 N9
Commonwealth Wy
HGDN/ICK UB10 .....171 H8
Como Rd AYL HP20 .....96 B7
Como Ga DUN/WHIP LU6 ....86 A2
The Comp DUN/WHIP LU6 ...85 P7
Compton Dr MDHD SL6 .....176 G7
Compton Rd HWYN HP13 ...191 H1
RAYLNE/WEN HP22 .....83 H6
Concorde Cl HGDN/ICK UB10 ..182 E5
Concorde Rd MDHD SL6 ....185 K3
Concord Wy SL SL1 * 187 L5
Concord Wy LBUZ LU7 .....75 J7
The Concourse WEAT MK2 *...53 K1
Concra Pk HHS/BOV HP3 ....44 G8
Conduit Hill Ri THAME OX9 ...118 C6
Conduit La DTCH/LGLY SL3 ..188 C6
Conegar Ct SL SL1 .....187 A8
Conegra Ct HWYN HP13 .....5 H5
Conegra Rd HWYN HP13 .....5 H5
Coneygere OLN MK46 .....15 N4
Coney Gv HGDN/ICK UB10 ...182 F6
Congreve EAG/OLD/WT MK6 ...43 K7
Conifer Ri HWYW HP12 .....152 B4
The Conifers HHW MK1 * 127 K7
MDHD SL6 .....176 G8
Conifer Wk WDSR SL4 * 186 G8
Conifer Wy HYS/HAR UB3 ...191 N1

Conigre CHNR OX39.....129 M6
Coningsby Cl MDHD SL6.....185 K4
Coningsby Ct HWYN HP13.....5 C1
Coningsby Rd LBUZ LU7.....186 A9
Coningsby Rd HWYN HP13.....5 C1
Coniston Crs SL1.....178 G8
Coniston Gdns PIN HA5.....171 N2
Coniston Rd AYL HP20.....95 M4
Coniston Rd LBUZ LU7.....74 A2
Connaught Cl MDHD SL6.....177 L7
  UX/CGN UB8 *.....183 J8
Connaught Gdns BERK HP4.....114 B7
Connaught Rd AYL HP20.....96 C8
  SL SL1.....188 D3
Conniburrow Bvd
  GTLIN MK14.....30 E9
Coniston Cl MLW SL7.....164 B7
Consort Wy DEN/HRF UB9.....169 P4
Constable Cl GTLIN MK14.....30 E9
  YEAD UB4.....183 J5
Constable Pl AYLW HP19.....95 H5
Constantine Wy BDWL MK13.....29 P8
Control Tower Rd
  HTHAIR TW6.....196 G2
Convent Rd WDSR SL4.....193 L1
  FLKWH HP10.....154 A9
Conway Cl AYLS HP21.....3 H7
Conway Crs BTCHLY MK3.....52 E3
Conway Dr WDSR SL4.....193 L4
Conway Rd MDHD SL6.....178 F9
Cook Cl WTR/OFPK MK7.....43 P8
Cookham Dean Bottom
  MDHD SL6.....165 J9
Cookham Rd MDHD SL6.....177 M7
Cookshall La SKCH HA14.....142 A9
Cooks La RMKS/WB MK17.....61 N1
Cook's Meadow
  DUN/WHIP LU6.....86 A4
Cooks Rd AYLW HP19.....95 H1
Coombe Av
  RAYLNE/WEN HP22.....122 G1
Coombe Cl
  RAYLNE/WEN HP22.....110 C4
Coombe Dr DUN/WHIP LU6.....86 C9
  RSLP HA4.....171 P6
Coombe Gdns BERK HP4.....114 B9
Coombe Hill Ct WDSR SL4.....193 H3
Coombe Hill Crs THAME OX9.....118 C6
Coombe La AYLW HP19.....95 H6
  SKCH HP14.....142 F5
Coombe V CFSP/GDCR SL9.....168 A2
Cooper Rd HEN RG9.....173 P5
Cooper's Court Rd
  SKCH HP14.....139 P6
Cooper's Hill La EGH TW20.....194 E9
Coopers Ms GTLIN MK14.....30 F6
Coopers Rw IVER SL0.....181 L7
Cooper's Yd AYL HP21.....2 D5
  SL SL1.....187 M4
Coots Cl BUCK/WIN MK18.....48 C4
Cope Ct MDHD SL6.....177 P4
Copeland Cl WTR/OFPK MK7.....44 A7
Copes Hvn SHEN MK5.....42 B9
Copes Rd HAZ/HG HP15.....143 C2
Copes Shroves
  HAZ/HG HP15.....143 M6
Copmans Wick
  RKW/CH/CXG WD3.....147 M7
Copners Dr HAZ/HG HP15.....144 A5
Copners Wy HAZ/HG HP15.....143 P5
Copper Beech Cl HHW HP1.....2 C6
  WDSR SL4.....187 H9
Copper Beech Wy LBUZ LU7.....64 G8
Copperdale Rd
  HYS/HAR UB3.....191 N3
Copperfields Av UX/CGN UB8.....182 C2
Copperfields BECG HP9.....153 B1
  HWYN HP12.....152 B1
Copperkins Gv AMS HP6.....135 M9
Copperkins La AMS HP6.....135 M9
Coppermill La
  RKW/CH/CXG WD3.....157 P2
Coppermill Lock
  DEN/HRF UB9 *.....158 A7
Coppermill Rd
  STWL/WRAY TW19.....195 K5
Copper Rdg CFSP/GDCR SL9.....157 P1
Coppice Cl AYL HP20.....96 C3
  RSLP HA4 *.....171 J4
Coppice Dr
  STWL/WRAY TW19.....194 D6
Coppice Farm Rd
  HAZ/HG HP15.....144 A9
The Coppice HAZ/HG HP15.....143 L2
  HWYN HP12.....152 B6
  SKCH HP14.....142 B6
  TRING HP23.....113 H5
  WDR/YW UB7.....182 C5
Coppice Wy AYL HP20.....3 J1
  SLN SL2.....167 P7
Coppidwell Dr AYLS HP21.....3 H1
Coppin La BDWL MK13.....43 M1
Coppins Cl BERK HP4.....126 A1
Coppins La IVER SL0.....181 P8
Copse Cl NTHWD HA6.....159 J4
  SL SL1.....187 K2
  WDSR SL4.....190 D4
Copse Ga BUCK/WIN MK18.....66 C6
Copse Hill Cl HHS/BOV HP3.....137 M1
Copse La BEAC HP9.....156 A7
The Copse AMSS HP7.....145 N2
  HHW HP1.....115 J4
  WDSR SL4 *.....192 F7
Copse Wy CSHM HP5.....125 L9
  SL SL1.....181 M4
Copse Wood Wy
  NTHWD HA6.....159 J8
Copthall Cl CFSP/GDCR SL9.....157 H7
Copthall La CFSP/GDCR SL9.....156 G7
Copthall Rd East
  HGDN/ICK UB10.....170 G7

Copthall Rd West
  HGDN/ICK UB10.....170 G7
Copthorn Cl MDHD SL6.....184 C3
Copthorne Ms HYS/HAR UB3.....191 L5
Copy Ground Ct HWYW HP12 *.....a A4
Coral Cl DUN/WHIP LU6 *.....86 A2
Coram Cl BERK HP4.....126 E2
Corbet Ride LBUZ LU7.....64 A3
Corbett Cl WLLN MK15.....31 K6
Cordelia Gdns
  STWL/WRAY TW19.....196 E6
Cordelia Rd
  STWL/WRAY TW19.....196 E6
Cordingley Rd RSLP HA4.....171 K6
Cordwainer Ct GTLIN MK14.....30 E9
Cordwallis Rd MDHD SL6.....177 L8
Cordwallis St MDHD SL6.....177 L8
Cores End Rd BNEND SL8.....165 N6
Corfe Cl AYLS HP21.....110 B1
Corfe Gdns SL SL1.....187 L1
Corfe Pl MDHD SL6.....177 P9
Coriander Ct WTR/OFPK MK7.....43 P7
Cork Wy WEAT MK2.....52 K6
Cork Pl BTCHLY MK3.....52 E1
Cornbrook Rd AYLS HP21.....109 L1
Cornbury Crs GTLIN MK14.....30 C7
Corncrake AYLW HP19.....95 N4
Cornel Cl HAZ/HG HP15.....145 H9
Cornelia Ct WEAT MK2.....52 F3
Corner Ct OLN MK46.....15 L4
Cornerstone PRRI HP27.....132 E1
Cornerwood
  GTMIS/PWD HP16 *.....123 P5
Cornfield Cl
  HGDN/ICK UB10.....182 D5
Cornfield Crs BERK HP4.....113 P7
Cornflower Pl
  BUCK/WIN MK18.....48 A4
Corn Hl CNH/GTH/TM MK8.....41 N3
Cornmarket THAME OX9.....118 D5
  WYM HP11.....5 F5
Cornwall Av SLN SL2.....179 N7
Cornwall Cl MDHD SL6.....177 L8
  WDSR SL4.....187 J6
Cornwall Gv BTCHLY MK3.....52 F3
Cornwall Rd BUCK/WIN MK18 *.....48 B2
Cornwall Rd HYS/HAR UB3.....191 M7
  UX/CGN UB8.....182 D2
Cornwalls Meadow
  BUCK/WIN MK18.....48 A5
Cornwell Rd WDSR SL4.....194 C5
Coronation Av
  DTCH/LGLY SL3.....188 A3
Coronation Cl RSLP HA4.....171 M5
  SL SL1.....179 H6
  WDSR SL4.....186 E4
Coronation Dr SKCH HP14.....151 K5
Coronation Pl
  BUCK/WIN MK18.....48 B8
Coronation Rd HWYW HP12.....152 D6
  SL SL1.....191 H5
  MDHD SL6.....188 A2
  RBEDW MK43.....33 M4
Coronation Vls AYLS HP21 *.....3 F5
Corporation St HWYN HP13.....5 F6
Corrigan Cl BTCHLY MK3.....52 C3
Corsair Cl STWL/WRAY TW19.....196 D6
Corsair Rd
  STWL/WRAY TW19.....196 E6
Corsham Ct
  CNH/GTH/TM MK8.....41 P3
Corwell Gdns UX/CGN UB8.....183 J9
Corwell La UX/CGN UB8.....183 J9
Cosgrove Rd RMKN MK19.....28 D6
Cotefield Dr LBUZ LU7.....74 A1
Coteford Cl PIN HA5.....171 H5
Cotesmore Rd HHW HP1.....127 N3
Cotes Wy LBUZ LU7.....74 A1
Cotman Cl WOLV MK12.....29 M4
Cotmans Cl HYS/HAR UB3.....191 N7
Cotmore Cl THAME OX9.....118 F6
Cotmore Gdns THAME OX9.....118 F6
Cotswold Cl MDHD SL6.....185 P1
  SL SL1.....187 M4
  UX/CGN UB8.....182 C4
Cotswold Dr LBUZ LU7.....74 A1
Cotswold Gn AYL HP20.....95 N5
Cotswolds Wy
  BUCK/WIN MK18.....67 G5
Cotswold Wy HWYN HP13.....4 B1
Cottage Common SHEN MK5.....42 A9
Cottage Grounds
  RAYLW HP18.....108 F1
Cottage Park Rd SLN SL2.....179 H1
Cottesbrooke Cl
  DTCH/LGLY SL3.....189 M9
Cottesloe Cl LBUZ LU7.....73 L6
Cottesloe Ct STSTR MK11.....29 H8
Cottesloe Rd AYLS HP21.....109 M1
Cottingham Cha RSLP HA4.....171 N3
Cottingham Gv BTCHLY MK3.....52 C4
Cottisford Crs BTCHLY MK3.....52 E4
Cottitand Clay HADM HP17.....107 L6
Coulson Av CNH/GTH/TM MK8.....41 N6
Coulson Ct
  GTMIS/PWD HP16.....133 K6
Coulson Wy SL SL1.....178 A9
Countess Cl DEN/HRF UB9.....158 C9
Countisbury EMV/FZ MK4.....52 L2
Country La HYS/HAR UB3.....191 J8
County Rd BRACKY NN13.....35 J4
Cours La Ville Cl
  BUCK/WIN MK18.....60 A7
Court Cl AYLS HP21.....3 E7
  HWYN HP13.....5 J8
  MDHD SL6.....184 A9
  PRRI HP27.....131 A5
Court Close Rd THAME OX9.....118 E5
Court Crs SL SL1.....179 P9
Court Dr HGDN/ICK UB10.....182 F4
  MDHD SL6.....178 A5
Courteney Ldg
  EMV/FZ MK4 *.....42 E9
Courtfield Dr MDHD SL6.....185 J1

Courtfield Gdns
  DEN/HRF UB9.....170 A8
  RSLP HA4.....171 M7
Courtfield Rd WHLY OX33.....102 C7
Courthouse Cl
  BUCK/WIN MK16 *.....60 B5
Courthouse Rd MDHD SL6.....177 J7
Courtlands MDHD SL6.....185 M1
Courtlands Av
  DTCH/LGLY SL3.....188 A3
Courtlands Cl RSLP HA4.....171 M5
Court La IVER SL0.....181 P9
  SL SL1.....179 H6
  WDSR SL4.....186 E4
Courtmoor Cl PRRI HP27.....121 L7
Courtneidge Cl LBUZ LU7.....72 E1
Courtney Rd HTHAIR TW6.....196 E2
Courtney Wy HTHAIR TW6.....196 E2
Court Rd HGDN/ICK UB10.....183 H1
  MDHD SL6.....185 L2
  RBEDW MK43.....33 N5
The Court RMKS/WB MK17.....44 A1
Courtyard Cft HADM HP17 *.....107 K9
Cousins Cl WDR/YW UB7.....190 C1
Cousins Dr AYL HP20.....95 P5
Cousins Piece AYLW HP18.....106 A4
Coventon Rd AYLW HP19.....95 K5
Coverack Pl EMV/FZ MK4.....52 B3
Coverdale BDWL MK13.....30 C8
Coverdale Wy SLN SL2.....179 J7
Covert Cl BERK HP4.....113 P7
Covert Rd HAZ/HG HP15.....144 H9
The Covert NTHWD HA6.....159 J8
Cowdray Cl WLLN MK15.....43 H1
Cowdray Rd HGDN/ICK UB10.....183 J4
Cow La BUCK/WIN MK18.....47 M7
  DUN/WHIP LU6.....86 A4
  TRING HP23.....113 H2
Cowleaze CHNR OX39.....129 M6
Cowley Cl RAYLNE/WEN HP22.....96 B4
Cowley Crs UX/CGN UB8.....182 C5
Cowley Mill Rd UX/CGN UB8.....182 A5
Cowley Rd UX/CGN UB8.....182 B5
Cowper Cl NPAG MK16.....30 C1
Cowper Rd BERK HP4.....126 D1
  CSHM HP5.....135 M2
  SLN SL2.....179 J8
Cowpers Orch OLN MK46.....14 C6
Cowslip Cl HGDN/ICK UB10.....182 G3
Cowslip Rd HAZ/HG HP15.....143 M5
Coxborrow Cl MDHD SL6.....177 J6
Coxfield Cl SKCH HP14.....140 F5
Cox Green La MDHD SL6.....185 H3
Cox Green Rd MDHD SL6.....185 K4
Coxwell Cl BUCK/WIN MK18.....48 D2
Crabbe Crs CSHM HP5.....135 P2
Crabs Gv RAYLNE/WEN HP22.....81 N1
Crab Tree Cl OLN MK46.....15 L4
Crabtree Cl AMSS HP7.....135 N9
Crabtree La RMKS/WB MK17 *.....44 C2
Crabtree Rd HADM HP17.....107 K9
Craddocks Cl BDWL MK13.....42 G1
Craddocks Dr LBUZ LU7.....64 B1
Cradley Wk AYL HP20.....95 N4
Crafton Rd AYLW HP20.....95 H9
Craig Dr UX/CGN UB8.....183 J9
Craigmore Av BTCHLY MK3.....52 F3
Craigwell Av AYLS HP21.....96 B1
  FELT TW13.....197 N9
Cranberry Cl WTR/OFPK MK7.....44 A6
Cranborne Av EMV/FZ MK4.....51 N1
Cranborne Waye HYS/HAR UB3.....191 P4
Cranborne Av WDSR SL4.....193 K1
Cranbourne Cl SL SL1.....179 H6
Cranbourne Rd NTHWD HA5.....171 J7
  SL SL1.....187 N2
Cranbrook Dr MDHD SL6.....177 F7
Cranbrook Rd DTCH/LGLY SL3.....188 G5
  HTHAIR TW6.....196 E2
Crane Cl SHEN MK5.....42 A9
Crane Gdns HYS/HAR UB3.....191 M5
Crane Lodge Rd HEST TW5.....191 P7
Crane Rd STWL/WRAY TW19.....196 E6
Cranesbill Pl GTLIN MK14.....30 D7
Cranes Cl RBEDW MK43.....31 H2
Craneswater HYS/HAR UB3.....191 M8
Crane Wy RBEDW MK43.....33 M3
Cranfield Rd NPAG MK16.....32 C5
  NPAG MK16.....32 C5
  RMKS/WB MK17.....44 C2
  RMKS/WB MK17.....44 C2
Cranford Av
  STWL/WRAY TW19.....196 E6
Cranford Cl
  STWL/WRAY TW19.....196 E6
Cranford Dr HYS/HAR UB3.....191 M5
Cranford La HYS/HAR UB3.....191 M5
Cranford Park Rd
  HYS/HAR UB3.....191 M5
Cranley Dr RSLP HA4.....171 J4
Cranmer Rd HYS/HAR UB3.....183 K9
Cranston Cl HGDN/ICK UB10.....171 K7
Cranwell Cl SHEN MK5.....42 B9
Cranwell Rd HTHAIR TW6.....196 C3
Cravan Av FELT TW13.....197 N8
Craven Cl YEAD UB4.....183 N9
The Craven BDWL MK13.....30 C9
Crawley Crossing
  RBEDW MK43.....45 N6
Crawley Rd RBEDW MK43.....33 N2
  RMKS/WB MK17.....55 K3
Crawley's La TRING HP23.....113 J2
Crayle St SLN SL2.....179 L6
Creden Cl MDHD SL6.....177 M8
Creed St WOLV MK12.....29 M4
Creighton Rd AYLW HP18.....106 C5
Crendon Rd RAYLW HP18.....106 C5
Crendon St HWYN HP13.....5 H6
Crescent Cl MDHD SL6.....185 M1
Crescent Dl MDHD SL6.....177 N9
Crescent Gdns RSLP HA4.....171 L1
Crescent Pde
  HGDN/ICK UB10 *.....182 D5
The Crescent HWYN HP13.....153 J2
  HYS/HAR UB3.....191 J8

LBUZ LU7.....98 G3
MDHD SL6.....177 L2
PRRI HP27.....131 A1
RMKN MK19.....29 N5
SKCH HP14 *.....140 A6
SL SL1.....188 A3
TRING HP23.....113 G1
WEAT MK2.....53 A2
Creslow Ct STSTR MK11.....29 H8
Creslow Wy HADM HP17.....108 D7
Cress End RKW/CH/CXG WD3.....158 A3
Cressex Rd HWYW HP12.....152 C6
Cressey Av SHEN MK5.....42 C8
Cressington Ct BNEND SL8.....165 N6
Cressington Pl BNEND SL8.....165 N5
Cresswell Rd CSHM HP5.....135 L3
Cress Rd SL SL1.....187 M3
Cresswells Md MDHD SL6.....185 H6
Cresswell Wy HAZ/HG HP15.....144 B4
Crest Rd WYM HP11.....152 D7
The Crest SL SL1.....187 M3
  WYM HP11.....141 H3
Creswick Meadow
  AYLS HP21.....110 A1
Crew Curve BERK HP4.....114 B7
Cricketers Rw
  BUCK/WIN MK18.....60 C6
Cricket Field Rd
  UX/CGN UB8.....182 C4
Cricketfield Rd
  WDR/YW UB7.....190 C5
Cricket Gnd SKCH HP14.....139 P6
Cricklebeck BDWL MK13.....30 B8
Crimp Hl WDSR SL4.....194 B6
Crispin Cl BEAC HP9.....154 G6
Crispin Fld LBUZ LU7.....98 G3
Crispin Rd BDWL MK13.....30 B6
Crispin Wy SLN SL2.....167 P7
  UX/CGN UB8.....182 C5
Crisp Rd HEN RG9.....173 N5
Criss Gv CFSP/GDCR SL9.....156 G9
Criss La CFSP/GDCR SL9.....156 G9
Crocketts La
  GTMIS/PWD HP16.....124 B8
Crocus Dr AYL HP21.....109 K1
Croft Cl HGDN/ICK UB10.....182 G3
  HYS/HAR UB3.....191 J8
Croft Ct AYLS HP21 *.....3 F6
Crofters WDSR SL4.....194 C5
Crofters Rd NTHWD HA6.....159 J4
The Crofters WDSR SL4 *.....194 C5
Croft Gdns RSLP HA4.....171 L1
Crofthill Rd SLN SL2.....179 L6
Croft Mdw LBUZ LU7.....84 F9
Croftie Cl AYLS HP21 *.....3 F6
  CFSP/GDCR SL9.....156 G9
  THAME OX9.....118 C6
Crofts End NPAG MK16.....21 M5
Crofts La RMKS/WB MK17.....52 B8
The Croft HADM HP17.....107 K9
  MDHD SL6.....164 G4
  MLW SL7.....164 C4
Croftwood HWYN HP13.....153 M3
Cromarty Ct BTCHLY MK3.....42 F9
Cromer Cl BERK HP4.....114 C2
  UX/CGN UB8.....183 J9
Cromer Rd HTHAIR TW6.....196 C2
Cromer Rd West
  HTHAIR TW6.....196 C2
Cromhamstone
  RAYLW HP18.....108 F1
Cromwell Av AYLW HP19.....95 M5
  NPAG MK16.....30 G2
  THAME OX9.....118 C6
Cromwell Ct CSTG HP8.....156 E3
  HEN RG9.....173 N6
Cromwell Cl BUCK/WIN MK18.....48 C1
  RMKS/WB MK17 *.....50 D3
Cromwell Gdns MLW SL7.....164 C4
Cromwell Rd FELT TW13.....197 P7
  HEN RG9.....174 A8
  HWYN HP13.....153 J3
  HYS/HAR UB3.....183 K9
  WDR/YW UB7.....190 B1
Cropredy Ct BUCK/WIN MK18.....48 C1
Cropton Ri EMV/FZ MK4.....52 A1
Cropwell Bishop EMV/FZ MK4.....52 A2
Crosby Cl AYL HP20.....96 B3
  SL SL1 *.....187 J7
Crosby Ct CNH/GTH/TM MK8.....41 N3
Crosier Rd HGDN/ICK UB10.....171 H9
Crosland Rd GTLIN MK14.....30 E9
Cross Cl NPAG MK16.....22 A1
Cross End RMKS/WB MK17.....44 A1
Crossfield Cl BERK HP4.....126 A1
Crossfield Rd PRRI HP27.....126 B1
Crosshills STSTR MK11.....29 H8
Crosslands GTLIN MK14.....30 D5
Cross La BEAC HP9.....167 K3
  BUCK/WIN MK18.....47 N5
  OLN MK46.....15 L4
Cross Lanes Cl
  CFSP/GDCR SL9.....157 H5
Cross Meadow CSHM HP5.....135 K2
Cross Oak WDSR SL4.....193 L1
Cross Oak Rd BERK HP4.....126 A3
Cross Rd HWYW HP12.....152 C1
Cross St NPAG MK16.....31 C3
  UX/CGN UB8.....182 C3
Cross Tree Rd RMKN MK19.....39 L1
Crossways CSHM HP5.....135 H5
  LBUZ LU7.....74 G2
  PIN HA5.....159 P9

Crossways BEAC HP9.....155 K9
  BERK HP4.....152 C6
  HWYW HP12 *.....152 C6
Crosthwaite Wy SL SL1.....179 C8
Crouch La WDSR SL4.....192 C7
Crowborough Ln
  WTR/OFPK MK7.....43 N4
Crowbrook Rd PRRI HP27.....121 C7
Crowell Rd CHNR OX39.....128 F2
Crowland Av HYS/HAR UB3.....191 L5
Crow La RBEDW MK43.....45 M8
  RMKS/WB MK17.....44 A8
Crownfield PRRI HP27.....131 C9
Crown La FLKWH HP10.....154 C3
  MDHD SL6.....177 N9
  SL SL1.....179 M3
  WYM HP11.....5 G6
Crown Leys AYL HP20.....2 C4
Crown Meadow
  DTCH/LGLY SL3.....189 K8
Crown Rd MLW SL7.....164 D7
Crown Sq MDHD SL6.....177 P9
Crown Wk WDR/YW UB7.....190 B1
Crow Piece La SLN SL2.....179 K3
Crowther Ct SHEN MK5.....42 A9
Croxley Ct LBUZ LU7 *.....74 D1
Croxley Rd MDHD SL6.....185 K1
Croyde Av HYS/HAR UB3.....191 L5
Croydon Cl EMV/FZ MK4.....52 A1
Cruickshank Cv
  CNH/GTH/TM MK8.....41 M4
Crummock Cl SL SL1.....178 G9
Crummock Pl WEAT MK2.....53 K5
Cryers Hill La HAZ/HG HP15.....143 K5
Cryers Hill Rd HAZ/HG HP15.....143 H5
Cubb Fld AYLW HP19.....95 H6
Cublington Rd LBUZ LU7.....82 C1
Cuddington Cl RAYLW HP18.....107 K3
Cuddington Hl RAYLW HP18.....107 J2
Cuddington Rd RAYLW HP18.....107 N3
Cuddsens Ct
  GTMIS/PWD HP16.....134 B5
Cuff La RMKS/WB MK17.....64 A1
Culbertson La BDWL MK13.....29 P9
Culham Dr MDHD SL6.....177 L6
Cullen Pl WEAT MK2.....53 K6
Cullera Cl NTHWD HA6.....159 L8
Culley Wy MDHD SL6.....184 E3
Cullyn Rd HWYW HP12.....152 C7
Culmstock Pl EMV/FZ MK4.....52 D1
Culrain Pl WOLV MK12.....29 M3
Culross Gv MKV MK10.....31 P3
Culverden Bd OXHEY WD19.....159 P3
Culvers Cft BEAC HP9.....155 H6
Culvert La UX/CGN UB8.....182 B5
Culverton La PRRI HP27.....131 J7
Cumberland Av SLN SL2.....179 N7
Cumberland Cl AMSS HP7.....146 B6
  AYLS HP21.....96 B8
Cumberland Rd ASHF TW15.....196 D9
Cumbrae Cl SL SL1 *.....179 L4
Cumbria Cl BTCHLY MK3.....52 F2
  MDHD SL6.....185 H1
Cumbrian Wy HWYN HP13.....4 D3
  UX/CGN UB8.....182 D4
Curfew Yd WDSR SL4 *.....187 P9
Curie Av AYLW HP19.....142 E2
Curls La MDHD SL6.....185 K6
Curran Ct UX/CGN UB8.....182 C7
Currier Dr GTLIN MK14.....30 E9
Curriers La SL SL1.....179 H1
Cursley Pth AYLW HP19.....95 N5
Curtis Cl RKW/CH/CXG WD3.....158 A1
Curtis Ct SHEN MK5.....42 B9
Curtis Wy BERK HP4.....126 F2
Curzon Av BEAC HP9.....155 H6
  HAZ/HG HP15.....144 A9
Curzon Cl HAZ/HG HP15.....144 A9
Curzon Gate Ct SKCH HP14 *.....140 A6
Curzon Pl WTR/OFPK MK7.....44 B6
Cutlers Ms GTLIN MK14.....30 F7
Cutlers Wy LBUZ LU7.....84 G9
Cut Throat Av DUN/WHIP LU6.....86 G9
Cuttsfield Ter HHW HP1.....127 J2
Cyclamen Pl AYLS HP21.....109 K1
Cygnet Cl NTHWD HA6.....159 J5
Cygnus Dr LBUZ LU7.....75 H1
Cypress NPAG MK16.....30 G2

D

Dacre Rd RAYLNE/WEN HP22.....111 L7
Dadbrook RAYLW HP18.....107 K4
Dadbrook Cl RAYLW HP18.....107 K4
Dadfield Cl RAYLW HP18.....107 K4
Dadford Rd BUCK/WIN MK18.....25 K7
  TOW NN12.....25 K2
Daggs Dell Rd HHW HP1.....115 N9
Dag La HYS/HAR UB3 *.....183 P1
Dagmar Rd WDSR SL4.....187 P8
Dagnall Crs UX/CGN UB8.....182 A3
Dagnall Rd DUN/WHIP LU6.....86 E6
  HHW HP1.....115 L1
  OLN MK46.....15 L4
Dairy Cl MDHD SL6.....185 K3
Dairy La HEN RG9.....162 D8
Dairymede PRRI HP27.....121 A9
Dale Cl BRACKY NN13.....35 J5
  HWYN HP12.....152 C6
Dale Dr YEAD UB4.....183 M7
Daleham Dr UX/CGN UB8.....183 H9
Dalesford Rd AYLS HP21.....3 A2
Dale Side CFSP/GDCR SL9.....168 G6
Dalgin Pl CMK MK9 *.....3 H1
Dallas Ter HYS/HAR UB3.....191 M4
Dallega Cl HYS/HAR UB3.....191 K1

Dalston Cl AYL HP20 .....95 P5
Dalton Ct WLW UB4 .....183 K7
Dalton Ga MKV MK10.....43 M1
Dalvina Pl WLW MK12 .....29 N9
Dalwood Ms AYLW HP19...95 H7
Daly Wy AYLS HP21 .....96 B8
Damar Gdns HEN RG9 ....174 A8
Damask Cl TRING HP23 ...112 G2
Damask Gn HHW HP1 .....127 N3
Damson Gv SL SL1 .....187 J8
Dancers End La TRING HP23 ..111 P8
Dandridge Ct DTCH/LGLY SL3 ...189 H7
Dandridge Dr BNEND SL8 ..166 A6
Dane Cl AMSS HP7 ....146 B5
Dane Rd DBCH MK1 ....53 K1
Danesborough Dr
  RMKS/WB MK17 .....54 E1
Danesbrook Cl HWW/FZ MK4 ..42 D8
Danesbury Rd FELT TW15 ..197 P7
Danes Gdns BNEND SL8 ...177 M2
Danes Wy LBUZ LU7 .....75 H2
Daniaud Ct BRACKY NN13 ..34 S4
Daniels Welch
  EAG/OLD/WT MK6 ....42 G6
Danstead Wy
  CNH/GTH/TM MK8 ....41 M5
  CNH/GTH/TM MK8 ....42 A2
  GTLIN MK14 .....30 F8
Danvers Cft TRING HP23 ...112 G1
Darby Ct SHEN MK5 .....42 B7
Darin Ct CNH/GTH/TM MK8 ..41 N4
Darin La RAYLNE/WEN HP22 ..80 E1
  RAYLNE/WEN HP22 ....83 K5
  RAYLW HP18 .....106 F4
Darley Cl AYLS HP21 ....96 B3
Darley La GTLIN MK14 ....30 F8
Darley's Cl RAYLW HP18 ...77 N5
Darling's La MDHD SL6 ....176 E8
Darnel Ct EAG/OLD/WT MK6 ..42 G7
Darrell Ct DTCH/LGLY SL3 ..189 H7
Darr's La BERK HP4 ....113 P9
Dart Cl AYLS HP21 ....109 L1
  DTCH/LGLY SL3 .....189 K7
  NPAC MK16 .....31 K1
Dartmouth Rd OLN MK46 ...15 H4
  RSLP HA4 .....171 N8
Darvell Dr CSHM HP5 ....135 L2
Darvill Rd RAYLW HP18 ....108 D1
Darvill's La SL SL1 ....187 L4
Darwin Ct SHEN MK5 ....41 N7
Darwin Rd DTCH/LGLY SL3 ..189 L3
Dashfield Gv HAZ/HG HP15 ..143 P7
Dashwood Av HWYW HP12 ..152 G2
Dashwood Cl DTCH/LGLY SL3 ..189 L5
Datchet Pl DTCH/LGLY SL3 ..188 D9
  WDSR SL4 .....187 P8
Daubeney Ga SHEN MK5 ....K1
Davenham Av NTHWD HA6 ..159 M4
Davenport Lea
  RMKS/WB MK17.....44 C7
Davenport Rd HWYW HP12 ..152 G2
Daventry Ct DTCH/LGLY SL3 ..189 P9
David Cl AYLS HP21 ....110 A3
  HYS/HAR UB3 .....191 K8
Davidge Pl BEAC HP9 ....154 D4
David Rd DTCH/LGLY SL3 ...189 P5
Davies Cl AYL HP21 ....2 C5
Davies Ct HWYW HP12 ....152 D5
Davis Cl MLW SL7 ....164 E8
Davy Av SHEN MK5 ....42 C5
Dawes Cl CSHM HP5 ....135 M5
  HGDN/ICK UB10 .....182 C5
Dawes East Rd SL SL1 ....178 C7
Dawes La RKW/CH/CXG WD3 ..187 M9
Dawes Moor Cl SL SL1 ....180 E9
Dawe's Rd HGDN/ICK UB10 ..182 C5
Dawley Av UX/CGN UB8 ....183 H8
Dawley Pde HYS/HAR UB3 ..191 J1
Dawley Ride DTCH/LGLY SL3 ..189 L5
Dawley Rd HYS/HAR UB3 ...191 K1
Dawlish Dr RSLP HA4 ....171 N7
Dawney Cl AYLW HP19 ....2 B1
Dawn Redwood Cl
  DTCH/LGLY SL3 .....195 J2
Daws Hill La WYM HP11 ....152 G6
Daws Lea WYM HP11 ....152 G6
Dawson Ct HYS/HAR UB3 ..183 K8
  WDSR SL4 .....193 L1
Dawson Rd DBGH MK1 ....43 J9
Daylesford Ct WLLN MK15 ..31 H1
Deacon Pl MKV MK10 ....31 N7
Deacons Ct PHA HP5 ....159 P9
Deadhearn La CSTG HP8 ...156 C1
Deal Av SL SL1 ....179 K9
Deanacre Ct CFSP/GDCR SL9 ..156 G6
Dean Cl AYLS HP21 ....110 A1
  HGDN/ICK UB10 .....182 F3
  WDSR SL4 .....193 H2
  WYM HP11 .....147 L4
Deancroft Rd
  CFSP/GDCR SL9 .....156 G6
Deane Av RSLP HA4 ....183 P1
Deane Ct NTHWD HA6 ....159 L8
Deane Wy RSLP HA4 ....172 A1
Dean Farm La LBUZ LU7....63 L5
Dean Fld HHS/BOV HP3 ...127 L5
Deanfield SKCH HP14 ....141 K3
Deanfield Av HEN RG9 ....173 N7
Deanfield Cl MLW SL7 ....164 E8
  MLW SL7 .....164 L2
Deanfield Rd HEN RG9 ....173 N7
Deangarden Ri WYM HP11 ..153 J4
Dean La MDHD SL6 ....165 H9
Dean Rd LBUZ LU7 ....71 D1
Dean St AMS HP6 146
  SLN SL2 .....180 D4
  TRING HP23 .....112 E2
Deansfield Cl MDHD SL6 ..177 J6
Deans Furlong TRING HP23 ..112 G3
Deanshanger Rd TOW NN12 ..27 J5
Deanshanger Rd RMKN NN13 ..25 H2
Deans Meadow BERK HP4 ..100 E3
Dean's Rd WOLV MK12 29

Dean St MLW SL7 .....164 D6
Deansway CSTH HP8.....135 M2
The Dean RAYLNE/WEN HP22 ..83 H5
Dean Vw MDHD SL6 ....177 L2
Dean Wy CSTC HP8 ....156 C3
  HAZ/HG HP15 .....143 P5
  RAYLNE/WEN HP22 ....111 M2
Dean Wood Rd BEAC HP9 ..155 P6
Dearing Cl AYL HP21 ....95 P5
Debbs Cl STSTR MK11 ....28 C8
Deben Cl RMKS/WB MK16 ..31 L2
De Clare Ct BUCK/WIN MK18 * ..48 C4
Dedmere Ct MLW SL7 ....164 F7
Dedmere Ri MLW SL7 ....164 F7
Dedmere Rd MLW SL7 ....164 F7
Dedworth Dr WDSR SL4 ...192 A1
Dedworth Rd WDSR SL4 ...192 F1
Deeds Gv HWW HP12 ....4 B6
Deena Cl SL SL1 ....187 J1
Deep Acres AMS HP6 ....135 L9
Deepdale BDWL MK13 ....30 C9
Deep Fld DTCH/LGLY SL3 ..188 D8
Deep Mill La
  CSHL/PWD HP16 .....134 B9
Deerfern Cl GTLIN MK14 ..30 E4
Deerfield Cl BUCK/WIN MK18 ..48 C4
Deerings Dr PIN HA5 ....171 N5
Deermead GTMIS/PWD HP16 ..133 P8
Dee Rd WDSR SL4 * 186 C8
Deer Park Wk CSHM HP5 ..135 L2
Deerswood MDHD SL6 ....177 N7
Deer Wk CMK MK9 * 7 D1
Deethe Rd RMKS/WB MK17 ..44 B6
De Havilland Dr
  HAZ/HG HP15 .....143 L9
De Havilland Wy
  STWL/WRAY TW19 .....196 D5
Delafield Cl SKCH HP14 ...140 B7
Delaford Cl IVER SLO * 181 P9
Delahay Ri BERK HP4 ....114 D8
Delamere Cl AYL HP20 ....95 P5
Delamere Gdns LBUZ LU7 ..74 A2
Delaware Dr WLLN MK15 ..31 J5
Delius Ct WTR/OFPK MK7 ..44 A8
Dellbow Rd
  EBED/NFELT TW14 .....197 P4
Dell Ct SLN SL2 ....179 N1
Dell Farm Rd RSLP HA4 ..171 N3
Dellfield CSHM HP5 ....135 L5
Dell Fld GTMIS/PWD HP16 ..133 N7
Dellfield Av BERK HP4 ....114 D6
Dellfield Crs UX/CGN UB8 ..182 C7
Dellfield Pde UX/CGN UB8 * ..182 C7
Dell Lees BEAC HP9 ....155 P7
Dell Rd BERK HP4 .....114 D6
  WDR/YW UB7 .....190 F4
Dells Cl SLN SL2 ....K3
Dellside DEN/HRF UB9 ....170 C5
The Dell AYL SL1 ....K1
  CFSP/GDCR SL9 .....156 G6
  EBED/NFELT TW14 .....197 P6
  FLWHH HP10 .....176 A5
  LBUZ LU7 .....64 F5
  MDHD SL6 * 177 L2
  NTHWD HA6 .....159 L2
  THAME OX9 .....140 B7
Dellwood Ct
  RKW/CH/CXG WD3 .....158 B3
Delmeade Rd CSHM HP5 ..135 L5
Deltic Av BDWL MK13 ....42 B2
De Montfort Ct BRACKY NN13 ..34 G3
Denbigh Dr WDR/YW UB7 ..191 J3
Denbigh Hall Dr BTCHLY MK3 ..42 F9
Denbigh Rd DBGH MK1 ....53 H1
  THAME OX9 .....118 C4
Denbigh Wy WEAT MK2 ....53 J2
Denby Wk AYL HP20 * 3 H4
Denchworth Ct EMV/FZ MK4 ..52 C1
Dene Ct BUCK/WIN MK18 ..60 C7
  RMKS/WB MK17 .....44 C6
Denecroft Crs
  HGDN/ICK UB10 .....183 H4
Dene Rd NTHWD HA6 ....159 J6
The Dene BUCK/WIN MK18 ..58 B7
Denewood HWYN HP13 ....153 L3
Denham Av DEN/HRF UB9 ..169 P7
Denham Ct BTCHLY MK3 ..52 D5
  DEN/HRF UB9 .....170 A4
  MDHD SL6 * 185 J1
Denham Court Dr
  DEN/HRF UB9 .....170 B8
Denham Green Cl
  DEN/HRF UB9 .....170 A5
Denham Green La
  DEN/HRF UB9 .....169 N5
Denham Ldg DEN/HRF UB9 ..157 N6
Denham Pde DEN/HRF UB9 * ..169 P8
Denham Pl DEN/HRF UB9 * ..170 A4
Denham Rd IVER SLO 181 M4
  SKCH HP14 .....140 B7
Denham Vw BUCK/WIN MK18 ..60 B8
  CFSP/GDCR SL9 .....157 P6
Denham Wy DEN/HRF UB9 ..170 A4
Denham Wy (North Orbital Rd)
  RKW/CH/CXG WD3 .....157 N5
Denison Ct ST MDHD SL6 ..177 L8
  WEAT MK2 .....53 J4
  WYM HP11 .....4 A6
Denmead CNH/GTH/TM MK8 ..41 M6
Denmead Cl CFSP/GDCR SL9 ..168 G5
Dennis Ct RAYLNE/WEN HP22 ..111 N2
Dennis Wy SL SL1 ....187 H1
Denny Rd DTCH/LGLY SL3 ..189 N8
Denny's La BERK HP4 ....126 B3
Denton Rd RNHPTN NN7 ...8 A1
Denziloe Av HGDN/ICK UB10 ..183 H6
De Pirenore HWYN HP15 ..143 N9
Depot Rd MDHD SL6 ....185 M1
De Quincey Ct BRACKY NN13 ..34 G3
Derby Rd UX/CGN UB8 ....182 C5

Derehams Av FLKWH HP10 ..154 A7
Derehams La FLKWH HP10 ..154 A8
Derek Rd MDHD SL6 ....178 A8
Dere Pl WEAT MK2 ....53 L7
Deri Dene Cl
  STWL/WRAY TW19 * 196 E5
Derwent Av HGDN/ICK UB10 ..170 E9
Derwent Cl AMSS HP7 ....146 D3
  EBED/NFELT TW14 .....197 M7
  NPAC MK16 .....31 K1
Derwent Dr BTCHLY MK3 ..52 E5
  HYS/HAR UB3 .....183 L3
  MDHD SL6 .....177 K8
  SL SL1 .....178 D8
  YEAD UB4 .....183 L8
Derwent Rd AYLS HP21 ....96 B9
  LBUZ LU7 .....73 P2
De Salis Rd HGDN/ICK UB10 ..183 J7
Desborough Cl BDWL MK13 ..185 J2
Desborough Gn AYL HP20 ..2 D1
Desborough Park Rd
  HWYW HP12 .....4 A4
Desborough Rd HWW HP12 ..4 A4
Desborough St WYM HP11 ..4 B3
Deseronto Est
  DTCH/LGLY SL3 * 188 C3
Desford Wy ASHF TW15 ...196 F8
Develin Cl GTLIN MK14.....30 F3
Devereux Pl AYLW HP19 ...95 J5
Devereux Rd WDSR SL4 ...193 P1
Deverill Rd AYLS HP21 ....109 L5
Deverills Wy DTCH/LGLY SL3 ..189 L5
Devon Av SL SL1 ....187 J5
Devon Cl AYLW HP19 ....95 J4
Devonshire Av AMS HP6 ..145 M1
Devonshire Gn SL SL1 ....179 M5
Devonshire Wy YEAD UB4 ..183 P9
Devon Wy HGDN/ICK UB10 ..182 F5
Dexter Av EAG/OLD/WT MK6 ..7 J2
Dexter Rd DEN/HRF UB9 ..158 C9
Dhoon Ri MDHD SL6 ....185 M1
Diamedes Av
  STWL/WRAY TW19 .....196 D6
Diamond Rd SL SL1 ....187 L8
Diana Cl DTCH/LGLY SL3 ..180 G9
Diane Cl AYLS HP21 ....110 A2
Diane Wk AYLS HP21 ....110 A2
Dibden Hi CSTG HP8 ....156 C3
Dickens Av UX/CGN UB8 ..183 P9
Dickens Cl HYS/HAR UB3 ..191 L5
  RBEDW MK45 .....11 K2
Dickens Dr RMKN MK19 ...19 K7
Dickens Pl DTCH/LGLY SL3 ..189 N9
Dickens Spinney OLN MK46 ..15 H4
Dickens Wy AYLW HP19 ...95 H5
Dick Wy AYLW HP19 ....95 H4
Dick Turpin Wy
  EBED/NFELT TW14 .....197 M3
Diddington Ct BTCHLY MK3 ..53 J8
Digby Cl THAME OX9 ....118 F4
Digby Ct MKV MK10 ....45 E1
Digby Rd LBUZ LU7 ....74 F4
Dingle Dell LBUZ LU7 ....64 D8
Dingleberry OLN MK46 ...15 H4
The Dingle HGDN/ICK UB10 ..182 F5
Dinmore HHS/BOV HP3 ...137 H1
Disraeli Ct DTCH/LGLY SL3 ..189 J7
Disraeli Crs HWYN HP13 ..152 F1
Disraeli Pk BEAC HP9 ....155 H4
Disraeli Sq AYLW HP19 ...95 J7
Diswell Brook Wy
  RMKN MK19 .....28 A3
Ditchingham Ct AYLW HP19 ..95 K8
Ditton Maze MDHD SL6 ...176 G7
Ditton Park Rd
  DTCH/LGLY SL3 .....188 A6
Ditton Rd DTCH/LGLY SL3 ..188 A6
Dixon Cl AYLS HP21 ....110 A4
Dixon Ct AYLS HP21 ....95 K9
Dixon's Gap Br TRING HP23 ..98 B5
Dobbins La
  RAYLNE/WEN HP22 ....110 C3
Dobsons La HEN RG9 ....161 N8
Dockwell Cl
  EBED/NFELT TW14 .....197 N3
Doctor's Commons Rd
  BERK HP4 .....126 D2
Dodds Cnr SKCH HP14 ...140 B7
Doddsfield Rd SLN SL2 ...179 L6
Dodkin EAG/OLD/WT MK6 ..43 H7
Dodman Gn EMV/FZ MK4 ..52 B3
Doggetts Farm Rd
  DEN/HRF UB9 .....169 L5
Doggett St BLUZ LU7 ....74 E2
Doggetts Wood Cl CSTG HP8 ..146 D9
Doggetts Wood La
  CSTG HP8 .....146 D9
Doghurst Av WDR/YW UB7 ..191 H6
Doghurst Dr WDR/YW UB7 ..191 H6
Dog Kennel La
  RKW/CH/CXG WD3 .....147 P7
Dog La HEN RG9 ....172 G9
Dog Rose Ramble
  NTHLT UB5 .....183 N4
Dog Rose Ramble &
  Hillingdon Trail YEAD UB4 ..183 M4
Doiben Ct WLLN MK15 ....31 K5
Dolesden La WDR/YW UB7 ..149 G9
Dollicot HADM HP17 ....100 D6
Dolphin Ct SL SL1 ....188 D3
Dolphin Ct North
  STWL/WRAY TW19 .....196 A9
Dolphin Rd SL SL1 ....188 D3
Dolphin Sq TRING HP23 ..112 D3
Donkey La BNEND SL8 ....165 N6
  TRING HP23 .....112 D3
  WDR/YW UB7 .....190 C5
Donlee Furlong LBUZ LU7 ..74 G2
Donnay Cl CFSP/GDCR SL9 ..168 G4
Donnington BDWL MK13 ..30 B7

Donnington Gdns MDHD SL6..177 M7
The Don BTCHLY MK3 ....52 D2
Doon Wy WEAT MK2 ....53 J6
Dorchester Av BTCHLY MK3 ..52 F7
Dorchester Ct MDHD SL6 ..177 H7
  RAYLNE/WEN HP22 ....110 B4
Dorchester Dr
  EBED/NFELT TW14 .....197 L5
Dorchester Pl THAME OX9 ..118 C5
Dorchester Waye YEAD UB4 ..183 P9
Doreen Cl WEAT MK2 ....53 J2
Dorking Pl BERK HP4 ....114 D8
Dormans Ct NTHWD *HA6..159 K7
Dormer Av LBUZ LU7 ....73 L6
Dormer Cl AYLW HP19 ....95 K9
Dormer La HAZ/HG HP15 ..143 P4
Dormers HHS/BOV HP3 ...127 N9
Dormywood RSLP HA4 ....171 M3
Dornels SLN SL2 ....180 E9
Dorney End CSHM HP5 ...135 L2
Dorney Hi North BEAC HP9 ..167 L4
Dorney Hi South BEAC HP9 ..167 L5
Dorney Pl BDWL MK13 ....41 N2
Dorney Reach Rd MDHD SL6 ..186 C6
Dorney Wood Rd SL SL1 ..166 G8
Dorrells Rd PRRI HP27 ....120 F7
Dorrien's Cft BERK HP4 ...114 A7
Dorset Cl BERK HP4 ....114 B9
  BTCHLY MK3 .....52 E7
  YEAD UB4 .....183 L6
Dorset Pl AYLS HP21 ....96 C9
Dorset Rd ASHF TW15 ....196 D9
  WDSR SL4 .....192 F1
Dorton Cl CNH/GTH/TM MK8 ..41 P5
Dorton Wy HGDN/ICK UB10 ..182 F5
Douglas Gdns BERK HP4 ..114 C9
Douglas La
  STWL/WRAY TW19 .....195 H4
Douglas Pl EAG/OLD/WT MK6 ..3 J2
Douglas Rd SLN SL2 ....179 P8
  STWL/WRAY TW19 .....196 D5
Dove Cl AYLS HP21 ....109 L1
  BUCK/WIN MK18 .....31 K1
  NPAC MK16 .....31 J1
Dovecote HADM HP17 ....107 K8
  PRRI HP27 .....121 E8
Dovecot Rd HWYN HP13 ..152 E1
Dove Ct BEAC HP9 ....155 H7
Dovedale Cl HGDN/ICK UB10 ..182 F4
Dove House Cl
  BUCK/WIN MK18 .....60 C6
  DUN/WHIP LU6 .....54 G5
Dove House Crs SLN SL2 ..179 J6
Dove House La
  BUCK/WIN MK18 .....60 C6
Dove La HEN RG9 ....87 L9
Dover Hedge AYLS HP21 ..96 B9
Dove Rd SL SL1 ....72 E1
Dove St LBUZ LU7 ....74 G3
Dovetail Cl HWYW HP12 ..152 C3
Dove Tree Rd LBUZ LU7 ..74 G3
Dowding Rd HGDN/ICK UB10 ..182 F3
Dower Ct BEAC HP9 ....155 G4
Dower Pk WDSR SL4 ....193 J5
Down Cl NTHLT UB5 ....183 P6
Downden Gdns EAG/OLD/WT MK6..7 M1
Downer Dr
  RKW/CH/CXG WD3 .....137 N9
Downfield La MDHD SL6 ..184 B9
Downham Rd
  RMKS/WB MK17 .....44 D6
Downings Wd
  RKW/CH/CXG WD3 .....157 M5
Downland CNH/GTH/TM MK8 ..41 P5
Downley Av BDWL MK13 ...42 C1
Downley Rd SKCH HP14 ..141 J4
Down Pl WDSR SL4 ....186 A1
Downs Barn Bvd GTLIN MK14 ..30 F9
Downs Pk HWYN HP13 ....152 E1
Downs Rd DTCH/LGLY SL3 ..188 B8
Downside AMSS HP7 ....145 P2
Down Wy NTHLT UB5 ....183 P6
Drake Av DTCH/LGLY SL3 ..195 K9
Drake Cl AYLS HP21 ....95 K9
Drakeloe Ct RMKS/WB MK17 ..44 B6
Drakes Dr NTHWD HA6 ...159 J7
  RAYLW HP18 118
Drakes Farm DEN/HRF UB9 ..170 F5
Drakes Ms CNH/GTH/TM MK8 ..41 N5
Drakewell Rd RMKS/WB MK17 ..54 D4
Dray's La HEN RG9 ....85 L7
Drayton Ct WDR/YW UB7 * ..190 F3
Drayton Gdns
  WDR/YW UB7 .....190 F3
Drayton Rd AYL HP20 ....2 C5
  WEAT MK2 .....53 J2
Drenon Sq HYS/HAR UB3 ..191 H1
Dresser Rd
  GTMIS/PWD HP16 .....133 J7
Drew Ct EAG/OLD/WT MK6 *..42 G7
Drew Meadow SL SL1 ....166 G8
Drews Pk BEAC HP9 ....155 G4
The Drey CFSP/GDCR SL9 ..156 C8
Drift Wy DTCH/LGLY SL3 ..189 H9
The Drive AMSS HP7 ....145 P2
  DTCH/LGLY SL3 .....188 C3

DTCH/LGLY SL3 .....188 C3
EBED/NFELT TW14 .....197 J4
HGDN/ICK UB10 .....170 E9
MDHD SL6 .....159 P8
RBEDW MK43 .....33 H5
STWL/WRAY TW19 .....194 F4
Dromore Pk SL SL1 ....166 F8
Dropmore Rd SL SL1 ....155 N6
Drovers La HEN RG9 ....161 N1
Drovers Wy BEAC HP9 ....155 M6
  RMKS/WB MK17 .....52 D9
Druce End TOW NN12 ....18 A8
Druids Wk CHNR OX39 ....129 N6
Drummond Ride
  TRING HP23 .....112 E1
Drummond Hay
  WLLN MK15 * 31 J6
Drydell La CSHM HP5 ....135 K4
Dryden Cl AYL HP20 ....95 N5
  NPAC MK16 .....30 G1
Drysdale Cl NTHWD HA6 ..159 J4
Duchess Gv WTR/OFPK MK7 ..44 A6
Duchess St SL SL1 ....187 P5
Duck Aly CSHM HP5 ....135 M5
Duck End BRACKY NN13 ..34 B6
  RMKS/WB MK17 .....64 B1
Duck Lake BUCK/WIN MK18 ..38 C9
Duck Lake Cl BUCK/WIN MK18 ..38 C8
Duck La RAYLW HP18 ....77 J8
  RAYLW HP18 .....77 M1
  SL SL1 .....55 K4
Duckmore La TRING HP23 ..112 C5
Ducks Hill Rd NTHWD HA6 ..159 J7
Duck Sq CHNR OX39 ....129 N6
Duckworth Ct
  EAG/OLD/WT MK6 .....42 E5
Dudley Br BUCK/WIN MK18 ..47 L4
Dudley Cl BUCK/WIN MK18 ..70 C7
Dudley Dr RSLP HA4 ....183 P1
Dudley Hi SHEN MK5 ....42 A6
Dudley La HEN RG9 ....162 C5
Dudley Pl HYS/HAR UB3 ..191 K5
Dudley Rd
  EBED/NFELT TW14 .....197 K3
  SL SL1 .....74 E3
Dudset La HEST TW5 ....191 N9
Dudswell Hi BERK HP4 ...113 N6
Dudswell La BERK HP4 ...113 N5
Duffield La SL SL1 ....180 B5
Duffield Pk SLN SL2 ....180 B6
Dukes Av CNH/GTH/TM MK8 ..41 M6
Dukes Cl CFSP/GDCR SL9 ..168 F6
  RAYLW HP18 .....117 J3
  WEAT MK2 .....53 J2
Dukes Kiln Dr
  CFSP/GDCR SL9 .....168 E7
Dukes Meadow BNEND SL8 * ..165 E6
Dukes Piece BUCK/WIN MK18 ..48 D5
Dukes Pl MLW SL7 ....55 K2
Dukes Ride CFSP/GDCR SL9 ..168 E6
  HGDN/ICK UB10 .....170 E9
  LBUZ LU7 .....64 C7
Duke St HEN RG9 ....174 A6
  HWYN HP13 .....5 J6
  PRRI HP27 .....121 K9
  RMKS/WB MK17 .....45 H8
  WDSR SL4 .....187 P5
Dukes Va BERK HP4 ....114 C2
  UX/CGN UB8 .....182 B4
Dukes Wood Av
  CFSP/GDCR SL9 .....168 E6
Dukes Wood Dr
  CFSP/GDCR SL9 .....168 E6
Dulverton Dr EMV/FZ MK4 ..42 D9
Dulverton Rd RSLP HA4 ..171 N7
Dulwich Cl NPAC MK16 ...31 J3
Dumas Cul-de-Sac
  BRACKY NN13 .....34 G4
Dumbletons
  RKW/CH/CXG WD3 .....157 N4
Dumfries Cl BTCHLY MK3 ..42 F9
  OXHEY WD19 .....159 N5
Dunbar Ct BTCHLY MK3 ..52 D2
  SLN SL2 .....188 D2
  YEAD UB4 .....183 N8
Dunbar Dr THAME OX9 ...118 G4
Duncan Gv SHEN MK5 ....41 P6
Duncannon Crs WDSR SL4 ..193 H2
Duncan Rd RBEDW MK43 ..33 J3
Dunchurch Dl WTR/OFPK MK7 ..44 A7
Duncombe Cl AMS HP6 ...146 A2
Duncombe Dr LBUZ LU7 ..74 A3
Duncombe St WEAT MK2 ..53 H4
Duncroft WDSR SL4 ....193 J2
Dundale Rd TRING HP23 ..112 E2
Dundee Rd SL SL1 ....179 K9
Dungeness Ct EMV/FZ MK4 ..51 P2
Dungrove Hill La MDHD SL6 ..176 C5
Dunholme End MDHD SL6 ..185 K4
Dunkery Beacon
  EMV/FZ MK4 .....42 D9
Dunnet Cl EMV/FZ MK4 ..52 A5
Dunnery Rd EAG/OLD/WT WD4 ..137 P5
Dunsby Rd EAG/OLD/WT MK6 ..42 D1
Dunsham La AYL HP20 ....2 D1
Dunsley Pl TRING HP23 ...112 F3
Dunsmore Rd PRRI HP27 ..121 G8
Dunsmore Ride PRRI HP27 ..121 G8
Dunstable Rd
  DUN/WHIP LU6 .....86 C3
  DUN/WHIP LU6 .....100 E1
Dunstall Av HEN RG9 ....173 M7
Dunster Cl DEN/HRF UB9 ..158 B9
Dunster Cl EMV/FZ MK4 ..42 D9
Dunster Gdns SL SL1 ....187 J1
Dunster Hi TRING HP23 ...112 E2
Dunthorpe Wy
  CNH/GTH/TM MK8 .....41 M6
Dunton Rd LBUZ LU7 ....72 C4
Dunvedin Pl WOLV MK12 ..29 K7
Dunvegan Cl WEAT MK2 ..53 K7
Dunwood Ri HWYN HP15 ..153 H1
Duparc Cl WTR/OFPK MK7 ..44 A7

Dupre Cl *SL* SL1......187 J3
Durgate *WTR/OFPK* MK7......43 N4
Durham Av *SL* SL1......179 L9
Durley Hollow *HWYN* HP13......5 H1
Durpe Crs *BEAC* HP9......155 M9
Durrans Ct *WEAT* MK4......53 L2
Durrants La *SLN* SL2......179 L4
Durrants Rd *BERK* HP4......114 B9
Durrell Cl *LBUZ* LU7......74 C2
Dutch Barn Cl
　STWL/WRAY TW19......196 D5
Dutton Wy *IVER* SL0......181 N9
Dyersdale MK13......30 C8
Dyers Ms *GTLIN* MK14......30 F7
Dyers Rd *DUN/WHIP* LU6......85 F9
Dyson Cl *WDSR* SL4......193 M2

E

Eagle Rd *HTHAIR* TW6......197 M2
Eagles Rd *AYL* HP20......3 J4
Eaglestone *EAG/OLD/WT* MK6......*
Eakley Lanes *RNWR/PK* MK7 *......13 N2
Ealing Cha *WTR/OFPK* MK7......43 M4
Eames Cl *AYL* HP20......95 P4
Eamont Cl *RSLP* HA4......171 H5
Earl Cl *HWYN* HP13......5 G1
Earl Howe Cl *HAZ/HG* HP15......144 A5
Earls Cl *WEAT* MK4......53 J3
Earlsfield *MDHD* SL6......186 D8
Earls La *SL* SL1......187 K2
Earls Willow *BDWL* MK13......30 A5
Eascote Rd *AYL* HP21......110 B2
Easedale Cl *DUN/WHIP* LU6......87 L2
Easington La *RAYLW* HP18......105 P5
East Av *HYS/HAR* UB3......191 N1
Eastbourne Rd *SL* SL1......179 L9
Eastbridge *SL* SL1......188 D3
Eastbrook Cl *RBICS/W* OX25......76 F9
East Burnham La *SLN* SL2......179 L4
Eastbury Av *NTHWD* HA6......159 L5
Eastbury Ct *EMV/FZ* MK4......52 D2
Eastbury Rd *BERK* HP4......114 C8
East Chapel *EMV/FZ* MK4......52 B3
Eastchurch Rd *HTHAIR* TW6......197 L2
East Claydon Rd
　BUCK/WIN MK18......59 N9
East Common
　CFSP/GDCR SL9......168 G4
Eastcote Rd *RSLP* HA4......171 L1
East Crs *WDSR* SL4......187 K9
Eastcroft *SLN* SL2......179 M7
East Dales *BDWL* MK13......30 D8
East Dr *HWYN* HP13......153 L2
　NTHWD HA6......159 L2
Eastergate *BEAC* HP9......154 G6
Eastern Dene *HAZ/HG* HP15......143 N6
East Dr *BNEND* SL8......166 A6
Eastern Perimeter Rd
　HTHAIR TW6......197 L1
Eastern St *AYL* HP20......3 F3
Eastern Wy *LBUZ* LU7......64 C9
Eastfield Cl *SL* SL1......188 C4
Eastfield Crs *TOW* NN12......18 E1
Eastfield Dr *RMKN* MK19......19 J3
Eastfield Rd *AYL* HP20......96 B7
　PRRI HP27......131 L1
　SL SL1......178 E8
Eastleigh Wy
　EBED/NFELT TW14......197 N7
East Hills *RD/BOV* HP3......137 J1
Easton St *HWYN* HP13......5 J6
East Paddock *MDHD* SL6......176 F2
East Rp *HTHAIR* TW6......191 H9
East Richardson St
　WYM HP11......4 D4
East Rdg *EBED/NFELT* TW14......197 K6
　MDHD SL6......177 L9
　RBEDW MK45......33 H5
　WDR/YW UB7......190 D7
East Stanley Gn
　DTCH/LGLY SL3......189 P9
East St *BUCK/WIN* MK18......59 K1
　CSHM MK5......135 M5
　LBUZ LU7......74 F1
　OLN MK46......15 M3
　THAME OX9......118 D6
East Wk *HYS/HAR* UB3......191 N5
East Wy *BEAC* HP9......154 G9
　HYS/HAR UB3......191 N2
　RSLP HA4......171 N5
Eastwick Crs
　RKW/CH/CXG WD3......157 P2
Eastwood Rd *SKCH* MK14......140 B8
Eaton Av *HWYN* HP12......152 C2
Eaton Bray Rd
　DUN/WHIP LU6......85 N3
Eaton Ga *NTHWD* HA6......159 N4
Eatongate Cl *DUN/WHIP* LU6......86 N3
Eaton Pk *DUN/WHIP* LU6......86 B2
Eaton Pl *HWYW* HP12 *......152 D2
Eaton Rd *AYLS* HP21......95 M9
Ebble Cl *AYLS* HP21......109 L2
Ebbsgrove *SHEN* MK5......135 J4
Ebsworth Cl *MDHD* SL6......186 D5
Ebury Rp *RKW/CH/CXG* WD3......158 D9
Ebury Cl *NTHWD* HA6......159 H5
Ebury Rd *RKW/CH/CXG* WD3......158 D1
Eddy St *BERK* HP4......114 C9
Eden Cl *AYLS* HP21......109 M2

　DTCH/LGLY SL3......189 J6
Eden Ct *LBUZ* LU7 *......74 F4
Edens La *RBEDW* MK43......11 M6
Edgar Rd *WDR/YW* UB7......190 E1
Edgcott Rd *RAYLW* HP18......77 L2
Edgecombe *AYLS* HP21......110 B1
Edgecote *CNH/GTH/TM* MK8......42 A4
Edgehill *THAME* OX9......118 D3
Edge Hill Ct *BUCK/WIN* MK18......48 C1
Edgewood *BEAC* HP9......155 H3
　WYM HP11......153 K5
Edinburgh Av *SL* SL1......179 L9
Edinburgh Cl
　HGDN/ICK UB10......171 H9
Edinburgh Dr *DEN/HRF* UB9......169 P4
　HGDN/ICK UB10......171 H9
Edinburgh Gdns *WDSR* SL4......193 P1
Edinburgh Pl *AYLS* HP21......95 L9
Edinburgh Rd *MDHD* SL6......177 L2
　MLW SL7......164 E6
Edison Rd *AYLW* HP19......94 G6
Edison Sq *SHEN* MK5......42 C7
Edith Rd *MDHD* SL6......176 D9
Edlyn Cl *BERK* HP4......114 B9
Edmonds Cl *BUCK/WIN* MK18......48 C1
Edmonds Rd *SKCH* HP14......111 K6
Edmund Ct *BEAC* HP9......166 E1
　SHEN MK5......41 P5
Edmunds Cl *HWYW* HP12......152 C5
Edmunds Gdns *HWYW* HP12......152 C5
Edmunds Wy *SLN* SL2......180 D8
Edrich Av *EAG/OLD/WT* MK6......7 C7
Edstone Pl *EMV/FZ* MK4......110 A2
Edward Rd
　EBED/NFELT TW14......197 K4
Edwards Ct *SL* SL1......188 A3
Edward St *LBUZ* LU7 *......74 E1
Edward Wy *ASHF* TW15......196 F8
Edwin Cl *RMKS/WB* MK17......54 B1
Edy Ct *SHEN* MK5......41 P8
Edzell Crs *EMV/FZ* MK4......51 N1
Eelbrook Av *BDWL* MK13......6 A2
Eeles Cl *AYL* HP19......95 L6
Egan Wy *HYS/HAR* UB3......191 L1
Egerton Cl *BRACKY* NN13......35 H5
　PIN HA5......171 N2
Egerton Ga *SHEN* MK5......42 A8
Egerton Rd *BERK* HP4......114 C8
　SLN SL2......179 L4
Egerton Wy *WDR/YW* UB7......191 H8
Egham Cl *BEAC* HP9......154 F6
Egham Ga *TRING* HP23......112 E1
Eghams Wood Rd *BEAC* HP9......154 F6
Egmont Av *STSTR* MK11......28 E1
Egremont Gdns *SL* SL1......187 L2
Egypt La *SLN* SL2......167 N8
Egypt Wy *AYLW* HP19......95 J7
Eider Cl *BUCK/WIN* MK18......59 K7
Eight Acres *SL* SL1......178 F7
　TRING HP23......112 E2
Eighth Av *HYS/HAR* UB3......191 L1
Elbow Meadow
　DTCH/LGLY SL3 *......189 P9
Elder Cl *WDR/YW* UB7......190 E1
　WYM HP11......153 P1
Elderdene *CHNR* OX39......129 P4
Elderfield Rd *SL* SL1......180 B2
Elder Cl *SHEN* MK5......41 N9
Elder Wy *DTCH/LGLY* SL3 *......189 H3
　HAZ/HG HP15......145 P8
Eldridge Cl
　EBED/NFELT TW14......197 N7
Eldridge La *HADM* HP17......122 C2
Eleanor Cl *RMKS/WB* MK17......55 J8
Eleanor Gdns *AYLS* HP21......95 N9
Eleanor Gv *HGDN/ICK* UB10......171 H8
Eleanor Rd *CFSP/GDCR* SL9......156 E3
Eleanors Gdn *LBUZ* LU7......62 C2
Electra Av *HTHAIR* TW6......197 M2
Elers Rd *HYS/HAR* UB3......191 J5
Elfords *EAG/OLD/WT* MK6......42 C6
Elgar Cl *HGDN/ICK* UB10......170 C7
Elgar Gv *WTR/OFPK* MK7......43 N4
Elgin Crs *HTHAIR* TW6......197 L1
Elgood Av *NTHWD* HA6......159 N2
Elham Wy *AYLS* HP21......110 A2
Eliot Cl *AYLW* HP19......95 H5
Elizabeth Wy *STWL/WRAY* TW19......196 D6
Elizabeth Av *AMS* HP6......146 E3
Elizabeth Cl *AYLS* HP21......110 B2
　HEN RG9......173 L7
Elizabeth Dr *HWYN* HP13 *......5 K6
Elizabeth Dr *AMS* HP6......146 E3
Elizabeth Rd *HEN* RG9......173 N8
　MLW SL7......164 D5
　SKCH HP14......111 K6
Elizabeth Sq *SLN* SL2......180 B4
Elkins Rd *SLN* SL2......180 B4
Ellen Pl *AYLS* HP21......109 L1
Ellenstow *BDWL* MK13......6 B5
Ellen Wk *AYLS* HP21 *......95 K9
Ellerburn Pl *EMV/FZ* MK4......42 B9
Ellery Ri *WDR/YW* UB7......190 D4
Ellesborough Gv
　CNH/GTH/TM MK8......41 M1
Ellesborough Rd
　HADM HP17......121 P3
Ellesmere Av *BRACKY* NN13......35 J5
Ellesmere Cl *BRACKY* NN13......35 J5
　DUN/WHIP LU6......86 B2
　RSLP HA4......171 H5
Ellesmere Crs *BRACKY* NN13......35 H5
Ellesmere Rd *BERK* HP4......126 F1
　BRACKY NN13......35 J5
Ellies Ms *ASHF* TW15......196 F8
Elliman Av *SL* SL1......188 A1
Ellington Ct *MDHD* SL6......178 A9

Ellington Gdns *MDHD* SL6......178 A9
Ellington Pk *MDHD* SL6......177 L7
Ellington Rd *MDHD* SL6......178 A9
Elliot Dr *MLW* SL7......164 A4
Elliott Av *RSLP* HA4......171 P7
Ellis Av *CFSP/GDCR* SL9......157 N8
　SL SL1......188 A3
Ellisgill Ct *BDWL* MK13......30 B9
Ellison Cl *WDSR* SL4......193 K2
Ellis Wy *SKCH* MK14......151 K6
Ellsworth Rd *HWYP* HP11......152 E3
Ellwood Ri *CSTG* HP8......156 E2
Ellwood Rd *BEAC* HP9......154 F9
Elmar Gn *SLN* SL2......179 L4
Elm Av *RSLP* HA4......171 N6
Elmbridge Cl *RSLP* HA4......171 N4
Elmbridge Dr *RSLP* HA4......171 N4
Elm Brook Cl *RAYLW* HP18......106 G5
Elm Cl *AMS* HP6......145 L2
　HADM HP17......122 C2
　HAZ/HG HP15......183 N8
　HYS/HAR UB3......183 N9
　RAYLNE/WEN HP22......110 F4
　RMKS/WB MK17......52 C9
　SLN SL2......179 L4
　STWL/WRAY TW19......196 D7
Elm Cft *HEN* RG9......173 P9
Elm Cft *DTCH/LGLY* SL3......188 E9
Elmcroft Cl
　EBED/NFELT TW14......197 M5
Elmcroft Ter *UX/CGN* UB8 *......182 C9
Elmdale Gdns *PRRI* HP27......131 K1
Elmdon Rd *HTHAIR* TW6......197 J5
Elm Dr *BRACKY* NN13......35 H5
　RMKN MK19......27 P9
　WDSR SL4......192 F7
Elm Gv *BERK* HP4......126 D1
　MDHD SL6......186 A6
　RMKS/WB MK17......44 F8
　WDR/YW UB7......190 F1
Elmhurst Cl *EMV/FZ* MK4......42 F8
　HWYN HP13......153 K1
Elmhurst Rd *AYL* HP20......95 M5
　HWYN HP13......153 N6
Elms Av *SLN* SL2......180 C3
Elms Rd *CFSP/GDCR* SL9......156 D8
　DUN/WHIP LU6......86 A1
　THAME OX9......118 F6
The Elms *BTCHLY* MK3......52 F5
　LBUZ LU7......74 C1
Elm St *BUCK/WIN* MK18......48 C1
Elms Wy *HEN* RG9......160 M6
Elmtree Gn
　CTMIS/PWD HP16......133 N4
Elmtree Hl *CSHM* HP5......135 J8
Elm Trees *RAYLW* HP18......105 P7
Elm Tree Wk
　RKW/CH/CXG WD3 *......147 P6
Elm Vw *HGDN/ICK* UB10......171 L8
Elm Wy *RKW/CH/CXG* WD3......158 B3
Elmwood *MDHD* SL6......177 H4
　RBEDW MK45......17 J1
Elmwood Av *FELT* TW13......197 N9
Elmwood Cl *RAYLW* HP18......105 P7
Elmwood Cv *CFSP/GDCR* SL9......156 D8
Elmwood Rd *SLN* SL2......188 D1
Elora Rd *HWYN* HP13......153 J6
Elruge Cl *WDR/YW* UB7......190 D4
Elsinore Av
　STWL/WRAY TW19 *......196 E6
Elsmore Cl *AYLS* HP21......110 B2
Elsworth Cl
　EBED/NFELT TW14......197 L1
Eltham Av *SL* SL1......179 L9
Elthorne Rd *UX/CGN* UB8......182 D5
Elthorne Wy *NPAG* MK16......51 N3
Elton *EAG/OLD/WT* MK6......43 M5
Elton Dr *MDHD* SL6......177 J2
Elwes Rd *SKCH* HP14......151 L6
Ely Av *SL* SL1......179 N6
Ely Cl *AMSS* HP7......158 C2
Ely Rd *HTHAIR* TW6......197 J5
The Embankment
　STWL/WRAY TW19......194 G6
Ember Rd *DTCH/LGLY* SL3......189 H4
Embleton Rd *OXHEY* WD19......159 N4
Embleton Wy
　BUCK/WIN MK18......48 A4
Emden Cl *WDR/YW* UB7......190 G3
Emerald Cl *BUCK/WIN* MK18......60 K2
Emerald Gt *SL* SL1......188 A3
Emerton Ct *BERK* HP4......114 A7
Emerton Gdns *STSTR* MK11......28 F3
Emerton Garth *BERK* HP4......114 A7
Emmanuel Rd *NTHWD* HA6......159 P8
Emma Rothschild Ct
　TRING HP23......112 E1
Emmett Cl *EMV/FZ* MK4......42 E8
Emperor Wy *BERK* HP4......114 A7
Empingham Cl *WEAT* MK4......53 F1
Emu Cl *LBUZ* LU7......64 E5
Enborne Rd *AYLS* HP21......109 M2

Enfield Cha *GTLIN* MK14......30 D8
Enfield Cl *UX/CGN* UB8......182 D5
Enfield Rd *HTHAIR* TW6......197 L1
Engaine Dr *SHEN* MK5......41 P6
Englehart Dr
　EBED/NFELT TW14......197 M5
English Gdns
　STWL/WRAY TW19......194 F3
Enmore Ga *CMK* MK9......42 A2
Ennell Gv *WEAT* MK2......53 J6
Ennerdale Av *DUN/WHIP* LU6......87 K1
Ennerdale Cl
　EBED/NFELT TW14......197 M5
　WEAT MK2......53 K5
Ennerdale Crs *SL* SL1......178 C8
Ensbury Pth *AYL* HP20......95 N5
Ensign Cl *STWL/WRAY* TW19......196 D2
Ensign Wy
　STWL/WRAY TW19......196 D2
Enstone Rd *HGDN/ICK* UB10......170 F8
Enterprise La *CMK* MK9......7 J1
Enterprise Wy *LBUZ* LU7......74 B3
Epsom Cl *LBUZ* LU7......74 B3
Epsom Gv *BTCHLY* MK3......52 D5
Epsom Sq *HTHAIR* TW6......197 M1
Erdioll Cl *LBUZ* LU7......73 P3
Eriboll Cl *SL* SL1......179 H6
Erica Rd *WOLV* MK12......29 L7
Eridge Gn *WTR/OFPK* MK7......43 N4
Errington Dr *WDSR* SL4......187 G8
Errol Gdns *YEAD* UB4......183 P7
Escarpment Av
　WHDN LU6......86 G8
Esker Crs *HTHAIR* TW6......197 M1
Eskdale Av *CSHM* HP5......135 P3
Eskdale Gdns *MDHD* SL6......185 P5
Eskdale Rd *IVER* SL0......182 B5
　RAYLNE/WEN HP22......110 B4
Essenden Ct *STSTR* MK11......28 F3
Essex Av *SLN* SL2......179 N8
Essex Cl *BTCHLY* MK3......52 C2
Essex Pl *AYLW* HP19......95 L3
Essex Rd *HWYN* HP13......153 L2
　THAME OX9......118 F6
Estover Wy *CHNR* OX39......129 M6
Etheridge Av *MKV* MK10......44 A4
Ethorpe Crs *CFSP/GDCR* SL9......168 G5
Eton Cl *DTCH/LGLY* SL3......188 C7
Eton Ct *WDSR* SL4......187 P8
Eton Pl *MLW* SL7......164 D7
Eton Rd *DTCH/LGLY* SL3......188 D7
　HYS/HAR UB3......191 H8
Eton Sq *WDSR* SL4......187 P8
Eton Wick Rd *WDSR* SL4......187 J5
Eunice Gv *CSHM* HP5......135 P6
Evans Ga *AYLS* HP21......110 A2
Evans Gv *EAG/OLD/WT* MK6......106 F4
Evelyn Av *RSLP* HA4......171 N4
Evelyn Pl *BDWL* MK13......30 A6
Evelyns Cl *UX/CGN* UB8......182 C9
Evenlode *MDHD* SL6......177 H8
Evenlode Cl *AYLS* HP21......109 L1
Evenlode Rd *BNEND* SL8......165 P5
Everard Av *SL* SL1......188 A3
Everest Cl *HWYN* HP13......153 K4
Everest Rd *HWYN* HP13......153 K4
　STWL/WRAY TW19......196 D3
Everglade Cl *EMV/FZ* MK4......42 F8
Evergreen Ct
　STWL/WRAY TW19......196 D6
Evergreen Oak Av *WDSR* SL4......194 C2
Evergreen Wy *HYS/HAR* UB3......191 N1
　STWL/WRAY TW19......196 D6
Everley Cl *EMV/FZ* MK4......42 F8
Eversley Crs *RSLP* HA4......171 N4
Evesham Gn *AYLW* HP19......95 L4
Evett Cl *AYL* HP20......3 G5
Evreux Cl *SHEN* MK5......41 P6
Exborne Pde *LBUZ* LU7 *......74 E2
Exchange Rd *AYLS* HP21......110 A2
Exchange St *AYLS* HP21......2 E4
Exeter Rd *HTHAIR* TW6......197 L2
Exford Av *HWYN* HP13......153 N6
Exmoor Ga *EMV/FZ* MK4......52 E1
Exmouth Rd *YEAD* UB3......183 L6
Explorer Av
　STWL/WRAY TW19......196 E7
Eynard Impasse
　BRACKY NN13......34 G3
Eynsford Ter *WDR/YW* UB7 *......182 F9
Eynsham Ct *WLM* MK15......43 J2
Eyre Cl *AYL* HP21......2 A3
Eythrope Rd *RAYLW* HP18......94 B7

Fairfield Av *DTCH/LGLY* SL3......188 E8
　RSLP HA4......171 J5
Fairfield Cl *BNEND* SL8......165 M4
　OLN MK46......15 N3
Fairfield Ct *RSLP* HA4......171 K6
Fairfield Rd *SL* SL1......178 G6
　TW19......194 B5
　UX/CGN UB8......182 D2
　WDR/YW UB7......190 E2
Fairfields *HAZ/HG* HP15......143 L2
Fairford Crs *GTLIN* MK14......30 G7
Fairford Leys Wy *AYLW* HP19......95 J3
Fairford Rd *MDHD* SL6......177 L8
Fairhaven Crs *OXHEY* WD19......159 N5
Fairholme
　EBED/NFELT TW14......197 K6
Fairholme Crs *YEAD* UB4......183 M7
Fairlawn Pk *WDSR* SL4......193 J3
Fairlea *MDHD* SL6......184 G3
Fair Leas *CSHM* HP5......135 L8
Fairlie Rd *SL* SL1......179 L9
Fairlight Av *WDSR* SL4......193 L9
Fairlight Dr *UX/CGN* UB8......182 D2
Fairmark Dr *HGDN/ICK* UB10......182 C2
Fair Meadow
　BUCK/WIN MK18......60 C6
Fair Mile *AYLS* HP21......3 M3
　HEN RG9......173 M3
Fair Rdg *WYM* HP11......153 J7
Fairthorn Cl *TRING* HP23......112 C3
Fairview *FLKWH* HP10 *......154 B8
Fairview La *FLKWH* HP10......153 N9
　SLN SL2......179 L9
Fairway *PRRI* HP27......131 J1
Fairway Av *WDR/YW* UB7......182 G1
Fairways *CNH/GTH/TM* MK8......41 L2
The Fairway *FLKWH* HP10......153 N9
　MDHD SL6......185 H4
　NTHWD HA6......159 L4
　SL SL1......178 G6
Faithful Cl *HADM* HP17......108 D1
Faithorn Cl *CSHM* HP5......135 L3
Falcon Cl *HAZ/HG* HP15......143 K2
Falcon Ct *HTHAIR* TW6......197 M1
Falcon Dr *STWL/WRAY* TW19......196 D5
Falcon Rdg *BERK* HP4......114 A7
Falcon Ri *HWYN* HP13......152 C1
Falcons Cft *FLKWH* HP10......154 C1
The Falcon *AYLW* HP19......95 P5
Falcon Wy *BRACKY* NN13......34 F2
Falklands Cl *BUCK/WIN* MK18......58 B8
Fall Cl *AYLW* HP19......95 M4
Falling La *WDR/YW* UB7......190 E1
Fallowfield *LBUZ* LU7......74 C2
Fallowfield Cl *AMS* HP6......158 C1
The Fallows *BNEND* SL8......177 N1
Falmouth Pl *EAG/OLD/WT* MK6......7 H5
Falmouth Rd *SL* SL1......185 K9
Fane Wy *MDHD* SL6......185 L9
Fanshawe Rd *THAME* OX9......118 D2
Faraday Cl *SL* SL1......179 L9
Faraday Dr *SHEN* MK5......42 C8
Faraday Rd *AYLW* HP19......95 J6
　SLN SL2......179 L9
Far Furlong Cl *AYLS* HP21......109 M5
Farinton *CNH/GTH/TM* MK8......41 P2
Farjeon Ct *WTR/OFPK* MK7......43 N4
Farmbrough
　EAG/OLD/WT MK6......43 J3
Farmbrough Cl *AYL* HP20......3 J3
Farm Cl *AMS* HP6......146 F3
　HGDN/ICK UB10......171 H9
　KID OX5......88 A5
　LBUZ LU7......74 E2
　MDHD SL6......186 A6
　RAYLW HP18......105 P7
Farm Crs *SLN* SL2......180 C1
Farm Dr *WDSR* SL4......194 D5
Farmers Cl *MDHD* SL6......186 L4
Farmers Wy *BEAC* HP9......184 G3
　MDHD SL6......184 G3
Farm Gv *BEAC* HP9......155 H2
Farmlands *PIN* HA5......159 N1
Farm La *BEAC* HP9......155 N2
Farm Lea *FLKWH* HP10......154 C1
Farm Pl *BERK* HP4......114 B9
Farm Rd *BNEND* SL8......165 P5
　BRACKY NN13......35 H6
　EDG HA8......159 N1
　MDHD SL6......186 E1
　NTHWD HA6......159 J3
　RKW/CH/CXG WD3......158 B3
　SKCH MK14......159 H4
　WDSR SL4......179 H9
Farnburn Av *SL* SL1......178 G6
Farndale Gdns *HYS/HAR* HP15......143 N5
Farnell Rd *SHEN* MK5......41 P6
Farnell Rd *STA* TW18......5 G7
Farnham Ct *HHS/BOV* HP3......137 J1
Farnham Cl
　CNH/GTH/TM MK8......41 N3
Farnham La *SLN* SL2......179 L4
Farnham Park La *SLN* SL2......179 N4
Farnley Rd *AYL* HP20......2 A3
Farrer Cl *UX/CGN* UB8......182 D3
Farrier Dr *GTLIN* MK14......30 F7
Farriers Cl *HHS/BOV* HP3......137 K1
Far Rd *HEN* RG9......173 K5
The Farthingales *MDHD* SL6......177 P5
Farthing Green La *SLN* SL2......180 C5
Farthinghoe Cl
　BRACKY NN13......34 F5
Farthings Cl *PIN* HA5......171 P4
Fassetts Rd *FLKWH* HP10......153 P8

Faugere Cl BRACKY NN13 ...... 34 C4
Faulkners Wy LBUZ LU7 ...... 74 D7
Faulkner Wy HWYN HP13 ...... 142 D9
Favell Dr EMV/FZ MK4 ...... 42 E8
Faversham Rd TRING HP23 ...... 112 E2
Fawcett Rd WDSR SL4 ...... 44 A5
Fawley Bottom La HEN RG9 ...... 161 L9
Fawley Cl NTHWD HA6 ...... 177 K6
Fawns Manor Rd
　EBED/NFELT TW14 ...... 197 N2
Fawsley Cl DTCH/LGLY SL3 ...... 189 N8
Fearney Md
　RKW/CH/CXG WD3 ...... 158 A1
Featherbed La
　GTMIS/PWD HP16 ...... 144 B5
Feathers La
　STWL/WRAY TW19 ...... 195 J8
Featherstone Rd WOLV MK12 ...... 29 J8
Fegans Ct STSTR MK11 ...... 28 F7
Felbridge WTR/OFPK MK7 ...... 45 N5
Felbridge La HEN RG9 ...... 106 B8
Felthambrook Wy
　FELT TW13 ...... 197 P9
Fennels La NPAG MK16 ...... 20 C4
Fencott Rd KID OX5 ...... 88 C3
Fennel Dr GTLIN OX5 ...... 30 E9
Fennels Farm Rd
　FLKWH HP10 ...... 153 N9
Fennels Rd WYM HP11 ...... 153 N6
Fennels Wy FLKWH HP10 ...... 153 N8
Fennemore Cl RAYLW HP18 ...... 104 D2
The Fennings AMS HP6 ...... 135 P9
Fennycroft Rd HHW HP1 ...... 115 P8
Fennymere
　CNH/GTH/TM MK8 ...... 41 M3
Fenny Rd RMKS/WB MK17 ...... 63 L2
Fenton Ct CNH/GTH/TM MK8 ...... 41 H4
Fenton Ri BRACKY NN13 ...... 34 F4
Fernan Dell RMKN MK19 ...... 41 M5
Fernborough Hvn
　EMV/FZ MK4 ...... 52 C1
Ferndale EAG/OLD/WT MK6 ...... 43 J4
Ferndale Cl SKCH HP14 ...... 140 F2
Ferndale Ct UX/CGN UB8 ...... 182 C6
Ferndale Pk MDHD SL6 * 186 C7
Ferndown NTHWD HA6 ...... 178 F9
Fern Dr MDHD SL6 ...... 186 D1
Ferne Furlong OLN MK46 ...... 15 M2
Fernes Cl UX/CGN UB8 ...... 182 C9
Fern Gv EBED/NFELT TW14 ...... 197 P6
Fernheath MK2 * 53 K6
Fernhill Cl THAME OX9 ...... 116 C7
Fernhurst Cl BEAC HP9 ...... 155 J8
Ferne Flds HWYN HP12 ...... 152 B6
Fern La HADM HP17 ...... 107 L8
　MLW SL7 ...... 165 L4
Fernlea Cl FLKWH HP10 ...... 155 L5
Fernleigh MDHD SL6 * 177 L2
Fernley Cl PIN HA5 ...... 171 N2
Fernley Ct MDHD SL6 ...... 177 K7
Fernside HAZ/HG HP15 ...... 143 L2
Fernsleigh Cl
　CFSP/GDCR SL9 ...... 156 C6
Ferrers Av WDR/YW UB7 ...... 190 D5
Ferrers Cl SL SL1 ...... 187 J2
Ferry La MDHD SL6 * 186 A3
　HEN RG9 ...... 174 F2
　MDHD SL6 ...... 177 P1
　MLW SL7 ...... 53 K6
　STWL/WRAY TW19 ...... 195 K8
Ferry Rd MDHD SL6 ...... 186 A3
Ferryside MDHD SL6 * 186 A3
Festival Cl HGDN/ICK UB10 ...... 183 H4
Fettiplace Rd HEAD OX3 ...... 102 A9
Fetty Pl MDHD SL6 ...... 185 K3
Fetch Cl AYL HP20 ...... 2 A4
　CSHM HP5 ...... 136 A1
　HGDN/ICK UB10 ...... 170 D7
　HSLWW TW4 ...... 191 P9
　HYS/HAR UB3 ...... 191 J8
　NPAG MK16 ...... 31 J5
　RAYLW HP18 ...... 116 C2
　RSLP HA4 ...... 171 J6
Field End RAYLW HP18 * 106 C9
Field End Rd PIN HA5 ...... 171 P3
Fieldfare AYLW HP19 ...... 95 N3
Fieldhead Gdns BNEND SL8 ...... 165 J7
Fieldhouse La MLW SL7 ...... 164 F1
Fieldhouse Wy MLW SL7 ...... 164 F1
Field Hurst DTCH/LGLY SL3 ...... 189 H5
Fielding Gdns
　DTCH/LGLY SL3 ...... 188 D3
Fielding Rd MDHD SL6 ...... 177 H9
The Fieldings MDHD SL6 ...... 185 M8
Field La WOLV MK12 ...... 29 K8
Field Rd DEN/HRF UB9 ...... 169 N9
　HWYN HP12 ...... 152 B5
Fields End TRING HP23 ...... 113 H5
Fields End Wd HWW HP1 ...... 115 M9
Field Wy AMSS HP7 ...... 145 K1
　AYL HP20 ...... 3 K1
　CFSP/GDCR SL9 ...... 156 F7
　HHW HP1 ...... 127 J9
　RKW/CH/CXG WD3 ...... 158 B1
　RSLP HA4 ...... 171 J6
　UX/CGN UB8 ...... 182 D7
Fieldway BERK HP4 ...... 126 C3
　TRING HP23 ...... 113 H5
Fifield La WDSR SL4 ...... 192 B2
Fifield Rd MDHD SL6 ...... 186 B3
Fifth St WYM HP11 ...... 153 H6
Filey Sp SL SL1 ...... 187 M4
Filey Waye RSLP HA4 ...... 171 N7
Filmer Rd WDSR SL4 ...... 192 A9
Fincham Rd HGDN/ICK UB10 ...... 171 J3
Finch Cl MKV MK10 ...... 39 L5
Finch Crs DTCH/LGLY SL3 ...... 188 F5
Finch Crs LBUZ LU7 ...... 74 D6
Finch End FLKWH HP10 ...... 155 K2
Finch Gn RKW/CH/CXG WD3 ...... 147 P6
Finch La AMSS HP7 ...... 146 C5
　BEAC HP9 ...... 154 C4
Finch Rd BERK HP4 ...... 126 C1

Findhorn Av YEAD UB4 ...... 183 P8
Findlay Wy WEAT MK2 ...... 53 J3
Fine Bush La DEN/HRF UB9 ...... 171 H4
Fingest La HEN RG9 ...... 150 D7
Fingle Dr BDWL MK13 ...... 23 N6
Finians Cl MDHD/ICK UB10 ...... 182 F3
Finings Rd SKCH HP14 ...... 151 H5
Finch La AYLS HP21 ...... 110 C1
Firbank Cl LBUZ LU7 ...... 74 E4
Firbank Wy LBUZ LU7 ...... 74 E4
Fircroft Cl SLN SL2 ...... 180 C2
Firecrest Wy AYLW HP19 ...... 95 H6
Fire La RMKS/WB MK17 ...... 142 A8
Firs Av WDSR SL4 ...... 192 B3
Firs Cl HAZ/HG HP15 ...... 143 P9
　HWYN HP13 ...... 153 L2
　IVER SLO 182 A1
　RAYLW/WEN HP22 ...... 81 J3
　SKCH HP14 ...... 151 K5
Firs La RAYLW/WEN HP22 ...... 96 C3
Firs Dr DTCH/LGLY SL3 ...... 189 H2
　HEST TW5 ...... 191 P8
Firs La MDHD SL6 ...... 184 F3
Firs Pth LBUZ LU7 ...... 64 E9
Firs Ri GTMIS/PWD HP16 ...... 155 L5
First Av AMSS HP7 ...... 145 J2
　DBCH MK1 ...... 53 H3
　DUN/WHIP LU6 ...... 89 K1
　HYS/HAR UB3 ...... 191 M2
　MLW SL7 ...... 164 C2
First Crs SL SL1 ...... 179 N8
The Firs EBED/NFELT TW14 * 197 L5
　RAYLW/WEN HP22 ...... 96 C3
　RAYLW HP18 ...... 153 H7
　TRING HP23 ...... 113 H5
First St WYM HP11 ...... 153 H7
Firs Vw Rd HAZ/HG HP15 ...... 143 P9
Firs Wk NTHWD HA6 ...... 160 B7
Fir Tree Av SLN SL2 ...... 180 G4
Firview Cl MLW SL7 ...... 164 F8
Fishermans Cl OLN MK46 ...... 15 L3
Fishermans Retreat
　MLW SL7 ...... 164 E8
Fisherman's Wy
　BNEND SL8 ...... 165 P5
Fishermead Bvd
　EAG/OLD/WT MK6 ...... 7 J3
Fishers Fld BUCK/WIN MK18 ...... 48 A3
Fishery Rd MDHD SL6 ...... 186 A2
Fishguard Sp SL SL1 ...... 188 D5
Fishwater LBUZ LU7 ...... 62 D9
Five Acres CSHM HP5 ...... 135 P6
Five Acre Wd HWYN HP12 ...... 152 C4
Flags Meadow OLN MK46 ...... 15 L5
Flag Wk PIN HA5 ...... 171 N4
Flambard Cl WLLN MK15 ...... 30 C5
Flamborough Sp SL SL1 ...... 187 L3
Flaunden Bottom
　CSHM HP5 ...... 146 C1
Flaunden Hi HHS/BOV HP3 ...... 137 H6
Flaunden La HHS/BOV HP3 ...... 137 K5
Flavius Ga BRACKY NN13 ...... 35 J5
Flaxbourne Ct
　RAYLW/WEN HP22 ...... 110 F4
Flaxley Ga MKV MK10 ...... 43 N2
Fleet Cl BUCK/WIN MK18 ...... 48 D1
　RSLP HA4 ...... 171 J4
　SKCH HP14 ...... 142 F4
Fleet St AYL HP20 ...... 2 C3
The Fleet EAG/OLD/WT MK6 ...... 43 H2
Fleetwood Ct CSTG HP8 ...... 156 C4
Fleetwood Rd SLN SL2 ...... 188 B2
Fleetwood Wy CFSP/GDCR SL9 ...... 156 F7
Fleming Dr
　EAG/OLD/WT MK6 ...... 43 H6
Fleming Wy HWYW HP12 ...... 152 D5
Flemming Av RSLP HA4 ...... 171 P6
Fletcher Cl AYLW HP19 ...... 95 H4
Fletchers Ms GTLIN MK14 ...... 30 F7
Flintergill Ct BDWL MK13 * 30 D2
Flint Hollow CHNR OX39 ...... 129 M6
The Flintings HHNE HP2 ...... 101 P7
Flintlock Ct
　STWL/WRAY TW19 ...... 196 A3
Flint Cl HADM HP17 ...... 107 K9
Flint Wy GTMIS/PWD HP16 ...... 155 J5
Flitcroft Lea HWYN HP13 ...... 4 E1
Flitton Ct STSTR MK11 ...... 29 H8
Flora Thompson Dr
　BRACKY NN13 ...... 34 F4
　NPAG MK16 ...... 20 F8
Florence Av MDHD SL6 ...... 177 M8
Florence Rd FELT TW13 ...... 197 P7
Florence Wy UX/CGN UB8 ...... 182 C3
Florida St WYM HP11 ...... 153 H6
Florin Cl WLLN MK15 ...... 30 C6
Floriston Av HGDN/ICK UB10 ...... 183 J3
Flowers Bottom La
　PRRI HP27 ...... 132 A8
Foinberg Cl LBUZ LU7 ...... 72 E1
Foley Cl BEAC HP9 ...... 154 C6
Foliejohn Wy MDHD SL6 ...... 185 H3
Folkestone Ct
　DTCH/LGLY SL3 ...... 189 J6
Follet Cl WDSR SL4 ...... 194 D5
Folly Farm RBEDW MK43 ...... 33 L5
Folly Rd RMKN MK19 ...... 41 H3
Fontmell Cl MDHD SL6 ...... 176 F9
Fontwell Rd RMKS/WB MK17 ...... 52 C6
Forbes Wy RSLP HA4 ...... 171 P7
Fordcombe Lea
　WTR/OFPK MK7 ...... 43 N4
Ford Dr BRACKY NN13 ...... 34 F4
Ford End DEN/HRF UB9 ...... 169 P7
Ford La IVER SLO 182 A3
Ford's Cl SKCH HP14 ...... 141 H3

Ford St BUCK/WIN MK18 ...... 48 B3
　WYM HP11 ...... 153 M6
Ford Wy HWYN HP13 ...... 142 E8
Forelands Wy CSHM HP5 ...... 135 L5
Forest Cl RAYLW/WEN HP22 ...... 123 H1
Foresters CHNR OX39 ...... 129 M6
　RAYLW HP18 ...... 90 D8
Forest Old RHPTN NN7 ...... 12 F5
Forest Gn MDHD SL6 ...... 192 B1
Forest Green Rd MDHD SL6 ...... 192 A1
Forest Pk WDSR SL4 * 193 J6
Forest Point HWYN HP13 ...... 153 M5
Fore St PIN HA5 ...... 171 N4
Forest Ri EAG/OLD/WT MK6 ...... 34 H3
Forest Rd RMKN MK19 ...... 19 H2
　RNHPTN NN7 ...... 12 F5
　WDSR SL4 ...... 193 H1
　WDSR SL4 ...... 193 H6
Forest Vw RNHPTN NN7 ...... 7 L1
Forest Wy HWYN HP13 ...... 153 N2
Forfar Dr BTCHLY MK3 ...... 52 F2
Forge Cl BUCK/WIN MK18 ...... 58 C8
　RAYLW HP18 ...... 92 C7
Forge La AYLW/WEN HP22 ...... 81 N3
Forge Rd SKCH HP14 ...... 142 C3
The Forge OLN MK46 ...... 15 M7
Forgetts Rd SKCH HP14 ...... 151 L6
Forlease Cl MDHD SL6 ...... 185 N1
Forlease Dr MDHD SL6 ...... 185 N1
Forlease Rd MDHD SL6 ...... 177 N9
Formby Cl BTCHLY MK3 ...... 52 C4
　DTCH/LGLY SL3 ...... 189 L5
Forrabury Av BDWL MK13 ...... 6 A1
Forrester Dr BRACKY NN13 ...... 34 G3
Forris Av HYS/HAR UB3 ...... 191 M2
Fortescue Dr SHEN MK5 ...... 42 A6
Fortuna Ct WTR/OFPK MK7 ...... 45 J4
Forty Gn PRRI HP27 ...... 130 B1
Forty Green Dr MLW SL7 ...... 164 A8
Forty Green Rd BEAC HP9 ...... 154 F6
Foscote Rd BUCK/WIN MK18 ...... 48 J1
Foscott Wy BUCK/WIN MK18 ...... 48 J1
Fossey Cl SHEN MK5 ...... 41 P9
Foster Av WDSR SL4 ...... 193 J2
Foster Cl AYL HP20 ...... 95 P5
Fosters La BDWL MK13 ...... 42 A1
Fosters Pth SLN SL2 ...... 179 K7
Fothergill Pl THAME OX9 ...... 116 B6
Fotheringay Gdns SL SL1 ...... 187 L1
Fotherby Rd
　RKW/CH/CXG WD3 ...... 158 D2
Founders Dr DEN/HRF UB9 ...... 169 P2
Founders Ms GTLIN MK14 ...... 30 G8
Foundry La DTCH/LGLY SL3 ...... 195 K2
　PRRI HP27 ...... 131 K6
Fountain Cl UX/CGN UB8 ...... 30 J8
Fountaine Cl GTLIN MK14 ...... 30 C3
Fountain Gdns WDSR SL4 ...... 193 P2
Four Ashes Rd HAZ/HG HP15 ...... 125 L9
Four Oaks CSHM HP5 ...... 135 M4
Fourth Av HYS/HAR UB3 ...... 191 M2
　MLW SL7 ...... 164 C2
Fourth St WYM HP11 ...... 153 H6
Fowler Rd AYLW HP19 ...... 95 K8
Foxborough Ct
　DTCH/LGLY SL3 ...... 189 J2
Foxborough Rd MDHD SL6 ...... 185 L3
Fox Cl TRING HP23 ...... 112 G5
Fox Cover CHNR OX39 ...... 129 M6
Fox Covert Rd RNHPTN NN7 ...... 12 A4
Foxcovert Rd SHEN MK5 ...... 41 P8
Foxdell NTHWD HA6 ...... 159 K6
Fox Dells DUN/WHIP LU6 ...... 87 L3
Foxdell Wy CFSP/GDCR SL9 ...... 156 F6
Foxes Piece MLW SL7 ...... 164 E7
Fox Fld HAZ/HG HP15 ...... 143 M6
Foxfield Cl NTHWD HA6 ...... 159 M6
Foxglade NPAG MK16 ...... 31 H1
Foxglove AYLS HP21 * 109 K1
Foxglove Cl
　BUCK/WIN MK18 ...... 48 A4
　STWL/WRAY TW19 ...... 196 D7
Foxgloves AYLS HP21 ...... 109 K1
The Foxgloves HHW HP1 ...... 127 N3
Foxherne DTCH/LGLY SL3 ...... 188 B2
Foxhill OLN MK46 ...... 15 L3
Foxhill Cl HWYN HP13 ...... 4 D7
Foxhollow Dr SLN SL2 ...... 180 D7
Fox La BRACKY NN13 ...... 34 G6
　HAZ/HG HP15 ...... 143 N5
Foxleigh WYM HP11 ...... 153 N4
Fox Rd DTCH/LGLY SL3 ...... 188 F5
　HAZ/HG HP15 ...... 143 N6
Foxton EAG/OLD/WT MK6 ...... 43 K6
Fox Wy BUCK/WIN MK18 ...... 48 A4
Foxwood Cl FELT TW15 ...... 197 P9
Framers Ct MLW SL7 ...... 164 E7
Framewood Rd
　DTCH/LGLY SL3 ...... 180 E3
Framingham Ct SHEN MK5 ...... 42 A7
France Furlong GTLIN MK14 ...... 30 F7
Frances Av MDHD SL6 ...... 185 H3
Frances Rd WDSR SL4 ...... 193 N2
Franche St CSHM HP5 ...... 135 N5
Francis Av FELT TW13 ...... 197 N9
Francis Ct SHEN MK5 ...... 42 A7
Francis Wy SL SL1 ...... 187 H1
Francis Wy CSHM HP5 ...... 135 M4
Frank Atter Cft WOLV MK12 ...... 29 J7
Franklin Av SLN SL2 ...... 180 B3
Franklin Cl HADM HP17 ...... 107 L7
Franklin Rd HADM HP17 ...... 107 L7
Frank Lunnon Cl BNEND SL8 ...... 166 A6
Franklyn Crs WDSR SL4 ...... 192 A3
Frankston Av STSTR MK11 ...... 28 G3
Frank Sutton Wy SL SL1 ...... 187 N1

Frankswood Av
　WDR/YW UB7 ...... 182 F9
Frascati Wy MDHD SL6 ...... 177 M9
Fraser Rd HWYW HP12 ...... 152 C5
Fraucup Cl HADM HP17 ...... 108 A7
Frays Av WDR/YW UB7 ...... 190 D5
Frays Cl WDR/YW UB7 ...... 190 D5
Fraysleia UX/CGN UB8 ...... 182 C4
Fray's Wave UX/CGN UB8 ...... 182 C4
Frederick Pl FLKWH HP10 ...... 153 P7
　LBUZ LU7 ...... 74 B9
Freeman Ct STSTR MK11 ...... 79 L9
Freeman Cl CSHM HP5 ...... 135 N5
Freemans Cl SLN SL2 ...... 180 B2
Freemans Gdns OLN MK46 ...... 15 M8
Freemans La HYS/HAR UB3 ...... 191 L1
Freestone Yd
　DTCH/LGLY SL3 * 189 M8
Freezeland Wy
　HGDN/ICK UB10 ...... 182 G2
Fremantle Rd AYLS HP21 ...... 109 N1
　HWYN HP13 ...... 143 K9
Frensham Gdns SL SL1 ...... 187 J2
Frensham Dr WLLN MK15 ...... 30 C5
Frensham Rd SLN SL2 ...... 179 N1
Friarage Rd AYLS HP21 ...... 2 D6
Friars Ct AYL HP20 ...... 2 B5
Friarscroft Wy AYL HP20 ...... 2 B5
Friars Fld BERK HP4 ...... 114 A7
Friars Furlong RAYLW HP18 ...... 106 A7
Friars Gdns NPAG MK16 ...... 31 J5
Friary Rd EAG/OLD/WT MK6 ...... 29 K8
Friary Gdns NPAG MK16 ...... 31 J5
The Friary STWL/WRAY TW19 ...... 194 F5
Friday Ct THAME OX9 ...... 118 D4
Friday St HEN RG9 ...... 174 F7
　LBUZ LU7 ...... 74 D7
Frieth Rd MLW SL7 ...... 163 M5
Frimley Rd HWYN HP11 ...... 127 N1
Fringewood Ct NTHWD HA6 ...... 160 A9
Frinton Cl OXHEY WD19 ...... 159 P2
The Frithe SLN SL2 ...... 180 D5
Frith Hl GTMIS/PWD HP16 ...... 135 K8
Frithsden Copse BERK HP4 ...... 115 H6
Frithwood Av NTHWD HA6 ...... 160 A9
Frithwood Crs
　WTR/OFPK MK7 ...... 43 P5
Frobisher Ct
　STWL/WRAY TW19 ...... 196 A3
Froggy La DEN/HRF UB9 ...... 169 M8
Frog La RAYLW HP18 ...... 107 K3
Frogmill Cl RSLP HA4 ...... 175 L5
Frogmill MDHD SL6 * 175 P4
Frogmill Spinnie MDHD SL6 ...... 175 D4
Frogmoor HWYN HP13 ...... 5 D5
Frogmoor La
　RKW/CH/CXG WD3 ...... 158 D2
Frogmore Av YEAD UB4 ...... 183 L7
Frogmore Cl SKCH HP14 ...... 142 F4
　SL SL1 ...... 187 L3
Frogmore Gdns YEAD UB4 ...... 183 L7
Frogmore La RAYLW HP18 ...... 106 A7
Frogmore St TRING HP23 ...... 112 E2
Fromer Rd FLKWH HP10 ...... 166 B5
The Front BERK HP4 ...... 115 K7
Froxfield Ct EMV/FZ MK4 ...... 52 C7
Fruen Rd EBED/NFELT TW14 ...... 197 K5
Fryday St EAG/OLD/WT MK6 ...... 42 G2
Fryer Cl CSHM HP5 ...... 135 N5
Fryers La HWYW HP12 ...... 152 D2
Frymley Vw WDSR SL4 ...... 187 M9
Fulford Gv OXHEY WD19 ...... 159 P2
Fulham Cl HGDN/ICK UB10 ...... 183 J7
Fullbrook Cl MDHD SL6 ...... 177 N8
Fuller's Cl CSHM HP5 ...... 135 N5
Fuller's Hi AMS HP6 ...... 135 N5
Fuller Wy HYS/HAR UB3 ...... 191 N3
Fullwell Rd BUCK/WIN MK18 ...... 46 A5
Fulmar Pl AYLW HP19 * 95 N3
Fulmer Common Rd
　DTCH/LGLY SL3 ...... 180 G2
Fulmer Cnr CFSP/GDCR SL9 * 180 F7
Fulmer Dr CFSP/GDCR SL9 ...... 168 G2
Fulmer La CFSP/GDCR SL9 ...... 168 G4
Fulmer Pl DTCH/LGLY SL3 ...... 168 G4
Fulmer Rd DTCH/LGLY SL3 ...... 168 G4
Fulmer Wy CFSP/GDCR SL9 ...... 168 G4
Fulton Cl HWYN HP13 ...... 5 D5
Fulwell Rd BRACKY NN13 ...... 36 A8
Fulwoods Dr
　EAG/OLD/WT MK6 ...... 7 J2
Furlong Cl BNEND SL8 ...... 165 P6
Furlong Crs HADM HP17 ...... 109 J5
Furlong La DUN/WHIP LU6 ...... 87 N9
Furlong Rd BNEND SL8 ...... 165 P6
The Furlong TRING HP23 ...... 112 E3
Furness WDSR SL4 ...... 192 D1
Furness Pl WDSR SL4 ...... 192 D1
Furnival Av SL SL1 ...... 179 N8
Furrow Wy MDHD SL6 ...... 184 G3
Furtho La TOW NN12 ...... 28 A2
Fury Ct CNH/GTH/TM MK8 ...... 41 M5
Furzefield Rd BEAC HP9 ...... 155 H6
Furzeground Wy
　STKPK UB11 ...... 191 H1
Furzeham Rd WDR/YW UB7 ...... 190 D5
Furze La BUCK/WIN MK18 ...... 49 H7
Furzen Cl DUN/WHIP LU6 ...... 87 M8
Furze Pl MDHD SL6 ...... 176 G6
Furze Rd HHW HP1 ...... 127 N1
Furze Vw
　RKW/CH/CXG WD3 ...... 147 L8
Furze Wy WOLV MK12 ...... 29 L7
Fuzzens Wk WDSR SL4 ...... 193 L5

Fyfield Barrow
　WTR/OFPK MK7 ...... 44 A6
Fyne Dr LBUZ LU7 ...... 74 A1

G

Gables Cl CFSP/GDCR SL9 ...... 156 G4
　DTCH/LGLY SL3 ...... 188 C7
　MDHD SL6 ...... 177 P8
　RAYLW/WEN HP22 ...... 122 G1
Gables Dr SKCH HP14 ...... 141 L2
Gables Meadow
　HAZ/HG HP15 ...... 143 M6
The Gables HADM HP17 ...... 107 L9
　LBUZ LU7 ...... 74 C3
Gable Thorne WTR/OFPK MK7 ...... 44 B6
Gabriel Cl WTR/OFPK MK7 ...... 44 A7
Gaddesden Crs
　WTR/OFPK MK7 ...... 44 A6
Gaddesden Turn LBUZ LU7 ...... 75 H7
Gade Cl HYS/HAR UB3 ...... 191 P2
Gadsden Cl THAME OX9 ...... 118 C2
Gadmore La TRING HP23 ...... 112 C7
Gadsden Cl RBEDW MK43 ...... 33 N3
Gadsden Ct RMKS/WB MK17 ...... 63 L3
Gage Cl MDHD SL6 ...... 185 L3
Gainsborough MDHD SL6 ...... 177 M3
Gainsborough Cl
　CNH/GTH/TM MK8 ...... 41 M6
Galleons La DTCH/LGLY SL3 ...... 180 F6
The Galleons AMSS HP7 * 145 N2
Galley La STSTR MK11 ...... 28 C8
Galley La RMKS/WB MK17 ...... 53 N6
Galleymead Rd
　DTCH/LGLY SL3 ...... 189 P3
Galloway Cha SL SLN SL2 ...... 188 C1
Galloway Ct BTCHLY MK3 ...... 52 E1
Gallows La HWYW HP12 ...... 152 C2
Gallys Rd WDSR SL4 ...... 187 M9
Galsworthy Pl AYLW HP19 ...... 95 H3
Galvin Rd SL SL1 ...... 187 N2
Ganton Cl HWYN HP13 ...... 4 A8
Ganton Cl BTCHLY MK3 ...... 52 D2
Garamonde Dr
　CNH/GTH/TM MK8 ...... 41 M3
Garbo Cl CNH/GTH/TM MK8 ...... 41 M5
Garden Cl MDHD SL6 ...... 186 C4
Garden Cl HWYN HP22 ...... 19 L4
　RSLP HA4 ...... 171 L7
Garden End AMS HP6 ...... 135 P9
Gardner Wk HAZ/HG HP15 ...... 144 A5
Garden Field La BERK HP4 ...... 127 H5
Garden Hedge LBUZ LU7 ...... 74 E1
Garden Leys LBUZ LU7 ...... 74 E1
Garden Reach CSTG HP8 ...... 146 F5
Garden Rd DUN/WHIP LU6 ...... 87 L1
Gardens Cl HAZ/HG HP15 ...... 140 B7
The Gardens BUCK/WIN MK18 ...... 59 K1
　EBED/NFELT TW14 ...... 197 K5
　HGDN/ICK UB10 ...... 29 N8
Gardner Cl BDWL MK13 ...... 29 N8
Gardner Ct AYLW HP19 ...... 95 J4
　HAZ/HG HP15 ...... 143 K2
Gardner House
　EBED/NFELT TW14 ...... 197 P9
Gardner Ri BRACKY NN13 ...... 34 F5
Gardner Rd MDHD SL6 ...... 177 L6
Gardner's Cl DUN/WHIP LU6 ...... 86 G1
Garfield Pl WDSR SL4 * 193 N1
Garland Ct CNH/GTH/TM MK8 ...... 41 N4
Garland Wy LBUZ LU7 ...... 74 G4
Garners Cl CFSP/GDCR SL9 ...... 156 G6
Garners End CFSP/GDCR SL9 ...... 156 G6
Garners La CFSP/GDCR SL9 ...... 156 G6
Garners Pl CFSP/GDCR SL9 ...... 156 G6
Garnet Cl SL SL1 ...... 187 L3
Garnet Ct MLW SL7 ...... 164 C8
Garrard Rd SLN SL2 ...... 179 J7
Garratt Wy HWYN HP13 ...... 4 A7
Garraways EAG/OLD/WT MK6 ...... 42 G6
Garrett Cl CSHM HP5 ...... 135 N6
　DUN/WHIP LU6 ...... 87 M3
Garron Ct AYLS HP21 ...... 109 N1
Garrowmore Gv WEAT MK2 ...... 53 K6
Garson Gv CSHM HP5 ...... 135 L2
Garson La STWL/WRAY TW19 ...... 194 F6
Garston CNH/GTH/TM MK8 ...... 41 P2
Garthlands MDHD SL6 ...... 176 F7
The Garth GTMIS/PWD HP16 ...... 135 K9
Garthwaite Crs SHEN MK5 ...... 41 P9
Garvin Av BEAC HP9 ...... 155 J2
Gascon's Gv SLN SL2 ...... 179 N1
Gas La MDHD SL6 ...... 185 N4
Gatcombe CNH/GTH/TM MK8 ...... 41 P3
Gate End NTHWD HA6 ...... 159 N7
Gatehill Rd NTHWD HA6 ...... 159 N9
Gatehouse Cl AYLW HP19 ...... 2 A4
　WDSR SL4 ...... 193 M2
Gatehouse Wy AYLW HP19 ...... 95 K4
Gatensbury Pl PRRI HP27 * 131 K1
Gatesden Cl BERK HP4 ...... 100 E7
Gates Orch
　RAYLW/WEN HP22 ...... 111 K1
Gateway Cl NTHWD HA6 ...... 159 J6
Gatewick La SL SL1 ...... 188 A2
Gatewick La WTR/OFPK MK7 ...... 43 N9
Gatting Wy HGDN/ICK UB10 ...... 182 G2
Gatward Av MDHD SL6 ...... 184 C4
Gaveston Dr BERK HP4 ...... 114 C9

Gaveston Rd SLN SL2 .....179 K6
Gaviots Cl CFSP/GDCR SL9 ...169 H6
Gaviots Gn CFSP/GDCR SL9 ...168 G5
Gaviots Wy CFSP/GDCR SL9 ...168 G5
Gawdrey Cl CSHM HP5 ......135 P6
Gayal Cft SHEN MK5 ....28 A4
Gayhurst Rd HWYN HP13 ...153 M3
Gayton Cl AMS HP6 ....75 H1
Gees Farm Cl RNHPTN NN7 ....8 G3
Gemini Cl LBUZ LU7 ....75 H1
Genesis Cl STWL/WRAY TW19 ...196 F4
George Cl MLW SL7 ....164 F5
George Ct RAYLW HP18 .....77 P3
George Green Dr
DTCH/LGLY SL3 ....181 H9
George Green Rd
DTCH/LGLY SL3 ....180 C8
George Rd SKCH HP14 ......140 A6
George's Dr FLKWH HP10 ...166 A2
George's HI HAZ/HG HP15 ...143 M5
George St AYL HP20 ....2 D4
BERK HP4 ....126 C1
CSHM HP5 ....135 N3
LBUZ LU7 ....3 D4
LBUZ LU7 ....74 F2
RMKS/WB MK17 ....55 K5
UX/CGN UB8 ....182 D3
WEAT MK2 ....53 L2
George Yd STSTR MK11 * ...7 E2
Geralds Rd HWYN HP13 ....153 K1
Gerard Cl BDWL MK13 .....29 P6
Germains Cl CSHM HP5 ....135 M5
Germain St CSHM HP5 .....135 N4
Germander Pl GTLIN MK14 ...30 D3
Gerrard Gdns PIN HA5 .....171 N3
Gerrards Cross Rd SLN SL2 ...180 C2
Gershwin Ct WTR/OFPK MK7 ...44 A3
Gervaise Cl SL SL1 ....187 K2
Ghibert Wy BERK HP4 ......126 C1
Ghyll Gdns BERK HP4 * 113 P7
Gibbings Cl BUCK/WIN MK18 ...70 C6
Gibbs Cl HWYN HP13 ....4 C5
Gibbwin GTLIN MK14 ......30 D5
Gib La RAYLNE/WEN HP22 ...96 D3
Gibraltar La MDHD SL6 ....165 H8
Gibson Ct DTCH/LGLY SL3 ...189 H6
Gibson Dr LBUZ LU7 ....74 C4
Gibson La HADM HP17 .....107 K2
Gibson Pl STWL/WRAY TW19 ...196 C5
Gibson Rd HGDN/ICK UB10 ...170 F9
HWYW HP12 ....152 B3
Gibsons Ct AYLS HP21 .....30 B9
Giffard Rd WEAT MK2 .....53 J3
Giffard Wy RAYLW HP18 ...106 A8
Gifford Ga GTLIN MK14 ....30 C6
Gifford Pl BUCK/WIN MK18 ...48 C2
Gig La LBUZ LU7 ....64 F5
Gilbert La BTCHLY MK3 .....53 H4
Gilbert Rd DEN/HRF UB9 ...158 D9
Gilbert Scott Rd
BUCK/WIN MK18 ....48 B1
Gilbert's HI TRING HP23 ....124 C2
Gilbey Rd HGDN/ICK UB10 ...171 H9
Gilchrist Wy MDHD SL6 ....184 B2
Gilded Acre CUN/HRF LU6 * ...87 L3
Gilders Ms GTLIN MK14 ....30 C6
Gilfrid Cl UX/CGN UB8 ....183 H9
Gillamoor Cl EMV/FZ MK4 ...42 D9
Gilletts La HWYW HP12 ...152 C1
Gillfield Cl HWYW HP12 ...152 E7
Gilliat Rd SL SL1 ....188 A1
Gilliat's Gn
RKW/CH/CXG WD3 ....147 N6
Gilliatt Cl IVER SL0 ....181 N9
Gillotts Cl HEN RG9 ....173 M9
Gillott's La HEN RG9 ......173 M9
Gilman Crs WDSR SL4 .....193 H2
Gilmore Cl HGDN/ICK UB10 ...170
SLN SL2 ....188 E3
Gilpin's Ride BERK HP4 ....114 C9
Gilpin Wy HYS/HAR UB3 ...191 K8
Gibson Ct STWL/WRAY TW19 ...194 D6
Gingers Cl
RAYLNE/WEN HP22 ......111 L1
Gipsy La LBUZ LU7 ....74 D9
Girling Wy EBED/NFELT TW14 ...197 L7
Gisburn Cl BDWL MK13 ...30 B8
Glade Rd MLW SL7 ....164 E7
The Glades HHW HP1 .....127 N1
Glade Vw HWYW HP12 ...152 C1
Gladsdale Dr PIN HA5 .....171 N2
Gladstone Av
EBED/NFELT TW14 ....197 N6
Gladstone Cl NPAC MK16 ...31 J2
Gladstone Ri HWYN HP13 ...153 N5
Gladstone Rd CSHM HP5 ...135 N4
Gladstone Wy SL SL1 .....187 L5
Glaisyer Wy IVER SL0 .....181 N5
Glamis Crs HYS/HAR UB3 ...191 J4
Glamorgan Cl BTCHLY MK3 ...52 F7
Glanmor Rd SLN SL2 ......188 D1
Glasgow Rd SL SL1 ....179 L9
Glasshouse Cl UX/CGN UB8 ...183 H8
Glastonbury Cl BTCHLY MK3 ...52 E7
Glaven Rd AYLS HP21 .....109 L2
Glazier Dr GTLIN MK14 ...30 C6
Glebe Av HGDN/ICK UB10 ...171 J4
RSLP HA4 ....183 P2
Glebe Cl BUCK/WIN MK18 ...38 D9
CFSP/GDCR SL9 ....159 M4
HAZ/HG HP15 ....143 P4
HGDN/ICK UB10 ....171 J9
LBUZ LU7 ....99 H2
MDHD SL6 ....186 D3
Glebe Dr BRACKY NN13 ...35 L5
Glebelands FLKWH HP10 ...154 A2
Glebelands Cl
GTMIS/PWD HP16 ....133 L8

Giebelands Rd
EBED/NFELT TW14 ....197 N6
Glebe La RMKN MK19 ....18 G1
Glebe Rd CFSP/GDCR SL9 ...156 E8
MDHD SL6 ....186 A5
RMKN MK19 ....29 A8
UX/CGN UB8 ....182 C5
WDSR SL4 ....194 D4
Glebe Ter BUCK/WIN MK18 ...38 C9
The Glebe GTMIS/PWD HP16 ...133 H5
HADM HP17 ....108 E1
HEN RG9 ....172 C3
OLN MK46 ....19 P6
RAYLNE/WEN HP22 ....110 F4
SKCH HP14 ....142 D5
WDR/YW UB7 ....190 E5
Glebe Wy AMS HP6 ....135 P9
Gledfield Pl WOLV MK12 ...29 L8
Gledwood Av YEAD UB4 ...183 N8
Gledwood Crs YEAD UB4 ...183 N8
Gledwood Gdns YEAD UB4 ...183 N8
Gleeman Cl WOLV MK12 ...29 J8
Glenalla Rd RSLP HA4 .....171 N5
Glenavon Gdns
DTCH/LGLY SL3 ....188 E5
Gleneagles Cl BTCHLY MK3 ...52 F4
HTHAIR TW6 ....196 E5
Glenfield Cl AYLS HP21 ...110 A1
Glenfield Crs RSLP HA4 ...171 L5
Glenham Rd THAME OX9 ...118 F4
Glenhurst Av RSLP HA4 ...171 J5
Glenister Rd GTLIN MK14 ...30 E5
HWYW HP12 ....152 N1
Glenisters Rd HWYN HP13 ...5 F4
Glenmore Cl FLKWH HP10 ...153 N8
Glenstall Pl CMK MK9 ......6 B4
The Glen DTCH/LGLY SL3 ...188 E5
MDHD SL6 * 157 L7
NTHWD HA6 ....159 K7
PIN HA5 ....159 K7
Glentworth Pl SL SL1 ......187 N2
Glimbers Cv CHNR OX39 ...129 N6
Glisson Rd HGDN/ICK UB10 ...182 C5
Globe La LBUZ LU7 ....64 F6
Glory Cl FLKWH HP10 .....166 D2
Glory Hill La BEAC HP9 ...166 D1
Glory Mill La FLKWH HP10 ...166 C2
Gloucester Av SL SL1 .....152 D2
Gloucester Dr
STWL/WRAY TW19 ....195 L9
Gloucester Pde
HYS/HAR UB5 * 191 J4
Gloucester Pl WDSR SL4 ...193 P6
Gloucester Rd MDHD SL6 ...177 L6
WOLV MK12 ....29 M8
Glovers Gv RSLP HA4 .....171 H5
Glovers La BDWL MK13 ....30 C8
Glyn St BDWL MK13 ....30 C8
Glynswood CFSP/GDCR SL9 ...159 H7
Glynswood Rd
BUCK/WIN MK18 ....48 A2
Goathland Cft EMV/FZ MK4 ...52 B1
Goddington Rd BNEND SL8 ...165 N4
Godolphin Rd BEAC HP9 ...155 N6
SL SL1 ....187 P1
Godwin Cl WTR/OFPK MK7 ...44 A4
Goffe Cl THAME OX9 ....118 F5
Gogh Rd AYLW HP19 ....94 D5
Gold Crest Ga AYLW HP19 ...95 P3
Goldcrest Rd BRACKY NN13 ...54 F3
Golden Ball La MDHD SL6 ...176 F5
Golden Crs HYS/HAR UB3 ...191 L2
Golden Dr EAG/OLD/WT MK6 ...43 J7
Golden Hills CHNR OX39 ...129 P6
Golden Oak Cl SL SL1 * ...179 N2
Golder's Cl RAYLW HP18 ...105 H9
Goldfield Rd TRING HP23 ...112 D3
Gold East CFSP/GDCR SL9 ...156 F9
Gold HI North
CFSP/GDCR SL9 ....156 E8
Goldicks WTR/OFPK MK7 ...43 P6
Goldmark Ct WTR/OFPK MK7 ...44 B7
Gold St RMKN MK19 ....19 J3
Goldsworthy Wy SL SL1 ...29 L9
Golspie Cft WOLV MK12 ...29 L9
Gomm Pl FLKWH HP10 ....153 N6
Gomm Rd HWYN HP13 .....153 L6
Gomms Wood Cl BEAC HP9 ...154 F6
Goodacres La PRRI HP27 ...131 N6
Goodall Cl HEN RG9 ......173 P7
Good Intent DUN/WHIP LU6 ...86 A4
Goodlake Ct DEN/HRF UB9 ...169 P5
Goodman Gdns
EAG/OLD/WT MK6 ....43 A4
Goodman Pk SLN SL2 .....188 E3
Goodwin Gv EMV/FZ MK4 ...52 B5
Goodwin Mdw FLKWH HP10 ...166 A3
Goodwin Rd AYLW HP19 ...2 B4
Goodvins Md LBUZ LU7 ...74 F4
Goodwood CNH/GTH/TM MK8...41 P4
Goodwood Ri MLW SL7 ....164 C1
Goose Acre CSHM HP5 ....136 C5
LBUZ LU7 ....74 E4
Goosecroft HHW HP1 .....127 J2
Goose Gn BRACKY NN13 ...54 G6
SLN SL2 ....187 J3
SLN SL2 ....179 M5
Goosemere RMKN MK19 ...28 A9
Goosen Gn AYLS HP21 ....96 C9
Goral Md RKW/CH/CXG WD3 ...158 F4
Goran Av STSTR MK11 .....28 C1
Gordale BDWL MK13 ....30 C8
Gordon Crs HYS/HAR UB3 ...191 N5
Gordon Rd ASHF TW15 ....196 B9
CSHM HP5 ....135 P5
HWYN HP13 ....5 K6
MDHD SL6 ....177 N9
WDR/YW UB7 ....190 E1
WDSR SL4 ....193 K1

Gordon Wy CSTG HP8 .....156 D3
Gore Cl DEN/HRF UB9 ....170 D2
Gore HI AMSS HP7 ....145 M6
Gorelands La CSTG HP8 ...156 C2
Gorell Rd BEAC HP9 ......156 B3
Gore Rd SL SL1 ....178 F6
Goring GTLIN MK14 ......30 C5
Gorman Pl WEAT MK2 ....53 L7
Gorrell Cl BUCK/WIN MK18 ...47 H1
Gorricks STSTR MK11 ....28 F9
Corse Meade SL SL1 .....187 M2
Gorse Rd MDHD SL6 .....177 L6
Gorse Wk WDR/YW UB7 ...182 F1
Gosforth La WDR/YW WD19 ...159 N3
Gosforth Pth OXHEY WD19 ...159 N3
Goshawk Gdns YEAD UB4 ...183 L6
Goslar Wy WDSR SL4 .....193 M4
Gosling Gn DTCH/LGLY SL3 ...188 C5
Gosling Gv HWYN HP15 ...142 D2
Gosling Rd DTCH/LGLY SL3 ...188 C4
Goslington DBGH MK1 ...53 J1
Gossage Rd HGDN/ICK UB10 ...182 F3
Goss Av RAYLW HP18 .....93 M1
Gossmore Cl MLW SL7 ...164 F8
Gossmore La MLW SL7 ...164 F8
Gossmore Wk MLW SL7 ...164 F8
Gossoms Ryde BERK HP4 ...114 C9
Goswell HI WDSR SL4 ....187 P6
Goswell Rd WDSR SL4 ...187 P6
Gothic Ct HYS/HAR UB3 ...191 K7
Goudhurst Ct WTR/OFPK MK7 ...43 P5
Gould Rd EBED/NFELT TW14 ...197 L6
Gould's Gn UX/CGN UB8 ...183 J9
Governors Av DEN/HRF UB9 ...169 P3
Governors Cl AMS HP6 ...146 B1
Gowers Fld AYL HP20 ...2 D7
The Gowers AMS HP6 ...146 A1
Gowings Gn SL SL1 .....186 F2
Goya Pl AYLW HP19 .....95 H5
Grace Cl EAG/OLD/WT MK6 ...43 J7
Grace Ct SL SL1 ....187 N2
Grace Reading Cl
HWYN HP13 ....153 L4
Graces Cl RBEDW MK43 ...33 N2
Graeme Av
GTMIS/PWD HP16 ....133 J6
Graemes Dyke Rd BERK HP4 ...126 C2
Grafham Cl GTLIN MK14 ...30 C5
Grafton Cl DTCH/LGLY SL3 ...180 C9
MDHD SL6 ....185 M9
RNHPTN NN7 ....12 F6
TOW NN12 ....28 A3
Grafton Ga CMK MK9 .....6 B4
Grafton Orch CHNR OX39 ...129 P5
Grafton Rd AYLW HP19 ...95 J5
TOW NN12 ....28 B4
Grafton St DBGH MK1 ....43 H9
EAG/OLD/WT MK6 ....7 M6
HWYW HP12 ....152 D2
RMKN MK19 ....29 N5
Graham Rd MDHD SL6 ....185 J2
Graham Dr HWYW HP12 ...152 D3
Graham HI TOW NN12 ...12 A3
Graham Rd DUN/HR/TOD LU5 ...87 N1
MDHD SL6 ....185 J2
Grampian Dr HYS/HAR UB3 ...191 K8
Grampian Ga
EAG/OLD/WT MK6 ....42 D5
Grampian Wy
DTCH/LGLY SL3 ....189 J6
Cramwell SHEN MK5 ......41 M1
The Granary LBUZ LU7 * ...74 D7
Granborough Rd
BUCK/WIN MK18 ....60 A8
BUCK/WIN MK18 ....70 C6
Grand Union Canal Wk
BDWL MK13 ....29 P7
BERK HP4 ....114 A7
DEN/HRF UB9 ....170 B1
DTCH/LGLY SL3 ....30 C5
GTLIN MK14 ....30 C5
HHW HP1 ....127 L4
LBUZ LU7 ....64 C5
NWDGN UB2 ....191 P4
RAYLNE/WEN HP22 .....122 A1
RKW/CH/CXG WD3 .....147 M2
RMKS/WB MK17 ....35 M2
SLN SL2 ....188 D2
STKPK UB11 ....191 H3
WLLN MK15 ....31 H5
WOLV MK12 ....43 J3
Granes End GTLIN MK14 ...30 E5
Grange Av HEN RG9 .....172 C4
Grange Cl BUCK/WIN MK18 ...38 C9
BUCK/WIN MK18 ....70 C6
CFSP/GDCR SL9 ....156 G8
HYS/HAR UB3 ....185 L8
LBUZ LU7 ....74 D7
STWL/WRAY TW19 ......194 C4
Grangedale Cl NTHWD HA6 ...159 M9
Grange Dr FLKWH HP10 ...166 A3
Grange Farm Rd SKCH HP14 ...140 C2
Grange Gdns LBUZ LU7 ...99 H2
Grange Ms FELT TW13 * ...197 K9
Grange Rd BTCHLY MK3 ...53 H8
CFSP/GDCR SL9 ....156 G8
HAZ/HG HP15 ....143 M7
HEN RG9 ....183 L6
HYS/HAR UB3 ....185 L8
LBUZ LU7 ....177 N5
MDHD SL6 ....177 A1
TRING HP23 ....112 A5
The Grange SL SL1 * 178 C6
WDSR SL4 ....194 D5
Grangewood DTCH/LGLY SL3 ...180 D9
Grangewood Cl PIN HA5 ...171 N3
Grant Av SL SL1 ....180 A9

Grantham Ct SHEN MK5 ...42 C7
Grantham Ms BERK HP4 ...126 C2
Granville Av FELT TW15 ...197 M9
SLN SL2 ....179 P8
Granville Dene
MDHD SL6 * HP3 ......127 J3
Granville PI AYL HP20 .....2 D4
Granville Rd HGDN/ICK UB10 ...183 H2
HYS/HAR UB3 ....191 M5
Granville Sq WLLN MK15 ...31 J6
Granville Wy AYL HP20 ...2 D4
Grapevine Cl WYM HP11 ...153 M6
Graphic Cl DUN/WHIP LU6 ...87 M2
Grasholm Wy
DTCH/LGLY SL3 ....189 L5
Grasmere Cl AYLS HP21 ...110 B1
Grasmere Av RSLP HA4 ...171 J5
DTCH/LGLY SL3 ....188 D9
DUN/WHIP LU6 ....87 N8
Grasmere Ct WTR/OFPK MK7 ...44 B7
EBED/NFELT TW14 ......197 M7
Grasmere Pde SLN SL2 * ...188 D1
Grasmere Wy LBUZ LU7 ...74 B3
Grass Croft EMV/FZ MK4 ...42 C9
Grass Hays AYLS HP21 ...96 E9
Grassingham End
CFSP/GDCR SL9 ....156 C7
Grassingham Rd
CFSP/GDCR SL9 ....156 C7
Grassington BDWL MK13 ...30 A8
Grasslands AYL HP20 .....2 D7
Grassy La MDHD SL6 ....177 J9
Gratton Ct EMV/FZ MK4 ...42 C9
Gratton Dr WDSR SL4 ...193 J3
Gravel Dr TRING HP23 ...111 P3
Gravel Hi CFSP/GDCR SL9 ...156 E7
UX/CGN UB8 ....182 D1
Gravel Pth BERK HP4 ....126 F1
Gravel Wk OLN MK46 ....15 H5
Graveney Pl
EAG/OLD/WT MK6 ....43 J5
Gravett Cl HEN RG9 .....173 N9
Grayburn Cl CSTG HP8 ...156 C2
Grayling Cl MLW SL7 ....164 C9
Grays Dormer SKCH HP14 * ...151 L6
Gray's La HWYN HP13 ...142 D9
TOW NN12 ....18 A3
Grays Park Rd SLN SL2 ...180 C5
Grays PI SLN SL2 ....188 D1
Gray's Rd HGDN/ICK UB10 ...182 E3
SL SL1 ....188 D1
Grays Wk CSHM HP5 ....135 M2
Great Benty WDR/YW UB7 ...190 B6
Great Brickhill La
RMKS/WB MK17 * 54 B6
Gratchesters BDWL MK13 ...30 A8
Great Denson
EAG/OLD/WT MK6 ....7 K7
Greatfields Dr UX/CGN UB8 ...182 G8
Great Gnd GTLIN MK14 ...30 E6
Greathead Dell
WTR/OFPK MK7 ....44 B8
Great Hill Crs MDHD SL6 ...185 H2
Great Hivings CSHM HP5 ...135 L2
Great Horwood Rd
RMKS/WB MK17 ....60 B2
Great La RAYLNE/WEN HP22 ...96 A3
Great Linch MK14 MK10 ...43 P2
Great Meadow Wy
AYLW HP19 ....95 J7
Great Monks St
CNH/GTH/TM MK8 ......41 N1
Great Northern Rd
DUN/WHIP LU6 ....87 L1
Great Ormes EMV/FZ MK4 ...52 A3
Great Slade BUCK/WIN MK18 ...48 B5
Great South-West Rd
EBED/NFELT TW14 ......197 J6
Great Stone Rd SKCH HP14 ...107 K3
Great Sturgess Rd HHW HP1 ...127 P2
Great Western St AYL HP20 ...2 C5
Greaves Rd HWYN HP13 ...153 K4
Greaves Wy LBUZ LU7 ...75 H3
Grecian St AYL HP20 ......3 J5
Green Acre AYLS HP21 * ...3 J5
Greenacre WDSR SL4 ....193 J1
Greenacres LBUZ LU7 ...98 C3
Greenacres Pk
DUN/WHIP LU6 * 87 P4
The Greenacres HWYN HP13 ...153 J1
Greenacres Cl
HGDN/ICK UB10 ....170 G8
Green Acres Ct
RAYLNE/WEN HP22 ......111 K1
Greenacres La HAZ/HG HP15 ...153 N1
Greenbury Ct
RKW/CH/CXG WD3 .....147 L5
Green Cl LBUZ LU7 ....64 C1
MDHD SL6 * 177 M7
MDHD SL6 ....178 E9
Green Common La
FLKWH HP10 ....167 H5
Green Crs FLKWH HP10 ...166 A2
Greendale Ms SLN SL2 ...188 C1
Green Dragon La
FLKWH HP10 ....165 P2
Green East Rd BEAC HP9 ...156 A7
Green Field Rd BERK HP4 ...126 C1
BUCK/WIN MK18 ....70 C6
Green End La HHW HP1 ...127 P2
RMKN MK19 ....19 J3
Green End Rd SKCH HP14 ...140 C5
Green End St
RAYLNE/WEN HP22 ......111 K1
Greens Ct BERK HP4 ....114 C9
Green Farm Rd NPAC MK16 ...31 N5
Greenfern Av SL SL1 ....178 C9
Greenfield End
CFSP/GDCR SL9 ....157 H7
Greenfield Rd NPAC MK16 ...30 G1
Greenfields BUCK/WIN MK18 ...59 K1

MDHD SL6 ....185 N1
Greenheys Cl NTHWD HA6 ...159 L8
Green HI HWYN HP13 .....153 H1
Greenhill LBUZ LU7 ....64 C9
Green Hill Cl HWYN HP13 ...153 H1
Greenhill Cl SHEN MK5 ...41 P4
Greenlands FLKWH HP10 ...165 P2
Greenlands Sq WLLN MK15 ...31 J6
Greenlands Cl HWYN HP13 ...153 H1
PRRI HP27 ....131 N7
Greenlands Cl NPAC MK16 ...30 G2
Greenlands La
GTMIS/PWD HP16 ....133 H5
Greenlane Cl AMS HP6 ...146 A2
AMS HP6 ....146 A2
DTCH/LGLY SL3 ....188 D9
DUN/WHIP LU6 ....85 P1
HEN RG9 ....173 P8
HHS/BOV HP3 ....137 J1
LBUZ LU7 ....99 J2
MDHD SL6 ....184 B2
MDHD SL6 ....185 P3
NTHWD HA6 ....159 K7
RMKS/WB MK17 ....45 J9
SKCH HP14 ....140 F5
SLN SL2 ....179 M2
TOW NN12 ....25 K1
UX/CGN UB8 ....183 J8
WDSR SL4 ....193 L1
Green Lane Ct SL SL1 ...178 D9
Greenlaw PI BTCHLY MK3 ...42 G9
Greenleaf Ct DTCH/LGLY SL3 ...188 C7
Green Leys HWYN HP13 ...142 C9
MDHD SL6 ....185 H1
Greenleys La WOLV MK12 ...29 L8
Green Man La
EBED/NFELT TW14 ......197 N3
Greenock Rd SL SL1 ......186 A7
Green Pk GTMIS/PWD HP16 ...133 K6
STA TW18 ....195 J1
Green Park Dr NPAC MK16 ...31 H2
Green Pth TRING HP23 ...112 A2
Greenridge FLKWH HP10 ...153 P3
Green Rd HWYN HP13 ...143 J9
Greensand Ridge Wk
LBUZ LU7 ....64 C9
RMKS/WB MK17 ....54 N6
Greenside BNEND SL8 ...165 N4
SLN SL2 ....179 L8
Greenside Hi EMV/FZ MK4 ...52 B3
Green St HAZ/HG HP15 ...143 M7
RKW/CH/CXG WD3 .....147 L4
WYM HP11 ....1 B4
DUN/WHIP LU6 ....86 B4
EAG/OLD/WT MK6 ......7 J7
FELT TW13 ....197 P8
FLKWH HP10 ....166 C4
HGDN/ICK UB10 ....171 J7
LBUZ LU7 ....3 L7
LBUZ LU7 ....64 B2
NPAC MK16 ....31 H2
PRRI HP27 ....120 F7
RAYLNE/WEN HP22 .....82 D4
RAYLW HP18 ....107 K3
RAYLW HP18 ....107 K3
RBEDW MK43 ....17 J2
RMKN MK19 ....19 J4
RMKN MK19 ....28 A9
RMKS/WB MK17 ....50 C8
SHEN MK5 ....41 N3
SL SL1 ....187 P3
STWL/WRAY TW19 .....194 D4
WDR/YW UB7 ....190 D4
WHLY CS3 ....151 H7
Green Tiles DEN/HRF UB9 * ...169 P5
Green Verges MLW SL7 ...164 E6
Green Vw AYL HP20 ......3 K1
Green View AYL HP20 ...3 K1
Greenview Cl CFSP/GDCR SL9 ...137 J2
Green Wk RSLP HA4 .....153 D7
Green Wy RMKS/WB MK17 ...52 D7
WHLY CS3 ....178 E5
Greenway BERK HP4 .....126 C1
CSHM HP5 ....135 M1
HADM HP17 ....107 K9
HHW HP1 ....159 P9
RMKS/WB MK17 ....50 C8
THAME OX9 ....118 D4
YEAD UB4 ....183 P7
Greenway Ct HWYN HP13 ...153 J1
Greenways DUN/WHIP LU6 ...85 P1
RMKS/WB MK17 ....A1
The Greenway
CFSP/GDCR SL9 ....168 F1
FLKWH HP10 ....165 P2
HGDN/ICK UB10 ....171 H7
HWYN HP13 ....5 J1
SL SL1 ....179 L2
TRING HP23 ....112 D1
UX/CGN UB8 ....182 D3
Greenwich Gdns NPAC MK16 ...31 H3
Greenwood SKCH HP14 ...142 D6
Greenwood Av CHNR OX39 ...129 N7
Greenwood Meadow
CHNR OX39 ....129 N6
Greenwood PI
BUCK/WIN MK18 ....58 B7
Greenwoods SKCH HP14 * ...142 D6
The Greenyard RNHPTN NN7 ...9 H1
Greetham Rd AYLS HP21 ...96 C9

Gregories Dr *WTR/OFPK* MK7....44 A6
Gregories Farm La
  BEAC HP9...................155 H8
Gregories Rd *BEAC* HP9.........154 G7
Gregory Dr *WDSR* SL4...........194 D5
Gregory Rd *SL* SL2.................2 A1
Grenadine Wy *THAME* OX39....112 E1
Grendon Rd *RAYLW* HP18.......67 M8
Grendon Wy
  RAYLNE/WEN HP22............96 A3
Grenfell Av *HWYW* HP12........152 D3
Grenfell Cl *SL* SL1.................185 M1
Grenfell Pl *MDHD* SL6............2 C1
Grenfell Rd *BEAC* HP9...........155 J7
  MDHD SL6.......................177 J9
Grenville Av
  RAYLNE/WEN HP22..........110 G8
Grenville Cl *SL* SL1...............178 F5
Grenville Gn *AYLS* HP21.......109 M2
Grenville Rd *AYLS* HP21.........109 L1
  BUCK/WIN MK18.................48 A2
Grenville Wy *THAME* OX9......118 F4
Gresham Ct *BERK* HP4...........126 D2
Gresham Rd *HGDN/ICK* UB10..182 C5
Greyhound La
  SL SL1............................179 L9
  BUCK/WIN MK18.................60 C6
  THAME OX9.....................118 D4
Greys Hl *HEN* RG9................173 P7
Grey's La *SKCH* HP14............149 N4
The Greys *EAG/OLD/WT* MK6...43 J4
Greystoke Cl *BEAC* HP9........126 C2
Greystoke Dr *RSLP* HA4.......171 H5
Greystoke Rd *SLN* SL2...........179 K8
Greystonley *EMV/FZ* MK4........52 C1
Griffin Cl *MDHD* SL6..............185 L2
  SL SL1............................187 N3
Griffin La *AYLW* HP19.............95 K6
Griffin Rd *THAME* OX9...........118 F5
Griffiths Acre *HADM* HP17.....108 C1
Griffon Cl *EAG/OLD/WT* MK6....7 K7
Griggs Orch *NPAG* MK16.........21 N4
Grimbold Ct *WLLN* MK15..........31 J6
Grimmer Cl *AYLW* HP19..........95 M4
Grimms Hl *GTMIS/PWD* HP16..133 M5
Grimms Meadow *SKCH* HP14...142 D2
Grimsdells Cnr *AMS* HP6 * ...145 P7
Grimsdell's La *AMS* HP6........145 P1
Grimsdyke Rd *TRING* HP23....115 H5
Gringer Hl *MDHD* SL6............177 K8
Grizedale *BDWL* MK13............30 B8
Groombridge *WTR/OFPK* MK7...45 H6
Groome Ct *FLKWH* HP10 * 166 A2
Groom Rd *GTMIS/PWD* HP16...133 J7
Groomsby Dr *LBUZ* LU7..........99 J2
Grooms Cottages *CSHM* HP5...136 D4
Grooms Dr *RSLP* HA4............171 N5
Groom Ct *EMV/FZ* MK4............52 B1
Grosvenor Av *YEAD* UB4.......185 M5
Grosvenor Crs
  HGDN/ICK UB10...............183 H3
Grosvenor Dr *MDHD* SL6.......177 P8
Grosvenor Rd *NTHWD* HA6.....159 K5
Grosvenor V *RSLP* HA4..........171 M7
Grounsel Cl *WTR/OFPK* MK7....45 H6
Grove Ash *DBGH* MK1 * 3 J3
Grovebury Cl *DUN/WHIP* LU6...87 M2
Grovebury Place Est
  LBUZ LU7..........................74 E3
Grovebury Rd *LBUZ* LU7.........74 E5
Grovebury Turn *LBUZ* LU7......74 A6
Grove Cl *CFSP/GDCR* SL9......156 E8
  HGDN/ICK UB10...............182 C1
  SL SL1............................188 C4
  WDSR SL4.......................194 D6
Grove Ct *RAYLNE/WEN* HP22...96 C2
  RBEDW MK43...................17 J1
Grove End *CFSP/GDCR* SL9...156 E8
Grove Farm Pk *NTHWD* HA6..159 K5
Grove Gdns *TRING* HP23.......112 F1
Grove Hl *CFSP/GDCR* SL9......156 D8
Grove La *CFSP/GDCR* SL9.....156 D8
  CSHM HP5........................126 D9
  HADM HP17....................121 N3
  UX/CGN UB8....................182 F7
The Grovelles *BERK* HP4 * ...101 H8
Grove Pk *TRING* HP23...........112 G1
Grove Pl *LBUZ* LU7.................74 E3
Grove Rd *AMS* HP6...............155 H8
  BEAC HP9........................155 K5
  DUN/HR/TOD LU5...............87 M1
  HAZ/HG HP15..................143 M8
  HEN RG9.........................174 A7
  HWYW HP12....................152 C2
  LBUZ SL6........................74 D2
  MDHD SL6.......................177 M9
  NTHWD HA6....................159 K5
  RBEDW MK43...................17 J1
  RKW/CH/CXG WD3............158 A2
  SL SL1............................179 J3
  TRING HP23....................112 G1
  UX/CGN UB8....................182 D3
  WDSR SL4.......................193 N1
Grovers Ct *PRRI* HP27..........131 J2
Grovesbrook *RMKS/WB* MK17..54 A1
Groves Cl *BNEND* SL8...........166 A6
Groves Rd
  RAYLNE/WEN HP22..........111 K9
Grovestile Waye
  EBED/NFELT TW14............197 K6
Groves Wy *MDHD* SL6...........177 L2
The Grove *AMS* HP6.............135 P8
  BDWL MK13.......................30 A9
  BTCHLY MK5......................52 F2
  CSHM HP5.......................136 F9
  HGDN/ICK UB10...............182 C1
  NPAG MK16......................31 D7
  RAYLW HP18.....................93 L1
  RMKS/WB MK17.................44 E7
  RNHPTN NN7.....................1 *
  SL SL1............................188 C3
  TRING HP23 * 112 G1

Grove Wy *RAYLW* HP18..........93 L1
  RKW/CH/CXG WD3............147 K6
  UX/CGN UB8....................182 D3
Groveway *BTCHLY* MK3............43 M6
  EAG/OLD/WT MK6...............43 M6
  WTR/OFPK MK7..................43 A5
Grovewood Cl
  RKW/CH/CXG WD3............147 K7
Grubbins La *PRRI* HP27........132 B6
Grubwood La *MDHD* SL6.......176 G1
Gryms Dyke
  GTMIS/PWD HP16.............133 J6
Guards Club Rd *MDHD* SL6....178 A3
Guards Rd *WDSR* SL4............192 G1
Guernsey Cl *AYLW* HP19.........95 J4
Guest Gdns *BDWL* MK13.........30 B5
Guildford Av *FELT* TW13........197 M8
Guildford Cl *BUCK/WIN* MK18..47 N7
Guillemot Wy *AYLW* HP19........95 N4
Guinea Orch *OLN* MK46...........15 L3
Guinions Rd *HWYN* HP13.......133 K9
Guinness Cl *HYS/HAR* UB3.....191 K4
Guise Ct *RMKS/WB* MK17........45 K8
Gull Wy *AYLW* HP19................95 P4
Gundale Ct *EMV/FZ* MK4..........52 A1
Gun La *NPAG* MK16.................21 M3
Gunmaker Ct *GTLIN* MK14........30 F7
Gunthorpe Rd *MLW* SL7..........176 A6
Gunver La *EMV/FZ* MK4...........52 A2
Gurnard Cl *WDR/YW* UB7.......190 D1
Gurnards Av *EAG/OLD/WT* MK6...7 J5
Gurnells Rd *BEAC* HP9..........155 N5
Gurney Cl *AYL* HP20................95 P5
  BEAC HP9.......................154 G8
Gurney Ct *DUN/WHIP* LU6.......86 B2
Gurney Rd *NTHLT* UB5..........183 P6
Gurneys Meadow
  HAZ/HG HP15..................144 B4
Gwendale *MDHD* SL6..............187 J7
Gwent Cl *MDHD* SL6..............185 H5
Gwynant Cl *WEAT* MK2..............5 J7
Gwynne Cl *TRING* HP23.........112 E1
  WDSR SL4.......................187 J9
Gynant Rd *HWYN* HP13..........153 M8
Gypsy La *MLW* SL7................164 E5
Gyspy La *WYM* HP11..............153 K5

H

H2 *WOLV* MK12........................29 L9
H3 *CNH/GTH/TM* MK8...............41 M1
H4 *BDWL* MK13.........................42 A2
H5 *CMK* MK9.............................6 B5
H6 *EAG/OLD/WT* MK6................6 D6
H7 *EMV/FZ* MK4.........................6 B9
H8 *BTCHLY* MK5.......................52 F2
H9 *WTR/OFPK* MK7....................43 N6
H10 *DBGH* MK1.........................43 J9
Haberley Md *BDWL* MK13..........42 B1
Hackett Pl *NPAG* MK16.............22 E8
Haddenham Rd *HADM* HP17....119 J3
Haddington Cl *BTCHLY* MK3......52 E1
  RAYLNE/WEN HP22............111 K9
Haddington Wy *AYLW* HP20........3 J2
Haddon Rd *MDHD* SL6............185 J9
  RKW/CH/CXG WD3............147 L7
Hadfield Rd
  STWL/WRAY TW19.............196 D5
Hadland Cl *HHW* HP1.............127 J8
Hadley Pl *BDWL* MK13..............6 B6
Hadlow Ct *SL* SL1..................187 N2
Hadrian Cl
  STWL/WRAY TW19.............196 E6
Hadrians Dr *BRACKY* NN13......29 J5
Hadrian's Ga *BRACKY* NN13......35 J5
Hadrian Wy
  STWL/WRAY TW19.............196 E6
Haggar St *HADM* HP17...........108 D1
Hag Hill La *MDHD* SL6............178 E9
Haglis Dr *RAYLNE/WEN* HP22..110 G8
Haig Dr *SL* SL1........................187 M3
Haig Rd *UX/CGN* UB8..............183 H8
Hainault Av *GTLIN* MK14..........30 G4
Haines Cl *AYLW* HP19..............95 H5
Haines Rd *HAZ/HG* HP15.........143 M5
Haithewaite
  CNH/GTH/TM MK8..............41 M5
Haldene *CNH/GTH/TM* MK8.......41 N2
Hale Av *STSTR* MK11...............28 G8
Hale End Cl *RSLP* HA4...........171 N4
Hale La *RAYLNE/WEN* HP22....123 J3
Hale Leys *AYL* HP20 * 2 D3
Hale Rd *RAYLNE/WEN* HP22....123 J1
Hales Cft *AYLS* HP21..............110 B2
Hale St *AYL* HP20.....................2 E4
Halfacre Hl *CFSP/GDCR* SL9...157 H8
Hall Moon La
  DUN/HR/TOD LU5...............87 M1
Hall Moon Pl
  DUN/WHIP LU6 * 87 M1
Halford Rd *HGDN/ICK* UB10....182 G1
Halifax Cl *MDHD* SL6..............176 C8
Halifax Rd *HWYW* HP12.........152 C5
  MDHD SL6.......................176 C8
  UX/CGN UB8....................182 D9
Halifax Wy *MDHD* SL6............176 C8
Halings La *DEN/HRF* UB9.......169 M2
Halkingcroft *DTCH/LGLY* SL3..188 E3
Halland Wy *NTHWD* HA6.........159 H6
Hall Cl *BUCK/WIN* MK18............47 L9
  HWYN HP13....................153 M5
  RBEDW MK43...................11 L2
  RKW/CH/CXG WD3............158 A2
  SL SL1............................179 J3
Hall Ct *DTCH/LGLY* SL3..........188 D8
Halldore Hl *MDHD* SL6...........177 J8
Hall Dr *DEN/HRF* UB9............158 D8
Hall La *HYS/HAR* UB3............191 K8

NPAG MK16............................22 A6
Hall Meadow *SL* SL1.............178 G5
Hallowell Rd *NTHWD* HA6.......159 J7
Hallowes Crs *OXHEY* WD19....159 N8
Hall Pk *BERK* HP4..................126 G2
Hall Park Av *BDWL* MK13..........6 G6
Hall Park Ga *BDWL* MK13..........6 F6
Hall Place La *AMS* HP6..........176 B8
Halls Cnr *FLKWH* HP10...........153 N9
Hall's La *BRACKY* NN13...........34 G6
Halls Ter *HGDN/ICK* UB10 *.....183 H7
The Hall Wk *BERK* HP4...........126 F1
Halsend *HYS/HAR* UB3...........191 P2
Halse Rd *BRACKY* NN13...........34 G3
Halsey Dr *HHW* HP1..............115 P9
Halsway *HYS/HAR* UB3...........191 N1
Halswell Pl *MKV* MK10.............43 N1
Haltonchesters *BDWL* MK13.....29 P7
Halton La
  RAYLNE/WEN HP22..........110 G7
Halton Wood Rd
  RAYLNE/WEN HP22..........111 K9
Haly Cl *BDWL* MK13.................30 A9
Hamberlins La *BERK* HP4.......113 M7
Hamble Cl *RSLP* HA4.............171 L7
Hambledon Cl *AYLS* HP21......110 B1
Hambledon Gv *EMV/FZ* MK4.....52 B1
Hambye Cl *PRRI* HP27............131 N8
Ham Croft Cl *FELT* TW13........197 N9
Hamer Cl *HHS/BOV* HP3..........137 J1
Hamfilton Av *SLN* SL2............179 M6
Hamilton Cl *BUCK/WIN* MK18....47 A7
Hamilton Ct *LBUZ* LU7 *...........74 E2
Hamilton Gdns *SL* SL1...........179 M6
Hamilton La *RMKS/WB* MK17....52 C5
Hamilton Md
  HHS/BOV HP3 * 127 J9
Hamilton Pk *MDHD* SL6............44 E7
Hamilton Rd *BERK* HP4...........126 D1
  HWYN HP13......................5 C2
  HYS/HAR UB3..................191 P1
  OXHEY WD19...................159 P3
  SL SL1............................179 L9
  THAME OX9.....................118 E5
  UX/CGN UB8....................182 D7
Ham La *WDSR* SL4.................194 E3
The Hamlet *BERK* HP4...........115 J7
Hamlins *EAG/OLD/WT* MK6.......41 H8
Hammersley La *FLKWH* HP10...153 P6
Hammerwood Ga
  WTR/OFPK MK7..................45 N5
Hammond Crs *WLLN* MK15.......31 H7
Hammond End *SLN* SL2..........167 M9
  THAME OX9.....................118 D6
Hampden Av *CSHM* HP5.........135 L3
Hampden Cl *AYLS* HP21..........95 M9
Hampden Gdns *AYLS* HP21......95 L9
Hampden Hl *BEAC* HP9...........154 F8
Hampden Rd *AYLS* HP21.........95 M9
  CFSP/GDCR SL9...............156 F8
  DTCH/LGLY SL3................189 H4
  GTMIS/PWD HP16.............153 M6
  HWYN HP13......................5 C5
  MDHD SL6.......................185 L2
  PRRI HP27......................132 C2
  RAYLNE/WEN HP22..........110 B5
  RAYLNE/WEN HP22..........123 J1
Hampermill La *OXHEY* WD19...159 L1
Hampshire Av *SL* SL1.............179 N8
Hampshire Cl *BTCHLY* MK5......52 F1
Hampson Cl *BDWL* MK13..........6 B1
Hampstead Ga *BDWL* MK13......6 B1
Hampton *CNH/GTH/TM* MK8.....41 H9
Hanbury Cl *SL* SL1.................178 B8
Hancocks La *RMKS/WB* MK17...44 C4
Handley Page Cl
  RBEDW MK43....................33 J3
Handsworth Cl *OXHEY* WD19...159 N3
Hangar Rd *DEN/HRF* UB9.......169 N2
Hanging Croft Cl
  HWYN HP13 * 153 M4
Hangings La
  GTMIS/PWD HP16.............132 C6
Hanley Cl *WDSR* SL4..............187 H9
Hanmer Rd *EAG/OLD/WT* MK6...43 J7
Hannibal Rd
  STWL/WRAY TW19.............196 E6
Hannon Rd *AYLS* HP21.............109 L1
Hanover Av *FELT* TW13...........197 N7
Hanover Cir *HYS/HAR* UB3.....183 J9
Hanover Cl *AYLW* HP19............95 J5
  SL SL1............................188 C4
  WDSR SL4.......................194 K9
Hanover Ct *LBUZ* LU7...............74 E2
  DUN *BRACKY* NN13.........34 C4
Hanover Ga *SL* SL1................178 F1
Hanover Md *WDSR* SL4............94 J4
Hanover Wy *WDSR* SL4..........193 K1
Hans Apel Dr *BRACKY* NN13....34 D4
Hanscomb Cl *WLLN* MK15........43 J2
Hanslope Circular Ride
  RMKN MK19......................12 C9
  RMKN MK19......................18 D4
Hanslope Rd *RMKN* MK19.........11 J9
Hanson La *WDR/YW* UB7........190 A1
Hanson Wy *AYLS* HP21..........110 A2
Hanworth Rd *FELT* TW13........197 P7
Harborne Ct
  CNH/GTH/TM MK8..............41 L2
Harbourne La *AYLS* HP21.......109 L5
Harby Cl *EMV/FZ* MK4..............52 A1
Harcourt *BDWL* MK13...............43 A1
  STWL/WRAY TW19.............194 D5
Harcourt Cl *HEN* RG9.............174 A7
  LBUZ LU7..........................74 C2
  MDHD SL6.......................185 K9
Harcourt Gdns *MLW* SL7 *.......95 K5
Harcourt Pl *MDHD* SL6...........185 K9
Harcourt Rd *MDHD* SL6..........186 D4
  TRING HP23....................112 G2

WDSR SL4.............................187 J9
Hardenwaye *HWYN* HP13........153 L1
Harding Rd *CSHM* HP5...........135 P5
  MKV MK10.........................44 A4
Hardings Rw *IVER* SL0............181 L6
Hardmead Rd *RBEDW* MK43....11 K8
Hardware Rd *MDHD* SL6.........176 F8
Hardwicke Gdns *AMS* HP6.....146 A4
Hardwick Ms *RMKS/WB* MK17...44 F7
Hardwick Pl *RMKS/WB* MK17....44 F7
Hardy Av *RSLP* HA4................186 A5
Hardy Cl *AYLS* HP21.................3 F7
  SL SL1............................187 L2
Hardy La *RAYLNE/WEN* HP22..111 L4
Hare Cl *BUCK/WIN* MK18...........48 C4
Hareden Cft *EMV/FZ* MK4.........52 B2
Harefield Rd *MDHD* SL6..........176 C9
  RKW/CH/CXG WD3............158 D3
  UX/CGN UB8....................182 D2
Harehatch La *SLN* SL2............167 L6
Hare La *GTMIS/PWD* HP16......133 P9
Harepark Cl *HHW* HP1............127 P1
Hare Shoots *MDHD* SL6..........185 L2
Harewood Ga *SLN* SL2............178 C1
  OXHEY WD19...................159 P2
Hargrave Rd *MDHD* SL6.........176 F9
Hargreaves Nook *GTLIN* MK14..31 H3
Harkness Cl *WEAT* MK2..........53 H5
Harkness Rd *SL* SL1...............178 F8
Harlans Cl *EAG/OLD/WT* MK6...43 H4
Harlech Pl *BTCHLY* MK5...........52 E4
Harlequin Pl *SHEN* MK5...........41 P9
Harle Stone Ct *GTLIN* MK14 *...30 E7
Harleyford *MLW* SL7 * 175 P2
Harleyford La *MLW* SL7............175 L4
Harling Rd *DUN/WHIP* LU6........86 C4
Harlington Cl *HYS/HAR* UB3....191 J3
Harlington Rd *UX/CGN* UB8.....182 C6
Harlington Rd East
  EBED/NFELT TW14............197 P6
Harlington Rd West
  EBED/NFELT TW14............197 P5
Harlyn Dr *PIN* HA5.................171 P1
Harmondsworth La
  WDR/YW UB7...................190 C1
Harmondsworth Rd
  WDR/YW UB7...................190 E1
Harmony Rw *LBUZ* LU7............75 J4
Harmon Dr *WOLV* MK12............29 H7
Harold Av *HYS/HAR* UB3.........191 N4
Harpers La *GTLIN* MK14...........30 F5
Harpsden Rd *HEN* RG9...........174 A3
Harrier Cl *AYLW* HP19.............95 P4
Harrier Dr *EAG/OLD/WT* MK6....7 K6
Harries Wy *HAZ/HG* HP15.......143 P5
Harriet Walker Wy
  RKW/CH/CXG WD3............147 P9
Harris Cl *WDSR* SL4...............193 K3
Harris Ct *AYL* HP20..................95 P5
Harris Gdns *SL* SL1................187 N3
Harrison Cl *NTHWD* HA6.........159 J7
  SHEN MK5.........................41 P9
Harrison Pl *THAME* OX9.........118 D4
Harrison Wy *SL* SL1...............178 F8
Harris Rd *HGDN/ICK* UB10......182 C5
Harroell *RAYLW* HP18..............67 L8
Harrogate Ct *DTCH/LGLY* SL3..189 H4
Harrow Cl *RBEDW* MK43..........17 J1
Harrow Ct *AYLS* HP21............109 N1
  MDHD SL6.......................177 L9
Harrowden *BDWL* MK13............42 B1
Harrow La *MDHD* SL6..............177 L9
Harrow Rd *ASHF* TW15...........196 A9
  DTCH/LGLY SL3................189 H4
  LBUZ LU7..........................74 D2
Harrow Vw *HGDN/ICK* UB10....183 J4
  HYS/HAR UB3..................191 N1
Harrow Yd *TRING* HP23..........112 F2
Hartdames *SHEN* MK5..............53 H5
Hartfield Av *RBEDW* MK43........33 L6
Hartfield Av *NTHLT* UB5...........183 L2
Hartfield Cl *MDHD* SL6............185 J9
Hartfield Rd *SL* SL1................188 C3
Hathaway Cl *RSLP* HA4..........171 M9
Hathaway Ct
  CNH/GTH/TM MK8..............41 N4
Hatherleigh Rd *RSLP* HA4......171 N7
Hatter's La *HWYN* HP13.........153 L5
Hatton Cl *EAG/OLD/WT* MK6.....43 K6
Hatton Av *SLN* SL2................179 P7
Hatton Ct *WDSR* SL4..............193 N1
Hatton Cross Est
  HTHAIR TW6 * 197 M3
Hatton Gn
  EBED/NFELT TW14............197 N3
Hatton Gv *WDR/YW* UB7 *.......190 D5
Hatton Rd
  EBED/NFELT TW14............197 J6
Hatton Rd North
  HTHAIR TW6....................191 K9
Hauksbee Gdns *SHEN* MK5......42 C7
Havelock Rd *MDHD* SL6..........177 H9
Havelock Rd *MDHD* SL6..........177 H9
Havelock St *AYLW* HP19..........95 H3
Haven Cl *YEAD* UB4................183 L8
Havenfield Rd *HWYW* HP12.....152 B6
Haven Shaw Cl *AYLS* HP21.....110 A1
Haversham Rd *RMKN* MK19......29 M4
Hawes Cl *NTHWD* HA6............159 M7
Hawfinch *AYLW* HP19...............95 P4
Hawkes Rd
  EBED/NFELT TW14............197 N6
Hawkesworth Cl
  NTHWD HA6....................159 L7
Hawkhurst Ga
  WTR/OFPK MK7..................45 M4
Hawkins Cl *HHW* HP1.............127 J9
Hawkins Cl *BRACKY* NN13........34 F4
  STSTR MK11......................28 F8
Hawkmoor Cl
  EAG/OLD/WT MK6...............43 H4
Hawkridge *EMV/FZ* MK4............42 B2
Hawkshead Dr *EMV/FZ* MK4.....42 C2
Hawks Hl *BNEND* SL8.............166 A7
Hawkshill Dr *HHW* HP1...........127 N5
Hawkshill Rd *SLN* SL2............179 L6
Hawksmoor Cl *HWYN* HP13.......4 E4
Hawkswaxy *STA* MK18............195 P9
Hawkswood *OLN* MK46............15 J2
Hawkswood La
  DTCH/LGLY SL3................181 H1
Hawkwell Dr *TRING* HP23.......112 G2
Hawkwell Est *RMKN* MK19.......28 D6
Haxby La *SKCH* HP14..............141 J2
Hawley's La
  RAYLNE/WEN HP22............81 J2
Hawridge La *CSHM* HP5..........125 J5
Hawridge V *CSHM* HP5...........125 K4
Hawthorn Av *THAME* OX9........118 C5
  WEAT MK2.........................5 J9
Hawthorn Cl *AYL* HP20..............2 E2
  DUN/WHIP LU6 * 87 M1
  HEST TW5.......................191 P8
  IVER SL0..........................181 L6
  RBEDW MK43...................17 J1
Hawthorn Crs *HAZ/HG* HP15...143 J2
Hawthorn Dr *BRACKY* NN13.....35 H5
  WDSR SL4.......................182 C2
Hawthorne Cl *LBUZ* LU7...........74 E5
  MLW SL7.........................164 E5
Hawthorne Ct
  STWL/WRAY TW19 *...........196 D6
  WDR/YW UB7...................182 C2
Hawthorne Dr *WDSR* SL4 *.....192 F7
Hawthorne Gdns
  MDHD SL6.......................153 N8
Hawthorne Rd *HWYN* HP13.....153 N4
The Hawthorns
  FLKWH HP10...................166 C9
Hawthorn Wy *RSLP* HA4.........186 E7
Hawthorn Gdns *MDHD* SL6.....153 E7
Hawthorn Rd *FELT* TW13........197 N9
Hawthorn Pl *HYS/HAR* UB3 *...191 M1
The Hawthorns *BERK* HP4......114 C9
  CSTG HP8.......................156 B3
  DTCH/LGLY SL3................188 E3
  FLKWH HP10...................165 P1
  HHS/BOV HP3..................127 P6
  PRRI HP27......................121 L6

RBEDW MK43 ....33 M4
RKW/CH/CXG WD3 * 157 M5
TOW NN12 ....25 K2
LBUZ LU7 ....73 L6
Hawthorn Wy CSHM HP5 ....135 P2
Hawtrey Gl SL SL1 ....188 D5
Hawtrey Dr RSLP HA4 ....171 N5
Hawtrey Rd WDSR SL4 ....193 N3
Haydock Cl RMKS/WB MK17 ....52 C5
Haydon Dr PIN HA5 ....171 N2
Haydon Rd AYLW HP19 ....2 A2
Hayes End Dr YEAD UB4 ....183 K8
Hayes End Rd YEAD UB4 ....183 K7
Hayes Rd NWDGN UB2 ....191 P5
RMKN MK19 ....28 B3
Hayfield Dr HAZ/HG HP15 ....143 P9
Hayling La DTCH/LGLY SL3 ....188 E7
Hayles Fld HEN RG9 ....150 C9
Hayling Rd OXHEY WD19 ....159 N3
Hayman Crs YEAD UB4 ....183 K5
Haymill Rd SL SL1 ....179 H7
Haynes Cl DTCH/LGLY SL3 ....188 B6
RMKS/WB MK17 ....54 B1
Haynes Md BERK HP4 ....114 C8
Hayse Hl WDSR SL4 ....187 H9
The Haystacks HWYN HP13 ....5 C4
Haystall Cl YEAD UB4 ....183 K7
Haythorp Cl WLN MK15 ....31 H7
Haywards Cl HEN RG9 ....173 N7
Haywards Md WDSR SL4 ....187 K6
Haywood
   RKW/CH/CXG WD3 * 147 P3
Haywood Pk LBUZ LU7 ....62 C7
   RKW/CH/CXG WD3 * 147 P7
Haywoods Dr HHW HP1 ....127 P5
Haywood Wy AYLW HP19 ....95 H4
Hazel Av THAME OX9 ....118 C5
   WDR/YW UB7 ....190 C4
Hazelbury Rd HWYN HP13 ....153 K4
Hazel Cl BRACKY NN13 ....35 L5
   MLW SL7 ....164 C5
   RNHPTN NN7 ....12 C5
Hazel Ct RKW/CH/CXG WD3 * 157 N4
Hazelcroft Cl
   HGDN/ICK UB10 ....182 F3
Hazeldell Link HHW HP1 * 127 N3
Hazeldell Rd HHW HP1 ....127 N3
Hazeldene
   RAYLNE/WEN HP22 ....123 J1
Hazeldene Gdns
   HGDN/ICK UB10 ....183 J4
Hazel Leaf WEAT MK2 53
Hazelhurst Rd SL SL1 ....178 C5
Hazell Av AYLS HP21 ....3 K6
Hazell Cl MDHD SL6 ....177 MB
Hazell Pk AMSS HP7 ....145 N5
Hazel Wy SL SL2 ....180 B2
Hazlemere Cl
   EBED/NFELT TW14 ....197 K5
Hazelrig Cl THAME OX9 ....118 C6
Hazel Rd BERK HP4 ....126 C4
Hazelton Cl THAME OX9 ....118 C5
Hazelwood Cl GTLIN MK14 ....30 F5
   TOW NN12 ....25 K2
Hazelwood Cl CSHM HP5 ....135 P2
Hazelwood Dr PIN HA5 ....159 P9
Hazely TRING HP23 ....112 C2
Hazlemere Dr AYLS HP21 ....110 A1
Hazlemere Rd FLKWH HP15 ....143 P6
   SLN SL2 ....188 D2
Hazlemere Vw HAZ/HG HP15 ....143 P6
Heacham Av
   HGDN/ICK UB10 ....171 J9
Headingham Ct SHEN MK5 ....42 A7
Headington Cl MDHD SL6 ....176 D9
Headington Rd MDHD SL6 ....176 D8
Headland Cl
Healey Av HWYN HP13 ....153 K3
Heaney Cl NPAG MK16 ....20 D9
Hearne Cl HAZ/HG HP15 ....143 N9
Hearne Dr MDHD SL6 ....185 N7
Hearne Pl EAG/OLD/WT MK6 ....7 G7
Hearnes Cl BEAC HP9 ....155 P5
Hearns Rd AYLS HP21 ....110 A5
Heart Br RIBCN OX27 ....76 C3
Heath Cl AYLS HP21 ....110 A4
   HAZ/HG HP15 ....143 P5
   HYS/HAR UB3 ....155 J6
   STWL/WRAY TW19 ....196 C5
Heathcote MDHD SL6 ....185 N4
Heathcote Wy WDR/YW UB7 ....190 C7
Heath Ct LBUZ LU7 ....64 C7
Heath End Cl CTLIN MK14 ....30 C6
Heath End Dr HAZ/HG HP15 ....143 N9
Heath End Rd FLKWH HP10 ....143 L2
   HAZ/HG HP15 ....143 L2
Heather Cl UX/CGN UB8 ....182 A6
Heatherden Gn IVER SLO 181 L4
Heatherfield Wy PIN HA5 ....171 M1
Heather La WDR/YW UB7 ....182 A1
Heatherside Gdns SLN SL2 ....167 P8
The Heathers
   STWL/WRAY TW19 ....196 F4
Heather Wy AYLS HP21 ....95 H3
Heatherwood Dr YEAD UB4 ....183 K5
Heathfield WOLV MK12 ....29 J1
Heathfield Ri HHW HP1 ....171 J5
Heathfield Wy HWYW HP12 ....152 B9
   MDHD SL6 ....166 D9
Heath Gn LBUZ LU7 ....64 C9
Heathlands Dr MDHD SL6 ....184 C1
Heath La RMKS/WB MK17 ....51 K1
Heath Park Dr LBUZ LU7 ....64 C8
Heath Park Rd LBUZ LU7 ....64 C8
Heath Rd AMS HP6 ....134 C4
   BEAC HP9 ....154 C4
   HGDN/ICK UB10 ....171 J8
   LBUZ LU7 ....64 E7
   LBUZ LU7 ....64 C8
   RMKS/WB MK17 ....64 B1

Heathrow Cl WDR/YW UB7 ....190 B9
Heathside Cl NTHWD HA6 ....159 K5
Heathside Rd NTHWD HA6 ....159 K4
The Heath LBUZ LU7 ....64 C7
Heath Wy IVER SLO 181 M5
Heathwood Cl LBUZ LU7 ....48 E7
Heavens Lea BNEND SL8 ....2 A7
Hedgerley CHNR OX39 ....129 M6
Hedgerley Hl SLN SL2 ....167 L9
Hedgerley La BEAC HP9 ....167 L1
The Hedgerows EMV/FZ MK4 ....42 E8
Hedges Ct SHEN MK5 ....42 A4
Hedgeside BERK HP4 ....115 J7
Hedingham Md MDHD SL6 * 177 K9
Hedley Cl
   RAYLNE/WEN HP22 ....111 N2
Hedley Rd FLKWH HP10 ....165 P1
Hedsor Hl MDHD SL6 ....166 B8
Hedsor La FLKWH HP10 ....166 D7
Hedsor Rd BNEND SL8 ....2 D7
Hele Ct WTR/OFPK MK7 ....43 M4
Helena Rd WDSR SL4 ....193 P1
Helen Av EBED/NFELT TW14 ....197 P6
Helford Cl RSLP HA4 ....171 L7
Hellyer Wy BNEND SL8 ....2 A6
Helston La WDSR SL4 ....187 M9
Helston Pl EAG/OLD/WT MK6 ....7 J7
Hemel Hempstead Rd
   BERK HP4 ....101 H6
Hemingway Cl NPAG MK16 ....30 F1
Hemingway Rd AYLW HP19 ....95 H5
Hemmen La HYS/HAR UB3 ....191 M1
The Hemmings BERK HP4 ....126 B2
Hemming Wy SLN SL2 ....179 M6
Hemp Hl AYLW HP19 ....95 J7
Hemp La TRING HP23 ....113 J5
Hempson Av DTCH/LGLY SL3 ....188 E4
Hempstead La BERK HP4 ....115 L8
Hempstead Rd
   HHS/BOV HP3 ....127 K8
Hemsdale MDHD SL6 ....177 H7
Hemwood Rd WDSR SL4 ....193 H2
Hencroft St North SL SL1 ....188 B3
Hencroft St South SL SL1 ....188 B4
Henders STSTR MK11 ....28 C8
Henderson Rd YEAD UB4 ....185 P6
Hendon Wy
   STWL/WRAY TW19 ....196 D4
Hendrix Dr CNH/GTH/TM MK8 ....41 M5
Hengistbury La HWYW HP12 ....152 C4
Hengrove Crs ASHF TW15 ....196 D9
Henley Gdns PIN HA5 ....171 P1
Henley Rd MDHD SL6 ....164 C8
   MLW SL7 ....164 C8
   WAR/TWY RG10 ....175 K6
Henmarton Wy HWYN HP13 ....153 L4
Henrietta Rd THAME OX9 ....118 E4
Henry Rd AYL HP20 ....96 B7
   SL SL1 ....187 P3
Henry St TRING HP23 ....112 E3
Henry Taunt Cl MEAD OX3 ....102 A3
Henson Cl RBDWH MK1 ....54 D5
Hepleswell CNH/GTH/TM MK8 ....41 N1
Hepplewhite Cl HWYN HP13 ....153 K2
Herbert Rd HWYN HP13 ....153 K1
Herberts Hole
   GTMIS/PWD HP16 ....134 D3
Hercies Rd HGDN/ICK UB10 ....182 F2
Hercules Cl LBUZ LU7 ....74 C1
Herdman Cl WOLV MK12 ....29 K3
Herd's Hl BUCK/WIN MK18 ....58 D6
Hereford Av AYLW HP19 ....95 J4
Heritage Cl UX/CGN UB8 ....182 A6
Heritage Wk
   RKW/CH/CXG WD3 * 147 N5
Herlwyn Av RSLP HA4 ....171 L8
Hermitage Cl DTCH/LGLY SL3 ....188 E4
Hermitage La WDSR SL4 ....193 L8
The Hermitage FELT TW15 * 197 M9
   GTMIS/PWD HP16 * 133 J8
Hermon Gv HYS/HAR UB3 ....191 N2
Heron Cl AYL HP20 ....96 C2
   RKW/CH/CXG WD3 ....158 D2
   DTCH/LGLY SL3 ....189 K3
Heron Dr BRACKY NN13 ....34 F3
   DTCH/LGLY SL3 ....189 K3
Heron Rd RKW/CH/CXG WD3 ....158 A6
Herons Elm BERK HP4 ....114 A7
Heronsgate Rd
   RKW/CH/CXG WD3 ....147 K8
The Heron AYLW HP19 ....95 L3
Heron Wk NTHWD HA6 ....159 L4
Heron Wy
   EBED/NFELT TW14 ....197 N3
Herrieffs Farm Rd
   BRACKY NN13 ....35 H6
Herriot Cl NPAG MK16 ....20 D9
Herschel Park Dr SL SL1 ....188 B8
Herschel St SL SL1 ....188 B5
Herston Cl AYLS HP21 ....110 B2
Hertford End Ct
   NTHWD HA6 * 159 L5
Hertford Pl BTCHLY MK3 ....52 F1
Hervines Cl AMS HP6 ....145 L4
Hervines Rd AMS HP6 ....145 L4
Hesa Rd HYS/HAR UB3 ....183 N1
Hesketh Rd TOW NN12 ....18 A8
Heswell Gn OXHEY WD19 * 159 N3
Hetherington Cl SLN SL2 ....179 K6
Hetherington Wy
   HGDN/ICK UB10 ....171 J8
Het's Orch PRRI HP27 ....131 N7
Hetton Cl WLN MK15 ....30 C9
Heusden Wy CFSP/GDCR SL9 ....169 K6
Hever Cl MDHD SL6 ....185 J1
Hewens Rd HGDN/ICK UB10 ....183 J5
Hexham Gdns BTCHLY MK3 ....52 D6
Heybridge Crs
   WTR/OFPK MK7 ....43 N9

Heydon Ct BDWL MK13 ....30 A6
Heynes Gn MDHD SL6 ....185 P3
Heythrop Dr HGDN/ICK UB10 ....170 F9
Heywood Av MDHD SL6 ....184 G6
Heywood Court Ct
   MDHD SL6 ....184 G6
Hibbert Rd MDHD SL6 ....185 P3
Hibberts Wy CFSP/GDCR SL9 ....168 G1
Hickmans Cl BUCK/WIN MK18 ....47 H5
Hickman St AYLW HP19 ....95 J5
Hickox Ct FLKWH HP10 ....166 D2
Hicks Farm Ri HWYN HP13 ....153 L6
The Hide EAG/OLD/WT MK6 ....43 J6
Higgs Ct SHEN MK5 ....42 A4
Higham Cross Rd RMKN MK19 ....18 G3
Higham Md CSHM HP5 ....135 N3
Higham Rd CSHM HP5 ....135 N3
High Banks LBUZ LU7 ....75 L5
High Beeches
   CFSP/GDCR SL9 ....168 F6
   HWYW HP12 ....152 C4
High Beeches Cl MLW SL7 ....164 C3
High Bois La AMS HP6 ....145 L2
Highbridge Rd AYLS HP21 ....3 F5
Highbridge Wk AYLS HP21 ....3 F5
Highbury La CMK MK9 ....2 K1
High Coppice AMSS HP7 ....145 N4
Highcroft LBUZ LU7 ....74 C3
Highcroft Cl TOW NN12 ....18 A8
Highcroft Trailer Gdns
   HHS/BOV HP3 ....127 K8
High Cross Wy HEAD OX3 ....102 A9
High Elms RBEDW MK43 ....11 J3
High Elms Cl NTHWD HA6 ....159 J6
Highfield CSTG HP8 ....156 A2
Highfield Av HWYW HP12 ....152 B5
Highfield Cl AMS HP6 ....145 P1
   BTCHLY MK3 ....52 F5
   NPAG MK16 ....31 L1
   NTHWD HA6 ....159 J6
   THAME OX9 ....118 A5
Highfield Ct RBCN NN13 ....34 A5
Highfield Crs NTHWD HA6 ....159 L8
   RBEDW MK43 ....45 N3
Highfield Dr HGDN/ICK UB10 ....170 F9
Highfield La MDHD SL6 ....184 G3
Highfield Pk MLW SL7 ....164 B9
Highfield Rd BERK HP4 ....126 F2
   BNEND SL8 ....2 B9
   BUCK/WIN MK18 ....60 B5
   CSHM HP5 ....135 M2
   FELT TW13 ....197 N1
   LBUZ LU7 ....74 C3
   MDHD SL6 ....177 H9
   NTHWD HA6 ....159 J6
   PRRI HP27 ....121 L9
   TRING HP23 ....112 C3
   WDSR SL4 ....193 H5
Highfield Wy HAZ/HG HP15 ....143 N8
   RNHPTN NN7 ....8 G2
Highgate Over
   WTR/OFPK MK7 ....43 P5
Highgrove Hl
   CNH/GTH/TM MK8 ....41 J1
Highgrove Pk MDHD SL6 ....177 P4
Highgrove Wy RSLP HA4 ....171 N4
High Halden WTR/OFPK MK7 ....43 P4
High Heavens Wd MLW SL7 ....164 C1
High Land Cl FLKWH HP10 ....90 G1
Highland Ms
   BUCK/WIN MK18 * 38 C9
Highland Rd AMSS HP7 ....145 N4
   NTHWD HA6 ....159 N9
Highlands FLKWH HP10 ....165 P2
Highlands Cl CFSP/GDCR SL9 ....157 H7
Highlands End
   HEN RG9 ....150 A2
Highlands La BEAC HP9 ....155 N5
   CFSP/GDCR SL9 ....157 H6
Highlands Rd BEAC HP9 ....155 N5
Highley Cl HWYN HP13 ....153 K2
The Highlands SL SL1 ....179 K9
Highlea Av FLKWH HP10 ....165 N1
High Meadow Cl PIN HA5 ....171 P3
Highmoor AMSS HP7 ....145 P3
High Moors
   RAYLNE/WEN HP22 ....111 N4
Highover Pk AMSS HP7 ....145 N4
High Park Dr WOLV MK12 ....29 J1
High Rd LBUZ LU7 ....63 L8
   MDHD SL6 ....175 L1
   UX/CGN UB8 ....182 C6
High Rd Ickenham
   HGDN/ICK UB10 ....171 J8
High St AMSS HP7 ....145 N4
   AYL HP20 ....2 E4
   AYLW HP19 ....95 G4
   BDWL MK13 ....30 B3
   BERK HP4 ....114 A8
   BRACKY NN13 ....35 H4
   BRACKY NN13 ....35 H4
   BUCK/WIN MK18 ....49 G3
   BUCK/WIN MK18 ....60 C7
   CFSP/GDCR SL9 ....157 H7
   CHNR OX39 ....129 K5
   CHNR OX39 ....129 P6
   CSHM HP5 ....135 N3
   CSTG HP8 ....156 C3
   DTCH/LGLY SL3 ....189 H3
   DTCH/LGLY SL3 ....189 K3
   DUN/WHIP LU6 ....86 A2
   FELT TW13 ....197 N8
   GTMIS/PWD HP16 ....133 J8
   HADM HP17 ....107 K8
   HADM HP17 ....108 A7

   HEAD OX3 ....102 C3
   HEN RG9 ....160 B7
   HEST TW5 ....191 P8
   HHS/BOV HP3 ....127 J9
   HWYN HP13 ....142 D6
   HYS/HAR UB3 ....155 J6
   IVER SLO 181 P9
   KID OX5 ....88 C3
   LBUZ LU7 ....73 K5
   LBUZ LU7 ....73 L6
   LBUZ LU7 ....75 M2
   LBUZ LU7 ....84 E9
   LBUZ LU7 ....99 J2
   MDHD SL6 ....177 N3
   MDHD SL6 ....178 D7
   MDHD SL6 ....186 A3
   MLW SL7 ....164 C3
   NPAG MK16 ....21 M4
   NPAG MK16 ....21 M5
   OLN MK46 ....14 C5
   OLN MK46 ....14 G5
   OLN MK46 ....15 K8
   PRRI HP27 ....131 K1
   RAYLNE/WEN HP22 ....81 J2
   RAYLNE/WEN HP22 ....81 J7
   RAYLNE/WEN HP22 ....123 H1
   RAYL HP18 ....77 H8
   RAYL HP18 ....90 D7
   RAYL HP18 ....106 B8
   RBEDW MK43 ....11 J3
   RBEDW MK43 ....17 J2
   RBEDW MK43 ....33 L5
   RKW/CH/CXG WD3 ....158 E1
   RMKN MK19 ....30 A2
   RMKN MK19 ....30 A2
   RMKS/WB MK17 ....44 B8
   RMKS/WB MK17 ....50 C8
   RMKS/WB MK17 ....51 K2
   RNHPTN NN7 ....9 J2
   RSLP HA4 ....171 L6
   SKCH HP14 ....141 P9
   SKCH HP14 ....151 K6
   SL SL1 ....187 P4
   SL SL1 ....188 C4
   STSTR MK11 ....28 C8
   STWL/WRAY TW19 ....194 D4
   STWL/WRAY TW19 ....196 D3
   THAME OX9 ....118 G4
   TOW NN12 ....18 B8
   TOW NN12 ....25 K2
   TOW NN12 ....26 A1
   TRING HP23 ....112 D3
   UX/CGN UB8 ....182 C8
   UX/CGN UB8 ....182 C8
   WDR/YW UB7 ....190 D7
   WDR/YW UB7 ....190 D7
   WDSR SL4 ....187 P4
   WEAT MK2 ....53 G4
   WTLGN OX49 ....138 F3
   WW HP11 ....9 J4
High St Harlington
   HYS/HAR UB3 ....191 K8
High St North LBUZ LU7 ....62 D8
High St South
   DUN/WHIP LU6 ....87 L1
   LBUZ LU7 ....72 E1
   OLN MK46 ....15 M4
The High St
   CNH/GTH/TM MK8 ....41 J1
High Town Rd MDHD SL6 ....185 L1
High Trees EAG/OLD/WT MK6 ....43 H4
High View Ap FLKWH HP10 ....166 C2
High Vw CSTG HP8 ....156 F2
   RMKN MK19 ....28 A8
High View Cl MLW SL7 ....164 C4
High View La LBUZ LU7 ....75 L7
High Wy AMSS HP7 ....145 M5
Highway RMKS/WB MK17 ....62 C4
Highway Rd MDHD SL6 ....176 D9
Highwood Av HWYW HP12 ....152 B5
Highwood Bottom
   PRRI HP27 ....132 A7
Highwood Crs HWYW HP12 ....152 B5
Highwoods Cl MLW SL7 ....164 C5
Highwoods Dr MLW SL7 ....164 C5
Highworth Cl HWYN HP13 ....153 L1
Hilda Whf AYL HP20 ....3 F5
Hildreth Rd GTMIS/PWD HP16 ....133 G6
Hiljon Crs CFSP/GDCR SL9 ....156 D8
Hillary Rd DTCH/LGLY SL3 ....188 E5
Hillbeck Cv HYS/HAR UB3 ....183 N1
Hillbottom Rd HWYW HP12 ....152 A5
Hillbury Cl AMS HP6 ....135 M4
Hill Cl FLKWH HP10 ....166 C2
Hill Ct BERK HP4 ....114 C9
Hillcrest AMD/WHLY OX33 ....102 B7
Hillcrest La CSTG HP8 ....156 F3
Hillcrest Cl SHEN MK5 ....42 A4
Hillcrest La BUCK/WIN MK18 ....58 D6
Hillcrest Crs OXHEY WD19 ....159 P1
Hillcroft Rd CSHM HP5 ....135 P2
   FLKWH HP10 ....154 A1

Hill End Rd DEN/HRF UB9 ....158 B6
Hillersdon SLN SL2 ....180 D8
Hillerston Cha
Hillesden Wy BUCK/WIN MK18 ....48 C2
Hill Farm Ap FLKWH HP10 ....166 C2
Hill Farm Cl CHNR OX39 ....129 P6
Hill Farm La CSTG HP8 ....156 B1
   RMKS/WB MK17 ....50 F9
Hillfield Cl CFSP/GDCR SL9 ....156 G7
   CSHM HP5 ....135 G7
   MDHD SL6 ....177 J8
   MLW SL7 ....164 E4
Hill Farm Wy HAZ/HG HP15 ....143 P9
Hillfield Rd CFSP/GDCR SL9 ....156 G7
Hillfield Sq CFSP/GDCR SL9 ....156 G7
Hilliard Dr BDWL MK13 ....42 A1
Hilliard Rd NTHWD HA6 ....159 L8
Hilliards Rd UX/CGN UB8 ....182 D9
Hilliers Av HGDN/ICK UB10 ....182 G6
Hillingdon Av
   STWL/WRAY TW19 ....196 E7
Hillingdon Hl
   HGDN/ICK UB10 ....182 E7
Hillingdon Pde
   HGDN/ICK UB10 * 183 H7
Hillingdon Rd
   DEN/HRF UB9 ....158 A7
   HGDN/ICK UB10 ....182 E4
Hillingdon Trail
   DEN/HRF UB9 ....158 A7
   HGDN/ICK UB10 ....182 E4
Hillington Cl AYLW HP19 ....95 K8
Hill La RSLP HA4 ....171 J6
Hillmead Ct MDHD SL6 ....178 D8
Hill Pl SLN SL2 ....179 M5
Hill Ri CFSP/GDCR SL9 ....156 G7
   RSLP HA4 ....171 J5
Hillrise DTCH/LGLY SL3 ....189 J7
Hill Rise Crs CFSP/GDCR SL9 ....156 G6
Hill Rd CHNR OX39 ....159 K6
   NTHWD HA6 ....159 K6
   WTLGN OX49 ....148 A1
Hillsborough Gn
   OXHEY WD19 * 159 N3
Hills Cl GTLIN MK14 ....30 E6
Hill Side LBUZ LU7 ....85 L5
   SKCH HP14 ....177 M1
   CSHM HP5 ....135 L1
   DEN/HRF UB9 ....170 C3
   MDHD SL6 ....185 K2
   SL SL1 ....188 A3
Hillside Cl CFSP/GDCR SL9 ....156 G6
   CSTG HP8 ....156 F3
Hillside Crs NTHWD HA6 ....159 M8
Hillside Gdns AMSS HP7 ....146 A4
   BERK HP4 ....115 K3
   HWYN HP13 ....153 K3
Hillside Ri NTHWD HA6 ....159 N7
Hillside Rd DUN/HR/TOD LU7 ....87 M1
   HAZ/HG HP15 ....143 L9
   LBUZ LU7 ....64 E8
   MLW SL7 ....164 D3
   NTHWD HA6 ....159 N7
   RKW/CH/CXG WD3 ....147 L7
Hills La MDHD SL6 ....185 H2
Hillslea NPAG MK16 ....21 N5
   SKCH HP14 ....141 L2
Hill View LBUZ LU7 ....75 H7
Hill View Rd HWYN HP13 ....153 K2
Hill View Rd
   STWL/WRAY TW19 ....196 F5
Hill Wy AMSS HP7 ....145 M5
Hillway AMSS HP7 ....145 M5
Hill Waye CFSP/GDCR SL9 ....169 H4
Hilltop RAYLW HP18 ....106 B9
Hilltop Av HAZ/HG HP15 ....143 L8
Hill Top Dr MLW SL7 ....164 D5
Hill Top La CHNR OX39 ....129 K6
Hilltop Rd BERK HP4 ....126 E2
Hill Vw BERK HP4 ....114 B8
   HADM HP17 ....121 M4
   RAYLW HP18 ....106 B9
Hillview NPAG MK16 ....21 N5
   SKCH HP14 ....141 L2
Hilversum Wy HYS/HAR UB3 ....191 N2
Hilyer Cl EAG/OLD/WT MK6 ....43 H2
Hillyfields DUN/WHIP LU6 ....87 L5
Hilperton Rd SL SL1 ....188 A3
Hilton Av AYL HP20 ....96 A1
   HGDN/ICK UB10 ....182 B6
Hilton Cl UX/CGN UB8 ....182 B6
Himley Gn LBUZ LU7 ....74 D1
Hindemith Gdns
   WTR/OFPK MK7 ....44 B7
Hindhay La MDHD SL6 ....177 H5
Hindhead Cl UX/CGN UB8 ....182 C4
Hindhead Knoll
   WTR/OFPK MK7 ....43 P6
Hinds Wy AYLS HP21 ....95 K9
Hinkley Cl DTCH/LGLY SL3 ....189 K4
Hinksey Cl DTCH/LGLY SL3 ....189 K4
Hinton Cl HWYN HP13 ....4 D1
   LBUZ LU7 ....75 M2
Hinton Ct BTCHLY MK3 ....52 F1
Hinton Rd BRACKY NN13 ....35 J1
   SL SL1 ....187 J1
   UX/CGN UB8 ....182 B4
Hipwell Cl OLN MK46 ....15 M4
Hitcham La SL SL1 ....178 E7
Hitcham Rd SL SL1 ....178 E7
Hitchens Cl HHW HP1 ....127 J4
Hitherbroom Rd
   HYS/HAR UB3 ....191 N2

Hithercroft Rd HWYN HP15 142 E9
Hither Meadow CFSP/GDCR SL9 * 156 G8
Hithermoor Rd STWL/WRAY TW19 196 A5
Hiving's Hill CSHM HP5 135 L1
Hivings Pk CSHM HP5 135 M1
Hoathly Ms WTR/OFPK MK7 43 P4
Hobart Cl HWYN HP13 153 K1
Hobart Crs WLLN MK15 31 H7
Hobart Rd HWYN HP13 153 K1
Hobbs Dr DEN/HRF UB9 169 P4
Hobbs Dr MDHD SL6 184 C1
Hobbs End HEN RG9 173 M8
Hobbshill Rd GTMIS/PWD HP16 133 P6
Hobbs Rd SKCH HP14 151 K6
Hobsons Wk TRING HP23 176 F2
Hockett La MDHD SL6 176 F2
Hockley La SL SL2 180 D3
Hockliffe Brae WTR/OFPK MK7 44 A7
Hockliffe Rd LBUZ LU7 74 F2
Hodder La EMV/FZ MK4 52 C1
Hodds Wood Rd CSHM HP5 135 N6
Hodge La WLLV SL4 * 193 N5
Hodgemoor Vw CSTG HP8 156 G6
Hodgemore Ct GTLIN MK14 30 D7
Hodges Ms HWYW HP12 152 C4
Hoe Meadow BEAC HP9 154 G6
Hogarth Cl SL SL1 187 J1
Hogarths Ct CNH/GTH/TM MK8 41 P9
Hogback Wood Rd BEAC HP9 154 F6
HogFair La SL SL1 178 G7
Hogg La HAZ/HG HP15 144 B5
Hog Hall La BERK HP4 100 C3
Hog La CSHM HP5 125 N4
Hogpits Bottom HHS/BOV HP3 137 J5
Hogshaw Rd BUCK/WIN MK18 69 D5
Hogtrough La RAYLNE/WEN HP22 123 J2
Holbein Cl RAYLNE/WEN HP22 110 F4
Holborn Crs EMV/FZ MK4 51 P4
Holdgate Cl BRACKY NN13 54 C5
Holdom Av BDWL MK1 15 M3
Holes La OLN MK46 15 M3
Holiday La RMKN MK19 19 H2
Holyhead La RAYLNE/WEN HP22 123 H1
Hollandbridge La WTLGN SL4 148 F3
Holland Rd AYLW HP19 95 K5
MLW SL7 164 F7
Holland Wy DTCH/LGLY SL3 * 31 J2
Hollick's La DUN/WHIP LU6 87 M6
Holliday Cl AYLW HP19 95 P4
Holliday St BERK HP4 126 F1
Holliers Cl CHNR OX39 129 H4
THAME OX9 118 C5
Hollies Ct LBUZ LU7 74 C2
The Hollies HHS/BOV HP3 137 J2
RKW/CH/CXG WD3 147 L9
TRING HP23 113 H5
Hollington Rd LBUZ LU7 63 K7
Hollington RAYLW HP18 105 P8
Hollin La WOLV MK12 30 A1
Hollinwell Cl EMV/FZ MK4 52 D2
Hollis Rd HWYN HP13 153 L2
Hollister Cha SHEN MK5 42 B8
Holloway Cl WDR/YW UB7 190 G6
Holloway Dr BUCK/WIN MK18 48 E3
Holloway La HEN RG9 149 L5
RKW/CH/CXG WD3 147 K2
WDR/YW UB7 190 E7
The Holloway PRRI HP27 121 M7
RAYLNE/WEN HP22 112 A2
Hollow Hill End BUCK/WIN MK18 70 A2
Hollow Hill La IVER SL0 189 K1
Hollow Wy AYLW HP19 95 H1
Hollow Wy CSHM HP5 135 J3
Hollow Way La AMS HP6 136 A8
Hollow Wd OLN MK46 15 L4
Hollyberry Gv HAZ/HG HP15 144 A4
Hollybush Cl BERK HP4 116 G5
Hollybush La AMS HP6 145 P1
DEN/HRF UB9 169 L1
HHW HP1 127 P1
IVER SL0 181 K9
MDHD SL6 177 H2
Hollybush Rd CSHM HP5 125 J1
Hollybush Rw TRING HP23 * 113 H6
Holly Cl BRACKY NN13 41 M6
CNH/GTH/TM MK8 41 M6
HEN RG9 172 C5
SLN SL2 180 B2
Holly Crs WDSR SL4 195 H1
Hollycroft Gdns WDR/YW UB7 190 G7
Holly Dr AYLS HP21 95 N9
BERK HP4 126 F2
MDHD SL6 177 M8
Holly End SKCH HP14 142 C5
Hollyfield TRING HP23 112 C5
Hollyfield Cl TRING HP23 112 C5
Holly Gdns WDR/YW UB7 190 G7
Holly Green La PRRI HP27 130 C1
Holly Hedges La HHS/BOV HP3 137 L5
Holly Pl WYM HP11 153 N7
Hollytree Cl CFSP/GDCR SL9 156 G6
CSHM HP5 135 N4
Holly Wk RMKS/WB MK17 54 F1
Hollywood Gdns YEAD UB4 185 P9

Holmanleaze MDHD SL6 177 N9
Holman St AYLW HP19 95 L4
Holmbury Gdns HYS/HAR UB3 * 191 M2
Holmdale SLN SL2 188 E1
Holmer Green Rd HWYN HP15 143 N7
Holmer La HWYW HP12 152 C7
Holmer Pl HAZ/HG HP15 144 A4
Holmers Ct HWYW HP12 * 152 B7
Holmers Farm Wy HWYW HP12 152 B7
Holmewood EMV/FZ MK4 42 E8
Holmfield Cl EAG/OLD/WT MK6 43 K7
Holmlea Rd DTCH/LGLY SL3 188 F9
Holmlea Wk DTCH/LGLY SL3 188 F9
Holmside Ri OXHEY WD19 159 P5
Holmsdale MDHD SL6 185 H2
Holst Crs WTR/OFPK MK7 44 A8
Holt La EMV/FZ MK4 52 C1
Holton Hl EMV/FZ MK4 52 C1
Holton Rd BUCK/WIN MK18 48 B1
Holtspur Av FLKWH HP10 166 D2
Holtspur Cl BEAC HP9 166 E1
Holtspur La FLKWH HP10 166 D3
Holtspur Pde BEAC HP9 166 E1
Holtspur Top La BEAC HP9 154 E9
Holtspur Wy BEAC HP9 154 E9
The Holt BUCK/WIN MK18 48 C4
Holyhead Crs EMV/FZ MK4 52 C1
Holyport Rd MDHD SL6 184 D8
Holyport St MDHD SL6 185 N1
Holyrood CNH/GTH/TM MK8 41 N4
Holy Thorn La SHEN MK5 41 P7
Holywell Cl DUN/WHIP LU6 101 K1
STWL/WRAY TW19 196 E2
Holywell Gdns HWYN HP13 * 153 L3
Holywell Pl EAG/OLD/WT MK6 43 J2
Holywell Rd DUN/WHIP LU6 87 K9
Holywell Wy STWL/WRAY TW19 196 E2
Home Cl BTCHLY MK3 53 H1
RAYLNE/WEN HP22 110 F4
TOW NN12 25 K1
Home Ct FELT TW15 * 197 H1
Home Farm RMKS/WB MK17 52 D8
TRING HP23 * 112 E4
Home Farm Ct CSTG HP8 * 156 C3
OLN MK46 15 L8
Home Farm La RMKS/WB MK17 54 B9
Home Farm Rd BERK HP4 113 P7
RKW/CH/CXG WD3 158 C4
Home Farm Wy DTCH/LGLY SL3 180 E4
Home Fld AYLW HP19 95 P4
WTR/OFPK MK7 44 A7
Homefield BERK HP4 115 K7
HHS/BOV HP3 137 K1
Homefield Cl SKCH HP14 140 A6
Homefield Rd RKW/CH/CXG WD3 147 M6
Homeground BUCK/WIN MK18 * 48 B5
Homelands Gdns HAZ/HG HP15 144 A4
Homelands Wy HEN RG9 173 P7
Home Meadow SLN SL2 179 N5
Home Meadow Dr FLKWH HP10 165 P2
Homers Rd WDSR SL4 187 H9
Homeside Cl MDHD SL6 177 L6
Homestall BUCK/WIN MK18 48 B5
Homestall Cl SHEN MK5 42 A5
Homestead Farm HADM HP17 108 C2
Homestead Pl AYLW HP19 95 J7
Homestead Rd MDHD SL6 185 K3
The Homestead HADM HP17 143 K2
HWYW HP12 152 C7
SHEN MK5 42 A6
Homestead Wy AYLW HP19 95 J8
TOW NN12 27 P2
Homeward Ct SHEN MK5 42 A5
Home Wy RKW/CH/CXG WD3 157 P1
Homewood DTCH/LGLY SL3 180 F9
Hondur Cl AYLW HP19 95 P5
Honey Banks RAYLNE/WEN HP22 123 J1
Honeycroft Hl HGDN/ICK UB10 182 E5
Honeycross Rd HHW HP1 127 J3
Honey Hl HGDN/ICK UB10 182 F1
OLN MK46 15 M8
Honey Hill Dr RMKN MK19 28 A3
Honey La MDHD SL6 175 N6
Honeypot Cl BDWL MK13 30 B9
Honeysuckle Cl IVER SL0 181 L9
Honeysuckle Fld CSHM HP5 135 N5
Honeysuckle Rd HAZ/HG HP15 143 M4
Honey Wy SKCH HP14 142 B3
Honiton Ct WTR/OFPK MK7 * 44 A6
Honor Rd GTMIS/PWD HP16 132 G3
Honorwood Cl GTMIS/PWD HP16 133 H6
Honour End La GTMIS/PWD HP16 132 G5
Honours Md HHW HP1 * 127 J9
Hoods Farm Cl RAYLNE/WEN HP22 96 C5
The Hooke WLLN MK15 31 N5
Hooper Dr UX/CGN UB8 183 H8
Hooper Ga WLLN MK15 31 J6
Hop Gdns HEN RG9 173 P6

Hopkins Cl MKV MK10 43 N2
Hopkins Ct AYL HP20 95 P5
Hoppers Meadow SHEN MK5 42 A4
Hoppers Wy HAZ/HG HP15 143 K3
Hoppner Rd YEAD UB4 185 K5
Hopton Rd THAME OX9 118 E4
Hordern Cl HADM HP17 107 K8
Hornbeam NPAG MK16 30 C9
Hornbeam Cl HWYW HP12 152 C8
LBUZ LU7 74 G1
Hornbeam Gdns SL SL1 188 C4
Hornbill Cl UX/CGN UB8 182 D9
Hornby Cha EMV/FZ MK4 52 B1
Hornhill Rd RKW/CH/CXG WD3 157 L5
Horn La STSTR MK11 28 F8
Horns La SKCH HP14 152 A6
Horn St BUCK/WIN MK18 60 G6
Horsefair Gn STSTR MK11 28 F8
Horseguards Dr MDHD SL6 177 P9
Horse Hl CSHM HP5 136 F5
Horsemoor Cl DTCH/LGLY SL3 195 H2
Horsemoor La AMSS MK7 144 A4
Horsemoor La PRRI HP27 131 K7
Horsenden Rd HWYN HP15 153 M5
Horsepool La RMKS/WB MK17 52 L9
Horseshoe Dr UX/CGN UB8 182 G9
Horseshoe Hl SL SL1 166 G9
Horseshoe Rd SKCH HP14 140 D4
Horseshoes Cl LBUZ LU7 74 B9
Horseshoes Pl THAME OX9 118 E6
Horsham Rd EBED/NFELT TW14 197 J5
Horsleys RKW/CH/CXG WD3 157 M5
Horton Av THAME OX9 118 C6
Horton Bridge Rd WDR/YW UB7 190 F2
Horton Cl AYLW HP19 95 P5
MDHD SL6 178 A7
WDR/YW UB7 190 F2
Horton Gdns DTCH/LGLY SL3 * 195 H2
Horton Ga GTLIN MK14 30 F3
Horton Pde WDR/YW UB7 * 190 E2
DTCH/LGLY SL3 189 K9
DTCH/LGLY SL3 194 G1
DTCH/LGLY SL3 195 N2
LBUZ LU7 74 A4
STWL/WRAY TW19 196 A4
WDR/YW UB7 190 F2
Hortonsfield Rd TOW NN12 18 B9
Horwood Ct DBGH MK1 53 K2
Hoskins Ct HHV/HAR UB3 191 M1
Hospital Hl CSHM HP5 135 N3
Hotch Cft RBEDW MK43 33 N2
Hotley Bottom La GTMIS/PWD HP16 133 J2
Houghton Ct CNH/GTH/TM MK8 41 P9
Hounslow Rd EBED/NFELT TW14 197 N5
Housman Cl NPAG MK16 20 C9
Howard Agne Cl HHW HP1 127 J9
Howard Av AYLS HP21 95 J9
SL SL1 179 P8
Howard Ct BNEND SL8 165 N6
Howard Crs BEAC HP9 155 N5
Howard Pl DUN/WHIP LU6 87 M7
Howard Rd BTCHLY MK3 53 H9
CSHM HP5 135 M1
Howards Cl PHN HA5 * 159 P8
Howards Dr HHW HP1 115 P8
Howards Thicket CFSP/GDCR SL9 168 C2
Howards Wood Dr CFSP/GDCR SL9 168 C2
Howard Wy NPAG MK16 31 M2
Howarth Rd MDHD SL6 185 N1
Howcut La RNHPTN NN7 6 E6
Howe Cl MKV MK10 43 N1
Howe Dr BEAC HP9 155 J5
Howell Hill Cl LBUZ LU7 86 B3
Howe Rd WTLGN OL49 148 B4
Howe Rock Pl EMV/FZ MK4 51 P4
Howland Pl RMKS/WB MK17 55 K4
Howland Rd THAME OX9 118 F6
Howletts Cl AYLW HP19 95 J5
Howletts La RSLP HA4 171 J4
How's Rd UX/CGN UB8 182 C4
Hoylake Cl BTCHLY MK3 52 D4
Hoylake Crs HGDN/ICK UB10 170 D6
Hoylake Gdns RSLP HA4 171 P6
Hoyton Ga CNH/GTH/TM MK8 41 N6
Hubbard Cl BUCK/WIN MK18 48 D2
Hubbards Cl UX/CGN UB8 182 A9
Hubbards Rd RKW/CH/CXG WD3 147 M7
Hubert Day Cl BEAC HP9 155 J6
Hubert Rd DTCH/LGLY SL3 188 F4
Huckleberry Cl WTR/OFPK MK7 44 A7
Hudnall La BERK HP4 100 F4
Hudson La DEN/HRF UB9 169 J6
Hudson Rd HYS/HAR UB3 191 K7
Hudsons Av OXHEY WD19 159 P8
Hughenden Av HWYN HP13 185 D2
Hughenden Cl MDHD SL6 185 L1
Hughenden Gn AYLS HP21 110 A4
Hughenden Rd SKCH HP14 143 H9
SL SL1 187 J5
Hughes Rd HYS/HAR UB3 191 P9
Hugh Park Cl SHEN MK5 42 A7
Hulbert End AYLS HP21 95 J9
Hulcombe Wk AYL HP20 * 95 N5
Hull Cl AYLS HP21 95 N9
SL SL1 187 H4
Hulton Dr OLN MK46 15 L8
Humber Dr AYLS HP21 109 L1
Humber Wy BTCHLY MK3 52 E2

DTCH/LGLY SL3 189 J5
Hume Wy RSLP HA4 171 N4
Humphreys Cl RAYLNE/WEN HP22 82 D3
Humphrey Talbot Av DUN/WHIP LU6 87 H9
Humphries Dr BRACKY NN13 54 C3
Hundred Acres La AMSS MK7 145 P4
Hungerford Av SL SL1 180 A8
Hungerford Dr MDHD SL6 177 L5
Hunsdon Cl GTLIN MK14 30 D7
Hunstanton Cl DTCH/LGLY SL3 189 L8
Hunstanton Wy BTCHLY MK3 52 D3
Huntercombe La North SL SL1 178 G8
Huntercombe La South SL SL1 186 F2
Hunter Dr WEAT MK2 53 J4
Hunters Cl CSHM HP5 135 L3
HHS/BOV HP5 137 J2
TRING HP23 112 F1
Hunters Gv HYS/HAR UB3 191 N2
Hunters Ms WDSR SL4 187 J3
Hunters Pk BERK HP4 114 C9
Hunters Point CHNR OX39 129 M6
Hunters Reach BDWL MK13 42 A1
Hunter St BUCK/WIN MK18 48 A4
Hunter Wy SL SL1 187 J3
Huntingbrooke CNH/GTH/TM MK8 41 P9
Huntingdon Crs BTCHLY MK3 52 C5
Huntington Pl DTCH/LGLY SL3 189 K4
Huntley Cl HWYN HP13 143 J9
Huntley Crs MDHD SL6 196 E6
STWL/WRAY TW19 196 E6
Hunters Gv CMK MK9 42 G2
Hunt Rd HWYN HP13 153 L4
THAME OX9 118 F6
Hunts Hill La SKCH HP14 142 D6
Hunt's La MDHD SL6 175 P5
Huntsman Gv GTLIN MK14 30 C2
Huntsmans Cl BERK HP4 100 E2
Huntsmill Rd HHW HP1 127 H5
Huntswood Cl SL SL1 178 D3
Hurley Cft WTR/OFPK MK7 43 P5
Hurley High St MDHD SL6 175 P4
Hurley Rd MDHD SL6 177 N8
Hurlock Cl DUN/WHIP LU6 87 L9
Hurlstone Gv EMV/FZ MK4 42 E8
Hurstfield Crs MDHD SL6 183 L8
Hurstfield Rd MDHD SL6 178 A8
Hurst Pl NTHWD HA6 158 E8
Hurst Rd SL SL1 179 H8
Hurworth Av DTCH/LGLY SL3 188 E5
Hutchings Cl SHEN MK5 42 A4
Hutton Av EAG/OLD/WT MK6 7 C1
Hutton Wy RMKS/WB MK17 54 F1
Huxley Cl NPAG MK16 30 F1
Huxtable Gdns MDHD SL6 183 N8
Hyacinth Dr HGDN/ICK UB10 182 E1
Hycliffe Gdns SKCH HP14 151 M5
Hyatts Yd CSHM HP5 135 M1
Hyde Av BTCHLY MK3 53 H5
Hyde Gn BEAC HP9 155 K6
MLW SL7 164 F6
Hyde Heath Rd GTMIS/PWD HP16 134 C5
Hyde La GTMIS/PWD HP16 134 B8
HHS/BOV HP3 127 J9
Hyde Mdw HHS/BOV HP3 137 J1
Hyde Rd HYS/HAR UB3 191 L4
The Hyde MDHD SL6 * 177 M8
RAYLNE/WEN HP22 110 F4
Hyde Vw HYS/HAR UB3 191 L5
Hylle Cl WDSR SL4 187 H1
Hylton Rd HWYW HP12 152 C3
Hyrons Cl AMS HP6 146 A2
Hyrons La AMS HP6 145 P2
Hythe End Rd STWL/WRAY TW19 195 J4
The Hythe CNH/GTH/TM MK8 41 M1

I

Ibstone Av BDWL MK15 30 C9
Ibstone Rd SKCH HP14 139 N6
Ickenham Cl RSLP HA4 171 K7
Ickenham Rd RSLP HA4 171 L6
Ickford Rd RAYLW HP18 104 F9
RAYLW HP18 98 J5
THAME OX9 116 F5
Icknield Cl CHNR OX39 129 L6
RAYLNE/WEN HP22 98 G9
Icknield Gn THAME OX9 118 C5
Icknield Wy BERK HP4 100 C2
BERK HP4 100 C2
DUN/WHIP LU6 86 G5
GTMIS/PWD HP16 132 G2
TRING HP23 112 C2
TRING HP23 113 K1
Icknieldway PRRI HP27 130 D5
Iffley Cl UX/CGN UB8 182 A3
Ilchester Cl MDHD SL6 185 L2
Illingworth WDSR SL4 193 N6
Illingworth Pl EAG/OLD/WT MK6 43 K4
Imperial Ct HEN RG9 * 174 B7
Imperial Rd EBED/NFELT TW14 197 L6
WDSR SL4 193 N6
Index Dr DUN/WHIP LU6 87 N1
India Rd SL SL1 187 N5
Ingleglen SLN SL2 179 N4
Ingleside DTCH/LGLY SL3 188 F6
Ingleton Cl BDWL MK13 30 A9
Ingram Av AYLS HP21 96 C9

J

Jackets La DEN/HRF UB9 158 F7
Jacks Cl OLN MK46 10 C9
Jacks La DEN/HRF UB9 158 A8
RBEDW MK43 17 J2
Jackson Ct HAZ/HG HP15 143 N8
Jackson Rd AYLW HP19 95 J4
HGDN/ICK UB10 182 E3
Jacksons Cl DUN/WHIP LU6 86 A4
Jacob Cl WDSR SL4 187 F9
Jacobs Ct GTLIN MK14 30 F8
Jakeman Wy AYLW HP19 95 K9
Jamaica EAG/OLD/WT MK6 43 L4
James Cl MLW SL7 164 F5
James Martin Cl DEN/HRF UB9 170 A4
James Rd CSHM HP5 135 K6
James St WDSR SL4 187 P9
Jane Cl AYLS HP21 110 A2
Jane Morbey Rd THAME OX9 118 C6
Jansel Sq AYLS HP21 96 B9
Jardine Wy DUN/WHIP/TOD LU5 87 N1
Jarman Cl BUCK/WIN MK18 48 A3
Jarvis Cl AYLS HP21 95 M9
Jasmin Cl NTHWD HA6 159 M8
Jasmine Cl AYLS HP21 95 N9
Jasmine Crs PRRI HP27 131 K1
Jasmine Ter WDR/YW UB7 190 G5
Jasmin Wy HHW HP1 127 H9
Jasons Hl CSHM HP5 136 D2
Jeeves Cl EAG/OLD/WT MK6 43 J5
Jefferies Rd RAYLW HP18 108 D1
Jefferson Cl DTCH/LGLY SL3 189 J5
Jefferson Wy THAME OX9 118 G2
Jeffrey Wk AYLW HP19 95 J8
Jeffries Ct BNEND SL8 165 M7
Jellicoe Cl SL SL1 187 M3
Jenkins Cl SHEN MK5 41 P6
Jenkins Ct RAYLNE/WEN HP22 83 J5
Jenkins La TRING HP23 124 C2
Jenna Wy NPAG MK16 31 N2
Jenner Rd AYLS HP21 109 L5

Jennery La SL SL1 ...178 G6
Jennings GTLIN MK14 ...30 C6
Jennings Fld FLKWH HP10 ...166 A9
Jerome CI MLW SL7 ...164 F5
Jerrard CI LBUZ LU7 ...74 G4
Jersey Rd WOLV MK12 ...29 L6
Jesse's La RAYLW HP18 ...106 B8
Job's La MDHD SL6 ...165 H9
Jocketts HI HHW HP1 ...127 P2
Jocketts Rd HHW HP1 ...127 P3
Joel St NTHWD HA6 ...159 N9
  PIN HA5 ...171 N1
John Bunyan Trail
  RBEDW MK43 ...45 P5
John Clare CI BRACKY NN13 ...35 H3
John Hall Wy HWYW HP12 ...152 C7
John Hampden Wy
  GTMIS/PWD HP16 * ...133 H5
Johns La OSHM MK5 ...125 P4
Johnson Av BRACKY NN13 ...34 G4
Johnson Rd SKCH HP14 * ...151 K5
Johnston PI EAG/OLD/WT MK6 ...7 H7
John Taylor Ct SL SL1 ...187 N2
Joiner's CI CFSP/GDCR SL9 ...157 H7
Joiners CI CFSP/GDCR SL9 ...159 C6
  OLN MK46 ...10 D8
Jonathans CI EAG/OLD/WT MK6 ...42 C6
Jonathans Ct
  RAYLNE/WEN HP22 * ...42 C6
Jones CI BRACKY NN13 ...34 F4
Jones Wy SLN SL2 ...167 P7
Jonson CI LBUZ LU7 ...183 N8
Jordans CI
  STWL/WRAY TW19 ...196 C6
Jordans La BEAC HP9 ...156 A7
Jordans Wy BEAC HP9 ...156 B6
Joules Ct SHEN MK5 ...42 C7
Journeys End SLN SL2 ...180 A8
Jubilee Arch STWL/WRAY SL4 * ...196 C6
Jubilee CI STWL/WRAY TW19 ...196 C6
Jubilee Gdns THAME OX9 ...118 B5
Jubilee Rd HWYN HP13 ...162 D7
  MDHD SL6 ...184 B3
  SKCH HP14 ...140 B8
  WYM HP11 ...4 B7
Jubilee Wy DTCH/LGLY SL3 ...188 L8
  EBED/NFELT TW14 ...197 N3
Judge Heath La
  HYS/HAR UB3 ...183 J9
Juniper CI HAZ/HC HP15 ...143 J9
Juniper Ct NTHWY HA6 * ...159 N8
Juniper Dr HWYW HP12 ...152 C5
Juniper Ga
  RKW/CH/CXG WD3 ...158 D2
Juniper Gn HHW HP1 ...127 N2
Juniper La FLKWH HP10 ...166 B2
Juniper Rd MLW SL7 ...164 D4
Juniper Wy HYS/HAR UB3 ...191 K1
Jupiter Dr LBUZ LU7 ...75 H1
Juson's Glebe
  RAYLNE/WEN HP22 ...111 J9

K

Kaduna CI PIN HA5 ...171 P3
Kalman Gdns WTR/OFPK MK7 ...44 B7
Kaplan CI SHEN MK5 ...42 B7
Karenza SKCH HP14 * ...140 A6
Katherine CI FLKWH HP10 * ...154 A3
  WTR/OFPK MK7 ...43 N8
Katrine PI WEAT MK2 ...53 K6
Kaybridge CI HWYN HP13 ...153 K6
Kay CI TRING HP23 ...112 C5
Kaywood Ct DTCH/LGLY SL3 ...188 E4
Keach CI BUCK/WIN MK18 ...60 C5
Keasden Pk EMV/FZ MK4 ...52 B1
Keaton CI CNH/GTH/TM MK8 ...41 M1
Keats CI AYLS HP21 ...95 P9
  NPAG MK16 ...30 C1
  WYM HP11 * ...4 E7
  YEAD UB4 ...183 N8
Keats La WDSR SL4 ...187 P7
  WDR/YW UB7 ...190 C5
Keble CI AYLW HP20 ...95 K4
Keble Rd BRACKY NN13 ...34 F4
Keel Dr SL SL1 ...187 N3
Keeler CI WDSR SL4 ...193 J2
Keen CI AYLW HP20 ...95 J2
Keen's La CHNR OX39 ...129 P6
Keepers CI LBUZ LU7 ...183 L5
Keepers Farm CI WDSR SL4 ...193 J2
Keep HI WYM HP11 ...153 J6
Keep HI Dr WYM HP11 ...153 K5
Keep Hill Rd WYM HP11 ...153 K6
Keilder CI HGDN/ICK UB10 ...182 C5
Keinches La
  RAYLNE/WEN HP22 ...81 J2
Keir Hardie Wy YEAD UB4 * ...183 N6
Keith Park Rd
  HGDN/ICK UB10 ...182 F3
Keith Rd HYS/HAR UB3 ...191 L4
Kelf CV HYS/HAR UB3 ...183 M9
Kellan Dr EAG/OLD/WT MK6 ...7 J4
Kelpatrick Rd SL SL1 ...179 N9
Kelsey Rd MDHD SL6 ...185 K4
Kelso CI RKW/CH/CXG WD3 ...52 D5
Kelso Rd RAYLW HP18 ...117 K3
Kelvin Dr NPAG MK16 ...22 C3
Kelvin Rd SHEN MK5 ...42 D6
Kemble Ct WLLN MK15 ...31 H7
Kempe Dr DTCH/LGLY SL3 ...189 C5
Kemps CI RKW/CH/CXG WD3 ...158 C2
Kempston Rd HGDN/ICK UB10 ...171 J9
Kempton Gdns BTCHLY MK3 ...52 D5
Kemsley Cha SLN SL2 ...179 N4

Kenbury CI HGDN/ICK UB10 ...170 G8
Kenchester BDWL MK13 ...29 P8
Kendal CI AYLS HP21 ...96 B9
  EBED/NFELT TW14 ...197 M7
  SLN SL2 ...188 C1
Kendal Dr SLN SL2 ...188 C1
Kendal Gdns LBUZ LU7 ...74 A2
Kendall PI SHEN MK5 ...41 M7
Kendalls CI HWYN HP13 ...153 M5
Kendals MS UX/CGN UB8 ...182 A4
Kendrick Rd DTCH/LGLY SL3 ...188 B4
Kenilworth Dr AYLW HP20 ...2 C1
  BTCHLY MK3 ...52 E4
Kenilworth Gdns YEAD UB4 ...183 M8
Kenmore CI YEAD UB4 ...183 M6
Kenneally WDSR SL4 ...192 G1
Kennedy Av WYM HP11 ...153 H6
Kennedy CI MDHD SL6 ...185 J1
  MLW SL7 ...164 E6
  SL SL1 ...179 N2
Kennel Rd TOW NN12 ...25 P2
Kennels Dr TOW NN12 ...25 L7
Kennet CI AYLS HP21 ...109 L2
  HWYN HP13 ...143 K9
Kennet Rd MDHD SL6 ...185 M8
Kennett CI BTCHLY MK3 ...52 E5
  DTCH/LGLY SL3 ...189 K4
Kennington CI NPAG MK16 ...31 H2
Kensington Dr
  CNH/GTH/TM MK8 ...41 P4
Kensworth Rd
  DUN/WHIP LU6 ...101 L3
Kent Av SLN SL2 ...188 C1
Kent CI UX/CGN UB8 ...182 C2
Kent Gdns RSLP HA4 ...171 N4
Kentmere Rd AYLS HP21 ...96 B9
Kenton CI MLW SL7 ...164 E7
Kenton's La WAR/TWY RG10 ...174 F8
  WDSR SL4 ...193 J1
Kenton Wy YEAD UB4 ...183 L6
Kents Rd GTLIN MK14 ...30 D5
Kent Wy MDHD SL6 ...185 L7
Kenway Dr AMSS HP7 ...146 D3
Kenwell CI WLLN MK15 ...43 J1
Kenwood CI MDHD SL6 ...185 K4
  WDR/YW UB7 ...190 C7
Kenwood Dr
  RKW/CH/CXG WD3 ...157 P2
Kenwood Ga
  RKW/CH/CXG WD3 ...43 H2
Keppel Av RMKN MK19 ...29 M3
Keppel Sp WDSR SL4 ...194 B6
Keppel St WDSR SL4 ...193 P1
Kepwick CNH/GTH/TM MK8 ...41 N5
Kercroft CNH/GTH/TM MK8 ...41 N5
Kernow Crs EAG/OLD/WT MK6 ...7 J5
Kerria PI BTCHLY MK3 ...52 F8
Kerry CI AYLW HP20 ...95 J4
Kersey Rd GTLIN MK14 ...30 C5
Kerstin CI HYS/HAR UB3 ...183 M1
Kesters Rd CSHM HP5 ...135 P5
Kestrel Av STA TW18 ...195 P9
Kestrel Ct BERK HP4 ...126 E1
  HWYN HP13 ...152 F1
Kestrel Crs BRACKY NN13 ...34 E2
Kestrel Dr HAZ/HC HP15 ...143 P6
  HYS/HAR UB3 ...191 K1
  RAYLNE/WEN HP22 * ...42 E4
Keswick CI DUN/WHIP LU6 ...87 K1
  SLN SL2 ...188 B1
Keswick Gdns RSLP HA4 ...171 K4
Keswick Rd RMKN MK19 ...19 J4
Ketchmere CI RAYLW HP18 ...106 A8
Ketelbey Nook
  WTR/OFPK MK7 ...44 B7
Ketton CI WLLN MK15 ...31 K6
Kew CI CNH/GTH/TM MK8 ...41 P5
Kewferry Dr NTHWD HA6 ...159 H5
Kewferry Rd NTHWD HA6 ...159 H6
Kew Gv WYM HP11 ...153 H6
Keyes Wy BUCK/WIN MK18 ...48 C1
Keynes CI NPAG MK16 ...31 L1
Keysham Av HEST TW5 ...191 N9
Khasiaberry WTR/OFPK MK7 ...43 P7
Kidd CI CNH/GTH/TM MK8 ...41 M1
Kidderminster Rd SLN SL2 ...179 L6
Kidwells CI MDHD SL6 ...177 M9
Kidwells Park Dr MDHD SL6 ...177 M9
Kildonan PI WOLV MK12 ...29 M3
Kilfillan Gdns BERK HP4 ...126 C2
Killarney Dr MDHD SL6 ...185 H1
Kiln Av AMS HP6 ...146 F2
Kiln CI BERK HP4 ...115 K9
  BUCK/WIN MK18 ...60 K6
  GTMIS/PWD HP16 ...133 K9
  HYS/HAR UB3 ...191 K7
Kiln Ct BEAC HP9 ...166 B1
Kiln Croft CI MLW SL7 ...164 C6
Kilner Rd AYLS HP21 ...95 M8
Kiln Flds MDHD SL6 ...166 E8
Kiln La CSHM HP5 ...136 D4
  FLKWH HP10 ...154 B1
  PRRI HP27 ...131 P7
  RAYLW HP18 ...107 L2
  SLN SL2 ...167 N6
Kilnwood SKCH HP14 ...142 B2
Kilpin Gn NPAG MK16 ...22 H9
Kilwinning Dr WRY MK15 ...31 J6
Kimbells CI RAYLW HP18 ...117 K3
Kimber CI WDSR SL4 ...189 K5
Kimberley Dr SL SL1 ...179 N6
Kimbers St SL SL1 ...179 N7
Kimber's La MDHD SL6 ...185 H1
Kimblewick Rd HADM HP17 ...121 L2
Kimbolton Ct GTLIN MK14 ...30 G5
Kinarstone Dr DUN/WHIP LU6 ...87 K2
Kincardine Rd BNEND SL8 ...42 E9

Kindermann Ct SHEN MK5 ...42 B7
Kindleton GTLIN MK14 ...30 F5
King Charles CI
  BUCK/WIN MK18 ...48 C1
King Edward Av AYLS HP21 ...3 K7
King Edward's Rd RSLP HA4 ...171 K6
King Edward St
  BDWL MK13 ...29 P6
  SL SL1 ...187 P3
King Edward VII Av
  WDSR SL4 ...188 A8
Kingfisher
  RAYLNE/WEN HP22 ...95 N3
Kingfisher CI NTHWD HA6 ...159 K9
Kingfisher Rd BRACKY NN13 ...34 C2
  BUCK/WIN MK18 ...48 C4
Kinghorn La MDHD SL6 ...177 K5
Kingham Dr MDHD SL6 ...177 P7
King James Wy HEN RG9 ...173 N6
King John's Ct
  STWL/WRAY TW19 ...194 E5
Kingsbridge EMV/FZ MK4 ...52 D1
Kingsbury AYLS HP21 ...95 M8
Kingsbury Dr WDSR SL4 ...194 C6
Kings CI BEAC HP9 ...166 E1
  CSTG HP8 ...156 F2
  NTHWD HA6 ...159 M6
  RAYLW HP18 ...104 D9
  THAME OX9 ...118 D5
Kings College Rd RSLP HA4 ...171 L6
King's Cross HADM HP17 ...107 L5
Kingsdale Rd BERK HP4 ...126 C2
Kingsend RSLP HA4 ...171 L6
Kingsend CI RSLP HA4 ...171 L6
Kingsey Rd THAME OX9 ...118 E7
Kings Farm Rd
  RKW/CH/CXG WD3 ...147 M8
Kingsfield WDSR SL4 ...187 H9
Kingsfield Piece TOW NN12 ...26 A1
Kingsfold BDWL MK13 ...29 N6
Kingsgate Rd MDHD SL6 ...185 L1
Kings Gv MDHD SL6 ...185 L1
Kings Head Pde
  RAYLNE/WEN HP22 * ...123 H1
Kingshill Av NTHLT UB5 ...183 P6
  YEAD UB4 ...183 L6
Kingshill Dr RMKN MK19 ...30 A5
Kingshill Rd HAZ/HC HP15 ...143 K8
Kingsland Rd AYLS HP21 ...95 M8
King's La CTMIS/PWD HP16 ...133 J1
  CTMIS/PWD HP16 ...134 B4
  MDHD SL6 ...165 H9
Kingsley CI NPAG MK16 ...30 C1
Kingsley Crs WYM HP11 ...153 H6
Kingsley Dr MLW SL7 ...164 C9
Kingsley Wk TRING HP23 ...112 E6
Kings Md DUN/WHIP LU6 ...86 A5
Kingsmead PRRI HP27 ...121 K7
Kings Meadow
  RAYLNE/WEN HP22 ...96 C3
Kingsmead Rd FLKWH HP10 ...154 A8
  WYM HP11 ...153 N7
Kings Oak CI PRRI HP27 ...121 L7
Kingsoge Leys MKV MK10 ...43 N2
Kings Ride FLKWH HP10 ...154 B1
Kings Rd AYLS HP21 ...95 P1
  BERK HP4 ...126 E2
  CSTG HP8 ...156 F2
  HEN RG9 ...173 P6
  SL SL1 ...188 A4
  THAME OX9 ...118 D5
  UX/CGN UB8 ...182 A4
  WDR/YW UB7 ...190 F1
  WDSR SL4 ...193 P1
  WYM HP11 ...153 P6
Kings Rw SKCH HP14 * ...140 A6
Kings St LBUZ LU7 ...183 M2
King Stable St WDSR SL4 ...187 P8
Kingston Av
  EBED/NFELT TW14 ...197 L5
  WDR/YW UB7 ...190 F1
Kingston CI RMKS/WB MK17 ...44 B2
Kingston HI CHNR OX39 ...139 L3
Kingston Rd HWYN HP13 ...153 K1
Kingston Rd HWYN HP13 ...155 K1
King St CSHM HP5 ...135 M5
  DUN/WHIP LU6 ...87 L1
  LBUZ LU7 ...183 M2
  SKCH HP14 ...140 A7
  SSTR MK17 ...151 L2
  TRING HP23 ...112 E3
Kingsway CFSP/GDCR SL9 ...168 L5
  HYS/HAR UB3 ...183 J8
  SL SL1 ...188 A2
  STWL/WRAY TW19 ...196 E5
Kingswear Rd RSLP HA4 ...171 N7
Kings Wd MLW SL7 ...155 C1
Kingswood Av FLKWH HP10 ...155 C1
Kingswood Ct MDHD SL6 ...185 M3
Kingswood Creek
  STWL/WRAY TW19 ...194 E4
Kingswood La RAYLW HP18 ...91 L2
Kingswood PI HWYN HP13 ...153 L1
Kingswood Rd HAZ/HC HP15 ...153 N1
Kings Yd RKW/CH/CXG WD3 ...158 C2
Kinloch PI WEAT MK2 ...53 K6
Kinnaird CI SL SL1 ...179 N6
Kinnear Ct CNH/GTH/TM MK8 ...41 M5
Kinross Dr BTCHLY MK3 ...52 D5
Kinson Gn AYL HP20 ...95 F1
Kipling Dr NPAG MK16 ...30 F1
Kipling Rd BTCHLY MK3 ...52 E6
Kippell HI OLN MK46 ...15 M2
Kirby CI NTHWD HA6 ...159 M6
Kirby Est WDR/YW UB7 * ...190 D1
Kirkeby CI GTLIN MK14 ...30 F5
Kirke CI SHEN MK5 ...42 C7
Kirkstall PI EAG/OLD/WT MK6 ...6 A7
Kirkstone Dr DUN/WHIP LU6 ...87 K2
Kirkwall Sp SL SL1 ...180 A6

Kirtle Rd CSHM HP5 ...135 N4
Kirtlington WLLN MK15 ...31 H8
Kitchener Rd WYM HP11 ...4 B5
Kite Fld BERK HP4 ...114 A7
Kite HI EAG/OLD/WT MK6 ...43 H4
Kitelee CI RMKN MK19 ...19 J5
Kiteleys Gn LBUZ LU7 ...74 A2
Kite Wood Rd FLKWH HP10 ...153 P8
Kitsbury Rd BERK HP4 ...126 C3
Kitsbury Ter BERK HP4 ...126 C3
Klondyke MLW SL7 ...164 D7
Knapp CI CNH/GTH/TM MK8 ...41 N5
Knapps Ct HEN RG9 ...173 N6
Knaves Beech Wy
  FLKWH HP10 ...154 A9
Knaves HI LBUZ LU7 ...74 B1
Knaves Hollow
  FLKWH HP10 ...154 B9
Knebworth Ga GTLIN MK14 ...30 C3
Knighton-Way La
  DEN/HRF UB9 ...182 B1
Knights CI DUN/WHIP LU6 ...86 A3
  RMKS/WB MK17 ...51 K3
  WDSR SL4 ...187 H9
Knightscote CI
  DEN/HRF UB9 ...158 D9
Knights HI WDSR SL4 ...4 A1
Knights Orch HHW HP1 ...115 P9
Knights Templar Wy
  WYM HP11 ...193 K1
Knoll CI NPAG MK16 ...21 M4
Knoll Crs NTHWD HA6 ...159 L9
Knolls CI RAYLNE/WEN HP22 ...83 P5
Knolls Vw DUN/WHIP LU6 * ...87 K1
The Knoll RMKS/WB MK17 * ...54 E2
Knolton Wy SLN SL2 ...188 C1
Knottocks CI BEAC HP9 ...155 M5
Knottocks Dr BEAC HP9 ...155 L5
Knottocks End BEAC HP9 ...155 L5
Knotts CI DUN/WHIP LU6 ...87 L3
Knowland Wy DEN/HRF UB9 ...169 P4
Knowles CI WDR/YW UB7 ...190 D1
Knowles Gn WEAT MK2 ...53 J4
Knowl Ga SHEN MK5 ...42 C5
Knowsley CI MDHD SL6 ...176 G7
Knox Br WTR/OFPK MK7 ...44 C6
Kop Hill Rd PRRI HP27 ...131 M4
Krohn CI BUCK/WIN MK18 ...48 C4
Krypton CI SHEN MK5 ...42 A7
Kynaston Av AYLS HP21 ...109 N2

L

Laburnham Rd MDHD SL6 ...185 K1
Laburnum Av WDR/YW UB7 ...190 F1
Laburnum CI MLW SL7 ...164 C6
Laburnum Ct LBUZ LU7 * ...74 B2
Laburnum Gv
  DTCH/LGLY SL3 ...189 J7
  WEAT MK2 ...53 L4
Laburnum Rd HWYW HP12 ...152 B6
  HYS/HAR UB3 ...191 M5
Laburnum Wy
  STWL/WRAY TW19 ...196 E5
Lacemaker Ct AMSS HP7 * ...145 N4
Lacemakers CHNR OX39 ...129 N6
  RAYLW HP18 ...
Lace Ms OLN MK46 ...15 M3
Lacey CI SKCH HP14 * ...142 B2
Laceys Dr HAZ/HC HP15 ...143 P6
Laceys Yd CSHM HP5 * ...135 M4
Lacy Dr WLLN MK15 ...30 G1
Ladbroke CI AYL HP20 ...2 D1
Ladbrooke Rd SL SL1 ...187 N4
Ladybridge Ter
  RBEDW MK43 * ...17 J2
Ladyday PI SL SL1 * ...187 N4
Ladygate La RSLP HA4 ...171 K3
Ladymead CI WTR/OFPK MK7 ...51 K3
Ladymeadow Ct MKV MK10 ...43 N1
Ladysmith Rd AYL HP20 ...99 H2
Lady Verney CI HWYN HP13 ...153 L1
Ladywalk RKW/CH/CXG WD3 ...157 M6
Laggan Rd MDHD SL6 ...177 N8
Laggan Sq MDHD SL6 ...177 N8
Lagger CI CSTG HP8 ...156 D2
Lagley Meadow BERK HP4 * ...185 N1
Lagonda CI NPAG MK16 ...31 H1
Laidon CI WEAT MK2 ...53 K6
Lake Av SL SL1 ...187 N1
Lake CI DUN/WHIP LU6 ...86 B1
Lake End CI MDHD SL6 ...186 B3
Lake End Rd WDSR SL4 ...186 B1
Laker CI EAG/OLD/WT MK6 ...43 J6
Lakeside AYLW HP20 ...95 K4
Lakeside CI RSLP HA4 ...171 P6
Lakeside Dr SLN SL2 ...180 B9
Lakeside Rd DTCH/LGLY SL3 ...189 H1
Lakes La BEAC HP9 ...167 K1
Lake St LBUZ LU7 ...183 M1
  NPAG MK16 ...21 H9
Lalande CI SHEN MK5 ...41 P9
Lamb CI WDR/YW UB7 ...190 D1
Lambert Av DTCH/LGLY SL3 ...188 F6
Lambert Wk MDHD SL6 ...177 N8
Lambeth Wk THAME OX9 ...118 D4
Lamb La WTR/OFPK MK7 ...44 A5
Lambourn CI HWYW HP12 ...152 A7
Lambourne Av AYLS HP21 ...109 N5
Lambourne CI UX/CGN UB8 ...185 K
Lambourne Dr MDHD SL6 ...185 K
Lambridge La HEN RG9 ...173 M4
Lambridge Wood Rd
  HEN RG9 ...173 M4

Lambscroft Wy
  CFSP/GDCR SL9 ...156 C9
Lambtons Wy
  BUCK/WIN MK18 ...60 D5
Lammas CI EAG/OLD/WT MK6 ...42 C7
Lammas Ct STA TW18 ...195 N9
Lammas HI EAG/OLD/WT MK6 ...43 H4
Lammas La RAYLW HP18 ...106 C3
Lammas Rd LBUZ LU7 ...179 H8
  SL SL1 ...179 H8
Lammas Wk SKCH HP14 ...151 J6
Lampitts Cross
  EAG/OLD/WT MK6 ...43 H6
Lamport CI EAG/OLD/WT MK6 ...42 A4
  CNH/GTH/TM MK8 ...41 A4
Lamva CI STSTR MK11 ...29 H8
Lancaster CI
  STWL/WRAY TW19 ...196 E5
Lancaster Ct HWYW HP12 * ...152 C6
Lancaster Dr BRACKY NN13 ...34 G4
  HHW HP1 * ...127 H9
Lancaster Rd UX/CGN UB8 ...182 D2
Lancaster Rd AYLS HP21 ...95 B9
Lancaster Ride FLKWH HP10 ...153 P2
  MDHD SL6 ...177 H8
Lanchester Rd RBEDW MK43 ...45 H3
Lancing Rd FELT TW13 ...197 M8
Lancot Av DUN/WHIP LU6 ...86 B1
Lancotbury CI DUN/WHIP LU6 ...86 E1
Lancresse CI UX/CGN UB8 ...182 D2
Lander Rd AYLS HP21 ...95 H4
Landford CI
  RKW/CH/CXG WD3 ...158 E2
Landrace Ct SHEN MK5 ...41 P9
Landsborough Ga
  WLLN MK15 ...31 J7
Lands End Gv EMV/FZ MK4 ...52 B1
The Lands LBUZ LU7 ...73 M7
Lane End BERK HP4 ...126 B1
Lane End Rd SKCH HP14 ...151 P5
Lanercost Crs WTR/OFPK MK7 ...43 J8
Lane's End LBUZ LU7 ...73 M7
The Lane CHNR OX39 ...129 P5
  RMKS/WB MK17 ...61 M4
Lanfranc Gdns WLLN MK15 ...31 J7
Langcliffe Dr BDWL MK13 ...28 L1
Langdale CI DUN/WHIP LU6 ...183 L5
Langdale Dr YEAD UB4 ...183 L5
  MDHD SL6 ...177 N9
  THAME OX9 ...118 D5
Langdale Rd DUN/WHIP LU6 ...87 K1
Langerstone La EMV/FZ MK4 ...52 B2
Langford PI WTR/OFPK MK7 ...43 N9
Langham CI RSLP HA4 ...183 P1
Langland CI NTHWD HA6 ...159 N6
Langland Rd
  EAG/OLD/WT MK6 ...43 J6
Langlands OLN MK46 ...10 D8
Langley Av RSLP HA4 ...171 P7
Langley Broom
  DTCH/LGLY SL3 ...189 H6
Langley Gm EMV/FZ MK4 ...52 B2
Langley Gv NTHWD HA6 ...159 H3
Langley Pk DTCH/LGLY SL3 * ...188 M8
Langley Park Rd IVER SL0 ...189 K1
Langley Quay
  DTCH/LGLY SL3 ...189 J3
Langley Rd DTCH/LGLY SL3 ...188 H8
Langston Gn HWYW HP12 ...152 C2
Langstone CI AYL HP20 * ...95 P4
Langton CI MDHD SL6 ...187 H2
Langton Dr
  CNH/GTH/TM MK8 ...41 N1
Langton Gv NTHWD HA6 ...159 H3
Langton's Meadow SLN SL2 ...159 N2
Langworth Dr YEAD UB4 ...183 P9
Langworthy End WDSR SL4 ...185 N1
Lanner Wk EAG/OLD/WT MK6 ...43 H4
Lannock Rd HYS/HAR UB3 ...183 M6
Lanrick Copse BERK HP4 ...114 C9
Lansbury Av
  EBED/NFELT TW14 ...197 M6
Lansbury Dr YEAD UB4 ...183 M5
Lansdell Av HWYW HP12 ...152 B6
Lansdowne CI SL SL1 ...188 A2
Lansdowne Rd AYL HP20 ...2 D1
  CSHM HP5 ...135 L2
  UX/CGN UB8 ...183 H9
Lansdowne Wk AYL HP20 ...2 D1
Lansdown Rd
  CFSP/GDCR SL9 ...156 F8
Lantern Wk MDHD SL6 ...177 N7
Lantern Wy WDR/YW UB7 ...190 E3
Lanthorn CI GTLIN MK14 ...30 E7
Lappetts La
  GTMIS/PWD HP16 ...134 C4
Larch CI AYL HP20 ...95 P3
  BTCHLY MK3 ...52 E8
  SLN SL2 ...188 M8
The Larches BERK HP4 ...115 H8
  HAZ/HC HP15 ...143 K9
  HGDN/ICK UB10 ...183 H5
Larchfield Rd MDHD SL6 ...185 K4
Larch Gv WEAT MK2 ...53 K4
The Larchlands FLKWH HP10 ...154 B1
Larchmoor Pk SLN SL2 ...180 C1
Larch Ri BERK HP4 ...114 C9

Larch Wd GTMIS/PWD HP16 ...133 P8
Lark Av STA TW18...........195 P9
Lark Cl BUCK/WIN MK18 ....48 C4
Larkfield Cl HWYN HP13 ....153 M1
Larkham Cl FELT TW13 ......197 L6
Larkin Cl NPAG MK16 ....20 C9
Larkings La RAYLNE/WEN SL3 ..180 D4
Lark Ri BRACKY NN13 ....34 C4
   HAZ/HG HP15 ....143 P6
Larkspur Av GTLIN MK14 ....30 E4
Larkspur Cl HWYN HP11.....127 N1
   RSLP HA4 ....171 H5
Larkspur Wy HAZ/HG HP15 ..143 P6
Larks Ri CSHM HP5 ....135 P6
Lark V AYL HP20 ....95 P4
Larne Rd RSLP HA4 ....171 M5
Larwood Pl EAG/OLD/WT MK6....7 C3
Lasborough Rd MKV MK10 ....44 A3
Lascelles Cl WLLN MK15 .....H5
Lascelles Rd DTCH/LGLY SL3 ..188 D4
Laser Cl SHEN MK5 ....42 C6
Lashlake Rd THAME OX9 .....118 D4
Lassell Gdns MDHD SL6 .....177 P9
Lastingham Gv EMV/FZ MK4 ..52 E7
Latchmoor Av
   CFSP/GDCR SL9 ....168 F2
Latchmoor Gv CFSP/GDCR SL9...168 F2
Latchmoor Wy
   RAYLNE/WEN SL9 ....168 F2
Lathbury Rd BRACKY NN13 ...34 F4
Latimer STSTR MK11 ....28 C9
Latimer Cl AMS HP6 ....146 E3
Latimer Rd AMS HP6 ....147 H2
   CSHM HP5 ....136 A4
Latimer Wy BEAC HP9 ....154 C4
Laud's Cl HEN RG9............2 B3
Launceston Ct SHEN MK5 .....42 B6
Launde WTR/OFPK MK7 ....43 P3
Launton Rd BIC OX26 ....66 A4
Laurel Av DTCH/LGLY SL3 ....188 C3
Laurel Bank HHS/BOV HP3 ....127 P5
Laurel Cl CNH/GTH/TM MK8 ..41 N5
   DTCH/LGLY SL3 ....189 N8
   PRRI HP27 ....132 C8
Laurel Ct AMS HP6 ....135 N9
   IVER SL0 * 181 M3
Laurel Dr FLKWH HP10 ......155 P7
   SKCH HP14 ....142 D4
Laurel La WDR/YW UB7 .....190 E5
Laurel Rd CFSP/GDCR SL9 ...156 F9
Laurels Rd SL1 ....181 M5
The Laurels BERK HP4 ......115 K8
   DBGH MK1 ....6 D7
   HHW HP1 * 152 C6
Laurel Wy AYLS HP21 ....3 G9
Lauries Cl HHW HP1..........142 A3
Lauser Rd STWL/WRAY TW19 ..196 C6
Lautrec Wy AYLW HP19 ....95 H5
Lautree Gdns MDHD SL6 .....177 L1
Lavender Cl AYLS HP21 ....3 G9
Lavender Gv WTR/OFPK MK7 ..43 N5
Lavender Ri WDR/YW UB7 ....190 G3
Lavender Rd UX/CGN UB8 ....182 E8
Lavender Wk AYLS HP21 * 95 K9
Lavric Rd OLN MK46 ....15 N7
Lavric Rd AYLS HP21 ....171 L5
Lawford Dr
   RKW/CH/CXG WD3 ....147 L8
Lawford Rd
   RKW/CH/CXG WD3 ....147 L8
Lawkland SLN SL2 ....179 N6
Lawn Av WDR/YW UB7 ....190 C3
Lawn Cl DTCH/LGLY SL3 .....188 C4
   RSLP HA4 ....171 M8
Lawn Hi RAYLW HP18 ....67 N7
Lawn House La RAYLW HP18 ..67 K4
Lawn Rd UX/CGN UB8 ....182 C7
The Lawns DTCH/LGLY SL3 ..189 N8
   FLKWH HP10 ....143 P9
   HHW HP1 ....127 N1
   RAYLW HP18 ....90 G6
The Lawn DTCH/LGLY SL3 * ..188 C3
Lawrence Cl AYL HP20 ....3 H1
Lawrence Dr
   HGDN/ICK UB10 ....171 J9
Lawrence Rd
   GTMIS/PWD HP16 ....133 K7
Lawrence Sq SL14 ....183 J5
Lawrence Wy SL SL1 ....178 C8
Laws Cl RBEDW MK43 ....33 L4
Laws Cft BRACKY NN13 ......34 F5
Lawsone Ri HWYN HP13 ......5 H1
Lawson Gdns PIN HA5 ....171 P1
Lawson Pl SHEN MK5 ....42 B7
Lawson Rd HEN RG9..........2 D8
Laxton Gn MDHD SL6 ....177 M4
Layburn Crs DTCH/LGLY SL3 ..189 K7
Lay Rd AYLW HP19 ....95 K6
Layter's Av CFSP/GDCR SL9 ..156 E9
Layter's Av South
   CFSP/GDCR SL9 ....156 E9
Layter's Cl CFSP/GDCR SL9 ..156 E9
Layters Grn La
   CFSP/GDCR SL9 ....156 D9
Layters Wy CFSP/GDCR SL9 ..168 E8
Leachcroft CFSP/GDCR SL9 ..156 E8
Leach Rd AYLS HP21 ....3 B6
Lea Cl MLW SL7 ....164 D3
Lea Crs RSLP HA4 ....171 M9
Leacroft Rd WDR/YW UB7 ...190 D4
Leacroft Rd IVER SL0 ....189 M1
Leaders Cl RAYLNE/WEN SL9 ..83 H5
Leaf Cl NTHWD HA6 ....147 K8
Leafield Rd CNH/GTH/TM MK8 ..41 N3
Leafy La TRING HP23 ....112 C5
Leaholme Cl MKV MK10 .....44 B5
Leaholme Waye RSLP HA4 ...171 H4
Lea La MLW SL7 * 118 C1
Leamington Pl YEAD UB4 ...183 N1
Leapingwell La

BUCK/WIN MK18 ....60 D5
Learoyd Wy LBUZ LU7 ....75 H3
Leary Crs NPAG MK16 ....31 M1
Leas Cl HWYN HP13 ....153 M2
Leas Dr IVER SL0 ....181 N9
Leasdale NPAC MK16 ....14 B9
Leaside Ct MDHD SL6 ....183 H6
Leasowe Pl BDWL MK13 ......6 A1
Leather La GTMIS/PWD HP16 ..133 M2
Leaver Rd HEN RG9...........173 N7
Leckhampstead Rd
   BUCK/WIN MK18 ....38 D4
   RMKN MK19 ....39 K2
Ledborough Ga BEAC HP9 ....155 H5
Ledborough La BEAC HP9 ....155 K6
Ledborough Wd BEAC HP9 ...155 J4
Ledburn Gv LBUZ LU7 ....74 C3
Ledger La MDHD SL6 ....186 B9
Ledger's Rd SL SL1 ....178 B3
Ledgemore La HHNE HP2 ....101 P9
Leeches Wy LBUZ LU7 ....84 E9
Lee Ct THAME OX9 ....118 B5
Lee Crs HADM HP17 ....108 F1
Leeds Rd SL SL1 ....181 N2
Lee Farm Cl CSHM HP5 ......136 B3
Lee La MDHD SL6 ....176 E5
Lee Rd AYLS HP21 ....131 M9
   PRRI HP27 ....131 K8
   RAYLNE/WEN SL9 ....79 R7
Lees Av AYL NTHWD HA6 ....155 L9
Lees Cl MDHD SL6 ....185 H2
   TOW NN12 ....155 G4
Lees Gdns MDHD SL6 ....185 H2
Leeson Gdns WDSR SL4 ......187 J5
Lees Pde HGDN/ICK UB10 * ..183 H7
Lees Rd UX/CGN UB8 ....185 H7
The Lee NTHWD HA6 ....159 M5
Leggfield Ter HHW HP1 ......127 P2
Leicester Cl HEN RG9.........173 P5
Leigh Hi EMV/FZ MK4 ....52 D1
Leigh Pk DTCH/LGLY SL3 * ..188 E8
Leigh Rd SL SL1 ....187 M1
Leigh Sq WDSR SL4 ....193 H1
Leigh St WYM HP11 ....4 C4
Leighton Buzzard Rd
   HHW HP1 ....115 N4
Leighton Gdns MDHD SL6 ...177 M8
Leighton Rd DUN/WHIP LU6 ..85 P2
   DUN/WHIP LU6 ....87 H1
   LBUZ LU7 ....63 N9
   LBUZ LU7 ....74 D2
   LBUZ LU7 ....75 J4
   RAYLNE/WEN HP22 ......85 L8
   RMKS/WB MK17 ....73 L5
Leighton St RMKS/WB MK17 ..55 J5
Leiston Sp SL SL1 ....180 A9
Leith Cl SL SL1 ....188 C2
Leith Rd AYLW HP19 ....95 J7
Lembrook Wk AYLS HP21 .....95 L9
Lenborough Cl
   BUCK/WIN MK18 ....48 A4
Lenborough Rd
   BUCK/WIN MK18 ....48 A4
Lennon Dr CNH/GTH/TM MK8 ..41 N5
Lennox Rd WEAT MK2 ....53 J2
Lent Green La SL SL1 ....178 F7
Lenthall Cl BDWL MK13 ......30 A8
Lent Rise Rd MDHD SL6 .....178 F9
Leominster Ga
   WTR/OFPK MK7 ....43 N3
Leonards Cl RAYLW HP18 ....90 M7
Leonards Lee EMV/FZ MK4 ...51 P1
Leon Av WEAT MK2 ....53 K3
Leopold Rd LBUZ LU7 ....74 B2
Lerwick Dr SLN SL2 ....180 A8
Le Sutton WTR/OFPK MK7 ...44 B9
Lester Gv HAZ/HG HP15 .....143 H2
Lesters Rd MDHD SL6 ....177 K2
Leston Cl DUN/WHIP LU6 ....87 M3
Letchfield CSHM HP5 ....136 M4
Letchworth Av
   EBED/NFELT TW14 ....197 M6
Letter Box La PRRI HP27 * ...132 C8
Leven Cl LBUZ LU7 ....73 P2
   WEAT MK2 ....53 K6
Leven Wy HYS/HAR UB3 .....183 L9
Levings Cl AYLW HP19 ....95 J4
Lewes Ct SL SL1 ....181 M4
Lewins Rd CFSP/GDCR SL9 ..168 F1
Lewins Wy SL SL1 ....187 K1
Lewis Cl DEN/HRF UB9 ......158 C9
   NPAG MK16 ....20 B7
Lewis La CFSP/GDCR SL9 ....156 D8
Lexham Gdns AMS HP6 ......145 N1
Lexington Av MDHD SL6 .....185 J2
Leybourne Rd
   HGDN/ICK UB10 ....183 J4
Leyburne Cl LBUZ LU7 ....74 A9
Leyburne Gdns CHNR OX39 ..129 N5
Leyfield Rd AYLS HP21 ....95 N9
Leyland Pl EAG/OLD/WT MK6 ..7 F5
Leylands La
   STWL/WRAY TW19 ....195 P4
Leys La DEN/HRF UB9 ....158 D4
Leys La BUCK/WIN SL18 .....57 H2
Leys Rd SHEN MK5 ....42 B7
   BUCK/WIN MK18 ....38 C9
   RMKS/WB MK17 ....44 F8
Leys Vw NPAG MK16 ....21 M5
Leywood Cl AMS HP6 ....145 P9
Lichfield Down
   MDHD SL6 ....177 M5
Lichfield Rd NTHWD HA6 ....170 H1
Liddall Wy WDR/YW UB7 ....190 F2
Liddell WDSR SL4 ....192 G2
Liddell Wy LBUZ LU7 ....75 H4
Liffre Dr RAYLNE/WEN HP22 ..111 H8
Lightfoot Ct WTR/OFPK MK7 ..43 N7
Lightlands La MDHD SL6 ....177 M3

Ligo Av RAYLNE/WEN HP22 ..110 C4
Lilac Av RAYLNE/WEN HP22 ..110 C4
Lilac Cl HWYN MK17 ....52 C8
Lilac Gdns HYS/HAR UB3 ....183 L9
Lilac Pl WDR/YW UB7 ....190 F1
Lilleshall Av MKV MK10 ......43 H5
Lilley Wy SL SL1 ....187 J2
Lillibrooke Crs MDHD SL6 ...184 C4
Lillyfee Farm La
   FLKWH HP10 ....166 C5
Lilly Bottom La PRRI HP27 ...132 A5
Lilly Hi OLN MK46 ....15 M3
Lily Rd WDR/YW UB7 ....190 D1
Lily's Wk WYM HP11 ....4 B9
Limbaud Cl WYM HP11 * 127 J5
Lime Av BUCK/WIN MK18 ....48 D4
   WDR/YW UB7 ....190 F1
   WDSR SL4 ....188 B3
   WYM HP11 * 153 K5
Lime Cl HAZ/HG HP15 ....143 N8
   NPAG MK16 ....31 H1
   RNHPTN NN7 ....12 G5
   RSLP HA4 ....171 M1
Lime Gv CNH OX39...........43 H1
   HYS/HAR UB3 ....191 K1
   LBUZ LU7 ....74 C1
   RMKS/WB MK17 ....44 F8
   RSLP HA4 ....171 M4
Limerick La SL SL1 ....43 H1
Lime Rd PRRI HP27 ....131 K1
   TOW NN12 ....155 G4
Limes Av AYLS HP21 ....96 B8
The Limes AMS HP6 ....135 M8
   RKW/CH/CXG WD3 * 158 C1
   STSTR MK11 ....28 C9
   WDSR SL4 ....192 E1
   WGM HP11 * 53 L3
Lime St DUN/WHIP LU6 ......87 K2
Limes Wy RAYLW HP18 ....117 K2
Lime Tree Cl HAZ/HG HP15 ..143 K4
Lime Tree Wk AMSS HP7 .....146 B3
Lime Wk DEN/HRF UB9 ......182 C1
Limmer La HWYW HP12 .....152 B7
Limmers Md HAZ/HG HP15 ..143 J3
Lincesdale Gv SHEN MK5 ....42 B5
Linchfield HWYN HP13 ......153 K4
Linchfield Rd DTCH/LGLY SL3 ..188 E4
Lincoln Ct AYLW HP19 ....95 K4
Lincoln Cl DUN/HR/TOD LU5 ..87 N2
   RAYLNE/WEN HP22 ......110 B4
Lincoln Ct BERK HP4 ....115 J2
Lincoln Hatch La SL SL1 .....178 D3
Lincoln Pk AMSS HP7 ....146 A3
Lincoln Pl THAME OX9 ....118 D5
Lincoln Rd CFSP/GDCR SL9 ..152 E5
   HWYW HP12 ....152 E5
   MDHD SL6 ....177 H8
   NTHWD HA6 ....170 G9
Lincoln's Inn HWYW HP12 * ..152 E5
The Lincolns
   GTMIS/PWD HP16 ....133 P8
Lincoln Wy SL SL1 ....187 H1
Lincombe Slade LBUZ LU7 ..74 A4
Lincroft RBEDW MK43 ....33 L4
Linden Av MDHD SL6 ....185 J1
   RSLP HA4 ....171 N6
Linden Cl RSLP HA4 ....171 N6
Linden Ct CFSP/GDCR SL9 ...156 C9
   SLN SL2 ....179 N4
Linden End AYLS HP21 ....95 P9
Linden Gv GTLIN MK14 ......30 E5
Linden Lea
   RAYLNE/WEN HP22 ......111 H9
Linden Sq DEN/HRF UB9 ....158 A6
The Lindens HHS/BOV HP3 ..127 P5
Linden Ter UX/CGN UB8 .....182 D9
Linden Wy HADM HP17 ......107 K8
Lindisfarne Dr MKV MK10 ...43 J4
Lindo Cl LBUZ LU7 ....74 E3
Lindlings HHW HP1 ....127 H5
Lindo Cl CSHM HP5 ....135 M5
Lindores Cft WTR/OFPK MK7 ..43 P5
Lindores Rd MDHD SL6 ......185 P7
Lindsay Av HWYW HP12 .....152 A4
Lindsay Cl STWL/WRAY TW19 ..196 D5
Lindsey Gdns
   EBED/NFELT TW14 ....197 K6
Lindsey Rd DEN/HRF UB9 ...170 A4
Lines Hi RAYLNE/WEN HP22 ..142 B5
Lines Rd SKCH HP14 ....151 K5
Linfields AMSS HP7 ....146 E4
Linford Av MKV MK10 ....30 C1
Linford La WLLN MK15 ....30 C1
Lingfield WOLV MK12 ....29 H3
Lingfield Cl HWYN HP13 .....115 K5
   NTHWD HA6 ....170 F8
Lingholm Cl MDHD SL6 .....185 J1
Linington Av CSHM HP5 .....136 A2
Link Cl HWYW HP12 ....152 D5
Link Rd DTCH/LGLY SL3 .....188 E7
   EBED/NFELT TW14 ....197 M6
   GTMIS/PWD HP16 ....133 P7
Links Ap FLKWH HP10 ....165 N1
Links Rd FLKWH HP10 ....165 N1
Links Wy FLKWH HP10 ......165 N1
   NTHWD HA6 ....170 F8
Linkswood Rd SL SL1 ....175 H8
Linnet Cl HWYW HP12 ....152 D5
Linnet Dr PRRI HP27 ....92 C5
Linney Head
   DNNY MK46 ....101 K1
Linslade Cl PIN HA5 ....171 N3
Linslade Rd LBUZ LU7 ....64 D1
Lintlaw Pl BTCHLY MK3 .....43 H7
Linton Cl BDWL MK13 ....30 C1
Lintott Ct STWL/WRAY TW19 ..196 B4
Linwood Gv LBUZ LU7 ....74 D3
The Linx BTCHLY MK3 ....52 G1

Lionel Av RAYLNE/WEN HP22 ..110 G9
Lionel Ct RAYLNE/WEN HP22 ..110 G9
Lion Meadow HEN RG9.......160 C7
Lipscombe Dr
   BUCK/WIN MK18 ....48 C2
Lipscomb La SHEN MK5 .....42 A5
Lisburn Pth AYL HP20 ....95 P5
Lisle Rd HWYN HP13 ....4 C1
Lisleys Fld HAZ/HG HP15 ....143 K4
Lismore Pk SLN SL2 ....180 B9
Lissel Rd EAG/OLD/WT MK6 ..52 B5
Lister Rd MDHD SL6 ....185 N1
Lister Ct AYLS HP21 * 109 N1
Liston Rd MLW SL7 ....164 D7
Litcham Sp SL SL1 ....179 P9
Lithgow's Rd HTHAIR TW6 ..197 J2
Little Balmer BUCK/WIN MK18 ..48 C1
Little Benty WDR/YW UB7 ...190 C3
Little Bridge Rd BERK HP4 ..126 F1
Little Britain RAYLW HP18 ...93 M1
Littlebrook Av SL SL1 ....179 J8
Little Buntings WDSR SL4 ...193 K6
Little Catherells HHW HP1 ..115 N9
Little Cl AYL HP20 ....2 D7
   FLKWH HP10 ....154 A8
   HWYW HP12 ....152 E7
Littlecote CNH/GTH/TM MK8 ..42 A3
Littledown Rd SL SL1 ....188 B2
Little Elms HYS/HAR UB3 ....191 K8
Littlefield Gn MDHD SL6 ....184 E3
Little Greencroft CSHM HP5 ..125 L9
Little Habton EMV/FZ MK4 * ..52 B1
Little Hame MKV MK10 ......43 M1
Little Ham La PRRI HP27 ....121 K8
Little Hampden Cl
   RAYLNE/WEN HP22 ......123 H1
Little Heath La BERK HP4 ...127 K3
Little Hill LBUZ LU7 ....75 J7
   RKW/CH/CXG WD3 ....147 L8
Little Hivings CSHM HP5 ....125 L9
Little Hollis
   GTMIS/PWD HP16 ....133 L5
Little Hoo TRING HP23 ......112 D2
Little Horwood Rd
   RMKS/WB MK17 ....50 E8
Little Hundridge La
   GTMIS/PWD HP16 ....135 L5
Little Kimble Hl HADM HP17 ..121 P4
Little La PRRI HP27 ....131 L8
   RNHPTN NN7 ....7 L9
Little Linford La RMKN MK19 ..30 L1
Little London
   RAYLNE/WEN HP22 ......81 J5
   RNHPTN NN7 ....29 F9
Little London Cl
   UX/CGN UB8 ....183 H8
Little London Gv RAYLNE/WEN HP18..90 G9
Little Marlow Rd MLW SL7 ..164 C6
Little Marsh Rd RBICN OX27 ..66 C6
Little Meadow WDSR SL4 ....42 B6
Little Mollards
   CNH/GTH/TM MK8 ....41 M1
Little Orchard Cl PRRI HP27 ..121 K8
Little Orchards
   RAYLNE/WEN HP22 ......95 P4
Little Pk HHS/BOV HP3 ......137 J1
Littleport Sp SL SL1 ....180 A9
Little Reeves Av AMSS HP7 ..146 B4
Little Rd HYS/HAR UB3 ......191 K5
   SL SL1 ....166 G4
Little Shardeloes AMSS HP7 ..145 L4
Little Spinney RBEDW MK43 ..33 N2
Little Spring CSHM HP5 .....135 M9
Little Stanton GTLIN MK14 ..30 D5
Little Stocking SHEN MK5 ...42 A9
Little Stream CE NTHWD HA6 ..159 L5
Little St RNHPTN NN7 ....8 C1
Little Sutton La
   DTCH/LGLY SL3 ....189 L6
Little Tring Rd TRING HP23 ..98 D2
Little Twye Rd TRING HP23 ..124 D2
Little Windmill Hl
   KGLGY WD4 ....137 N5
Little Wd SKCH HP14 ....140 A9
Little Woodlands WDSR SL4 ..193 K6
Littleworth LBUZ LU7 ....73 L6
Littleworth Rd HWYN HP15 ..142 F9
Liverpool Rd SL SL1 ....179 M9
Livesey Hi SHEN MK5 ....42 B7
Livingstone Dr WLLN MK15 ..31 J8
Llanbury Cl CFSP/GDCR SL9 ..156 C9
Llandores Cft WTR/OFPK MK7 ..43 P5
Lloyds EAG/OLD/WT MK6 ....7 H4
Loakes Rd WYM HP11 ....4 C5
Lochinvar Cl SL SL1 ....187 M3
Lochnell Rd BERK HP4 ....114 E8
Locke Dr LBUZ LU7 ....74 B2
Locke Gdns DTCH/LGLY SL3 ..178 A9
Locke Rd WEAT MK2 ....53 J4
Lockes Cl WDSR SL4 ....187 H4
Lockhart Cl DUN/WHIP LU6 ..87 M2
Lock Island MLW SL7 ....164 E6
Lock La MDHD SL6 ....185 N2
   RMKN MK19 ....28 C3
Lock Rd MLW SL7 ....164 D4
Lockton CE EMV/FZ MK4 .....52 E8
Lock View La DBGH MK1 ....53 J1
Locomotive Dr
   EBED/NFELT TW14 ....197 M6
Loddon Cl AYLS HP21 ....109 M5
Loddon Dr MDHD SL6 ....178 A4
Loddon Rd BNEND SL8 ......165 N5
Loddon Sp SL SL1 ....180 A9
Lodge BUCK/WIN MK18 .....48 C4
   MLW SL7 ....164 C6
   SL SL1 ....164 G3
   UX/CGN UB8 ....182 C7

Lodge Farm Ct RMKN MK19 ..19 H8
Lodge Ga MDHD SL6 ....14 D6
Lodge La CSTG HP8 ....147 H4
   GTMIS/PWD HP16 ....133 J7
   HHS/BOV HP3 ....65 L5
Lodge Pk TOW NN12 ....26 A2
Lodge Rd RBEDW MK43 .....33 J8
Lodge Wy ASHF TW15 ......196 E8
   WDSR SL4 ....193 J2
Lodore Gn HGDN/ICK UB10 ..170 A4
Logan Rock EMV/FZ MK4 ....52 B5
Lollards Cl AMS HP6 ....145 N1
Lombardy Dr BERK HP4 .....126 F2
Lomond Dr LBUZ LU7 ....53 J8
   WEAT MK2 ....53 J8
London End La
   RMKS/WB MK17 ....54 B2
London Rd BERK HP4 ....126 F2
   BUCK/WIN MK18 ....48 C4
   CSTG HP8 ....147 H4
   DTCH/LGLY SL3 ....188 E3
   DUN/WHIP LU6 ....87 N5
   FLKWH HP10 ....154 A8
   GTMIS/PWD HP16 ....133 J7
   HHW HP1 ....127 K4
   MKV MK10 ....31 M2
   RAYLNE/WEN HP22 ......111 N2
   RAYLNE/WEN HP22 ......123 H2
   RKW/CH/CXG WD3 ....158 E1
   RMKN MK19 ....19 P8
   RMKS/WB MK17 ....42 B5
   SHEN MK5 ....42 B5
   STWL/WRAY TW19 ....116 F9
   THAME OX9 ....116 F9
   TRING HP23 ....112 F3
   WYM HP11 ....53 J7
London Rd East AMSS HP7 ..145 L4
London Rd West AMSS HP7 ..145 N4
Long Ayres WTR/OFPK MK7 ..43 N9
Longbottom La BEAC HP9 ...155 M7
Longbourn WDSR SL4 ....193 L2
Longbournes RBEDW MK43 ..33 L4
Longbridge Cl TRING HP23 ..98 B5
Long Bridge UX/CGN UB8 ..182 B5
Long Chaulden HHW HP1 ...127 H3
Long Chaulden HHW HP1 ...127 H3
Longcliffe Pth OXHEY WD19 ..159 N5
Long Crendon Rd
   RAYLW HP18 ....117 K2
Longcroft
   RAYLNE/WEN HP22 ......111 M1
Longcroft Av
   RAYLNE/WEN HP22 ......111 K8
Longcroft La HHS/BOV HP3 ..137 L1
Long Croft Rd
   STWL/WRAY TW19 ....157 M5
Longcross WLLN MK15 ......30 D7
Longdown Hl PRRI HP27 .....121 P7
Long Dr SL SL1 ....154 D4
   WDR/YW UB7 ....190 E3
Longfellow Dr NPAG MK16 ..7 P7
Longfield Dr AMS HP6 ....133 P8
   SLN SL2 ....167 P8
Longfield Gdns TRING HP23 ..112 C3
Longfield Rd CSHM HP5 .....125 L9
   TRING HP23 ....112 C3
Longfield Wy
   STWL/WRAY TW19 ....196 E7
Longford Wy
   STWL/WRAY TW19 ....196 E7
Long Furlong HADM HP17 ...107 K8
   HADM HP17 ....121 P4
Long Gv BEAC HP9 ....155 N6
Long Hale LBUZ LU7 ....98 G4
Long Half Acre MDHD SL6 ..184 B3
Long Hedge LBUZ LU7 ......74 B2
Longhedge HHW HP1 ....127 K4
Long Hide PRRI HP27 ....121 C9
Longhook Gdns NTHLT UB5 ..183 L8
Longlands Ct
   BUCK/WIN MK18 ....60 C5
Longland Wy WDSR SL4 ....193 K6
Long La HGDN/ICK UB10 ...182 G5
   HHS/BOV HP3 ....137 L8
   MDHD SL6 ....177 J5
   OLN MK46 ....15 M5
   RKW/CH/CXG WD3 ....196 E7
   STWL/WRAY TW19 ....196 F7
Longleat Ct
   CNH/GTH/TM MK8 ....41 P3
Longleat Gdns MDHD SL6 ...177 J6
Longleat Wy
   EBED/NFELT TW14 ....197 L6
Long Ley LBUZ LU7 ....74 E9
Long Leys AYLW HP19 ....95 J5
Long Marston La LBUZ LU7 ..98 C7
Long Marston Rd TRING HP23 ..98 C5
Long Massey OLN MK46 ....15 N6
Longmead La SL SL1 ....179 H5
Long Meadow AYLS HP21 ...95 P4
   CSHM HP5 ....135 N1
Long Meadow CW PRRI HP27 ..121 L8
Long Mdw HYS/HAR UB3 ....191 N1
Longmire OLN MK46 ....10 D8
Longmore Cl
   RKW/CH/CXG WD3 ....157 P4
Long Orchard Dr
   FLKWH HP10 ....154 A2
Long Pk AMS HP6 ....135 N8
Long Park Cl AMS HP6 ......135 N8
Long Park Wy AMS HP6 .....135 N8
Longpeak Cl EMV/FZ MK4 ..52 E8
Long Readings La SLN SL2 ..179 M6
Long Rw GTMIS/PWD HP16 * ..133 G6

Longstone Rd *IVER* SL0 ....181 L5
Long Street Rd *RMKN* MK19 ....19 H2
Longview *BEAC* HP9 ....166 D9
Long Vw *BERK* HP4 ....114 C8
Longville *WOLV* MK12 ....29 L8
Long Wk *CSTG* HP8 ....146 G5
  WDSR SL4 * 193 P4
The Long Wk *WDSR* SL4 ....193 P7
Long Wall *HADM* HP17 ....107 K9
Longwick Rd *PRRI* HP27 ....21 J7
Long Wood Dr *BEAC* HP9 ....156 B6
Longwood La *AMSS* HP7 ....145 K9
Longworth Dr *MDHD* SL6 ....178 A7
Lonsdale Cl
  UX/CGN UB8 ....183 J9
Lonsdale Wy *MDHD* SL6 ....186 A6
Loosen Dr *MDHD* SL6 ....184 G4
Loosley Hl *PRRI* HP27 ....131 M6
Lord Knyvett Cl
  STWL/WRAY TW19 ....196 D5
Lord Knyvetts Ct
  STWL/WRAY TW19 * 196 E5
Lord Mayors Dr *SL* SL2 ....179 K2
Lords Cl *WEAT* MK2 ....53 J2
Lords Md *DUN/WHIP* LU6 ....86 A2
Lordsmead *RBEDW* MK43 ....33 N5
Lords Mill Ct *CSHM* HP5 ....135 N5
Lords Ter *DUN/WHIP* LU6 * 86 A2
Loriner Pl *GTLIN* MK14 ....9 L5
Loring Rd *BERK* HP4 ....126 C2
  WDSR SL4 ....187 K9
Lorne Cl *SL* SL1 ....187 M4
Lorraine Cl *HWYN* HP13 ....153 L2
Loseley Ct
  CRIN/GTH/TM MK8 ....41 P5
Losfield Rd *WDSR* SL4 ....187 J9
Lossie Dr *IVER* SL0 ....189 K1
Lothersdale *BDWL* MK15 ....30 B8
Lothian Av *YEAD* UB4 ....183 P8
Lothian Cl *BTCHLY* MK5 ....52 E1
Lott Meadow *AYLS* HP21 ....109 M5
Louches La *SKCH* HP14 ....142 D5
Loudhams Rd *AMSS* HP7 ....146 E3
Loudhams Wood La
  CSTG HP8 ....146 E4
Loughborough Rd *BDWL* MK15 .....30 A9
Louise Wk *HHS/BOV* HP3 ....137 J2
Lovatt St *NPAC* MK16 ....11 J1
Lovatt Dr *BTCHLY* MK5 ....52 D3
Love Green La *IVER* SL0 ....181 M8
Love Hill La *DTCH/LGLY* SL3 .....189 J1
Lovejoy La *WDSR* SL4 ....193 H1
Lovelace Cl *MDHD* SL6 ....185 L1
Love La *WYM* SL0 ....181 M9
Lovel End *CFSP/GDCR* SL9 ....156 F7
Lovell Cl *HEN* RG9 ....173 N8
Lovel Rd *CFSP/GDCR* SL9 ....156 F7
Lovett Cl *DUN/WHIP* LU6 ....74 F3
Lovett Gdns *MDHD* SL6 ....178 A5
Lovett Rd *DEN/HRF* UB9 ....170 C1
Lovetts End *LBUZ* LU7 ....72 C1
Lovibonds Av *WDR/YW* UB7 ......182 F9
Lowbrook Cl *AYLS* HP21 ....110 A2
Lowbrook Dr *MDHD* SL6 ....184 G4
Lowdell Cl *WDR/YW* UB7 ....182 E9
Lowdon Cl *WYM* HP11 ....153 L3
Lower Boyndon Rd
  MDHD SL6 ....185 K1
Lower Britwell Rd *SL* SL1 ....179 H7
Lower Church St
  RAYLW HP18 ....107 K3
  SKCH HP14 ....140 K4
Lower Cippenham La *SL* SL1 ......49 K3
Lower Cl *WYM* HP19 ....95 K8
Lower Cookham Rd
  MDHD SL6 ....178 A5
Lower Dr *BEAC* HP9 ....155 H5
Lower End *BUCK/WIN* MK18 ....49 K3
  RAYLNE/WEN HP22 ....83 H6
  RAYLW HP18 ....92 G4
  RBICS/W OX25 ....76 E8
  RMKS/WB MK17 ....52 C8
  RNHPTN NN7 ....12 C6
Lower End Rd
  RMKS/WB MK17 ....44 F4
Lower Farm La *RAYLW* HP18 ......117 K2
Lower Farm Ga *HADM* HP17 .....108 C3
Lower Fourth St *CMK* MK9 6
Lower Furney Cl
  HWYN HP13 ....153 K2
Lower Gn *RAYLW* HP18 ....92 F1
Lower Green La
  RAYLW HP18 ....106 F4
Lower Icknield Wy
  CHNR OX39 ....129 G5
  HADM HP17 ....121 K6
  PRRI HP27 ....130 E1
  RAYLNE/WEN HP22 ....111 N1
  TRING HP23 ....98 A3
Lower Kings Rd *BERK* HP4 ....114 C9
Lower Lees Rd *SLN* SL2 ....179 L6
Lower Lodge La
  HAZ/HG HP15 ....143 N5
Lower Md *IVER* SL0 ....181 M6
Lower Ninth St *CMK* MK9 7
Lower Pound La *MLW* SL7 ....176 C1
Lower Rdg *BNEND* SL8 ....145 N5
Lower Riding *BEAC* HP9 ....154 F9
Lower Rd *AYLS* HP21 ....109 P3
  CFSP/GDCR SL9 ....156 G8
  CHNR OX39 ....129 G5
  DEN/HRF UB9 ....158 D1
  MDHD SL6 ....177 M7
  PRRI HP27 ....130 A1
  RAYLNE/WEN HP22 ....111 J3
  TRING HP23 ....98 A1
Lower Sales *HHW* HP1 ....127 P5
Lower Second St *CMK* MK9 6
Lower Stonehayes
  GTLIN MK14 ....22 A3
Lower St *RAYLNE/WEN* HP22 .....79 L3
Lower Tenth St *CMK* MK9 ....7 F2
Lower Third St *CMK* MK9 ....6 C4
Lower Twelfth St *CMK* MK9 ....7 H1
Lower Wk *MDHD* SL6 ....48 C9
  RMKS/WB MK17 ....54 A9
Lower Whf *BUCK/WIN* MK18 ....48 C2
Lowes Cl *SKCH* HP14 ....139 N6
Lowestoft Dr *SL* SL1 ....178 C9
Lowfield Cl *HAZ/HG* HP15 ....141 M4
Lowfield Wy *HAZ/HG* HP15 ....143 P8
Lowick Pl *HAZ/HG* HP15 ....143 P8
Lowland Rd *HAZ/HG* HP15 ....52 D5
Lowlands Crs *HAZ/HG* HP15 .....143 K2
Lowlands Rd
  STWL/WRAY TW19 ....196 D4
Lowman Wy *AYLS* HP21 ....109 M2
Lowndes Av *CSHM* HP5 ....135 M8
Lowndes Wy *BUCK/WIN* MK18 .....60 C5
Lownes Gv *SHEN* MK5 ....41 P5
Lowswood Rd *NTHWD* HA6 ....159 J8
Lowther Rd *DUN/WHIP* LU6 ....87 L2
Loxboro Dr *EMV/FZ* MK4 ....42 C8
Loxboro Hl *SKCH* HP14 ....42 C8
Loxley Rd *BERK* HP4 ....114 A8
Loxwood Cl
  EBED/NFELT TW14 ....197 K7
Loyne Cl *LBUZ* LU7 ....98 B4
Lucas Rd *LEAG/OLD/WT* MK6 .....41 L6
Lucas La *HWYN* HP13 ....5 J4
Lucas Wood Cl *HAZ/HG* HP15 ....153 K5
Luccombe *EMV/FZ* MK4 ....42 D9
Lucks Hl *HHW* HP1 ....127 N1
Lucy La *SHEN* MK5 ....42 B4
Ludgate *EAG/OLD/WT* MK6 ....42 C5
Ludgershall Rd *RAYLW* HP18 ......91 H4
  RBICS/W OX25 ....76 B9
Ludlow Cl *BTCHLY* MK3 ....52 F4
Ludlow Dr *THAME* OX9 ....118 C4
Ludlow Md *OXHEY* WD19 ....159 P3
Ludlow Wk *FLKWH* HP10 ....153 N6
Ludlow Pl *AYLS* HP21 ....109 K1
Ludlow Rd *FELT* TW13 ....197 N9
  MDHD SL6 ....185 L2
Ludsden Gv *THAME* OX9 ....118 B4
Luff Cl *WDSR* SL4 ....193 J2
Lufford Rd *GTLIN* MK14 ....10 F3
Luke Pl *MKV* MK10 ....43 M1
Luker Av *HEN* RG9 ....175 N5
Lukes Lea *TRING* HP23 ....98 E6
Lullingston Dr *BDWL* MK15 ....29 N8
Lulworth Waye *YEAD* UB4 ....183 P9
Lundy Dr *HYS/HAR* UB3 ....191 L5
Lupin Cl *WDR/YW* UB7 ....190 D6
Lupin Ct *AYLS* HP21 * 9 K9
Lupin Wk *AYLS* HP21 ....109 K1
Lupton Rd *THAME* OX9 ....118 C4
Lych Gate Wk *HYS/HAR* UB3 .....191 M1
Lycrome La *CSHM* HP5 ....135 H1
Lycrome Rd *CSHM* HP5 ....136 A1
Lydford Av *SLN* SL2 ....179 P8
Lydiard *CNH/GTH/TM* MK8 ....41 N3
Lydiard Cl *AYLS* HP21 ....110 B2
Lydsey Cl *SLN* SL2 ....179 L6
Le Green Rd *CSHM* HP5 ....136 A5
Lyell Rd *BERK* HP4 ....100 C9
The Lye *BERK* HP4 ....100 C9
Lyme Av *BERK* HP4 ....115 P7
Lymington Dr *RSLP* HA4 ....171 P7
Lynch Cl *UX/CGN* UB8 ....182 C5
Lynchen Cl *NELT* TW5 ....195 J1
Lynch Hill La *SLN* SL2 ....179 J7
The Lynch *UX/CGN* UB8 ....182 D5
Lynden Cl *MDHD* SL6 ....185 P7
Lyndhurst Av *MDHD* SL6 * 177 L2
  PIN HA5 ....159 P8
Lyndhurst Cl *HCDN/ICK* UB10 ....183 J3
Lyndhurst Gdns *PIN* HA5 ....159 P8
Lyndon Cl *GTMIS/PWD* HP16 .....135 J5
Lyndon Gdns *HAZ/HG* HP15 ......153 L2
Lyndwood Pde *WDSR* SL4 * 194 C5
Lyneham Gdns *MDHD* SL6 ....177 H7
Lyne Wy *HHW* HP1 ....137 J2
Lynford Pde *HAZ/HG* HP15 * 144 A4
Lynher Cl *AYLS* HP21 ....109 L2
Lynhurst Crs
  HCDN/ICK UB10 ....183 J3
Lynhurst Rd *HCDN/ICK* UB10 .....183 H3
Lynmouth Crs *EMV/FZ* MK4 ....42 C8
Lynmouth Dr *RSLP* HA4 ....171 P7
Lynott Cl *CNH/GTH/TM* MK8 ......41 N6
Lynton Cl *AYLS* HP21 ....110 C1
Lynton Rd *CSHM* HP5 ....135 M1
Lynwood Av *DTCH/LGLY* SL3 .....188 F4
Lynwood Dr *NTHWD* HA6 ....159 J8
Lynwood Rd *AYLS* HP21 ....109 P1
Lyon Rd *DBGH* MK1 ....53 J8
Lysa Gdns *LBUZ* LU7 ....75 H5
Lysander Cl *HHW* HP1 ....127 H9
Lysander Rd *RSLP* HA4 ....171 K7
Lywood Rd *LBUZ* LU7 ....74 C3

M

Macdonald Cl *AMS* HP6 ....135 N8
Mackenzie St *SL* SL1 ....188 B3
Maclaren Ct *EAG/OLD/WT* MK6 .....2 F7
Madeira Av *MLW* SL7 ....187 P9
Madeira Rd *AYLS* HP21 ....109 N9
Mafeking Rd
  STWL/WRAY TW19 ....195 K8
Mafeking Rw *WTLGN* OX49 ....138 C7
Magdalen Cl *BRACKY* NN13 ....24 C5
Magdalen Mdw
  BRACKY NN13 ....34 C3
Magenta Cl *WEAT* MK2 ....53 K5

Magna Carta La
  STWL/WRAY TW19 ....194 G7
Magnolia Ct
  HCDN/ICK UB10 * 183 H2
Magnolia Dene
  HAZ/HG HP15 ....143 M9
Magnolia Gdns
  DTCH/LGLY SL3 ....188 D4
Magnolia St *WDR/YW* UB7 ....190 D6
Magnolia Wy *FLKWH* HP10 ....153 N9
  RAYLNE/WEN HP22 ....42 D5
  SHEN MK5 ....88 D5
Magpie La *AMSS* HP7 ....145 K9
  BRACKY NN13 ....34 G6
  FLKWH HP10 ....153 N9
Magpie Wy *BUCK/WIN* MK18 .....60 C5
Mahler La *WTR/OFPK* MK7 ....44 A1
Mahlon Av *RSLP* HA4 ....183 P7
Maidenhead Rd *BDWL* MK13 ....6 C1
Maidenhead Ct Pk
  MDHD SL6 ....177 P5
Maidenhead Rd *MDHD* SL6 ....177 M8
Maidstone Rd *MKV* MK10 ....44 B2
Main Av *NTHWD* HA6 ....159 K2
Main Dr *CFSP/GDCR* SL9 ....168 F3
  IVER SL0 ....189 N4
  TOW NN12 ....27 L3
Main Rd *BRACKY* NN13 ....23 J3
  NPAC MK16 ....23 A5
  PRRI HP27 ....131 N7
  RAYLW HP18 ....78 A4
  RAYLW HP18 ....93 L6
  RMKS/WB MK17 ....62 B5
  SKCH HP14 ....142 C3
  WDSR SL4 * 44 F3
Main Rd North *BERK* HP4 ....8 F3
Main Rd South *BERK* HP4 ....100 E2
Main St *BRACKY* NN13 ....35 L4
  BRACKY NN13 ....36 A7
  BUCK/WIN MK18 ....37 N8
  BUCK/WIN MK18 ....38 C9
  BUCK/WIN MK18 ....38 D3
  BUCK/WIN MK18 ....47 N8
  BUCK/WIN MK18 ....47 H5
  BUCK/WIN MK18 ....58 D7
  BUCK/WIN MK18 ....57 J9
  BUCK/WIN MK18 ....57 E1
  RAYLNE/WEN HP22 ....110 E4
  RAYLW HP18 ....77 M2
  RAYLW HP18 ....92 C4
  RBICN OX27 ....66 C2
  RBICN OX27 ....67 L4
  RMKN MK19 ....40 C3
  RMKN MK19 ....19 J3
  RMKS/WB MK17 ....61 M4
Maise Webster Cl
  STWL/WRAY TW19 * 196 D6
Maitland Dr *RAYLW* HP18 ....11 K3
Maitland Rd
  RAYLNE/WEN HP22 ....111 K7
Major's Farm Rd
  DTCH/LGLY SL3 ....188 G8
Makins Rd *HEN* RG9 ....175 P6
Malbons Ct *EAG/OLD/WT* MK6 .....42 E5
Malcolm Rd *HCDN/ICK* UB10 ......170 F9
Malders La *MDHD* SL6 ....177 L6
Malet Cl *SKCH* HP14 ....140 B6
Malins Ga *GTLIN* MK14 ....30 E5
Malkin Dr *BEAC* HP9 ....155 G7
Mallard Cl *RAYLNE/WEN* HP22 .....95 N3
Mallard Cft *HADM* HP17 ....3 F5
Mallard Dr *BUCK/WIN* MK18 ....48 C3
  SL SL1 ....187 K1
Mallard Wy *NTHWD* HA6 ....159 J7
Mallets End
  RAYLNE/WEN HP22 ....79 M4
Mallett Cl *STSTR* MK11 ....28 C8
Mallow Ga *GTLIN* MK14 ....30 E9
Mallow Pk *MDHD* SL6 ....177 H8
The Mallows *HCDN/ICK* UB10 ....183 H3
Malm Cl *RKW/CXG* WD3 ....158 D2
Malpas Rd *SLN* SL2 ....179 L6
Malt House Cl *WDSR* SL4 ....194 D4
Malthouse Ms
  DEN/HRF UB9 158
Malthouse Sq *BEAC* HP9 ....167 K1
Malthouse Wy *MLW* SL7 ....164 D8
Malting Cl *NPAC* MK16 ....22 A5
Malting La *TRING* HP23 ....113 P1
Maltings Cl *LBUZ* LU7 ....72 C1
  RBEDW MK43 ....34 A3
Maltings Rd *RMKN* MK19 ....19 H9
The Maltings *AMSS* HP7 * 145 L4
  BUCK/WIN MK18 ....37 N8
  BUCK/WIN MK18 ....48 H5
  LBUZ LU7 ....72 C1
  OLN MK46 * 15 N4
Malting Wy *RNHPTN* NN7 ....12 C4
Malt La *BRACKY* NN13 ....24 C5
Maltmans Av *CFSP/GDCR* SL9 ....168 F1
Malton Av *SL* SL1 ....179 M9
Malton Cl *MKV* MK10 ....43 N1
Malvern Cl *HCDN/ICK* UB10 ......170 C1
  HWYN HP13 ....4 A2
Malvern Dr *LBUZ* LU7 ....75 J5
Malvern Rd *AYLS* HP21 ....96 C1
  HYS/HAR UB3 ....191 L2
  STSTR MK11 ....29 H9
Malvern Wk *BUCK/WIN* MK18 .....58 C7
Mandelvis Dr *MKV* MK10 ....42 G4
Mandeville Dr *AYLS* HP21 ....109 N1
Mandeville Rd
  GTMIS/PWD HP16 ....135 J5
  RAYLNE/WEN HP22 ....111 J3
Manditt Cl *SHEN* MK5 ....42 B4
Manningtree Rd *RSLP* HA4 ....171 N9
Mannock Wy *LBUZ* LU7 ....75 H4

Manor Cl *BERK* HP4 * 126 E1
  HAZ/HG HP15 ....143 N9
  MKV MK10 ....43 M1
  RBEDW MK43 ....11 L5
  RMKN MK19 ....28 G3
  RMKS/WB MK17 ....63 L3
  RNHPTN NN7 ....12 A3
  RSLP HA4 ....171 M6
Manor Cottages
  NTHWD HA6 ....159 M8
Manor Ct *BRACKY* NN13 ....35 H5
  DEN/HRF UB9 ....158 C9
  MLW SL7 ....164 C6
  SL SL1 ....187 K2
Manor Court Yd *HWYN* HP13 ....5 F1
Manor Crs *BEAC* HP9 ....155 P5
  RAYLNE/WEN HP22 ....111 P4
Manor Dr *AMS* HP6 ....135 M9
  AYL HP20 ....3 G1
  LBUZ LU7 ....72 E1
  RAYLNE/WEN HP22 ....110 E4
  WDSR SL4 ....193 K2
Manor Farm Cottages
Manor Farm La *LBUZ* LU7 ....74 A9
Manorfields Rd *RMKN* MK19 ....28 G3
Manor Gdns *BUCK/WIN* MK18 .....60 B3
  FLKWH HP10 ....166 C4
Manor Gv *MDHD* SL6 ....186 B9
Manor House Cl *AYL* HP20 ....3 G3
Manor House Dr
  NTHWD HA6 ....159 H7
Manor House La
  DTCH/LGLY SL3 ....188 D9
Manor La *CFSP/GDCR* SL9 ....168 G5
  FELT TW13 ....197 N8
  HYS/HAR UB3 ....191 K7
  WDSR SL4 ....193 K2
Manor Park Av *PRRI* HP27 ....131 J2
Manor Pk *BUCK/WIN* MK18 ....38 D6
  STA TW18 ....195 M4
Manor Pl *EBED/NFELT* TW14 .....197 N8
Manor Pound Rd *LBUZ* LU7 ....84 E9
Manor Rd *AYL* HP20 ....3 F2
  BEAC HP9 ....154 G5
  BRACKY NN13 ....34 C5
  BUCK/WIN MK18 ....38 C9
  CSHM HP5 ....135 M2
  HAZ/HG HP15 ....143 N9
  HYS/HAR UB3 ....191 K7
  LBUZ LU7 ....84 D9
  MDHD SL6 ....185 L3
  NPAC MK16 ....30 A7
  PRRI HP27 ....131 J2
  RAYLNE/WEN HP22 ....80 E1
  RAYLW HP18 ....92 C4
  RAYLNE/WEN HP22 ....111 J3
  RAYLW HP18 ....104 D1
  RMKS/WB MK17 ....61 M4
  RSLP HA4 ....171 K6
  THAME OX9 ....119 H6
  TRING HP23 ....113 L2
  WDSR SL4 ....193 K2
  WEAT MK2 ....53 L4
  WOLV MK12 ....29 H6
Manor St *BERK* HP4 * 126 F1
  BUCK/WIN MK18 ....48 A3
Manor Vw *HAZ/HG* HP15 ....143 N9
Manor Wy *CSHM* HP5 ....135 M2
  MDHD SL6 ....185 N1
  RSLP HA4 ....171 M6
  TOW NN12 ....18 A4
Manor Waye *UX/CGN* UB8 ....182 C5
Mansard Cl *TRING* HP23 ....113 P3
Mansel Cl *HYS/HAR* UB3 ....191 K1
Manse Cl *HYS/HAR* UB3 ....191 K7
  STSTR MK11 ....28 F7
Mansell Cl *CSHM* HP5 ....135 M1
Mansel St *SHEN* MK5 * 180 D8
  WDSR SL4 ....193 J1
Mansfield Av *RSLP* HA4 ....171 P6
Mansfield Cl *DR* YEAD* UB4 ......183 L7
Manshead Ct *STSTR* MK11 ....29 H9
Manson Ter *HYS/HAR* UB3 * 191 L1
Mansion Hl
  RAYLNE/WEN HP22 ....111 K6
Mansion La East *SL* SL1 ....189 L2
  RBEDW MK43 ....11 L5
The Mansions *OLN* MK46 * 15 N4
Manton Cl *HYS/HAR* UB3 ....191 L1
Manton Rd *DUN/WHIP* LU6 ....86 F9
Maple Av *WDR/YW* UB7 ....190 E1
Maple Cl *BRACKY* NN13 ....23 P3
  HAZ/HG HP15 ....143 N9
  HWYN HP13 ....152 C5
  MDHD SL6 ....185 L4
  RBEDW MK43 ....11 H5
Maple Crs *SLN* SL2 ....188 D1
Mapledean *WOLV* MK12 ....29 L8
Mapledurham
  WTR/OFPK MK7 ....43 M9
Maplefield La *CSTG* HP8 ....146 D5
Maple Gdns *ASHF* TW15 ....196 B6
Maple Gv *AYLS* HP21 ....96 C1
  RMKS/WB MK17 ....61 M4
Maple Leys *BUCK/WIN* MK18 ......58 C7
Maple Lodge Cl
  RKW/CXG WD3 ....157 N4
  RKW/CXG WD3 ....166 E1
Maple Rd *THAME* OX9 ....118 C4
The Maples *BNEND* SL8 * 165 H6
  RAYLNE/WEN HP22 ....111 J3
Maple Wy *DUN/WHIP* LU6 ....87 L2
  FELT TW13 ....197 P8
  RBEDW MK43 ....11 L5
Maplewood Gdns *BEAC* HP9 ......154 F9
Maplin Pk *DTCH/LGLY* SL3 ....189 K4

Mapridge Green La
  GTMIS/PWD HP16 ....133 K3
Mara Pl *CMK* MK9 ....42 C1
Marbeck Cl *WDSR* SL4 ....187 H9
March Meadow
  RMKS/WB MK17 ....44 B5
March Pl *AYLW* HP19 ....95 K7
Marcia Ct *SL* SL1 ....187 K2
Marcourt Rd *BERK* HP4 * 140 B7
Mardale Av *DUN/WHIP* LU6 ....87 L2
Mardle Rd *AYLS* HP21 ....110 A4
Maree Cl *LBUZ* LU7 ....74 A2
Marefield Rd *MLW* SL7 ....164 D7
Mare Lees *BUCK/WIN* MK18 ....48 A3
Marescroft Rd *SLN* SL2 ....179 J7
Margam Crs *WTR/OFPK* MK7 ....43 N3
Marigold Pl *GTLIN* MK14 ....9 L5
Marigold Wk *HAZ/HG* HP15 ......143 M5
Marina Dr *DUN/WHIP* LU6 ....86 G1
  WOLV MK12 ....29 M8
Marina Wy *IVER* SL0 ....189 H1
  SL SL1 ....187 H1
Marios La *DEN/HRF* UB9 ....158 L2
Marish Whf *DTCH/LGLY* SL3 * 188 L3
Marjoram Pl *GTLIN* MK14 ....30 E9
Mark Dr *CFSP/GDCR* SL9 ....156 F8
Markenfield Pl *EMV/FZ* MK4 ....51 N2
Market Ct *LBUZ* LU7 * 74 A2
Market Hl *BUCK/WIN* MK18 ....48 B2
  EAG/OLD/WT MK6 ....43 H4
  RAYLNE/WEN HP22 ....79 L2
Market La *DTCH/LGLY* SL3 ....189 L4
  CFSP/GDCR SL9 ....156 F8
  DTCH/LGLY SL3 * 188 D4
  HEN RG9 ....15 M4
  OLN MK46 ....15 N4
Market Sq *AYL* HP20 ....3 F4
  BUCK/WIN MK18 ....48 B2
  LBUZ LU7 ....74 A2
  RMKN MK19 ....19 J3
The Market Square Ml
  WYM HP11 ....5 F6
Market St *AYL* HP20 ....3 F4
  MDHD SL6 ....185 M9
Market Wk *AMSS* HP7 * 145 M4
Markham Cl *AYLW* HP19 ....95 J8
Marks Orch *BUCK/WIN* MK18 .....70 B2
Marlborough Av *RSLP* HA4 ....171 L3
Marlborough Crs
  HYS/HAR UB3 ....191 K8
Marlborough Cft
  BRACKY NN13 ....35 H6
Marlborough Ga *CMK* MK9 ....42 F7
Marlborough Pde
  HCDN/ICK UB10 ....183 H7
Marlborough Rd *AYLS* HP21 ......109 N2
  DTCH/LGLY SL3 ....188 D4
  HCDN/ICK UB10 ....183 H7
  HYS/HAR UB3 ....191 K8
  SL SL1 ....184 L1
Marlborough St
  EAG/OLD/WT MK6 ....43 K7
  GTLIN MK14 ....10 C9
Marley Flds *LBUZ* LU7 ....75 H3
Marley Gv *CNH/GTH/TM* MK8 .....41 N5
Marlin Cl *DUN/WHIP* LU6 ....114 B9
Marlin Copse *BERK* HP4 ....126 C2
Marlin Ct *MLW* SL7 ....164 B6
Marlin Hl *TRING* HP23 ....112 E5
Marlins Cl *RKW/CXG* WD3 ....147 N4
Marlins End *BERK* HP4 ....126 C2
Marlins Mdw *WATW* WD18 ....164 C5
Marlow Bottom *MLW* SL7 ....164 C2
Marlow Common *MLW* SL7 ....163 P7
Marlow Dr *NPAC* MK16 ....30 A8
Marlow Gdns *HYS/HAR* UB3 ......191 K4
Marlow Hl *WYM* HP11 ....152 F7
Marlow Ml *MLW* SL7 ....164 A5
Marlow Rd *HEN* RG9 ....174 A8
  MDHD SL6 ....184 D1
  MLW SL7 ....164 A3
  MLW SL7 ....164 J4
  MLW SL7 ....176 D2
  SKCH HP14 ....141 L7
  WYM HP11 ....152 F6
Marmion Rd *HEN* RG9 ....174 A8
Marquis Cl *RMKS/WB* MK17 ....54 K4
Marram Ct *EAG/OLD/WT* MK6 ......30 E9
Marrans Ter *HYS/HAR* UB3 * 191 L1
Marriott Cl
  EBED/NFELT TW14 ....197 K5
Marriotts Av
  GTMIS/PWD HP16 ....135 C4
Marriott's Cl *HADM* HP17 ....107 M3
Marriott's La *HADM* HP17 ....107 K9
Marriott's Wy *HADM* HP17 ....107 K9
Marriott Ter
  RKW/CXG WD3 ....147 P6
Marrod's Bottom
  AMSS HP7 ....154 C9
Marron La *WOLV* MK12 ....29 L8
Marroway
  RAYLNE/WEN HP22 ....110 D5
Marshall Dr *YEAD* UB4 ....183 M8
Marshalls La *MLW* SL7 ....164 A5
Marshalls Lea
  RAYLNE/WEN HP22 ....96 C3
Marsham La *AYLS* HP21 ....110 A2
Marsham Lg *CFSP/GDCR* SL9 ....156 H3
Marsham Lo
  CFSP/GDCR SL9 ....168 G4
Marsham Wy
  CFSP/GDCR SL9 ....168 G5
Marsh Dr *EMV/FZ* MK4 ....54 C3
Marshcroft La *TRING* HP23 ....99 H9
Marsh Gn *MKV* MK14 ....10 F3
Marsh Rd *AYLS* HP21 ....63 L3
Marsh Gibbon Rd *RAYLW* HP18 ..92 D4
Marsh La *MDHD* SL6 ....177 N5
  RAYLNE/WEN HP22 ....109 N6
Marsh Rd *HADM* HP17 ....121 M1
  RAYLW HP18 ....117 J2

The Marsh *RBEDW* MK43 ....11 K5
Marshworth
   EAG/OLD/WT MK6 ....43 K6
Marston Cl *CSHM* HP5 ....125 L9
Marston Ct *TRING* HP25 * 97 F7
Marstonfields Rd
   BUCK/WIN MK18 ....70 D7
Marston Hl
   RAYLNE/WEN HP22 ....70 E9
Marston Rd *BUCK/WIN* MK18 ....70 B3
   THAME OX9 ....118 E4
Marsworth Rd *LBUZ* LU7 ....99 H3
Martell Cl *WTR/OFPK* MK7 ....43 N8
Martial Daire Bvd
   BRACKY NN13 ....34 C4
Martin Cl *BUCK/WIN* MK18 ....48 D4
   GTLIN MK14 ....30 F7
Martindale *IVER* SL0 ....181 L7
Martindale Rd *HHW* HP1 ....127 P1
Martingale Pl *GTLIN* MK14 ....30 F8
Martin Rd *MDHD* SL6 ....177 M8
   SL SL1 ....188 A4
The Martins Dr *LBUZ* LU7 ....74 D1
Martinsend La
   GTMIS/PWD HP16 ....133 L5
Martin's Pln *SLN* SL2 ....180 B6
Marunden Gn *SLN* SL2 ....179 K6
Marvell Av *YEAD* UB4 ....183 N8
Marwood Cl *EMV/FZ* MK4 ....42 D9
Marygold Wk *AMS* HP6 ....146 E3
Maryland Rd *WLLN* MK15 ....31 H5
Maryside *DTCH/LGLY* SL3 ....188 C3
Mary's Mdl *HAZ/HG* HP15 ....143 M7
Masefield Cl *NPAG* MK16 ....30 C1
Masefield Gv *BTCHLY* MK5 ....52 C4
Masefield La *YEAD* UB4 ....183 P7
Masefield Wy
   STWL/WRAY TW19 ....196 F7
Maslin Dr *EAG/OLD/WT* MK6 ....43 J1
Mason Cl *GTLIN* MK14 ....30 C5
Masons Cl *GTMIS/PWD* HP16 ....133 J1
Mason's Ct *AYLW* HP19 ....95 K8
Masons Rd *SL* SL1 ....187 J1
Massie Cl *WLLN* MK15 ....31 H4
Mathiesen Rd *BDWL* MK13 ....30 A7
Mathisen Wy *DTCH/LGLY* SL3 ....189 N4
Matilda Gdns *SHEN* MK5 ....42 B6
Matlock Rd *AYL* HP20 ....95 P5
Matthew Ct *SHEN* MK5 ....42 B6
Maude Cl *BEAC* HP9 ....155 L9
Maude Rd *BEAC* HP9 ....155 L9
Maud Jane's Cl *LBUZ* LU7 ....99 J2
Maudsley Cl *SHEN* MK5 ....42 B6
Mauduit Cl *RMKN* MK19 ....19 J5
Maulden Gdns *GTLIN* MK14 ....30 C4
Maundsey Cl *DUN/WHIP* LU6 ....87 L3
Maurice Mt *HAZ/HG* HP15 ....143 M5
Mavoncliff Dr *EMV/FZ* MK4 ....52 A3
Maxham *SHEN* MK5 ....42 A9
Maxwell Cl *HYS/HAR* UB3 ....191 N1
   RKW/CH/CXG WD3 ....158 A2
Maxwell Dr *HAZ/HG* HP15 ....143 P6
Maxwell Rd *BEAC* HP9 ....155 J7
   NTHWD HA6 ....159 K7
   WDR/YW UB7 ....190 E5
Maybank Gdns *PIN* HA5 ....171 N3
Maybrook Gdns *HWYN* HP13 ....5 J3
Maybury Ct *SL* SL1 ....179 H8
Maybush Gdns
   GTMIS/PWD HP16 ....133 J6
Maybush Wk *DUN/MR* MK46 ....15 M8
May Cl *DUN/WHIP* LU6 ....86 A2
Maycock Gv *NTHWD* HA6 ....159 P9
Maycroft *PIN* HA5 ....159 P9
Mayditch Pl *BDWL* MK13 ....42 C7
Mayer Gdns *SHEN* MK5 ....42 C7
Mayfield Cl *HGDN/ICK* UB10 ....163 K6
Mayfield Dr *WDSR* SL4 ....193 L2
Mayfield Rd
   DUN/HR/TOD LU5 ....87 M1
   FLKWH HP10 ....166 C3
Mayflower Wy *SLN* SL2 ....179 N1
Mayflower Rd *SL* HADM HP17 ....109 H1
   RSLP HA4 ....171 J4
Maygoods *UX/CGN* UB8 * 182 C8
Mayhall La *AMS* HP6 ....135 M8
Mayhew Crs *HWYN* HP13 ....5 K2
Maylands Dr *UX/CGN* UB8 ....182 D2
Maynard Cl *BDWL* MK13 ....42 A1
Maypole Rd *MDHD* SL6 ....178 A8
Mays Rd *RBEDW* MK45 ....17 J1
Mays Wy *TOW* NN12 ....2 C4
McConnell Dr *WOLV* MK12 ....29 M6
McDougall Rd *BERK* HP4 ....126 F1
McEwen Ride
   RAYLNE/WEN HP22 ....111 K9
McKenzie Cl *BUCK/WIN* MK18 ....48 B3
McLellan Pl *HWYW* HP12 ....152 D5
McLernon Wy
   BUCK/WIN MK18 ....60 B6
Mead Acre *PRRI* HP27 ....121 K8
Mead Av *DTCH/LGLY* SL3 ....189 N8
Meade Cl *DEN/HRF* UB9 ....170 A7
   DTCH/LGLY SL3 ....164 K5
   MLW SL7 ....164 C8
   PRRI HP27 ....121 K7
Meades La *CSHM* HP5 ....135 M5
Meadfield Av *DTCH/LGLY* SL3 ....189 J4
Meadfield Rd
   DTCH/LGLY SL3 ....189 K4
Mead House La *YEAD* UB4 ....183 K7
Meadoway *BUCK/WIN* MK18 ....58 D3
   HADM HP17 ....109 H3
Meadowbank Cl
   RAYLW HP18 ....106 A4
Meadowbank Gdns
   HEST TW5 ....191 N9

   HSLWW TW4 ....197 N1
Meadowbrook *TRING* HP25 ....98 F9
Meadowbrook Cl
   DTCH/LGLY SL3 ....195 N1
Meadow Cl *CSHM* HP5 * 135 M2
   LBUZ LU7 ....72 C8
   MLW SL7 ....164 F8
   RAYLW HP18 ....104 D2
   RSLP HA4 ....171 M4
   TRING HP23 ....112 E2
   WDSR SL4 ....194 D4
   WYM HP11 ....153 M6
Meadowcot La *AMSS* HP7 ....145 K8
Meadowcroft *AYLW* HP19 ....95 K5
   BERK HP4 ....113 P7
   CFSP/GDCR SL9 ....156 F9
Meadow Dr *AMS* HP6 ....146 E4
   PRRI HP27 ....120 F7
Meadow Gdns
   BUCK/WIN MK18 ....48 C5
Meadow Ga *BUCK/WIN* MK18 ....48 F9
Meadow La *AMSS* HP7 ....145 K7
   GTMIS/PWD HP16 ....133 J9
Meadow Hl *AMSS* HP7 ....145 K7
Meadow La *BEAC* HP9 ....155 K8
   GTMIS/PWD HP16 ....134 C3
   LBUZ LU7 ....99 J4
   MKV MK10 ....43 M3
   WDSR SL4 ....187 N8
Meadow Rd *BERK* HP4 ....114 B8
   CHNR OX39 ....129 P6
   DTCH/LGLY SL3 ....189 J4
   HEN RG9 ....174 A4
Meadow Road Cl *BERK* HP4 ....114 C8
Meadowside *BERK* HP4 ....156 B7
Meadow Spring *RAYLW* HP18 ....91 N6
The Meadows *AMSS* HP7 ....146 A3
   RSLP HA4 ....155 P5
   FLKWH HP10 ....165 P1
   RAYLNE/WEN HP22 ....81 H1
Meadowsweet
   WTR/OFPK MK7 ....43 P7
Meadow Vw *CSTG* HP8 ....156 C5
   MLW SL7 ....164 E5
   RAYLW HP18 * 118 C1
   RMKS/WB MK17 ....45 H6
   STWL/WRAY TW19 ....195 P4
   TOW NN12 ....2 C8
   UX/CGN UB8 * 182 C2
Meadow View La *MDHD* SL6 ....168 D1
Meadow View Rd *YEAD* UB4 ....183 K7
Meadow Wk *BNEND* SL8 ....165 N4
   FLKWH HP10 ....154 A1
Meadow Wy *AMS* HP6 ....134 G8
   AYL HP20 ....3 K2
   HHS/BOV HP3 ....27 P5
   LBUZ LU7 ....72 C4
   LBUZ LU7 ....75 H7
   MDHD SL6 ....186 B9
   MDHD SL6 ....186 D3
   RSLP HA4 ....171 P4
   THAME OX9 ....118 C4
   WDSR SL4 ....194 B1
Mead Pl *RKW/CH/CXG* WD3 ....158 B1
Mead Platt *SKCH* HP14 ....139 P6
Mead Rd *UX/CGN* UB8 ....182 D2
Meads Cl *BDWL* MK13 ....30 A5
Meadslade *RNHPTN* NN7 ....12 F5
The Meads *BERK* HP4 ....114 B8
   DUN/WHIP LU6 ....86 A3
   UX/CGN UB8 ....182 E7
Mead St *FLKWH* HP10 ....153 N6
The Mead *BEAC* HP9 * 155 J8
   HGDN/ICK UB10 ....170 C7
   LBUZ LU7 ....63 L7
Mead Wk *DTCH/LGLY* SL3 ....188 C3
Meadway *BERK* HP4 ....114 C9
   BUCK/WIN MK18 ....48 B5
   DUN/WHIP LU6 ....87 J1
   RAYLNE/WEN HP22 ....70 C8
   RBEDW MK45 ....11 L4
Mead Wy *RSLP* HA4 ....171 L5
   SL SL1 ....179 H8
   WYM HP11 ....153 M6
Meadway Dgls *RSLP* HA4 ....171 K4
Meadway Pk
   CFSP/GDCR SL9 ....168 F6
The Meadway *SHEN* MK5 ....42 A4
Meadle Rd *EAG/OLD/WT* MK6 * 42 C7
Medallion Pl *MDHD* SL6 ....177 P9
Mede Cl *STWL/WRAY* TW19 ....195 N4
Medeswell *EMV/FZ* MK4 ....42 E9
Medhurst *CNH/GTH/TM* MK8 ....41 N1
Medland Cl *EAG/OLD/WT* MK6 ....43 K5
Medley Cl *DUN/WHIP* LU6 ....86 B9
Medman Cl *UX/CGN* UB8 ....182 C5
Medway Cl *NPAG* MK16 ....31 L2
Meeting Oak La
   BUCK/WIN MK18 ....60 D5
Melbourne Av *SL* SL1 ....179 N9
Melbourne Rd *HWYN* HP13 ....153 M4
Melford Gn *AYLW* HP19 ....95 K8
Melfort Dr *LBUZ* LU7 ....75 P2
   WEAT MK2 ....53 K7
Melick Rd *EAG/OLD/WT* MK6 ....42 G8
Melina Cl *HYS/HAR* UB3 ....183 K8
Mellow La East *YEAD* UB4 ....183 J7
Mellow La West *YEAD* UB4 ....183 H7
Melrose Av *BTCHLY* MK3 ....52 F1
Melrose Ct *YEAD* UB4 ....183 N6
Melrose St *HWYN* HP13 ....153 N1
Melrose Wk *AYLS* HP21 ....109 P1
Melton *GTLIN* MK14 ....30 C5
Melton Rd *MDHD* SL6 ....185 M1
Melville Pl *HGDN/ICK* UB10 ....171 K9
Mendelssohn Gv
   WTR/OFPK MK7 ....44 A8

Mendip Cl *DTCH/LGLY* SL3 ....189 J6
   HYS/HAR UB3 ....191 K8
Mendip Wy *HWYN* HP13 ....4 C2
Mendy St *WYM* HP11 ....4 A9
Menmarsh Rd *RAYLW* HP18 ....104 D7
Mentmore Cl *HWYW* HP12 ....152 B4
Mentmore Crs
   CNH/GTH/TM MK8 ....41 P4
Mentmore Gdns *LBUZ* LU7 ....74 C4
Mentmore Rd *HWYW* HP12 ....152 B4
   LBUZ LU7 ....74 C4
   LBUZ LU7 ....74 D1
Mentmore Vw *TRING* HP23 ....112 D1
Mentone Av *RMKS/WB* MK17 ....45 H9
Menzies Ct *SHEN* MK5 ....42 B8
Mercers Dr *BDWL* MK13 ....30 D7
Mercers Meadow
   RAYLNE/WEN HP22 ....111 H8
Merchant La *RBEDW* MK43 ....33 L4
Merchant Pl *MKV* MK10 ....43 L1
Mercian Wy *SL* SL1 ....187 J2
Mercia Rd *MDHD* SL6 ....185 H1
Mercury Gv
   CNH/GTH/TM MK8 ....41 N5
Mercury House
   HYS/HAR UB3 * 191 M5
Mercury Wy *LBUZ* LU7 ....75 H1
Meredith Dr *AYLW* HP19 ....95 H5
Mere La *BUCK/WIN* MK18 ....46 E5
Mere Pk *MLW* SL7 * 164 F7
Mere Rd *BUCK/WIN* MK18 ....46 E5
   SL SL1 ....188 B4
Merle Av *DEN/HRF* UB9 ....169 L5
Merlewood Cl *HWYN* HP11 ....152 G6
Merlewood Dr *SHEN* MK5 ....41 N8
Merlin Cl *DTCH/LGLY* SL3 * 189 K7
Merling Cft *BERK* HP4 ....114 A4
Merlins Ct *LBUZ* LU7 * 74 C5
Merlin Wk *EAG/OLD/WT* MK6 ....43 H2
Merrivale Ms *WDR/YW* UB7 * 190 D2
Merrow Dr *HHW* HP1 ....127 N1
Merrows Cl *NTHWD* HA6 ....159 J6
Merry Down *HWYN* HP13 ....5 K3
Merryfields *HGDN/ICK* UB10 ....182 D5
Mersey Cl *BTCHLY* MK3 ....52 E2
Mersey Wy *BTCHLY* MK3 ....52 E3
Merthen Gv *EMV/FZ* MK4 ....52 B3
Merton Av *HGDN/ICK* UB10 ....183 H5
Merton Cl *HHW* HP1 ....127 K7
   MDHD SL6 ....185 J4
Merton Dr *EAG/OLD/WT* MK6 ....42 G8
Merton Rd *PRRI* HP27 ....121 J7
   SL SL1 ....188 A4
Merton Wy *HGDN/ICK* UB10 ....183 H5
Merwin Wy *WDSR* SL4 ....193 H3
Messenger Cl *AYLS* HP21 ....96 A9
Metcalfe Gv *GTLIN* MK14 ....31 H5
Mews Gammel *TRING* HP23 ....112 D1
Mezen Cl *NTHWD* HA6 ....159 K5
Micawber Av *UX/CGN* UB8 ....182 C7
Michael Cl *MDHD* SL6 ....185 J2
Michigan Dr *WEAT* MK2 ....53 J5
Nicholls Av *CFSP/GDCR* SL9 ....156 C5
Micklefield Rd *HWYN* HP13 ....153 M2
Middle Dr *HHW* HP1 * 127 L6
Mickleton *WLLN* MK15 ....30 G7
Midcot Wy *BERK* HP4 ....114 A8
Midcroft *RSLP* HA4 ....171 L6
   SLN SL2 ....180 C7
Mid Cross La *CFSP/GDCR* SL9 ....157 H5
Middle Cl *AYLS* HP21 ....109 N1
Middle Culham *HEN* RG9 * 174 F4
Middle Dr *BEAC* HP9 ....155 H5
Middle Fld
   RAYLNE/WEN HP22 ....110 F5
Middlefield Cl
   HGDN/ICK UB10 ....48 C2
Middle Gn *DTCH/LGLY* SL3 ....188 C1
   LBUZ LU7 ....74 D1
Middlegreen Rd
   DTCH/LGLY SL3 ....188 F3
Middlehill *HHW* HP1 ....127 N1
Middle La *HHS/BOV* HP3 ....137 J2
Middle Meadow *CSTG* HP8 ....156 C4
Middle Rd *AYLS* HP21 ....96 B8
   BERK HP4 ....114 D1
   DEN/HRF UB9 ....169 L1
   WHLY OX33 ....102 F7
Middlesex Dr *BTCHLY* MK3 ....52 F1
Middle Slade *BUCK/WIN* MK18 ....48 B5
Middleton Cl *HHW* HP1 ....127 M1
Middleton *GTLIN* MK14 ....30 G6
Middleton Dr *PIN* HA5 ....171 N1
Middleton Rd *HYS/HAR* UB3 ....183 H5
   RKW/CH/CXG WD3 ....158 A3
Middleton Wy *LBUZ* LU7 ....75 H1
Middle Wk *SL* SL1 ....164 C8
Middle Wy *CHNR* OX39 ....129 M6
The Middleway *HWYW* HP12 ....152 C4
Midhurst Cl *AYLS* HP21 ....110 B1
Midhurst Gdns
   HGDN/ICK UB10 ....183 J3
Midhurst Ms *BDWL* MK15 ....15 M2
Midshires Wy *BDWL* MK15 ....30 D6
   BUCK/WIN MK18 ....70 D6
   CHNR OX39 ....130 A5
   CNH/GTH/TM MK8 ....41 M7
   HADM HP17 ....109 M2
   RAYLNE/WEN HP22 ....79 M2
   RAYLW HP18 ....91 N6
   RMKN MK19 ....19 J5
   RMKS/WB MK17 ....50 C5
   RMKS/WB MK17 ....51 J9
   RNHPTN NN7 ....12 C1
   SLN SL2 ....167 M9
Midsummer Av *RMKS/WB* MK43 * 7 L1
Midsummer Bvd *CMK* MK9 ....6 C4
Midway *LBUZ* LU7 ....74 D1
Midway Ct *STA* TW18 ....196 B9
Miersfield *WYM* HP11 ....4 B8
Milbourne Cl *WEAT* MK2 ....53 J4
Milburn Av *EAG/OLD/WT* MK6 ....6 E6
Milburn Dr *WDR/YW* UB7 ....190 E1
Mildenhall Rd *SL* SL1 ....180 A9

Mildred Av *HYS/HAR* UB3 ....191 K5
Milebush *LBUZ* LU7 ....74 A1
Milecastle *BDWL* MK13 ....30 A8
Mile Elm *MLW* SL7 ....164 F6
Miles Av *LBUZ* LU7 ....74 B1
Miles Cl *AYLS* HP21 ....96 B8
   GTLIN MK14 ....30 C2
Miles End *AYLS* HP21 ....95 K9
Milesmere *CNH/GTH/TM* MK8 ....41 M3
Milestone Cl *SKCH* HP14 ....140 A6
Milestone Ct *LBUZ* LU7 * 74 D1
Miletree Cl *LBUZ* LU7 ....74 A1
Miletree Crs *DUN/WHIP* LU6 ....87 H2
Mile Tree Rd *LBUZ* LU7 ....65 H7
Milfoil Av *GTLIN* MK14 ....30 C9
Milford Av *STSTR* MK11 ....28 C3
Milk Hall *BERK* HP4 ....113 P6
Millards Cl *RBEDW* MK45 ....33 M2
Millars Cl *RAYLW* HP18 * 92 C1
Millbank *LBUZ* LU7 ....74 D1
Millbank Pl *WTR/OFPK* MK7 ....43 P4
Millboard Rd *BNEND* SL8 ....165 P6
Mill Bridge Pl *UX/CGN* UB8 ....182 B5
Millbrook Cl *HWYW* HP12 ....152 D2
Millbrook Wy
   DTCH/LGLY SL3 ....195 N1
Mill Cl *CSHM* HP5 ....136 A7
   HEN RG9 ....161 K9
   KID OX5 ....4 C3
   RAYLNE/WEN HP22 * 82 C5
   WDR/YW UB7 ....190 D4
Mill Ct *WOLV* MK12 ....29 J8
Milldun Wy *HWYW* HP12 ....152 D5
Mill End Cl *DUN/WHIP* LU6 ....86 B4
Mill End Rd *HWYW* HP12 ....152 C3
Millennium Ct *UX/CGN* UB8 * 182 B5
Millennium Point
   AYLW HP19 * 95 J6
Millennium Whf
   RKW/CH/CXG WD3 * 158 B1
Millers Cl *LBUZ* LU7 ....68 F3
Millers Ct *LBUZ* LU7 ....75 H2
Millers Turn *CHNR* OX39 ....129 M6
Millers Wy *AYLW* HP19 ....95 J7
   WOLV MK12 ....29 K9
Millfield *BERK* HP4 ....114 F9
Millfield Av *RBICN* OX27 ....24 A1
Millfields *RMKS/WB* MK43 ....33 M5
   RBICN OX27 ....24 A1
Millfields *CSHM* HP5 ....135 M6
Millfield Gdns *TRING* HP23 ....112 F2
Millhayes *GTLIN* MK14 ....30 F5
Millington Cl *EAG/OLD/WT* MK6 ....43 L1
Millington Dr *HYS/HAR* UB3 ....191 L4
Mill La *AMSS* HP7 ....145 L3
   BDWL MK13 ....30 A5
   BRACKY NN13 ....35 J6
   BRACKY NN13 ....36 A8
   BUCK/WIN MK18 ....48 C9
   CFSP/GDCR SL9 ....169 J4
   CHNR OX39 ....129 M6
   CSTG HP8 ....156 C2
   GTMIS/PWD HP16 ....134 A5
   HADM HP17 ....118 F2
   HEN RG9 ....174 B8
   KID OX5 ....4 C3
   MDHD SL6 ....175 P4
   MDHD SL6 ....176 P9
   PRRI HP27 ....121 L7
   RAYLNE/WEN HP22 ....83 J6
   RAYLNE/WEN HP22 ....83 H6
   RBEDW MK45 ....17 H4
   RMKS/WB MK17 ....44 F7
   RMKS/WB MK17 ....53 M9
   SKCH HP14 ....139 N6
   STSTR MK11 ....28 B5
   WDSR SL4 ....187 J8
   WHLY OX33 ....49 J9
Mill Meadow *AYLW* HP19 ....95 K7
Mill Ri *DTCH/LGLY* SL3 ....194 F1
Mill Rd *HEN* RG9 ....160 C6
   LBUZ LU7 ....74 E1
   LBUZ LU7 ....75 H1
   LBUZ LU7 ....99 K1
   MLW SL7 ....164 E8
   RAYLW HP18 ....104 C4
   RBEDW MK45 ....33 M5
   RBEDW MK43 ....33 H4
   SKCH HP14 ....139 N7
   WDR/YW UB7 ....190 D4
   WEAT MK2 ....53 J4
Mills Cl *HGDN/ICK* UB10 ....182 D5
Millside *BNEND* SL8 ....165 N4
Mill Sq *WDSR* SL4 ....193 H1
Millstone Cl *NPAG* MK16 ....31 M3
Millstream
   RAYLNE/WEN HP22 ....110 F4
Millstream *SL* SL1 ....187 J1
Millstream Wy *FLKWH* HP10 ....165 P1
   LBUZ LU7 ....74 D2
Mill St *AYL* HP20 ....2 A3
   BERK HP4 ....126 E1
   DTCH/LGLY SL3 ....189 M8
   NPAG MK16 ....32 B2
   SLN SL2 ....188 B2
   WHLY OX33 ....49 J9
   WYM HP11 ....4 A9
Millsum Av *RMKS/WB* MK43 * 7 L1
Mill Vw *RMKN* MK19 ....19 J5
Mill View Rd *TRING* HP23 ....112 F2
Mill Wy *NTHWD* HA6 ....159 N6
   WTR/OFPK MK7 ....44 A7
   EBED/NFELT TW14 ....197 P3
   RKW/CH/CXG WD3 ....158 A6
   RMKS/WB MK17 ....45 H7

Milner Rd *SL* SL1 ....178 E8
Milneway *DEN/HRF* UB9 ....158 B8
Milton Cl *CFSP/GDCR* SL9 ....168 F2
   DTCH/LGLY SL3 ....195 P1
   HEN RG9 ....173 P6
   YEAD UB4 ....183 N9
Milton Ct *HGDN/ICK* UB10 ....171 H8
   SLN SL2 ....181 L1
Milton Dr *NPAG* MK16 ....31 L2
Milton Flds *CSTG* HP8 ....156 D5
Milton Gdns *PRRI* HP27 ....131 H1
   STWL/WRAY TW19 ....196 F7
Milton Gv *BTCHLY* MK3 ....52 F1
Milton Hl *CSTG* HP8 ....156 D5
Milton Keynes Boundary Wk
   EMV/FZ MK4 ....51 N4
   NPAG MK16 ....13 N6
   OLN MK46 ....14 F1
   RBEDW MK45 ....10 C5
   RMKS/WB MK17 ....47 J2
   RMKN MK19 ....21 H6
   RMKS/WB MK17 ....52 E7
   RMKS/WB MK17 ....54 D2
   RNHPTN NN7 ....12 F5
Milton Lawns *AMS* HP6 ....135 P9
Milton Rd *AYLS* HP21 ....95 M2
   CSHM HP5 ....135 M2
   HGDN/ICK UB10 ....171 H9
   MKV MK10 ....43 M1
   RAYLNE/WEN HP22 ....111 M1
   SLN SL2 ....179 P7
   SL SL1 ....187 J1
   WLLN MK15 ....31 K6
   WTR/OFPK MK7 ....44 A7
Milton Wy *WDR/YW* UB7 ....190 F5
Milverton Cl *MDHD* SL6 ....185 J4
Milverton Dr
   HGDN/ICK UB10 ....171 J9
Mimosa Cl *AYLS* HP21 * 95 K9
Mina Av *DTCH/LGLY* SL3 ....188 F3
Mineral La *CSHM* HP5 ....135 N5
Minerva Cl
   STWL/WRAY TW19 ....196 A4
Minerva Gdns
   WTR/OFPK MK7 ....44 A5
Minerva Wy *BEAC* HP9 ....155 L9
Mines Cl *HWYN* HP13 ....4 C3
Minet Dr *HYS/HAR* UB3 ....191 P2
Minet Gdns *HYS/HAR* UB3 ....191 P2
Minimax Cl
   EBED/NFELT TW14 ....197 N5
Ministry Whf *SKCH* HP14 * 141 L2
Minniecroft Rd *SL* SL1 ....178 F6
Minorca Gv *SHEN* MK5 ....42 B8
Minshull Cl *BUCK/WIN* MK18 ....48 B2
Minster Wy *DTCH/LGLY* SL3 ....189 H1
Minstrel Ct *BDWL* MK13 ....30 B6
Mint Cl *HGDN/ICK* UB10 ....183 H6
Minton Ri *MDHD* SL6 ....185 L4
Minton Rd *MDHD* SL6 ....185 J3
Mirador Crs *SLN* SL2 ....188 D1
Mirrie La *DEN/HRF* UB9 ....169 H3
Misbourne Av
   CFSP/GDCR SL9 ....156 G5
   HWYN HP13 ....5 K3
Misbourne Cl *AYLS* HP21 ....109 M3
Misbourne Ct *AMSS* HP7 * 145 M4
Misbourne Dr
   GTMIS/PWD HP16 ....133 P6
Misbourne Mdw
   DEN/HRF UB9 ....169 L6
Misbourne Rd
   HGDN/ICK UB10 ....182 C5
Missenden Cl
   BUCK/WIN MK18 ....60 B6
   EBED/NFELT TW14 ....197 M7
Missenden Gdns *SL* SL1 ....178 F9
Missenden Ms
   GTMIS/PWD HP16 * 133 N5
Missenden Rd
   AMS HP6 ....135 K5
   CSHM HP5 ....135 K5
   GTMIS/PWD HP16 ....133 K1
   HADM HP17 ....122 C3
Miss Joans Ride
   DUN/WHIP LU6 ....86 D9
Miswell La *TRING* HP23 ....112 D3
Mitcham Pl *BDWL* MK13 ....6 C1
Mitcham Wk *AYLW* HP19 ....95 J5
Mitchell Cl *HHW* HP1 ....127 L4
   SL SL1 ....187 L4
   THAME OX9 ....118 C5
Mitchell Rd *RBEDW* MK43 ....33 J6
Mitchell Wk *AMS* HP6 ....146 A2
Mithras Gdns
   WTR/OFPK MK7 ....44 A5
Moat Dr *BUCK/WIN* MK18 ....48 A4
Moat La *GTMIS/PWD* HP16 ....133 J5
   RSLP HA4 ....171 L5
   SLN SL2 ....180 B2
Moat Rd
   RAYLNE/WEN HP22 ....96 B3
Moat La *GTMIS/PWD* HP16 ....133 J5
   RAYLNE/WEN HP22 ....82 C4
   RAYLNE/WEN HP22 ....83 H1
   RBICN OX27 ....24 A1
Moat Pl *DEN/HRF* UB9 ....170 B9
Moat's Crs *THAME* OX9 ....118 E5
Mobwell Ter
   GTMIS/PWD HP16 * 133 N4
Moeran Cl *WTR/OFPK* MK7 ....44 A7
Moffy Hl *MDHD* SL6 ....177 L6
Mole Run *HWYN* HP13 ....5 J3
Molyns Ms *SL* SL1 ....187 J2
Monarch Cl
   EBED/NFELT TW14 ....197 L6
Monarch's Wy *RSLP* HA4 * 171 K6
Monastery Gdns
   DTCH/LGLY SL3 ....194 D2
Mondial Wy *WDR/YW* UB7 ....191 J8
Monellan Gv *WTR/OFPK* MK7 ....43 N9
Monet Pl *AYLW* HP19 ....95 J6
Moneyhill Ct
   RKW/CH/CXG WD3 * 158 B1

Money Hill Rd
RKW/CH/CXG WD3 ....158 C4
Money La *WDR/YW* UB7 ....190 D4
Moneyrow Gn *MDHD* SL6 .....185 N8
Monkey Island La
MDHD SL6 ....186 L5
Monksfield Wy *SLN* SL9 ....179 L7
Monks Hollow *MLW* SL7 .....164 L4
Monks Pth *AYLW* HP19 ....95 J7
Monks Rd *WDSR* SL4 ....193 H1
Monks Wy *BDWL* MK13 ....29 P9
CNH/GTH/TM MK8 ....41 L2
GTLIN MK14 ....35 J5
WLLN MK15 ....31 H4
Monkswood *TOW* NN12 ....25 J1
Monkton Waye *PRRI* HP27 ....132 C2
Monmouth Cl *AYLW* HP19 ......95 J5
Monmouth Rd *HYS/HAR* UB3 ...191 L5
Monro Av *CNH/GTH/TM* MK8 ....41 N5
Montabaur Rd *BRACKY* NN13 ...35 J5
Montagu Dr
EAG/OLD/WT MK6 ....43 H4
Montague Cl *AYLS* HP21 ....2 D7
BERK HP4 ....126 D1
SL SL1 ....188 B1
UX/CGN UB8 ....182 D5
Montagu Rd
DTCH/LGLY SL3 ....188 D9
Montcalm Cl *YEAD* UB4 ....185 P6
Montem La *SL* SL1 ....187 P5
Montford Ms *HWYN* HP13 ......143 L9
Montgomerie Cl *BERK* HP4 ....114 C8
Montgomery Cl *LBUZ* LU7 ......85 L2
Montgomery Crs *WLLN* MK15 ...30 G6
Montgomery Pl *SLN* SL2 ......180 E9
Montpelier Cl
HGDN/ICK UB10 ....182 C4
Montpellier Ct *WDSR* SL4 ....193 N1
Montrose Av *DTCH/LGLY* SL3 ..188 E8
SL SL1 ....179 M9
Montrose Dr *MDHD* SL6 ....184 C1
Montrose Rd
EBED/NFELT TW14 ....197 K5
Montrose Wy
DTCH/LGLY SL3 ....188 F9
Monument La
CFSP/GDCR SL9 ....156 C6
Monycrower Dr *MDHD* SL6 ....177 L9
Moon St *WOLV* MK12 ....19 P1
Moorbridge Rd *MDHD* SL6 ....177 N9
Moor Cl *RMKN* MK19 ....28 E8
Moorcroft La *UX/CGN* UB8 ....182 C8
Moore Cl *SL* SL1 ....187 N5
Moore End *DUN/WHIP* LU6 ....86 A6
Moore End La *DUN/WHIP* LU6 ...86 B6
Moorend La *TOW* NN12 ....18 A8
Moorend Rd *THAME* OX9 ....118 A3
Moore Rd *BERK* HP4 ....114 B8
Moor Furlong *SL* SL1 ....186 E5
Moorgate *EAG/OLD/WT* MK6 .....42 F5
Moorhall Rd *DEN/HRF* UB9 ....170 A5
Moor Hart Cl *SKCH* HP14 .....140 F7
Moorhen Wy
BUCK/WIN MK18 * 48 C1
Moorhills Crs *LBUZ* LU7 ....73 M6
Moorhouse Wy *LBUZ* LU7 ....75 H4
The Moorings
BUCK/WIN MK18 * 48 A3
STWL/WRAY TW19 ....194 G6
WDSR SL4 * 187 H8
Moorland Rd *HHW* HP1 ....142 F7
WDR/YW UB7 ....190 C8
Moorlands *LBUZ* LU7 ....73 L1
Moorlands Rd *LBUZ* LU7 ....75 H6
Moor La *HWYN* HP13 ....142 D8
MDHD SL6 ....177 N7
RKW/CH/CXG WD3 ....158 D4
RKW/CH/CXG WD3 ....158 E2
STWL/WRAY TW19 ....195 J1
WDR/YW UB7 ....190 C7
Moor Pk *BTCHLY* MK3 ....52 D5
RAYLNE/WEN HP22 ....111 H7
Moor Park Gdns
NTHWD HA6 * 159 J2
Moor Park Rd *NTHWD* HA6 ....159 N6
Moors Cl *RMKN* MK19 ....28 A9
Moorside *FLKWH* HP10 ....110 H1
Moorside Cl *MDHD* SL6 ....177 M7
Moorstown Ct *SL* SL1 ....188 A3
The Moor *MLW* SL7 ....165 J5
RBEDW MK43 ....11 L4
Morar Cl *LBUZ* LU7 ....74 A2
Moray Av *HYS/HAR* UB3 ....191 M2
Moray Dr *SLN* SL2 ....180 C9
Morcom Rd
DUN/HR/TOD LU5 ....87 N2
Mordaunt Cl *RBEDW* MK45 .....17 J1
Mordaunts Ct *WLLN* MK15 .....43 J2
Moreau Wk *DTCH/LGLY* SL3 ...180 A9
More Av *AYLS* HP21 ....2 C4
Morebath Gv *EMV/FZ* MK4 .....42 C8
Morefields *TRING* HP23 ....98 F9
Moreland Cl *DTCH/LGLY* SL3 ..189 L8
Moreland Dr
CFSP/GDCR SL9 ....169 H5
Morello Av *UX/CGN* UB8 ......183 H8
Morello Dr *DTCH/LGLY* SL3 ...189 H2
Moretaine Rd *ASHF* TW15 .....196 B9
Moreton Dr *BUCK/WIN* MK18 ...38 C9
Moreton La *HADM* HP17 ....109 J5
THAME OX9 ....118 C9
Moreton Rd
BUCK/WIN MK18 ....48 B1
Moreton Wy *SL* SL1 ....187 H2

Morford Cl *RSLP* HA4 ....171 P5
Morford Wy *RSLP* HA4 ....171 P5
Morgan Cl *NTHWD* HA6 ....159 M5
Morgan's La *HYS/HAR* UB3 ....183 L9
Morland Dr *DUN/WHIP* LU6 .....87 J2
Morland Dr
CNH/GTH/TM MK8 ....41 M6
Morley Cl *DTCH/LGLY* SL3 ....189 H3
Morley Crs *WTR/OFPK* MK7 ....44 E8
Mornington Crs *HEST* TW5 ....191 P9
Morrell Cl *SHEN* MK5 ....42 B7
Morrice Cl *DTCH/LGLY* SL3 ....189 H5
Morris Cl *AYLS* HP21 ....109 M2
Morrison Ct
CNH/GTH/TM MK8 ....41 N6
Morrison Rd *YEAD* UB4 ....185 N9
Morse Cl *DEN/HRF* UB9 ....170 D7
Mortain Cl *WTR/OFPK* MK7 .....43 C9
Mortain Dr *BERK* HP4 ....114 B8
Morten Gdns *DEN/HRF* UB9 ...170 A5
Mortens Wd *AMSS* HP7 ....145 J9
Mortimer Hl *TRING* HP23 ......112 F2
Mortimer Rd *TRING* HP23 ......112 F2
Mortimer Rd *DTCH/LGLY* SL3 ..188 F4
Morton Cl *BUCK/WIN* MK18 .....70 D8
LBUZ LU7 ....84 E7
Mortons Fk *BDWL* MK13 ....29 P7
Moseley Rd *SKCH* HP14 ....142 C4
Moses Plat La *PRRI* HP27 ....132 B7
Moss Cl *RKW/CH/CXG* WD3 ...158 D2
Mossdale *BDWL* MK13 ....30 B8
Mossendew Cl
DEN/HRF UB9 ....158 D8
Moss Gdns *FELT* TW13 ....197 N8
Mossy V *MDHD* SL6 ....177 K7
Moston Cl *HYS/HAR* UB3 ....191 M9
Mountain Ash *MLW* SL7 ....164 D3
Mount Av *DBGH* MK1 ....43 K9
Mountbatten Cl *SL* SL1 ....188 C4
Mountbatten Gdns *LBUZ* LU7 ..64 F9
Mountbatten Sq *WDSR* SL4 * ..192 F7
Mount Cl *HWW* HP1 ....127 P2
SLN SL2 ....167 N9
Mounthill Av *RMKN* MK19 ....28 E8
Mount Hill La
CFSP/GDCR SL9 ....168 D6
Mount La *DEN/HRF* UB9 ....169 M7
Mount Nugent *CSHM* HP5 .....125 L9
Mount Park Rd *PIN* HA5 ....171 N3
Mount Pleasant
DEN/HRF UB9 ....158 A8
OLD/WT MK6 ....63 L7
LBUZ LU7 ....63 L7
NPAC MK16 ....15 H4
RAYLNE/WEN HP22 ....81 H2
RMKS/WB MK17 ....65 K8
RMKS/WB MK17 ....65 L5
TOW NN12 ....18 B8
Mount Pleasant Cl
BUCK/WIN MK18 * 48 A4
Mount Rd *HYS/HAR* UB3 ....191 M9
Mountsfield Cl *LBUZ* LU7 ......73 J2
Mount Vw *WDSR* SL4 ....192 C4
Mount St *AYL* HP20 ....2 C3
The Mount *EAG/OLD/WT* MK6 ...43 L8
RMKS/WB MK17 ....45 H8
Mount Vw *HEN* RG9 ....173 P5
RKW/CH/CXG WD3 ....158 B1
Mountview *NTHWD* HA6 ....159 N6
Mountview Av
DUN/HR/TOD LU5 ....87 M2
Mount Wy *PRRI* HP27 ....131 J9
Mowbray Dr *LBUZ* LU7 ....74 B2
Mowbray Rd *AYL* HP20 ....20 F5
Mowhills *RBEDW* MK43 ....11 K2
Mow Mdw *OLN* MK46 ....15 M2
Moyleen Ri *MLW* SL7 ....164 C9
Mozart Cl *WTR/OFPK* MK7 ......44 F9
Muddiford La *EMV/FZ* MK4 .....42 D9
Muirfield Dr *BTCHLY* MK3 ....52 F9
Muirfield Rd *OXHEY* WD19 ....159 P4
Mulberry Av
STWL/WRAY TW19 ....194 E7
WDSR SL4 ....194 B2
Mulberry Cl *HAZ/HC* HP15 ....144 A4
Mulberry Crs *WDR/YW* UB7 ...190 C7
Mulberry Ct *DTCH/LGLY* SL3 ..188 G6
Mulberry Pde
WDR/YW UB7 ....190 D8
Mulberry Wk *MDHD* SL6 ....177 J8
Mullen Av *GTLIN* MK14 ....35 J5
Mullins Wy *AYLW* HP19 ....94 C5
Mullion Pl *EAG/OLD/WT* MK6 * ..7 J2
Mumfords La
CFSP/GDCR SL9 ....168 C3
Munces Rd *MLW* SL7 ....164 D3
Mundaydean La *MLW* SL7 .....163 P4
Mundesley Sp *SL* SL1 ....188 A3
Murcott Rd *RBICS/W* OX25 ....39 M1
Murray Rd *BERK* HP4 ....114 E9
NTHWD HA6 * 172 B9
Murrey Cl *SHEN* MK5 ....42 C7
Murrin Rd *MDHD* SL6 ....177 J9
Mursley Ct *STSTR* MK11 ....29 J8
Mursley Rd *RMKS/WB* MK17 ...62 G7
RMKS/WB MK17 ....61 K1
Murswell La *TOW* NN12 ....25 K1
Musgrave La *TOW* NN12 ....25 K1
Musgrave Rd *CHNR* OX39 .....129 P5
Musgrave Wk *SKCH* HP14 .....140 B6
Muski Hl *HWW* HP1 ....128 C9
Myddleton Rd *UX/CGN* UB8 ...182 C4
Mylne Cl *HWYN* HP13 ....143 J9
Mynchen End *BEAC* HP9 ......155 H4
The Myrke *DTCH/LGLY* SL3 ....180 E4
Myrtle Av
EBED/NFELT TW14 ....197 L3
RSLP HA4 ....171 N5
Myrtle Bank *WOLV* MK12 ....29 M8

Myrtle La *DTCH/LGLY* SL3 ....189 N9
UX/CGN UB8 ....182 F8
WDR/YW UB7 ....190 F5
Myrtle Crs *SLN* SL2 ....188 B1
Myrtleside Cl *NTHWD* HA6 ....159 K7

N

Nag's Head La
GTMIS/PWD HP16 ....133 M8
Nailzee Cl *CFSP/GDCR* SL9 ...168 G5
Nairdwood Cl
GTMIS/PWD HP16 ....133 L8
Nairdwood La
GTMIS/PWD HP16 ....133 L8
Nairdwood Wy
GTMIS/PWD HP16 ....133 L8
Nairn Cl *BTCHLY* MK3 ....52 E1
Nairn Gn *OXHEY* WD19 ....159 N3
Naisby Dr *RMKS/WB* MK17 .....44 E9
Nalders Rd *CSHM* HP5 ....5 P2
Nancarrow *RAYLNE/WEN* HP22 ..82 C5
Nancy Hall Ct *HWYW* HP12 * ..152 C1
Naphill Pl *MDHD* SL6 ....42 C1
Napier Cl *WDR/YW* UB7 ....185 H1
WDR/YW UB7 ....190 A8
Napier Rd *MDHD* SL6 ....185 H1
Napier Sq *WEAT* MK2 ....53 K5
Nappin Cl *AYLW* HP19 ....95 J4
Nappins Cl *RAYLW* HP18 ......106 D9
Narbeth Dr *AYL* HP20 ....96 C7
Narborough Cl
HGDN/ICK UB10 ....171 J7
Narcot Cl *CSTG* HP8 ....156 C4
Narcot Rd *CSTG* HP8 ....156 C6
Narcot Wy *CSTG* HP8 ....156 C6
Narrow La *HWYN* HP13 ....142 E8
Narrow Pth *RMKS/WB* MK17 ....44 E8
Naseby Cl *MDHD* SL6 ....30 G2
Naseby Ct *BDWL* MK13 ....30 B7
BUCK/WIN MK18 ....48 C1
Nash Cl *AYLS* HP21 ....110 A2
RAYLNE/WEN HP22 ....79 L3
Nashdom La *SL* SL1 ....178 E3
Nash Lee End
RAYLNE/WEN HP22 ....110 E8
Nash Lee La *HADM* HP17 ......110 E8
Nash Lee Rd *HADM* HP17 .....110 F7
Nashleigh Hl *CSHM* HP5 ....135 P2
Nashmead *SHEN* MK5 ....42 A7
Nash Rd *BUCK/WIN* MK18 ....49 M5
DTCH/LGLY SL3 ....189 H6
RMKS/WB MK17 ....50 C7
RMKS/WB MK17 ....51 J2
Nashs Farm
RAYLNE/WEN HP22 ....82 D4
Natalie Cl *EBED/NFELT* TW14 .197 K6
Nathaniel Cl *SHEN* MK5 ....42 A7
Nathaniel Wk *TRING* HP23 ....112 F1
Natwoke Cl *BEAC* HP9 ....155 H5
Neal Cl *CFSP/GDCR* SL9 ......169 K6
NTHWD HA6 ....159 N8
Neapland *EAG/OLD/WT* MK6 ....43 L4
Nearton End *RMKS/WB* MK17 ...61 J8
Neath Crs *BTCHLY* MK3 ....52 E1
Neats Acre *RSLP* HA4 ....171 K5
Nebular Ct *LBUZ* LU7 ....74 A2
Needham Cl *WDSR* SL4 ....187 J3
Needlemakers *RAYLW* HP18 ...106 B7
Neild Wy *RKW/CH/CXG* WD3 ..147 N9
Nellgrove Rd *HGDN/ICK* UB10 .183 J7
Nelson Cl *AMSS* HP7 ....144 Q3
CSTG HP8 * 146 G5
DTCH/LGLY SL3 ....188 F5
EBED/NFELT TW14 ....197 M7
HGDN/ICK UB10 ....183 J7
HWYN HP13 ....153 M5
Nelson La *HGDN/ICK* UB10 ....183 J7
Nelson Rd *BERK* HP4 ....100 A3
HGDN/ICK UB10 ....183 H6
LBUZ LU7 ....64 F9
WDR/YW UB7 ....190 B7
Nelson St *BUCK/WIN* MK18 .....48 A3
THAME OX9 ....118 C2
Nelson Ter *AYL* HP20 * 2 D3
Nene Dr *BTCHLY* MK3 ....52 E1
Nene Rd *HTHAIR* TW6 ....191 N6
Nene Gdns *LBUZ* LU7 ....73 J1
Neptune Rd *HTHAIR* TW6 * 191 J9
Ness Wy *WEAT* MK2 ....53 K5
Nestle's Av *HYS/HAR* UB3 ....191 M4
Netherby Cl *TRING* HP23 ....98 E5
Nether Cl *BRACKY* NN13 ....35 J3
Nethercote La *WTLGN* OX49 ...126 E8
Nether Gv *SHEN* MK5 ....42 A5
Netherwood Rd *BEAC* HP9 ....155 H5
Netley Ct *MKV* MK10 ....43 L1
Nettlecombe *EMV/FZ* MK4 ......42 C9
Nettleden Rd *BERK* HP4 ....100 B5
HHW HP1 ....115 J4
Nettleton Rd
HGDN/ICK UB10 ....170 D9
HTHAIR TW6 ....191 H7
Nevil Cl *NTHWD* HA6 ....159 N5
Nevill Cl *RMKN* MK19 ....19 N4
Neville Cl *SLN* SL2 ....180 F7
Nevis Cl *LBUZ* LU7 ....74 A2
Nevis Gv *WEAT* MK2 ....53 K5
Newall Rd *HTHAIR* TW6 ....191 J9
New Ar *UX/CGN* UB8 * 46 J9
Newark Ct *WTR/OFPK* MK7 .....43 N9
Newark Rd *SL* SL1 ....153 M6
Newbarn La *BEAC* HP9 ....156 N4
Newberry Crs *WDSR* SL4 ......186 E5

Newbery Cl *BRACKY* NN13 .....34 F4
Newboult Rd *SL* SL1 ....187 P5
Newbolt Cl *NPAC* MK16 ....20 D7
New Bvd *MDHD* SL6 ....185 H7
New Broadway
HGDN/ICK UB10 * 183 H7
Newbury Cl *BTCHLY* MK3 ....52 E1
Newbury Dr *MDHD* SL6 ....185 P1
Newbury Rd *WDR/YW* UB7 .....190 F5
Newby Pl *EMV/FZ* MK4 ....42 B9
New Chilterns *AMSS* HP7 ......146 A3
New College St
BUCK/WIN MK18 ....37 P1
Newcombe Ri *WDR/YW* UB7 ...182 E9
New Ct *MLW* SL7 ....164 D7
Newcourt *UX/CGN* UB8 ....182 C8
Newcroft Cl *UX/CGN* UB8 .....182 D8
Newdigate Gn *DEN/HRF* UB9 ..158 E8
Newdigate Rd *DEN/HRF* UB9 ..158 D8
Newdigate Rd East
DEN/HRF UB9 ....158 D8
New Dr *HWYN* HP13 ....153 L2
New Rd *AMSS* HP7 ....145 K6
Newells Hedge *LBUZ* LU7 ......99 H9
New Farm La *NTHWD* HA6 ....159 N8
Newfield Gdns *MLW* SL7 ......164 F6
Newfield Rd *MLW* SL7 ....164 E7
New Garden Dr
WDR/YW UB7 ....190 E3
Newgate Rd *KID* SL6 ....88 C2
Newground Rd *TRING* HP23 ...113 M9
New Hall Cl *HHS/BOV* HP3 ....127 J9
Newhall Cl *HHS/BOV* HP3 .....127 J9
Newham Ct *MKV* MK10 ....44 A4
Newhaven Sp *SL* SL1 * 179 M7
Newhouse Rd *HHW* HP1 ....127 J8
New Inn La *BUCK/WIN* MK18 ...47 P7
New Inn Rd *HEAD* OX5 ....102 C7
Newlands Dr *DTCH/LGLY* SL3 .195 N2
MDHD SL6 ....176 C9
Newlands Rd *HHW* HP1 ....142 F5
Newlyn Pl *EAG/OLD/WT* MK6 .....7 M7
Newman Wy *LBUZ* LU7 ....74 A2
Newman Rd *HYS/HAR* UB3 ....183 M1
Newmarket Ct *MKV* MK10 ....44 A4
New Meadow *AYLS* HP21 ....96 C9
Newmer Rd *HWYN* HP12 ......152 B9
New Pde *WDR/YW* UB7 * 190 E2
New Park Rd *DEN/HRF* UB9 ...158 C8
New Peachey La *UX/CGN* UB8 .182 D9
New Pond La *KID* SL6 ....88 C2
New Pond Rd *RSLP* HA4 * 171 N4
New Pond Rd *HGDN/ICK* UB10 .144 H4
Newport Pagnell Rd
RBEDW MK43 ....23 M7
BDWL MK13 ....30 B5
EAG/OLD/WT MK6 ....43 H4
HTHAIR TW6 ....191 N9
NPAC MK16 ....15 M7
NPAC MK16 ....32 A5
OLN MK46 ....15 M7
SLN SL2 ....179 J2
WLLN MK15 ....43 J3
YEAD UB4 ....185 P8
Newquay Gdns
OXHEY WD19 ....159 P2
New Ark Ms *NWPG* MK16 ......146 A1
AMSS HP7 ....145 K6
BERK HP4 ....114 B7
BERK HP4 ....114 C9
BNEND SL8 ....165 P5
BRACKY NN13 ....34 G5
CSTG HP8 ....146 G5
DTCH/LGLY SL3 ....188 F5
DTCH/LGLY SL3 ....189 L8
EBED/NFELT TW14 ....197 K5
FLKWH HP10 ....154 A1
GTMIS/PWD HP16 ....133 M8
HADM HP17 ....108 A2
HAZ/HC HP15 ....143 K7
HGDN/ICK UB10 ....183 J7
HWYW HP12 ....152 C4
HYS/HAR UB3 ....191 J8
LBUZ LU7 ....84 D7
MDHD SL6 ....175 J9
MDHD SL6 ....185 H7
MLW SL7 ....164 B3
PRRI HP27 ....131 J9
PRRI HP27 * 131 P9
RAYLNE/WEN HP22 ....81 H2
RAYLNE/WEN HP22 ....111 K3
RBEDW MK43 ....11 J2
RKW/CH/CXG WD3 ....147 P3
RMKN MK19 ....19 N4
RMKS/WB MK17 ....62 D7
SKCH HP14 ....140 B7
SKCH HP14 ....142 C5
SKCH HP14 ....151 J4
TRING HP23 ....98 E7
UX/CGN UB8 ....182 C8
New Road Cl *HWYW* HP12 ....152 C4
New Road Gdns
HWYW HP12 ....152 C4
New Rw *OLN* MK46 ....10 C8
New Sq *SL* SL1 ....188 C3
New St *AYL* HP20 ....2 C3
BERK HP4 ....126 D1
BUCK/WIN MK18 ....47 N5
HEN RG9 ....174 A6
LBUZ LU7 ....84 D7
RAYLW HP18 ....79 L8
STSTR MK11 ....28 E5
Newton Cl *DTCH/LGLY* SL3 ...189 H3

Newton Ct *WDSR* SL4 ....194 C5
Newton La *WDSR* SL4 ....194 C5
Newton Rd *BTCHLY* MK3 ....52 E5
RBEDW MK43 ....11 J8
RMKS/WB MK17 ....62 D2
RMKS/WB MK17 ....63 K2
SL SL1 ....190 E9
Newtonside Orch
WDSR SL4 * 194 C5
Newtown Gdns *HEN* RG9 ......174 A8
Newtown Rd *DEN/HRF* UB9 ...182 B2
HEN RG9 ....174 A8
MLW SL7 ....164 F6
Newville *BRACKY* NN13 * 81 L7
New Woodfield Gn
DUN/HR/TOD LU5 ....87 N2
Newyears Green La
DEN/HRF UB9 ....170 F4
New Zealand Gdns *LBUZ* LU7 ..73 L7
Neyland Dr *AYLW* HP19 ....95 J4
Niagara Rd *HEN* RG9 ....174 A8
Nicholas Gdns *HWYN* HP13 ...153 K2
SL SL1 ....187 J2
Nicholas Rd *HEN* RG9 ....174 A8
Nicholas Wy *NTHWD* HA6 .....159 J8
Nicholls *WDSR* SL4 ....192 G3
Nicholls Av *UX/CGN* UB8 ......182 G7
Nicholls Wk *MDHD* SL6 ....177 M9
Nicholsons Wk *MDHD* SL6 * ..185 H9
Nickleby Cl *UX/CGN* UB8 ......183 H9
Nicol Cl *CFSP/GDCR* SL9 .....156 E8
Nicol End *CFSP/GDCR* SL9 ...156 E8
Nicol Rd *CFSP/GDCR* SL9 .....156 E8
Nicolson Dr *LBUZ* LU7 ....75 H4
Nield Rd *HYS/HAR* UB3 ....191 J2
Nightingale Cl *BRACKY* NN13 ..34 G2
HAZ/HC HP15 ....143 P6
Nightingale Crs *BDWL* MK13 ...29 P6
Nightingale La *MDHD* SL6 ....177 K8
Nightingale Pk *SL* SL1 ....179 K3
Nightingale Pl
BUCK/WIN MK18 ....37 C2
MDHD SL6 ....177 M9
CSHM HP5 * 135 M2
Nightingale Rd *AYLS* HP21 .....95 N9
RAYLNE/WEN HP22 ....111 P8
Nightingales La *CSTG* HP8 ...146 F7
The Nightingales
STWL/WRAY TW19 ....195 N2
Nightingale Wk *WDSR* SL4 ....193 N2
Nightingale Wy
DEN/HRF UB9 ....169 P4
Nine Acres *SL* SL1 ....187 K2
Nine Elms Cl
EBED/NFELT TW14 ....197 M7
UX/CGN UB8 ....182 D8
Nine Stiles Cl *DEN/HRF* UB9 ..182 B2
Ninnings Rd *CFSP/GDCR* SL9 .157 H7
Ninnings Wy *CFSP/GDCR* SL9 .157 H7
Ninth Av *HYS/HAR* UB3 ....191 J2
Nithsdale Gv
HGDN/ICK UB10 ....171 J8
Nixey Cl *SL* SL1 ....188 D3
Nixons Cl *EAG/OLD/WT* MK6 ...42 E6
Noble Cl *WLLN* MK15 ....30 G6
Noble Rd *HEN* RG9 ....174 B8
Nook Pk *RMKS/WB* MK17 * 50 C8
Noon Layer Dr *MKV* MK10 ......43 L1
Norbrek *CNH/GTH/TM* MK8 .....41 N2
Norbury Rd *FELT* TW13 ....197 M1
Norcotts Kiln *RAYLW* HP18 .....78 B9
Norden Cl *MDHD* SL6 ....185 J3
Norden Mdw *MDHD* SL6 ......185 J3
Norden Rd *MDHD* SL6 ....185 J3
Norelands Dr *SL* SL1 ....178 G5
Norfolk Av *SLN* SL2 ....179 N8
Norfolk House
RKW/CH/CXG WD3 * 158 E1
Norfolk Park Cottages
MDHD SL6 ....177 M8
Norfolk Rd *DUN/HR/TOD* LU5 ..87 N2
RBEDW MK43 ....17 J1
RKW/CH/CXG WD3 ....158 E1
UX/CGN UB8 ....182 B2
Norfolk Ter *AYL* HP20 ....3 F3
Norgrove Pk *CFSP/GDCR* SL9 .168 G2
Norman Av *FELT* TW13 ....198 A7
Norman Crs *MKV* MK10 ....43 L1
Normandy Dr *BERK* HP4 ....114 C9
HYS/HAR UB3 ....183 J9
Normandy Wy *BTCHLY* MK3 ....52 E1
The Normans *SLN* SL2 ....180 D3
Norreys Dr *MDHD* SL6 ....185 K3
Norrington
CNH/GTH/TM MK8 ....41 N2
Norris Acre *BRACKY* NN13 ......34 B6
Norris Cl *FLKWH* HP10 ....110 F5
Northall Cl *DUN/WHIP* LU6 .....86 A7
Northall Rd *DUN/WHIP* LU6 .....86 A7
Northampton Av *SL* SL1 ....179 N9
Northampton Rd
BRACKY NN13 ....35 J3
OLN MK46 ....10 C8
RMKN MK19 ....28 E4
RNHPTN NN7 ....9 G2
North Ap *RKW/CH/CXG* WD3 ..159 J2
North Av *HYS/HAR* UB3 ....191 N1
Northborough Rd *SL* SL1 .....179 L7
North Bridge Rd *BERK* HP4 ...114 B7
Northbrook Dr *NTHWD* HA6 ...159 M8
North Buckinghamshire Wy
HADM HP17 ....109 H7
HADM HP17 ....109 H7
RAYLW HP18 ....79 L8
RAYLW HP18 ....94 E7
RMKS/WB MK17 ....50 C1

RMKS/WB MK17	51	L2
STSTR MK11	41	K2
WOLV MK12	29	K6
North Burnham CI SL SL1	178	F5
Northchurch La CSHM MK5	125	N3
Northcliffe DUN/WHIP LU6	86	A2
North CI EBED/NFELT TW14	197	K5
RMKS/WB MK17	62	C5
THAME OX9	116	F6
WDSR SL4	187	K9

North Common Rd
UX/CGN UB8	182	D1
Northcourt LBUZ LU7	64	E9
RKW/CH/CXG WD5	158	A1
North Crawley Rd NPAC MK16	31	M2
North Crft BUCK/WIN MK18	166	C2
FLKWH HP10	166	C2

Northcroft
RAYLNE/WEN HP22	81	L7
SHEN MK5	42	B6
THAME OX9	116	E5
North Dean MDHD SL6	177	M8
Northdown CI RSLP HA4	171	M8

Northdown Rd
CFSP/GDCR SL9	156	G6
BEAC HP9	155	K8
HWYN HP13	153	K2
RSLP HA4	171	L5
North Eastern Rd AYLW HP19	2	E3
North Eighth St CMK MK9	6	E1
North Eleventh St CMK MK9	42	L1

North End Pde
BUCK/WIN MK18	58	B7
RAYLNE/WEN HP22	79	L3
Northend Sq BUCK/WIN MK18	48	B2
Northern Hts BNEND SL8	165	P4

Northern Perimeter Rd
HTHAIR TW6	191	J9

Northern Perimeter Rd (West)
HTHAIR TW6	190	C9
Northern Rd AYLW HP19	2	B2
SLN SL2	179	P7

Northern Woods
FLKWH HP10	166	A2
Northfield CI HYS/HAR UB3	191	M4
Northfield Dr WLLN MK15	31	M9
Northfield End HEN RG9	173	P5

Northfield Pde
HYS/HAR UB3	191	M4
Northfield Ri AYL HP20	96	B7
MDHD SL6	177	M7
PRRI MK27	121	L9
TRING HP23	99	J7
WDSR SL4	187	K5
North Fifth St CMK MK9	6	C2

North Fourteenth St
CMK MK9	30	F9
Northgate NTHWD HA6	159	J7
North Grafton BDWL MK13	63	A3
North Gv ON MDHD SL6	177	M7
SL SL1	188	A1
North HI RKW/CH/CXG WD3	147	N4

North Hyde Gdns
HYS/HAR UB3	191	N4

North Hyde Rd
HYS/HAR UB3	191	L4

Northlands Rd
BUCK/WIN MK18	59	K1
North La WTR/OFPK MK7	43	L5

North Lee La
RAYLNE/WEN HP22	109	P7
Northleigh EMV/FZ MK4	52	D1
North Links Rd FLKWH HP10	153	F4
North Ldg LBUZ LU7 *	64	D7

North Marston La
RAYLNE/WEN HP22	80	C3
Northmead Rd SLN SL2	179	K7
Northmill PRRI MK27	131	H1
North Mill Rd PRRI MK27	120	C8
North Ninth St CMK MK9	6	E1
Northolt Av RSLP HA4	183	P1
Northolt Rd WDR/YW UB7	190	D9

North Orbital Rd
DEN/HRF UB9	169	P2
North Pk CFSP/GDCR SL9	168	G2
IVER SL0	189	N4
Northrdg Wy HHW HP1	127	P3
North Rd AMS HP6	135	N9
EBED/NFELT TW14	197	L5
HAZ/HG HP15	143	K6
HYS/HAR UB3	183	K8
MDHD SL6	177	L9
RKW/CH/CXG WD3	147	M7
WDR/YW UB7	190	F4
Northrop Rd HTHAIR TW6	191	L9
North Rw CMK MK9	6	A5
DTCH/LGLY SL3	158	A7
North Saxon GTLIN MK14	6	D1
North Secklow GTLIN MK14	42	A2
North Second St CMK MK9	6	B5
North Seventh St CMK MK9	6	E1
North Sixth St CMK MK9	6	D2
North Sq NPAC MK16	21	K9
North Star Dr LBUZ LU7	74	C1
North Star La MDHD SL6	185	J1
North St BDWL MK13	30	A6
AYL HP20	2	E2
RMKN MK19	19	J8
THAME OX9	118	D3
WDSR SL4	192	D9
WEAT MK2	53	J2
North Tenth St CMK MK9	42	E1
North Third St CMK MK9	6	C2
North Thirteenth St CMK MK9	30	F9
North Town CI MDHD SL6	177	M7
North Town Rd MDHD SL6	177	M7

North Town Moor
MDHD SL6	177	M6
North Town Rd MDHD SL6	177	M7
North Twelfth St CMK MK9	42	E1

Northumberland Av
AYLS HP21	96	B9

Northumberland CI
STWL/WRAY TW19	196	E5

Northumberland Crs
EBED/NFELT TW14	197	L5
Northumbria Rd MDHD SL6	185	H3
North Wy HGDN/ICK UB10	182	E3
RMKN MK19	28	A3
TOW NN12	27	K6

Northwood Rd
DEN/HRF UB9	158	E8
HTHAIR TW6	190	D9

Northwood Wy
DEN/HRF UB9	158	D8
NTHWD HA6	159	N8
Nortoft Rd CFSP/GDCR SL9	157	H6
Norton Leys WTR/OFPK MK7	44	A5
Norton Rd UX/CGN UB8	182	D6
The Nortons WTR/OFPK MK7	43	P9
Norvic Rd TRING HP23	98	E6
Norway Dr SLN SL2	180	D6
Norwich Rd PIN HA5	171	M1
Norwood CI AYL HP20	95	P5
Norwood Ct AMSS HP7 *	145	M4
Norwood Crs HTHAIR TW6	191	J9
Norwood La IVER SL0	181	M7
SHEN MK5	31	J2
Norwood Rd FLKWH HP10	153	P8
Nottingham Gv BTCHLY MK5	52	E2

Nottingham Rd
RKW/CH/CXG WD3	157	L1
Nova Ldg EMV/FZ MK4	52	B1
Novello Cft WTR/OFPK MK7	44	B8
Nutfield CI BRACKY NN13	34	F4

Nup End CI
RAYLNE/WEN HP22	83	H5

Nup End La
RAYLNE/WEN HP22	82	G5
The Nurseries DUN/WHIP LU6	86	A2
Nursery CI AMSS HP7	146	A3
AYLS HP21	109	L1
EBED/NFELT TW14	197	P6
FLKWH HP10	154	A2
Nursery Dr SKCH HP14	151	K5
Nursery Gdns BDWL MK13	30	A9
TRING HP23	112	F2
Nursery La DTCH/LGLY SL3	188	E2
FLKWH HP10	154	A2
Nursery PI WDSR SL4	194	D5
Nursery Rd MDHD SL6	178	F9

Nursery Wy
STWL/WRAY TW19	194	H5
Nursery Waye UX/CGN UB8	182	D4
Nutfield La WYM HP11	4	C3
Nutkins Wy CSHM MK5	135	N2
Nutmeg CI WTR/OFPK MK7	43	P7
Nye Wy HHS/BOV HP3	137	L5

Oak Av HGDN/ICK UB10	171	J7
WYM HP11	190	G4
Oak Bank Dr LBUZ LU7	64	E7
Oak CI RNHFFTN NN7	12	C5
Oak Crs HWYW HP12	152	C6
Oakcroft CI PIN HA5	159	P9
Oakdale Av NTHWD HA6	159	N9
Oakdene BEAC HP9	155	J2
Oakdene Rd HGDN/ICK UB10	183	H5
Oakdown Crs OLN MK46	15	M4
Oak Dr BERK HP4	126	F2
Oak End Dr IVER SL0	181	L5
Oak End Wy CFSP/GDCR SL9	169	H5
SHEN MK5	129	N7
Oaken Gv MDHD SL6	177	J7

Oakengrove CI
HAZ/HG HP15	144	A5

Oakengrove Rd
HAZ/HG HP15	143	N6
Oaken Head EMV/FZ MK4	52	C1
Oakeshott Av SKCH HP14	142	E5
Oak Fld CSHM HP5	135	M3
Oakfield Ar SL SL1	187	M2
BNEND SL8	165	N6
Oak Gld NTHWD HA6	159	H8
Oak Gn AYLS HP21	2	B7
Oakham Ri EMV/FZ MK4 *	51	N2
Oakhill CI RKW/CH/CXG WD3	157	N4
SHEN MK5	41	P6

Oakleigh Rd
HGDN/ICK UB10	183	J3
Oakley CI FLKWH HP10 *	166	D2
Oakley Crs SL SL1	188	A1
Oakley Gdns GTLIN MK14	30	E8
Oakley Gn CL LBUZ LU7	74	F1
Oakley Green Rd WDSR SL4	193	M6
Oakley La CHNR OX39	129	N6
Oakley Rd CHNR OX39	129	N6
RAYLW HP18	90	C7
WHLY OX35	103	M2
Oakridge EMV/FZ MK4	42	F8
Oakridge Pk LBUZ LU7 *	74	F4

Oakridge PI SLN SL2	167	N9
Oakridge Rd WYM HP11	4	A4
Oak Rd BRACKY NN13	35	H3
PRRI MK27	131	L1
Oakside DEN/HRF UB9	182	M3
Oaks Rd STWL/WRAY TW19	196	D4
The Oaks BERK HP4	126	C1
LBUZ LU7 *	64	E6
RSLP HA4	171	K5
YEAD UB4	183	J5
Oak St WYM HP11	153	J6
Oak Stubbs La MDHD SL6	186	D3
Oak Tree Av MLW SL7	164	D6
Oaktree CI FLKWH HP10	153	P1
Oak Tree CI SL SL1	187	P3
Oak Tree Dr SKCH HP14	151	L5
Oak Tree Rd HAZ/HG HP15	164	D5
Oak Vw HAZ/HG HP15	143	K3
Oakway AMS HP6	135	M8
DUN/WHIP LU6	87	K9
Oakwell CI DUN/WHIP LU6	87	H1
Oak Wd BERK HP4	126	B2
Oakwood FLKWH HP10	153	M8

Oakwood Av
DUN/HRF/TOD LU5	87	N1
Oakwood Dr WEAT MK2	53	L4
Oakwood Rd PIN HA5	159	P9

Oast House CI
STWL/WRAY TW19	194	G6
Oat CI AYLS HP21	109	L3
Oatfield Gdns LBUZ LU7	75	H2
Oatlands Dr SL SL1	179	P9
Oban Ct SL SL1	187	P3
The Observatory SL SL1 *	188	C3
Ockwells Rd MDHD SL6	185	H4
Octagon Ar WYM HP11	5	F5
Octagon Ct WYM HP11	5	F5
Octagon Pde WYM HP11	5	F5
Octavian Dr BDWL MK13	29	P8
Octavian Wy BRACKY NN13	35	J6
Ocastle CPk EMV/FZ MK4	52	A2
Odacres MDHD SL6	177	P9

Odds Farm Est
FLKWH HP10 *	166	F5
Odell Wy TRING HP23	112	C3
Odell CI EAG/OLD/WT MK6	43	J4
Odencroft Rd SLN SL2	179	L6

Odeon Pde
RKW/CH/CXG WD3 *	158	E1
Offas La BUCK/WIN MK18	60	D5
Ogilvie Rd HWYW HP12	4	A4
O'Grady Wy AYLW HP19	95	J4
Okeford CI TRING HP23	112	D2
Okeford Dr TRING HP23	112	D3
Okeley La TRING HP23	112	C3
Olcaste CPk EMV/FZ MK4 *	52	A2
Olcaste Off EMV/FZ MK4	52	A2

Old Amersham Rd
CFSP/GDCR SL9	168	G2
Old Barn CI BUCK/WIN MK18	47	N7
Old Belle CI RMKS/WB MK17	63	L8
Old Beds Rd CSHM HP5	135	M5
Old Brewery La AYLS HP21	2	D3

Old Brewery Wk
BRACKY NN13	35	H6

Oldbrook Bvd
EAG/OLD/WT MK6	7	F7
Old Burrs AYLS HP21	109	K4
Oldbury Gv BEAC HP9	155	H5

Old Chapel CI
RAYLNE/WEN HP22	121	N2
Old Chapel Ms LBUZ LU7 *	74	D3
Old Coach Dr FLKWH HP10	155	N6
Old Court CI MDHD SL6	185	H4
Old Croft CI CHNR OX39	129	K8
Old Crown SL SL1 *	188	B5

Old Dashwood HI
SKCH HP14	140	G9
Old Dean HHS/BOV HP3	127	J9
Olde Bell La SHEN MK5	42	A5
Old End BUCK/WIN MK18	58	F1

Old English CI
RMKS/WB MK17	50	E2
Oldershaw Ms MDHD SL6	177	H8
Old Farm LBUZ LU7	99	H3
Old Farm CI BEAC HP9	155	H3
LBUZ LU7	84	E5
RAYLW HP18	79	L4
Old Farm Rd HWYN HP13	142	E9
WDR/YW UB7	190	D3

Old Ferry Dr
STWL/WRAY TW19	194	E5
Old Field CI AMS HP6	145	P6
Oldfield Rd HWYW HP12	127	N5
MDHD SL6	185	P1
Oldfield Vw MDHD SL6	186	A3
Old Fishery La HHW HP1	127	P4
Old Fives Ct SL SL1	178	C6

Old Forge Ct
BUCK/WIN MK18	48	A4
MDHD SL6 *	185	N4

Old Forge Gdns
RAYLNE/WEN HP22	96	B3
Old Gannon CI NTHWD HA6	159	J4

Old Groveway
EAG/OLD/WT MK6	43	K7
Oldhams Meadow AYL HP20	95	P5

Old Hardenware
HWYN HP13	153	L1
Oldhill DUN/WHIP LU6	87	L2
Old Horns La SKCH HP14	142	F7
Oldhouse CI HWYW HP12	152	E7

Old House Ct
DTCH/LGLY SL3 *	158	B7
Old Howlett's La RSLP HA4 *	171	K4
Old Kiln Rd FLKWH HP10	144	A9
Old Kiln La AYLW HP18	91	N1
The Old Kiln HEN RG9	160	C7
Old Linslade Rd LBUZ LU7	64	B6
Old Lodge Dr BEAC HP9	155	H9
Old London Rd THAME OX9	116	F9

The Old Maltings
BUCK/WIN MK18	48	A4

Old Manor CI RMKS/WB MK17	51	K2
Old Manor Ct LBUZ LU7 *	72	E1
Old Marsh La MDHD SL6	186	D3
Old Md CFSP/GDCR SL9	156	G6
Old Meadow CI BERK HP4	126	C5
The Old Ms OLN MK46 *	15	M3
Old Mill CI HADM HP17	107	L8

Old Mill Furlong
BUCK/WIN MK18	60	C5
Old Mill La MDHD SL6	186	B4
UX/CGN UB8	182	B8
Old Mill PI STWL/WRAY TW19	195	K5
Old Mill Rd DEN/HRF UB9	170	B8
Old Moor La FLKWH HP10	166	C1
Old Nursery Ct SLN SL2	167	N7
Old Oak Dr TOW NN12	25	K1
Old Oak Gdns BERK HP4 *	114	A7
Old Orch CHNR OX39	130	A2
Old Orchard CI UX/CGN UB8	182	G9
Old Orchard Ms BERK HP4	126	E2

The Orchards
RAYLNE/WEN HP22	96	A4
Old Oxford Rd SKCH HP14	151	L1
Old Papermill CI HAZ/HG HP15	166	C1
Old Plough CI RAYLW HP18	106	F4

Old Post Office La
MDHD SL6 *	177	M9
Old Priory DEN/HRF UB9	171	H5

Old Rectory La
DEN/HRF UB9	169	N5

Old Risborough Rd
RAYLNE/WEN HP22	110	A6
Old Rd LBUZ LU7	74	C2
Old Sax La CSHM MK5	125	H9

Old School CI
RAYLNE/WEN HP22	111	J5

Old School Ct
BUCK/WIN MK18 *	48	A3
DUN/WHIP LU6	86	B2
LBUZ LU7 *	74	E2
STWL/WRAY TW19	194	D5

The Old School La
BUCK/WIN MK18 *	60	B6
Old School Rd UX/CGN UB8	182	F7

The Old School
FLKWH HP10 *	166	B5
Old's CI WATW WD18	159	H1
Old Shire La CFSP/GDCR SL9	157	K3
Old School St MK5	147	K8

Old Shire Lane Circular Wk
RKW/CH/CXG WD3	147	L9
Old Slade La DTCH/LGLY SL3	189	P6

Old Station La
STWL/WRAY TW19	195	H5
Old Station Rd HYS/HAR UB3	191	M4
Old Station Wy FLKWH HP10	166	C4
Old Stoke Rd AYLS HP21	95	N9

Old Tan Yard CI
BUCK/WIN MK18 *	60	B6
Old Town BRACKY NN13	35	J5

Old Uxbridge Rd
RKW/CH/CXG WD3	157	N7

Old Vicarage Wy
FLKWH HP10	166	B5
Old Watery La FLKWH HP10	166	C1
Oldway La SL SL1	187	H2

Old Windmill Wy
RAYLNE/WEN HP22	106	A7

Old Wolverton Rd
WOLV MK12	29	J6
Oliffe CI AYLW HP19	95	M4
Oliffe Wy AYLW HP19	95	M4
Oliver Rd WEAT MK2	53	J3
Olivers CI BERK HP4	115	J2
Oliver's Paddock MLW SL7	164	D4
Olivia Gdns DEN/HRF UB9	158	C8
Olivier Wy AYL HP20	3	A7

Olleberrie La
RKW/CH/CXG WD3	137	N5
Olney Rd OLN MK46	10	C5
OLN MK46	15	M7
Omega Ct LBUZ LU7	74	C1
One Pin La SLN SL2	167	N9
One Tree La BEAC HP9	155	H5
One Tree PI AMS HP6 *	145	N2
Onslow St WTR/OFPK MK7	43	M8
Onslow Dr THAME OX9	118	E4
Onslow Gdns HWYN HP13	153	L3
Opal Ct DTCH/LGLY SL3	180	C2
Opendale Rd SL SL1	178	F8
Oram Ct MLW SL7	164	D7
Orbison Ct CMK/CTM/TM MK3	41	M5
Orchard Av BERK HP4	126	C1
EBED/NFELT TW14	197	K4
SL SL1	179	H8
WDSR SL4	187	J3
Orchard CI BTCHLY MK3	52	F2
DEN/HRF UB9	171	H5
HEN RG9	174	A7
MDHD SL6	185	J6
PRRI MK27	120	F6
RAYLNE/WEN HP22	96	A4
RAYLNE/WEN HP22	95	P4
RAYLNE/WEN HP22	110	A6
RAYLW HP18	79	L9
RAYLW HP18	90	G8
RBEDW MK43	33	L4
RKW/CH/CXG WD3	147	M5
RMKS/WB MK17	52	C8
SKCH HP14	142	A8
THAME OX9	118	C5
TOW NN12	25	M5
Orchard Ct BEAC HP9	155	N5

Orchard Dene
RAYLNE/WEN HP22	96	B5
Orchard Dr FLKWH HP10	166	B5
HAZ/HG HP15	143	K8
LBUZ LU7	74	C2
RAYLNE/WEN HP22	111	J6
RKW/CH/CXG WD3	147	L5
UX/CGN UB8	182	D7

Orchard End DUN/WHIP LU6	86	A9
AYL HP20 *	3	A5
Orchard End Av AMSS HP7	146	B3
Orchard Est LBUZ LU7	75	H5
Orchard Ga SLN SL2	179	N1
Orchard Gv CFSP/GDCR SL9	156	G6
FLKWH HP10	165	P2
MDHD SL6	177	J9

The Orchard Lake Vw
WDSR SL4	192	D7
Orchard La AMS HP6	145	J2
GTMKS/PWD HP16	133	J6
LBUZ LU7	63	J2
RBEDW MK43	11	K1
Orchard MI BNEND SL8	165	P8
Orchard Pk HAZ/HG HP15	36	A8
SKCH HP14	182	C8
UX/CGN UB8 *	182	C8
Orchard Rd BEAC HP9	155	K9
BERK HP4	126	N5
CSTG HP8	156	E2
FLKWH HP10	156	C2
HYS/HAR UB3	183	M1
WDSR SL4	194	D6
The Orchards DUN/WHIP LU6	86	A2
GTMKS/PWD HP16	143	N1
HADM HP17	108	E1
TRING HP23	112	D3
Orchardville SL SL1	178	F7
Orchard Wy ASHF TW15	196	F8
AYL HP20	95	P5
BUCK/WIN MK18	69	J3
CHNR OX39	129	N6
DTCH/LGLY SL3 *	188	B7
DUN/WHIP LU6	86	A9
HAZ/HG HP15	144	A5
HHS/BOV HP3	137	J1
LBUZ LU7	75	H2
NPAC MK16	14	B9
NPAC MK16	22	E8
RBEDW MK43	33	L4
Orchard Waye UX/CGN UB8	182	D5
Orchehill Av CFSP/GDCR SL9	168	F2
Orchehill Ri CFSP/GDCR SL9	168	G2
Ordnance CI FELT TW15	197	N8
Oregano CI WDR/YW UB7	190	F1
Orford Ct SHEN MK5	42	A5
Oriel CI WOLV MK12	29	K7
Oriel Wy BRACKY NN13	35	J6
Orion Wy LBUZ LU7	75	H1
NTHWD HA6	159	M4
Orkney CI BTCHLY MK3	52	F1
LBUZ LU7 *	72	E1
Ormesby CI AYLS HP21	110	A1
Ormonde GTLIN MK14	30	D6
Ormonde Rd NTHWD HA6	159	K4
Ormond Rd THAME OX9	118	E4
Ormsgill CI BDWL MK13	30	G6
Orne Gdns WLLN MK15	30	G6
Orpington Gv SHEN MK5	42	B8
Ortensia Dr WTR/OFPK MK7	44	A5
Orwell CI AYLS HP21	109	M2
HYS/HAR UB3	191	M2
NPAC MK16	14	D9
WDSR SL4	193	P2
Orwell Dr AYLS HP21	109	M2

Osborne Av
STWL/WRAY TW19	196	E7
Osborne Ct WDSR SL4	193	N1
Osborne Ms WDSR SL4	193	N1
Osborne St SL SL1	188	B3
WEAT MK2	53	J4
Osborne Wy TRING HP23	111	J6
Osborn Rd UX/CGN UB8 *	182	C5
Osborn St SL SL1	15	M4
Osbourne St WOLV MK12	29	M7
Osier La SHEN MK5	42	B8
Osier Wy AYL HP20	3	G4
BUCK/WIN MK18	48	A4
Osmington PI FRHG HP23	112	D2
Osney Rd MDHD SL6	177	J6
Osprey Ct EAG/OLD/WT MK6	7	K9
Osprey Wk BUCK/WIN MK18	48	A8
Ostler Ga MDHD SL6	177	J7
Ostlers La STSTR MK11	28	D8
Otmoor La HEAD OX3	102	D2
KID OX5	88	C3
Otter CI BTCHLY MK3	52	D2
Otterfield Rd WDR/YW UB7	190	E1
Otters Brook BUCK/WIN MK18	48	A8
Otway CI AYLS HP21	109	N3
Oulton CI AYLS HP21	110	A1
Ousebank St NPAC MK16	21	K9
Ousebank Wy STSTR MK11	28	F8
Ouseley Rd STWL/WRAY TW19	194	E6
Outfield Rd CFSP/GDCR SL9	156	F9
Outlook Dr CSTG HP8	156	E5
Ouzel CI BTCHLY MK3	52	F6
The Oval EAG/OLD/WT MK6	42	E5
Oval Wy CFSP/GDCR SL9	168	G2
Overdale Rd CSHM HP5	135	M1
Overdales LBUZ LU7	75	H2
Overend CI BDWL MK13	30	A9
Overend Green La LBUZ LU7	64	G4
Overgate CMK MK9	31	H9

Over Hampden
GTMKS/PWD HP16	133	H5
Overhills OLN MK46	15	L3
Overn Av BUCK/WIN MK18	48	B6

Overn Cl *BUCK/WIN* MK18....48 B2
Overn Crs *BUCK/WIN* MK18 ....48 A2
Oversley Ct *GTLIN* MK14 * 30 C4
Overstrand
  RAYLNE/WEN HP22....111 L1
Overstreet *GTLIN* MK14 ....30 C7
Over The Misbourne
  CFSP/GDCR SL9....169 J4
Over the Misbourne Rd
  DEN/HRF UB9....169 J4
Overton Dr *THAME* OX9....118 F4
Oville Ct *SHEN* MK5....42 A7
Oving Rd *RAYLNE/WEN* HP22....80 C1
Ovitts Cl *BUCK/WIN* MK18....60 C5
Owen Cl *NTHLT* UB5 *....183 H6
Owl Cl *AYLV* HP19 *....95 F4
Owlsears Cl *BEAC* HP9....155 H6
Oxendon Ct *LBUZ* LU7....64 D8
Oxfield Cl *BERK* HP4....126 C2
Oxfield Park Dr *RMKN* MK19....26 E8
Oxford Av *HYS/HAR* UB3....191 M8
  SL SL1....178 C5
  SL SL1....179 K8
Oxford Ct *NTHWD* HA6....159 J4
Oxford Gdns *DEN/HRF* UB9....170 A8
Oxford Rd *AYLW* HP19....95 J7
  BRACKY NN13....34 C7
  CFSP/GDCR SL9....168 C2
  CFSP/GDCR SL9....169 K6
  DEN/HRF UB9....182 B1
  HADM HP17....108 F1
  HWYN HP13....104 D3
  MLW SL7....164 C7
  RAYLW HP18....104 D3
  SKCH HP14....139 M5
  THAME OX9....116 F7
  THAME OX9....118 A5
  WDSR SL4....187 N9
Oxford Rd East *WDSR* SL4....187 N9
Oxfordshire Wy *HEN* RG9....161 H2
  THAME OX9....128 A8
  WHLV QX35....103 K8
  WTLGN OX49....159 P4
Oxford St *GTMIS/PWD* HP16....124 B8
  WEAT MK2....53 J3
  WOLV MK12....29 M7
  WYM HP11....95 H2
Oxhey Dr *OXHEY* WD19....159 P4
Oxhey Dr South
  OXHEY WD19....159 N5
Oxhey Ridge Cl
  OXHEY WD19....159 N5
Oxhouse Ct *SHEN* MK5....42 A9
Oxleys *OLN* MK46....15 L3
Oxman La *WOLV* MK12....29 J8
Oxwich Gv *EMV/FZ* MK4....52 B3

P

Pacific Cl *EBED/NFELT* TW14....197 M7
Packet Boat La *UX/CGN* UB8....182 B7
Packhorse Rd
  CFSP/GDCR SL9....168 G4
Pack & Prime La *HEN* RG9....173 N6
Padbury Br *BUCK/WIN* MK18....48 C7
Padbury Cl
  EBED/NFELT TW14....197 K7
Padcroft Rd *WDR/YW* UB7....190 D2
Paddock Cl *GTLIN* MK14....30 C5
The Paddock Lake Vw
  WDSR SL4 *....192 C6
The Paddocks
  BUCK/WIN MK18....58 C7
  HADM HP17....107 L9
  HWYW HP12....152 A9
  LBUZ LU7....74 F2
  MLW SL7 *....164 F7
  RAYLNE/WEN HP22....111 H9
  RKW/CH/CXG WD3....147 P6
The Paddock *AYLS* HP21....96 C5
  BUCK/WIN MK18....38 C8
  CFSP/GDCR SL9....156 G5
  DTCH/LGLY SL3....188 D4
  HGDN/ICK UB10....171 H9
  OLN MK46....15 L4
  WDSR SL4 *....186 D8
  WDSR SL4 *....192 F7
Paddock Wy
  WAR/TWY RG10 *....184 A9
Paddock Wy *WEAT* MK2....53 K2
Padstow Cl *AYL* HP20....3 D2
  DTCH/LGLY SL3 *....188 D4
Padstow Wk
  EBED/NFELT TW14....197 M8
Page Hill Av *BUCK/WIN* MK18....48 C2
Page Rd *EBED/NFELT* TW14....197 K5
Pages Cft *BERK* HP4....114 C8
Pages La *UX/CGN* UB8....182 C2
Pages Wlf *MDHD* SL6 *....178 A9
Paget Cl *MLW* SL7....164 F7
Paget Rd *DTCH/LGLY* SL3....189 H5
  HGDN/ICK UB10....183 J7
The Pagoda *MDHD* SL6....177 P7
Paignton Rd *RSLP* HA4....171 N8
Paines Orch *LBUZ* LU7....88 E8
Palace Cl *SL* SL1....187 L2
Palace Sq *EAG/OLD/WT* MK6....7 H4
Paley St *MDHD* SL6....185 H9
Palladian Br *WRAY* SL4....171 M3
Palliser Rd *CSTG* HP8....156 C3
Palmers Moor *BUCK/WIN* MK18....49 G1
Palmer's Moor La *WER* SLO....182 B7
Palmers Rd *OLN* MK46....15 N4
Palmerston Av
  DTCH/LGLY SL3....188 D4

Pamela Gdns *PIN* HA5....171 P3
Pamela Rw *MDHD* SL6 *....185 N7
Pankridge Dr
  GTMIS/PWD HP16....133 J5
Pannier Pl *GTLIN* MK14....30 C8
Pantile Rw *DTCH/LGLY* SL3....189 J5
Paprika Ct *WTR/OFPK* MK7....45 J7
Parade Ct *BNEND* SL8....165 N5
The Parade *BNEND* SL8....165 N5
  UX/CGN UB8 *....182 C8
  WYM HP11....4 C7
Paradise *RMKS/WB* MK17....52 D7
Parchment Cl *AMS* HP6....146 A1
Parish La *SLN* SL2....167 N8
Park Av *DUN/WHIP* LU6....86 B1
  NPAG MK16....31 H1
  RSLP HA4....171 L4
  STWL/WRAY TW19....194 F4
Park Cl *BUCK/WIN* MK18....71 N4
  RKW/CH/CXG WD3....159 H4
  RMKN MK19....28 C3
  SKCH HP14....26 A1
  TOW NN12....26 A1
  WDSR SL4....187 N9
Park Cnr *MDHD* SL6....176 F5
  WDSR SL4....195 J2
Parker Cl *BDWL* MK13....30 A7
Parker Knoll Wy *HWYN* HP15....5 F3
Parker Wk *AYLW* HP19....95 M4
Park Farm Rd *HWYW* HP12....152 B1
Park Farm Wy *RKW/CH/CXG* WD3....147 P6
Parkfield *RKW/CH/CXG* WD3....147 P6
Parkfield Crs *FELT* TW13....197 N9
Parkfield Pde *FELT* TW13....197 N9
Parkfield Rd *FELT* TW13....197 N9
  HGDN/ICK UB10....171 H7
Park Gdns *BTCHLY* MK3....57 G2
Park Ga *LBUZ* LU7....73 L7
Parkgate *SL* SL1....178 C7
Park Gv *CSTG* HP8....146 C5
Parklands *BTCHLY* MK3....188 F6
  GTLIN MK14....30 D4
Park La *BEAC* HP9....155 K9
  DEN/HRF UB9....158 A4
  DTCH/LGLY SL3....188 D4
  DUN/WHIP LU6....195 J2
  HAZ/HG HP15....143 N7
  HEN RG9....161 J3
  HYS/HAR UB3....191 N8
  SKCH HP14....151 K5
  SL SL1....179 J1
  WDSR SL4....192 F7
  YEAD UB4....183 L8
Park Ms *STWL/WRAY* TW19....196 F6
Parkminster Rd *AYLS* HP21....14 N5
Park Pde *HYS/HAR* UB3....183 L9
Park Pl *AMS* HP6....146 A2
  DEN/HRF UB9....158 A4
Park Ri *BERK* HP4....114 A8
Park Rd *AMS* HP6....146 B1
  BUCK/WIN MK18....70 B3
  DUN/HR/TOD LU5....87 L1
  HEN RG9....173 M4
  HGDN/ICK UB10....182 D5
  NPAG MK16....21 N4
  RAYLW HP18....104 D3
  RMKN MK19....19 K4
  RNHPTN NN7....21 L4
  SLN SL2....179 P5
  STSTR MK11....28 F8
  STWL/WRAY TW19....196 C5
  TRING HP23....112 D4
  WYM HP11....95 F2
  YEAD UB4....183 L8
Park Rd East
  BUCK/WIN MK18....70 B6
Park Rd South
  HYS/HAR UB3 *....191 N1
Parkside *CFSP/GDCR* SL9....156 H3
  EMV/FZ MK4....42 E9
  SKCH HP14....26 A1
  SLN SL2....179 N8
  WDSR SL4....142 B2
Parkside Wk *DTCH/LGLY* SL3....188 M5
Park Sq *WDSR* SL4 *....192 F7
Park St *AYL* HP20....3 D4
  BERK HP4....114 B8
  DTCH/LGLY SL3....189 M9
  MDHD SL6....177 M9
  PRRI HP27....55 K1
  RMKS/WB MK17....55 K4
  SL SL1....188 B4
  THAME OX9....118 E6
  TRING HP23....112 E5
  WDSR SL4....192 F7
Park Ter *THAME* OX9....118 E6
Park Vw *MDHD* SL6....177 M9
Parkview *FLKWH* HP10....165 N2
  WDR/YW UB7 *....181 J9
Parkview Cha *SL* SL1....179 J6
Park View Ct *HWYW* HP12....152 D2
Park View Rd *BERK* HP4....114 A8
  PIN HA5....159 P6
  UX/CGN UB8....182 C1
Park Wy *EBED/NFELT* TW14....197 L4
  RKW/CH/CXG WD3....158 C1
  RSLP HA4....171 L6
Parkway *HGDN/ICK* UB10....182 D5
  IVER SLO....181 L4

Parkwood *SKCH* HP14....141 P1
Parkwood Dr *HHW* HP1....127 P2
Parlaunt Rd *DTCH/LGLY* SL3....189 K5
Parliament Cl
  GTMIS/PWD HP16....133 H5
Parliament La *SL* SL1....178 D3
Parliament Rd *THAME* OX9....118 D4
Parmiter Cl *AYLW* HP19....95 K7
Parmoor La *HEN* RG9....163 H1
Parneleys *MKV* MK10....43 M2
Parrishs Piece
  RAYLNE/WEN HP22....111 J1
Parrot Cl *AYLS* HP21....95 K9
Parrott's La *TRING* HP23....124 F2
Parrs Rd *SKCH* HP14....140 A7
Parry Gn North
  DTCH/LGLY SL3....189 H5
Parry Gn South
  DTCH/LGLY SL3....189 J5
Parsley Cl
  RAYLNE/WEN HP22....111 J1
  WTR/OFPK MK7....43 P7
Parslow Cl *AYLS* HP21....96 A6
Parsonage Cl *HWYN* HP13....5 J1
  MLW SL7....164 D3
  THAME OX9....118 A5
  TRING HP23....112 E2
Parsonage Farm
  RAYLNE/WEN HP22....110 C3
Parsonage Gdns *MLW* SL7....164 E8
Parsonage La *SLN* SL2....167 L9
Parsonage Pl *AMSS* HP7 *....145 N3
  TRING HP23....112 E5
Parsonage Rd *CSTC* HP8....156 D3
Parson Cl *BUCK/WIN* MK18....60 B6
Parsons Cl *SHEN* MK5....42 C7
Parson's Fee *AYL* HP20....2 C4
Parsons La *RAYLNE/WEN* HP22....96 C4
Parsons Rd *DTCH/LGLY* SL3....189 P7
Parsons Wk *HAZ/HG* HP15....144 A5
Parson's Wood La *SLN* SL2....179 P7
Parton Cl
  RAYLNE/WEN HP22....110 C9
Parton Rd *AYL* HP20....2 D6
Partridge Cl *BUCK/WIN* MK18....48 D4
  CSHM HP5....136 A1
Partridge Md *MDHD* SL6....177 H6
Partridge Piece *RBEDW* MK43....35 N2
Partridge Wy *AYLW* HP19....95 J4
Pasadena Cl *HYS/HAR* UB3....191 N1
Pascal Dr *SHEN* MK5....41 N7
Passalewe La *WTR/OFPK* MK7....45 J4
Passmore *EAG/OLD/WT* MK6....43 K4
Pastern Pl *GTLIN* MK14....30 C8
Pastures Md *HGDN/ICK* UB10....182 G2
The Pastures *AYL* HP20....3 K1
  DUN/WHIP LU6....86 B3
  HHW HP1....127 N1
Patches Fld *MLW* SL7....164 E4
Patemore La *HEN* RG9....148 C8
Paterson Rd *AYLS* HP21....95 J4
Pates Manor Dr
  EBED/NFELT TW14....197 K6
Patrick Cl *SL* SL1....187 J1
Patrick Haugh Rd
  RBICS/WB OX5....76 A9
Patricks La *RMKN* MK19....28 A8
Patrick Wy *AYLS* HP21....110 A1
Patrington Cl *UX/CGN* UB8....182 C6
Patron Dr *BDWL* MK13....30 A7
Patrons Dr *DEN/HRF* UB9....169 P4
Patterdale Cl *DUN/WHIP* LU6....87 K9
Patterson Rd *FLKWH* HP10....166 C2
Patterson Rd *CSHM* HP5....135 L9
Pattison La *WLLN* MK15....43 J2
Paul's Rw *WYM* HP11....4 D3
Pavenham Rd *RBEDW* MK45....11 M4
Pavers Ct *AYLS* HP21 *....109 M3
Pavilion Cl *AYL* HP20....2 D9
Pavilion Wy *AMS* HP6....146 A2
Pavilions Wy *BRACKY* NN13....34 F5
Pawley Cl *SL* SL1....187 N4
Paxton Cl *OLN* MK46....15 N4
Paxton Crs *SHEN* MK5....42 B7
Paynes Dr *SHEN* MK5....42 A4
Paynes Field Cl *BERK* HP4....113 P8
Peace La *MDHD* SL6....177 M9
Peachey Cl *UX/CGN* UB8....182 D9
Peachey La *UX/CGN* UB8....182 D8
Peach Rd *FELT* TW13....197 N7
Peach's Cl *RBEDW* MK43....11 L1
Peacock Av
  EBED/NFELT TW14....197 K7
Peacock Hay *EMV/FZ* MK4....52 C1
Peacocks Cl *MLW* SL7....164 C8
Pea La *BERK* HP4....114 C8
Pearce Dr *AYLS* HP21....109 N5
Pearce Dr *MDHD* SL6....177 M9
Pearce Rd *CSHM* HP5....135 M4
  MDHD SL6....177 M9
Pearces Meadow *HEN* RG9....161 H8
Pearce's Orch *HEN* RG9....173 P9
Pearl Gdns *SL* SL1....187 M2
Pear Gv *UX/CGN* UB8....182 C1
Pearson Cl *AYLW* HP19....95 K9
Pear Tree Av *WDR/YW* UB7....182 K9
Pearson Rd *WDR/YW* UB7....190 F4
Pear Tree Cl *AMSS* HP7....155 N6
Pear Tree La *LBUZ* LU7....74 C1
The Pear Trees
  WDR/YW UB7....190 D1
Peascod St *WDSR* SL4....187 P4
Peascroft *RAYLW* HP18....197 M8
Peatey Ct *HWYN* HP13....153 N4
Pebble La *AYL* HP20....2 D4

  BRACKY NN13....35 H5
Pebblemoor *DUN/WHIP* LU6....86 B5
Peckover Ct
  RAYLNE/WEN HP22....96 C3
Pecks Farm Cl
  RAYLNE/WEN HP22....96 C3
Pedley Hi *DUN/WHIP* LU6....101 L6
Pednor Bottom *CSHM* HP5....134 F1
Pednordmead End *CSHM* HP5....135 M4
Pednor Rd *CSHM* HP5....135 J2
Peebles Pl *BTCHLY* MK3....42 F9
Peel Cl *WLLN* MK15....43 J2
Peel Rd *WOLV* MK12....29 L7
Peel Wy *UX/CGN* UB8....182 E8
Peerless Dr *DEN/HRF* UB9....170 C3
Peers Dr *RMKS/WB* MK17....45 J9
Pegasus Rd *LBUZ* LU7....74 E6
Peggotty Wy *UX/CGN* UB8....182 E8
Peggs La *RAYLNE/WEN* HP22....111 H1
Pelham Rd *GTLIN* MK14....30 F8
  THAME OX9....118 D4
Pelham Rd *CSHM* HP5....135 M4
Pelling *HP29* *....30 A1
Pelton Ct *SHEN* MK5....42 A9
Pemberton Cl *AYLS* HP21....109 P1
Pemberton Rd *SLN* SL2....179 K7
Pembridge Cl *HHS/BOV* HP5....137 H1
Pembridge Gv *EMV/FZ* MK4....51 N2
Pembridge Rd
  HHS/BOV HP5....137 J1
Pembroke Rd *AYL* HP20....3 C1
  NTHWD HA6....159 J3
  RSLP HA4....171 L6
Pembury Cl *HYS/HAR* UB3....191 K7
Pemerich Ct *HYS/HAR* UB3 *....191 M6
Pencarrow Pl
  EAG/OLD/WT MK6....7 J3
Pendell Av *HYS/HAR* UB3....191 M8
Pendennis Pl *EMV/FZ* MK4....52 A3
Pendle Cl *HGDN/ICK* UB10 *....183 H4
Penfold *RAYLNE/WEN* HP22....110 C4
Pengelly Ct *EAG/OLD/WT* MK6....7 J3
Penhale Cl *EMV/FZ* MK4....52 B5
Penina Cl *BTCHLY* MK3....52 D2
Penington Rd *BEAC* HP9....166 F1
Peninsular Cl
  EBED/NFELT TW14....197 K5
Penlee Rl *EMV/FZ* MK4....52 A3
Penley Cl *CHNR* OX39....139 M6
Penley Wy *LBUZ* LU7....74 E4
Penling Cl *MDHD* SL6....177 L2
Penmon Cl *MKV* MK10....43 M5
Penn Cl *RKW/CH/CXG* WD3....147 M6
  UX/CGN UB8....182 D7
Pennefather Dr *AYLS* HP21....3 P7
Penn Gaskell La
  CFSP/GDCR SL9....157 H5
Pennine Rd *SLN* SL2....179 L5
Pennine Wy *HYS/HAR* UB3....191 L8
The Pennings
  RAYLNE/WEN HP22....111 H9
Pennington Pl *THAME* OX9....118 F4
Pennington Rd
  CFSP/GDCR SL9....156 F7
  HWYN HP13....5 J3
The Penningtons *AMS* HP6....146 A3
Pennivale Cl *LBUZ* LU7....74 E7
Penn Meadow *SLN* SL2....180 B4
Penn Rd *AYLS* HP21....3 P7
  BEAC HP9....154 G5
  DTCH/LGLY SL3....188 D3
  HAZ/HG HP15....143 N8
  RKW/CH/CXG WD3....147 M6
  SLN SL2....179 P7
  WEAT MK2....53 L3
Penn Wv *RKW/CH/CXG* WD3....147 M6
Pennycress Wy *NPAG* MK16....31 H6
Pennycuik *RMKS/WB* MK17....64 A1
Pennylets Gn *SLN* SL2....180 B3
Pennyroyal *WTR/OFPK* MK7....45 P5
Penpont Cl *EAG/OLD/WT* MK6....7 J3
Penrose Dr *EAG/OLD/WT* MK6....7 J3
Penryn Av *EAG/OLD/WT* MK6....7 J3
Penshurst Cl *CFSP/GDCR* SL9....156 F9
Penshurst Rd *MDHD* SL6....185 K2
Pentelow Gdns
  EBED/NFELT TW14....197 N5
Pentewan Ga
  EAG/OLD/WT MK6....7 J3
Pentland Rd *AYLS* HP21....109 P1
  SLN SL2....179 L5
Pentlands *STSTR* MK11....29 H7
The Pentlands *FLKWH* HP10....153 P6
Pentland Wy
  HGDN/ICK UB10....171 J8
Penwood Ct *CSHM* HP5....135 M4
Penwood La *MLW* SL7....164 C8
Penyston Rd *MDHD* SL6....176 G7
Penzance Cl *DEN/HRF* UB9....169 P4
Penzance St *SLN* SL2....179 M7
Pepler Wy *SL* SL1....178 F6
Peplow Cl *WDR/YW* UB7....190 D2
Peppard Cl *HEN* RG9....161 H8
Peppard La *HEN* RG9....173 P9
Peppard Meadow
  GTMIS/PWD HP16....133 A7
Peppett's Gn *CSHM* HP5....125 H5
Peppiatts Cl *DUN/WHIP* LU6....189 A7
Pepys Cl *DTCH/LGLY* SL3....189 K7
  HGDN/ICK UB10....171 J9
Perch Cl *MKV* MK10....43 M5
Perch La *LBUZ* LU7....74 C1
Percheron Pl *GTLIN* MK14....30 C8
Perch Mdw
  RAYLNE/WEN HP22....111 H6
Percival Rd *FELT* TW13....197 M8
Percy Bush Rd
  WDR/YW UB7....190 F4

Percy Gdns *YEAD* UB4....183 L6
Percy Ter *AYLS* HP21....156 C3
Peregrine *AYLW* HP19....95 N4
Peregrine Cl
  EAG/OLD/WT MK6....43 H4
Periam Cl *HEN* RG9....173 L7
Periwinkle La *DUN/WHIP* LU6....87 L1
Perivale Av
  DUN/WHIP LU6 *....183 H1
Perks La *GTMIS/PWD* HP16....133 H9
Permayne *BNEND* SL8....29 P6
Perracombe *EMV/FZ* MK4....52 E9
Perry Cl *UX/CGN* UB8....188 H9
Perryacre *WDSR* SL4....193 K2
Perryfields Wy *SL* SL1....178 F7
Perry Hl *RAYLW* HP18....97 N6
Perry La *PRRI* HP27....127 J3
Perry Manor Cl *BTCHLY* MK3....57 G2
Perry Md *RAYLNE/WEN* HP22....111 J1
Perry Oaks Dr *WDR/YW* UB7....196 B1
Perry St *RAYLNE/WEN* HP22....111 J1
Pershore Rd *MKV* MK10....43 N5
Perth Av *BDWL* MK13....30 A1
Perth Cl *BTCHLY* MK3....52 D2
Perth Rd *HWYN* HP13....153 K2
Peterborough Av
  HWYN HP15....15 J5
Peterborough Ga
  WLLN MK15....31 J7
Peterhead Ms
  DTCH/LGLY SL3....189 J6
Peterhill Cl *CFSP/GDCR* SL9....156 C5
Peterley Av
  GTMIS/PWD HP16....133 L8
Peterley Ct *SKCH* HP14 *....151 K6
Peterley La
  GTMIS/PWD HP16....133 L8
Peter's Cl *GTMIS/PWD* HP16....133 L8
Petersfield
  RAYLNE/WEN HP22....110 C3
Petersfield Av *SLN* SL2....179 J4
Petersham Cl *NPAG* MK16....31 J3
Peters La *MDHD* SL6....121 H8
Peter's Cl *BERK* HP4....114 M8
Pether Av *BRACKY* NN13....34 B4
Pettifer Wy *HWYW* HP12....152 D5
Pettingrew Cl
  WTR/OFPK MK7....45 P6
Petty Cross *SL* SL1....179 H9
Petworth *CH/GTH/TM* MK8....41 N3
Petworth Gdns
  HGDN/ICK UB10....183 J4
Pevensey Cl *AYLS* HP21....110 B1
  BTCHLY MK3....52 E4
Peverel Dr *DBGH* MK1....43 N3
Peverel Dr *DBGH* MK1....43 N3
Peveril Cl *AYL* HP20....52 L3
  WDSR SL4....179 L8
Pevers La *OLN* MK46....14 G6
Pheasant Cl *BERK* HP4....126 E2
  TRING HP23....98 F9
Pheasant Hl *CSHM* HP5....152 E2
Pheasant Ri *CSHM* HP5....156 E2
Pheasants Cft *MDHD* SL6....164 C8
Pheasants Dr *HAZ/HG* HP15....143 P6
Pheasant Wk
  RAYLNE/WEN HP22....111 H9
Phelps Wy *HYS/HAR* UB3....191 K5
Philbye Ms *SL* SL1....187 K3
Philip Dr *FLKWH* HP10....166 A2
Philip Rd *HWYN* HP13....153 L3
Philips Cl *AYLW* HP19....95 J7
Philip Ct *SHEN* MK5....42 A9
Philpots Cl *WDR/YW* UB7....190 D1
Philps Rd *SKCH* HP14....151 L6
Phipps Cl *AYL* HP20....3 J1
  MDHD SL6....179 H8
Phoebe La *RMKS/WB* MK17....44 A3
Phoebe's Orch
  RMKS/WB MK17....63 L3
Phoenix Cl *LBUZ* LU7....99 H4
  NTHWD HA6....159 M4
Phoenix Dr *EAG/OLD/WT* MK6....42 E8
The Phygtle *CFSP/GDCR* SL9....156 G6
Phyllis Court Dr *HEN* RG9....174 A5
Picasso Pl *AYL* HP20....3 J1
Pickenfield *THAME* OX9....118 F6
Pickering Dr *EMV/FZ* MK4....52 B5
Pickford Dr *DTCH/LGLY* SL3....188 G2
Pickfords Gdns *SL* SL1....188 B3
Pickins Piece *DTCH/LGLY* SL3....195 J1
Picton St *EMV/FZ* MK4....51 N2
Picts La *PRRI* HP27....131 J3
Piddington La *SKCH* HP14....151 K3
Piddington Rd *RAYLW* HP18....76 D8
Pield Heath Av *UX/CGN* UB8....182 C2
Pield Heath Rd *UX/CGN* UB8....182 C3
Pier Rd *EBED/NFELT* TW14....197 K3
Pierson Rd *WDSR* SL4....193 H3
Pigeon Farm Rd
  SKCH HP14....140 A6
Piggott's Mt *SKCH* HP14....151 J9
Piggotts Orch *AMSS* HP7....145 M4
Pightle Crs *BUCK/WIN* MK18....48 C8
Pightle End
The Pightle *BUCK/WIN* MK18....48 B2
  LBUZ LU7....99 H4
  RAYLNE/WEN HP22....79 L3
Pigott Dr *SHEN* MK5....42 A7
Pigott Orch
  RAYLNE/WEN HP22....79 L3
Pike Cl *UX/CGN* UB8....182 C1
Pike Cnr *AYLS* HP21....110 C1
Pike's End *PIN* HA5....171 D2
Pilch La *RMKS/WB* MK17....49 D6
Pilgrims Cl *PRRI* HP27....121 K8
Pilgrim St *GTLIN* MK14....30 D6
Pimms Gv *FLKWH* HP10....153 N5
Pimpernel Gv *WTR/OFPK* MK7....43 P6

Pinchfield
 RKW/CH/CXG WD3 ....157 M5
Pineapple Rd AMSS HP7 .146 B8
Pine Cha HWYW HP12 ......152 B7
Pine Cl BERK HP4 ....126 D1
 HAZ/HG HP15 ....143 P8
 LBUZ LU7 ....64 C8
 MDHD SL6 ....177 H9
Pinecroft MLW SL7 ....164 C6
Pine Gdns RSLP HA4 ......171 H8
Pine Gv RMKS/WB MK17 ...44 E8
Pine Hl HAZ/HG HP15 .....143 M8
Pinels Wy HWYW HP12 ....152 E7
Pine Rd DUN/WHIP LU6 .....86 B8
Pines Cl AMS HP6 ....145 M1
 GTMIS/PWD HP16 ....133 P8
 NTHWD HA6 ....159 L6
The Pines FLKWH HP10 ...153 P1
 HHW HP1 ....127 P6
Pine St AYLW HP19 ....95 N3
Pinetree Cl CFSP/GDCR SL9 ..156 F8
Pine Tree Cl HEST TW5 ...191 N9
Pine Trees Dr
 HGDN/ICK UB10 ....170 A4
Pine Wk BERK HP4 ....113 P7
Pinewood Av UX/CGN UB8 .182 F9
Pinewood Cl
 CFSP/GDCR SL9 ....168 G5
 IVER SL0 ....181 L3
 NTHWD HA6 ....159 N5
Pinewood Gn IVER SL0 ....181 L3
Pinewood Ms
 STWL/WRAY TW19 ....196 D6
Pinewood Rd FELT TW13 ..197 P9
 HWYW HP12 ....152 C3
Pinfold WTR/OFPK MK7 .....43 P6
Pinglestone Cl WDR/YW UB7 .190 E8
Pinions Rd HWYW HP12 ...152 C3
Pinkard Ct EAG/OLD/WT MK6 ..43 J4
Pinkcoat Cl FELT TW13 ...197 P9
Pink Hl SL SL1 ....178 F5
Pinkle Hill Rd LBUZ LU7 ....64 E5
Pinkneys Dr MDHD SL6 ...176 F8
Pinkneys Rd MDHD SL6 ...176 G8
Pink Rd PRRI HP27 ....131 M6
Pinks Cl SHEN MK5 ....6 A1
Pinkwell Av HYS/HAR UB3 .191 K5
Pinkwell La HYS/HAR UB3 .191 K5
Pinkworthy EMV/FZ MK4 ....42 A8
Pinn Cl UX/CGN UB8 ....182 D9
Pinner Hl PIN HA5 ....159 P7
Pinner Rd NTHWD HA6 ....159 M8
Pinstow Wy CFSP/GDCR SL9 .169 K7
Pintail Cl AYLW HP19 ....95 N3
Pipard GTLIN MK14 ....30 E6
Pipers Cl SL SL1 ....178 C6
Pipers Cft DUN/WHIP LU6 ..87 H1
Pipers La HAZ/HG HP15 ...143 J5
Pipers Ct WDR/YW UB7 ...190 D8
The Pippins DTCH/LGLY SL3 .189 H2
Pipston Gv WTR/OFPK MK7 ..43 P5
Pitchcott Rd
 RAYLNE/WEN HP22 ....80 D7
Pitcher La SHEN MK5 ....6 D2
Pitchford Av BUCK/WIN MK18 ..48 C1
Pitch Pond Cl BEAC HP9 ..154 F4
The Pitch SKCH HP14 .....140 F8
Pitfield STSTR MK11 ....41 L1
Pitters Piece RAYLW HP18 .105 P5
Pitt Gn BUCK/WIN MK18 .....48 D2
Pitts Cl RAYLNE/WEN HP22 * .110 C3
Pitts Rd SL SL1 ....187 N2
Pix Farm La HHW HP1 .....127 K3
Pixies Hill Crs HHW HP1 ..127 K4
Pixies Hill Rd HHW HP1 ...127 K4
Plackett Wy SL SL1 ....187 H2
Plaines Cl SL SL1 ....187 K2
Plaiters Cl TRING HP23 ...112 E2
Plaitford Cl
 RKW/CH/CXG WD3 ......158 E2
Plane Tree Crs FELT TW13 .197 P9
Plantagenet Cl BRACKY NN13 ..34 E4
Plantain Ct WTR/OFPK MK7 ..43 P6
Plantation Cl SHEN MK5 ...42 A8
Plantation Pl SHEN MK5 ...42 A8
Plantation Rd AMS HP6 ...146 A1
 HWYN HP13 ....153 N6
 LBUZ LU7 ....64 D6
Plantation Wy BUCK/WIN MK18 .36 A1
The Platt AMSS HP7 ....145 M4
Playing Rd BRACKY NN13 ..36 A8
Pleasant Mt BUCK/WIN MK18 .58 D8
Pleasant Pl
 RKW/CH/CXG WD3 * 157 N7
The Pleasaunce
 RAYLNE/WEN HP22 ....111 L1
Pleck La CHNR OX39 ......129 L1
Pleshey Cl SHEN MK5 ......42 B6
Plested Ct
 RAYLNE/WEN HP22 ....110 C4
Plewes Cl DUN/WHIP LU6 ..87 N8
Plomer Green Av
 HWYN HP13 ....142 D9
Plomer Green La
 HWYN HP13 ....142 D9
Plomer Hl HWYN HP13 ....152 D1
Plough Cl AYLS HP21 .....109 N3
 RBEDW MK43 ....33 K5
Plough Cnr CHNR OX39 ...129 K3
Plough Farm Cl RSLP HA4 .171 K4
Plough La BERK HP4 ....126 K2
 DEN/HRF UB9 ....158 C6
 RKW/CH/CXG WD3 ......157 P6
 SLN SL2 ....180 D4
Ploughlees La SL SL1 .....188 L1
Plover Cl BERK HP4 ....126 E2
 BUCK/WIN MK18 ....48 D1
 NPAG MK16 ....31 M2
 STA TW18 ....195 P9

The Plover AYLW HP19 .....95 N3
Plowden Pk CHNR OX39 ..129 H9
Plowman Cl WOLV MK12 ...29 K8
Plum Cl FELT TW13 ....197 N1
Plumer Rd WYM HP23 ....HP1 B5
Plumer Ter WYM HP23 ......B1
Plumstead Av BDWL MK13 ...6 C1
Plum Tree La LBUZ LU7 .....74 E1
Plym Cl AYLS HP21 ....109 L1
Pocock Av WDR/YW UB7 ..190 F4
Pococks La WDR/YW UB7 .190 A6
Poets Cha AYLS HP21 ......95 P9
The Points MDHD SL6 .....185 H4
Polecat End La WHLY OX53 .103 H9
Polehanger La HHW HP1 ..115 N9
Pole Hill Rd HGDN/ICK UB10 .183 H7
Poles Hl CSHM HP5 ....135 L3
 RKW/CH/CXG WD3 ......156 E4
Polidoris La HAZ/HG HP15 .144 A4
Polish Av RAYLNE/WEN HP22 .111 L6
Pollard Av DEN/HRF UB9 .169 P4
Pollard Cl WDSR SL4 ......194 D4
Pollards RKW/CH/CXG WD3 .157 M5
Pollywick Rd TRING HP23 .113 H5
Polmartin Ct
 EAG/OLD/WT MK6 ....7 J3
Polruan Pl EAG/OLD/WT MK6 ...7 J3
Pomander Crs
 WTR/OFPK MK7 ....43 P5
Pomeroy Cl AMSS HP7 ....145 P4
Pond Ap HAZ/HG HP15 ...144 A5
Pond Cl AMSS HP7 ....144 C8
 DEN/HRF UB9 ....158 C9
 RMKS/WB MK17 ....52 C9
Pondgate WTR/OFPK MK7 ..43 P6
Pond Gn AYL HA4 ....171 L7
Pond La CFSP/GDCR SL9 .156 D8
Pond Park Rd CSHM HP5 .135 M2
Pondside Cl HYS/HAR UB3 .191 K8
Pondwicks AMSS HP7 .....145 M3
Poole Cl RSLP HA4 ....171 H4
Poole Wy YEAD UB4 ......183 L6
Pool La SL SL1 ....188 A1
Poolmans Rd WDSR SL4 .193 H2
Pope Cl EBED/NFELT TW14 .197 M7
Popes Acre HADM HP17 ..107 K9
Popes Cl DTCH/LGLY SL3 .189 L8
Popes La MDHD SL6 ......177 J1
Poplar Av AMSS HP7 ......145 B3
 WDR/YW UB7 ....190 F1
Poplar Cl CSHM HP5 ......155 N1
 DTCH/LGLY SL3 ....189 N9
 EAG/OLD/WT MK6 ....43 L7
Poplar Rd HYS/HAR UB3 ..191 N1
Poplar Rd AYL HP20 ....3 J1
 DEN/HRF UB9 ....182 C2
 DUN/WHIP LU6 ....87 N8
Poplars Cl HADM HP17 ...108 E1
Poplars Gv MDHD SL6 ....171 L6
Poplars Rd BUCK/WIN MK18 .48 B5
The Poplars DEN/HRF UB9 * .158 C8
 RAYLNE/WEN HP22 ....111 J9
Poppy Cl HHW HP1 ....127 N1
Poppy Rd PRRI HP27 ......131 L2
Porlock La EMV/FZ MK4 ....42 C8
Portal Rd
 RAYLNE/WEN HP22 ......111 K8
Portchester Ct
 CNH/GTH/TM MK8 ....41 P7
Porter's Cl RMKN MK19 ....28 A9
Portfield Cl BUCK/WIN MK18 .48 B3
Portfields Rd NPAG MK16 ..30 C1
Portfield Wy BUCK/WIN MK18 .48 C4
Porthcawl Gn EMV/FZ MK4 .52 C5
Porthleven Pl
 EAG/OLD/WT MK6 ....7 J3
Porthmellin La EMV/FZ MK4 .52 B4
Portishead Dr EMV/FZ MK4 .51 P2
Portland Cl SL SL1 ....179 H7
Portland Dr WLLN MK15 ...31 H6
Portland Gdns MLW SL7 ..164 D8
Portland Pk CFSP/GDCR SL9 .168 F4
Portland Rd ASHF TW15 ..196 B9
 YEAD UB4 ....183 L6
Portlock Rd MDHD SL6 ...177 J9
Portman Gdns
 HGDN/ICK UB10 ....182 G3
Portmarnock Cl BTCHLY MK3 .52 C6
Portobello Cl GTMIS/PWD HP16 ..135 M2
Portrush Ct BTCHLY MK3 ..52 D5
Portway BUCK/WIN MK18 ...70 D8
 CMK MK9 ....2 A1
 CNH/GTH/TM MK8 ....41 N6
 SHEN MK5 ....42 B3
 WLLN MK15 ....31 H8
Portway Dr HWYW HP12 ..152 B1
Portway Rd BUCK/WIN MK18 .70 D8
 HADM HP17 ....108 G2
Post Meadow IVER SL0 ...181 M6
Post Office La
 DTCH/LGLY SL3 ....180 F9
 RAYLNE/WEN HP22 ....81 J2
Potash La TRING HP23 .....97 M3
Potkiln La BEAC HP9 ......167 P1
Potten End Hl HHW HP1 ..115 N6
Potter Rw GTMIS/PWD HP16 .134 A2
Potters Cl RAYLNE/WEN HP22 .111 J6
Potters Cross IVER SL0 ...181 M6
Potters Cross Crs
 HWYN HP13 ....143 L9
Potters Gln BUCK/WIN MK18 .58 B1
Potters Heights Cl PIN HA5 .159 P7
Potters La STSTR MK11 ...29 K9
Potter St NTHWD HA6 .....159 N6
Potter Street Hl NTHWD HA6 .159 N6
Pottery Cl AYLW HP19 ......95 J8
Pottery Flds HEN RG9 ....160 C2
Potts Pl MLW SL7 * 164 D7

Pouchen End La HHW HP1 .127 M3
Poulcott STWL/WRAY TW19 .194 G5
Pound Cl BUCK/WIN MK18 ..58 B7
 RMKN MK19 ....27 L9
Pound Crs MLW SL7 ....164 C8
Pound Field Cl HEAD OX3 ....A9
Poundfield La MDHD SL6 ..177 M1
Poundfield Rd TOW NN12 ...28 A3
Pound Hl RMKS/WB MK17 ..44 C8
Pound La BUCK/WIN MK18 ..57 H2
 MLW SL7 ....164 C8
 NPAG MK16 ....22 F7
 WHLY OX53 ....102 E7
Pounds Cl RBEDW MK43 ...33 M4
Pound St RAYLNE/WEN HP22 .123 H1
Pound La South MLW SL7 .191 N1
The Pound BRACKY NN13 ..24 B5
 SLN SL2 ....177 M1
Powell Hvn WLLN MK15 ....43 M1
Powis Cl MDHD SL6 ....185 H5
Powis La EMV/FZ MK4 ......41 N9
Powney Rd MDHD SL6 ....177 J9
Poyle La SL SL1 ....178 F4
Poyle Pk DTCH/LGLY SL3 .195 N2
Poyle Rd DTCH/LGLY SL3 .195 N2
The Poynings IVER SL0 ...189 P5
Prebendal Av AYLS HP21 ....2 B7
Prebendal Ct AYL HP20 * 2 C4
Precedent Dr BDWL MK13 ...42 B2
Precinct Rd HYS/HAR UB3 .191 N1
The Precincts SL SL1 * ...178 F7
Prentice Gv SHEN MK5 .....42 B9
Prescott Rd DTCH/LGLY SL3 .195 N1
Presley Wy CNH/GTH/TM MK8 .41 N5
Press Rd UX/CGN UB8 ....182 D3
Preston Hl CSHM HP5 .....135 P2
Prestwick Cl BTCHLY MK3 .52 D4
Prestwold Wy AYLW HP19 ..95 J8
Prestwood SLN SL2 ....180 D9
Prestwood La HWYW HP12 .152 D2
Prestwood Pl
 GTMIS/PWD HP16 * 133 J9
Pretoria Rd HWYN HP13 ...53 K3
Prices Wy BRACKY NN13 ...34 F3
Priest Cl HEN RG9 ....160 B6
Priestend THAME OX9 ....118 C4
Priest Hl ECH TW20 ....194 B8
Priestley Ct AYLS HP21 ...95 P9
Priests Paddock BEAC HP9 .154 F5
Primatt Crs SHEN MK5 ....6 B6
Primrose Cl AYLS HP21 * ..95 N2
Primrose Dr AYLS HP21 ..109 K1
Primrose Hl HAZ/HG HP15 .185 N9
Primrose La MDHD SL6 ...185 N9
Primrose Lea MLW SL7 ...164 A8
Primrose Rd BDWL MK13 ...30 A9
Primrose Wy BUCK/WIN MK18 .48 A4
Prince Andrew Cl
 MDHD SL6 ....177 P7
Prince Andrew Rd
 MDHD SL6 ....177 P7
Prince Consort Cottages
 WDSR SL4 ....193 P1
Prince Consort's Dr
 WDSR SL4 ....193 K6
Prince Edward St BERK HP4 .126 E1
Prince Philip Av BEAC HP9 .MK45 H3
Princes Ct BERK HP4 .....126 E1
 RAYLW HP18 ....105 P3
 WDSR SL4 ....193 P3
Princes Cl LBUZ LU7 ....74 D1
Princes Gdns PRRI HP27 .131 K1
Princes Ga HWYN HP13 ..153 K4
Prince's La
 GTMIS/PWD HP16 ....124 B8
Princes Park Av
 HYS/HAR UB3 ....191 K1
Princes Park Cir
 HYS/HAR UB3 ....191 K1
Princes Park Cl
 HYS/HAR UB3 ....191 K1
Princes Park La
 HYS/HAR UB3 ....191 K1
Princes Park Pde
 HYS/HAR UB3 ....191 K1
Prince's Rd AYLS HP21 * 3 F5
 BNEND SL8 ....161 N1
 FELT TW15 ....197 M9
Princess Av WDSR SL4 ...193 M2
Princess La RSLP HA4 ...171 L6
Princess St SKCH HP14 ...151 K2
 SL SL1 ....188 D1
Princes Wy AYLW HP19 ....95 K7
Printers End AYLW HP19 ...95 K7
Printinghouse La
 HYS/HAR UB3 ....191 L3
Priors Cl MDHD SL6 ....185 P5
 SL SL1 ....188 C1
Priors Pk EMV/FZ MK4 ....52 C8
Priors Rd WDSR SL4 ......193 H2
Priors Wy MDHD SL6 .....185 P5
Priory Cl AYLW HP19 ......95 N1
 DEN/HRF UB9 ....169 P6
 HYS/HAR UB3 ....170 D3
 NPAG MK16 ....11 L2
 RBEDW MK43 ....45 H7
 RSLP HA4 ....171 M6
Priory Crs AYLW HP19 ....95 N1
Priory Gdns BERK HP4 ...126 E1
 HWYN HP13 ....153 L5
 SL SL1 ....188 D1
Priory Rd AYLW HP19 .....95 N1
 CFSP/GDCR SL9 ....168 C1
 DTCH/LGLY SL3 ....188 D1
 WDR/YW UB7 ....182 C2
Proctors Cl
 EBED/NFELT TW14 ....197 N7

Progress Rd HWYW HP12 .152 B3
Prospect Cl RMKS/WB MK17 .62 C4
Prospect Ct SKCH HP14 ..151 K5
 TOW NN12 ....18 B8
Prospect Pl LBUZ LU7 .....73 L7
 MDHD SL6 ....175 P5
 RMKN MK19 ....19 H9
Prospect Rd MLW SL7 ....164 C7
 STSTR MK11 ....29 K8
Protheroe Fld
 WTR/OFPK MK7 ....44 B8
Providence La HYS/HAR UB3 .191 K8
Providence Pl MDHD SL6 .177 M9
Providence Rd
 WDR/YW UB7 ....190 D2
Pudseys Cl MDHD SL6 ...177 H2
Puers La BEAC HP9 ....156 A6
Puffin Wy AYLW HP19 ....95 P4
Pulborough Cl BTCHLY MK3 .52 C6
Pulford Rd LBUZ LU7 ....74 D3
Pulleys Cl HHW HP1 ......127 P1
Pulleys La HHW HP1 ......127 P1
Pullfields CSHM HP5 .....135 L5
Pulpit Cl CSHM HP5 ......135 L2
Pump La RAYLNE/WEN HP22 .72 F9
Pumpkin Hl SL SL1 ....179 J2
Pump La CSHM HP5 ....136 A6
 HYS/HAR UB3 ....191 N5
Pump La North MLW SL7 .164 F5
Pump La South MLW SL7 .164 G4
Pump Meadow
 GTMIS/PWD HP16 ....133 N5
Pumpus Gn BUCK/WIN MK18 .60 C6
Punch Bowl La CSHM HP5 .135 N5
Purbeck GTLIN MK14 ....30 C6
Purbeck Cl AYLS HP21 ...110 B1
Purcel Dr MLW SL7 ....164 C6
Purse La NPAG MK16 ....19 L3
Pursers Ct SL SL1 ....188 A1
Purssell Cl MDHD SL6 ....184 G4
Purssell Pl PRRI HP27 ...121 K9
Purssells Meadow
 WDR/YW UB7 ....142 C4
Purton Ct SL SL2 ....179 N3
Purton La SL SL2 ....179 N5
Pusey Wy SKCH HP14 ....151 L5
Putlowes Dr RAYLW HP18 ..94 E4
Putman Cl THAME OX9 ....118 C5
Putnams Dr
 RAYLNE/WEN HP22 ......111 K1
Puxley Rd RMKN MK19 ....27 P4
Pyebush La BEAC HP9 ...167 L2
The Pyghtles
 RAYLNE/WEN HP22 ......164 D8
 RBEDW MK43 ....15 M4
Pyke Hayes
 CNH/GTH/TM MK8 ....41 M1
Pymcombe Cl PRRI HP27 .121 K8
Pym Wk THAME OX9 ......118 C4
Pynchester Cl
 HGDN/ICK UB10 ....170 G7
Pyxe Ct WTR/OFPK MK7 ...43 P6

P

The Quadrangle HWYN HP13 .153 L3
Quadrans Cl WLLN MK15 * ..30 E6
The Quadrant HWYN HP13 .153 L1
Quainton Rd BUCK/WIN MK18 .70 B8
 RAYLW HP18 ....93 L1
Quaker's Md
 RAYLNE/WEN HP22 ......110 F3
Quakers Mede HADM HP17 .107 L8
Quantock Cl DTCH/LGLY SL3 .189 K8
 HYS/HAR UB3 ....191 K8
Quantock Crs EMV/FZ MK4 .52 D1
Quarrendon Av AYLW HP19 .95 K5
Quarrendon Rd AMSS HP7 .145 P4
Quarry Cl RAYLW HP18 ....94 A7
Quarry Wk DTCH/LGLY SL3 ....M6
Quarry Wood Rd MLW SL7 .164 A8
Quaves Rd DTCH/LGLY SL3 .188 D4
Quebec Rd HWYN HP13 ..153 L4
Queen Alexandra Rd
 WYM HP14 ....5 E4
Queen Anne's Cl WDSR SL4 .193 M9
Queen Anne's Ride
 WDSR SL4 ....193 N6
Queen Anne's Rd WDSR SL4 .193 N9
Queen Anne St BDWL MK13 .29 P6
Queen Catherine Rd
 BUCK/WIN MK18 ....57 J4
Queen Elm RG9 ....174 ...
Queen Eleanor St
 STSTR MK11 ....28 D7
Queen Elizabeth's Wk
 WDSR SL4 ....194 B1
Queen Mother's Dr
 WDR/YW UB7 ....169 P6
Queens Acre WDSR SL4 ..193 P9
Queens Av NPAG MK16 ...31 J1
Queens Cl THAME OX9 ...118 C4
 WDSR SL4 ....194 C4
Queens Ct SL SL1 * 188 B1
Queen's Dr DTCH/LGLY SL3 .181 H4
The Queen's Dr
 RKW/CH/CXG WD3 ......147 P9
Queensgate AYLW HP19 ...95 J7
Queens Md AYLS HP21 ....96 C3
Queensmead
 DTCH/LGLY SL3 ....188 D3
Queensmead Rd
 FLKWH HP10 ....154 C1
Queensmere Rd SL SL1 ..188 B3
Queen's Pde AYLW HP19 ..3 J6
Queens Park Gdns
 FELT TW13 ....197 M9
Queens Rd BERK HP4 .....114 C9

 CSHM HP5 * 135 N3
 DTCH/LGLY SL3 ....189 D9
 FELT TW13 ....197 P7
 HAZ/HG HP15 * 183 K6
 HYS/HAR UB3 ....183 L8
 LBUZ LU7 ....64 D1
 LBUZ LU7 ....99 H5
 MDHD SL6 ....177 M9
 RAYLW HP18 ....93 K1
 SKCH HP14 ....151 K1
 SL SL1 ....188 B1
 THAME OX9 ....118 C6
 UX/CGN UB8 ....182 C6
 WDR/YW UB7 ....187 J6
 WDSR SL4 ....193 N4
Queens Sq PRRI HP27 ....131 K1
Queen St AYL HP20 ....3 J5
 HEN RG9 ....174 A7
 HWYN HP13 ....153 K5
 LBUZ LU7 ....64 D1
 LBUZ LU7 ....99 H5
 MDHD SL6 ....177 M9
 RAYLW HP18 ....93 K1
 SKCH HP14 ....151 K1
 SL SL1 ....188 B1
 STSTR MK11 ....112 E3
 TRING HP23 ....112 E3
The Queensway
 CFSP/GDCR SL9 ....168 F2
Queen Victoria Rd WYM HP15 ..5 G6
Queen Victoria's Wk
 WDSR SL4 ....188 A8
Quickberry Pl AMSS HP7 * .145 N3
Quickley Brow
 RKW/CH/CXG WD3 * 147 K8
Quickley La
 RKW/CH/CXG WD3 ....147 L8
Quickley Ri
 RKW/CH/CXG WD3 * 147 L8
Quickly Brow
 RKW/CH/CXG WD3 * 147 K8
Quickwood Cl
 RKW/CH/CXG WD3 * 147 P8
Quill Hall La AMS HP6 ....146 B1
Quilter Meadow
 WTR/OFPK MK7 ....44 C8
Quilters Wy
 RAYLNE/WEN HP22 ......110 D6
Quinbrookes SLN SL2 ....180 E9
Quinton Cl HEST TW5 ....191 P8
Quinton Dr BDWL MK13 ...42 A1
Quoitings Dr MLW SL7 * ..164 C7
Quoiting Sq MLW SL7 * ...164 D8

R

Raans Rd AMS HP6 ....146 B2
Rabans Cl AYLW HP19 .....94 C5
Rabans La AYLW HP19 .....95 H6
Rackstraw Gv
 WTR/OFPK MK7 ....44 B7
Radcliffe St WOLV MK12 ...29 M1
Radclive Rd BUCK/WIN MK18 .47 N5
Radcot Av DTCH/LGLY SL3 .189 L4
Radcot Cl MDHD SL6 ......177 L5
Radian Ct SHEN MK5 ......42 C5
Radius Pk
 EBED/NFELT TW14 * 197 M4
Radley Cl EBED/NFELT TW14 .197 M7
Radman Ov WOLV MK12 ...29 K8
Radnage Common Rd
 SKCH HP14 ....140 F6
Radnage La SKCH HP14 ..140 E1
Radnor End AYL HP20 * 95 N5
Radnor Wy DTCH/LGLY SL3 .188 F5
Radstone Rd BRACKY NN13 .35 H2
Radworthy EMV/FZ MK4 ...42 C5
Raeburn Rd YEAD UB4 ...183 K5
Raeside Cl BEAC HP9 .....155 N6
Raglan Gdns OXHEY WD19 .159 P1
Ragmans Cl MLW SL7 ....164 ...
Ragmans La MLW SL7 ....152 D9
Ragnall's La WHLY OX53 ..89 H7
Ragstone Rd SL SL1 ....187 P4
Ragstones FLKWH HP10 * .153 N9
Railway St FELT TW13 ....197 N2
Railway Ter FELT TW13 ...197 N1
Railway Vw
 DTCH/LGLY SL3 * 195 H2
Rainbow Dr
 EAG/OLD/WT MK6 ....7 H7
Rainsborough Ctn
 MDHD SL6 ....185 H4
Raisins Hl PIN HA5 ....171 P1
Rake Wy AYLS HP21 ......109 N3
Raleigh Av YEAD UB4 ....183 P5
Raleigh Cl RSLP HA4 ......171 M7
Raleigh Ct SL SL1 * 187 L2
Raleigh Rd FELT TW13 ...197 M8
Ralphs Retreat
 HAZ/HG HP15 ....143 M7
Ram Aly NPAG MK16 ....14 E9
Rambler Cl MDHD SL6 ...178 F9
Rambler La DTCH/LGLY SL3 .188 D4
Rambling Wy BERK HP4 ..115 L8
Ramsay Cl BDWL MK13 ....42 B1
Ramscote La CSHM HP5 ..125 K7
Ramsey Ct SL SL1 ....179 M7
Ramsgill Ct BDWL MK13 ...30 C9
Ramshaw Cl MLW SL7 ....164 ...
Ramsons Av GTLIN MK14 ..30 D9
Ramsthorn Gv
 WTR/OFPK MK7 ....43 P6
Ramworth Wy AYLS HP21 ..96 A9
Randall Cl DTCH/LGLY SL3 .189 H6
Randolph Cl BDWL MK13 ...18 B3
Randolph Rd DTCH/LGLY SL3 .188 G5
Ranelagh WDSR SL4 * 192 F7
Ranelagh Gdns NPAG MK16 .31 J3

Rangers Ct CNH/GTH/TM MK8....41 P3
Rannal Dr CHNR OX39.....129 N6
Rannoch Cl WEAT MK2.....53 K6
Rannock Gdns LBUZ LU7.....74 A2
Rashleigh Pl
  CNH/GTH/TM MK6.....42 E8
Ratcliffe Ct LBUZ/CGN UB8....182 D6
Rathbone Cl
  CNH/GTH/TM MK6.....41 N5
Ravel Cl WTR/OFPK MK7.....44 B7
Raven Crs RAYLW HP18.....92 G1
Raven Rd SKCH HP14.....140 B7
Ravensbourne Av
  STWL/WRAY TW19.....196 E7
Ravensbourne Pl
  EAG/OLD/WT MK6.....43 H2
Ravensbourne Rd
  AYLS HP21.....109 M2
Ravenscar Ct EMV/FZ MK4.....52 C2
Ravenscroft Rd HEN RG9.....173 P6
Ravensdell HHW HP1.....127 P5
Ravens Fld DTCH/LGLY SL3.....188 F3
Ravenside Cl BNEND SL8.....165 N6
Ravens La BERK HP4.....126 F1
Ravensmead
  CFSP/GDCR SL9.....157 N5
  CHNR OX39.....129 N6
Ravenswood Pk
  OLN MK46.....14 C2
Ravensworth Rd SLN SL2.....179 L6
Ravigill Pl WOLV MK12.....29 M9
Rawlings Ct
  RMKS/WB MK17 *.....55 K4
Rawlings La BEAC HP9.....155 P5
Rawlins Rd BDWL MK13.....30 A9
Ray Dr MDHD SL6.....177 P9
Raylands Rd CFSP/GDCR SL9.....168 G3
Ray Lea Cl MDHD SL6.....177 P8
Ray Lea Rd MDHD SL6.....177 P8
Rayleigh Cl SHEN MK5.....42 B6
Ray Lodge Ms MDHD SL6.....177 P8
Ray Mead Ct MDHD SL6.....178 A7
Ray Mead Rd MDHD SL6.....178 A8
Ray Mead Rd East MDHD SL6.....177 N7
Ray Mill Rd West MDHD SL6.....177 M7
Raymond Cl DTCH/LGLY SL3.....189 N9
  MDHD SL6.....177 M9
Rayners Av FLKWH HP10.....154 A7
Rayners Cl DTCH/LGLY SL3.....189 N9
Rayners Gdns NTHLT UB5.....183 A7
Raynton Cl YEAD UB4.....183 M7
Raynton Dr YEAD UB4.....183 L5
Ray Park Av MDHD SL6.....177 P7
Ray Park La MDHD SL6.....177 P7
Rays Av WDSR SL4.....183 K8
Ray's Hl CSHM HP5.....124 C3
Rays La FLKWH HP10.....154 A1
Ray St WDR/YW UB7.....191 J8
Raywood Cl WDR/YW UB7.....191 J8
Reach Gn LBUZ LU7.....64 D4
Reach La LBUZ LU7.....64 D3
Read Dr RAYLNE/WEN HP22.....96 C3
Reading Cl AYLW HP19.....95 N4
Reading Rd HEN RG9.....174 A8

Red Lion Ct RBEDW MK43.....33 M4
Red Lion Dr SKCH HP14.....139 H8
Red Lion St CSHM HP5.....135 M5
Red Lodge Gdns BERK HP4.....126 C8
Redman Rd HWYW HP12.....152 B7
Redmead Rd HYS/HAR UB3.....191 L5
Redpitch Pk FLKWH HP10 *.....166 C3
Redriff Cl MDHD SL6.....185 K1
Redshaw Cl BUCK/WIN MK18....48 C2
Redthorn Cl MLW SL7.....164 E5
Redvers Ga WLLN MK15.....31 H6
Red Wing AYLW HP19.....95 N4
Redwood SL SL1.....178 C2
Redwood Cl HAZ/HC HP15.....143 P8
  HGDN/ICK UB10.....185 H5
  LBUZ LU7.....73 L7
Redwood Dr AYLS HP21.....3 F6
  LBUZ LU7.....73 L7
Redwood Gdns SL SL1.....187 P1
Redwood Ga SHEN MK5.....42 C8
Redwood Gld LBUZ LU7.....64 D7
Redwood Pl BEAC HP9.....155 M9
The Redwoods WDSR SL4.....195 P3
Reed Cl IVER SL0.....181 N9
Reedsfield Cl ASHF TW15.....197 H8
Reeve Cl MDHD SL6.....185 P7
Reform Rd MDHD SL6.....185 N1
Regal Ct MDHD SL6.....185 P5
Regatta Pl BNEND SL8 *.....165 N6
Regency Ct AYLS HP21.....96 B8
  DUN/WHIP LU6.....87 L1
Regency Dr RSLP HA4.....171 L6
Regent Av HGDN/ICK UB10.....183 H3
Regent St HEST TW5.....191 P9
Regents Cl YEAD UB4.....183 L8
Regent St LBUZ LU7.....73 J7
  WEAT MK2.....53 J5
Reginald Rd NTHWD HA6.....159 M8
Reid Av MDHD SL6.....185 K2
Reid Cl PIN HA5.....191 K1
Reliance La CMK MK9.....43 H1
Rembrandt End AYLW HP19 *.....94 C5
  HEN RG9.....174 C4
Remenham Church La.....174 C4
Remenham La HEN RG9.....174 B6
Remenham Rw HEN RG9.....174 B6
Remenham Ter HEN RG9.....174 B6
Remus Ga BRACKY NN13.....35 J3
Rendlesham WLLN MK15.....31 J1
Rendlesham Wy
  RKW/CH/CXG WD3.....147 L8
Rennie Cl ASHF TW15.....196 D9
  HWYN HP13.....1 D1
Repton Av HYS/HAR UB3.....191 K5
Repton Cl MDHD SL6.....185 J4
Repton Pl AMSS HP7.....146 C3
Reservoir Rd RSLP HA4.....171 J3
Retreat La SKCH HP14.....140 F1
The Retreat AMS HP6.....146 A4
  MDHD SL6.....186 B8
  PRRI HP27.....121 K9
  STSTR MK11 *.....28 B7
Revel Rd FLKWH HP10.....166 B1
Revesby Cl MDHD SL6.....185 K4
Reynes Gn
  GTMIS/PWD HP16.....133 J6
Reynold Dr AYL HP20.....96 A5
Reynolds Cl HWYN HP13.....153 L2
  RBEDW MK43.....33 M3
Reynolds Rd BEAC HP9.....154 G7
Reynolds Wd CSHM HP5.....135 J3
Rhodes Pl EAG/OLD/WT MK6.....6 E7
Rhondda Cl DBGH MK1.....53 H5
Rhoscolyn Dr EMV/FZ MK4.....52 C2
Rhuddlan Cl SHEN MK5.....41 P5
Rhymer Cl RMKN MK19.....19 H2
Ribble Cl RPAG MK16.....31 L7
Ribble Crs BTCHLY MK3.....52 D3
Ribstone Rd MDHD SL6.....185 M2
Ricardo Rd WDSR SL4.....194 D4
Richard Gdns HWYN HP13.....153 L2
Richards Cl HGDN/ICK UB10.....182 G4
  HYS/HAR UB3.....191 L5
Richardson Dr
  EAG/OLD/WT MK6.....7 F5
Richardson St WYM HP11 *.....4 L2
Richards Wy SL SL1.....187 L2
Richborough BDWL MK13.....30 A7
Richmond Av WDR/YW UB7.....189 P4
Richmond Cl
  EBED/NFELT TW14.....197 L5
  HGDN/ICK UB10.....183 H2
Richmond Ct BTCHLY MK3.....52 D2
Richmond Crs HWYN HP13.....? J5
Richmond Crs SL SL1.....188 C8
Richmond Rd AYL HP20.....96 C7
  LBUZ LU7.....74 A2
Richmond Wy NPAG MK16.....31 K2
Rickard Cl AYLS HP21.....109 M3
Ricketts Rd HWYN HP13.....153 K4
Rickford's Hl AYL HP20.....2 C5
Rickley La DTCH/LGLY SL3.....52 D3
Rickman's La SLN SL2.....180 A2
Rickmansworth La
  CFSP/GDCR SL9.....156 G6
Rickmansworth Rd
  DEN/HRF UB9.....169 K6
  NTHWD HA6.....159 H6
  PIN HA5.....159 L9
  RKW/CH/CXG WD3.....147 N5
Rickman Wk AYLW HP19.....95 J8
Rickyard Cl BDWL MK13.....30 A9
Riders Wy CHNR OX39.....130 B9
The Ride DUN/WHIP LU6.....96 A7
Ridgebank SL SL1.....187 K1
Ridge Cl AYLS HP21.....109 L4
  SKCH HP14.....151 L6
Ridge Lea HHW HP1.....127 K4
Ridgemead Rd EGH TW20.....194 D9
Ridgemount End
  CFSP/GDCR SL9.....156 C5
Ridge Side SKCH HP14.....141 K8

Ridge Vw TRING HP23.....112 G1
Ridge Wy HWYN HP13.....153 J1
  IVER SL0.....189 N1
  RAYLW HP18.....106 D9
Ridgeway BERK HP4.....126 B5
  CHNR OX39.....129 N7
  DUN/WHIP LU6.....87 N8
  GTMIS/PWD HP16.....123 H4
  HADM HP17.....122 B6
  LBUZ LU7.....73 M1
  PRRI HP27.....121 N8
  PRRI HP27.....121 K9
  PRRI HP27.....131 H1
  RMKN MK19.....29 H9
  TRING HP23.....99 L5
  TRING HP23.....112 B8
Ridgeway Cl CSHM HP5.....135 M1
Ridgeway Ct AYL HP20.....3 F2
Ridgeway Meads PRRI HP27.....130 D2
Ridgeway Rd CSHM HP5.....135 M1
The Ridgeway AMSS HP7.....146 A4
  HEN RG9.....160 B3
  MLW SL7.....164 E5
  RSLP HA4.....171 N5
Ridgmont Av RMKN MK19.....27 P8
Ridgmont Rd RBEDW MK45.....45 M6
Ridgway DTCH/LGLY SL3.....188 H6
Ridgway Rd RBEDW MK45.....45 P3
Riding Court Rd
  DTCH/LGLY SL3.....188 F7
Riding La BEAC HP9.....154 D8
Riding Rd BRACKY NN13.....35 H7
Ridings Cottages
  HAZ/HC HP15.....144 B5
The Ridings AMS HP6.....135 P8
  CSHM HP5.....136 F9
  IVER SL0.....181 P8
  MDHD SL6.....176 F9
  WDSR SL4 *.....186 D6
The Riding RMKN MK19.....27 P8
Rigby La HYS/HAR UB3.....191 K3
Rignall Rd GTMIS/PWD HP16.....133 L4
Riley Cl AYL HP20.....3 K2
Riley Rd MLW SL7.....164 D7
Rillington Gdns EMV/FZ MK4.....42 B9
Rimsdale Ct WEAT MK2.....53 K8
Ring Rd FLKWH HP10.....153 M8
Ring Rd East WTR/OFPK MK7.....43 L5
Ring Rd North
  WTR/OFPK MK7.....43 L5
Ring Rd West WTR/OFPK MK7.....43 L5
Ringshall Dr BERK HP4.....100 D7
Ringshall Rd BERK HP4.....100 D4
Ringstead Wy AYLS HP21.....109 P1
Ripley Cl DTCH/LGLY SL3.....189 N7
  HEN RG9.....160 B3
Ripley Wy HHW HP1.....127 N1
Ripon St AYL HP20.....2 D3
Risborough Rd MDHD SL6.....177 L8
  RAYLNE/WEN HP22.....110 A3
Rise Nag Hl MDHD SL6.....178 E9
Riseley Rd MDHD SL6.....177 J9
The Rise AMSS HP7.....146 A4
  BUCK/WIN MK18.....47 M7
  FLKWH HP10.....153 P6
  HGDN/ICK UB10.....182 F5
Rising Hill Cl SLN SL2 *.....159 J6
The Riverbank WDSR SL4.....187 M4
River Ct RSLP HA4.....171 M4
River Gdns
  EBED/NFELT TW14.....197 L3
River Gates EBED/NFELT TW14.....197 P4
  MDHD SL6.....186 B3
Riverpark Rd MLW SL7.....164 D7
Rivers Edge WWF MK3.....52 D9
River Side RPAG MK16.....31 K4
Riverside BNEND SL8.....165 P6
  LBUZ LU7.....74 C1
  MDHD SL6.....186 A3
  STWL/WRAY TW19.....194 C6
Riverside Cl CSHM HP5 *.....135 N4
Riverside Dr
  RKW/CH/CXG WD3.....158 D1
Riverside Gdns BERK HP4.....114 C9
Riverside Ms
  BUCK/WIN MK18 *.....48 B3
Riverside Pl
  STWL/WRAY TW19.....196 D6
Riverside Rd
  STWL/WRAY TW19.....196 C6
Riverside Wk WDSR SL4.....187 L...
Riverside Wy UX/CGN UB8.....182 A4
River St WDSR SL4.....187 H3
River Vw FLKWH HP10.....165 P2
River Wk DEN/HRF UB9.....182 C1
Riverwood Av MLW SL7.....164 C8
Riverwoods Dr MLW SL7.....164 C8
Rivets Cl AYLS HP21.....95 N5
Rivets Ct AYLS HP21.....95 M5
Rixband Ct WTR/OFPK MK7.....43 M8
Rixman Cl MDHD SL6.....185 K2
Rixon Cl DTCH/LGLY SL3.....180 C3
Rixons Meadow AYLW HP19.....95 J8
Roade Hl RNHPTN NN7.....12 B9
Robarts Cl PIN HA5.....171 J3
Robert Rd SLN SL2.....159 J9
Roberts Cl STWL/WRAY TW19.....196 A5
  WDR/YW UB7.....190 C7
Roberts La CFSP/GDCR SL9.....157 J3
Robertson Cl SHEN MK5.....41 P5
Robertson Rd BERK HP4.....126 C5
Roberts Ride HAZ/HC HP15.....143 M5
Roberts Rd HADM HP17.....107 L7
Roberts Wy AYLS HP21.....95 N5
Roberts Wood Dr
  CFSP/GDCR SL9.....157 J5

Robeson Pl
  CNH/GTH/TM MK6.....41 N4
Robina Cl NTHWD HA6.....159 M9
Robin Cl AYLW HP19.....95 P4
  BUCK/WIN MK18.....48 D4
Robin Hi BERK HP4.....126 E2
Robin Hood Cl SL SL1.....187 M6
Robin Ride BRACKY NN13.....34 G3
Robins Cl UX/CGN UB8.....182 C3
Robins Orch CFSP/GDCR SL9.....156 C6
Robins Platt CHNR OX39.....129 N6
Robins Wy STA TW18.....195 P9
Robin Willis Wy WDSR SL4.....194 C5
Robinson Crs BRACKY NN13.....34 F5
Robinson Dr BRACKY NN13.....34 F5
Robinson Rd FLKWH HP10.....153 P6
Robinswood Cl BEAC HP9.....154 E6
  LBUZ LU7.....64 D8
Robin Wy STA TW18.....195 P9
Robinwood Gv UX/CGN UB8.....182 F7
Roblin Cl AYLS HP21.....109 N2
Robson Cl CFSP/GDCR SL9.....156 E6
Roche Gdns BTCHLY MK3.....52 E3
Rochester Av FELT TW13.....197 M8
Rochester Cl SHEN MK5.....42 A7
Rochester Ms FELT TW13 *.....74 C...
Rochester Pde FELT TW13 *.....197 N8
Rochford Rd NTHWD HA6.....171 M1
Rochfords EAG/OLD/WT MK6.....42 F6
Rochfords Gdns SLN SL2.....22 C2
Rochford Wy MDHD SL6.....186 E1
Rockall Ct DTCH/LGLY SL3.....189 K4
Rockingham Cl
  UX/CGN UB8 *.....182 C4
Rockingham Dr GTLIN MK14.....30 E9
Rockingham Rd
  UX/CGN UB8.....182 C3
Rock La LBUZ LU7.....74 B2
Rockspray Gv WTR/OFPK MK7.....43 P5
Rocky La HEN RG9.....172 D4
Rodney Gdns PIN HA5.....171 P3
Rodney Wy DTCH/LGLY SL3.....189 N9
Rodwell Gdns WTR/OFPK MK7.....43 P6
Rodwell Yd TRING HP23 *.....112 E3
Roebuck Av HWYN HP13.....153 M5
Roebuck Gn SL SL1.....187 J2
Roeburn Crs EMV/FZ MK4.....52 B2
Roger Ct NTHWD HA6.....159 N9
Rogers Cft EAG/OLD/WT MK6.....43 K5
Rogers La SLN SL2.....180 A3
Rogers Ruff NTHWD HA6.....159 J9
Roker Park Av
  HGDN/ICK UB10.....170 E9
Rokesby Rd SLN SL2.....179 N9
Rolfe Cl BEAC HP9.....155 J9
Rolls La MDHD SL6.....185 L7
Rolvenden Gv
  GTMIS/PWD HP16.....133 J7
Roman Ct DBGH MK1.....53 J1
Roman Lea MDHD SL6.....177 M1
Roman Wy AYL HP20.....3 L6
  BRACKY NN13.....35 J3
  HEAD OX3.....102 A3
Romar Ct DBGH MK1.....53 J1
Romney Lock Rd WDSR SL4.....187 K3
Romney Ct AYLS HP21.....109 P1
  YEAD UB4.....183 K3
Romsey Cl DTCH/LGLY SL3.....189 N4
Romsey Dr SL SL1.....167 P8
Romsey Wy HWYN HP13.....153 J...
Romulus Wy BRACKY NN13.....35 J3
Ronald Rd BEAC HP9.....155 K8
Ronaldsay Sp SLN SL2.....180 A8
Rookeries Cl FELT TW13.....197 P9
Rookery Ct MLW SL7.....164 D7
Rookery Meadow
  HAZ/HC HP15.....144 A4
Rookery Rd BUCK/WIN MK18.....48 D7
Rook Rd FLKWH HP10.....166 B6
Rooks La THAME OX9.....118 E5
Rooksley BDWL MK13.....42 B1
Rooks Ter WDR/YW UB7 *.....190 E1
Rook Wood Wy
  GTMIS/PWD HP16.....133 J7
Roosevelt Av LBUZ LU7.....74 C1
The Roperies HWYN HP13.....153 L4
The Rosary HAZ/HC HP15.....144 A4
Roseary Cl WDR/YW UB7.....190 D5
Rose Av AYLW HP19.....2 A1
Rosebank Cl MDHD SL6.....177 L1
Rosebarn La TRING HP23.....99 N6
Rosebay Cl WTR/OFPK MK7.....43 P5
Rosebery Av HWYN HP13.....153 L5
  LBUZ LU7.....74 D2
Rosebery Ct LBUZ LU7.....74 D2
  SL SL1.....?
Rosebery Rd
  RAYLNE/WEN HP22.....111 H4
Rosebery V RSLP HA4.....171 H7
Rose Ct RNHPTN NN7 *.....8 A1
Rose Cft BERK HP4.....114 A8
Rosecomb Pl SHEN MK5.....42 A6
Rose Crs DUN/WHIP LU6.....85 P7
Rosecroft Ct WTR/OFPK MK7 *.....43 M9
Rosedale Av HYS/HAR UB3.....183 K8
Rose Dr CSHM HP5.....135 L...
Rose Gdns FELT TW13.....197 M8
  STWL/WRAY TW19.....196 A6
Roseheath HHW HP1.....127 N1
Rosehill BERK HP4.....114 A8
Rose Hl SL SL1.....187 J1
Rose Hill Crs BUCK/WIN MK18.....58 B8
Rose La WAR/TWY RG10.....175 J8
Roseleigh Cl MDHD SL6.....176 G9

Rosemary Cl HWYW HP12.....152 B1
  UX/CGN UB8 *.....182 G8
Rosemary Ct WTR/OFPK MK7.....43 N7
Rosemary La HADM HP17.....107 L7
Rosemead
  RAYLNE/WEN HP22.....111 L5
Rosemead Av FELT TW13.....197 M8
Rosemont Wy THAME OX9.....118 E5
Rosemullion Av EMV/FZ MK4.....52 B3
The Rosery BNEND SL8.....165 N6
Roses Cl LBUZ LU7.....72 B8
Rose La WDSR SL4.....193 H1
Rose Ter RAYLW HP18.....93 L1
Rosetree Cl
  GTMIS/PWD HP16.....133 J6
Roseville Rd HYS/HAR UB3.....191 N6
Rose Wk SLN SL2.....179 N8
Rosewood Gdns
  HWYW HP12.....152 C6
Rosewood Wy SLN SL2.....179 N1
Roslyn Ct SLN SL2.....31 K6
Rossal Pl WOLV MK12.....29 K6
Rosse Cl HYS/HAR UB3.....191 K5
Rossendale GTLIN MK14 *.....30 D8
Rossetti Pl HAZ/HC HP15.....144 A4
Rossini Pl WTR/OFPK MK7.....44 B7
Rossiter Cl DTCH/LGLY SL3.....188 C3
Rosslyn Av
  EBED/NFELT TW14.....197 N5
Rosslyn Cl HYS/HAR UB3.....183 K8
Ross Rd RAYLNE/WEN HP22.....82 D3
Ross Wy BTCHLY MK5.....159 M4
  NTHWD HA6.....159 M4
Rossway La TRING HP23.....113 L6
Rostrevor Gdns IVER SL0.....181 L2
  HYS/HAR UB3.....191 L2
Rotherfield Rd HEN RG9.....173 P9
Rothersthorpe GTLIN MK14.....30 C5
Rothesay Cl AYL HP20.....2 E2
Rothschild Av
  RAYLNE/WEN HP22.....111 L1
Rothschild Rd LBUZ LU7.....73 L7
  LBUZ LU7.....74 C1
Rotten Rw RMKS/WB MK17.....54 A9
The Roughs NTHWD HA6.....159 L5
Roughwood La CSTG HP8.....146 G8
Roundel Dr LBUZ LU7.....75 H4
Roundhead Dr THAME OX9.....118 E5
Roundheads End BEAC HP9.....154 F6
Round Hl HADM HP17 *.....107 L7
Roundhill Ct RAYLW HP18.....107 K5
Roundways RSLP HA4.....171 N7
Roundwood Av STKPK UB11.....191 J5
Roundwood Cl RSLP HA4 *.....171 N5
Round Wood Gdns AMS HP6.....146 B1
Rouse Ct CFSP/GDCR SL9.....169 H3
Routs Gn SKCH HP14.....140 C1
Rovers Cft WOLV MK12.....29 K9
Rowan Av HWYN HP13.....153 K2
Rowan Cl AYLS HP21.....109 N2
  BRACKY NN13.....35 J3
  HAZ/HC HP15.....143 N6
Rowan Dr RMKN MK19.....29 H3
Rowan Gdns IVER SL0.....181 L5
Rowanhurst Dr SLN SL2.....159 N1
Rowan Pl HYS/HAR UB3.....191 M1
Rowan Rd WDR/YW UB7.....190 C1
The Rowans CFSP/GDCR SL9.....168 G1
Rowan Wk CSHM HP5.....135 M1
Rowan Wy RBEDW MK45.....45 M6
  SLN SL2.....179 M8
Rowborough Rd
  RAYLNE/WEN HP22.....111 K7
Rowcroft HHW HP1.....127 H5
Rowland Cl WDSR SL4.....193 H2
Rowland Pl NTHWD HA6 *.....159 L7
Rowlands Cl WEAT MK2.....53 J5
Rowland Wy AYLW HP19.....95 K8
Rowle Cl GTLIN MK14.....30 D6
Rowley Furrows LBUZ LU7.....74 C1
Rowley La DTCH/LGLY SL3.....180 C5
Rowlheys Pl WDR/YW UB7.....190 D1
Rowliff Rd HWYW HP12.....152 C4
Rowsham Dell GTLIN MK14.....30 D8
Rowsham Rd
  RAYLNE/WEN HP22.....96 C1
The Row AMSS HP7 *.....145 J...
Roxborough Wy BTCHLY MK3.....52 E3
Roxburn Wy RSLP HA4.....171 J...
Roxwell Cl SL SL1.....187 J2
Roxwell Pth AYL HP20 *.....2 C...
Royal Cl WDR/YW UB7.....190 D3
Royal La WDR/YW UB7.....190 D1
Royal Mel HADM HP17 *.....107 L7
Royal Wk DUN/WHIP LU6.....87 L1
Royce Cl DUN/WHIP LU6.....85 P...
Royle Cl CFSP/GDCR SL9.....157 H5
Royston Cl HEST TW5.....191 P9
Royston Wy SL SL1.....167 J...
Rubbra Cl WTR/OFPK MK7.....44 A7
Rubens Cl AYLW HP19.....95 J...
Ruby Cl SL SL1.....187 L5
Ruckles Wy AMSS HP7.....145 N4
Rudchesters BDWL MK13.....29 P8
Ruddlesway WDSR SL4.....186 F4
Rudds Cl BUCK/WIN MK18.....60 L7
Rudd's La HADM HP17.....107 L7
Rudsworth Cl
  DTCH/LGLY SL3.....189 M5
Ruffle Cl WDR/YW UB7.....190 D3
Rugwood Rd FLKWH HP10.....153 M9
Ruislip Ct RSLP HA4 *.....171 M4

Rumptons Paddock
RAYLW HP18 ....77 M2
Runford Ct SHEN MK5 ....42 C7
Run Furrow HADM HP17 ....107 L7
Runnymede GTLIN MK14 ....30 F4
Runrig HI AMS HP6 ....136 M8
The Runway RSLP HA4 ....183 P1
Rupert Av HWYW HP12 ....152 E6
Rupert CI HWYN RC9 ....174 A5
Rupert Wy THAME OX9 * 118 U2
Ruscombe Gdns
DTCH/LGLY SL3 ....188 C8
Ruscombe Wy
EBED/NFELT TW14 ....197 N6
Rushall Rd THAME OX9 ....118 E4
Rushbrooke CI HWYN HP15 ......143 M9
Rush Burn FLKWH HP10 ....166 D2
Rush Ct RNHPTN NN7 ....12 C5
Rushdene Crs NTHLT UB5 ....183 P5
Rushendon Furlong
LBUZ LU7 ....99 J2
Rushes Md UX/CGN UB8 ....182 C4
The Rushes MDHD SL6 ....185 P1
Rushington Av MDHD SL6 ....185 M2
Rushleys CI SHEN MK5 ....41 N4
Rushmere La CSHM HP5 ....156 C1
Rushmere CI RMKS/WB MK17 .....54 H1
Rushmoor Av HAZ/HG HP15 ......143 P9
Rushmoor Ct PIN HA5 ....171 P2
RKW/CH/CXG WD3 ....158 D2
Rushton Ct CNH/GTH/TM MK8 ....41 P4
Ruskin Av EBED/NFELT TW14 ....197 M6
Ruskin CI NPAG MK16 ....31 J3
Ruskin Wy AYL HP21 ....2 D1
Russell Av AYLS HP21 ....95 L9
Russell Ct AMS HP6 ....146 F5
DUN/WHIP LU6 ....87 N8
FLKWH HP10 ....153 P1
NTHWD HA6 ....159 J5
Russell Dr STWL/WRAY TW19 ....196 D5
Russell Gdns WDR/YW UB7 ......190 C6
Russell Rd NTHWD HA6 ....159 J3
Russell St RMKS/WB MK17 ......44 F8
WDSR SL4 ....187 P9
Russell Wy LBUZ LU7 ....75 H2
Russet Ct HGDN/ICK UB10 ......183 J7
STWL/WRAY TW19 ....195 P5
Russet Rd MDHD SL6 ....185 J1
The Russets CFSP/GDCR SL9 ....156 F9
Russett HI CFSP/GDCR SL9 .....168 G1
Rustics CI BUCK/WIN MK18 .....67 P4
Rustlings Ga SKCH HP14 ....151 L5
Rutherford Ct UX/CGN UB8 .....182 F7
WDSR SL4 ....187 K9
Rutherford Ga SHEN MK5 ....42 C7
Rutherford Rd AYLS HP21 ......109 N2
Ruthven Ct WEAT MK2 ....53 J8
Rutland Av HYS/HAR UB3 ....189 K5
SL SL1 ....179 N8
Rutland Ga MDHD SL6 ....185 J1
Rutland PI MDHD SL6 ....185 J1
Rutland Rd HYS/HAR UB3 ....191 K5
MDHD SL6 ....185 K1
Rutland Wy WDR/YW UB7 ....190 E6
Rutters CI WDR/YW UB7 ....190 C5
Ryan CI RSLP HA4 ....171 P6
Ryans Mt MLW SL7 ....164 C4
Rycote La THAME OX9 ....119 X9
Rycroft EMV/FZ MK4 ....51 E9
Rycroft CI EMV/FZ MK4 ....51 E9
WEAT MK2 ....53 K5
Rydal Wy HWYW HP12 ....152 I5
WEAT MK2 ....53 K5
Ryder CI HHS/BOV HP3 ....137 J1
Rydings SHEN MK5 ....193 K2
The Ryding SHEN MK5 ....41 P9
Rye CI AYLS HP21 ....109 M2
LBUZ LU7 ....75 H2
MDHD SL6 ....184 C3
Rye Ct SL SL1 * 188 C4
Ryecroft Rd CSHM HP5 ....156 C4
Ryefield Av HGDN/ICK UB10 ....183 L4
Ryefield Crs PIN HA5 * 159 N9
Ryefield Pde NTHWD HA6 * 159 N9
Ryeland STSTR MK17 ....28 C7
Ryeland CI WDR/YW UB7 ....182 E9
Ryemead La WDSR SL4 ....192 A9
The Rye LBUZ LU7 ....75 K8
Rye Vw HWYN HP12 ....5 J4
Rylands Ms LBUZ LU7 ....74 E2
Rylstone CI BDWL MK13 ....42 B1
MDHD SL6 ....185 J4
Rymill CI HHS/BOV HP3 ....137 J1
Ryton PI EMV/FZ MK4 ....42 C9
Ryvers End DTCH/LGLY SL3 .....189 H4
Ryvers Rd DTCH/LGLY SL3 ......189 H4

S

Sabina CI HWYW HP12 ....4 A1
Sacombe Rd HHW HP1 ....115 P9
Saddlers PI GTLIN MK14 ....30 C6
Sadleirs Gn RMKS/WB MK17 .....44 F7
Sadlers Ms MDHD SL6 ....177 N9
Saffron CI DTCH/LGLY SL3 .....188 A2
Saffron Rd DUN/WHIP LU6 ......86 A2
Saffron St WEAT MK2 ....53 K4
Saham Croft CI
BUCK/WIN MK18 ....60 A6
Sailing Club Rd BNEND SL8 ....166 H4
Saimon CI BRACKY NN13 ....34 A4
St Adrian's CI MDHD SL6 ......185 H3
St Agnes Ga
RAYLNE/WEN HP22 ....110 C9
St Aidan's CI BTCHLY MK3 .....52 E5
St Albans CI WDSR SL4 * 187 H9
St Alban's Rd
BUCK/WIN MK18 ....60 A6
St Alban's St WDSR SL4 ....187 H1

St Andrews Av WDSR SL4 ....193 K1
St Andrew's CI HWYN HP13 .....153 P1
LBUZ LU7 ....74 E2
STWL/WRAY TW19 ....194 C5
St Andrews Ct THAME OX9 ......118 D5
St Andrews Ct WDSR SL4 ....193 K1
CHNR OX59 ....129 N7
HEN RC9 ....173 P8
HGDN/ICK UB10 ....182 C4
St Andrew's St LBUZ LU7 ......74 E2
St Andrew's Wy SL SL1 ....187 H1
St Anne's Av
STWL/WRAY TW19 ....196 D6
St Annes CI BRACKY NN13 ......34 F4
HEN RC9 ....173 P8
RAYLNE/WEN HP22 ....111 H9
St Anne's Rd AYLW HP19 ....95 K7
DEN/HRF UB9 ....170 C1
St Anselms Rd RMKS/WB MK17 ...191 M5
St Anthony's CI AYLW HP19 ....95 K7
St Anthony's Wy
EBED/NFELT TW14 ....197 M8
St Bartholomews MKV MK10 .....43 N3
St Bees WTR/OFPK MK7 ....43 P5
St Bernards Rd
DTCH/LGLY SL3 ....188 E4
St Birinus FLKWH HP10 ....153 N6
St Botolphs HTR/OFPK MK7 .....43 P5
St Brides EAG/OLD/WT MK6 .....43 J2
St Catherine's Av BTCHLY MK3 .52 D5
St Catherine's Ct AYLW HP19 ..95 K7
FELT TW13 ....197 N7
St Catherines Rd RSLP HA4 ....171 J3
St Chad's Rd MDHD SL6 ....185 J1
St Christopher Rd
UX/CGN UB8 ....182 D9
St Christopher's CI
GTMIS/PWD HP16 ....133 P9
St Christophers Ct
RKW/CH/CXG WD3 * 147 M6
St Christophers Dr
HYS/HAR UB3 ....191 P1
St Clement CI UX/CGN UB8 .....182 D9
St Clement's Dr BTCHLY MK3 ...52 D5
Saint-Cloud Wy MDHD SL6 ......177 K9
St Columba's CI MDHD SL6 .....185 J1
St David CI UX/CGN UB8 ....182 D9
St David's Rd IVER SL0 ....181 M4
MDHD SL6 ....184 C3
St David's Rd BTCHLY MK3 .....52 E5
St Dunstans
EAG/OLD/WT MK6 ....42 G6
St Dunstans CI HYS/HAR UB3 ...191 M5
St Dunstan's Rd FELT TW13 ....197 M9
HSLWW TW4 ....197 P1
St Edmunds BERK HP4 ....126 E2
St Edmunds Av RSLP HA4 ....171 J3
St Edmund's CI AYLW HP19 .....95 K7
St Edwards Ct GTLIN MK14 * ...30 F6
St Elmo CI SLN SL2 ....179 P7
St Elmo Crs SLN SL2 ....179 P7
St Faith's CI RMKS/WB MK17 ...122 D8
St Francis CI OXHEY WD19 .....159 P7
St Francis Rd DEN/HRF UB9 ....169 P4
SKCH HP14 ....140 F8
St George's CI HWYN HP13 .....153 K5
WDSR SL4 ....187 J9
St Georges Ct HWYW HP12 * 152 D2
LBUZ LU7 ....74 E1
St George's Crs SL SL1 ....187 H1
St George's Dr
HGDN/ICK UB10 ....170 F8
St Georges Rd BTCHLY MK3 .....52 E5
St Georges Wv WOLV MK12 ......29 M6
St Giles Av HGDN/ICK UB10 ....171 J9
St Giles Ms STSTR MK17 ....28 F7
St Giles St NPAG MK16 ....31 H6
St Govans CI EMV/FZ MK4 ......52 C3
St Helen CI UX/CGN UB8 ....182 D9
St Helens Gv WTR/OFPK MK7 ....43 M5
St Hilda's CI AYLW HP19 ......95 K7
St Hilda's Wy FLKWH HP10 .....153 N6
St Huberts CI
CFSP/GDCR SL9 ....168 G7
St Huberts La
CFSP/GDCR SL9 ....169 H7
St Hugh's Av HWYN HP13 ....153 K4
St Hugh's PI SKCH HP14 ....140 B7
St Ives Crs HWY/FZ MK4 ....52 A3
St Ives Rd MDHD SL6 ....177 N9
St James CI RMKN MK19 ....19 J4
St James Ctyd MLW SL7 * 164 E2
St James Gn BRACKY NN13 ......34 C2
St James St BDWL MK13 ....29 P6
St James Wk IVER SL0 ....189 N3
St James Wy
RAYLNE/WEN HP22 ....96 B4
St Jerome's CI
HYS/HAR UB3 ....183 J9
St John's Av FLKWH HP10 ......153 P1
St Johns CI FLKWH HP10 ....153 P1
LBUZ LU7 ....75 H4
UX/CGN UB8 * 182 B4
St John's Crs WOLV MK12 ......29 M6
St John's Dr HADM HP17 ....108 D2
WDSR SL4 ....193 K1
St John's La RMKN MK19 ....27 M9
St John's Rd AYL HP20 ....2 E1
BTCHLY MK3 ....52 D5
FLKWH HP10 ....153 P1
SLN SL2 ....180 C5
UX/CGN UB8 ....182 B5
WDSR SL4 ....193 L1
St John's St AYL HP20 ....2 D1
St John St NPAG MK16 ....31 K1
St John's Well Ct BERK HP4 ...114 D9
St Josephs CI OLN MK46 ....15 M3
St Josephs Ms BEAC HP9 ....155 K8

St Katherine's Rd HEN RC9 ....173 P9
St Katherine's Wy BERK HP4 ...114 B7
St Laurence CI UX/CGN UB8 ....182 C8
St Laurence Rd
BUCK/WIN MK18 ....60 B6
St Laurence Wy SL SL1 ....188 C4
St Lawrence Dr
HHS/BOV HP3 ....127 J9
St Lawrence Dr PIN HA5 ....171 J4
St Lawrence Vw BDWL MK13 .....30 A4
St Leger Dr GTLIN MK14 ....30 D4
St Leonard's Av WDSR SL4 .....193 N1
St Leonard's CI LBUZ LU7 .....64 F7
St Leonard's HI WDSR SL4 .....193 H3
St Leonards Rd AMS HP6 ....136 A9
WDSR SL4 ....193 H3
WDSR SL4 ....193 M5
St Leonards Wk IVER SL0 ......189 P4
St Luke CI UX/CGN UB8 ....182 D9
St Luke's Rd
HGDN/ICK UB10 * 182 E3
MDHD SL6 ....177 M9
SL SL1 ....188 B5
St Margaret CI WEAT MK2 ......53 L5
St Margarets Av UX/CGN UB8 ...182 C7
St Margaret's CI BERK HP4 ....126 E7
FLKWH HP10 ....154 A2
HAZ/HG HP15 ....143 L2
MDHD SL6 ....181 M5
NPAG MK16 ....31 L1
St Margaret's Gv
HAZ/HG HP15 ....143 L2
St Margaret's Rd MDHD SL6 ....176 D9
RSLP HA4 ....171 K4
St Mark's CI AYLW HP19 ....95 K7
St Mark's Dr WDR/YW UB7 ......190 C4
St Mark's Rd AYLS HP21 ....1 B7
HEN RC9 ....173 P8
MDHD SL6 ....177 K9
WDSR SL4 ....193 N1
St Martin CI UX/CGN UB8 ......182 E3
St Martins NTHWD HA6 ....159 K5
St Martin's Ap RSLP HA4 ......159 J5
St Martin's La WDR/YW UB7 ....190 C4
St Martin's St WEAT MK2 ......53 J5
St Mary's Av BERK HP4 ....113 P8
BTCHLY MK3 ....52 E5
NTHWD HA6 ....159 J5
STSTR MK11 ....28 F7
STWL/WRAY TW19 ....196 D6
St Marys CI BUCK/WIN MK18 ....69 K1
DEN/HRF UB9 ....170 B1
GTMIS/PWD HP16 ....176 D4
HEN RC9 ....173 L8
MDHD SL6 ....184 C5
RMKS/WB MK17 ....44 C5
RMKS/WB MK17 ....61 M4
St Marys Ct BUCK/WIN MK18 ....52 H4
St Mary's Crs HYS/HAR UB3 ....191 M1
STWL/WRAY TW19 ....196 D6
St Mary's Dr
EBED/NFELT TW14 ....197 J6
St Mary's Glebe
DUN/WHIP LU6 ....86 A5
St Marys La WDSR SL4 ....192 B9
St Marys Rd BUCK/WIN MK18 ....69 K1
DEN/HRF UB9 ....169 P4
DTCH/LGLY SL3 ....188 G3
HYS/HAR UB3 ....191 M1
St Marys Rw AYL HP20 * 2 D4
St Mary's Sq AYL HP20 * 2 E1
St Mary's St BDWL MK13 ....29 P6
St Mary's Wk HYS/HAR UB3 .....191 M1
MDHD SL6 ....177 M9
St Mary's Wy
CFSP/GDCR SL9 ....156 F9
CSHM HP5 ....155 M5
LBUZ LU7 ....74 C2
St Matthew CI UX/CGN UB8 .....182 D9
St Matthews Ct BTCHLY MK3 ....52 E5
St Michaels CI LBUZ LU7 ......62 E9
RAYLNE/WEN HP22 ....111 J4
RAYLW HP18 ....67 M7
St Michaels Dr
WTR/OFPK MK7 ....43 M6
St Michael's Gn BEAC HP9 .....155 J7
St Michaels Wy
BUCK/WIN MK18 ....67 P4
LBUZ LU7 ....74 C2
UX/CGN UB8 ....182 D9
St Nicholas Mt HHW HP1 ....127 P2
St Nicholas CI AMS HP7 ....146 D3
LBUZ LU7 ....74 E2
UX/CGN UB8 ....182 D9
St Patrick's CI LBUZ LU7 .....74 C2
St Patrick's Wy BTCHLY MK3 ...52 E5
St Paul CI UX/CGN UB8 ....182 D8
St Pauls Av SLN SL2 ....188 B1
St Pauls CI HYS/HAR UB3 ......191 K6
St Paul's Rd BTCHLY MK3 .....52 D5
St Peter's Av AYLW HP19 ......95 L4
St Peters Ct PRRI NN7 ....8 A5
RKW/CH/CXG WD3 ....158 B2
SL SL1 ....188 C2
WDSR SL4 ....194 C3
WYM NN12 ....18 D5
St Peters Ct
CFSP/GDCR SL9 * 156 G8
St Peter's Ga BRACKY NN13 ....35 J5
St Peters HI TRING HP23 ......112 E2
St Peter's Rd BRACKY NN13 ....35 H5
MDHD SL6 ....177 K6
UX/CGN UB8 ....182 D8
St Peter St MLW SL7 ....164 E2
St Peter's Wk AYLW HP19 ......95 L4
St Peters Wy HYS/HAR UB3 .....183 J9
RKW/CH/CXG WD3 ....147 K6
St Rumbolds La
BUCK/WIN MK18 ....48 A3
St Stephen's Rd
WDR/YW UB7 ....190 D2
St Teresas Ct PRRI NN7 ....12 D3
St Theresa's Rd
EBED/NFELT TW14 ....197 M3

St Thomas Ct EMV/FZ MK4 ......51 P2
St Thomas Wk
DTCH/LGLY SL3 ....189 MB
St Vincents RMKS/WB MK17 .....44 C8
Salcey Av RNHPTN NN7 ....12 C5
Salcey CI RNHPTN NN7 ....12 C5
Salcombe Wy RSLP HA4 ....171 N7
Salden CI RMKS/WB MK17 ....62 D1
RMKS/WB MK17 ....45 H5
Salford Rd RMKS/WB MK17 ......45 H5
RMKS/WB MK17 ....61 M4
Salisbury Av SLN SL2 ....179 N2
Salisbury CI AMSS HP7 ....146 A3
PRRI NN7 ....131 C1
Salisbury Gv GTLIN MK14 ......30 F3
Salisbury Rd HWYN HP13 ....153 K1
PIN HA5 ....171 N2
UX/CGN UB8 ....182 D5
Sallowsprings
DUN/WHIP LU6 ....87 H7
Salmons La
GTMIS/PWD HP16 ....133 K6
Saltash CI FLKWH HP10 ....153 P6
Salter's CI BERK HP4 ....114 B8
MDHD SL6 ....177 N9
Salters La RAYLW HP18 ....77 J8
Salters Ms GTLIN MK14 ....30 F7
Salters Rd MDHD SL6 ....177 K6
Salters Rw FLKWH HP10 * 166 E5
Salt Hill Av UX/CGN UB8 ......187 N2
Salt Hill CI UX/CGN UB8 ......182 D1
Salt Hill Dr SL SL1 ....187 N2
Salt Hill Wy SL SL1 ....187 N2
Salt La THAME OX9 ....138 C1
Salton Link EMV/FZ MK4 ....42 C9
Saltwood Av EMV/FZ MK4 ....51 N2
Samphire Ct WTR/OFPK MK7 .....43 N5
Sampsons Dr SLN SL2 ....179 K6
Sampsons HI AMSS HP7 ....145 J9
Sanctuary Rd HAZ/HG HP15 .....158 C7
Sanctuary Rd HAZ/HG HP15 .....143 M5
Sandage Rd SKCH HP14 ....151 K5
Sandal Ct SHEN MK5 ....42 C7
Sandals Spring HHW HP1 ....115 P9
Sandalwood Dr RSLP HA4 ....171 J3
Sandalwood Rd FELT TW13 ......197 M9
Sandbrier CI WTR/OFPK MK7 ....43 N6
Sandbrook La TRING HP23 ......98 A6
Sandelswood Ms CSHM HP5 ......155 H5
Sandelswood Wy BEAC HP9 ......155 H6
Sanders La TOW NN12 ....27 D2
Sanderson Rd UX/CGN UB8 ......182 C7
Sandford Gdns HWY HP11 * 153 K1
Sandhill Rd BUCK/WIN MK18 ....69 K1
Sandhills LBUZ LU7 ....64 E9
Sandhill Wy AYLW HP19 ....95 J9
Sandholme BUCK/WIN MK18 ......48 A4
Sandlepit HI MDHD SL6 ....184 G1
Sandlespiatt Rd MDHD SL6 ....184 A5
Sand La HEAD OX3 ....102 C4
Sandlers End SLN SL2 ....179 M7
Sandleswood CI BEAC HP9 ......155 H6
Sandon CI TRING HP23 ....112 D2
Sandow Crs HYS/HAR UB3 ....183 J9
Sandown Ct HEST TW5 ....191 N9
Sandown Ct BTCHLY MK3 ....52 E8
Sandown Rd SLN SL2 ....180 C6
Sandpit La PRRI NN7 ....120 D9
Sandpits La FLKWH HP10 ....154 A3
Sandringham
BRACKY NN13 ....34 G5
Sandringham Ct SL SL1 ....179 H9
Sandringham Gdns
HEST TW5 ....191 N9
Sandringham PI WEAT MK2 ......53 L5
Sandringham Rd
HTHAIR TW6 ....196 E4
MDHD SL6 ....177 L6
Sands Farm Dr SL SL1 ....178 D7
Sandstone CI
BUCK/WIN MK18 ....67 P4
Sandwick CI CNH/GTH/TM MK8 ...41 L2
Sandwood Ms CSHM HP5 ....135 K4
Sandy CI CLTH/HET TW14 ....30 D5
Sandycombe Rd
EBED/NFELT TW14 ....197 N7
Sandycroft Rd AMS HP6 ....146 C4
Sandy Dr EBED/NFELT TW14 ....197 L7
Sandygate Rd MLW SL7 ....164 D6
Sandy La LBUZ LU7 ....64 D8
NTHWD HA6 ....159 J4
RAYLW HP18 ....78 B8
RBEDW MK43 ....45 M7
RMKN MK19 ....19 K3
RMKS/WB MK17 ....63 K2
RNHPTN NN7 ....12 F5
SHEN MK5 ....42 B7
SLN SL2 ....180 D5
TOW NN12 ....18 A8
Sandy Lodge Ct
NTHWD HA6 ....159 L5
Sandy Lodge La NTHWD HA6 .....159 K2
Sandy Lodge Rd
RKW/CH/CXG WD3 ....159 H2
Sandy Lodge Wy NTHWD HA6 .....159 J5
Sandy Ri CFSP/GDCR SL9 ......156 G9
San Remo Rd RMKS/WB MK17 ....30 G7
Santen Gv WEAT MK2 ....53 L5
Saracens' Whf WEAT MK2 ....59 K1
Sargeant Ct UX/CGN UB8 ....182 E5
Sarsby Dr STWL/WRAY TW19 ....195 P5
Sarum Complex
UX/CGN UB8 * 182 B5
Saturn Ct LBUZ LU7 ....75 D1
Satwell Ct HEN RC9 ....173 L6
Saunders Ct WTR/OFPK MK7 .....43 N5
Saunders La AMS HP6 ....144 B3
Saunders PI AYLW HP19 ....95 J9
Saunders Rd HGDN/ICK UB10 ....171 J9
Saunders Wood Copse
SKCH HP14 ....140 D2

Saunderton V SKCH HP14 ....141 L2
Saunton Av HYS/HAR UB3 ....191 M8
Savage Cft WLLN MK15 ....43 L1
Savay CI DEN/HRF UB9 ....170 A5
Savay La DEN/HRF UB9 ....170 A5
Sawmake Rd AYLW HP19 ....95 L5
Savill Wy MLW SL7 ....164 D6
Savoy Av DEN/HRF UB9 ....191 L6
Savoy CI DEN/HRF UB9 ....158 D9
Savoy Crs St MDHD SL6 ....177 K7
Savoy Crs CMK MK9 ....7 H1
Sawmill Rd PRRI NN7 ....11 K4
Sawpit HI HAZ/HG HP15 ....143 N6
Sawyers CI MDHD SL6 ....184 F5
WDSR SL4 ....187 J8
Sawyers Crs MDHD SL6 ....184 F5
Saxhorn Rd SKCH HP14 ....151 L6
Saxon Av EMV/FZ MK4 ....51 N2
Saxon CI AMS HP6 ....135 H5
DTCH/LGLY SL3 ....189 H3
SL SL1 ....188 E8
Saxon Gdns MDHD SL6 ....177 J8
Saxon Ga CMK MK9 ....6 E2
Saxon Ga West CMK MK9 ....6 E2
Saxons CI LBUZ LU7 ....74 C2
Saxon St BDWL MK13 ....30 C6
EAG/OLD/WT MK6 ....7 H6
WEAT MK2 ....53 J4
Saxon Wy WDR/YW UB7 ....190 C7
WDSR SL4 ....194 D5
Sayers Gdns BERK HP4 ....114 C7
Saye & Sele CI RAYLW HP18 ...77 M2
Sayward CI CSHM HP5 ....155 P2
Scafell Rd SLN SL2 ....180 D5
Scampton Rd HTHAIR TW6 ......196 F5
Scarborough Rd
HTHAIR TW6 ....197 J5
Scarborough Wy SL SL1 ....187 M3
Scardale BDWL MK13 ....30 B8
Scarlett Av
RAYLNE/WEN HP22 ....111 L3
Scatterdells La KGLGY WD4 ....137 P3
Scatterill CI BDWL MK13 .....30 A3
Scholars Wk CFSP/GDCR SL9 ...156 G6
DTCH/LGLY SL3 ....189 J3
Scholars Wy AMS HP6 ....145 J5
School CI HAZ/HG HP15 ....143 J5
HAZ/HG HP15 ....144 A4
HWYN HP13 ....142 D9
RAYLW HP18 ....116 G2
WYM NN12 ....152 N6
School Ms RMKS/WB MK17 ......52 D8
School End RMKS/WB MK17 .....50 D7
School HI BUCK/WIN MK18 .....70 D7
RBICN OX27 ....27 M3
School La AMSS HP7 ....145 L5
AMSS HP7 ....145 L5
BEAC HP9 ....156 P6
BUCK/WIN MK18 ....48 A5
BUCK/WIN MK18 ....57 H2
CFSP/GDCR SL9 ....156 K9
CHNR OX59 ....129 J9
DUN/WHIP LU6 ....86 A2
HEN RC9 ....150 B7
MDHD SL6 ....177 H1
MDHD SL6 ....184 B3
MLW SL7 ....175 K2
NPAG MK16 ....21 N4
RAYLNE/WEN HP22 ....111 H4
RAYLW HP18 ....93 L1
RAYLW HP18 ....91 H9
RAYLW HP18 ....106 H4
RBEDW MK43 ....117 X3
RMKN MK19 ....11 G6
RMKS/WB MK17 ....63 K2
RNHPTN NN7 ....12 F5
SHEN MK5 ....41 J2
SLN SL2 ....180 D3
SLN SL2 ....188 B1
TOW NN12 ....18 A8
School Pde DEN/HRF UB9 * 158 D9
School Rd FLKWH HP10 ....154 B2
FLKWH HP10 ....166 C9
WDR/YW UB7 ....190 D7
School Rw HHW HP1 ....127 P3
School Wk MDHD SL6 ....29 P6
School Wy HWY HP11 ....153 P8
Schumann CI WTR/OFPK MK7 ....44 A5
Scotlands Dr SLN SL2 ....179 M3
Scotney Gdns BTCHLY MK3 .....52 E5
Scots CI STWL/WRAY TW19 .....196 D7
Scotsgrove HI HADM HP17 .....118 F2
Scotswood CI BEAC HP9 ....155 H5
Scott Dr NPAG MK16 ....21 N4
Scott End AYLW HP19 ....95 H5
Scotts CI RBICN OX27 ....63 L2
Scotts Farm Ct
BUCK/WIN MK18 ....38 C4
Scotts La BUCK/WIN MK18 .....38 C4
Scrubbs La SHEN MK5 ....141 K5
Scylla Crs HTHAIR TW6 ....197 H5
Scylla Rd HTHAIR TW6 ....197 J5
Seacourt Rd DTCH/LGLY SL3 ...189 K5
Seaford Rd RSLP HA4 ....171 L7
Seaford Rd HTHAIR TW6 ....196 F4
Seagrave Ct WTR/OFPK MK7 ....43 N6
Seamans CI DUN/WHIP LU6 .....85 M3
Seamoons CI DUN/WHIP LU6 ....85 M3
The Sears DUN/WHIP LU6 ......85 M3
Seaton Dr ASHF TW15 ....196 B2
AYLS HP21 ....109 M2

Seaton Gdns *RSLP* HA4 ....171 N8
Seaton Rd *HYS/HAR* UB3 ....191 K5
Secklow Ga *CMK* MK9 ....7 G2
Secklow Ga East *CMK* MK9 * 7 J2
Secklow Ga West *CMK* MK9 ....7 J2
Second Av *DBGH* MK1 ....53 J1
  HYS/HAR 191 M2
Second Crs *SL* SL1 ....179 N8
Second St *WYM* HP11 ....153 J6
Sedgemere
  CNH/GTH/TM MK8 ....41 M3
Sedgemoor Dr *THAME* OX9 ....118 E4
Sedgmoor La *FLKWH* HP10 ....165 N2
Sedgmoor Gdns
  FLKWH HP10 ....165 N2
Sedgmoor La *FLKWH* HP10 ....165 P2
Sedgmoor Rd *FLKWH* HP10 ....165 N1
Sedgwick Av
  HGDN/ICK UB10 ....183 H3
Sedley Gv *DEN/HRF* UB9 ....170 G4
Sedrup La *HADM* HP17 ....109 H2
Seeleys Ct *BEAC* HP9 * 8 E7
Seer Green La *BEAC* HP9 ....158 A7
Seer Rd *BEAC* 155 P5
Sefton Cl *SL* SL1 ....180 B4
Sefton Paddock *SLN* SL2 ....180 C3
Sefton Pk *SLN* SL2 ....180 C3
Selan Gdns *YEAD* UB4 ....182 C9
Selbourne Av *BTCHLY* MK3 ....52 F4
Selby Cha *RSLP* HA4 ....171 P7
Selby Gv *SHEN* MK5 ....42 A7
Selkirk Av *AYLW* HP19 ....2 C1
Selway Cl *PIN* HA5 ....171 P2
Selwood Cl
  STWL/WRAY TW19 * 196 C5
Selwood Gdns
  STWL/WRAY TW19 ....196 C5
Selwood Wy *HWYN* HP13 ....142 G9
Selwyn Cl *WDSR* SL4 ....193 H1
Serjeants Gn *GTLIN* MK14 ....30 F7
Serles Cl *EAG/OLD/WT* MK6 ....42 G6
Seven Acres *NTHWD* 159 N6
  THAME OX9 ....118 E5
Sevenhills Rd *IVER* SL0 ....K1
Seventh Av *HYS/HAR* UB3 ....191 N2
Severalls Av *CSHM* HP5 ....135 N4
Severn Crs *DTCH/LGLY* SL3 ....189 K6
Severn Dr *NPAG* MK16 ....31 K1
Severn Wy *BTCHLY* MK3 ....J5
Sewell Cl *AYLW* HP19 ....95 H5
Sewell's La *CHNR* OX39 ....129 J4
Seymour Cl *FLKWH* HP10 ....165 M8
  MDHD 185 H4
Seymour Court La *MLW* SL7 ....164 B4
Seymour Court Rd *MLW* SL7 ....164 A4
Seymour Park Rd *MLW* SL7 ....164 D6
Seymour Pln *MLW* SL7 ....164 C5
Seymour Rd *BERK* HP4 ....114 A8
  CSTG HP8 ....156 E4
  SL SL1 ....187 N3
Shackleton Pl
  EAG/OLD/WT MK6 ....7 J5
Shackleton Rd *HWYW* HP12 ....152 D5
  SL SL1 ....188 B1
Shaftesbury Av
  EBED/NFELT TW14 ....197 N5
Shaftesbury Cl
  BUCK/WIN MK18 ....60 B5
Shaftesbury Crs *BTCHLY* MK3 ....52 G2
Shaftesbury Rd *HEAD* OX3 ....102 A3
Shaftesbury St *WYM* HP11 ....4 B7
Shaftesbury Waye
  YEAD UB4 ....183 D8
Shaggy Calf La *SLN* SL2 ....188 C1
Shakespeare Av
  EBED/NFELT TW14 ....197 N5
  YEAD UB4 ....183 N9
Shakespeare Cl *NPAG* MK16 ....20 C9
Shakespeare Orch
  RAYLW HP18 ....77 M2
Shakespeare Wy *AYL* TW20 ....2 D9
Shallowford Gv *EMV/FZ* MK4 ....42 D8
Shamrock Cl *WTR/OFPK* MK7 ....45 J4
Shannon Cl *GTLIN* MK14 ....30 C7
Shantock Hall La
  HHS/BOV HP3 ....136 G2
Shantock La *HHS/BOV* HP3 ....136 G3
Shantung Pl *CSHM* HP5 * 135 N6
Sharkham Cl *EMV/FZ* MK4 ....52 B2
Sharman Beer Ct
  THAME OX9 ....118 C6
Sharman Wk *BDWL* MK13 ....42 A1
Sharnlake Rd *DTCH/LGLY* SL3 ....189 K4
Sharp Cl *AYLS* HP21 ....109 N1
Sharpes La *HHW* HP1 ....127 K3
Sharp's Av *RAYLW* HP18 ....93 M1
Sharp's Cl *RAYLW* HP18 ....93 M1
Sharps La *RSLP* HA4 ....171 K6
Sharrow V *HWYW* HP12 ....A4
Sharvel La *NTHLT* UB5 ....183 N4
Shaw Cl *AYLS* HP21 ....3 J5
  NPAG MK16 ....20 P9
Shaw Ct *AYLS* HP21 * 109 N3
Shaw Cl *GTMIS/PWD* HP16 * T5
The Shaw *MDHD* SL6 ....179 L5
Shearmans *STSTR* MK11 ....29 J5
Sheehy Wy *SL* SL1 ....188 D1
Sheelin Gv *WEAT* MK2 ....53 P3
Sheepcoat Cl *SHEN* MK5 ....42 A7
Sheepcote Cl *BEAC* HP9 ....154 C4
  HEST TW5 ....191 P5
Sheepcote Crs *LBUZ* LU7 ....64 E5
Sheepcote Dell Rd
  HAZ/HG HP15 ....144 B4
Sheepcote Gdns
  DEN/HRF UB9 ....A4
Sheepcote Rd *WDSR* SL4 ....166 G8
  WDSR SL4 ....187 L6
Sheepfold La *AMSS* HP7 ....145 P3

Sheephouse Rd *MDHD* SL6 ....177 P6
Sheepridge La *FLKWH* HP10 ....165 M1
Sheep St *BUCK/WIN* MK18 ....60 C6
Sheerness Ct *EMV/FZ* MK4 ....52 A3
Sheerstock *HADM* HP17 ....107 J9
Sheet St *WDSR* SL4 ....193 P1
Sheet Street Rd *WDSR* SL4 ....193 J9
Sheffield Ga *AYLS* HP21 ....95 N9
Sheffield Rd *HTHAIR* TW6 ....197 J5
  SL SL1 ....187 L1
Sheffield Wy *HTHAIR* TW6 ....197 K4
Shefton Ri *NTHWD* HA6 ....159 J7
Shelburne Ct *HWYW* HP12 ....152 E6
Shelburne Rd *HWYW* HP12 ....152 E6
Sheldon Cl *CNH/GTH/TM* MK8 ....41 P3
Sheldon Rd *RAYLW* HP18 ....116 D2
Shelley Cl *DTCH/LGLY* SL3 ....189 J6
  FLKWH HP10 ....166 C1
  MLW SL7 ....175 M1
  NPAG MK16 ....31 H1
  NTHWD HA6 ....159 M5
  YEAD UB4 ....188 N8
Shelley Dr *BTCHLY* MK3 ....52 F5
Shelley La *DEN/HRF* UB9 ....158 A7
  MLW SL7 ....164 F6
  WYM HP11 ....F7
Shelley Rd *CSHM* HP5 ....135 M2
  MLW SL7 ....164 F6
  WYM HP11 ....F7
Shellfield Cl
  STWL/WRAY TW19 ....196 A4
Shelsmore *GTLIN* MK14 ....30 C5
Shelson Av *FELT* TW13 ....197 M9
Shelson Pde *FELT* TW13 * 197 M9
Shenley Av *RSLP* HA4 ....171 M7
Shenley Church End 41 N8
Shenley Hill Rd *LBUZ* LU7 ....64 F4
Shenley Rd *BTCHLY* MK3 ....52 F5
  RMKS/WB MK17 ....51 L3
  SHEN MK5 ....42 A6
Shenstone Dr *SL* SL1 ....179 H7
Shenstone Hl *BERK* HP4 ....114 A8
Shepherd Cl *AYL* HP20 ....J1
Shepherds *STSTR* MK11 ....29 J5
Shepherds Cl *MDHD* SL6 ....177 P5
  UX/CGN UB8 * 182 C7
Shepherds Fold
  HAZ/HG HP15 ....144 B8
Shepherds Ga
  GTMIS/PWD HP16 ....143 M1
Shepherds Gn *HHW* HP1 ....127 L5
Shepherds La *FLKWH* HP10 ....155 K9
  HAZ/HG HP15 ....145 M6
  MDHD SL6 ....178 D6
  RKW/CH/CXG WD3 ....156 E9
Shepherds Rw
  BUCK/WIN MK18 ....60 C6
Shepherds Wy *CSHM* HP5 ....135 N6
Shepiston La *WDR/YW* UB7 ....191 H5
Shepperds Cl
  BUCK/WIN MK18 ....70 C7
Shepperds Gn *SHEN* MK5 ....42 C7
Shepperton Ct *RMKN* MK19 ....18 D1
Sheraton Dr *HWYN* HP13 ....153 K1
Sherborne Pl *NTHWD* HA6 ....159 K6
Sherborne Rd
  EBED/NFELT TW14 ....197 J5
  WDSR SL4 ....193 K3
  WTR/OFPK MK7 ....45 J4
Sherbourne Wk *SLN* SL2 ....167 N9
Shereway *AYLW* HP19 ....95 K7
Sherfield Av
  RKW/CH/CXG WD3 ....158 D3
Shergold Wy *MDHD* SL6 ....177 M2
Sherington Rd *AYLS* HP21 ....109 M8
  HGDN/ICK UB10 ....183 H7
Sheriff Cl *AYLW* HP19 ....95 K7
Sherman Rd *SL* SL1 ....180 A8
Shernfold *WTR/OFPK* MK7 ....45 K8
Sherringham Av *FELT* TW13 ....197 N9
Sherwood Av *RSLP* HA4 ....171 L4
  YEAD UB4 ....183 P7
Sherwood Cl
  DTCH/LGLY SL3 ....188 G4
Sherwood Dr *BTCHLY* MK3 ....52 H2
Sherwood Gdns *HEN* RG9 ....173 N6
Shifford Crs *MDHD* SL6 ....177 L6
Shilling Cl *AYLS* HP21 ....30 C6
Shillingridge Pk *MLW* SL7 * 163 N6
Shinfield Cl *MDHD* SL6 ....168 B8
Ship Hl *SL* SL1 ....167 J6
Shiplake Bottom *HEN* RG9 ....172 C9
Ship La *LBUZ* LU7 ....99 H4
Shipley Rd *NPAG* MK16 ....30 B8
Shipman Ct *WLLN* MK15 ....31 J4
Ship Rd *LBUZ* LU7 ....74 C3
Ship St *HWYN* HP13 ....4 B5
Shipton Rd *BDWL* MK13 ....30 B8
Shipton Rd *HGDN/ICK* UB10 ....170 F9
Shirburn Rd *WTLGN* OX49 ....138 B4
Shire La *CFSP/GDCR* SL9 ....157 K8
  NPAG MK16 ....20 P9
  RKW/CH/CXG WD3 ....147 K2
  TRING HP23 ....112 C7
Shires Rd *BDCKY* NN13 ....35 J6
Shirley Moor
  WTR/OFPK MK7 ....45 P4
Shirley Rd *MDHD* SL6 ....185 J2
Shirwell Crs *EMV/FZ* MK4 ....42 D7
Shogmoor La *HEN* RG9 ....162 D1
Shootacre La *PRRI* HP27 ....151 H8
Shootersway *BERK* HP4 ....113 M8
Shootersway La *BERK* HP4 ....126 B3
Shootersway Pk *BERK* HP4 ....126 B2
Shoppenhangers Rd
  MDHD SL6 ....185 H4
Shop Rd *WDSR* SL4 * 186 C8
Shop Ter *BUCK/WIN* MK18 * 38 D9

Shore Cl *EBED/NFELT* TW14 ....197 N6
Shorediche Cl
  HGDN/ICK UB10 ....170 F9
Shoreham Ri *SLN* SL2 ....179 H7
Shoreham Rd (East)
  HTHAIR TW6 ....196 A6
Shoreham Rd (West)
  HTHAIR TW6 ....196 A6
Shorham Ri
  CNH/GTH/TM MK8 ....41 N2
Shortborough Av *PRRI* HP27 ....121 K9
Short Ditch *HADM* HP17 ....107 L7
Shortfern *SLN* SL2 ....180 E9
Shortlands *HYS/HAR* UB3 ....191 N7
Short La *STWL/WRAY* TW19 ....196 F6
Short Massey *OLN* MK46 ....15 L2
Short Rd *STWL/WRAY* TW19 ....196 F6
Short St *WYM* HP11 ....4 C4
Shortway *CSHM* HP5 ....135 M2
Shortwood Av *STA* TW18 ....196 M3
Shotfield Rd *SKCH* HP14 ....151 L6
Shothanger Wy
  DUN/WHIP HP3 ....127 N7
Shottesbrooke Pk
  MDHD 184 D9
Shouler Cl *SHEN* MK5 ....42 A7
Showers Wy *HYS/HAR* UB3 ....191 N1
Shrewsbury Cl *MKV* MK10 ....43 J7
Shrewsbury Rd
  EBED/NFELT TW14 ....197 J5
Shrimpton Cl *BEAC* HP9 ....155 H4
Shrimpton Rd *BEAC* HP9 ....155 H4
  HWYW HP12 ....J1
Shropshire Ct *BTCHLY* MK3 ....52 E2
Shrubbery Cl *HWYN* HP11 ....5 H5
Shrubbery Rd *HWYN* HP11 ....5 H3
The Shrubbery *HHW* HP1 ....127 N1
Shrub Hill Rd *HWYW* HP12 ....J1
Shrublands Av *BERK* HP4 ....126 C1
Shrublands Rd *BERK* HP4 ....126 B1
Shucklow Hl *RMKS/WB* MK17 ....36 F8
Shugars Gn *TRING* HP23 ....112 F1
Shupp's La *RAYLW* HP18 ....106 F4
Shuttleworth Gv
  WTR/OFPK MK7 ....44 B6
Sibley Ct *UX/CGN* UB8 ....183 J4
Sible Ri *GTMIS/PWD* HP16 ....134 F4
Side Rd *DEN/HRF* UB9 ....169 M5
Sidford Cl *HHW* HP1 ....135 P1
Sidlaw Ct *STSTR* MK11 ....29 L8
Sidmouth Cl *OXHEY* WD19 ....159 P2
Sidmouth Rd *RSLP* HA4 ....171 N8
Sidney Cl *UX/CGN* UB8 ....182 C3
Sidney Ct *SL* SL1 ....192 C2
Sidney Ter
  RAYLNE/WEN HP22 ....111 H9
The Sigers *RSLP* HA4 ....171 P4
Silbury Ar *CMK* MK9 * 7 F1
Silbury Bvd *CMK* MK9 ....6 D1
Silbury Rd *EBED/NFELT* TW14 ....185 L1
Silicon Ct *SHEN* MK5 ....42 C7
Silk Mill Wy *TRING* HP23 ....112 E1
Silk St *RAYLW* HP18 ....93 L1
Sillswood *OLN* MK46 ....15 L5
Silverbeck Wy
  STWL/WRAY TW19 ....196 A4
Silver Birch Cl
  HGDN/ICK UB10 ....170 D9
Silver Birch Dr *PRRI* HP27 ....121 N7
Silverbirches La
  RMKS/WB MK17 ....54 L1
Silver Cl *MDHD* SL6 ....184 C2
Silverdale *AYL* HP20 ....2 G2
Silverdale Gdns
  HYS/HAR UB3 ....191 N5
Silverdale Rd *HYS/HAR* UB3 ....191 N5
Silver Hl *CSTG* HP8 ....156 C2
Silvermead *RAYLW* HP18 ....104 D9
Silver St *AYL* HP20 * 2
  LBUZ LU7 ....72 B8
  NPAG MK16 ....31 K1
Silvertrees Dr *MDHD* SL6 ....184 C2
Silver Wy *HGDN/ICK* UB10 ....183 H5
Silverweed Ct
  WTR/OFPK MK7 ....43 P7
Silverwood Cl *NTHWD* HA6 ....159 J4
Simdims *RBEDW* MK43 ....33 L4
Simmons Cl
  DTCH/LGLY SL3 * 189 J5
Simmons Ct *AYLS* HP21 * 109 M1
Simmons Wy *HEN* RG9 ....173 P5
Simmons Wy *SKCH* HP14 ....151 L1
  THAME OX9 ....118 D2
Simon Ct *MKV* MK10 ....43 L6
Simmei *EAG/OLD/WT* MK6 ....43 H6
Simon Dean *HHS/BOV* HP3 ....127 J4
Simonsbath *EMV/FZ* MK4 ....52 B2
Simons Lea *BDWL* MK13 ....30 D8
Simpson Cl *MDHD* SL6 ....177 P8
Simpson Dr *EAG/OLD/WT* MK6 ....43 K4
Simpson Rd *AYLS* HP21 ....109 N6
  WEAT MK2 ....53 N5
Simpson Rd
  EAG/OLD/WT MK6 ....43 J7
Sinclair Ct *DBGH* MK1 ....53 J3
Singers Cl *HEN* RG9 ....174 A9
Singleborough La
  RMKS/WB MK17 ....50 B3
Singleton Dr
  CNH/GTH/TM MK8 ....41 M6
Singleton Wy *AYLW* HP19 ....95 J1
Singret Pl *UX/CGN* UB8 * 182 C7
Sion Ter *BUCK/WIN* MK18 * 47
Sipson Cl *WDR/YW* UB7 ....191 L9
Sipson La *HYS/HAR* UB3 ....191 L8
Sipson Rd *WDR/YW* UB7 ....190 L6
Sipson Wy *WDR/YW* UB7 ....190 M9
Sipthorp Cl *WTR/OFPK* MK7 ....44 A6
Sir Henry Peakes Dr *SLN* SL2 ....167 K4
Sir Peter's Wy
  DUN/WHIP HP3 100
Sirus Rd *NTHWD* HA6 ....159 N5
Sitwell Cl *NPAG* MK16 ....20 C9

Sixth Av *HYS/HAR* UB3 ....191 M2
Sixth St *WYM* HP11 ....153 J6
Sixty Acres Rd
  GTMIS/PWD HP16 ....133 J2
Skeats Whf *HWYN* HP13 ....30 G6
Skeldon Ga *GTLIN* MK14 ....30 D5
Skelton Cl *BEAC* HP9 ....166 E1
Skene Cl *WEAT* MK2 ....53 J7
Skidmore Wy
  RKW/CH/CXG WD3 ....158 C1
Skimmers Cl *HAZ/HG* HP15 ....144 A3
Skimmers End *HAZ/HG* HP15 ....144 A3
Skimmers Fld *HAZ/HG* HP15 ....144 A3
Skippon Wy *THAME* OX9 ....118 D3
Skipton Cl *WLLN* MK15 ....31 J7
Skipton Dr *HYS/HAR* UB3 ....191 J2
Skittle Gm *PRRI* HP27 ....136 C2
Skylark Rd *DEN/HRF* UB9 ....169 L4
Skyport Dr *WDR/YW* UB7 ....190 D8
Slade Hl *AYLW* HP19 ....95 H3
Slade La *STSTR* MK11 ....29 J5
Slade Oak La *DEN/HRF* UB9 ....169 L4
Slade Rd *SKCH* HP14 ....52 D6
The Slades *HAZ/HG* HP15 ....142 D2
Slad La *PRRI* HP27 ....131 P8
Slapton La *DUN/WHIP* LU6 ....85 J2
Slated Rw *WOLV* MK12 ....29 L6
Slater St *HWYN* HP11 ....5 H3
Slattenham Cl *AYLW* HP19 ....95 K9
Slave H *HADM* HP17 107
Slayter Rd *SKCH* HP14 ....151 L6
Slickett's La *DUN/WHIP* LU6 86
The Slipe *LBUZ* LU7 ....84 E9
The Slipway *WDSR* SL4 * 192 D2
Slough La *SKCH* HP14 151
Slough Rd *IVER* SL0 ....181 M6
  SL SL1 ....188 A5
  WDSR SL4 ....187 P6
Sly Cnr *GTMIS/PWD* HP16 ....124 C9
Smabridge Wk *MLW* SL7 ....31 M8
Smaldon Cl *WDR/YW* UB7 ....190 C4
Small Acre *HHW* HP1 ....135 N1
Small Crs *BUCK/WIN* MK18 ....48 D3
Smaldean La *PRRI* HP27 ....141 M1
Smarden Bell *WTR/OFPK* MK7 45
Smart's Cl *BRACKY* NN13 34
Smeaton Cl *AYLW* HP19 ....95 J6
  GTLIN MK14 30
Smewins Rd *MDHD* SL6 ....184 D9
Smith Cl *AYLS* HP21 96
Smithergill Ct *BDWL* MK13 30
Smithfield Cl *MDHD* SL6 ....184 H4
Smithfield End
  RMKS/WB MK17 61
Smithfield Rd *MDHD* SL6 ....184 D9
Smith's La *RAYLW* HP18 ....103 P7
  SKCH HP14 ....193 J1
Smithsons Pl *CMK* MK9 ....43 H1
Snaith Crs *SHEN* MK5 ....42 A5
Snakeley Cl *FLKWH* HP10 ....154 A9
Snape Sp *SL* SL1 ....188 A4
Snells La *AMSS* HP7 ....146 E3
Snells Wood Ct *AMSS* HP7 ....146 E4
Snelshall St *EMV/FZ* MK4 ....51 P5
Snowball Hl *MDHD* SL6 ....185 H6
Snowberry Cl *WOLV* MK12 ....29 L6
Snowcrete *DTCH/LGLY* SL3 * 180
Snowden Av
  EAG/OLD/WT MK6 ....7 H4
Snowden Cl *WDSR* SL4 ....193 H5
Snowdon Crs *HYS/HAR* UB3 ....191 J4
Snowdon Dr
  EAG/OLD/WT MK6 ....42 G5
Snowdon Rd
  West *HTHAIR* TW6 ....197 J5
Snowdrop Wy *HAZ/HG* HP15 ....143 M4
Snowhill Cottages
  CSHM HP5 ....126 B6
Snowhill Ct *GTLIN* MK14 ....30 F5
Soames Ct *OLN* MK46 ....10 D9
Soane Wk *HWYN* HP13 4
Soho Crs *FLKWH* HP10 ....166 B5
Sokeman Cl *WOLV* MK12 ....29 J8
Solesbridge Ct
  RKW/CH/CXG WD3 ....147 P5
Solesbridge La
  RKW/CH/CXG WD3 ....147 P5
Solters Ri *RAYLW* HP18 ....77 J8
Somerford Cl *MDHD* SL6 ....177 P8
  PIN HA5 ....N...
Somerford Pl *BEAC* HP9 8
Someries Rd *HWYW* HP11 ....115 P9
Somersby Crs *MDHD* SL6 ....185 K4
Somerset Cl *BTCHLY* MK3 ....52 E2
Somerset Rd *IVER* SL0 ....189 P9
Somers Lees *AYLW* HP19 95
Somerville Rd *BRACKY* NN13 34
  WDSR SL4 ....187 N6
Somerville Wy *AYLW* HP19 ....95 J1
Sorensen Ct *SHEN* MK5 ....42 A5
Sorrell Dr *NPAG* MK16 ....31 H1
Soskin Dr *GTLIN* MK14 ....30 C5
Sospel Ct *SLN* SL2 ....180 D3
Soudan Av *BRACKY* NN13 ....34 B2
Soulbury Rd *LBUZ* LU7 ....62 F9
  LBUZ LU7 ....73 K1
  LBUZ LU7 ....74 B1
Southall La *HEST* TW5 ....191 P6
Southampton Rd
  HTHAIR TW6 ....196 C4
South Ap *NTHWD* HA6 ....159 N3
South Bank Rd *BERK* HP4 174
Southbourne Dr
  BNEND SL8 ....165 N6
Southbourne Gdns
  RSLP HA4 ....171 N6
Southbridge Gv
  WTR/OFPK MK7 ....45 N5
South Bucks Wy
  CFSP/GDCR SL9 ....157 J9
  DEN/HRF UB9 ....170 A6
  GTMIS/PWD HP16 ....122 E8
  GTMIS/PWD HP16 ....133 P8

Southcliffe Dr
  CFSP/GDCR SL9 ....156 G5
South Cl *MLW* SL7 ....175 M1
  SL SL1 ....
  WDR/YW UB7 190
Southcote Av *FELT* TW15 ....197 N8
Southcote Ri *RSLP* HA4 ....171 K5
Southcote Wy *FLKWH* HP10 ....153 N1
South Cottage Dr
  RKW/CH/CXG WD3 ....147 P7
South Cottage Gdns
  RKW/CH/CXG WD3 ....147 P7
Southcott La *LBUZ* LU7 ....74 B3
Southcourt Av *LBUZ* LU7 ....74 B3
Southcourt Rd *LBUZ* LU7 ....74 B3
South Dr *BEAC* HP9 ....166 F1
  HWYN HP13 ....153 K2
  RSLP HA4 ....171 L6
South Eighth St *CMK* MK9 ....7 F3
South End *HHW* HP1 ....127 N1
South End La *DUN/WHIP* LU6 ....85 M5
Southern Av
  EBED/NFELT TW14 ....197 N7
Southern Perimeter Rd
  HTHAIR TW6 ....196 C4
Southern Rd *AYLW* HP19 ....2 B2
  THAME OX9 ....118 C5
Southern Wy
  DUN/WHIP LU6 ....101 L3
South Field Cl *WDSR* SL4 ....186 A5
Southfield Cl *UX/CGN* UB8 ....182 C3
  WLLN MK15 ....31 L6
Southfield Ct *BRACKY* NN13 * 34 A3
Southfield Gdns *SL* SL1 ....178 F8
Southfield Rd *AYL* HP20 ....95 N7
  FLKWH HP10 ....153 N9
  HWYN HP13 ....
  PRRI HP27 ....131 L1
Southfields Rd
  DUN/WHIP LU6 ....87 M2
South Fifth St *CMK* MK9 ....6 E4
South Fourth St *CMK* MK9 6
South Grafton
  EAG/OLD/WT MK6 ....6 D6
South Gn *SL* SL1 ....188 A1
South Hall *BUCK/WIN* MK18 38
South Hl *NTHWD* HA6 * 159 L8
Southill Ga *PIN* HA5 ....171 N2
Southlands Rd *IVER* SL0 ....181 M6
South La *LBUZ* LU7 ....72 E2
South Lawne *BTCHLY* MK3 ....52 F3
Southlea Rd *WDSR* SL4 ....194 E2
South Maundin *SKCH* HP14 ....142 G3
South Meadow La *WDSR* SL4 ....187 N8
South Ninth St *CMK* MK9 ....7 F3
South Pk *CFSP/GDCR* SL9 ....169 H5
South Park Av
  RKW/CH/CXG WD3 ....147 P7
South Park Crs
  CFSP/GDCR SL9 ....169 H3
South Park Dr
  CFSP/GDCR SL9 ....168 G2
South Park Gdns *BERK* HP4 ....114 D9
South Park Vw
  CFSP/GDCR SL9 ....169 H2
South Pl *MLW* SL7 ....175 M1
South Rd *AMS* HP6 ....135 N9
  MDHD SL6 ....185 L1
  RKW/CH/CXG WD3 ....147 L4
  WDR/YW UB7 ....190 C4
South Rw *CMK* MK9 6
  DTCH/LGLY SL3 ....168 G9
South Saxon
  EAG/OLD/WT MK6 ....7 F4
South Secklow *CMK* MK9 * 7 H3
South Second St *CMK* MK9 ....6 E5
South Seventh St *CMK* MK9 ....6 E4
South Side *CFSP/GDCR* SL9 ....168 G1
South Sixth St *CMK* MK9 ....6 E4
South St *LBUZ* LU7 72
  RAYLNE/WEN HP22 ....123 H1
  RMKN MK19 ....19 J3
South Tenth St *CMK* MK9 ....7 F3
South Ter *WEAT* MK2 ....53 J3
South V *RNHPTN* NN7 ....4 J3
South Vw *HWYN* HP13 ....142 D9
  WDSR SL4 ....193 N6
South View Rd
  CFSP/GDCR SL9 ....168 G2
  PIN HA5 ....171 P6
Southview Rd *MLW* SL7 ....164 G5
Southville Cl
  EBED/NFELT TW14 ....197 L6
Southville Rd
  EBED/NFELT TW14 ....197 L7
South Wy *BEAC* HP9 ....166 E1
Southwick Ct
  EAG/OLD/WT MK6 ....41 P4
South Witan *CMK* MK9 ....6 E5
Southwold Sp
  DTCH/LGLY SL3 ....189 L3
Southwood Gdns *MDHD* SL6 ....177 L3
Southwood La
  HLW/TOD LU5 ....87 N2
Sovereign Ct *BUCK/WIN* MK18 ....70 B2
  RSLP HA4 ....171 L4
Sovereign Dr *HWYN* HP13 ....143 K6
Sovereign Wy *WLLN* MK15 ....30 G6
Space Waye
  EBED/NFELT TW14 ....197 N4
Spackmans Wy *SL* SL1 ....187 N4
Spa Cl *RAYLW* HP18 ....93 L1
Spade Oak Meadow
  BNEND SL8 ....165 L5
Spark Wy *NPAG* MK16 ....20 P9
Sparrow Cl *AYLW* HP19 ....95 P4
Sparsholt Cl *EMV/FZ* MK4 ....52 C4
Spearing Rd *HWYW* HP12 ....152 C4

Spearmint Cl WTR/OFPK MK7 ..44 A7
Specklands SHEN MK5 ....42 A5
Speedbird Wy WDR/YW UB7 ...190 B6
Speedwell Cl HHW HP1 ....127 N3
Speedwell Pl GTLIN MK14 ....30 E9
Speen Rd GTMIS/PWD HP16 ....132 C8
Spelhurst Ct WTR/OFPK MK7 ...48 A7
Spencer GTLIN MK14 ....30 C5
Spencer Av YEAD UB4 ....185 N8
Spencer Cl UX/CGN UB8 ....182 C5
Spencer Gdns BRACKY NN13 ....34 C6
Spldna OX27 ....67 L4
Spencer Rd DTCH/LGLY SL3 ....189 H4
Spencers La HADM HP17 ....177 J8
Spencers Cl MDHD SL6 ....177 L2
Spencers Rd MDHD SL6 ....177 J8
Spenlows Rd BTCHLY MK3 ....42 C9
Spenser Rd AYLS HP21 ....99 M8
The Spens MDHD SL6 * 177 M7
Sperling Rd MDHD SL6 ....177 M7
Spickett's La RAYLW HP18 ......107 J3
Spiers Dr BRACKY NN13 ....34 F5
Spier's La RBICN OX27 ....66 F7
The Spiert HADM HP17 ....108 F1
Spindle Cl HAZ/HG HP15 ....143 N8
Spinfield La MLW SL7 ....164 B8
Spinfield La West MLW SL7 .....164 C8
Spinfield Mt MLW SL7 ....164 C8
Spinfield Pk MLW SL7 ....164 B8
Spinners Wk MLW SL7 ....164 B8
WDSR SL4 ....187 N9
Spinney Cl SL1 ....187 M2
Spinney Cl BUCK/WIN MK18 ....58 C8
WDR/YW UB7 ....190 E1
Spinney Dr
Spinney Hill Rd OLN MK46 .....15 J8
Spinney La BRACKY NN13 * 45 J8
WDSR SL4 ....192 F7
The Spinneys FLKWH HP10 .....153 P2
The Spinney BDWL MK13 ....30 A9
BEAC HP9 ....155 J9
BERK HP4 ....126 B2
BUCK/WIN MK18 ....60 C4
CFSP/GDCR SL9 ....168 F6
CSHM HP5 ....135 P2
HAZ/HG HP15 ....144 B4
WYM HP11 ....152 C6
Spittal Ct DTCH/LGLY SL3 .....189 J6
Spittal St MLW SL7 ....164 D7
Spoondell DUN/WHIP LU6 ......87 P2
Spoonley Wd BDWL MK15 ....29 N8
Sportsfield Ap BEAC HP9 ......155 P5
Sportsman Cl
BUCK/WIN MK18 ....58 B7
Spout La STWL/WRAY TW19 ....196 A4
Spout La North
STWL/WRAY TW19 ....196 A4
Spratts La DUN/WHIP LU6 ......87 P7
Sprigs Holly La SKCH HP14 ....140 C2
Springate Fld
DTCH/LGLY SL3 ....188 C3
Springbank Cl NPAG MK16 ......14 D7
Spring Cl CSHM HP5 ....136 F9
DEN/HRF UB9 ....158 D8
HWYN HP15 ....153 M3
MDHD SL6 ....177 L6
RMKS/WB MK17 ....50 D9
Spring Coppice SKCH HP14 ....151 P5
Spring Coppice La
PRRI HP27 ....132 C8
Spring Dr FELT TW13 * 197 N9
Spring Dr PIN HA5 ....171 N4
Springett Pl AMS HP6 ....146 B8
Springfield EAG/OLD/WT MK6 ..7 J7
Springfield Bvd
EAG/OLD/WT MK6 ....43 H2
Springfield Cl AYLW HP19 ......3 M6
CSHM HP5 ....135 N6
WDSR SL4 ....193 M1
WTLGN OX49 ....148 A1
Springfield Gdns CHNR OX39 ..129 N5
RMKN MK19 ....28 A9
RSLP HA4 ....171 P6
Springfield Pk MDHD SL6 .....185 J4
Spring Field Rd BERK HP4 ....114 B7
Springfield Rd CSHM HP5 .....135 N5
DTCH/LGLY SL3 ....189 K8
DUN/WHIP LU6 ....86 F3
LBUZ LU7 ....74 B2
OLN MK46 ....15 M4
SKCH HP14 ....140 B7
WDSR SL4 ....193 M1
Springfields AMS HP6 ....145 N1
BUCK/WIN MK18 ....58 C1
FLKWH HP10 * 144 A3
Springfields Cl
BUCK/WIN MK18 ....48 C9
Springfields Ct
BUCK/WIN MK18 ....58 C1
Springfields Wy
BRACKY NN13 ....34 C3
RBEDW MK43 ....33 N3
Spring Gdns FLKWH HP10 .....166 C5
MLW SL7 ....164 D6
NPAG MK16 ....31 J3
Spring Gardens Rd
HWYN HP15 ....153 L5
Spring Gdns BNED SL6 ....165 N5
Spring Gv RMKS/WB MK17 .....42 A8
Springhill Rd RAYLW HP18 ....107 K9
Spring La FLKWH HP10 ....155 N8
MDHD SL6 ....177 L2
OLN MK46 ....16 A4
RMKS/WB MK17 ....50 C9
SL SL1 ....187 M2
SLN SL2 ....179 M3
WTLGN OX49 ....148 A1
Spring Pth THAME OX9 ....118 C5
Spring Rd FELT TW13 * 197 M9
Springs Cl HADM HP17 ....122 B3

Springs La HADM HP17 ....122 B3
Spring Valley Dr SKCH HP14 ..142 G4
Springwater Ml WYM HP11 * ..153 L6
Springwell Av
RKW/CH/CXG WD3 * 158 A2
Springwell Ct
RKW/CH/CXG WD3 * 158 A2
Springwell La
RKW/CH/CXG WD3 * 158 A2
Springwood La HEN RG9 ....172 D8
Spruce Dene HAZ/HG HP15 ....148 M9
Spurgrove La HEN HP27 ....150 C8
Spurlands End Rd
HAZ/HG HP15 ....143 L2
Spur Rd EBED/NFELT TW14 ....197 P4
The Spur SL SL1 ....179 H8
Spurt St RAYLW HP18 ....107 J2
The Square
GTMIS/PWD HP16 ....133 P5
RAYLW HP18 ....107 J2
RAYLW HP18 ....106 A8
RNHPTN NN7 ....8 G1
STKPN UB11 ....191 J2
WDR/YW UB7 ....190 B9
WOLV MK12 ....29 M7
Squires Ct EAG/OLD/WT MK6 ..42 G6
Squirrel Cha HHW HP1 ....127 N1
Squirrel La BUCK/WIN MK18 ..57 N7
Squirrel La HWYW HP12 ....152 B6
Squirrel Ri MLW SL7 ....164 D3
Squirrels Cl HGDN/ICK UB10 ..182 G3
Squirrels Wy
BUCK/WIN MK18 ....48 C4
Stablebridge Rd
RAYLW/WEN HP22 * 111 M3
Stable Cl BUCK/WIN MK18 .....46 C5
Stable Ct BRACKY NN13 * 35 H5
Stable La BEAC HP9 ....155 N6
Stable Rd
RAYLW/WEN HP22 * 111 K7
Stables Ct MLW SL7 ....164 B8
Stacey Av WOLV MK12 ....29 M7
Staddie Stones PRRI HP27 ....121 K9
Stafferton Wy MDHD SL6 ......185 N1
Stafford Av SLN SL2 ....179 N7
Stafford Cl MDHD SL6 ....177 L7
Stafford Gv SHEN MK5 ....42 B6
Stafford Rd RSLP HA4 ....171 M9
Stag La BERK HP4 ....114 B4
HAZ/HG HP15 ....145 K2
RKW/CH/CXG WD3 * 157 M8
Stag Pl FLKWH HP10 * 166 B5
Stagshaw Pl EMV/FZ MK4 ......52 B3
Stainby Cl WDR/YW UB7 ....190 E4
Staines By-Pass
STWL/WRAY TW19 ....195 P6
Staines Rd
EBED/NFELT TW14 ....197 K6
EBED/NFELT TW14 ....195 H7
Staines Sq DUN/WHIP LU6 .....87 L1
Stainton Dr BRACKY NN13 .....30 C9
Stamford Av
EAG/OLD/WT MK6 ....43 H2
Stamford Rd MDHD SL6 ....185 J1
Stanbridge Cl HADM HP17 ....107 L7
Stanbridge Rd HADM HP17 ....107 M7
LBUZ LU7 ....74 F3
LBUZ LU7 ....75 J8
LBUZ LU7 ....75 P6
Stanbridge Road Ter
LBUZ LU7 ....74 F3
Stanbrook Pl WTR/OFPK MK7 ..43 N3
Standale Gv RSLP HA4 ....171 J3
Standfield Cl AYLW HP19 ....95 J7
Standing Wy BTCHLY MK3 ......52 B4
MKV MK10 ....44 A3
Standring Pl AYL HP20 * 3 J7
Stanford Cl RSLP HA4 ....171 J4
Stanhope Cl
RAYLW/WEN HP22 ....110 C7
Stanhope Heath
STWL/WRAY TW19 ....196 C5
Stanhope Rd AYL HP20 ....3 L3
SL SL1 ....179 H9
Stanhope Wy
STWL/WRAY TW19 ....196 C5
Stanier Rd BERK HP4 ....114 B7
Stanley Av CSHM HP5 ....135 N5
Stanley Ct MLW SL7 ....164 F6
UX/CGN UB8 ....182 D5
Stanley Cottages SL1 ....188 B2
Stanley Gdns TRING HP23 .....112 D3
Stanley Gn West
DTCH/LGLY SL3 ....189 H5
Stanley Hi AMSS HP7 ....146 A4
Stanley Hill Av AMSS HP7 ....145 P3
Stanley Rd HWYW HP12 ....152 B3
NTHWD HA6 ....159 N4
Stanmore Gdns NPAG MK16 ....31 H5
Stansfield Rd HLNWW TW4 ....195 P7
Stanstead Pl AMSS HP7 * 145 N3
Stansted Rd HTHAIR TW6 ......196 F5
Stanton Av BDWL MK13 ....30 C5
Stanton Ga GTLIN MK14 ....30 D5
Stanton Rd WHLY OX35 ....102 G3
The Stile LBUZ LU7 ....74 G4
Stanwell Cl
STWL/WRAY TW19 ....196 C5
Stanwell Gdns
STWL/WRAY TW19 ....196 D5
Stanwell Moor Rd
STWL/WRAY TW19 ....196 B8
WDR/YW UB7 ....190 B9
Stanwell Pl
STWL/WRAY TW19 * 196 C5
Stanwell Rd ASHF TW15 ....196 D6
DTCH/LGLY SL3 ....195 K2
EBED/NFELT TW14 ....197 J6

Staple Hall Rd DBGH MK1 ......53 K2
Stapleton Cl MLW SL7 ....164 F5
Star Rd HGDN/ICK UB10 ......183 J7
Stars La HADM HP17 ....108 A4
Startins La MDHD SL6 ....165 J9
Starveall Cl WDR/YW UB7 ....190 F4
Starwood Ct DTCH/LGLY SL3 ..188 F6
Staters Pound WLLN MK15 .....30 C4
Statham Pl EAG/OLD/WT MK6 ...7 J4
Station Ap CFSP/GDCR SL9 ...168 G3
DEN/HRF UB9 ....169 M5
GTMIS/PWD HP16 ....133 N5
HWYN HP15 * 3 J2
HYS/HAR UB3 ....191 M4
MDHD SL6 * 185 M1
MLW SL7 ....164 E7
NTHWD HA6 ....159 L7
RAYLW/WEN HP22 ....123 H1
RKW/CH/CXG WD3 ....147 L6
RSLP HA4 ....171 L6
RSLP HA4 ....183 P1
WDR/YW UB7 ....190 E2
Station Ct AMSS HP7 * 145 N2
Station Estate Rd
EBED/NFELT TW14 ....197 P4
Station Hi MDHD SL6 ....185 M1
Station Pde DEN/HRF UB9 ....170 A5
EBED/NFELT TW14 * 197 P6
MDHD SL6 * 177 M1
RSLP HA4 ....171 J7
Station Ri MLW SL7 ....164 E7
Station Rd AMSS HP7 ....145 N3
BEAC HP9 ....155 J8
BERK HP4 ....114 F9
BIC OX26 ....66 A5
BNEND SL8 ....165 N6
BUCK/WIN MK18 ....60 B5
CFSP/GDCR SL9 ....168 G3
CHNR OX39 ....129 N5
CSHM HP5 ....135 M4
DTCH/LGLY SL3 ....189 J3
FLKWH HP10 ....154 A8
HADM HP17 ....107 J4
HEN RG9 ....174 A1
HWYN HP15 ....3 J6
HYS/HAR UB3 ....191 M4
LBUZ LU7 ....74 C3
LBUZ LU7 ....75 P5
LBUZ LU7 ....74 E4
LBUZ LU7 ....99 J2
MDHD SL6 ....177 M1
MDHD SL6 ....178 D9
MLW SL7 ....164 E8
NPAG MK16 ....31 J1
PRRI HP27 ....131 J2
RAYLW/WEN HP22 ....79 L5
RAYLW/WEN HP22 ....110 B4
RBEDW MK43 ....45 M2
RBEDW MK43 ....45 H6
RBICN OX27 ....66 F7
RBICS/W OX25 ....66 A5
RMKN MK19 ....18 D3
RMKS/WB MK17 ....44 F4
RMKS/WB MK17 ....53 P1
RMKS/WB MK17 ....61 H5
RMKS/WB MK17 ....61 N5
SL SL1 ....179 J9
STWL/WRAY TW19 ....195 H5
THAME OX9 ....118 A6
TRING HP23 ....97 N3
TRING HP23 ....112 F3
UX/CGN UB8 ....182 C7
WDR/YW UB7 ....190 E2
Station Ter BUCK/WIN MK18 ...48 M4
Station Wy AYL HP20 ....2 G3
Station Yd RSLP HA4 * 171 K7
THAME OX9 ....118 E6
Staunton Rd SL SL1 ....179 P8
Staveley Rd DUN/WHIP LU6 ....87 K2
Stavordale WTR/OFPK MK7 .....43 L5
Steam Farm La
EBED/NFELT TW14 ....197 M3
Steane Vw BRACKY NN13 ....34 F5
Stedman Cl HGDN/ICK UB10 ...170 A7
Steeple Cl EMV/FZ MK4 ....52 A3
Steinbeck Crs EMV/FZ MK4 ....51 N4
Stephenson Cl AYLW HP19 .....95 K8
HWYN HP15 ....3 C1
LBUZ LU7 ....74 C1
Stephenson Ct SL SL1 ....188 D3
Stephenson Dr WDSR SL4 .....187 M8
Stepnells TRING HP23 ....98 E6
Steppingstone Pl LBUZ LU7 ...74 B5
Stert Rd CHNR OX39 ....129 K8
Stevens Cl GTMIS/PWD HP16 ..133 K7
HAZ/HG HP15 ....143 P4
Stevens Fld WTR/OFPK MK7 ...44 B8
Stevens La HEN RG9 ....172 B8
Stevenson Rd SLN SL2 ....167 M5
Stewart Av SL SL1 ....179 H4
Stewart Cl MDHD SL6 ....186 A9
Stewart Dr TOW NN12 ....25 K1
Stewart Dr SLN SL2 ....179 M1
Stewarts Wy MLW SL7 ....164 D9
Stewkley La RMKS/WB MK17 ....61 N6
Stewkley Rd LBUZ LU7 ....73 G1
LBUZ LU7 ....72 G5
LBUZ LU7 ....72 C3
Stilebrook Rd OLN MK46 ....15 M4
Stile Rd DTCH/LGLY SL3 ......188 F5
Stilewell Gv UX/CGN UB8 .....182 F7
Stirling Av AYL HP20 ....2 F5
Stirling Cl UX/CGN UB8 ......182 F7
WDSR SL4 ....193 H1
Stirling Gv MK5 ....42 G9
Stirling Rd HAZ/HG HP15 .....144 B8
Stirling Rd HWYW HP12 ....152 B3
HYS/HAR UB3 ....191 P1
SLN SL2 ....179 J1
Stockaway
RAYLW/WEN HP22 ....81 L8
Stockdale BDWL MK15 * 30 B5
Stockdales Rd WDSR SL4 .....187 K5
Stocken Cl OLN MK46 ....15 L3

Stockers Farm Rd
RKW/CH/CXG WD3 ....158 D3
Stock Field Cl HAZ/HG HP15 ..143 P9
Stockhall Crs LBUZ LU7 ....62 D8
Stocking Cl RNHPTN NN7 ....12 F6
Stocking Green Cl
RMKN MK19 ....19 J3
Stocking La SKCH HP14 ....142 D4
Stocklake RD 3 G3
RAYLW/WEN HP22 ....96 B6
Stocklands Wy
GTMIS/PWD HP16 ....133 K7
Stock La RMKS/WB MK17 ....51 K2
Stockley Cl WDR/YW UB7 .....191 H5
Stockley Farm Rd
WDR/YW UB7 ....191 H4
Stockley Rd UX/CGN UB8 ......182 C9
WDR/YW UB7 ....191 H4
Stockleys La
BUCK/WIN MK18 ....47 H5
Stockport Rd
RKW/CH/CXG WD3 ....147 L9
Stocks Hi HGDN/ICK UB10 ....182 C4
Stocks Rd TRING HP23 ....99 P3
The Stocks RMKN MK19 ....28 C3
Stockwell HADM HP17 * 107 L9
Stockwell Furlong
HADM HP17 ....107 L8
Stockwell La HADM HP17 .....121 J4
Stockwell Rd AYLW HP19 * 3 M4
Stockwells MDHD SL6 ....178 B2
Stoke Common Rd SLN SL2 ...168 C9
Stoke Court Dr SLN SL2 ......180 A4
Stoke Farm La AYLS HP21 * ..109 H3
Stoke Gdns SL SL1 ....188 A2
Stoke Gn SLN SL2 ....180 C7
Stoke La AYLS HP21 * 3 H3
Stokenchurch Rd BDWL MK13 ..42 C7
Stoke Park Av SLN SL2 ....179 N6
Stoke Poges La SL SL1 ....188 A2
Stoke Rd AYLS HP21 ....3 C7
LBUZ LU7 ....64 C9
RMKS/WB MK17 ....52 E8
RNHPTN NN7 ....9 F3
SLN SL2 ....180 C8
WEAT MK2 ....53 K6
Stoke Row Rd HEN RG9 ....172 C8
Stokesay SLN SL2 ....180 C9
Stokesay Ct EMV/FZ MK4 ......51 N4
Stokes Cft HADM HP17 * 107 L8
Stokes End HADM HP17 ....107 L8
Stokesley Ri FLKWH HP10 ....166 B6
Stolford Ri EMV/FZ MK4 ....52 B2
Stompits Rd MDHD SL6 ....185 K7
Stonebridge Fld WDSR SL4 ...187 M6
Stonebridge Rd AYLW HP19 ....95 K4
Stonechat WDR/YW UB7 ....190 F2
Stone Crs EBED/NFELT TW14 ..197 M6
Stonecroft AMS HP6 ....134 G8
Stonecroft Av IVER SLO 181 N9
Stonecrop Pl MDHD SL6 ....177 J9
Stone Cft HADM HP17 ....108 F1
Stonegate BDWL MK15 ....30 A8
Stonehaven Rd AYLW HP19 .....95 K4
Stonehurst Ct EMV/FZ MK4 ....41 M8
Stone House La MDHD SL6 ....165 J8
Stoneleigh Ct EMV/FZ MK4 ....51 N1
Stone Pit Cl OLN MK46 ....15 M4
Stonepitts Pk RAYLW HP18 ...105 P5
Stones Rw WYM HP11 * 153 M6
Stoney Ct RKW/CH/CXG WD3 ..147 L9
Stone Vw RAYLW/WEN HP22 ....80 F1
Stoney Cft TRING HP23 ....113 N1
Stoney Gv CSHM HP5 ....135 P3
Stoney La HHW HP1 ....127 K5
KGLGY WD4 ....148 L9
Stoney Mdw MLW SL7 ....187 M2
Stoney Ware MLW SL7 ....164 C6
Stonor Ct CNH/GTH/TM MK8 ...41 M9
Stony La CSHM HP5 ....146 C1
Stookslade
RAYLW/WEN HP22 ....82 G5
Stopps Orch PRRI HP27 ....121 L8
Stork Cl AYLW HP19 * 95 J4
Stormount Dr HYS/HAR UB3 ..191 J3
Stornaway Rd
DTCH/LGLY SL3 ....189 L3
Stotfold Ct STSTR MK11 ....28 C3
Stour Cl AYLS HP21 ....109 J2
BTCHLY MK3 ....53 H5
NPAG MK16 ....31 L2
Stourhead Ga EMV/FZ MK4 ....51 N2
Stoveld Rd WDSR SL4 ....187 M8
Stowe Av BUCK/WIN MK18 .....37 H9
Stowe Cl BUCK/WIN MK18 ......48 A9
Stowe Crs RSLP HA4 ....171 H4
Stowe Rd BUCK/WIN MK18 .....48 A9
Stowe Rd MDHD SL6 ....178 B8
Strafford Wy THAME OX9 .....118 A5
Straight Bit FLKWH HP10 ....165 N9
Straight Rd WDSR SL4 ....194 C5
Strande La MDHD SL6 ....185 K9
Strande View Wk MDHD SL6 ..177 M8
The Strand
RAYLW/WEN HP22 ....79 L5
Strangers La BUCK/WIN MK18 ..46 G5
Stranraer Gdns SL SL1 ....188 A2
Stratfield Ct
CNH/GTH/TM MK8 ....41 P3
Stratfield Rd SL SL1 ....188 C3

Stratford Ar STSTR MK11 ....28 FB
Stratford Av HGDN/ICK UB10 ..182 F3
Stratford Cl SLN SL2 ....179 H7
Stratford Dr AYLS HP21 ....95 P8
FLKWH HP10 ....166 B5
Stratford Rd
BUCK/WIN MK18 ....48 B2
HTHAIR TW6 ....197 H5
RMKN MK19 ....28 B9
RMKS/WB MK17 ....41 J8
RMKS/WB MK17 ....50 D2
WOLV MK12 ....29 J7
YEAD UB4 ....185 N8
Stratfords Wy HADM HP17 ....107 K8
Strathcona Cl FLKWH HP10 ...166 A2
Strathcona Wy FLKWH HP10 ..166 A2
Strathearn Av HYS/HAR UB3 ..191 M8
Strathmore Pl WOLV MK12 ....29 L8
Stratton Chase Dr CSTG HP8 .156 C2
Stratton Dr BRACKY NN13 .....34 F5
Stratton Gn AYLS HP21 ....96 C9
Stratton Ms LBUZ LU7 ....74 F7
Stratton Pl AMSS HP7 * 54 B8
Stratton Rd BEAC HP9 ....154 F8
PRRI HP27 ....131 J1
Strauss Gv WTR/OFPK MK7 ....44 A8
Strawberry Cl
GTMIS/PWD HP16 ....133 K7
Strawberry Rd
RAYLW/WEN HP22 * 83 H6
Streamside SL SL1 ....187 K2
Streamside Wk AYLS HP21 .....95 L9
Streatham Pl BDWL MK13 ......6 A2
Street Cl RBEDW MK43 ....11 L5
Stretton Cl FLKWH HP10 * 53 J3
Stringfellow Cl RBEDW MK43 ..33 J5
Stroma Ct SL SL1 ....187 H1
Stroud Cl WDSR SL4 ....193 H2
Stroud Farm Rd MDHD SL6 ...185 P7
Strudwick Dr
EAG/OLD/WT MK6 ....7 C6
Stuart Cl HGDN/ICK UB10 ....182 C1
WDSR SL4 ....193 K1
WEAT MK2 ....53 J7
Stuart Ct AMS HP6 * 145 P2
Stuart Crs HYS/HAR UB3 .....183 J9
Stuart Rd BRACKY NN13 ....34 F4
HWYN HP15 ....3 J7
Stuart Wy THAME OX9 ....138 E5
WDSR SL4 ....193 K1
Stubble Hl AYLW HP19 ....95 J7
Stubbles La MDHD SL6 ....176 G2
Stubbs End Cl AMS HP6 ....146 A5
Stubbs Fld SHEN MK5 ....42 B8
Stubbs Wd AMS HP6 ....136 A9
Stuchbury Cl AYLW HP19 ......95 J7
Studdridge Ct SKCH HP14 ....139 N7
Studham La AMS HP4 ....100 C3
Studio Ct WEAT MK2 * 53 K5
Studley Knapp
WTR/OFPK MK7 ....43 P6
Studridge La PRRI HP27 ......132 C7
Sturges Cl WTR/OFPK MK7 ....43 N7
Sturt Gn MDHD SL6 ....185 J7
Stylecroft Rd CSTG HP8 ......156 F5
Styles Cl RBICN OX27 ....66 E7
Suffield Rd WYM HP11 * 4 D6
Suffolk Cl SL SL1 ....179 H9
Suffolk Ct RBICN OX27 * 66 F7
Suffolk Rd LTN LU1 ....87 P2
WDSR SL4 ....187 H9
Sugar La HHW HP1 ....127 K4
Sulby Ct AYLS HP21 ....96 D2
Sulgrave Ct
CNH/GTH/TM MK8 ....41 P4
Sulgrave Crs TRING HP23 ....112 C1
Sullivan Crs DEN/HRF UB9 ...158 D9
Sultan Crt SHEN MK5 ....42 A4
Sumburgh Wy SL SL1 ....179 H8
Summergill Ct BDWL MK13 ....30 C9
Summerhayes GTLIN MK14 ....30 F6
Summerhouse La
DEN/HRF UB9 ....158 A7
WDR/YW UB7 ....190 D7
Summerlea SL SL1 ....187 M2
Summerleaze Rd MDHD SL6 ..177 M1
Summerleys DUN/WHIP LU6 ...86 A4
Summerleys Rd PRRI HP27 ...120 C9
Summerson Rd
EAG/OLD/WT MK6 ....42 F7
Summers Rd SL SL1 ....178 C6
Summer St LBUZ LU7 ....74 F2
Sumner Cl SHEN MK5 ....42 A4
Sunbury Cl BDWL MK13 ....30 J2
Sunbury Rd FELT TW13 ....197 M9
WDSR SL4 ....187 P7
Sun Cl WDSR SL4 ....187 J7
Sun Crs RAYLW HP18 ....104 C9
Sunderland Ct EMV/FZ MK4 ...51 P2
Sunderland Rd MDHD SL6 ....177 H8
Sundew Rd HHW HP1 ....127 N1
Sundown Av
DUN/HR/TOD LU5 ....87 M1
Sun La MDHD SL6 ....185 M1
Sunningdale Cl HWYW HP12 ..152 B5
Sunningdale Wy BTCHLY MK3 ..52 C3
Sunny Bank HAZ/HG HP15 ....143 M5
Sunrise Av NPAG MK16 ....14 G7
Sunnybank MLW SL7 ....164 C6
Sunny Brook Cl
RAYLW/WEN HP22 ....97 K9
Sunny Cft HWYN HP13 ....142 C9
Sunnydene Av RSLP HA4 ......171 N4
Sunnyhill Rd
RKW/CH/CXG WD3 ....157 M6
Sunnymede Av CSHM HP5 .....135 M3
Sunnyside Rd AYLS HP21 ....95 L9
Sunray Av WDR/YW UB7 ......190 D3
Sunridge Cl NPAG MK16 ....14 F5
Sunrise Pkwy GTLIN MK14 ......30 E7
Sunset Cl WEAT MK2 * 53 J4
Sunset Wk CMK MK9 * 6 C7

Sunters Wood Cl
 HWYW HP12 ....152 B5
Sun Vw BUCK/WIN MK18 * ...46 C5
Surly Hall Wk WDSR SL4 ....187 K3
Surrey Av SLN SL2 ....179 N8
Surrey Pl BTCHLY MK3 ......52 F1
 TRING HP23 ....112 E3
Surrey Rd BTCHLY MK3 ......52 F1
Sussex Cl AYLW HP19 ....95 J4
 CSTG HP8 ....113 J3
 HWYN HP13 ....153 K1
 SL SL1 ....188 D3
Sussex Keep SL SL1 * 188 D3
Sussex Pl CFSP/GDCR SL9 * ..156 G6
 DTCH/LGLY SL3 ....188 D3
Sussex Rd BTCHLY MK3 ......52 F2
Sussex Wy DEN/HRF UB9 .....169 P3
Sutcliffe Av EAG/OLD/WT MK6 ...6 E5
Sutherland Av HYS/HAR UB3 ..191 N5
Sutherland Gv BTCHLY MK3 ....42 F9
Sutherland Wy AYLS HP21 * ...109 P1
Sutleye Ct SHEN MK5 ....42 E3
Sutton Av DTCH/LGLY SL3 ....188 E3
Sutton Cl MDHD SL6 ....177 P2
 MDHD SL6 ....185 J2
 PIN HA5 ....171 N5
Sutton Ct EMV/FZ MK4 ....52 C2
Sutton Court Rd
 HGDN/ICK UB10 ....183 H4
Sutton La DTCH/LGLY SL3 ....189 H1
Sutton Rd MDHD SL6 ....177 P2
Swabey Rd DTCH/LGLY SL3 ....189 J5
Swains Cl WDR/YW UB7 ....190 E3
Swains Ct OLN MK46 * 15 M3
Swains La FLKWH HP10 ....153 P9
Swakeleys Dr
 HGDN/ICK UB10 ....170 G9
Swakeleys Rd
 HGDN/ICK UB10 ....170 G9
Swale Rd AYLS HP21 ....109 L1
Swales Dr LBUZ LU7 ....75 H3
Swallow Cl BRACKY NN13 .....34 C3
 BUCK/WIN MK18 ....48 C4
Swallowdale SLN SL2 ....181 M6
Swallow Dr HAZ/HG HP15 .....143 P6
Swallowfield
 CNH/GTH/TM MK8 ....41 N5
Swallowhall Wy
 HYS/HAR UB3 ....191 K3
Swallow La AYLW HP19 ....95 H1
 RAYLNE/WEN HP22 ....110 A4
Swallow St IVER SL0 ....181 M6
Swanbourne Rd
 BUCK/WIN MK18 * 60 D7
 RMKS/WB MK17 ....61 M5
Swan Cl AYLW HP19 ....95 H1
 BRACKY NN13 ....34 F2
 BUCK/WIN MK18 ....48 C5
 CSHM HP5 ....125 M9
 LBUZ LU7 ....85 L7
 RAYLNE/WEN HP22 ....81 K3
Swan Ct OLN MK46 ....15 M3
Swanells Wd DUN/WHIP LU6 ...101 K3
Swan Hl RAYLU HP18 ....107 K5
Swan La RBICN QX27 ....66 C6
Swan Ms RAYLNE/WEN HP22 ...111 H4
Swann Rd
 RAYLNE/WEN HP22 * 123 J1
Swan Rd IVER SL0 ....181 N9
 WDR/YW UB7 ....190 D3
Swansea Rd HTHAIR TW6 .....197 J3
Swansons Rd DUN/WHIP LU6 ...86 B5
Swan's Wy CHNR OX39 ....129 P7
 WTLGN OX49 ....148 C1
Swanwick La AMSS HP7 ....43 N2
Swayne Rd MKV MK10 ....43 N2
Sweetcroft La
 HGDN/ICK UB10 ....182 F3
Sweetlands Cnr
 WTR/OFPK MK7 ....43 P8
 YEAD UB4 ....20 D9
Swift Cl NPAG MK16 ....30 C9
 YEAD UB4 ....21 J9
Swift Wy BRACKY NN13 ......34 F3
Swimbridge La EMV/FZ MK4 ...42 A4
Swinden Ct BDWL MK15 * 39 N7
Swindon Rd HTHAIR TW6 .....197 J5
Swinnertons Yd STSTR MK11 * ...28 D2
Swing Br LBUZ LU7 ....64 A4
Swing Gate La BERK HP4 .....126 F2
Switchback Rd MDHD SL6 ....177 K6
Switchback Rd North
 MDHD SL6 ....177 M6
Switchback Rd South
 MDHD SL6 ....177 L6
The Switchback MDHD SL6 * ...177 K6
Swyncombe Gn RNHPTN NN7 ...12 K6
Sycamore Av HYS/HAR UB3 ....191 L1
 WEAT MK2 ....53 L3
Sycamore Cl AMS HP6 ....145 P1
 BNEND SL8 ....165 J4
 BUCK/WIN MK18 ....48 D4
 FELT TW13 ....197 N9
 LBUZ LU7 ....62 D8
 RAYLU HP18 ....106 A3
 WDR/YW UB7 ....190 D1
Sycamore Ct AYLW HP19 * 2 C2
 HWYW HP12 ....152 C6
Sycamore Dene CSHM HP5 ....135 P1
Sycamore Dr MLW SL7 ....164 D4
 THAME OX9 ....118 B3
 TRING HP23 ....112 F2
Sycamore Leys
 BUCK/WIN MK18 ....58 C7
Sycamore Pl AMS HP6 ....145 N2
 BERK HP4 ....126 F4
 CSTG HP8 ....156 C3
Sycamore Rd AMS HP6 ....145 N1
 CSTG HP8 ....156 C3
 HWYW HP12 ....152 C6
The Sycamores HHS/BOV HP3 ...127 P5
Sycamore Wk
 DTCH/LGLY SL3 ....180 G9

Sycamore Wy HAZ/HG HP15 ...143 N8
Sydenham Gv CHNR OX39 ....129 J4
Sydney Gv SLN SL2 ....179 N9
Sydney Rd
 EBED/NFELT TW14 ....197 N7
Syke Cluan IVER SL0 ....189 N1
Syke Ings IVER SL0 ....189 N1
Sykes Cft EMV/FZ MK4 ....52 C2
Sykes Rd SL SL1 ....179 M9
Sylvana Cl HGDN/ICK UB10 ...182 C1
Sylvester Rd MDHD SL6 .....177 L6
Sylvester St LBUZ LU7 ......64 A6
Sylvia Cl GTMIS/PWD HP16 ...133 P8
Symington Ct SHEN MK5 .....42 P7
Synergy Pk
 EAG/OLD/WT MK6 * 42 E6
Syon Gdns NPAG MK16 ....31 J5
Syowe Ct GTLIN MK14 ....30 C5

T

Tabard Gdns NPAG MK16 .....31 J5
Tachbrook Rd
 EBED/NFELT TW14 ....197 M6
 SL SL1 ....188 C5
Tacknell Dr SHEN MK5 ....42 A8
Tacks La HADM MK17 ....43 K8
Tadmarton GTLIN MK14 ......30 C7
Tadmere IVER SL0 ....189 N1
Talbot Av DTCH/LGLY SL3 ....189 H4
 HWYN HP13 ....142 C9
Talbot Ct LBUZ LU7 ....74 E1
Talbot Pl DTCH/LGLY SL3 ....188 E3
Talbot Rd
 RAYLNE/WEN HP22 ....111 L1
 RKW/CH/CXG WD3 ....58 E9
Talbots Dr MDHD SL6 ....184 C1
Talbots Hyde OLN MK46 ......15 L3
Talland Av EAG/OLD/WT MK6 ...7 H4
Tallis La WTR/OFPK MK7 .....44 A7
Tall Oaks AMS HP6 ....145 P1
Tall Pines LBUZ LU7 * 64 D8
Tall Trees DTCH/LGLY SL3 ...189 H4
Tamar Cl AYLS HP21 ....109 L2
 FLKWH HP10 ....153 P6
Tamarisk Ct WTR/OFPK MK7 ...43 P7
Tamarisk Wy SL SL1 ....187 M3
Tamar Wy DTCH/LGLY SL3 ....189 K6
Tamworth Stubb
 WTR/OFPK MK7 ....43 P7
Tancred Rd HWYN HP13 ......4 E1
Tandra Cl RBEDW MK43 ......17 J2
Tandys Ct RBEDW MK43 * 17 J2
Tanfield La MKV MK10 ....43 N1
Tanglewood Wy FELT TW13 ...197 P7
Tank House Rd
 BUCK/WIN MK18 ....60 D5
Tanners Dr GTLIN MK14 ......30 G3
Tannery Rd FLKWH HP10 .....153 N6
Tansman La WTR/OFPK MK7 ...44 A7
Tanworth Cl NTHWD HA6 .....155 P9
Tanworth Gdns PIN HA5 .....159 P9
The Tanyard
 RAYLNE/WEN HP22 * 123 J1
Taplin Wy FLKWH HP10 ......95 J1
Taplow Common Rd SL SL1 ...178 D2
Taplow Rd MDHD SL6 ....178 E9
Tapping Rd SKCH HP14 ......151 L6
Taranis Cl WTR/OFPK MK7 ....44 A5
Tarbay La WDSR SL4 ....192 F1
Target Cl EBED/NFELT TW14 ...197 L8
Tarmac Wy WDR/YW UB7 .....190 B4
Tarnbrook Cl EMV/FZ MK4 ....52 E1
Tarnside Cl DUN/WHIP LU6 ...87 K2
Tarragon Cl WTR/OFPK MK7 ...43 N6
Tasker Cl HYS/HAR UB3 .....191 J8
Taskers Rw DUN/WHIP LU6 ...86 B5
The Task OLN MK46 ....15 M3
Tatchbrook Cl MDHD SL6 ....177 P4
Tate Rd CFSP/GDCR SL9 .....157 H5
Tatling Gv WTR/OFPK MK7 ...43 N6
Tattam Cl WLLN MK15 ....43 J2
Tattams La RMKS/WB MK17 ...61 K7
Tattenhoe La BTCHLY MK3 ....52 E4
Tattenhoe Pk EMV/FZ MK4 ...52 A2
Tattershall St SHEN MK5 ....42 A6
Tattlers Hl RAYLNE/WEN HP22 ...83 H5
Taunton Deane EMV/FZ MK4 ...52 D1
Taurus Cl BUCK/WIN MK18 ...58 B8
Tavelhurst CNH/GTH/TM MK8 ...41 N3
Taverner Ct WTR/OFPK MK7 ...44 A6
Tavistock Ms HWYW HP12 ....4 C1
Tavistock Rd
 HGDN/ICK UB10 ....183 K1
 WDR/YW UB7 ....190 C1
Tavistock St WEAT MK2 .....53 L2
Tavistock Wk AYL HP20 * 95 N5
Tawny Cl FELT TW13 ....197 N9
Tayfield Cl HGDN/ICK UB10 ..171 J8
Taylor Rd AYLS HP21 ....109 M2
Taylors Cl SL SL1 ....179 M7
Taylors Ct FELT TW13 ....197 N8
Taylors La AMSS HP7 ....144 F1
 TRING HP23 ....124 A2
Taylors Ms GTLIN MK14 .....30 C5
Taylor's Ride LBUZ LU7 .....64 E8
Taylors Rd CSHM HP5 ......135 P2
Taymouth Pl CMK MK9 ....43 H1
Tay Rd BTCHLY MK3 ....53 J2
Teal Ct NTHWD HA6 ....159 J2
Teasel Av GTLIN MK14 ......30 E8
Tedder Ct HGDN/ICK UB10 ...182 F3
Tedder Rd
 RAYLNE/WEN HP22 ....111 N9
Teesdale Rd SLN SL2 ....179 K8
Tees Rd AYLS HP21 ....109 L1
Tees Wy BTCHLY MK3 ....52 D2

Teign Cl NPAG MK16 ....31 K1
Telford Cl AYLW HP19 ....95 H6
Telford Dr SL SL1 ....187 L3
Telford Wy GTLIN MK14 .....31 H1
 HWYN HP13
Telston Cl BNEND SL8 ....165 N4
Temple Gdns
 RKW/CH/CXG WD3 ....159 H8
Temple La MLW SL7 ....176 D2
Temple Mill Island MLW SL7 ...176 C3
Temple Orch HWYN HP13 * ...5 F5
Temple Pk MDHD SL6 ....175 P5
 UX/CGN UB8 ....182 G1
Temple Rd WDSR SL4 ....193 N1
Temple Sq AYL HP20 ....2 D4
Temple St AYL HP20 ....91 H4
Temple Wy SLN SL2 ....179 N1
Templewood La SLN SL2 ....179 M1
Tene Acres SHEN MK5 ....41 P6
Tennis La BUCK/WIN MK18 ...60 E7
Tennyson Cl
 EBED/NFELT TW14 ....197 N5
Tennyson Dr NPAG MK16 ....30 G1
Tennyson Gv BTCHLY MK3 ....52 F4
Tennyson Rd AYLS HP21 .....109 P9
 WYM HP11 ....152 E5
Tennyson Wy SLN SL2 ......179 N7
Tenterden Crs
 WTR/OFPK MK7 ....43 P5
Tenzing Dr HWYN HP13 .....152 L4
The Terrace TRING HP23 ....112 E3
Terrington Cl BRACKY NN13 ...34 G1
Terrington Hl MLW SL7 .....164 B7
Terry Orch HWYN HP13 .....153 K3
Terry Rd HWYN HP13 ....153 K3
Terry's La UX/CGN UB8 * 182 C5
Testwood Rd WDSR SL4 .....187 J4
Tewkesbury La MKV MK10 ...43 M3
Thackeray Cl UX/CGN UB8 ...182 C5
Thackeray End AYLW HP19 ...95 H5
Thame Br THAME OX9 ....118 D9
Thame Pk Rd THAME OX9 ....118 D9
Thame Rd AYLS HP21 ....2 B7
 CNH OX39 ....129 L4
 HADM HP17 ....43 F7
 PRRI HP27 ....91 F7
 RAYLU HP18 ....91 J3
 RAYLU HP18 ....105 J3
 RAYLU HP18 ....106 J3
 RBICS/W OX25 ....90 C7
 THAME OX9 ....119 H6
Thame Rd South AYLW HP19 ...95 H5
Thamesbourne Ms
 BNEND SL8 * 165 N6
Thames Cl BNEND SL8 ....165 N5
 BTCHLY MK3 ....53 E3
Thames Dr NPAG MK16 ......31 L2
 RSLP HA4
Thamesfield Gdns MLW SL7 ...164 D6
Thames Md WDSR SL4 ....187 J9
Thames Pth EGH TW20 ......194 D8
 HEN RG9 ....175 J5
 MDHD SL6 ....184 C7
 STA TW18 ....195 M9
Thames Reach MLW SL7 .....175 M2
Thames Rd
 DTCH/LGLY SL3 ....189 K5
 WDSR SL4 ....186 C8
Thames Side HEN RG9 ....174 A6
 WDSR SL4 ....187 J6
Thames St WDSR SL4 ....187 J5
Thame Valley Wk
 RAYLU HP18 ....94 F7
 RAYLU HP18 ....106 F9
 THAME OX9 ....117 J7
Thane Ct GTLIN MK14 ....30 C6
Thanestead Copse
 FLKWH HP10 ....154 A8
Thatchers Dr MDHD SL6 ....184 C2
Thellusson Wy
 RKW/CH/CXG WD3 ....147 P9
Theodora Wy PIN HA5 ....171 M4
Theydon Av RMKS/WB MK17 ...44 F8
Thicket Gv MDHD SL6 ....176 P9
The Thicket FLKWH HP10 ....95 E9
 HYS/HAR UB3 ....191 M2
 MLW SL7 ....164 F7
Third Av DBGH MK1 ....53 H1
Third St SL SL1 ....190 G9
Third St WYM HP11 ....153 H6
Thirkleby Cl SL SL1 ....187 N2
Thirlby La SHEN MK5 ....42 A7
Thirlmere Av SL SL1 ....178 C4
Thirlmere Cl EGH TW20 ....194 B2
Thirsk Gdns RMKS/WB MK17 ...52 L5
Thistle Cl HHW HP1 ....127 H3
Thomas Crewe Cl
 BRACKY NN13 ....34 E4
Thomas Dr NPAG MK16 ......20 D9
Thomas Rd FLKWH HP10 .....166 C2
Thomas St LBUZ LU7 ....64 A5
Thompkins La SLN SL2 * 179 K9
Thompson Cl DTCH/LGLY SL3 ...189 H3
Thompson Rd
 HGDN/ICK UB10 ....182 D3
Thompson St BDWL MK13 ...39 N5
Thomson Cl AYLS HP21 .....95 M9
Thomson Wk AYLS HP21 * ...95 M9
Thornaby Pl FLKWH HP10 ...166 C1
Thornborough Br
 BUCK/WIN MK18 ....49 H4

Thornborough Rd
 RMKS/WB MK17 ....50 B3
Thornbridge Rd IVER SL0 ...181 L4
Thorncliffe CNH/GTH/TM MK8 ...41 M4
Thorndike SL SL1 ....179 L8
Thorn Dr DTCH/LGLY SL3 ...180 D3
Thorne Cl HEN RG9 ....173 M9
Thorne Wy AYL HP20 ....96 A5
 RAYLNE/WEN HP22 ....111 K5
Thorneycroft La WLLN MK15 ...31 H7
Thorney La North IVER SL0 ...181 P9
Thorney La South IVER SL0 ...189 P3
Thornhill BUCK/WIN MK18 ...49 M5
Thornhill Rd IVER SL0 .....190 B4
 NTHWD HA6 ....159 J4
Thornlea Cft OLN MK46 .....15 M4
Thornley Cft EMV/FZ MK4 ...52 C1
Thorns Cl PRRI HP27 ....121 M8
Thorns La PRRI HP27 ....121 N7
Thornton Av WDR/YW UB7 ...190 F4
Thornton Cl WDR/YW UB7 ...190 F4
Thornton Crs
 RAYLNE/WEN HP22 ....110 G9
Thornton Rd RMKN MK19 ....40 B6
 RMKS/WB MK17 ....50 B1
Thorn Tree Dr TRING HP23 ...112 D5
Thorpe Cl AYLS HP21 ....109 M2
Thorpeness Cft EMV/FZ MK4 ...51 P3
Thorpland Av
 HGDN/ICK UB10 ....171 J8
Thorwold Pl SHEN MK5 .....42 B7
Thrasher Rd AYLS HP21 ....95 M9
Three Castles Pth WDSR SL4 ...186 F7
Three Close La BERK HP4 ...126 C5
Three Households CSTG HP8 ...156 B4
Three Oaks Cl
 HGDN/ICK UB10 ....170 F8
Three Points La
 BUCK/WIN MK18 ....68 A4
Three Shires Wy
 BOZ/IR/WOL NN29 ....10 C3
 NPAG MK16 ....16 A6
 OLN MK46 ....16 A6
 RMKN MK19 ....19 P5
Thresher Gv WOLV MK12 ....39 H4
Thrift Cl AYLS HP21 ....109 M2
Thrift La MDHD SL6 ....185 K6
Thrupp Cl RMKN MK19 ......40 A2
Thrush Cl AYLW HP19 * 95 H4
Thruxton Dr EMV/FZ MK4 ...52 A1
Thurby Wy MDHD SL6 ......185 K6
Thurlestone Rd RSLP HA4 ...171 N8
Thurne Cl NPAG MK16 ......31 L2
Thursby Cl WLLN MK15 .....31 H6
Thurston Rd SL SL1 ....179 P9
Thyme Cl NPAG MK16 ......20 D9
Tibbett Cl DUN/WHIP LU6 ...87 J2
Tibbys La RAYLW HP18 .....107 K5
Ticehurst Cl WTR/OFPK MK7 ...43 P5
Tichborne
 BUCK/WIN MK18 ....38 C8
 TOW MK11 ....28 D6
Tickford Gdns RSLP HA4 ....159 P9
Tickford St NPAG MK16 ....31 K1
Tickford Street
 BUCK/WIN MK18 * 38 C8
Tidbury Cl RMKS/WB MK17 ...44 D7
Tidbury Rd RMKS/WB MK17 ...53 L5
Tilburywood Cl HWYN HP13 ...142 C9
Tilehouse La DEN/HRF UB9 ...169 N4
 RKW/CH/CXG WD3 ....157 N9
Tilehouse Wy DEN/HRF UB9 ...169 N5
Tilers Rd WTR/OFPK MK7 ....41 K2
Tilley Rd FELT TW13 ....197 L9
Tilling Crs HWYN HP13 .....153 N5
Tilman Cl WOLV MK12 ......29 J8
Tilstone Av WDSR SL4 ......187 J6
Tilstone Cl WDSR SL4 ......187 J6
Tilsworth Rd BEAC HP9 ....154 C7
Timber La RMKS/WB MK17 ...55 J5
Timberscombe EMV/FZ MK4 ...52 D1
Timbers Wy MDHD SL6 .....185 H2
Timbold Dr WTR/OFPK MK7 ...44 B6
Timpson La OLN MK46 ......16 A4
Timpsons Rw OLN MK46 ....16 A4
Tindall Av LBUZ LU7 ....75 L3
Tindal Rd AYL HP20 ....3 F1
Tingewick Rd
 BUCK/WIN MK18 ....47 L4
 BUCK/WIN MK18 ....60 B7
Tinkers La TRING HP23 ....113 L8
 WDSR SL4 ....193 H1
Tinkers Wood Rd
 HWYN HP13 ....152 E1
Tintagel Ct EAG/OLD/WT MK6 ...7 H4
Tintern Cl SL SL1 ....187 N4
Tippett Cl AYLW HP19 .....95 H6
Tippet Cl WTR/OFPK MK7 ...44 B6
Tippings SKCH HP14 ....140 E6
Tiptree Rd RSLP HA4 ......171 P8
Titchmarsh Ct
 EAG/OLD/WT MK6 ....6 D7
Tithe Barn Dr MDHD SL6 ...185 H5
Tithe Barn Wy NTHLT UB5 ...183 P2
Tithe Cl MDHD SL6 ....184 D8
 YEAD UB4 ....183 N8
Tithe Ct DTCH/LGLY SL3 ....189 K6
Tithe La STWL/WRAY TW19 ...195 N6
Tithe Rd FLKWH HP10 ......95 J1
Titmus Rd
 RAYLNE/WEN HP22 ....111 L1
Tiverton Crs AYLW HP19 ....95 H6
 EMV/FZ MK4 ....51 P2
Tiverton Rd RSLP HA4 ......171 N8
Tockley Rd SL SL1 ....178 D1
Todd Cl AYLS HP21 ....109 M2
Tofrek Ter HWYN HP13 * ...145 P3
Tolcarne Av EAG/OLD/WT MK6 ...7 J3
Tolcarne Dr PIN HA5 ......159 N8
Toll Bar Cnr PRRI HP27 ....120 F6

Tollgate MDHD SL6 ....184 G1
Tollgate Cl
 RKW/CH/CXG WD3 ......147 P6
Tolman Ct AYLS HP21 ....95 K9
Tomlin Rd SL SL1 ....179 J7
Tompion Rd AYLW HP19 ....95 H6
Tompkins Cl
 RAYLNE/WEN HP22 ....111 M2
Tompkins La RBICN OX27 ...66 A5
Toms Hill Cl TRING HP23 ...113 P1
Toms Hill Rd TRING HP23 ...113 P1
Toms Turn HAZ/HG HP15 ...143 M6
Tongwell La NPAG MK16 ....31 L5
Tongwell St MKV MK10 .....31 L5
Toonagh WDSR SL4 * 192 A8
Toot Hill Cl SHEN MK5 .....42 A7
Topaz Cl SL SL1 ....187 M2
Top Farm Cl BEAC HP9 .....154 E8
Topland Rd CFSP/GDCR SL9 ...156 F7
Top Meadow WTR/OFPK MK7 ...44 A9
Top Pk CFSP/GDCR SL9 .....156 E6
Topping La UX/CGN UB8 ....182 D6
Top Station Rd BRACKY NN13 ...15 P5
Torbay RAYLNE/WEN HP22 ...79 P8
Torcross Rd RSLP HA4 ......171 P8
Tornay Ct LBUZ LU7 ....75 H3
Torquay Sp SLN SL2 ....179 M6
Torre Cl BTCHLY MK3 ......53 K7
Torridge Rd AYLS HP21 ....109 M2
 DTCH/LGLY SL3 ....189 K7
Torridon Cl WEAT MK2 .....53 K3
Torrington Rd BEAC HP9 ...126 D1
Torrs Cl HADM MK17 ....43 H5
Tortoiseshell Wy BERK HP4 ...114 B8
Torwood Cl BERK HP4 ......126 E6
Totteridge Cl HWYN HP13 ...153 K4
Totteridge Dr HWYN HP13 ...153 L9
Totteridge La HWYN HP13 ...143 L9
Totteridge Pde
 HWYN HP13 * 153 L2
Totteridge Rd HWYN HP13 ...153 J5
Totternhoe Rd
 DUN/WHIP LU6 ....101 G1
 DUN/WHIP LU6 ....86 G1
Towan Av EAG/OLD/WT MK6 ...7 J3
Towcester Dr TOW NN12 ....27 M2
Towcester Rd
 BUCK/WIN MK18 ....38 C8
 TOW NN12 ....27 K1
Tower Cl BERK HP4 ....126 C2
 FLKWH HP10 ....166 A2
Tower Crs GTLIN MK14 .....30 A2
Tower Dr GTLIN MK14 ......30 A2
Towergate Cl UX/CGN UB8 ...182 N2
Tower Hl KGLCY WD4 ....137 N2
Towerage La HWYW HP12 ...152 C1
 SKCH HP14 ....151 P1
Tower Rd AMSS HP7 ....43 P1
Towers Av HGDN/ICK UB10 ...183 J6
Towers Cft HGDN/ICK UB10 * ...183 J6
Towersey Dr THAME OX9 ....118 F6
Towersey Rd THAME OX9 ....118 G6
Towersey St HWYN HP13 ....143 K9
Town Bridge Ct CSHM HP5 ...135 M3
Town End Crs NPAG MK16 ...30 B1
Town End Rd SKCH HP14 ...140 F3
Town Farm LBUZ LU7 ......64 A4
Town Farm Cl THAME OX9 ...118 F4
 WTLGN OX49 ....138 F4
Town Farm Wy
 STWL/WRAY TW19 ......196 B4
Townfield CSHM HP5 ....135 M5
Town Field La CSTG HP8 ...156 E3
Townfield Rd HWYN HP13 ...5 J5
 HYS/HAR UB3 ....191 N2
Townfield Sq HYS/HAR UB3 ...191 M2
Town Hall Ar BERK HP4 * ...126 C1
Town La FLKWH HP10 ......166 C4
 STWL/WRAY TW19 ......196 C6
Townsend RBICN OX27 .....50 B8
Townsend Cottages
 RMKS/WB MK17 ....50 B5
Townsend Gn BDWL MK15 ...39 B5
Townsend La OLN MK46 ....27 B2
Townsend Piece AYLW HP19 ...2 B3
Townsend Rd CSHM HP5 ....135 M3
 NTHWD HA6 ....159 M7
Townside DUN/WHIP LU6 ...86 B5
 HADM HP17 ....107 K3
Townson Av NTHLT UB5 ....183 N5
Townson Rd NTHLT UB5 ....183 N5
Trafalgar Av BTCHLY MK3 ...52 E1
Trafford Cl
 CTMIS/PWD HP16 ....133 N5
Trafford Rd
 GTMIS/PWD HP16 ....133 N5
Tramhill RAYLW HP18 ......91 H5
Tranlands Brigg BDWL MK13 ...30 B9
Trapp's La CSHM HP5 ......135 N6
Travell Ct BDWL MK13 .....42 C2
Travel Rd SLN SL2 ....179 K6
Travis Ct SLN SL2 ....179 M6
Travis Gv BTCHLY MK3 .....53 J2
Travistock Ms HWYW HP12 ...4 B4
Treacher's Cl CSHM HP5 ...135 M4
Treadaway Hl FLKWH HP10 ...153 N9
Treadaway Rd FLKWH HP10 ...95 N1
Trebah Sq AYLW HP19 .....95 H1
Treborough EMV/FZ MK4 ....52 D1
Tredington Gv
 WTR/OFPK MK7 ....43 P8
Treehanger Cl TRING HP23 ...112 F2
Trees Av HWYN HP13 ....152 G2
Treeside Cl WDR/YW UB7 ...190 B3
Treesmill Dr MDHD SL6 ....185 H6
Trees Rd BNEND SL8 ....165 P6
 SKCH HP14 ....140 E6
Treetops Cl NTHWD HA6 ...159 K5

Trelawney Av
DTCH/LGLY SL3 ......188 G4
Tremayne Cr
EAG/OLD/WT MK6 ......7 M1
Trenchard Av
RAYLNE/WEN HP22 ......111 K8
RSLP HA4 ......183 P1
Trenchard Rd MDHD SL6 ......185 P7
Trenchard St AYLW HP19 ......95 J7
Trenches La DTCH/LGLY SL3 ......189 J2
Trent Dr NPAG MK16 ......31 K1
Trentishoe Crs EMV/FZ MK4 ......42 D2
Trent Rd BTCHLY MK3 ......52 E2
DTCH/LGLY SL3 ......189 K7
Trent Wy YEAD UB4 ......185 N5
Tresco Rd BERK HP4 ......114 D9
Tresham Ct SHEN MK5 ......41 K2
The Tressell MDHD SL6 ......185 N1
Trevelyan Wy BERK HP4 ......114 D8
Treves Gn AYLS HP21 ......109 N1
Trevithick Cl
Trevithick La SHEN MK5 ......42 B7
Trevone Ct EAG/OLD/WT MK6 ......7 M4
Trevor Crs RSLP HA4 ......171 M9
Trevor Rd HYS/HAR UB3 ......191 L3
Trewarden Av IVER SL0 ......181 M5
Tring HI NWDCN UB2 ......191 P4
Tring Ford Rd TRING HP23 ......98 F9
Tring HI TRING HP23 ......112 A3
Tring Rd AYL HP20 ......3 J9
BERK HP4 ......113 N7
DUN/WHIP LU6 ......86 A9
DUN/WHIP LU6 ......86 C2
RAYLNE/WEN HP22 ......83 J7
RAYLNE/WEN HP22 ......111 J9
TRING HP23 ......98 J4
Tring Rd (Icknield Wy)
DUN/WHIP LU6 ......86 E5
Trinity Av MLW SL7 ......2 A6
Trinity Cl NTHWD HA6 ......159 L6
RMKN MK19 ......28 D6
STWL/WRAY TW19 ......196 C5
Trinity Ct
RKW/CH/CXG WD3 * 158 E2
Trinity Pl WDSR SL4 * 6 C5
Trinity Rd HAZ/HG HP15 ......143 M8
MLW SL7 ......164 D7
WOLV MK12 ......29 K6
Trispen Ct EAG/OLD/WT MK6 ......7 P
Triumph Cl HYS/HAR UB3 ......191 J9
Troutbeck Cl DEN/HRF UB9 ......170 C2
Troutbeck Cl SLN SL2 ......188 C1
Trout Ct MLW SL7 ......164 C9
Trout Hollow PRRI HP27 ......131 H4
Trout La WDR/YW UB7 ......*
Trout Rd WDR/YW UB7 ......*
Trubys Gdn EAG/OLD/WT MK6 ......42 C5
Trueman Pl EAG/OLD/WT MK6 ......42 D5
Truesdale Dr DEN/HRF UB9 ......170 C2
Trumper Wy SL SL1 ......187 K2
Trumpton La WTR/OFPK MK7 ......44 A5
Truro Cl MDHD SL6 ......176 C9
Truro Wy YEAD UB4 ......185 L3
Trust Cnr HEN RG9 ......174 A3
Trustees Wy DEN/HRF UB9 ......169 P9
Tubwell Rd SLN SL2 ......180 C4
Tucker Ct HWYN HP13 ......*
Tudeley Hale WTR/OFPK MK7 ......43 P4
Tudor Cl PIN HA5 ......171 N3
Tudor Ct AMS HP6 * 177 K4
MDHD SL6 ......178 A6
STSTR MK11 ......28 C9
Tudor La WDSR SL4 ......54 E6
Tudor Mi FLKWH HP10 * 166 B1
Tudor Orch BERK HP4 * 114 A8
Tudor Pk AMS HP6 ......145 N1
HYS/HAR UB3 ......144 A9
Tudors Cl BUCK/WIN MK18 ......67 P5
Tudor Sq HYS/HAR UB3 ......183 K9
Tudor Wy BRACKY NN13 ......34 H4
HGDN/ICK UB10 ......182 G2
RKW/CH/CXG WD3 ......158 A1
WDSR SL4 ......187 J9
Tuffnell Cl WLLN MK15 ......31 L6
Tulip Wy WDR/YW UB7 ......190 D5
Tulkers Cl CTMIS/PWD HP16 ......133 J7
Tulla Ct WEAT MK7 ......53 J7
Tummell Wy WEAT MK7 ......53 J7
Tunbridge Gv WTR/OFPK MK7 ......43 N4
Tunners End
CFSP/GDCR SL9 ......
Tunnel Link Rd HTHAIR TW6 ......196 C4
Tunnel Rd East
WDR/YW UB7 ......191 H8
Tunnel Rd West
WDR/YW UB7 ......190 C9
Tuns La SL SL1 ......187 N4
Turks Cl UX/CGN UB8 ......182 C6
Turnberry Cl BTCHLY MK3 ......52 C4
Turner Cl AYL HP20 ......95 P4
Turner Rd DTCH/LGLY SL3 ......188 B2
Turners Dr HWYN HP13 ......153 L2
Turners Fld HWYN HP13 ......142 E9
Turners Meadow
RAYLNE/WEN HP22 ......97 H9
Turners Ms MGTLN MK14 ......30 F7
Turners Wk CSHM MK5 ......135 N3
Turners Wood Dr CSTG HP8 ......156 F4
Turner Wk AYL HP20 * 95 P4
Turneys Dr WOLV MK12 ......29 J5
Turneys Orch
RKW/CH/CXG WD3 ......147 N2
Turnfields RAYLW HP18 ......106 C9
Turnfurlong AYLS HP21 ......3 H7
Turnfurlong La AYLS HP21 ......3 J7
Turnfurlong Rw AYLS HP21 ......3 J7
Turnham Wy AYLW HP19 ......95 K8
Turnip Cl RAYLW HP18 ......106 F4
Turnmill Av EAG/OLD/WT MK6 ......43 H1

Turnoak Pk WDSR SL4 ......193 J3
Turnpike Cl DUN/WHIP LU6 ......86 C7
Turnpike End AYLS HP21 ......95 P9
Turnpike La HGDN/ICK UB10 ......182 D6
Turnpike Rd HWYW HP12 ......152 C6
RMKS/WB MK17 ......55 M1
The Turnpike HHNE HP2 ......118 D4
Turnpike Wy HWYW HP12 ......152 C6
Turnstone Rd AYLW HP19 ......95 N4
Turpin Rd BEAC HP9 * 154 A1
Turpins Gn MDHD SL6 ......184 C2
Turpin St EAG/OLD/WT MK6 ......7 L3
Turton Wy SL SL1 ......187 P4
Turvey Cl
RAYLNE/WEN HP22 ......111 L1
Turvey Rd NPAG MK16 ......17 K8
RBEDW MK45 ......11 J7
Turvill End SHEN MK5 ......42 B4
Turville Rd AYLS HP21 ......96 C9
Turweston Rd BRACKY NN13 ......35 J3
Tuscans Cl BUCK/WIN MK18 ......67 P4
Tweedale Cl RMKS/WB MK17 ......61 L5
Tweed Cl BERK HP4 ......114 D9
Tweeddale Gv
HGDN/ICK UB10 ......171 J8
Tweed Dr BTCHLY MK3 ......52 D2
Tweed Rd DTCH/LGLY SL3 ......189 K7
Tweenways CSHM MK5 ......135 P5
Twelve Leys
RAYLNE/WEN HP22 ......82 G5
Twinches La SL SL1 ......187 M2
Twinflower Rd CSHM MK5 ......43 P6
The Twist TRING HP23 ......113 H4
Twitchell La
RAYLNE/WEN HP22 ......111 L1
Twitchen La EMV/FZ MK4 ......42 D9
Two Dells La CSHM MK5 ......126 B6
Two Gates La CSHM HP5 ......125 J6
Two Ridges Link
DUN/WHIP LU6 ......85 L5
LBUZ LU7 ......84 F2
Two Ridges Link (Grand Union Canal Wk) LBUZ LU7 ......74 D9
Two Tree HI HEN RG9 ......173 M8
Twyford La WTR/OFPK MK7 ......44 A7
Twynham Rd MDHD SL6 ......177 M9
Tyle HI WDSR SL4 ......194 C4
Tylers Crs HAZ/HG HP15 ......143 P9
Tylers Gn BDWL MK13 ......42 D1
Tylers Hill Rd CSHM HP5 ......136 B5
Tylers Rd HAZ/HG HP15 ......143 P9
Tyler Wk DTCH/LGLY SL3 ......189 H6
Tynan Cl EBED/NFELT TW14 ......197 N1
Tyneham Cl AYLS HP21 ......110 B2
Tynemouth Ri
WTR/OFPK MK7 ......43 N1
Tyne La AYLS HP21 ......109 M2
Tyne Sq BTCHLY MK3 ......52 D2
Tyrefields SHEN MK5 ......48 C5
Tyrell Cl BUCK/WIN MK18 ......48 A4
Tyrell Gdns WDSR SL4 ......193 K2
Tyrells Gdns RMKS/WB MK17 ......63 L2
Tyrells Rd RMKS/WB MK17 ......61 L3
Tyrill GTLIN MK14 ......30 C6
Tyson St EAG/OLD/WT MK6 ......6 E1
Tythe Cl LBUZ LU7 ......72 E1
Tyzack Rd HWYN HP13 ......143 L9

U

Ullswater Cl SL SL1 ......178 G8
YEAD UB4 ......185 L5
Ullswater Dr LBUZ LU7 ......74 A2
Ullswater Rd DUN/WHIP LU6 ......87 K2
Ulverscroft MKV MK10 ......43 N7
Ulverston Rd DUN/WHIP LU6 ......87 J2
Ulyett Pl EAG/OLD/WT MK6 ......7 L1
Umberville Wy SLN SL2 ......179 N7
Underhill Cl MDHD SL6 ......185 L1
Underwood Pl
EAG/OLD/WT MK6 ......7 L7
Underwood Rd HWYN HP13 ......153 K3
Union St NPAG MK16 * 21 H9
University Wy RBEDW MK45 ......33 H5
Unwin Av EBED/NFELT TW14 ......197 N4
Up Cnr CSTG HP8 ......156 D2
Upcroft WDSR SL4 ......193 M2
Upland Av CSHM MK5 ......135 N1
Uplands MLW SL7 ......164 C5
Uplands Ct CFSP/GDCR SL9 ......168 A6
Uplatt Rd EAG/OLD/WT MK6 ......7 N3
The Uplands CFSP/GDCR SL9 ......168 A7
RSLP HA4 ......171 N6
Upper Abbotts HI AYLW HP19 ......95 N6
Upper Ashlyns Rd BERK HP4 ......126 D2
Upper Belmont Rd
CSHM HP5 ......135 M1
Upper Bourne End La
HHW HP1 ......127 K5
Upper Bray Rd MDHD SL6 ......186 A5
Upper Church St
RAYLW HP18 ......107 K3
Upper Coombe LBUZ LU7 ......74 C1
Upper Dr BEAC HP9 ......155 H5
Upper Fifth St CMK MK9 ......6 B3
Upper George St CSHM MK5 ......135 N3
Upper Gladstone Rd
CSHM HP5 * 135 N1
Upper Green St WYM HP11 ......4 B5
Upper Hall Pk BERK HP4 ......126 C3
Upper High St THAME OX9 ......118 D5
Upper Hollis
CTMIS/PWD HP16 ......133 L5
Upper Hundreds Wy
AYL HP20 ......2 E4
Upper Icknield Wy
PRRI HP27 ......121 M8
PRRI HP27 ......130 G5

RAYLNE/WEN HP22 ......111 K7
TRING HP23 ......99 H7
Upper Lees Rd SLN SL2 ......179 L6
Upper Lodge La
HAZ/HG HP15 ......143 M5
Upper Meadow CSHM HP5 ......135 M5
Upper Riding BEAC HP9 ......154 F4
Upper Rd DEN/HRF UB9 ......169 M5
Upper Sales HHW HP1 ......117 H1
Upper Second St CMK MK9 ......6 B4
Upper Stonehayes
GTLIN MK14 ......30 F5
Upper St BUCK/WIN MK18 ......46 G5
RAYLNE/WEN HP22 ......79 J3
Upper Third St CMK MK9 ......6 B3
Upper Wy RMKS/WB MK17 ......64 A1
Upper Wood Cl SHEN MK5 ......41 M4
Upton Cl HEN RG9 ......174 A7
SL SL1 ......188 B4
Upton Court Rd
DTCH/LGLY SL3 ......188 C4
Upton Gv SHEN MK5 ......42 C8
Upton Lea Pde SLN SL2 * 188 D1
Upton Pk SL SL1 ......188 A3
Upton Rd HADM HP17 ......108 C2
Upton Rd SLN SL2 * 188 D1
Uxbridge Rd
HGDN/ICK UB10 ......183 J7
RKW/CH/CXG WD3 ......158 B2
SL SL1 ......180 F9
SLN SL2 ......180 F9
YEAD UB4 ......183 N9

V

V2 SHEN MK5 ......41 N9
V3 SHEN MK5 ......41 L9
V4 STSTR MK11 ......41 J1
V5 WOLV MK12 ......42 C5
V6 CMK MK9 ......6 C5
V7 EAG/OLD/WT MK6 ......7 G5
V8 CMK MK9 ......7 C5
V10 WLIN MK15 ......31 J8
V11 WLLN MK15 ......31 J4
WTR/OFPK MK7 ......44 A7
Vache La CSTG HP8 ......156 C1
SHEN MK5 ......41 P6
Vache Ms CSTG HP8 * 156 C1
Vale Cl CFSP/GDCR SL9 ......146 F9
Vale Gv SL SL1 ......188 A4
Valence End DUN/WHIP LU6 ......87 J8
Valency Cl NTHWD HA6 ......159 M4
Valens Cl CNH/GTH/TM MK8 ......41 N5
Valentine Ct
CNH/GTH/TM MK8 ......41 M5
Valentine Wy CSTG HP8 ......156 F3
Vale Park Dr AYL HP20 ......3 F4
Valerian Pl NPAG MK16 ......30 F1
Vale Ri CSHM MK5 ......135 N1
Vale Rd AYL HP20 ......3 F2
CSHM HP5 ......125 N9
WDSR SL4 ......187 N9
The Vale CFSP/GDCR SL9 ......146 F9
EBED/NFELT TW14 ......197 P5
Valley Cl BRACKY NN13 ......35 H4
DUN/WHIP LU6 ......86 C9
PIN HA5 ......159 P9
Valley Crs BRACKY NN13 ......35 H4
Valley End DTCH/LGLY SL3 ......35 H4
Valley Ri BRACKY NN13 ......35 H4
Valley Rd BERK HP4 ......114 B8
BRACKY NN13 ......35 H3
BUCK/WIN MK18 ......46 G5
BUCK/WIN MK18 ......58 D7
DUN/WHIP LU6 ......101 K3
HEN RG9 ......173 M8
HGDN/ICK UB10 ......182 G5
UX/CGN UB8 ......182 C5
WEAT MK7 ......53 J5
Valleyside HHW HP1 ......127 P2
Valley Vw CSHM HP5 ......135 L2
Valley Wy CSHM MK5 ......135 L2
Vancouver Rd YEAD UB4 ......183 P7
Van Der Bilt Ct BDWL MK13 ......29 P7
Van Diemans Rd
THAME OX9 ......118 D6
Van Diemens Cl CHNR OX39 ......129 N5
Vandyke Cl RMKS/WB MK17 ......44 C8
Vandyke Rd LBUZ LU7 ......74 C9
LBUZ LU7 ......74 E2
Vane Rd THAME OX9 ......118 D5
Vanguard Cl BDWL MK13 ......29 L8
Vanguard Wy HTHAIR TW6 ......197 L1
Vansittart Est WDSR SL4 * 187 M9
Vansittart Rd MLW SL7 ......176 E1
WDSR SL4 ......187 M9
Vantage Ct NPAG MK16 ......31 H4
Vanwall Rd MDHD SL6 ......185 J3
Varney Cl HHW HP1 ......127 P2
Varney Pl HWW HP1 ......127 P2
Vaughan Gdns WDSR SL4 ......187 K5
Vaughan Wy SLN SL2 ......179 J7
Vauxhall BDWL MK13 ......29 P6
Vauxhall Dr AYLW HP19 ......95 L8
Veldan Av EAG/OLD/WT MK6 ......43 H5
Venables La WLLN MK15 ......30 D1
Venetian Ct WTR/OFPK MK7 ......44 C5
Venus HI HHS/BOV HP3 ......136 A1
Verbena Ct WDR/YW UB7 ......190 D6
Ver-Colne Valley Wk
HHS/BOV HP3 ......
Verdi Cl WTR/OFPK MK7 ......44 F1
Verdon Dr WLLN MK15 ......31 H6
Verity Pl EAG/OLD/WT MK6 ......131 H6
Verley Cl EAG/OLD/WT MK6 ......43 H5
Vermont Pl WLLN MK15 ......179 J4
Vermont Rd SLN SL2 ......2 J7
Verney Av HWYW HP12 ......152 D3
Verney Rd BERK HP4 ......114 B9
BUCK/WIN MK18 ......58 D7
MLW SL7 ......164 D7

TRING HP23 ......112 G1
Verney Farm Ct
BUCK/WIN MK18 ......69 K2
Verney Rd BUCK/WIN MK18 ......60 A6
DTCH/LGLY SL3 ......189 J5
Verney Wk AYLS HP21 ......95 M9
Vernier Crs SHEN MK5 ......41 N7
Vernon Dr DEN/HRF UB9 ......158 C9
Vernon Rd FELT TW13 ......197 M8
Verona Cl UX/CGN UB8 ......182 B7
Verwood Rd AYLW HP19 ......95 N5
Veryan Pl EAG/OLD/WT MK6 ......7 P2
Vibia Cl STWL/WRAY TW19 ......196 E6
Vicarage Cl BEAC HP9 ......155 N7
MDHD SL6 ......177 N1
RAYLNE/WEN HP22 ......110 D9
RSLP HA4 ......171 K5
TOW NN12 ......18 A8
Vicarage Dr MDHD SL6 ......186 A3
Vicarage Gdns BDWL MK13 ......30 A9
BERK HP4 ......115 K7
LBUZ LU7 ......73 H2
MDHD SL6 ......186 A3
TRING HP23 ......98 C8
Vicarage La BUCK/WIN MK18 ......58 D8
HHS/BOV HP3 ......127 K8
LBUZ LU7 ......73 H2
LBUZ LU7 ......99 K2
RBICS/W OX25 ......90 E1
STWL/WRAY TW19 ......194 G7
Vicarage Rd SRMKS/WB MK17 ......44 C8
Vicarage Wy AYLS HP21 ......109 M1
DTCH/LGLY SL3 ......188 B8
Vicarage Wk RMKS/WB MK17 ......44 C8
Vickery Cl AYLS HP21 ......109 N1
Vicarage Wk MDHD SL6 ......184 A9
STSTR MK11 ......28 C9
Vicarage Wy HGDN/ICK UB10 ......183 J1
Victoria Av HYS/HAR UB3 ......183 K8
Victoria Cl IVER SL0 ......190 A1
Victoria Crs MLW SL7 ......164 C7
WYM HP11 ......152 D7
Victoria Ms MLW SL7 ......164 C7
Victoria Rd BERK HP4 ......118 C6
Victoria St AYL HP20 ......3 F3
SL SL1 ......188 B3
WDSR SL4 ......187 P3
WOLV MK12 ......29 K6
Victor Rd WDSR SL4 ......4 C4
Victory Rd BERK HP4 ......58 D7
BUCK/WIN MK18 ......58 D7
Vienna Gv BDWL MK15 ......29 N7
Viking Cl WTR/OFPK MK7 ......44 B1
Village Cl LBUZ LU7 ......74 B8
Village La SLN SL2 ......167 P6
Village Rd AMS HP6 * 145 K8
DEN/HRF UB9 ......170 A6
IVER SL0 ......190 B1
Village Wy AMS HP6 ......146 F4
DTCH/LGLY SL3 ......188 C8
Villiers Cl BUCK/WIN MK18 ......58 D7
Villiers Rd SLN SL2 ......179 N2
Villier St UX/CGN UB8 ......182 C6
Vimy Rd LBUZ LU7 ......74 D7
Vincent Av CNH/GTH/TM MK8 ......41 N7
Vincent Rd AYLW HP19 ......95 L8
Vincent Rd AYLW HP19 * 95 L8
Vine Cl HAZ/HG HP15 ......143 N9
STWL/WRAY TW19 ......194 E6
WDR/YW UB7 ......190 C5
Vine Gv HGDN/ICK UB10 ......183 J1
Vine La HGDN/ICK UB10 ......182 F4
Vineries Cl WDR/YW UB7 ......190 F6
Vine Rd RSLP HA4 ......171 H7
Vine Rw RBEDW MK45 * 17 J1
Vineyard Dr BNEND SL8 ......165 H1
Vineyard Rd FELT TW13 ......197 H7
Viney La AYLW HP19 ......95 H7
The Vine RAYLW HP18 ......106 C9
Vinetrees RAYLNE/WEN HP22 ......83 H1
Vineyard Cl BNEND SL8 ......165 N6
Viola Av STWL/WRAY TW19 ......196 E6
Violet Av UX/CGN UB8 ......182 A8
Violet Cl PRRI HP27 ......131 M6
Violets Cl NPAG MK16 ......30 A9
Violet Tee UX/CGN UB8 * 182 A8
Virginia Cl LBUZ LU7 ......73 J6
Virginia Gdns SKCH UB9 ......95 L8
Viscount Cl AYL HP20 ......95 P4
Viscount Rd
STWL/WRAY TW19 ......196 D6

Viscount Wy HTHAIR TW6 ......197 L3
Vivaldi Cl WTR/OFPK MK7 ......44 M4
Vivash Cr HYS/HAR UB3 ......53 J2
Vivian Cl OXHEY WD19 ......159 N2
Vivian Gdns OXHEY WD19 ......159 N4
Vivien Cl MDHD SL6 ......177 M2
Volta Ri SHEN MK5 ......42 C8
Vyne Crs CNH/GTH/TM MK8 ......41 P3
Vyners Wy HGDN/ICK UB10 ......182 C1
The Vyne LBUZ LU7 * 74 G4

W

Waborne Rd BNEND SL8 ......165 P5
Waddesdon Cl
CNH/GTH/TM MK8 ......41 P4
Waddesdon HI RAYLW HP18 ......93 N4
Wade Dr SL SL1 ......187 L2
Wadesmill La WTR/OFPK MK7 ......43 N8
Wadhurst La WTR/OFPK MK7 ......43 N3
Wagner Cl MDHD SL6 ......184 F4
WTR/OFPK MK7 ......44 A8
Waine Cl BUCK/WIN MK18 ......48 B4
Wainwrights RAYLW HP18 ......106 A3
Wakefield Cl GTLIN MK14 ......110 A1
Wakefield Crs SLN SL2 ......180 B3
Wakelins End MDHD SL6 ......117 K3
Wakeman Rd BNEND SL8 ......165 N6
Walbank Gv SHEN MK5 ......42 B5
Walbrook Av
EAG/OLD/WT MK6 ......43 H1
Waldeck Rd MDHD SL6 ......177 N9
Waldens Cl BNEND SL8 ......165 N6
Walducks Cl LBUZ LU7 ......72 E1
Walford Rd UX/CGN UB8 ......182 C5
Walgrave Cl EBED/NFELT TW14 ......197 M6
Walgrove Gdns MDHD SL6 ......184 D9
Walker Cl EBED/NFELT TW14 ......197 M6
Walker Dr MDHD SL6 ......185 N3
Walker Rd PRRI HP27 ......127 F6
Walkham Cl FLKWH HP10 ......153 P6
Walkhampton Av
BDWL MK13 ......42 B1
Walk House Cl RBEDW MK45 ......33 H4
The Walk BUCK/WIN MK18 ......60 B7
Walkwood End BEAC HP9 ......154 C9
Walk Wood Ri BEAC HP9 ......155 J8
Wall Cl HGDN/ICK UB10 ......182 C5
MLW SL7 ......164 F5
Wallace End AYLS HP21 ......95 A9
Wallace Ms WYM HP11 ......29 N6
Wallace St DTCH/LGLY SL3 ......29 N6
Wallasey Crs
HGDN/ICK UB10 ......170 G7
Wallbridge Cl AYLW HP19 ......95 N8
Waller Dr NTHWD HA6 ......159 N3
Waller Rd BEAC HP9 ......155 K8
Wallinger Dr SHEN MK5 ......42 N3
Wallingford BDWL MK13 ......29 P8
Wallingford Gdns
WYM HP11 ......4 H6
Wallingford Cl RSLP HA4 ......171 J4
Wallington Cl RSLP HA4 ......171 J4
Walney Pl EMV/FZ MK4 ......51 P2
Walnut Av DTCH/LGLY SL3 ......190 G4
Walnut Cl BRACKY NN13 ......35 H3
CTMIS/PWD HP16 ......133 L5
NPAG MK16 ......30 A9
RAYLNE/WEN HP22 ......110 C4
TOW NN12 ......25 K1
Walnut Crs PRRI HP27 ......127 F6
Walnut Dr BUCK/WIN MK18 ......58 D8
Walnut Gv FLKWH HP10 ......153 L8
The Walnuts LBUZ LU7 ......64 B8
Walnut Tree La PRRI HP27 ......127 F6
Walnut Wy AMS HP6 ......134 G8
RSLP HA4 ......165 P7
Walpole Rd SL SL1 ......179 H9
WDSR SL4 ......194 D6
Walsham Rd
EBED/NFELT TW14 ......197 P6
Walsh's Mnr GTLIN MK14 ......30 C6
Walsingham Ca WYM HP11 ......152 D6
Waltham Av HYS/HAR UB3 ......191 J4
Waltham Dr WTR/OFPK MK7 ......45 N3
Walton Av RSLP HA4 ......171 H3
Walton Dene AYLS HP21 * 3 H7
Walton Dr HWYN HP13 ......153 L1
WTR/OFPK MK7 ......43 H6
Walton End WTR/OFPK MK7 ......43 A6
Walton Gv AYLS HP21 ......3 J7
Walton Heath BTCHLY MK3 ......52 D5
Walton La SL SL1 ......179 K5
Walton Rd AYLS HP21 ......109 M1
MKV MK10 ......43 M2
WTR/OFPK MK7 ......44 A6
Walton St AYL HP20 ......2 D5
Walton Wy AYLS HP21 ......3 J7
Wanbourne La HEN RG9 ......160 B7
Wandlebury GTLIN MK14 ......30 C6
Wandsworth Pl BDWL MK13 ......30 A8
Wannions Cl CSHM HP5 ......136 A5
Wantage Cl LBUZ LU7 ......73 L6
Wantage Crs LBUZ LU7 ......73 L6
Wappenham Rd
BRACKY NN13 ......24 C2

Wapping RAYLW HP18 ......106 B8
Wapseys La SLN SL2 ......168 A4
Wapseys Wd
  CFSP/GDCR SL9 * 168 A3
Ward Cl IVER SL0 ......189 P1
Wardes Cl GTMIS/PWD HA0 ...133 J7
Ward Gdns SL1 SL1 ......187 J2
Wardle Pl EAG/OLD/WT MK6 ...6 E6
Ward Pl AMS HP7 * 145 M4
Ward Rd BRACKY NN13 ......35 J7
  DBGH MK1 9
Wardrobes La PRRI HP27 ......131 M4
Ward Royal WDSR SL4 * 187 N9
Ward Royal Pde WDSR SL4 * ...187 N9
Wardstone End EMV/FZ MK4 ...52 B1
Ware Leys Cl RBICN OX27 ......66 E6
Warfield Rd
  EBED/NFELT TW14 ......197 L6
Wargrave Rd HEN RG9 ......174 C8
Warley Av YEAD UB4 ......183 N9
Warley Rd YEAD UB4 ......183 N9
Warmark Rd HHW HP1 ......115 N9
Warmington Gdns
  WLLN MK15 ......31 H8
Warmstone Cl RAYLW HP18 ...93 M1
Warmstone La RAYLW HP18 ...93 M1
Warneford Av
  RAYLNE/WEN HP22 ......111 K9
Warnford Wy LBUZ LU7 ......74 C6
Warner Cl HYS/HAR UB3 ......191 K8
  SL SL1 ......187 J2
Warners Cl RMKS/WB MK17 ...64 B1
Warners Hl MDHD SL6 ......177 M1
Warners Rd RMKS/WB MK17 ...52 D8
Warren Cl BUCK/WIN MK18 ...48 C4
  DTCH/LGLY SL3 ......188 C4
  HADM HP17 ......108 D1
Warrendene Rd SKCH HP14 ...142 C3
Warrender Rd CSHM HP5 ...136 C4
Warrender Wy RSLP HA4 ......171 N5
Warren Fld IVER SL0 ......181 C5
Warren Pde SLN SL2 * 188 E2
Warren Rd HGDN/ICK UB10 ...170 E9
  RMKS/WB MK17 ......51 H5
  TOW NN12 ......18 B8
Warren Row Rd
  WAR/TWY RG10 ......175 J9
The Warren CFSP/GDCR SL9 ...157 H7
  CSHM HP5 ......135 J1
  HAZ/HG HP15 ......145 N6
  YEAD UB4 ......183 N9
Warren Vw MDHD SL6 * 177 M1
Warren Wood Dr WYM HP11 ...153 J5
Warrington Av SL SL1 ......179 P8
Warrington Rd DLIN MK46 ...15 M2
Warrington Sp WDSR SL4 ...194 D6
Warsaw Cl RSLP HA4 ......183 P2
Warwick Av HWWY HP12 ......152 E4
  SLN SL2 ......179 N7
Warwick Cl MDHD SL6 ......185 H5
  RAYLNE/WEN HP22 ......111 L1
Warwick Ct
  RKW/CH/CXG WD3 ......147 P5
Warwick Crs YEAD UB4 ......183 M7
Warwick Dr LBUZ LU7 ......73 L7
Warwick Pl BTCHLY MK3 * ...52 E1
  UX/CGN UBB 182 C5
Warwick Rd BEAC HP9 ......155 H7
  BTCHLY MK3 ......52 E4
  HSLWW TW4 ......197 P2
  RMKN MK19 ......19 J3
  WDR/YW UB7 ......190 D2
Warwick Rw AYL HP20 2
Warwick Ter OLN MK46 * 15 K9
  RAYLNE/WEN HP22 ......111 L1
Washfield EMV/FZ MK4 ......42 D9
Wash Hl HWW HP4 ......126 C7
Wash Hill Lea FLKWH HP10 ...166 C6
Washington Dr SL SL1 ......187 H1
  WDSR SL4 ......193 J2
Wastel EAG/OLD/WT MK6 ......43 H7
Watchcroft Dr
  BUCK/WIN MK18 ......48 C1
Watchet Cl EMV/FZ MK4 ......42 D9
Watchet La HAZ/HG HP15 ......145 P3
Waterbeach Rd SL SL1 ......179 P9
Water Cl RMKN MK19 ......28 D6
Waterdell LBUZ LU7 ......74 C2
Water Eaton Rd BERK HP4 ...53 H4
  SKCH HP14 ......140 E6
Waterford Cl BTCHLY MK3 ...52 E1
Waterhouse Cl NPAC MK16 ...31 K1
Water La BERK HP4 ......126 E1
  HADM HP17 ......108 D7
  HHS/BOV HP3 ......115 P2
  LBUZ LU7 ......74 D2
  NPAC MK16 ......21 L5
  PRRI HP27 ......132 C8
Waterlily AYLW HP19 ......95 N3
Waterloo Cl
  EBED/NFELT TW14 ......197 M7
Waterloo Ct BTCHLY MK3 ...52 E1
Waterloo Rd LBUZ LU7 ......74 C3
  UX/CGN UBB 182 C4
Waterlow Cl NPAC MK16 ......31 J3
Waterman St SL SL1 ......187 J2
Waterman's Rd HEN RG9 ...174 A8
Watermead AYLW HP19 ......95 M4
  EBED/NFELT TW14 ......197 L7
Watermeadow AYLW HP19 ...95 N4
Water Meadow CSHM HP5 ...135 M5
Water Meadow Wy
  RAYLNE/WEN HP22 ......111 H8
Watermill Wy
  RAYLNE/WEN HP22 ......111 K8
Waterperry Rd RAYLW HP18 ...104 D3
Waters Dr
  RKW/CH/CXG WD3 ......158 C4
Waterside RMKS/WB MK17 ...135 N5
  DUN/WHIP LU6 ......86 B4
  EAG/OLD/WT MK6 ......43 J4
  FLKWH HP10 ......166 C2
  UX/CGN UBB 182 C8

Waterside Dr DTCH/LGLY SL3...189 H3
Waterside Ms
  RKW/CH/CXG WD3 ......158 A6
Watersplash La
  HADM HP17 ......107 J8
Watersmeet Cl EMV/FZ MK4 ...42 D8
Watersplash La
  HYS/HAR UB3 ......191 N5
Water Stratford Rd
  BUCK/WIN MK18 ......47 H2
Water Tower Cl UX/CGN UBB ...182 E1
Watery La BRACKY NN13 ......35 J5
  FLKWH HP10 ......166 C1
  HEN RG9 ......185 J5
  RBICN OX27 ......191 K6
  RMKN MK19 ......40 C6
  THAME OX9 ......98 D6
Watford Rd NTHWD HA6 ......159 M7
Watling St CNH/GTH/TM MK8 ...41 N4
  DBGH MK1 ......53 K2
  EMV/FZ MK4 ......52 D1
Watling Ter WEAT MK2 ......53 L2
Watlington Rd WTLGN OX49 ...138 B8
Watlow Gdns
  BUCK/WIN MK18 ......48 C1
Wattleton Rd BEAC HP9 ......166 C1
Watts Cl RMKN MK19 ......19 J3
Watts Gn RAYLW HP18 ......106 F4
Wavell Ct WLN MK15 ......31 H6
Wavell Gdns SLN SL2 ......179 K6
Wavell Rd BEAC HP9 ......155 M9
  MDHD SL6 ......185 H1
Wavendon House Dr
  RMKS/WB MK17 ......44 E4
Wavendon Rd
  RMKS/WB MK17 ......44 G2
Waveney Cl HYS/HAR UB3 ......191 K4
Waverley Cl HYS/HAR UB5 ...191 K5
Waverley Cft MKV MK10 ......35 M8
Waverley Gdns NTHWD HA6 ...159 N8
Waverley Rd SLN SL2 ......179 N8
Waverley Wk AYL HP20 2
Waxwing Cl AYL HP20 ......95 N4
Waybourne Gv RSLP HA4 ......183 N1
Waye Av HEST TW5 ......191 N9
Wayfarers Pk BERK HP4 ......126 B1
Waylands HYS/HAR UB5 ......183 K8
  STWL/WRAY TW19 ......194 C5
Waynflete Av BRACKY NN13 ...34 C5
Waynflete Cl BRACKY NN13 ...34 C5
Wayside DUN/WHIP LU6 ......87 M3
  HWYN HP13 ......153 K3
  PRRI HP27 ......132 C8
Wayside Gdns
  CFSP/GDCR SL9 ......168 F5
Wayside Ms MDHD SL6 ......177 M8
Weald Dr HGDN/ICK UB10 ...182 D5
Wealdstone Pl
  EAG/OLD/WT MK6 ......7 K2
Weald Wy YEAD UB4 ......183 L6
Weasel Wy RMKS/WB MK17 ...52 B5
Webber Heath
  WTR/OFPK MK7 ......44 B8
Webbs Home Cl MKV MK10 ...43 N2
Webbs Meadow AYLW HP19 ...95 J7
Webbs Rd YEAD UB4 ......183 N6
Webster Cl MDHD SL6 ......184 G2
  THAME OX9 ......118 D4
Webster Rd AYLS HP21 ......96 A9
Websters Meadow
  EMV/FZ MK4 ......42 D8
Wedgewood Av AYLW HP19 ...95 J7
Wedgewood Cl
  NTHWD HA6 * 159 J7
Wedgewood St AYLW HP19 ...95 J7
Wedgwood Av CTLIN MK14 ...31 H5
Wedgwood Dr SKCH HP14 ...142 C5
Weedon Cl CFSP/GDCR SL9 ...156 D8
Weedon Hi AMS HP6 ......135 H6
Weedon Hill AMS HP6 ......135 L9
Weedon Rd AYLW HP19 2
Weekes Dr SL SL1 * 187 M3
Weill Rd AYLS HP21 ......110 A2
Weir La BUCK/WIN MK18 ......69 J4
  RAYLNE/WEN HP22 ......96 B7
  RBICS/W OX25 ......78 A3
Weirside Gdns WDR/YW UB7 ...190 D2
Welbeck Av AYLS HP21 ......96 C9
  YEAD UB4 ......183 P7
Welbeck Cl MKV MK10 ......43 M5
Welbeck Rd MDHD SL6 ......185 K2
Welby Cl MDHD SL6 ......184 C3
Welden SLN SL2 ......180 E9
Welders La CFSP/GDCR SL9 ...156 B7
Weldon Cl RSLP HA4 ......183 P2
Weldon Rd SHEN MK5 ......42 B4
Weldon Wy THAME OX9 ......118 E3
Welford Wy RAYLW HP18 ...107 K5
Welland Cl AYLS HP21 ......109 L2
  DTCH/LGLY SL3 ......189 J7
Welland Dr NPAC MK16 ......31 J2
Wellbank AYLW HP19 * 2
Wellbank MDHD SL6 ......178 C2
Wellbrook Ms TRING HP23 * ...112 F2
Wellcroft LBUZ LU7 ......99 K2
Wellcroft Cl SL SL1 ......187 M2
Weller Cl AMS HP6 ......146 A1
Weller Rd AMS HP6 ......146 A1
Wellesbourne Gdns
  HWYN HP13 ......143 K9
Wellesley Av IVER SL0 ......189 P4
  NTHWD HA6 ......159 M5
Wellesley Pth SL SL1 ......188 C3

Wellesley Rd SL SL1 ......188 C3
Welles Rd HWYN HP13 ......153 M5
Welley Av STWL/WRAY TW19 ...194 C3
Welley Rd STWL/WRAY TW19 ...194 C4
Wellfield HAZ/HG HP15 ......143 P9
Wellfield St WLLN MK15 ......31 K5
Wellfield Rd SKCH HP14 ......151 K2
Wellhayes GTLIN MK14 ......30 F5
Well Head Rd DUN/WHIP LU6 ...86 E2
Wellhouse La HAZ/HG HP15 ...145 M6
Wellhouse Wy SKCH HP14 ...142 E5
Wellingborough Rd
  OLN MK46 ......15 M2
Wellington Av PRRI HP27 ......121 K9
Wellington Cl MDHD SL6 ......177 H8
Wellington Pl AYLS HP21 ......109 N2
  BTCHLY MK3 ......52 E5
Wellington Rd AYLS HP21 ...109 N2
  EBED/NFELT TW14 ......197 L4
  MDHD SL6 ......177 H9
  UX/CGN UBB 182 C4
Wellington St SL SL1 ......187 J2
  THAME OX9 ......118 D5
Well La LBUZ LU7 ......73 N8
Wellmore RMKS/WB MK17 * ...38 D7
Wellonhead Br
  RAYLNE/WEN HP22 ......111 M3
Wells Cl WDSR SL4 ......187 L8
Wells Ct LBUZ LU7 * 74 E2
Well St BUCK/WIN MK18 ......48 B3
Welsh La BUCK/WIN MK18 ......37 H1
Welsumer Gv SHEN MK5 ......42 A9
Welton Rd AYLS HP21 ......96 B9
Welwyn Wy
  EBED/NFELT TW14 ......197 M5
Welwyn Wy YEAD UB4 ......183 L7
Wendover Hts
  RAYLNE/WEN HP22 ......111 K9
Wendover Rd AYLS HP21 ......109 P9
  BNEND SL8 ......165 N5
  HADM HP17 ......122 D2
  RAYLNE/WEN HP22 ......110 F7
  SL SL1 ......178 F8
Wendover St WYM HP11 ......4 D3
Wendover Wy AYLS HP21 ......95 P9
  WYM HP11 ......5 H7
Wenlak Cl DEN/HRF LU9 ......170 A8
Wenman Rd THAME OX9 ......118 E2
Wenning La EMV/FZ MK4 ......52 B1
Wensum Wy
  RKW/CH/CXG WD3 ......158 D1
Wentworth Av SLN SL2 ......179 L6
Wentworth Cl HWYN HP13 ...5 L6
Wentworth Crs
  HYS/HAR UB3 ......191 K4
  MDHD SL6 ......185 J1
Wentworth Dr LBUZ LU7 ......64 E9
  PRRI HP4 ......31 N3
Wentworth Pl CSHM HP5 * ...155 H5
Wentworth Rd THAME OX9 ...118 E5
Wentworth Wy BTCHLY MK3 ...52 C4
Wenwell Cl
  RAYLNE/WEN HP22 ......111 N9
Werner Ct AYLS HP21 ......109 N2
Werth Dr RMKS/WB MK17 ...54 F1
Wescott Wy UX/CGN UBB ...181 P5
Wesley Cl AYL HP20 ......3 J1
Wesley Dene HWYN HP13 ...5 J5
Wesley Pl MDHD SL6 ......197 F8
Wesley Rd HYS/HAR UB3 ...191 N1
Wessex Rd BNEND SL8 ......165 P7
Wessex Wy MDHD SL6 ......185 L8
Westacott YEAD UB4 ......183 L8
Westacott Wy MDHD SL6 ...184 D3
West Acres AMS HP7 ......145 P4
Westanley Av AMS HP7 ......145 P5
West Av FLKWH HP10 ......166 C1
  HYS/HAR UB3 ......191 M1
Westborough Ct MDHD SL6 ...185 J1
Westborough Rd MDHD SL6 ...185 J1
Westbourne Pde
  HGDN/ICK UB10 * 170 F3
Westbourne St WYM HP11 ...4 D5
Westbrook MDHD SL6 ......186 C6
Westbrook End
  RMKS/WB MK17 ......52 C8
Westbury Circular Ride
  BRACKY NN13 ......36 D4
Westbury La NPAC MK16 ......31 H5
Westbury Rd NTHWD HA6 ...159 L4
Westcliffe CNH/GTH/TM MK8 ...41 L5
West Common
  CFSP/GDCR SL9 ......168 F3
West Common Rd
  UX/CGN UBB 182 D1
Westcote Ri RSLP HA4 ......171 J5
West Ct HWYN HP13 ......142 C4
West Crs WDSR SL4 ......187 K9
Westcroft SL SL1 ......187 M2
West Dales BDWL MK13 ......30 B8
West Dean MDHD SL6 ......177 M6
Westdean La CSHM HP5 ...134 C1
West Dene DUN/WHIP LU6 ...101 P7
Westdown Gdns
  DUN/WHIP LU6 ......87 H1
West Drayton Park Av
  WDR/YW UB7 ......190 E4
West Drayton Rd
  UX/CGN UBB 183 J8
West Dr HWYN HP13 ......153 K2
West Edge RBICN OX27 ......66 E7
West End
  RAYLNE/WEN HP22 ......110 E4
  TOW NN12 ......25 J2
West End Cl BUCK/WIN MK18 ...48 A8
West End La HYS/HAR UB3 ...191 M3
  SLN SL2 ......180 A4
West End Rd LBUZ LU7 ......84 D9
  RSLP HA4 ......171 N9

Westend Rd WYM HP11 ......4 C5
Westend St WYM HP11 ......4 C5
Western Av BUCK/WIN MK18 ...48 C4
  DEN/HRF LU9 ......170 A9
  HEN RG9 ......174 A8
  HGDN/ICK UB10 ......182 C2
  NTHLT UB5 ......183 P5
Western Cl HEN RG9 * 174 A8
Western Dene HAZ/HG HP15 ...145 K6
Western Dr FLKWH HP10 ......166 C4
  RMKN MK19 ......19 J5
Western La BUCK/WIN MK18 ...60 A7
Western Pde
  HGDN/ICK UB10 * 183 H2
Western Perimeter Rd
  HTHAIR TW6 ......196 B2
Western Rd HEN RG9 ......174 A8
  RMKS/WB MK17 ......50 C8
  TRING HP23 ......112 D5
  WEAT MK2 ......53 J2
  WOLV MK12 ......21 P1
Western Vw HYS/HAR UB3 ...191 H4
Westfield AMS HP6 ......154 G8
  AYLS HP21 ......109 N3
Westfield Av RMKN MK19 ...27 P3
Westfield Rd BEAC HP9 ......154 G9
  BERK HP4 ......114 D8
  LBUZ LU7 ......98 C4
  MDHD SL6 ......185 H1
  SLN SL2 ......179 M7
  WEAT MK2 ......53 J4
Westfields BUCK/WIN MK18 ...47 P5
  PRRI HP27 ......121 M9
Westfield Wk HWYW HP12 ...152 D4
Westfield Wy RSLP HA4 ......171 L8
West Furlong
  BUCK/WIN MK18 ......58 E1
Westgate Crs SL SL1 ......187 K1
Westgate Est
  EBED/NFELT TW14 * 197 H7
West Hatch Mnr RSLP HA4 ...171 M6
West Hl DUN/WHIP LU6 ......87 L3
  RMKS/WB MK17 ......45 H8
Westhill SL SL1 * 34 D5
Westhill Cl BRACKY NN13 ...34 C5
Westhill Gdns BRACKY NN13 ...34 C5
Westholme Gdns RSLP HA4 ...171 N6
Westhorpe Pk MLW SL7 * ...165 H6
Westhorpe Rd MLW SL7 ......164 F6
Westland Ct
  STWL/WRAY TW19 * 196 E5
Westland Cl
  CFSP/GDCR SL9 ......157 H7
Westlands Av SL SL1 ......178 F9
Westlands Cl HYS/HAR UB3 ...191 N5
  SL SL1 ......178 F9
Westlands Rd PRRI HP27 ......121 N9
West La HEN RG9 ......173 P6
  OLN MK46 ......15 J7
West Lieth TRING HP23 ......112 C5
Westlington La HADM HP17 ...107 H7
Westmacott Dr
  EBED/NFELT TW14 ......197 N1
West Md MDHD SL6 ......177 M6
Westmead PRRI HP27 ......121 K8
  WDSR SL4 ......193 M2
Westminster Cl
  EBED/NFELT TW14 ......197 M7
  WYM HP11 ......153 H6
Westminster Crs
  BRACKY NN13 ......35 H5
Westminster Cft
  BRACKY NN13 ......35 H5
Westminster Dr AYLS HP21 ...95 P9
  BTCHLY MK3 ......52 C4
Westminster Rd
  BRACKY NN13 ......35 H5
Westmorland Rd MDHD SL6 ...177 P8
Weston Cl THAME OX9 ......74 C4
Weston La THAME OX9 ......117 M5
Weston Rd OLN MK46 ......15 K9
  OLN MK46 ......15 J2
  RAYLNE/WEN HP22 ......111 J2
  SL SL1 ......179 K8
  THAME OX9 ......138 C2
  WTLGN OX49 ......138 E3
Weston Wy
  RAYLNE/WEN HP22 ......110 A4
Westover Ct HYS/HAR UB3 ...143 C9
Westover Rd HWYN HP13 ...152 D1
West Point SL SL1 ......187 H2
West Rd HTHAIR TW6 ......196 B3
West Richardson St
  WYM HP11 ......4 D5
West Rdg BNEND SL8 ......165 P5
Westridge Cl HWW HP1 ......127 P2
West Rd BERK HP4 ......114 E8
  EBED/NFELT TW14 ......197 K6
  MDHD SL6 ......177 H9
  RBEDW MK43 ......137 J3
  WDR/YW UB7 ......190 F4
West Side LBUZ LU7 * 98 E4
Westside La HWYN HP13 ......152 C4
West Side Ri OLN MK46 ......15 K9
West St AYLW HP19 2
  BUCK/WIN MK18 ......48 A4
  BUCK/WIN MK18 ......37 J2
  BUCK/WIN MK18 ......59 K1
  DUN/WHIP LU6 ......87 H1
  HEN RG9 ......173 P6
  LBUZ LU7 ......74 E2
  MDHD SL6 ......177 H9
  OLN MK46 ......15 K9
West Vw CSHM HP5 ......135 K2
West Wy HYS/HAR UB3 ......191 N2
West Wy BEAC HP9 ......154 D9

  RKW/CH/CXG WD3 ......158 B1
  RSLP HA4 ......171 M6
West Waye HWYN HP13 ......143 J9
West Well La BUCK/WIN MK18 ...46 C5
Westwick Gdns HEST TW5 ...197 P3
Westwood Cl AMS HP6 ......146 F3
  CNH/GTH/TM MK8 ......41 N4
  RSLP HA4 ......171 H4
Westwood Dr AMS HP6 ......146 F3
Westwood Gn MDHD SL6 ......177 M2
Westwood Rd MLW SL7 ......164 C8
Westwood Wk AYL HP20 * ...95 N5
West Wycombe Hill Rd
  SKCH HP14 ......141 P9
West Wycombe Rd
  SKCH HP14 ......142 B9
Wetherby Gdns BTCHLY MK3 ...52 D5
Wethered Pk MLW SL7 ......164 D5
Wethered Rd MLW SL7 ......164 C8
  SL SL1 ......178 F9
Wexham Park La
  DTCH/LGLY SL3 ......180 E7
Wexham Pl DTCH/LGLY SL3 * ...180 F2
Wexham Rd SL SL1 ......180 C8
  SLN SL2 ......180 D8
Wexham St SL SL1 ......180 E8
Wexham Woods
  DTCH/LGLY SL3 ......180 E8
Wey La CSHM HP5 ......135 M5
Weymouth Rd YEAD UB4 ...183 L6
Whaddon Cha AYLW HP19 ...2
Whaddon Rd EMV/FZ MK4 ...51 N2
  NPAC MK16 ......31 N2
  RMKS/WB MK17 ......50 E1
  RMKS/WB MK17 ......51 K6
  RMKS/WB MK17 ......52 F7
  RMKS/WB MK17 ......61 M2
  SHEN MK5 ......42 A9
Whaddon Wy BTCHLY MK3 ...52 D6
Whales La RBICN OX27 ......66 E7
Whalley Dr BTCHLY MK3 ......52 D5
Wharf Cl RAYLNE/WEN HP22 ...111 H9
Wharfe La HEN RG9 ......174 A6
Wharf La BERK HP4 ......113 N5
  BNEND SL8 ......165 N6
  RMKN MK19 ......28 E6
Wharf Rd
  RAYLNE/WEN HP22 ......111 H9
  STWL/WRAY TW19 ......194 E6
Wharf Rw
  RAYLNE/WEN HP22 ......111 J2
Wharfside WEAT MK2 * 53 L2
Wharfside Pl BUCK/WIN MK18 ...48 C2
The Wharf GTLIN MK14 ......30 F3
  WEAT MK2 ......53 L2
Wharf Vw BUCK/WIN MK18 ...48 C2
Whatmore Cl
  STWL/WRAY TW19 ......196 A5
The Wheatbolts WDSR SL4 ...187 P3
Wheatcroft Cl
  EAG/OLD/WT MK6 ......42 G7
Wheatfield Cl LBUZ LU7 ......73 H2
  MDHD SL6 ......184 C3
Wheathouse Copse
  RMKS/WB MK17 ......50 C8
Wheatlands Rd
  DTCH/LGLY SL3 ......188 D4
Wheatley Cl EMV/FZ MK4 ...52 C1
Wheatley Crs HYS/HAR UB3 ...191 N1
Wheatley Wy
  CFSP/GDCR SL9 ......156 G6
Wheatsheaf Pde
  WDSR SL4 ......194 C3
Wheatstone Cl
  DTCH/LGLY SL3 ......188 C4
Wheeler Cl AYLS HP21 ......95 J8
Wheeler Dr RSLP HA4 ......171 J4
Wheelers End CHNR OX39 ...129 N6
Wheelers La BDWL MK13 ......30 A7
Wheelers Orch
  CFSP/GDCR SL9 ......156 C8
Wheelers Pk HWYN HP13 ...153 K3
Wheelwright Ms GTLIN MK14 ...30 F7
Wheelwright Rd PRRI HP27 ...120 F7
Wheelwrights
  RAYLNE/WEN HP22 ......110 F3
Wheelwrights Pl
  DTCH/LGLY SL3 * 189 L8
Wheelwrights Wy
  RMKN MK19 ......28 C6
Wheelwrights Yd
  RAYLNE/WEN HP22 ......79 L3
Whetstone Cl BDWL MK13 ...30 B8
Whichert Cl BEAC HP9 ......154 G4
Whielden Gate CSHM HP5 ...145 H4
Whielden La AMS HP7 ......145 H4
Whielden St AMS HP7 ......145 M5
Whinchat AYLW HP19 ......95 N4
Whincup Cl WYM HP11 ......152 E6
Whinneys Rd FLKWH HP10 ...154 A7
Whipsnade Rd
  DUN/WHIP LU6 ......87 H1
Whirlpool Arch RAYLW HP18 ...116 F4
Whitby Cl BTCHLY MK3 ......52 F1
Whitby Rd RSLP HA4 ......171 P8
  SL SL1 ......187 N1
Whitchurch Cl MDHD SL6 ...177 L5
Whitchurch La
  RAYLW HP18 ......70 F9
Whitchurch Rd LBUZ LU7 ......72 B9
White Alder WOLV MK12 ......29 N8
Whitebaker Ct GTLIN MK14 ...30 F7
White Bridge Cl
  EBED/NFELT TW14 ......197 M5
Whitebrook Pk 178 A4
Whitebroom Rd HHW HP1 ...115 N5
White Cl HWYN HP13 ......152 D1
  SL SL1 ......187 P2
White Crs
  RAYLNE/WEN HP22 ......111 K8
Whitecross Rd HADM HP17 ...107 J8

Whitefield La
GTMIS/PWD HP16 ....133 N6
Whiteford Rd SLN SL2 ......180 A8
Whitegate Ct
EAG/OLD/WT NK6 ....43 H6
Whitehall Av MKV MK10 ......44 B3
Whitehall La
STWL/WRAY TW19 ....195 J5
Whitehall Rd UX/CGN UB8 ....182 D4
Whitehall St AYL HP20 ....2 C4
White Hart Ct CSTG HP8 ....156 C5
RAYLW HP18................77 H8
White Hart Fld
RAYLW/WEN HP22 ....79 M4
White Hart La HADM HP17 ...107 K9
White Hart MI WYM MK18 ......5 F5
White Hart Meadow
BEAC HP9 ....155 J9
White Hart Rd MDHD SL6 * ..177 M9
SL SL1.....................187 P4
White Hart St WYM HP11 ....5 F5
Whitehaven SL SL1 ....187 N7
Whitehead Wy AYLS HP21 .....95 N9
White Heart Av UX/CGN UB8 ..38 A8
Whiteheath Av RSLP HA4 .....171 C5
White Hermitage
STWL/WRAY TW19 * 194 E4
White HI BERK HP4 ....126 E6
CSHM HP5 ....135 N4
FLKWH HP10...............154 C9
HEN RG9 ....174 C6
HHW HP1 ....127 P3
NTHWD HA6 ....158 D6
White HI OLN MK46 ....15 L2
White Hill CI CSHM HP5 .....135 N3
Whitehill Ct MLW SL7 ....164 C3
Whitehill Ct BERK HP4 ......114 F9
Whitehorn PI WDR/YW UB7 ....190 E1
White Horse Ct LBZU LU7 * ...74 E2
White Horse Dr EMV/FZ MK4...52 C1
White Horse La
RAYLW/WEN HP22 ....81 J2
White Horse Rd WDSR SL4....193 H2
White House La
CFSP/GDCR SL9 ....156 C9
Whitehouse Wy IVER SL0 .....181 M6
Whitelands Av
RKW/CH/CXG WD3 ....147 K5
Whitelands Rd HWYW HP12 ...152 C4
Whitelands Wy HWYW HP12 ...152 D5
White La HEN RG9 ....173 J1
Whiteleaf Wy PRRI HP27 .....127 M4
Whiteley WDSR SL4 ....187 J8
Whiteley Crs BTCHLY MK5 .....52 C5
Whiteleys Pde
HGDN/ICK UB10 * 183 H7
White Lilies Island WDSR SL4 187 M8
White Lion Rd AMSS HP7 .....135 L5
White Lion Yd CSHM HP5 .....135 N5
White Lodge CI MLW SL7 .....164 C3
White Paddock MDHD SL6.....184 C5
Whitepit La FLKWH HP10 .....166 B3
White Rock MDHD SL6 ....177 P7
Whites La DTCH/LGLY SL3....188 D7
Whitethorn Av
WDR/YW UB7 ....190 E1
Whitethorn CI
RAYLW/WEN HP22 ....110 A6
Whitethorns NPAG MK16 ......31 H2
White Vw AYL HP20 ....95 H4
Whitewood Rd BERK HP4 .....126 C1
Whitfield Rd SKCH HP14 .....142 C5
Whitfield Wy
RKW/CH/CXG WD3 ....157 P1
Whitley CI STWL/WRAY TW19 .196 H4
Whitmees CI OLN MK46 ....15 L3
Whitsun Pasture
WLLN MK15 * 31 H6
Whittaker Rd SLN SL2 ....179 J7
Whittenham CI SLN SL2 .....188 C2
Whittington Av YEAD UB4 ....183 M8
Whittle Pkwy SL SL1.........179 H9
The Wittle Rd THAME OX9 ....118 B5
Whitton Wy NPAG MK16 ....31 J2
Whitworth La SHEN MK5 ......42 B5
Whurley Wy MDHD SL6 ....177 L6
Whyteladyes La MDHD SL6 ...164 G8
Whytingham Rd TRING HP23..112 C2
Wicken Park Rd SHEN MK5 ....42 B5
Wicken Rd BUCK/WIN MK18....39 M4
The Wickets MDHD SL6.......177 P9
Wickham CI DEN/HRF UB9 ....158 D8
Wick Rd DUN/WHIP UL6 ....87 P8
Wick Rd TRING HP23 ....112 C6
Wicksteed Av
CNH/GTH/TM MK8............41 M4
Widbrook Rd MDHD SL6.......177 P5
Widdenton Vw SKCH HP14 ....151 L3
Widecroft Rd IVER SL0 ......181 N9
Widewater PI
DEN/HRF UB9 * 170 C3
Widmere Fld
GTMIS/PWD HP16 ....133 J7
Widmere La MLW SL7 ....164 A2
Widmore CI CSHM HP5 ....125 J3
Widmill La RBICS/W OX25.....76 B9
Wieland Rd NTHWD HA6 ......159 N7
Wigan's La PRRI HP27 ....130 E9
Wigginton Bottom
TRING HP23 ....113 H6
Wiggles La TRING HP23 ....98 C8
Wigmore Ct AYLW HP19 ....95 J3
Wigmore Rd AYLW HP19 ....95 J3
Wigwell Gdns RMKS/WB MK17..50 C9
Wilberforce Ms RMKS/WB.....177 M9
Wildacre Rd SHEN MK5 ....41 P8
Wildlands NTHWD HA6 ....159 M4
Wilder CI RSLP HA4 ....171 H4
The Wilderness BERK HP4 ....114 C7
Wildgreen North
DTCH/LGLY SL3 ....189 J5

Wildgreen South
DTCH/LGLY SL3 ....189 J5
Wild Oaks CI NTHWD HA6 ....159 M6
Wildwood NTHWD HA6 ....159 M7
Wilford Ct NTHWD HA6 ....159 K7
WLLN MK15................43 J2
Wilford Rd DTCH/LGLY SL3 ..188 G5
Wilfrids Wood CI
FLKWH HP10...............165 P5
Wilkes Cft SHEN MK5 ....41 P5
Wilkins CI HYS/HAR UB3 .....191 M6
Wilkinson CI HGDN/ICK UB10..183 H4
Willant CI MDHD SL6 ....184 F5
Willenhall Dr HYS/HAR UB3 ..191 L1
Willen La GTLIN MK14 ....30 C5
Willen Park Av MLW SL7......31 H6
Willen Rd MKV MK10 ....43 M1
NPAG MK16................31 K2
Willets Ri SHEN MK5 ....42 A8
Willetts La DEN/HRF UB9 ....169 P9
William Bandy CI LBZU LU7 ...73 M6
William Burt Ct
RAYLW/WEN HP22 ....110 F5
William Ellis CI WDSR SL4 ..194 C4
William Harding CI AYLS HP21...3 F1
William Hartley Yd SLN SL2 *..180 D7
William Hill Dr
RAYLW/WEN HP22 ....96 C3
William Moulder Ct
CSHM HP5 ....135 M1
Williams Cir WTR/OFPK MK7 ..43 N8
Williams CI AYLW HP19 ....2 C2
RMKN MK19...............19 H3
William Smith CI WLLN MK15 ..43 J1
William St BERK HP4 ....126 F1
SL SL1...................188 B3
WDSR SL4.................187 P9
Williams Wy PRRI HP27 ......120 C3
Willis Rd HADM HP17 ....107 L9
Willoners SLN SL2 ....179 L8
Willoughby Ct DUN/WHIP LU6 ..87 L1
Willoughby Rd
DTCH/LGLY SL3 ....189 K4
Willoughby's Wk
HWYW HP13 ....142 D9
Willow Av DEN/HRF UB9 .....189 J2
HWYW HP12...............152 B6
WDR/YW UB7 ....190 D4
Willow Bank MLW SL7 ....164 D4
Willow Bank Ter AYLS HP21 ....3 F5
Willow Bank Wk LBZU LU7 ....74 C1
Willowbrook
RAYLW/WEN HP22 ....111 H7
WDSR SL4.................187 P5
Willowbrook Rd
STWL/WRAY TW19 ....196 E7
Willow Cha HAZ/HG HP15 ....143 L8
Willow CI DTCH/LGLY SL3 ....189 L8
FLKWH HP10...............166 C3
NPAG MK16................32 C5
Willow Ct SKCH HP14 ....142 C5
WYM HP11................153 L6
Willow Crs East
DEN/HRF UB9 ....182 C1
Willow Crs West
DEN/HRF UB9 ....182 C1
MDHD SL6.................185 P5
Willow Dr BUCK/WIN MK18 ....49 M7
Willow Herd AYLW HP19 ......95 N5
Willow La AMSS HP7 ....146 B5
STSTR MK11...............28 E8
Willowmead HADM HP17 .....109 H1
Willowmead Gdns MLW SL7 ..164 F6
Willowmead Rd MLW SL7 .....164 F6
Willowmead Sq MLW SL7 .....164 F6
Willow Pk SLN SL2 ....179 L8
Willow PI WDSR SL4 ....187 N7
Willow Ri HADM HP17 ....107 L7
WYM HP19.................2 C2
Willow Springs RBEDW MK45 ..33 L5
Willows Rd BNEND SL8 ......165 P6
The Willows AMS HP6 ....135 M6
BNEND SL8 * 165 P6
DUN/WHIP LU6 ....86 B5
HWYW HP12 * A3
PRRI HP27 ....120 C3
RKW/CH/CXG WD3 ....158 A2
Willowtree CI
HGDN/ICK UB10 ....171 J8
Willow Wy FLKWH HP10 ......155 P9
LBZU LU7.................74 A5
PRRI HP27................131 J1
WEAT MK2.................53 J4
Willow Wood CI SL SL1 ......178 F5
Willow Wren Whf GTLIN MK14..30 E6
Willow Wren Whf
NWDGN UB2 * 191 P5
Wilmar CI UX/CGN UB8 ....182 D4
YEAD UB4.................183 K7
Wilmin Gv SHEN MK5 ....42 B5
Wilmot Rd SL SL1 ....178 C9
Wilsley Pound
WTR/OFPK MK7 ....43 P8
Wilson Av HEN RG9 ....174 A8
Wilson Ct CNH/GTH/TM MK8 ...41 N5
Wilstone Br TRING HP23 ......98 B6
Wilton Av BTCHLY MK5 ....52 C5
Wilton Rd WDR/YW UB7 ......190 D7
Wilton Crs BEAC HP9 ....155 J7

WDSR SL4 ....193 H3
Wilton La BEAC HP9 ....155 P7
Wilton Rd BEAC HP9 ....155 J6
Wilton Wk FELT TW13 ....197 P8
Wilton Wk SLN SL2 ....179 N7
Wiltshire Av SLN SL2 ....179 N7
Wiltshire La PIN HA5 ....171 N2
Wiltshire Rd MLW SL7 ......166 A6
Wimbledon PI MLW MK13 ....6 B1
Wimbington Dr
EAG/OLD/WT MK6 ....42 G8
Wimborne Av YEAD UB4 ......183 M6
Wimborne Crs EMV/FZ MK4...51 P1
Wimpole Rd WDR/YW UB7 ....190 D2
Winbury Ct MDHD SL6 ....177 L9
Wincanton HI BTCHLY MK3 ....52 C5
Winchbottom La
FLKWH HP10...............152 G9
MLW SL7 ....165 H3
Winchendon Rd
RAYLW HP18...............79 L3
Winchester Cir MKV MK10 .....43 P5
Winchester Ct AMSS HP7 ....146 A5
DTCH/LGLY SL3 ....188 F5
Winchester Dr MDHD SL6.....185 H4
Winchester Rd
HYS/HAR UB3..............191 L8
Windermere CI AYLS HP21 ...191 L8
Windermere Ct MLW SL7 .....166 A6
Windermere Dr WEAT MK2 ....53 K6
Windermere Gdns LBZU LU7 ..74 A2
Windermere Wy SL SL1 ......178 G8
WDR/YW UB7...............190 E2
Windmill CI AYLW HP19 ....95 K7
BUCK/WIN MK18............48 D2
LBZU LU7.................99 K2
THAME OX9................119 J6
Windmill Dr HAZ/HG HP15 ...145 M5
Windmill HI AMSS HP7 ......145 M5
KGLCY WD4................137 P5
PRRI HP27................131 K2
RSLP HA4.................171 M6
Windmill HI Dr BTCHLY MK5...52 C4
Windmill La HAZ/HG HP15 ...143 M4
Windmill Pth LBZU LU7 * 74 E2
Windmill Rd CFSP/GDCR SL9..156 F7
DTCH/LGLY SL3 ....180 F1
HADM HP17................107 K8
MDHD SL6.................185 H3
SL SL1...................187 P2
THAME OX9................118 D6
THAME OX9................119 J5
Windmill St RAYLW HP18 ......65 H8
Windmill St RBEDW MK43 .....33 N2
RSLP HA4.................171 M6
TRING HP23...............112 C6
Windmill Wd AMS HP6 ....145 L1
Windrush Av DTCH/LGLY SL3..188 A5
Windrush CI HGDN/ICK UB10..170 F9
WLLN MK15................30 C7
Windrush Ct HWYN HP13 .....153 M4
Windrush Dr HWYN HP13 .....153 M4
Windrush Wy MDHD SL6 .....164 E7
Windsor Av HGDN/ICK UB10 ..183 H5
LBZU LU7.................99 J2
NPAG MK16................31 J1
Windsor Br WDSR SL4 ....187 P8
Windsor CI HHS/BOV HP3 ....137 J1
NTHWD HA6 ....159 N9
SL SL1...................178 D9
Windsor Ct AMS HP6 * 145 P2
BRACKY NN13..............34 B3
HWYN HP13................153 K1
Windsor Dr BRACKY NN13 ....34 B3
Windsor End BEAC HP9 ......155 K1
Windsor Gdns HYS/HAR UB3..191 K4
Windsor HI FLKWH HP10 .....166 C1
PRRI HP27................121 J3
Windsor La
GTMIS/PWD HP16 ....143 N1
SL SL1...................178 D7
Windsor Park Rd
HYS/HAR UB3..............191 M8
Windsor Rd AYLS HP21 ....3 K7
CFSP/GDCR SL9 ....168 E6
CSHM HP5.................135 M1
DTCH/LGLY SL3 ....188 C8
EGH TW20.................195 H9
HSLWW TW4................98 C4
LBZU LU7.................98 C4
MDHD SL6.................185 H3
SL SL1...................187 P2
STWL/WRAY TW19 ....194 F7
Windsor St UX/CGN UB8 ......38 A8
WEAT MK2.................53 J3
WOLV MK12................29 J8
Windsor Wy
RKW/CH/CXG WD3 ....158 A1
Winemar CI RMKN MK19 ....19 J3
Winfold La EMV/FZ MK4 ....52 B2
Wingate Av HWYN HP13 ......153 L3
Wingate Cir WTR/OFPK MK7...43 N8
Wingate Wk AYL HP20 ....3 K4
Wing CI MLW SL7 ....164 C9
Wing Ga West CMK MK9 ....6 C4
Wingfield Gv RSLP HA4 .....183 M7
Wingrave Cross Roads
RAYLW/WEN HP22 ....82 E4
Wingrave Rd
RAYLW/WEN HP22 ....79 L3
TRING HP23...............98 E9
TRING HP23...............112 F1
Wing Rd LBZU LU7 ....72 F3
LBZU LU7.................72 E3
Winkers CI CFSP/GDCR SL9 ..157 H6
Winkfield La WDSR SL4 ......192 A7
Winkfield Pln WDSR SL4 .....192 H3
Winkfield Rd WDSR SL4 .....192 A7
Winkfield St WDSR SL4 .....192 M4

Winnock Rd WDR/YW UB7 ....190 D2
Winsford HI EMV/FZ MK4 .....42 E9
Winslow CI PIN HA5 ....171 P4
Winslow Fld
GTMIS/PWD HP16 ....133 M4
Winslow Gdns HWYN HP13 ...153 N3
Winslow Rd BUCK/WIN MK18...70 B1
RAYLW/WEN HP22 ....82 G4
RMKS/WB MK17............50 E4
RMKS/WB MK17............50 E4
WDR/YW UB7...............61 J7
Winstanley WYM HP11 * 7 C7
Winstanley La SHEN MK5 .....42 C8
Winston CI LBZU LU7 ....64 E9
Winston Ct MDHD SL6 ....177 H8
Winston Crs BRACKY NN13 ....35 H6
RMKS/WB MK17............135 M7
Winston Gdns BERK HP4 .....126 B6
Winterburn BDWL MK13 ....30 B8
Winter HI MDHD SL6 ....165 J8
Winter Hill Rd MDHD SL6 ....176 D2
Winterton Dr AYLS HP21 ....109 N2
Winton Dr RKW/CH/CXG WD3..147 N3
Winton Gdns BERK HP4 ......126 B6
Winwood SLN SL2 ....180 E9
Winwood CI RMKN MK19 ....35 A8
Winwood Dr
RAYLW/WEN HP22 ....79 L3
Wise La WDR/YW UB7 ....190 D5
Wisewood Rd EMV/FZ MK4 ....41 M8
Wishart Gn RMKS/WB MK17....44 C7
Wisley Av BDWL MK13 ....29 N8
Wistmans EMV/FZ MK4 ....42 D9
Witan Ct CMK MK9 ....6 C6
Witan Ga CMK MK9 ....6 C4
Witan Ga West CMK MK9 ....6 C4
Witchell RAYLW/WEN HP22 ..123 H1
Witham Ct BTCHLY MK3 ....52 B5
Witham Wy AYLS HP21 ....109 L2
Witheridge La BEAC HP9 ....154 F9
Withey CI WDSR SL4 ....187 J9
Withington BDWL MK13 ....30 A8
Withycombe EMV/FZ MK4 .....42 D9
Withy Cft DTCH/LGLY SL3 ...180 G9
Witley La RSLP HA4 ....171 J3
Witney CI HGDN/ICK UB10 ...170 F9
Wittington Gn MLW SL7 .....175 M7
Wittmills Oak
RAYLW/WEN HP22 ....48 C2
Wivelsfield DUN/WHIP LU6 ....86 A3
Woad La GTLIN MK14 ....30 B5
Woburn Av WOLV MK12 ....29 K7
Woburn Av RMKS/WB MK17....45 J5
Woburn PI LBZU LU7 ....64 E9
Woburn Rd RMKS/WB MK17....54 C5
Woburn Sands Rd
RMKS/WB MK17............54 D5
Wodhams Dr BRACKY NN13 ...34 G3
Wolfe CI YEAD UB4 ....183 P6
Wolfe La WDSR SL4 ....193 H2
Wolfscote La EMV/FZ MK4 ....42 D9
Wolsey Gdns BDWL MK13 .....30 A9
Wolsey Rd
RKW/CH/CXG WD3 ....159 J2
Wolstan CI DEN/HRF UB9 ....170 A3
Wolston Meadow MKV MK10 ...43 H1
Wolverton Rd GTLIN MK14 ....30 D6
NPAG MK16................31 H1
RMKN MK19...............19 H3
STSTR MK11...............28 C3
Wooburn CI UX/CGN UB8 .....183 H7
Wooburn Common Rd
FLKWH HP10...............166 C1
Wooburn Ct FLKWH HP10 ....166 E2
FLKWH HP10 * 166 B6
Wooburn Green La
FLKWH HP10...............166 E2
Wooburn Md FLKWH HP10 ....166 E2
Wooburn Mnr FLKWH HP10 ...166 E1
Wooburn Town FLKWH HP10..166 D5
Woodbank PRRI HP27 ....131 C1
Woodbank Av
CFSP/GDCR SL9 ....168 F4
Woodbank Dr CSTG HP8 .....156 F5
Woodbine CI PRRI HP27 .....120 C8
Woodchester Pk BEAC HP9 ..154 C6
Wood CI DUN/WHIP LU6 ....87 N6
WDSR SL4.................193 N3
Woodcock Av SKCH HP14 ....142 B3
Woodcock HI
RKW/CH/CXG WD3 ....158 G5
Woodcote Gdns MKV MK10 ...185 K1
Woodcote Gn HWYN HP13 ...142 D9
Woodcroft Crs
HGDN/ICK UB10 ....183 H4
Woodcroft Rd CSHM HP5 ....135 P1
Woodfield CI PRRI HP27 .....120 B8
RBEDW MK43..............33 L6
RMKS/WB MK17............50 C9
Wood End CI SLN SL2 ....167 P8
Wood End Rd YEAD UB4 .....183 M8
Wood End Green Rd
HYS/HAR UB3..............183 K8
Wood End La NPAG MK16 ......32 C4
Woodfield Rd PRRI HP27 ....159 L4
Woodfield Dr MDHD SL6 ....184 C1
Woodfield Ga
DUN/HR/TOD LU5 ....87 N2
Woodfield Pk HSLWW TW4 * ..191 P7
Woodfield Rd HSLWW TW4 *..191 P7
PRRI HP27................131 L1
Woodford CI UX/CGN UB8 .....95 J8
Woodford Crs PIN HA5 ......159 H5
Woodford Wy SLN SL2 ....179 L4
Woodgate Crs NTHWD HA6 ..159 N6
Woodhall Av UX/CGN UB8 ....182 F5
Woodhill Av CFSP/GDCR SL9..168 E6
Woodhouse CI HYS/HAR UB3.191 L4
Woodhouse EMV GTLIN MK14 ..30 E7
Woodhouse Eaves
NTHWD HA6 ....159 N5
Woodhurst North
MDHD SL6 * 178 A7
Woodhurst Rd MDHD SL6 ....177 P7

Woodhurst South
MDHD SL6 * 178 A7
Woodland Av LBZU LU7 ....64 D8
SL SL1...................187 J1
WDSR SL4.................195 K3
Woodland CI
HGDN/ICK UB10 ....171 H7
HWYW HP12...............152 C4
MLW SL7 ....164 D5
TRING HP23...............112 D4
Woodland Qld SLN SL2 ......167 P8
Woodland La
RKW/CH/CXG WD3 ....147 M5
Woodland Ri
DUN/WHIP LU6 ....87 K9
Woodland Rd
RKW/CH/CXG WD3 ....157 M5
Woodlands
CFSP/GDCR SL9 ....126 F2
HADM HP17 * 107 L8
Woodlands Av BERK HP4 ....126 F2
Woodlands CI BUCK/WIN MK18..48 B1
Woodlands Gld BEAC HP9 ...154 C6
Woodlands Gld BEAC HP9 ...167 J4
Woodlands Park Av
MDHD SL6 ....184 C5
Woodlands Park Rd
MDHD SL6 ....184 G5
The Woodlands AMS HP6 .....135 N8
HAZ/HG HP15.............143 M8
TOW NN12.................25 K1
Woodland Vw CSHM HP5 .....135 P6
WOLV MK12................29 M8
Woodlands CI
FLKWH HP10...............153 M9
Woodlands Gdns
FLKWH HP10...............153 M9
Woodlea Gv NTHWD HA6 .....159 J6
Woodley CI AMSS HP7 * 145 P5
Woodley Headland
EAG/OLD/WT MK6 ....43 J5
Woodman HI CSHM HP5 ......135 P8
Woodman CI LBZU LU7 ....73 M6
LBZU LU7.................74 F2
Woodmans CI RMKN MK19 .....19 J5
Woodmans Dr AYLW HP19 .....95 J7
Woodmoor End MDHD SL6 ...177 P7
Woodpeery Rd HA4 ....102 D4
Woodpiece Rd RBICS/W OX25..80 H1
Wood Pond CI BEAC HP9 ....155 N6
Woodridge Wy NTHWD HA6 ...159 J4
Wood Ri PIN HA5 ....171 N3
Woodrow Av YEAD UB4 ......183 M8
Woodruff Av
EAG/OLD/WT MK6 ....43 H8
Woods CI DEN/HRF UB9 .....170 A3
Woodside Av AMS HP6 ....135 P9
BEAC HP9.................155 G9
FLKWH HP10...............166 A3
Woodside CI BEAC HP9 ......154 C6
CFSP/GDCR SL9 ....171 K4
RSLP HA4.................171 K4
WYM HP11.................153 C9
Woodside HI CFSP/GDCR SL9.168 A3
Woodside Rd BEAC HP9 .....145 P1
HADM HP17 * 107 L8
NTHWD HP13..............159 M7
Woodside Wy LBZU LU7 ....74 B5
Woods La TOW NN12 ....18 C8
Woods PI
RAYLW/WEN HP22 * 123 H1
TRING HP23...............112 E3
Woodspring Ct
WTR/OFPK MK7 ....131 H3
The Woods HGDN/ICK UB10 ..171 H9
NTHWD HA6 ....159 N5
Woodstock Av
DTCH/LGLY SL3 ....188 C5
Woodstock CI AYLS HP21 ....95 M7
MDHD SL6.................177 M7
Woodstock Ct BDWL MK13 ....30 B9
Woodstock Dr
HGDN/ICK UB10 ....170 E9
Wood Stoke SLN SL2 ....168 B9
Wood St BDWL MK13 ....29 P6
RAYLW HP18...............79 L3
The Wood LBZU LU7 ....74 C5
Woodvale CI SLN SL2 ....179 K3
Woodview Ct HWYN HP13 ....142 D9
Woodview Dr PRRI HP27 .....132 C7
Woodville CMK OX39 ....29 N6
Woodville CI BEAC HP9 ......18 A4
Woodville Gdns RSLP HA4 ...171 K5
Woodward PI
CNH/GTH/TM MK8 ....42 A3
Woodway BEAC HP9 ....154 C9
Woodway PRRI HP27 ....131 K4

Woodways *HADM* HP17 ....107 L8
Woodwicks
  RKW/CH/CXG WD3 .....157 M5
Woolacombe Wy
  HYS/HAR UB3 ....191 L5
Woollerton Crs
  RAYLNE/WEN HP22 ....111 J9
Woolmans *STSTR* MK11 ....29 J9
Woolpack Cl *DUN/WHIP* LU6 ...87 L1
Woolrich Gdns *STSTR* MK11 ....28 C8
Wooster Rd *BEAC* HP9 ....154 G6
Wootton Dr *FLKWH* HP10 ....166 C1
Wootton Gn *RBICN* OX27 ....67 L3
Wootton Rd *HEN* RG9 ....173 N8
Wootton Wy *HADM* HP17 ....185 J1
Worcester Cl *MDHD* SL6 ....185 J4
  NPAC MK16 ....30 C1
Worcester Gdns *SL* SL1 ....187 P3
Worcester Rd *UX/CGN* UB8 .....182 C8
Wordsworth Av *NPAC* MK16 .....20 F9
Wordsworth Cl *BRACKY* NN13 ....35 H5
Wordsworth Dr *BTCHLY* MK3 ....52 F4
Wordsworth Rd *SLN* SL2 ....179 N7
  WYM HP11 ....152 C5
Wordsworth Wy
  WDR/YW UB7 ....190 E6
World's End La
  RAYLNE/WEN HP22 ....110 F6
Worminghall Rd
  RAYLW HP18 ....104 D2
  RAYLW HP18 ....116 F2
Wormsley Crs *SKCH* HP14 ......139 N1
Wormal Pk *RAYLW* HP18 ....104 L8
The Worple
  STWL/WRAY TW19 ....195 M5
Worrelle Av *MKV* MK10 ....43 M1

Worster Rd *MDHD* SL6 ....177 L2
Wotton End *RAYLW* HP18 ....77 J9
Wotton Rd *RAYLW* HP18 ....92 C6
Wray Ct *EMV/FZ* MK4 ....52 A1
Wraysbury Rd
  STWL/WRAY TW19 ....195 L9
Wren Cl *BUCK/WIN* MK18 ....48 D4
Wren Dr *WDR/YW* UB7 ....190 D4
Wren Rd
  GTMIS/PWD HP16 ....133 J7
Wrensfield *MLW* SL7 ....164 C8
Wrens Pk *MKV* MK10 ....43 N2
Wrenswood Wy *PIN* HA5 ....5 J8
Wright *WDSR* SL4 ....192 C2
Wrights Cl *SKCH* HP14 ....151 K5
Wright's La
  GTMIS/PWD HP16 ....133 J7
Wyatt Cl *HWYN* HP13 ....4 E3
  YEAD UB4 ....183 N8
Wyatt's Rd
  RKW/CH/CXG WD3 ....147 P6
Wychwood
  GTMIS/PWD HP16 ....133 P8
Wychwood Gdns
  HWYW HP12 ....152 C5
Wychwood Ri
  GTMIS/PWD HP16 ....133 N8
Wychwood Wy
  NTHWD HA6 ....159 M7
Wycombe Abbey
  WYM HP11 ....153 H5
Wycombe Cl *AYLS* HP21 ....110 B2
Wycombe End *BEAC* HP9 ....167 H1
Wycombe La *FLKWH* HP10 .....166 C2

Wycombe Rd
  GTMIS/PWD HP16 ....133 J8
  HAZ/HG HP15 ....143 P5
  MLW SL7 ....152 E8
  PRRI HP27 ....131 J2
  SKCH HP14 ....140 C7
Wycombe Vw *FLKWH* HP10 ....153 M8
Wye Cl *AYLS* HP21 ....109 L1
  BTCHLY MK3 ....52 E2
Wye Rd *FLKWH* HP10 ....166 B1
Wyevale Cl *PIN* HA5 ....171 N1
Wyfold La *HEN* RG9 ....172 C8
Wykeham Cl *WDR/YW* UB7 .....190 C7
Wykeham Ga *HADM* HP17 ....107 K9
Wykeham Pk *THAME* OX9 ....118 E5
Wykeham Ri *CHNR* OX39 ....129 P6
Wykeham Wy *HADM* HP17 ....107 K9
Wykeridge Cl *CSHM* HP5 ....125 M9
Wylands Rd *DTCH/LGLY* SL3 ...189 J6
Wylchin Cl *PIN* HA5 ....171 M2
Wylie End *BDWL* MK13 ....30 A6
Wymering Rd *AYLS* HP21 ....96 C9
Wymers Cl *SL* SL1 ....178 E5
Wymers Wood Rd *SL* SL1 ....178 E4
Wymondham
  WTR/OFPK MK7 ....43 P7
Wynbury Dr *HWYN* HP13 ....15 B3
Wyncote Cl *HEN* RG9 ....174 A7
Wyndham Av *HWYN* HP13 ......142 F9
Wyndham Crs *SL* SL1 ....178 E5
Wyness Av *RMKS/WB* MK17 ....54 B6
Wynford Gn *AYLS* HP21 ....109 P1
Wyngates *LBUZ* LU7 ....74 C4
Wyngrave Pl *BEAC* HP9 ....154 C5
Wynlie Cdns *PIN* HA5 ....159 P9
Wynn Gv *HAZ/HG* HP15 ....143 P8
Wynnstay Gdns *MLW* SL7 ....164 C8

Wynnswick Rd *BEAC* HP9 ......155 N5
Wynyard Ct
  EAG/OLD/WT MK6 ....42 E5
Wyre Cl *HADM* HP17 ....107 L9
Wye Gv *HYS/HAR* UB3 ....191 N5
Wyteleaf Cl *RSLP* HA4 ....171 J4
Wyvern Wy *UX/CGN* UB8 ....182 B3

Y

Yalts Brow *EMV/FZ* MK4 ....52 B1
Yardley Av *LBUZ* LU7 ....98 C5
Yardley Gn *AYL* HP20 ....3 F1
Yardley Rd *OLN* MK46 ....15 L1
  RMKN MK19 ....28 A1
  RNHPTN NN7 ....9 J5
  TOW NN12 ....28 A1
Yarmouth Rd *SL* SL1 ....179 N9
Yarrow Pl *GTLIN* MK14 ....30 E9
Yarrowside *AMSS* HP7 ....146 D6
Yeading Gdns *YEAD* UB4 ....183 P6
Yeading La *YEAD* UB4 ....183 P9
Yeates Cl *THAME* OX9 ....118 C4
Yeatman Cl *THAME* OX9 ....118 D4
Ye Meads *MDHD* SL6 ....186 D2
Yeomans Acre *RSLP* HA4 ....171 N4
Yeomans Cl *BRACKY* NN13 ....35 J4
Yeomans Dr *GTLIN* MK14 ....30 C5
Yeoveney Cl
  STWL/WRAY TW19 ....195 M8
Yeovil Rd *SL* SL1 ....179 J8
Yew Av *WDR/YW* UB7 ....190 E1
Yew Tree Cl *BEAC* HP9 ....155 K9
  CSHM HP5 ....136 C3

DUN/WHIP* LU6 ....86 B3
  LBUZ LU7 ....99 J3
  MDHD SL6 ....177 L8
  RAYLNE/WEN HP22 ....110 A5
  RMKS/WB MK17 ....52 C8
Yew Tree Dr *HAZ/HG* HP15 .....145 M5
  HHS/BOV HP3 ....137 K1
Yew Tree Rd
  HGDN/ICK UB10 ....182 F4
  SL SL1 ....188 C4
Yewsan Cl *HADM* HP17 ....183 J9
Yonder Slade
  231*BUCK/WIN* MK18 ....48 B5
York Av *HYS/HAR* UB3 ....183 J9
  SL SL1 ....179 P9
  WDSR SL4 ....193 M1
York Dr *BRACKY* NN13 ....34 C4
Yorke Cl *RAYLNE/WEN* HP22 .111 L1
York Pl *AYLS* HP21 ....3 G6
York Rd *HEN* RG9 ....173 P6
  MDHD SL6 ....164 D7
  MLW SL7 ....164 D7
  NTHWD HA6 ....159 N9
  STSTR MK11 ....29 L8
  UX/CGN UB8 ....182 D3
  WDSR SL4 ....193 M1
York Wy *HWYW* HP12 ....152 E6
Youens Dr *THAME* OX9 ....118 E6
Youens Rd *HWYW* HP12 ....152 C5
Young Cl *AYLS* HP21 ....96 A9
Youngfield Rd *HHW* HP1 ....127 P1

Z

Zealand Av *WDR/YW* UB7 ....190 D8

Index - featured places

Abbey Hill Golf Club
  CNH/GTH/TM MK8 ....41 M2
Abbeys Combined School
  BTCHLY MK3 ....52 G1
Abbotsfield School for Boys
  HGDN/ICK UB10 ....183 H5
Abergele Industrial Estate
  HYS/HAR UB3 ....191 K3
Acorn Business Centre
  LBUZ LU7 ....72 F7
Acorn Medical Centre
  HGDN/ICK UB10 ....182 G4
Adler Industrial Estate
  HYS/HAR UB3 ....191 K3
Airbase Valley Elementary
  School *HCDN/ICK* UB10 .....171 J7
Airbus Coach Station
  HTHAIR TW6 ....196 F2
Airport Gate Business Centre
  WDR/YW UB7 ....190 H8
Akeley CE First School
  BUCK/WIN MK18 ....38 D4
Akeley Wood Junior School
  RMKN MK19 ....39 L3
Akeley Wood School at
  Charmandean
  BUCK/WIN MK18 ....38 A4
Akeman Business Park
  TRING HP23 ....112 E3
Aldbury Primary School
  TRING HP23 ....99 N9
Alexander First School
  WDSR SL4 ....192 G2
Alfriston Special School
  BEAC HP9 ....154 G4
Allan Shaw Co Combined
  School *BUCK/WIN* MK18 ....58 C7
Alton Business Park
  AYLW HP19 ....95 K6
Altwood CE School
  MDHD SL6 ....185 H7
Alwyn Infant School
  MDHD SL6 ....177 J8
Ambassador Court Hotel
  HWYW HP12 ....4 B3
American Community School
  HGDN/ICK UB10 ....182 F4
Amersham & Chiltern RFC
  AMS HP6 ....135 L9
Amersham Hill CC
  AMS HP6 ....146 A2
The Amersham School
  AMSS HP7 ....146 A4
Amersham Town FC
  AMSS HP7 ....145 L3
Amersham & Wycombe College
  AMSS HP7 ....125 P9
  CSHM HP5 ....125 P9
  FLKWH HP10 ....153 L8
Aqua Vale Swimming &
  Fitness Centre *AYL* HP20 ....3 G4
Arbour Vale Special School
  Sports College *SLN* SL2 ....180 C9
Ardley Hill Lower School
  DUN/WHIP LU6 ....87 L2
Arts Centre
  AMS HP6 ....193 N1
The Arts Educational School
  TRING HP23 ....112 F3
Ascott House (NT)
  LBUZ LU7 ....73 N7
Ashbrook First School
  MDHD SL6 ....41 M3
Ashleigh Road Industrial
  Estate *CSHM* HP5 ....135 L2
Ashfold School
  RAYLW HP18 ....91 M7

Ashford Clinic
  ASHF TW15 ....196 E9
Ashford High School
  ASHF TW15 ....196 E9
Ashford Hospital A & E
  ASHF TW15 ....196 E8
Ashford Sports Club
  STWL/WRAY TW19 ....196 F7
Ash Hill Primary School
  HWYN HP13 ....153 P3
Ashlyns School
  BERK HP4 ....126 E5
Ashmead Combined School
  AYLS HP21 ....109 L1
Ashridge Estate (NT)
  BERK HP4 ....100 A9
Ashridge Golf Club
  BERK HP4 ....100 D8
Ashton CE Primary School
  RNHPTN NN7 ....12 B6
Aspect Park Golf Centre
  HEN RG9 ....174 F7
Asplands Medical Centre
  RMKS/WB MK17 ....44 F8
Aspley Guise Lower School
  RMKS/WB MK17 ....45 K8
Aspley Guise & Woburn Sands
  Golf Club*RMKS/WB* MK17 ....45 H8
Aston Clinton School
  RAYLNE/WEN HP22 ....111 K1
Aston Rowant CE Primary
  School *WTLGN* OX49 ....129 J9
Aston Rowant CC
  CHNR OX39 ....129 J9
Aurora Garden Hotel
  WDSR SL4 ....193 P2
Avant Business Centre
  DBGH MK1 ....53 H1
Avenue Medical Centre
  SLN SL2 ....179 L6
Avocet Trading Estate
  WYM HP11 ....4 C1
Aylesbury Business Centre
  AYLW HP19 ....95 K6
Aylesbury College
  AYL HP21 ....2 B6
  RAYLNE/WEN HP22 ....110 C3
Aylesbury & District Sports
  Club *AYLS* HP21 ....96 A9
Aylesbury Golf Centre
  RAYLNE/WEN HP22 ....96 D2
Aylesbury Grammar School
  AYLS HP21 ....3 G6
Aylesbury High School
  AYLS HP21 ....3 G6
Aylesbury Industrial Centre
  AYLW HP19 ....2 A2
Aylesbury Magistrates Court
  AYLS HP21 ....2 E7
Aylesbury RFC
  RAYLNE/WEN HP22 ....110 C3
Aylesbury United FC
  AYLW HP19 ....95 M4
Aylesbury Vale Golf Club
  LBUZ LU7 ....72 G3
Aysgarth Medical Centre
  IVER SL0 ....181 M5
BAA Heathrow Visitor Centre
  HTHAIR TW6 ....191 H9
Badgemore Park Golf Club
  HEN RG9 ....173 M5
Badgemore Primary School
  HEN RG9 ....173 N6
Balloon Flights
  RAYLNE/WEN HP22 ....111 L2
Barbara Batson Clinic
  AYL HP20 ....2 C3
Barley Hill Primary School
  THAME OX9 ....118 D4

Barnhill Community
  High School *YEAD* UB4 ......183 P6
Barn Hotel
  RSLP HA4 ....171 L7
Barton Village First School
  BDWL MK13 ....30 A4
Batchworth Park Golf Club
  RKW/CH/CXG WD3 ....158 F4
Bayhurst Wood Country Park
  DEN/HRF UB9 ....170 F3
Baylis Business Centre
  SLN SL2 ....187 P1
Baylis Court School
  SLN SL2 ....179 P8
Beachampton Business Park
  RMKN MK19 ....40 E8
Beachborough School
  BRACKY NN13 ....36 A4
The Beacon School
  AMS HP6 ....135 M4
Beaconsfield CC
  BEAC HP9 ....155 K9
Beaconsfield Golf Club
  BEAC HP9 ....155 N8
Beaconsfield High School
  BEAC HP9 ....155 H9
Beaconsfield RFC
  BEAC HP9 ....167 K1
Beaconsfield School
  BEAC HP9 ....155 J9
Beaudesert Lower School
  LBUZ LU7 ....75 H1
Beckley CE Primary School
  HEAD OX3 ....102 C3
The Beck Theatre
  HYS/HAR UB3 ....183 M9
Bedfont Health Clinic
  EBED/NFELT TW14 ....197 L5
Bedfont Industrial Park
  FELT TW13 ....197 K9
Bedfont J & I School
  EBED/NFELT TW14 ....197 L5
Bedfont Lakes Country Park
  EBED/NFELT TW14 ....197 J3
The Bedford Arms Hotel
  RKW/CH/CXG WD3 ....147 K2
Bedgrove Health Centre
  AYLS HP21 ....96 B9
Bedgrove Junior School
  AYLS HP21 ....96 C9
Beechview Junior School
  HWYN HP13 ....153 L5
Beechwood School
  SLN SL2 ....179 M6
Bekonscot Model Village
  BEAC HP9 ....155 H7
Bell Business Centre
  MDHD SL6 ....185 M1
Bell Business Park
  AYLW HP19 ....95 H6
Bell Lane Combined School
  AMS HP6 ....146 D2
Belmont Medical Centre
  UX/CGN UB8 ....182 D7
Belmore Primary School
  NTHLT UB5 ....183 P6
Berber Business Centre
  WYM HP11 ....4 B4
Berkeley Clinic
  RKW/CH/CXG WD3 ....158 C1
Berkhamsted Castle (Remains)
  BERK HP4 ....114 F9
Berkhamsted Collegiate
  Preparatory School
  BERK HP4 ....126 D1
Berkhamsted Collegiate
  School *BERK* HP4 ....126 E1
Berkhamsted FC
  BERK HP4 ....114 D9

Berkhamsted Golf Club
  BERK HP4 ....114 C7
Berkhamsted Health Centre
  BERK HP4 ....114 C9
Berkhamsted House
  BERK HP4 ....126 E1
Berkhamsted Tennis Club
  BERK HP4 ....114 C9
The Bharani Medical Centre
  SL SL1 ....179 H9
Bierton CE Combined School
  RAYLNE/WEN HP22 ....96 B4
Bigham's Park Farm
  HHW HP1 ....115 N6
Bisham Abbey National
  Sports Centre *MLW* SL7 .....176 D1
Bisham CE Primary School
  MLW SL7 ....176 D1
Bishophalt School
  UX/CGN UB8 ....182 F6
Bishop Parker RC Combined
  School *WEAT* MK2 ....53 J5
Bishop Ramsey CE School
  (Upper) *RSLP* HA4 ....171 N5
Bishop Ramsey CE School
  RSLP HA4 ....171 N5
Bishopsgate School
  ECH TW20 ....194 C9
Bishops Wood Hospital
  RKW/CH/CXG WD3 ....158 C5
Bishop Winnington-Ingram
  CE Primary School
  RSLP HA4 ....171 K5
Bishop Wood School
  TRING HP23 ....112 E3
Blackberry Farm
  Animal Centre
  RAYLNE/WEN HP22 ....80 A6
Blackburn Trading Estate
  STWL/WRAY TW19 ....196 F5
Black Park Country Park
  DTCH/LGLY SL3 ....181 J5
Bledlow CC
  PRRI HP27 ....130 C3
Bledlow Ridge School
  SKCH HP14 ....141 H5
Bletchley Leisure Centre
  WEAT MK2 ....53 K2
Bletchley Park Museum
  BTCHLY MK3 ....53 H5
Blind Pond Industrial Estate
  RMKS/WB MK17 ....54 B1
Blue Lagoon Park
  BTCHLY MK3 ....53 H5
Blue Max Museum
  SKCH HP14 ....152 A8
Boarstall Duck Decoy (NT)
  RAYLW HP18 ....90 A4
The Bobsleigh Hotel
  HHS/BOV HP3 ....127 K8
Bon Secours Hospital
  BEAC HP9 ....155 J8
Booker Hill Combined School
  HWYW HP12 ....152 B5
The Bossard Centre
  LBUZ LU7 ....74 E2
Botwell RC Primary School
  HYS/HAR UB3 ....191 M3
Boulter's Lock
  MDHD SL6 ....178 A7
Bourbon Tower
  BUCK/WIN MK18 ....37 N4
Bourne End Business Centre
  BNEND SL8 ....165 P6
Bourton Meadow School
  BUCK/WIN MK18 ....48 D3

Bovingdon Primary School
  HHS/BOV HP3 ....127 K9
Bow Brickhill First School
  RMKS/WB MK17 ....54 B1
Bowling Alley *FELT* TW13 ......197 M8
  MDHD SL6 ....177 MB
  NTHWD HA6 ....159 M7
Boxmoor Golf Club
  HHW HP1 ....127 N6
Boxmoor House School
  HHS/BOV HP3 ....127 P5
Boyne Hill CE I & N School
  MDHD SL6 ....185 K1
Boyn Valley Industrial Estate
  MDHD SL6 ....185 L1
Bracken Leas Primary School
  BRACKY NN13 ....34 F5
Brackley CE Junior School
  BRACKY NN13 ....34 G4
Brackley Cottage Hospital
  BRACKY NN13 ....35 H5
Brackley Recreation Centre
  BRACKY NN13 ....34 F5
Brackley RFC
  BRACKY NN13 ....34 F4
Brackley Swimming Pool
  BRACKY NN13 ....34 G5
Brackley Town FC
  BRACKY NN13 ....34 F4
Bradenham CC
  SKCH HP14 ....141 P5
Bradwell Priory (Remains)
  BDWL MK13 ....29 P9
Bradwell Village Middle School
  BDWL MK13 ....30 A9
Braintree Road Industrial
  Estate *RSLP* HA4 ....171 P9
Braywick Cemetery
  MDHD SL6 ....185 P5
Braywood CE First School
  WDSR SL4 ....192 D1
Breakspear Crematorium
  RSLP HA4 ....171 J3
Breakspear Primary School
  HGDN/ICK UB10 ....170 G7
Brent Park Industrial Estate
  NWDGN UB2 ....191 P4
Bridgegate Business Centre
  AYLW HP19 ....95 K6
The Brigidine School
  WDSR SL4 ....193 P2
Brill CE Combined School
  RAYLW HP18 ....91 H6
Britannia Industrial Estate
  DTCH/LGLY SL3 ....195 N1
Britannia Industrial Park
  HWYW HP12 ....152 D3
Britwell Health Clinic
  SLN SL2 ....179 L6
Broadfields Retail Park
  AYLW HP19 ....95 J5
Brook Business Centre
  IVER SL0 ....182 A5
Brook Fox FC
  YEAD UB4 ....183 M6
Brooklands Middle School
  LBUZ LU7 ....74 G3
Brookmead School
  LBUZ LU7 ....99 J2
Brookside Clinic
  AYLS HP21 ....2 E6
Brooksward Combined School
  GTLIN MK14 ....30 F5
Broomstick Industrial Estate
  DUN/WHIP LU6 ....86 A4

Broughton Fields Combined School
MKV MK10 ....31 N9
Broughton Infant School
AYL HP20 ....96 C7
Broughton Junior School
AYL HP20 ....96 B7
Broughton Manor Business
Park *MKW* MK16 ....31 P9
Brunel Bus Station
SL SL1 ....188 B2
Brunel Shopping Centre
WEAT MK2 ....53 H3
Brunel University
UX/CGN UB8 ....182 E6
Brushwood Junior School
CSHM HP5 ....136 A2
Buckingham Beales Hotel
BUCK/WIN MK18 ....48 B5
Buckingham Centre
(Queens Hall)
BUCK/WIN MK18 ....48 B4
Buckingham Community
Hospital *BUCK/WIN* MK18 ....48 B2
Buckingham County Junior
School *BUCK/WIN* MK18 ....48 C1
Buckingham Golf Club
BUCK/WIN MK18 ....47 M3
Buckingham Road Industrial
Estate *BRACKY* NN13 ....35 J6
Buckingham RUFC
BUCK/WIN MK18 ....38 C8
Buckingham School
BUCK/WIN MK18 ....48 B4
Buckinghamshire Chilterns
University College
CSTG HP8 ....157 J2
Buckinghamshire County
Museum *AYL* HP20 ....2 C4
Buckinghamshire Golf Club
DEN/HRF UB9 ....170 C7
Buckinghamshire Railway
Centre *RAYLW* HP18 ....79 K6
Buckingham Town FC
BUCK/WIN MK18 ....48 B3
Bucks Chilterns University
College *WYN* HP11 ....5 F6
Bucks University College
HWYN HP13 ....143 K8
Bull Hotel
CFSP/GDCR SL9 ....168 F3
Bullsbridge Industrial Estate
NWDGN UB2 ....191 P5
Burchetts Green CE Infant
School *DHD* SL6 ....176 B9
Burford School
MLW SL7 ....164 C4
Burnham Abbey
MDHD SL6 ....186 F2
Burnham Beeches Golf Club
SL SL1 ....179 H4
Burnham Beeches Hotel
SLN SL2 ....179 H5
Burnham Beeches
(Nature Reserve) *SLN* SL2 ...179 L1
Burnham FC
SL SL1 ....178 F6
Burnham Grammar School
SL SL1 ....179 H7
Burnham Health Centre
SL SL1 ....178 F6
Burnham Upper School
SL SL1 ....178 F7
Bury Lawn School
GTLIN MK14 ....30 D6
Bushfield Middle School
WOLV MK12 ....29 M7
The Business Village
SLN SL2 ....188 D2
Butlers Court County First &
Middle School *BEAC* HP9 ....155 J9
Byfleet Industrial Estate
WATW WD18 ....159 J1
C & L Golf & Country Club
NTHLT UB5 ....183 P5
C & L Leisure Centre
NTHLT UB5 ....183 P3
Cadmore End CE Combined
School *SKCH* HP14 ....150 E4
Calcot Medical Centre
CFSP/GDCR SL9 ....156 F8
Caldicott School
SL SL3 ....179 M3
California Industrial Estate
AYLS HP21 ....2 D6
Calvert Jubilee Nature Reserve
BUCK/WIN MK18 ....67 N2
Cambridge Close Retail Park
AYL HP20 ....2 E2
Campanile Hotel
WEAT MK2 ....53 L3
Camp Industrial Estate
THAME OX9 ....117 H9
Capswood Business Centre
CFSP/GDCR SL9 ....169 L6
Cardinal Road Infant School
FELT TW13 ....197 P7
Carlton VC Lower School
RBEDW MK43 ....11 L4
Caroline Haslett Combined
School *SHEN* MK5 ....42 B8
Carrington Primary School
FLKWH HP10 ....153 N9
Castlefield Foundation School
HWYN HP13 ....152 C4
The Castle Hotel
WDSR SL4 ....187 P9
Castle Montessori School
BERK HP4 ....126 F1
Castle Street Clinic
HWYN HP13 ....5 G5
Castleview First School
RMKN MK19 ....19 H8
Castleview Combined School
DTCH/LGLY SL3 ....188 F5
Cattle Market
TRING HP23 ....112 F2

Caxton Trading Estate
HYS/HAR UB3 ....191 L3
Cedar Park School
HAZ/HG HP15 ....143 M6
Cedars Combined School
NPAG MK16 ....31 K1
Cedars First School
HAZ/HG HP15 ....143 M6
The Cedars Primary School
HEST TW5 ....191 N8
The Cedars Upper School
LBUZ LU7 ....74 C4
Centenary Business Park
HEN RG9 ....174 B7
Central Bus Station
....6 B5
Central Milton Keynes
Medical Centre *CMK* MK9 ....6 D2
Central Park Business Centre
....4 E3
the centre:mk
CMK MK9 ....7 F2
Chackmore CE School
NPAG MK18 ....37 P8
Chailey Industrial Estate
HYS/HAR UB3 ....191 N3
Chalfont Leisure Centre
CSHM HP5 ....156 E8
Chalfont St Giles Infant
School *CSTG* HP8 ....156 D2
Chalfont St Giles Junior
School *CSTG* HP8 ....156 D3
Chalfont St Peter FC
CFSP/GDCR SL9 ....156 F7
Chalfont St Peter Infant
School *CFSP/GDCR* SL9 ......156 E7
Chalfont St Peter Junior
School *CFSP/GDCR* SL9 ......156 F7
The Chalfonts Community
College *CFSP/GDCR* SL9 .....156 E7
Chalfonts & Gerrards Cross
Health Clinic
CFSP/GDCR SL9 ....156 F8
Chambers Business Park
WDR/YW UB7 ....190 G7
Chantry School
WDR/YW UB7 ....182 E9
Charlton on Otmoor Primary
School *KID* OX5 ....88 C2
Charville Primary School
YEAD UB4 ....183 L5
Chartridge Combined School
CSHM HP5 ....124 C9
Chartridge Park Golf Club
CSHM HP5 ....135 H1
Chaulden Primary School
HHW HP1 ....127 P3
Cheddington Combined School
LBUZ LU7 ....84 E9
Chenies CC
RKW/CH/CXG WD3 ....147 L3
Chenies Combined School
RKW/CH/CXG WD3 ....147 J2
Chequers Inn
BNEND SL8 ....166 B7
Cherrycourt Way Industrial
Estate *LBUZ* LU7 ....75 H3
Cherry Lane Primary School
WDR/YW UB7 ....190 F5
Chesham Bois CE Combined
School *AMS* HP6 ....136 A8
Chesham Community Hospital
CSHM HP5 ....135 N5
Chesham Health Centre
CSHM HP5 ....135 M5
Chesham High School
CSHM HP5 ....135 P5
Chesham Leisure Centre
CSHM HP5 ....135 P4
Chesham & Ley Hill Golf Club
CSHM HP5 ....136 E4
Chesham Park Community
College *CSHM* HP5 ....135 L3
Chesham Preparatory School
CSHM HP5 ....126 C9
Chesham United FC
CSHM HP5 ....135 M6
Chestnut Combined School
BTCHLY MK3 ....52 D4
Chestnut Lane First School
AMS HP6 ....136 A9
Chicheley Hall
NPAG MK16 ....22 B6
Chiltern Brewery
HADM HP17 ....110 C9
Chiltern Business Village
IVER SL0 ....182 B5
Chiltern Forest Golf Club
RAYLNE/WEN HP22 ....111 M5
Chiltern Gate Special School
HWYN HP12 ....152 E6
The Chiltern Hospital
GTMIS/PWD HP16 ....134 A8
Chiltern House Medical Centre
HWYN HP13 ....5 F4
Chiltern Open Air Museum
CFSP/GDCR SL9 ....157 H2
Chiltern Pools
AMS HP6 ....145 P2
The Chilterns Crematorium
AMSS HP7 ....145 K5
The Chilterns Shopping Centre
HWYN HP13 ....5 F5
Chiltern Trading Estate
HAZ/HG HP15 ....144 B5
LBUZ LU7 ....74 E4
The Chimes Shopping Centre
UX/CGN UB8 ....182 C5
Chinnor & Princes Risborough
Railway *CHNR* OX39 ....130 A6
Chinnor RFC
THAME OX9 ....118 G4
Chorleywood Golf Club
RKW/CH/CXG WD3 ....147 M6
Chorleywood Health Centre
RKW/CH/CXG WD3 ....147 L6

Chorleywood Primary School
RKW/CH/CXG WD3 ....147 L8
Christ Church CE Primary
School *RKW/CH/CXG* WD3 ...147 P6
Christopher Hotel
WDSR SL4 ....187 N7
Christ the King RC First School
STWL/WRAY TW19 ....196 D5
Churchmead School
DTCH/LGLY SL3 ....188 D3
Church of Christ
the Cornerstone *CMK* MK9 ....6 E2
Cineworld Cinema
CMK MK9 ....7 H2
TRING HP23 ....197 P8
Cippenham Infants School
SL SL1 ....187 H1
Cippenham Junior School
SL SL1 ....187 H1
Cippenham Medical Centre
SL SL1 ....187 M2
City Square
CMK MK9 ....6 E2
Claires Court School
MDHD SL6 ....177 P7
Claires Court School College
MDHD SL6 ....177 L9
Clarendon Primary School
ASHF TW15 ....196 F9
Claycots Primary School
SLN SL2 ....179 L7
Claydon House (NT)
BUCK/WIN MK18 ....68 F2
Claytons Combined School
BNEND SL8 ....165 N4
Clewer Green CE First School
WDSR SL4 ....95 J6
Clifton Business Park
AYLW HP19 ....95 J6
Clipstone Brook Industrial
Estate *LBUZ* LU7 ....75 J2
Cliveden Hotel
MDHD SL6 ....178 C1
Cliveden (NT)
MDHD SL6 ....178 C1
Clockhouse Industrial Estate
EBED/NFELT TW14 ....197 H1
Coach Museum
WDSR SL4 ....188 A9
Cold Harbour CE Combined
School *BTCHLY* MK3 ....42 F9
Colehill CC
AMSS HP7 ....145 L7
Coleshill CE First School
AMSS HP7 ....145 K8
Colham Manor Primary School
UX/CGN UB8 ....182 F9
College Lake Wildlife Centre
TRING HP23 ....98 G5
Colnbrook CE Primary School
DTCH/LGLY SL3 ....189 M9
Colnbrook Sports Club
DTCH/LGLY SL3 ....189 N9
Coln Industrial Estate
DTCH/LGLY SL3 ....189 P8
Combermere Barracks
WDSR SL4 ....193 M2
Comfort Inn
HYS/HAR UB3 ....191 L6
Commerce Way Industrial
Estate *LBUZ* LU7 ....75 J3
Commonwealth War Graves
Commission *MDHD* SL6 ......177 M9
Compass Theatre
HGDN/ICK UB10 ....171 J8
The Compleat Angler Hotel
MLW SL7 ....164 E8
Convent of St John the Baptist
WDSR SL4 ....193 L1
Cookham Dean CE Primary
School *MDHD* SL6 ....177 H1
Cookham Medical Centre
MDHD SL6 ....165 N8
Cookham Reach Sailing Club
MDHD SL6 ....165 N9
Coppthorne Hotel
SL SL1 ....187 N3
Corinium Industrial Estate
AMS HP6 ....146 B2
Corinthian Arch
BUCK/WIN MK18 ....37 N7
Cosgrove Lodge Park
RMKN MK19 ....29 J3
Cosgrove Primary School
RMKN MK19 ....28 G5
Coterford Infant School
RSLP HA4 ....171 N3
The Cottesloe School
LBUZ LU7 ....73 K8
Court Farm Industrial Estate
STWL/WRAY TW19 ....196 F5
Court Garden Leisure Centre
MLW SL7 ....164 D8
Courthouse Junior School
MDHD SL6 ....177 H8
Court Industrial Park
DBGH MK1 ....53 H2
Courtyard by Marriott Hotel
NPAG MK16 ....31 P9
NPAG MK16 ....31 N5
SL SL1 ....187 N3
Cowley Business Park
UX/CGN UB8 ....182 C6
Cowley Mill Industrial Estate
IVER SL0 ....182 A5
Cowper & Newton Museum
OLN MK46 ....15 N4
Cox Green School
MDHD SL6 ....184 G3
Cranfield Airfield
RBEDW MK43 ....33 K4
Cranfield Lower School
RBEDW MK43 ....33 M4
Cranfield University
RBEDW MK43 ....33 J8

Cranford Community College
HEST TW5 ....191 P7
Cranford Infant School
HSLWW TW4 ....197 N1
Cranford Junior School
HSLWW TW4 ....197 P1
Cranford Park Junior School
HYS/HAR UB3 ....191 M5
Cranford Park Primary School
HYS/HAR UB3 ....191 M3
CR Bates Industrial Estate
SKCH HP14 ....140 A6
Cressex Business Park
HWYW HP12 ....152 D6
Cressex Industrial Estate
HWYW HP12 ....152 E5
The Cressex School
HWYW HP12 ....152 C7
Cromwell Business Centre
WDR/YW UB7 ....190 F2
Crown Business Centre
CSHM HP5 ....135 N3
Crowne Plaza Hotel
WDR/YW UB7 ....190 G5
Crownhill Crematorium
CNH/GTH/TM MK8 ....41 N4
The Crown Hotel
AMSS HP7 ....145 M4
Crown Trading Centre
HYS/HAR UB3 ....191 L3
Crusader Industrial Estate
HWYW HP12 ....152 D5
Cuddington CE School
RAYLW HP18 ....107 K3
Curzon CE Primary School
AMSS HP7 ....144 F6
Dagnall County First School
BERK HP4 ....100 E2
D'Albiac House
HTHAIR TW6 ....196 C1
Danesfield House Hotel
MLW SL7 ....175 M3
Danesfield School
MLW SL7 ....175 N1
Dashwood Works Industrial
Centre *HWYW* HP12 ....152 D2
Datchet Golf Club
DTCH/LGLY SL3 ....188 C8
Datchet St Marys Primary
School *DTCH/LGLY* SL3 ....188 D8
Datchet Sports Club
DTCH/LGLY SL3 ....188 D8
Davenies School
BEAC HP9 ....155 J8
David Lloyd Centre
WLLN MK15 ....31 J8
Days Inn
WHLY OX33 ....116 A7
Deanshanger Primary School
RMKN MK19 ....40 A1
Debworth Green First School
WDSR SL4 ....193 J1
Dedworth County Middle
School *WDSR* SL4 ....193 J1
De Montfort University
WTR/OFPK MK7 ....43 M5
Denbigh East Industrial Estate
DBGH MK1 ....53 L1
Denbigh Hall Industrial Estate
BTCHLY MK3 ....42 F8
Denbigh Industrial Estate
DBGH MK1 ....53 H1
Denbigh School
SHEN MK5 ....42 A6
Denbigh West Industrial Estate
DBGH MK1 ....53 H1
Dene House Hospital
WDSR SL4 ....193 N2
Denham Aerodrome
DEN/HRF UB9 ....169 N3
Denham Country Park
DEN/HRF UB9 ....170 D7
Denham County Infant School
DEN/HRF UB9 ....169 P7
Denham Golf Club
DEN/HRF UB9 ....169 M4
Desborough Castle
HWYW HP12 ....152 D3
Desborough Industrial Park
HWYW HP12 ....4 A2
Desborough School
WDSR SL4 ....185 L2
De Vere Bellhouse Hotel
BEAC HP9 ....168 A2
Different Drummer Hotel
STSTR MK11 ....28 E7
Dinton Castle
RAYLW HP18 ....108 B2
Dinton CE School
HADM HP17 ....108 B4
The Disraeli School
HWYN HP13 ....4 C1
Dockwell's Industrial Estate
EBED/NFELT TW14 ....197 P4
Dorney County Combined
School *MDHD* SL6 ....186 A1
Dorney Court
WDSR SL4 ....186 F4
Douay Martyrs RC School
HGDN/ICK UB10 ....171 J9
Downe Manor Primary
School *NTHLT* UB5 ....183 P6
The Downley School
HWYN HP13 ....142 D9
Downs Barn First School
GTLIN MK14 ....30 F6
Downside Lower School
DUN/HR/TOD LU5 ....87 N1
Drayton Park Combined School
WEAT MK2 ....53 J6
Drayton Parslow Village School
RMKS/WB MK17 ....62 B4

Dr Challoners Grammar School
AMS HP6 ....145 N2
Dr Challoners High School
AMSS HP7 ....146 D4
Dropmore Infant School
SL SL1 ....166 C8
Dr Triplett's CE J & I School
HYS/HAR UB3 ....183 M9
Dryleas Sports Ground
HEN RG9 ....173 P5
Dry Ski Slope
HGDN/ICK UB10 ....182 F1
Dundale JM School
TRING HP23 ....112 E1
Dundale Primary School
TRING HP23 ....112 E1
Dunstable Downs Country
Park *DUN/WHIP* LU6 ....87 H4
Dunstable Downs Golf Club
DUN/WHIP LU6 ....87 H3
Dunstable Town CC
DUN/WHIP LU6 ....86 E1
Eaglestone Health Centre
EAG/OLD/WT MK6 ....42 C6
East Berkshire College
DTCH/LGLY SL3 ....189 H3
DTCH/LGLY SL3 ....185 K1
WDSR SL4 ....193 N1
Eastbury Farm JMI School
NTHWD HA6 ....159 M4
East Clayton School
BUCK/WIN MK18 ....69 J2
Eastcote CC
PIN HA5 ....171 P5
Eastern Business Park
HTHAIR TW6 ....197 M1
Eaton Bray Lower School
DUN/WHIP LU6 ....86 A2
Eaton Mill Combined School
WEAT MK2 ....53 K5
Edison Business Centre
AYLW HP19 ....94 C6
Edlesborough School
DUN/WHIP LU6 ....86 A5
Edon Business Park
WHLY OX33 ....116 A7
Education Centre
UX/CGN UB8 ....182 C2
Edward Pauling School
FELT TW13 ....197 L8
Egerton Rothesay School
BERK HP4 ....126 B1
Elangeni Junior School
AMS HP6 ....136 A9
Elers Clinic
HYS/HAR UB3 ....191 K5
Ellesborough Golf Club
HADM HP17 ....122 D2
Ellington Primary School
MDHD SL6 ....177 M7
Elmhurst Primary School
AYL HP20 ....2 E1
Elmtree Infant School
CSHM HP5 ....135 M3
Elva Lodge Hotel
MDHD SL6 ....177 L9
Emberton (Country Park)
OLN MK46 ....15 L3
Emberton School
OLN MK46 ....15 M7
Emerson Valley Combined
School *EMV/FZ* MK4 ....52 C1
Equestrian Centre
NTHWD HA6 ....159 H7
The Ethorpe Hotel
CFSP/GDCR SL9 ....168 G3
Eton College
WDSR SL4 ....187 P6
Eton Porny CE First School
WDSR SL4 ....187 P7
Eton Wick CE First School
WDSR SL4 ....187 L6
Eton Wick FC
WDSR SL4 ....187 K6
Europa Business Park
MKV MK10 ....44 B2
Evelyns Community School
WDR/YW UB7 ....182 F9
Express by Holiday Inn
WDSR SL4 ....31 J9
Fairacres Industrial Estate
WDSR SL4 ....192 G1
Fairholme Primary School
EBED/NFELT TW14 ....197 K7
Fairview Estate
WYM HP11 ....153 N6
Fairview Industrial Estate
AMS HP6 ....146 B2
HYS/HAR UB3 ....191 M3
Fairview Trading Estate
HEN RG9 ....174 B8
Falconhurst Combined
School *EAG/OLD/WT* MK6 ....43 H4
Farnham Common Infant
School *SLN* SL2 ....167 N9
Farnham Common Junior
School *SLN* SL2 ....167 N9
Farnham Common Middle
School *SLN* SL2 ....167 N9
Farnham Park Golf Club
SLN SL2 ....180 A4
Farnham Royal CE Combined
School *SLN* SL2 ....179 N6
Farnham Royal Cricket Club
SLN SL2 ....179 N6
Feltham Athletics Arena
EBED/NFELT TW14 ....197 N6
Felthambrook Industrial
Estate *FELT* TW13 ....197 P5
Feltham Hill Infant School
FELT TW13 ....197 M9
Feltham Hill Junior School
FELT TW13 ....197 M9
Feltham & Hounslow
Boro FC
EBED/NFELT TW14 ....197 N6

Fernwood School
  RMKS/WB MK17 ....**54** F1
Field Farm Business Centre
  BIC OX26 ....**66** A4
Filgrave School
  NPAC MK16 ....**21** J1
Finmere CE Primary School
  BUCK/WIN MK18 ....**46** D5
Fishermead Medical Centre
  EAG/OLD/WT MK6 ....**7** H4
Five Ways Business Centre
  FELT TW15 ....**197** P9
Flackwell Heath Golf Club
  FLKWH HP10 ....**153** P9
Foxes Piece Combined School
  MLW SL7 ....**164** E6
Francis Edmonds CP School
  SKCH HP14 ....**151** K6
Fredrick's Hotel
  MDHD SL6 ....**185** L2
Friars Square Shopping Centre
  AYL HP20 ....**2** D5
Frieth CE Combined School
  HEN RG9 ....**151** H9
Frithwood Primary School
  NTHWD HA6 ....**159** M6
Frogmore House
  WDSR SL4 ....**194** B2
Frogmore Industrial Estate
  HYS/HAR UB5 ....**191** L5
Fulbrook Middle School
  RMKS/WB MK17 ....**44** F7
Fulmer Infant School
  DTCH/LGLY SL3 ....**168** G9
Furze Down Special School
  BUCK/WIN MK18 ....**60** A6
Furze Platt J & I School
  MDHD SL6 ....**177** J7
Furze Platt Senior School
  MDHD SL6 ....**177** J7
Future School
  HYS/HAR UB3 ....**133** N5
The Gatehouse School
  GTLIN MK14 ....**30** D6
Gateway School
  GTMIS/PWD HP16 ....**133** N4
Gawcott Infant School
  BUCK/WIN MK18 ....**47** M7
Gayhurst House
  NPAC MK16 ....**20** D5
Gayhurst School
  CFSP/GDCR SL9 ....**168** E2
Germander Park First School
  GTLIN MK14 ....**30** A5
Gerrards Cross CE School
  CFSP/GDCR SL9 ....**168** G5
Gerrards Cross Golf Club
  CFSP/GDCR SL9 ....**169** H1
Gerrards Cross Sports Centre
  CFSP/GDCR SL9 ....**168** F5
Giffard Park Combined School
  GTLIN MK14 ....**30** C3
Gilbert Inglefield Middle School
  LBUZ LU7 ....**64** C9
Gilesbrook Combined School
  EMV/FZ MK4 ....**52** A4
Gilletts School
  HEN RG9 ....**173** M9
Gladstone Industrial Estate
  MDHD SL6 ....**177** L8
Glastonbury Thorne
  First School *SHEN* MK5 ....**42** A6
Glebe Primary School
  HGDN/ICK UB10 ....**171** K9
Glenwood School
  DUN/WHIP LU6 ....**87** N3
Globeside Business Park
  MLW SL7 ....**164** F7
Goat Centre
  RAYLNE/WEN HP22 ....**110** A7
Godolphin Infant School
  SL SL1 ....**179** N8
Godolphin Junior School
  SL SL1 ....**179** P8
Godstowe Preparatory School
  HWYN HP13 ....**5** J5
Goldfield Infant School
  TRING HP23 ....**112** D3
Goodson Industrial Mews
  THAME OX9 ....**118** D5
Grafton Medical Centre
  CMK MK9 ....**6** B3
Grange Park Clinic
  YEAD UB4 ....**183** M7
Grange Park Primary School
  YEAD UB4 ....**183** M7
The Grange School
  AYLS HP21 ....**3** H7
Grangewood School
  RSLP HA4 ....**171** N3
Great Brickhill CC
  RMKS/WB MK17 ....**54** A9
Great Gaddesden JMI School
  HHW HP1 ....**115** M3
Great Horwood CE Combined
  School *RMKS/WB* MK17 ....**50** B8
Great Kimble CE Infant School
  HADM HP17 ....**121** N4
Great Kingshill CE Combined
  School *HAZ/HG* HP15 ....**143** J4
Great Linford Combined
  School *GTLIN* MK14 ....**30** C5
Great Marlow School
  MLW SL7 ....**164** F5
Great Missenden CE Combined
  School *GTMIS/PWD* HP16 ....**133** P6
Greaves Way Industrial Estate
  LBUZ LU7 ....**74** G3
Greenleas Lower School
  LBUZ LU7 ....**74** A2
Greenleys First School
  WOLV MK12 ....**29** L8
Greenleys Middle School
  WOLV MK12 ....**29** L8
Green Park Combined School
  NPAC MK16 ....**31** H2

Green Street County
  First School *WYM* HP11 ....**4** C4
Grendon Underwood
  Combined School
  RAYLW HP18 ....**77** N2
Grenville Combined School
  BUCK/WIN MK18 ....**48** B3
Greys Court (NT)
  HEN RG9 ....**172** C5
Griffin Lane Industrial Estate
  AYLW HP19 ....**95** K6
Grovebury Road Industrial
  Estate *LBUZ* LU7 ....**74** D5
Grovefield Hotel
  BURN SL1 ....**178** E5
The Grove Independent School
  SHEN MK5 ....**42** C5
Grove Lock
  LBUZ LU7 ....**74** C7
Grove Park Industrial Estate
  MDHD SL6 ....**184** E7
  MDHD SL6 ....**184** F3
Grove Road Primary School
  TRING HP23 ....**112** F1
The Grove Surgery
  EAG/OLD/WT MK6 ....**43** H6
Grove Village Medical Centre
  EBED/NFELT TW14 ....**197** L7
Gulliver's Land
  WLLN MK15 ....**31** J9
Haddenham Business Park
  HADM HP17 ....**107** K7
Haddenham Health Centre
  HADM HP17 ....**107** L8
Haddenham Infant School
  HADM HP17 ....**107** L8
Haddenham Junior School
  HADM HP17 ....**107** L8
Hale Leys Shopping Centre
  AYL HP20 ....**2** D4
Halls Business Centre
  HYS/HAR UB3 ....**191** N4
Halton Camp
  RAYLNE/WEN HP22 ....**111** L7
Halton Combined School
  RAYLNE/WEN HP22 ....**111** K7
Hamilton Combined School
  HWYN HP13 ....**5** H2
Hamilton School
  HWYN HP13 ....**5** F4
Hannah Ball Infant School
  HWYN HP13 ....**153** K5
Hanslope Combined School
  RMKN MK19 ....**19** J5
Harefield CC
  DEN/HRF UB9 ....**158** D9
Harefield Health Centre
  DEN/HRF UB9 ....**158** C8
Harefield Hospital
  DEN/HRF UB9 ....**158** C8
Harefield Infant School
  DEN/HRF UB9 ....**158** B8
Harefield Junior School
  DEN/HRF UB9 ....**158** C8
Harefield Road
  Industrial Estate
  RKW/CH/CXG WD3 ....**158** E4
Haresfoot School
  BERK HP4 ....**126** D4
Haresfoot Senior School
  BERK HP4 ....**115** J8
Harewood Down Golf Club
  CSTG HP8 ....**146** D6
Harleyford Golf Club
  MLW SL7 ....**175** N2
Harlington Community
  School *WDR/YW* UB7 ....**191** K5
Harlyn Primary School
  PIN HA5 ....**171** J7
Harmill Industrial Estate
  LBUZ LU7 ....**74** E5
Harrold Lower School
  RBEDW MK43 ....**11** K2
Harrold-Odell Country Park
  RBEDW MK43 ....**11** M2
Hartwell CE Primary School
  RNHPTN NN7 ....**12** F6
Hartwell House Hotel
  HADM HP17 ....**109** H1
Haslemere Industrial Estate
  EBED/NFELT TW14 ....**197** N4
Haste Hill Golf Club
  NTHWD HA6 ....**159** L9
Haversham First School
  RMKN MK19 ....**29** N3
Hawridge & Cholesbury CE
  Combined School
  CSHM HP5 ....**125** J3
The Hay Barn Business Park
  RAYLNE/WEN HP22 ....**82** C2
Haydon Abbey Combined
  School *AYLW* HP19 ....**95** K5
Haydon School
  PIN HA5 ....**171** M1
Hayes CC
  HYS/HAR UB3 ....**183** M9
Hayes FC
  HYS/HAR UB3 ....**191** M1
The Hayes Manor School
  HYS/HAR UB3 ....**183** K9
Hayes Park J & I School
  YEAD UB4 ....**183** M7
Hayes Pool
  HYS/HAR UB3 ....**191** M2
Hayes Social & Sports Club
  HYS/HAR UB3 ....**191** M1
Hayes Stadium Sports Centre
  HYS/HAR UB3 ....**183** K9
Hayward House Day Hospital
  HWYN HP13 ....**5** K6
Hazlemere CE Combined
  School *HAZ/HG* HP15 ....**143** M8
Hazlemere Golf Club
  HAZ/HG HP15 ....**143** P7
Heathpark Golf Club
  WDR/YW UB7 ....**190** G4

Heathrow Airport
  HTHAIR TW6 ....**197** H1
Heathrow Airport Central
  Bus & Coach Station
  HTHAIR TW6 ....**196** C2
Heathrow International
  Trading Estate
  HSLWW TW4 ....**197** P2
Heathrow Medical Centre
  HYS/HAR UB3 ....**191** K6
Heathrow Primary School
  WDR/YW UB7 ....**190** F7
Heathrow Spectators
  Viewing Area *HTHAIR* TW6 .....**197** H2
Heathrow Terminal 1
  HTHAIR TW6 ....**197** H2
Heathrow Terminal 2
  HTHAIR TW6 ....**197** H3
Heathrow Terminal 3
  HTHAIR TW6 ....**197** C2
Heathrow Terminal 4
  HTHAIR TW6 ....**197** H4
Heathrow Terminal 5
  (Under Construction)
  HTHAIR TW6 ....**196** C2
Heathrow World Cargo Centre
  HTHAIR TW6 ....**196** F4
Heathwood Lower School
  LBUZ LU7 ....**64** F7
Hedgewood School
  YEAD UB4 ....**183** L6
Hedsor School
  BNEND SL8 ....**166** B7
Heelands First School
  BDWL MK13 ....**30** B9
Hemel Hempstead (Camelot)
  RFC HHW HP1 ....**127** P4
Hengrove School
  TRING HP23 ....**124** A1
The Henley College
  HEN RG9 ....**173** N7
Henley & District Indoor
  Sports Centre *HEN* RG9 ....**173** M9
Henley Town FC
  HEN RG9 ....**174** B8
Heritage Centre
  RMKS/WB MK17 ....**55** K4
Heritage House Special School
  CSHM HP5 ....**135** P3
Hermitage Primary School
  UX/CGN UB8 ....**182** D5
Hernes Estate
  HEN RG9 ....**173** K8
Heronsgate Middle School
  WTR/OFPK MK7 ....**43** N7
Heronshaw First School
  WTR/OFPK MK7 ....**43** P7
Herries School
  MDHD SL6 ....**165** H9
Herschel Grammar School
  SL SL1 ....**179** N9
High Ash CE Combined School
  RMKS/WB MK17 ....**54** B9
Highbridge Industrial Estate
  DEN/HRF UB9 ....**182** C2
Highclere Farm Country
  Touring Park *BEAC* HP9 ....**156** A4
Highcrest Community School
  HWYN HP13 ....**153** L3
Highfield PNEU School
  MDHD SL6 ....**177** L9
Highfield School
  HGDN/ICK UB10 ....**183** H6
Highgrove Pool
  RSLP HA4 ....**171** N5
High March School
  BEAC HP9 ....**155** J6
Highworth Combined School
  HWYN HP13 ....**143** L9
High Wycombe CE Combined
  School *WYM* HP11 ....**4** E6
High Wycombe RUFC
  WYM HP11 ....**153** N7
High Wycombe Squash Club
  MLW SL7 ....**152** A8
High Wycombe Tennis Club
  WYM HP11 ....**153** K5
Hill Fort
  LBUZ LU7 ....**99** N1
Hillingdon Borough FC
  RSLP HA4 ....**171** H3
Hillingdon Cemetery
  HGDN/ICK UB10 ....**182** E6
Hillingdon Golf Club
  HGDN/ICK UB10 ....**182** F5
Hillingdon Hospital
  UX/CGN UB8 ....**182** F7
Hillingdon Primary School
  HGDN/ICK UB10 ....**182** G6
Hillside Primary School
  HWYN HP13 ....**159** N7
Hill Top First School
  BDWL MK13 ....**193** J2
Hilltops Medical Centre
  CNH/GTH/TM MK8 ....**7** M4
HM Customs
  HTHAIR TW6 ....**191** H9
HM Prison
  CSHM HP5 ....**127** H8
  EMV/FZ MK4 ....**41** M8
  RAYLW HP18 ....**67** N9
HM Young Offender Institution
  AYL HP20 ....**2** D6
  FELT TW13 ....**197** K9
HM Young Offender Institution
  (Grendon)
  RAYLW HP18 ....**67** N8
Holiday Inn
  CMK MK9 ....**6** E3
  HYS/HAR UB3 ....**191** K9
  MDHD SL6 ....**185** L3
  RAYLNE/WEN HP22 ....**96** E9
  WDR/YW UB7 ....**190** G6
Holland & Holland Shooting
  School *DEN/HRF* UB9 ....**158** C9

Holmer Green First School
  HAZ/HG HP15 ....**143** P4
Holmer Green Junior School
  HAZ/HG HP15 ....**144** B4
Holmer Green Senior School
  HAZ/HG HP15 ....**144** A4
Holmwood First School
  HSLWW TW4 ....**41** N3
Holne Chase Combined School
  BTCHLY MK3 ....**52** C4
Holtspur Primary School
  BEAC HP9 ....**154** E9
Holy Cross Convent School
  CFSP/GDCR SL9 ....**156** F8
Holy Family Catholic School
  DTCH/LGLY SL3 ....**189** H6
Holyport CE Primary School
  MDHD SL6 ....**185** P7
Holyport Manor School
  MDHD SL6 ....**185** L9
Holy Trinity CE (A) School
  MLW SL7 ....**164** D6
Holy Trinity CE Primary School
  MLW SL7 ....**177** N1
  MDHD SL6 ....**159** J6
Holywell School
  RBEDW MK45 ....**33** M4
Homers First School
  WDSR SL4 ....**187** H9
Horton Industrial Park
  WDR/YW UB7 ....**190** F2
Horton Trading Estate
  DTCH/LGLY SL3 ....**195** K2
Hotel Ibis
  SL SL1 ....**191** L9
Household Cavalry Museum
  WDSR SL4 ....**193** M2
Howard Industrial Estate
  CSHM HP5 ....**135** N2
Howe Park School
  EMV/FZ MK4 ....**52** B2
HRH Princess Christians
  Hospital *WDSR* SL4 ....**187** N9
Hughenden Infant School
  SKCH HP14 ....**142** F4
Hughenden Manor (NT)
  SKCH HP14 ....**142** G8
Huntercombe Manor Hospital
  WDSR SL4 ....**186** G1
Hunters Farm Industrial Estate
  RAYLW HP18 ....**94** C1
Hurley Riverside Park
  MDHD SL6 ....**175** P4
Husborne Crawley Lower
  School *RBEDW* MK43 ....**45** N8
Hyde Heath Infant School
  AMS HP6 ....**134** G7
Ibstone CE School
  SKCH HP14 ....**149** P4
Ickenham Clinic
  HGDN/ICK UB10 ....**171** J8
Ickford Combined School
  RAYLW HP18 ....**116** F2
Icknield County Middle
  School *PRRI* HP27 ....**121** K8
Icknield Way Industrial Estate
  TRING HP23 ....**112** C2
Imperial College Athletic
  Ground *WDR/YW* UB7 ....**191** J7
Independent Business Park
  SKCH HP14 ....**139** N6
Independent Industrial Estate
  WDR/YW UB7 ....**190** F2
Industrial Farm Mount Estate
  DBGH MK1 ....**43** K9
Industrial Health Clinic
  UX/CGN UB8 ....**182** B6
The Inn at Woburn Hotel
  RMKS/WB MK17 ....**55** K4
Innkeeper's Lodge
  BEAC HP9 ....**155** J9
  DTCH/LGLY SL3 ....**189** H6
  RAYLNE/WEN HP22 ....**110** F4
  RAYLNE/WEN HP22 ....**111** L2
  WDSR SL4 ....**194** C4
The Inn on the Green
  MDHD SL6 ....**177** N1
International Trading Estate
  NWDGN UB2 ....**191** P4
Iver Golf & Leisure Centre
  IVER SL0 ....**189** K2
Iver Heath First School
  IVER SL0 ....**181** M6
Iver Heath Health Centre
  IVER SL0 ....**181** M5
Iver Primary School
  IVER SL0 ....**181** N5
Iver Village Infant School
  IVER SL0 ....**181** P9
Iver Village Junior School
  IVER SL0 ....**181** N9
Ivinghoe Golf Club
  LBUZ LU7 ....**99** K1
Ivyleaf WM Club
  MDHD SL6 ....**177** N9
Jackson Industrial Estate
  HTHAIR TW6 ....**191** H9
James Elliman School
  SL SL1 ....**180** A9
John Colet School
  RAYLNE/WEN HP22 ....**111** J9
John F Kennedy RC School
  HWYN HP13 ....**127** P1
John Hamden Primary School
  THAME OX9 ....**118** D6
John Hampden Grammar
  School *WYM* HP11 ....**152** E6
The John Hampden
  Wendover School
  RAYLNE/WEN HP22 ....**111** J9
John Hellins Primary School
  TOW NN12 ....**27** P2
John Penrose School
  DEN/HRF UB9 ....**158** D8
John Penrose Sports Centre
  DEN/HRF UB9 ....**158** D8

Johnsons Industrial Estate
  HYS/HAR UB3 ....**191** N4
Jordans School
  BEAC HP9 ....**156** B6
Juniper Hill School
  FLKWH HP10 ....**165** P2
Kart Circuit
  CNH/GTH/TM MK8 ....**42** A2
Kensworth Lower School
  DUN/WHIP LU6 ....**87** P8
Kenton Theatre
  HEN RG9 ....**174** A6
Kents Hill First School
  WTR/OFPK MK7 ....**43** N5
Kiln Farm Industrial Estate
  STSTR MK11 ....**41** K1
King Edward Court Shopping
  Centre *WDSR* SL4 ....**187** N9
King Edwards Road Clinic
  RSLP HA4 ....**171** K6
King Edward VII Hospital
  WDSR SL4 ....**193** N2
The Kings Arms Hotel
  SKCH HP14 ....**139** P6
Kingsbrook School
  RMKN MK19 ....**28** B9
The Kings Centre
  WYM HP11 ....**4** D5
Kings College Sports Ground
  RSLP HA4
Kingsceote School
  CFSP/GDCR SL9 ....**168** G1
Kings Court First School
  WDSR SL4 ....**194** C6
Kings Grove Industrial Estate
  MDHD SL6 ....**185** L1
Kingsmead Business Park
  WYM HP11 ....**153** P7
Kingston Centre
  MKV MK10 ....**44** A3
Kingston Leisure Centre
  MKV MK10 ....**44** A3
Kings Wood Primary School
  HWYN HP13 ....**153** M2
Knaves Beech Business Centre
  FLKWH HP10 ....**154** B9
Knaves Beech Industrial
  Estate *FLKWH* HP10 ....**154** A9
Knowles First & Middle School
  WEAT MK2 ....**53** K3
Lady Bankes Primary School
  RSLP HA4 ....**171** N6
Lakeside Industrial Estate
  DTCH/LGLY SL3 ....**188** N8
  DTCH/LGLY SL3 ....**190** A7
Lambourne Golf Club
  SL SL1 ....**178** F2
Lancaster Business Park
  LBUZ LU7 ....**72** F6
Lane End Industrial Park
  SKCH HP14 ....**151** K6
Langland Combined School
  EAG/OLD/WT MK6 ....**43** J6
Langley Business Centre
  DTCH/LGLY SL3 ....**189** J5
Langley Business Park
  DTCH/LGLY SL3 ....**189** H3
Langley Grammar School
  DTCH/LGLY SL3 ....**189** H5
Langley Health Centre
  DTCH/LGLY SL3 ....**189** H5
Langley Manor School
  DTCH/LGLY SL3 ....**188** G2
Langley Park Country Park
  DTCH/LGLY SL3 ....**181** J7
Langleywood School
  DTCH/LGLY SL3 ....**188** G4
Lansdowne Middle School
  HWYN HP13 ....**152** D7
Lark Rise Lower School
  DUN/WHIP LU6 ....**87** K2
Lavendon Combined School
  OLN MK46 ....**10** D8
Lawn Farm Business Centre
  RAYLW HP18 ....**78** B4
Lawn Tennis Club
  WDSR SL4 ....**192** F2
Lawn Tennis School
  BEAC HP9 ....**155** J7
Lea Infant School
  SLN SL2 ....**188** D1
Lea Junior School
  SLN SL2 ....**188** C1
Learning Difficulties Unit
  AMS HP6 ....**146** A2
Lee Common CE First School
  CTMIS/PWD HP16 ....**124** B8
Leedon Lower School
  LBUZ LU7 ....**74** G3
Le Flaive Business Park
  SKCH HP14 ....**142** E5
Legoland Windsor
  WDSR SL4 ....**193** H4
Leighton Buzzard Golf Course
  LBUZ LU7 ....**64** D7
Leighton Buzzard Railway
  LBUZ LU7 ....**64** G8
  LBUZ LU7 ....**74** F4
Leighton Buzzard Theatre
  Cinema *LBUZ* LU7 ....**74** E3
Leighton Industrial Park
  LBUZ LU7 ....**74** E3
Leighton Middle School
  LBUZ LU7 ....**74** D3
Leisure Plaza
  CMK MK9 ....**6** B6
Lent Rise Combined School
  SL SL1 ....**178** F8
Lent Rise School
  BURN SL1
Leon School & Sports College
  WEAT MK2 ....**53** J2
Lewknor CE School
  WTLGN OX49 ....**138** E3
Ley Hill CC
  CSHM HP5 ....**136** E4
Ley Hill School
  CSHM HP5 ....**136** D3

Light Industrial Estate
  WDSR SL4 ...192 F8
Limelight Theatre
  AYLS HP21 ...3 G5
Lincolns Park Business Centre
  HWYW HP12 ...4 A7
Linden Medical Centre
  MDHD SL6 ...177 J7
Linslade Lower School
  LBUZ LU7 ...74 B2
Little Chalfont CP School
  AMS HP6 ...146 G5
Little Chalfont Golf Club
  CSTG HP8 ...146 G4
Littledown Special School
  SL8 ...188 B1
Little Furze JMI School
  OXHEY WD19 ...159 P3
Little Gaddesden CE Primary
  School BERK HP4 ...100 E7
Little Hay Golf Complex
  HHW HP1 ...127 L6
Little Kingshill Combined
  School GTMIS/PWD HP16 ...143 P1
Little Marlow CE Infant School
  MLW SL7 ...165 K4
Little Missenden CE Infant
  School AMSS HP7 ...144 D1
Little St Helens School
  NTHWD HA6 ...159 L6
Lodge Farm Industrial Estate
  RMKN MK19 ...29 K2
Lodge Industrial Centre
  RMKS/WB MK17 ...62 C4
Lombardy Retail Park
  HYS/HAR UB3 ...191 P1
London Area Terminal Control
  Centre WDR/YW UB7 ...190 F3
London Bible College
  NTHWD HA6 ...159 K6
London Central High School
  WYM HP11 ...153 J5
London Wasps RFC
  SKCH HP14 ...152 A4
Long Close School
  DTCH/LGLY SL3 ...188 C5
Long Crendon
  Courthouse (NT)
  RAYLW HP18 ...106 B7
Long Crendon School
  RAYLW HP18 ...106 A7
Longford Community School
  EBED/NFELT TW14 ...197 M6
Long Marston JMI School
  TRING HP23 ...97 P3
Long Meadow School
  SHEN MK5 ...41 P9
Longmead Primary School
  WDR/YW UB7 ...190 D5
Longwick CE Combined
  School PRRI HP27 ...120 F7
The Lord Grey School
  BTCHLY MK5 ...52 C2
Lord Williams Lower School
  THAME OX9 ...118 F5
Lord Williams School
  THAME OX9 ...118 B5
Loudwater Combined School
  WYM HP11 ...153 P8
Loughton Manor Equestrian
  Centre SHEN CMK MK9 ...42 B5
Loughton Manor First School
  SHEN MK5 ...42 A4
Loughton Middle School
  SHEN MK5 ...42 A5
Lovat Middle School
  NPAC MK16 ...31 K2
Lynch Hill School
  SLN SL2 ...179 K6
Lyons Industrial Estate
  WDR/YW UB7 ...182 C9
Macintyre School
  RAYLNE/WEN HP22 ...83 J5
Magdalen College School
  BRACKY NN15 ...34 C5
The Magnet Leisure Centre
  MDHD SL6 ...177 M9
Maidenhead Clinic
  MDHD SL6 ...177 M9
Maidenhead Golf Club
  MDHD SL6 ...185 M2
Maidenhead Rowing Club
  MDHD SL6 ...178 A9
Maidenhead RFC
  MDHD SL6 ...185 N2
Maidenhead Sailing Club
  MDHD SL6 ...177 N6
Maidenhead United FC
  MDHD SL6 ...185 N1
Maids Moreton CE School
  BUCK/WIN MK18 ...38 C9
Maltmans Green School
  CFSP/GDCR SL9 ...168 E1
Mandeville Upper School
  AYLS HP21 ...109 M2
Manor Farm Primary School
  HAZ/HG HP15 ...143 P9
Manor House Hospital
  AYL HP20 ...3 G3
Manor Park Medical Centre
  SLN SL2 ...179 P8
Manshead CE School
  LTN LU1 ...87 P3
Maple Cross Industrial Estate
  RKW/CH/CXG WD3 ...157 N4
Maple Cross JMI School
  RKW/CH/CXG WD3 ...157 N5
Maple Industrial Estate
  FELT TW13 ...197 N8
Maplewood School
  HWYN HP15 ...142 C9
  HWYW HP12 ...152 D7
Marish Infant School
  DTCH/LGLY SL3 ...189 H4
The Marjory Kinnon School
  EBED/NFELT TW14 ...197 L4

Market Trading Estate
  NWDGN UB2 ...191 P5
Marlborough Trading Estate
  WYM HP11 ...4 C3
Marlin Montessori School
  MLW SL7 ...126 D1
Marlow CE Infants School
  MLW SL7 ...164 D6
Marlow Community Hospital
  MLW SL7 ...164 E7
Marlow FC
  MLW SL7 ...164 E6
Marlow RFC
  MLW SL7 ...164 G8
Marlow Rowing Club
  MLW SL7 ...164 E8
Marlow Sports Club Pavilion
  Ground MLW SL7 ...164 D9
Marriott Hotel
  DTCH/LGLY SL3 ...189 H6
  HTHAIR TW6 ...191 K9
Marsh Gibbon CE School
  RBICN OX27 ...66 F6
Marsh Infant School
  WYM HP11 ...153 M6
Marsworth CE Infant School
  TRING HP23 ...98 E5
Martin Baker Sports Ground
  DEN/HRF UB9 ...169 P5
Martindale JMI School
  HHW HP1 ...127 P1
The Mary Bassett Lower
  School LBUZ LU7 ...74 D2
Maryland College
  RMKS/WB MK17 ...55 J5
Mary Towerton First School
  SKCH HP14 ...140 F8
McKay Trading Estate
  DTCH/LGLY SL3 ...195 N1
McMillan Clinic
  HYS/HAR UB3 ...191 J1
The Meacham Clinic
  WOLV MK12 ...29 K6
Meadowcroft First School
  AYLW HP19 ...95 J4
Meadow High School
  UX/CGN UB8 ...182 E8
The Meadows Combined
  School FLKWH HP10 ...166 C2
Meadow Walk Shopping
  Centre BUCK/WIN MK18 ...48 B2
Mellow Lane School
  YEAD UB4 ...183 J7
Menmarsh Guide Post
  WHLY OX33 ...103 L5
Mentmore Golf & Country Club
  LBUZ LU7 ...84 A6
Merchant Taylors School
  NTHWD HA6 ...159 L1
Merebrook First School
  EMV/FZ MK4 ...42 C9
Micklem JMI School
  HHW HP1 ...127 P1
Midas Industrial Estate
  UX/CGN UB8 ...182 B5
Middlegreen Trading Estate
  DTCH/LGLY SL3 ...188 F3
Middleton Swimming Pool
  NPAC MK16 ...31 L2
Midsummer Place Shopping
  CMK MK9 ...7 F2
Milbarn Medical Centre
  BEAC HP9 ...155 K9
Millbrook Combined School
  HWYW HP12 ...152 D2
Mill Lane CP School
  CHNR OX39 ...129 M5
Milton Keynes Central
  Business Exchange
  CMK MK9 ...6 E3
Milton Keynes College
  BTCHLY MK3 ...53 H5
Milton Keynes Gallery
  CMK MK9 ...42 F1
Milton Keynes Hospital
  EAG/OLD/WT MK6 ...43 H5
Milton Keynes Museum of
  Industry & Rural Life
  WOLV MK12 ...29 N8
Milton Keynes Preparatory
  School BTCHLY MK3 ...52 D3
Milton Keynes RFC
  WOLV MK12 ...29 J8
Milton Keynes Stadium
  EAG/OLD/WT MK6 ...43 J8
Milton Keynes Theatre
  CMK MK9 ...7 H1
Milton Medical Centre
  WEAT MK2 ...53 J3
Milton's Cottage
  CSTG HP8 ...156 D5
Minet Clinic
  HYS/HAR UB3 ...191 N2
Minet J & I School
  HYS/HAR UB3 ...191 P2
Misbourne Swimming Pool
  HAZ/HG HP15 ...133 P6
Monkey Island Hotel
  MDHD SL6 ...186 C4
Monks Risborough CE
  Combined School
  PRRI HP27 ...121 M8
Montem Primary School
  SL1 SL1 ...187 M3
Montem Sports Centre
  SL1 SL1 ...187 P3
Moorcroft School
  UX/CGN UB8 ...183 H8
Moore Place Hotel
  RMKS/WB MK17 ...45 J8
Moorland First School
  RMKS/WB MK17 ...45 J8
Moor Park Golf Club
  RKW/CH/CXG WD3 ...159 H5
The Motorsports Centre
  BRACKY NN13 ...36 B7

Mount Farm Industrial Estate
  DBGH MK1 ...43 K8
Mount Vernon Hospital
  RKW/CH/CXG WD3 ...159 H5
Mursley CE School
  RMKS/WB MK17 ...61 M4
Naphill, Walters Ash School
  SKCH HP14 ...142 B2
National Badminton Centre
  CNH/GTH/TM MK8 ...42 A3
The National Bowl
  SHEN MK5 ...42 E7
National Film & TV School
  BEAC HP9 ...155 J8
National Hockey Stadium (MK
  Dons FC) CMK MK9 ...6 A4
Neath Hill Health Centre
  GTLIN MK14 ...30 F6
Nettlebed Community School
  HEN RG9 ...160 B7
New Bradwell Combined
  School BDWL MK13 ...29 P6
New Chapter Combined
  School EAG/OLD/WT MK6 ...42 G7
The New College
  WDSR SL4 ...187 P8
New Elgiva Theatre
  CSHM HP5 ...135 M4
Newlands Girls School
  MDHD SL6 ...176 C9
Newport Pagnell Medical
  Centre NPAC MK16 ...31 J1
New Regal Cinema
  HEN RG9 ...174 A6
Newton Blossomville CE First
  School RBEDW MK43 ...16 F3
Newton Longville CE
  Combined School
  RMKS/WB MK17 ...52 C8
Nicholsons Shopping Centre
  MDHD SL6 ...177 M9
Northchurch CC
  BERK HP4 ...113 P7
North Crawley CE First School
  NPAC MK16 ...22 EB
North Feltham Trading Estate
  EBED/NFELT TW14 ...197 P3
North Maidenhead CC
  MDHD SL6 ...177 N6
North Marston CE School
  BUCK/WIN MK18 ...70 D7
Northolt Aerodrome
  RSLP HA4 ...183 N2
Northwood Cemetery
  NTHWD HA6 ...159 M9
Northwood College
  NTHWD HA6 ...159 K7
Northwood FC
  NTHWD HA6 ...159 M9
Northwood Golf Club
  NTHWD HA6 ...159 K7
Northwood & Pinner
  Community Hospital
  NTHWD HA6 ...159 N8
Northwood Preparatory
  School RKW/CH/CXG WD3 ...159 J2
Northwood School
  NTHWD HA6 ...159 P8
Northwood Sports Centre
  PIN HA5 ...159 P8
Notley Abbey
  RAYLW HP18 ...106 F7
Novotel BDWL MK13 ...30 C8
  WDR/YW UB7 ...190 G5
Oak Farm Clinic
  HGDN/ICK UB10 ...183 H4
Oak Farm J & I School
  HGDN/ICK UB10 ...183 H3
Oakfield First School
  WDSR SL4 ...193 M1
Oak Green School
  AYLS HP21 ...2 C7
Oakland Park Golf Club
  CSTG HP8 ...156 B4
Oakley CE Combined School
  RAYLW HP18 ...104 D2
Oakridge CP School
  WYM HP11 ...4 B5
The Observatory Shopping
  Centre SL1 SL1 ...188 C3
Octagon Shopping Centre
  WYM HP11 ...5 F5
Odeon Cinema AYL HP20 ...2 E5
  CFSP/GDCR SL9 ...168 G3
  UX/CGN UB8 ...182 C3
Odyssey Business Park
  RSLP HA4 ...183 P1
Officers Lawn Tennis Club
  RAYLNE/WEN HP22 ...111 J5
Old Airfield Industrial Estate
  LBUZ LU7 ...98 B2
Oldfield First School
  EAG/OLD/WT MK6 ...7 F6
Oldfield Primary School
  MDHD SL6 ...185 P1
Oldfield Road Industrial Estate
  MDHD SL6 ...177 P9
Old Gaol Museum
  BUCK/WIN MK18 ...48 A2
Old Kiln Industrial Estate
  MDHD SL6 ...176 C5
Old Luxters Farm Brewery
  HEN RG9 ...162 B2
Old Stratford Primary School
  RMKN MK19 ...28 D6
Olney First School
  OLN MK46 ...15 L3
Olney Middle School
  OLN MK46 ...15 M2
Open Air Swimming Pool
  WYM HP11 ...153 J5
Open Air Theatre
  CMK MK9 ...42 G1
The Open University
  DBGH MK1 ...53 L1
  SHEN MK5 ...42 B5

STSTR MK11 ...28 F8
  WTR/OFPK MK7 ...43 M5
Orchard House Industrial
  Estate CSHM HP5 ...135 N5
Our Lady of Peace RC
  Primary School SL1 SL1 ...188 C5
Our Ladys Catholic Primary
  School AMS HP6 ...135 M8
Ousedale School
  NPAC MK16 ...31 H2
Overstone Combined School
  LBUZ LU7 ...73 K7
The Oxford Belfry Hotel
  THAME OX9 ...116 G9
Oxford & Cherwell College
  THAME OX9 ...118 C5
Oxford Crematorium
  HEAD OX3 ...102 B9
The Oxfordshire Golf Club
  THAME OX9 ...117 N9
Padbury CE First School
  BUCK/WIN MK18 ...48 C9
Paddocks Hospital
  PRRI HP27 ...121 L9
Pages Industrial Park
  LBUZ LU7 ...74 E4
Parkhouse Business Centre
  HWYW HP12 ...4 A3
The Park Inn Heathrow
  WDR/YW UB7 ...191 H8
Park School
  AYL HP20 ...3 G5
Parkside Hotel
  EAG/OLD/WT MK6 ...43 K4
Park Street Industrial Estate
  AYL HP20 ...3 H5
Parlaunt Park Combined
  School DTCH/LGLY SL3 ...189 K4
Pavilions Shopping Centre
  UX/CGN UB8 ...182 C4
Pear Tree Farm Industrial Units
  RBICN OX27 ...66 E7
Pebble Brook Special School
  AYLS HP21 ...2 A7
Pendley Manor Hotel
  TRING HP23 ...113 J2
Penn School BEAC HP9 ...154 E5
  FLKWH HP10 ...154 B5
Penwith First School
  EAG/OLD/WT MK6 ...7 H5
Peppard CE Primary School
  HEN RG9 ...172 E8
Pepper Hill First School
  BDWL MK13 ...30 A6
Peregrine Business Park
  FLKWH HP10 ...153 N5
Perth Trading Estate
  SLN SL2 ...179 M8
Peter James Business Centre
  HYS/HAR UB3 ...191 N3
Phoenix Business Centre
  CSHM HP5 ...135 M3
Pield Heath School
  UX/CGN UB8 ...182 E7
Pilot Trading Estate
  HWYW HP12 ...4 A3
Pinewood Film Studios
  IVER SL0 ...181 K3
Pinkwell Primary School
  WDR/YW UB7 ...191 J5
Pinner Hill Golf Club
  PIN HA5 ...159 P6
Pipers Corner School
  HAZ/HG HP15 ...143 H5
Pippins School
  DTCH/LGLY SL3 ...189 P7
Pixies Hill JMI School
  HHW HP1 ...127 P5
The Place Retail Park
  CMK MK9 ...42 B3
Planet Ice
  CMK MK9 ...6 B6
The Players Theatre
  THAME OX9 ...118 D5
The Point Entertainment
  Centre CMK MK9 ...7 G2
Polygon Business Centre
  DTCH/LGLY SL3 ...195 P1
Portfields Combined School
  NPAC MK16 ...20 C9
Portland Business Centre
  DTCH/LGLY SL3 ...188 D9
Potten End First School
  BERK HP4 ...115 K8
Prehistoric Monument
  MDHD SL6 ...184 D1
Premier Lodge
  BRACKY NN13 ...24 F5
  EAG/OLD/WT MK6 ...43 M8
  EMV/FZ MK4 ...42 D7
  SL1 SL1 ...188 D5
Prestwood Infant School
  CTMIS/PWD HP16 ...133 J5
Prestwood Junior School
  CTMIS/PWD HP16 ...133 J6
Prestwood Lodge Special
  School CTMIS/PWD HP16 ...133 K7
Princes Industrial Estate
  PRRI HP27 ...131 H1
Princes Risborough Golf Club
  PRRI HP27 ...131 H6
Princes Risborough
  Health Clinic PRRI HP27 ...121 J9
Princes Risborough Primary
  School PRRI HP27 ...121 L9
Princes Risborough Station
  PRRI HP27 ...131 K2
Princess Margaret Hospital
  WDSR SL4 ...193 P1
The Princess Marina Centre
  BEAC HP9 ...193 P3
Priors Way Industrial Estate
  MDHD SL6 ...185 P5
Priory Common First School
  BDWL MK13 ...30 B9

Priory School
  HADM HP17 ...179 H8
Progress Business Centre
  SL1 SL1 ...179 H9
Pronto Trading Estate
  YEAD UB4 ...183 L8
Prospect Industrial Estate
  HYS/HAR UB3 ...135 N5
Providence Road School
  WDR/YW UB7 ...190 E2
Provident Industrial Estate
  HYS/HAR UB3 ...191 N3
Pulfords Lower School
  LBUZ LU7 ...74 D5
Pulpit Hill
  HADM HP17 ...122 A6
Pump Lane Industrial Estate
  HYS/HAR UB3 ...191 P5
Quainton CE Combined School
  RAYLNE/WEN HP22 ...79 M5
Quality Hotel
  CNH/GTH/TM MK8 ...41 M1
  DTCH/LGLY SL3 ...189 K7
Quarrendon Upper School
  AYLW HP19 ...95 L5
The Queen Anne Royal Free
  First School
  WDSR SL4 ...193 P2
Queen Eleanor Combined
  School STSTR MK11 ...29 H9
Queen's Building
  HTHAIR TW6 ...197 H2
Queensbury School
  DUN/WHIP LU6 ...87 J2
Queensmere Shopping Centre
  SL1 SL1 ...188 B3
Queens Schools
  WEAT MK2 ...187 N7
Queensway Clinic
  WEAT MK2 ...53 K5
Rabbsfarm Primary School
  WDR/YW UB7 ...182 D9
Racecourse Yacht Basin
  WDSR SL4 ...187 K8
Radcliffe Centre
  BUCK/WIN MK18 ...48 A3
The Radcliffe School
  WOLV MK12 ...29 K7
Radisson Edwardian Hotel
  HYS/HAR UB3 ...191 J8
Radnage CE First School
  SKCH HP14 ...140 F5
RAF Edlesborough
  DUN/WHIP LU6 ...86 B9
RAF Stanbridge
  LBUZ LU7 ...75 H4
RAF Uxbridge
  HGDN/ICK UB10 ...182 E4
Rainbow Industrial Estate
  WDR/YW UB7 ...190 D1
Randolph Medical Centre
  DTCH/LGLY SL3 ...188 D8
Rare Breeds Centre
  FLKWH HP10 ...166 F3
Rare Breeds Park
  FLKWH HP22 ...96 C6
Rebellion Brewery
  MLW SL7 ...164 E4
Red Lion Hotel
  HEN RG9 ...174 A6
The Redway School
  EAG/OLD/WT MK6 ...43 J5
Regent Business Centre
  HYS/HAR UB3 ...191 P3
The Renaissance Hotel
  HTHAIR TW6 ...191 J9
Replica Locomotive
  CMK MK9 ...6 B5
Richings Park Golf & Country
  Club DTCH/LGLY SL3 ...189 H5
Richings Park Sports Club
  IVER SL0 ...189 P4
Rickley Middle School
  BTCHLY MK3 ...52 F3
Rickmansworth Public Golf
  Club RKW/CH/CXG WD3 ...158 F2
Ridgeway School
  MDHD SL6 ...184 E2
River Gardens Business Centre
  EBED/NFELT TW14 ...197 P3
River Park Industrial Estate
  BERK HP4 ...114 C9
River & Rowing Museum at
  Henley & Wind in the
  Willows HEN RG9 ...174 B7
Rivers County First School
  BTCHLY MK3 ...52 E3
Riverside Business Centre
  WYM HP11 ...4 C4
Riverside First School
  NPAC MK16 ...31 K2
Roade Primary School
  RNHPTN NN7 ...12 A3
Robertswood Combined
  School CFSP/GDCR SL9 ...157 H7
Romans Field School
  SHEN MK5 ...52 E2
Rook Tree Farm Industrial
  Estate RMKS/WB MK17 ...45 L1
The Rose & Crown Hotel
  PRRI HP27 ...131 K8
  TRING HP23 ...112 F3
Rose Industrial Estate
  MLW SL7 ...164 D4
Ross Road Medical Centre
  MDHD SL6 ...185 L3
Rowing Lake
  WDSR SL4 ...186 G7
Royal Adelaide Hotel
  WDSR SL4 ...193 P1
The Royal Bucks Hospital
  AYLW HP19 ...2 E3
Royal Grammar School
  HWYN HP13 ...153 J1
The Royal Latin School
  BUCK/WIN MK18 ...48 B4

Royal Mews
WDSR SL4 ....187 P9
Royal Windsor Racecourse
WDSR SL4 ....187 L7
RSPB Site
SLN SL2 ....167 P6
Ruislip Gardens Primary
School *HGDN/ICK* UB10 ....171 L9
Ruislip Golf Club
RSLP HA4 ....171 J7
Ruislip Manor FC
RSLP HA4 ....171 M7
Ruislip RFC
RSLP HA4 ....171 L7
Ruislip Woods National
Nature Reserve
NTHWD HA6 ....171 J1
RSLP HA4 ....171 L3
Runnymede Hotel & Spa
EGH TW20 ....195 K9
Runnymede (NT)
STWL/WRAY TW19 ....194 E7
Rupert House School
HEN RG9 ....174 A6
Rushmere Retail Park
DBCH NN5 ....53 K1
The Russell School
RKW/CH/CXG WD3 ....147 K6
Russell Street First School
STSTR MK11 ....28 F7
Rycote Chapel
THAME OX9 ....117 K7
Ryefield Primary School
HGDN/ICK UB10 ....183 K4
The Rye
WYM HP11 ....5 H6
Ryvers School
DTCH/LGLY SL3 ....188 F4
Sacred Heart RC Primary
School *HEN* RG9 ....173 P7
RSLP HA4 ....171 L7
St Andrews CE First School
GTLIN MK14 ....30 E1
St Andrews CE J & I School
UX/CGN UB8 ....182 D4
St Andrews CE Primary School
CHNR OX39 ....117 M2
St Andrews Industrial Estate
AYLW HP19 ....2 B3
St Annes CP School
STWL/WRAY TW19 ....196 E6
St Anthonys RC Primary
School *SLN* SL2 ....179 N6
St Augustines RC Primary
School *WYM* HP11 ....152 C6
St Bartholomewes CE School
TRING HP23 ....113 H5
St Bernadettes RC Primary
School *HGDN/ICK* UB10 ...183 H4
St Bernards Convent School
DTCH/LGLY SL3 ....188 D3
St Bernards RC School
WYM HP11 ....152 C7
St Catherines RC J & I School
WDR/YW UB7 ....190 D3
St Clement Danes School
RKW/CH/CXG WD3 ....147 M4
St Davids Health Centre
STWL/WRAY TW19 ....196 D6
St Davids School
ASHF TW15 ....196 F9
St Edmund Campion RC
Primary School *MDHD* SL6 ...185 H1
St Edwards CE First School
WDSR SL4 ....187 L9
St Edwards CE Junior School
AYLS HP21 ....3 K7
St Edwards Royal Free
Ecumenical School
WDSR SL4 ....187 L9
St Ethelberts Catholic Primary
School *SLN* SL2 ....180 C9
St Georges CE Infant School
AMS HP6 ....146 A2
St George's Chapel
WDSR SL4 ....187 P8
St Georges Industrial Estate
AMSS HP7 ....146 B2
St Georges Preparatory
School *WDSR* SL4 ....187 P8
St Helens College
HGDN/ICK UB10 ....182 G3
St Helens Junior School
for Girls *NTHWD* HA6 ......159 L6
St Johns Beaumont School
EGH TW20 ....194 D8
St Johns CE Combined School
PRRI HP4 ....131 P8
St Johns RC Primary School
RKW/CH/CXG WD3 ....158 B1
St Johns School
NTHWD HA6 ....159 P6
St Josephs Catholic High
School *SLN* SL2 ....180 C9
St Josephs Catholic Infant
School *AYLS* HP21 ....3 K6
St Josephs Catholic Primary
School *THAME* OX9 ....118 C4
St Josephs CE Combined
School *CFSP/GDCR* SL9 ...168 L1
St Josephs RC Primary School
OXHEY WD19 ....159 P3
St Laurence CE Junior School
UX/CGN UB8 ....182 C8
St Lawrence Business Centre
FELT TW13 ....197 P6
St Lawrence Catholic School
FELT TW13 ....197 P8
St Leonards Heath & Reach
VA School *LBUZ* LU7 ....64 E5
St Louis Catholic Combined
School *AYL* HP20 ....95 P5
St Lukes CE Primary School
MDHD SL6 ....177 M8
St Marks Hospital
MDHD SL6 ....177 J9

St Martins Medical Centre
RSLP HA4 ....171 L5
St Martins Pre-Preparatory
School *NTHWD* HA6 ....159 K5
St Mary & All Saints CE
Primary School *BEAC* HP9 ...155 J8
St Mary Magdalene RC
Combined School
WOLV MK12 ....29 J8
St Mary & St Giles CE Middle
School *STSTR* MK11 ....28 F7
St Marys CE Combined School
AMSS HP7 ....145 M3
St Mary CE Junior School
STWL/WRAY TW19 ....196 E5
St Marys CE Primary School
SL SL1 ....188 C4
St Marys CE School
AYLW HP19 ....95 J7
HADM HP17 ....119 L1
St Marys First School
BERK HP4 ....114 A8
St Marys Lower School
LTN LU1 ....87 P2
St Marys RC Primary School
MDHD SL6 ....177 M6
UX/CGN UB8 ....182 C4
St Marys School
CFSP/GDCR SL9 ....168 C2
HEN RG9 ....174 A8
St Matthews CE Primary
School *WDR/YW* UB7 ....190 E2
St Michaels CE Combined
School *LBUZ* LU7 ....62 D9
St Monicas RC Combined
School *GTLIN* MK14 ....30 E7
St Nicholas CE Combined
School *MDHD* SL6 ....178 B7
St Pauls Catholic School
EAG/OLD/WT MK6 ....42 F5
St Pauls CE Combined School
FLKWH HP10 ....166 B5
St Peters Catholic School
MLW SL7 ....164 C6
St Peters CE Combined School
SL SL1 ....178 F6
St Peters CE Middle School
WDSR SL4 ....194 B5
St Peters JMI School
RKW/CH/CXG WD3 ....158 B1
St Raphaels RC Primary School
NTHLT UB5 ....183 P5
St Teresas School
PRRI HP4 ....121 K9
St Thomas Aquinas RC
Combined School
BTCHLY MK3 ....52 E4
St Thomas More RC Primary
School *BERK* HP4 ....126 C1
St Vincents Hospital
RSLP HA4 ....171 L1
Sands County First School
HWYW HP12 ....152 C3
Sands Industrial Estate
HWYW HP12 ....152 A3
Sandy Lodge Golf Club
NTHWD HA6 ....159 K2
Saxeways Business Centre
CSHM HP5 ....135 J1
Saxon Clinic
EAG/OLD/WT MK6 ....43 H5
Secklow Centre
EAG/OLD/WT MK6 ....42 C5
Seer Green CE Combined
School *BEAC* HP9 ....155 N6
Sheeji Medical Centre
SL SL1 ....187 P1
Shelburne County First
School *HWYW* HP12 ....152 D7
Shenley Brook End School
SHEN MK5 ....52 A1
Shenley Leisure Centre
SHEN MK5 ....41 P5
Shepherd Primary School
RKW/CH/CXG WD3 ....158 A1
Shepherdswell First School
EAG/OLD/WT MK6 ....43 H2
Sheraton Skyline Hotel
HYS/HAR UB3 ....191 K8
Sherington CE First School
NPAG MK16 ....21 N4
Shire Horse Centre
CFSP/GDCR SL9 ....157 J3
Shortwood Infant School
STA TW18 ....196 B9
Silchester House School
MDHD SL6 ....178 B9
Silverdale Industrial Estate
HYS/HAR UB3 ....191 N2
Silverstone CE Junior School
TOW NN12 ....25 K1
Silverstone Golf Club
BRACKY NN13 ....25 J7
Silverstone Infant School
TOW NN12 ....25 K1
Silverstone Motor Racing
Circuit *TOW* NN12 ....25 M3
Simpson Combined School
EAG/OLD/WT MK6 ....43 K7
Simpson Health Centre
BEAC HP9 ....154 G7
Sir Christopher Wren's
House Hotel *WDSR* SL4 ...187 P8
Sir Frank Markham
Community School
EAG/OLD/WT MK6 ....42 F5
Sir Henry Floyd Grammar
School *AYLW* HP19 ....2 A6
Sir William Borlases Grammar
School *MLW* SL7 ....164 C8
Sir William Ramsay School
HAZ/HG HP15 ....145 N8
Skidmore Clinic
RKW/CH/CXG WD3 ....158 E1
Ski Slopes
WYM HP11 ....153 K7

Ski & Watersport Centre
RAYLNE/WEN HP22 ....95 M3
Slapton Lock
LBUZ LU7 ....84 F3
Slated Row Special School
WOLV MK12 ....29 J6
Slough Cemetery
SLN SL2 ....180 B9
Slough Community Mental
Health Centre
DTCH/LGLY SL3 ....189 J5
Slough Crematorium
SLN SL2 ....180 B9
Slough & Eton CE School
SL SL1 ....187 P4
Slough Grammar School
SLN SL2 ....188 D4
Slough Ice Arena
SL SL1 ....187 P3
Slough Museum
SL SL1 ....188 C3
Slough RFC
DTCH/LGLY SL3 ....188 D5
Slough Sports Club
SL SL1 ....188 A4
Slough Town FC
SLN SL2 ....180 C8
Slough Trading Estate
SL SL1 ....179 L8
Soho Mills Industrial Estate
FLKWH HP10 ....166 B5
Southcott Lower School
LBUZ LU7 ....74 B2
Southfield CP School
BRACKY NN13 ....34 C6
Southville Infant School
EBED/NFELT TW14 ....197 M7
Sovereign Medical Centre
GTLIN MK14 ....30 E8
Spearmans Industrial Estate
HWYW HP12 ....152 B4
Spearmast Industrial Park
HWYW HP12 ....152 B4
Speedway Industrial Estate
HYS/HAR UB3 ....191 K5
Speen CE School
PRRI HP27 ....132 B8
Spinfield School
MLW SL7 ....164 B7
Spinney Park Industrial Estate
LBUZ LU7 ....74 F5
Sports Ground Pavilion
HGDN/ICK UB10 ....183 K5
Spread Eagle Hotel
THAME OX9 ....118 D5
Springfield Middle School
EAG/OLD/WT MK6 ....7 K3
Springfield Surgery
BRACKY NN13 ....34 G3
Squirrels Trading Estate
HYS/HAR UB3 ....191 M4
Stanbridge Lower School
LBUZ LU7 ....75 P4
Stantonbury Campus
GTLIN MK14 ....30 C7
Stantonbury Campus Leisure
Centre *GTLIN* MK14 ....30 C6
Stantonbury Health Centre
GTLIN MK14 ....30 C6
Stantonbury Stadium
GTLIN MK14 ....30 D6
Stanton Middle School
BDWL MK13 ....30 A4
Station Road Industrial Estate
BUCK/WIN MK18 ....60 B5
Stockgrove Country Park
LBUZ LU7 ....64 D3
Stocklake Industrial Estate
AYL HP20 ....3 C4
Stocklake Park Industrial
Estate *AYL* HP20 ....3 C4
Stockley Park Business Centre
STKPK UB11 ....191 J2
Stockley Park Golf Club
STKPK UB11 ....191 J1
Stocks Hotel Golf & Country
Club *TRING* HP23 ....99 M3
Stoke Goldington CE First
School *NPAG* MK16 ....14 B9
Stoke Green Cricket Club
SNL SL3 ....180 D7
Stoke Mandeville Combined
School *RAYLNE/WEN* HP22 ...110 A5
Stoke Mandeville Hospital
AYLS HP21 ....109 P2
Stoke Mandeville Sports
Stadium *AYLS* HP21 ....109 P2
Stokenchurch County First
School *SKCH* HP14 ....140 A7
Stokenchurch Health Centre
SKCH HP14 ....140 A6
Stokenchurch Primary School
SKCH HP14 ....140 A6
Stoke Park House
SLN SL2 ....180 A6
Stoke Poges Golf Club
SLN SL2 ....179 P6
Stoke Poges School
SLN SL2 ....180 B3
SLN SL2 ....180 D3
Stone CE Combined School
HADM HP17 ....108 F1
Stonor Hotel
HEN RG9 ....161 K3
Stonor House & Park
HEN RG9 ....161 L2
Stony Dean Special School
AMSS HP7 ....146 B3
Stony Stratford Health Centre
STSTR MK11 ....28 F8
Stony Stratford Sports Club
STSTR MK11 ....28 F7
Stowe Castle Business Park
BUCK/WIN MK18 ....37 P5

Stowe House
BUCK/WIN MK18 ....37 L5
Stowe Landscape Gardens (NT)
BUCK/WIN MK18 ....37 M5
Stowe School
BUCK/WIN MK18 ....37 L5
Streetfield Middle School
DUN/HR/TOD LU5 ....87 H7
Studham Lower School
DUN/WHIP LU6 ....101 K3
Studley Priory Hotel
WHLY OX33 ....103 K1
Studley Wood Golf Club
WHLY OX33 ....103 J2
Summerfield Combined
School *BDWL* MK13 ....42 C1
Sun Life Trading Estate
EBED/NFELT TW14 ....197 N2
Sunshine House School
NTHWD HA6 ....159 K6
Swakeleys School
HGDN/ICK UB10 ....183 J5
Swallowfield School
RMKS/WB MK17 ....44 F7
Swanbourne CE First School
RMKS/WB MK17 ....61 J7
Swanbourne House School
RMKS/WB MK17 ....61 H7
The Swan Pool & Leisure
Centre *BUCK/WIN* MK18 .....48 B4
Swan Revived Hotel
NPAG MK16 ....31 K1
Swan Wharf Business Centre
UX/CGN UB8 ....182 C5
Swing Gate First School
BERK HP4 ....126 F2
Swiss Farm International
Camping *HEN* RG9 ....173 P4
The Symonds Medical Centre
MDHD SL6 ....177 K9
Syresham St James CE
Primary School
BRACKY NN13 ....24 C6
Tannery Road Industrial Estate
WYM HP11 ....153 M6
Tapling Trading Estate
WDR/YW UB7 ....190 D1
Taplow Health Centre
MDHD SL6 ....178 F9
Taplow House Hotel
MDHD SL6 ....178 B8
Technology Park
RBEDW MK43 ....33 H5
Teikyo School
DTCH/LGLY SL3 ....180 F3
Temple Golf Club
MDHD SL6 ....176 B6
Thame Health Centre
THAME OX9 ....118 E5
Thame Park Business Centre
THAME OX9 ....118 E6
Thames Industrial Estate
MLW SL7 ....164 F7
Thame Sports Club
THAME OX9 ....118 F5
Thames Riviera Hotel
MDHD SL6 ....178 A9
Thames Valley Athletics
Centre *WDSR* SL4 ....188 A6
Thames Valley Community
Infant School *SL* SL1 ....187 N3
The Thames Valley
Nuffield Hospital
DTCH/LGLY SL3 ....180 E4
Thames Valley University
SL SL1 ....188 A2
Thame United FC
THAME OX9 ....118 D6
Theatre Royal
WDSR SL4 ....187 P8
The Thomas Coram Middle
School *BERK* HP4 ....126 F3
Thomas Harding Junior
School *CSHM* HP5 ....135 M5
Thornborough Infant School
BUCK/WIN MK18 ....49 L3
Thorney Park Golf Club
IVER SL0 ....190 B4
Thornton College Convent
of Jesus & Mary
RMKS/WB MK17 ....39 N7
Three Locks Golf Club
RMKS/WB MK17 ....63 N4
Tiddenfoot Leisure Centre
LBUZ LU7 ....74 C4
Tilehouse Combined School
DEN/HRF UB9 ....169 P4
Tingewick Infant School
BUCK/WIN MK18 ....46 G5
Tingewick Road Industrial
Estate *BUCK/WIN* MK18 ....47 P3
Top Station Road Industrial
Estate *BRACKY* NN13 ....35 J4
Totternhoe FC
DUN/WHIP LU6 ....86 E1
Totternhoe Lower School
DUN/WHIP LU6 ....86 D1
Tower Hill Business Park
RBICN OX27 ....66 D2
Town Farm Primary School
STWL/WRAY TW19 ....196 D6
Townlands Hospital
HEN RG9 ....173 P6
Tramway Business Park
RAYLW HP18 ....91 H4
Travel Inn
AYLW HP19 ....95 M4
CMK MK9 ....7 G3
FLKWH HP10 ....154 B8
HHW HP1 ....127 K5
HTHAIR TW6 ....191 L9
TRING HP23 ....112 A3
WLLN MK15 ....31 K9
YEAD UB4 ....183 P9

Travelodge
CMK MK9 ....6 B4
RMKN MK19 ....5 G6
SL SL1 ....188 A3
Treadaway Business Centre
FLKWH HP10 ....154 A9
Tree Cathedral (NT)
DUN/WHIP LU6 ....87 H7
Trevelyan Middle School
WDSR SL4 ....193 L1
WDSR SL4 ....193 N3
Triangle Business Park
RAYLNE/WEN HP22 ....110 D6
Trident Industrial Estate
DTCH/LGLY SL3 ....195 N2
Tring Business Centre
TRING HP25 ....112 C2
Tring Health Centre
TRING HP25 ....112 F2
Tring School
TRING HP23 ....112 F2
Tring Sports Centre
TRING HP25 ....112 C2
Trinity CE Primary School
HEN RG9 ....174 A7
Trinity St Stephen CE First
School *WDSR* SL4 ....187 N9
Trinity Trading Estate
HYS/HAR UB3 ....191 N4
Tudor Lodge Hotel
PIN HA5 ....171 P4
Turnfurlong Primary School
AYLW HP19 ....96 A9
Turvey Lower School
RBEDW MK43 ....17 J1
Turweston Airfield
BRACKY NN15 ....35 P5
Two Mile Ash Middle School
CNH/GTH/TM MK8 ....41 N2
Twyford CE First School
BUCK/WIN MK18 ....57 J8
Tylers Green Infant School
FLKWH HP10 ....154 B2
Tylers Green Middle School
FLKWH HP10 ....153 P2
Tyringham Health Clinic
NPAG MK16 ....20 F4
UCI Cinema
CMK MK9 ....7 F2
MDHD SL6 ....185 M1
WYM HP11 ....5 L4
UGC Cinema Slough
SL SL1 ....188 B3
Union Business Park
UX/CGN UB8 ....182 C3
The University of Buckingham
BUCK/WIN MK18 ....48 A3
Upper Wingbury Courtyard
Business Centre
RAYLNE/WEN HP22 ....83 K3
Upton Hospital
SL SL1 ....188 A4
Upton House School
WDSR SL4 ....195 N1
Uxbridge CC
HGDN/ICK UB10 ....182 E2
Uxbridge Cemetery
HGDN/ICK UB10 ....182 F6
Uxbridge College
UX/CGN UB8 ....182 E3
HYS/HAR UB3 ....191 N1
Uxbridge County Court
UX/CGN UB8 ....182 C2
YEAD UB4 ....183 L8
Uxbridge FC
WDR/YW UB7 ....190 G1
Uxbridge Golf Club
HGDN/ICK UB10 ....170 E7
Uxbridge Health Centre
UX/CGN UB8 ....182 D3
Uxbridge High School
UX/CGN UB8 ....182 D5
Uxbridge Industrial Estate
UX/CGN UB8 ....182 B5
Uxbridge Swimming Pool
HGDN/ICK UB10 ....182 E2
The Vale Industrial Centre
AYLW HP19 ....2 B2
Vale Industrial Estate
AYLW HP19 ....95 J1
Vale Retail Park
AYL HP20 ....3 F4
The Valley Centre
(Trading Estate)
HWYN HP15 ....5 K6
Valley Road Primary School
HEN RG9 ....173 N8
Vandyke Upper School &
Community College
LBUZ LU7 ....64 C9
The Van Straten Clinic
FELT TW13 ....84 E7
Vanwall Business Park
MDHD SL6 ....185 J2
Verney Avenue School
HWYW HP12 ....152 D6
Victoria Barracks
WDSR SL4 ....187 P9
Victoria CE First School
BERK HP4 ....126 C1
Victoria Junior School
FELT TW13 ....197 P7
The Village Medical Centre
SL SL1 ....187 H2
Village Shopping Centre
SL SL1 ....188 B3
Villiers Hotel
BUCK/WIN MK18 ....48 A3
Viscount Industrial Estate
DTCH/LGLY SL3 ....195 N2
Vitalograph Business Park
BUCK/WIN MK18 ....38 C7
Vyners School
HGDN/ICK UB10 ....170 F9
Waddesdon CE School
RAYLW HP18 ....93 L1

Waddesdon Manor (NT)
  RAYLW HP18 ....93 J1
Wallbrook Business Centre
  HSLW TW4 ....197 P2
The Walnuts School
  EAG/OLD/WT MK6 ....43 L7
Walnut Tree Health Centre
  WTR/OFPK MK7 ....43 P6
The Walter Rothschild
  Zoological Museum
  TRING HP23 ....112 F3
Walton High School
  WTR/OFPK MK7 ....44 A6
Warnford Industrial Estate
  HYS/HAR UB3 ....191 L3
Warrender School
  RSLP HA4 ....171 M5
The Warren Medical Centre
  YEAD UB4 ....183 P9
Washington House Surgery
  BRACKY NN13 ....35 H4
Water Eaton Health Centre
  WEAT MK2 ....53 K7
Water Hall Combined School
  WEAT MK2 ....53 K7
Watermill Hotel
  HHW HP1 ....127 L4
Waterperry Gardens
  WHLY OX33 ....116 C4
Waterperry Horticultural
  Centre WHLY OX33 ....116 C4
Waterside Combined School
  CSHM HP5 ....135 P6
Waterstock Golf Course
  WHLY OX33 ....116 C7
Waterways Heritage
  Museum
  RKW/CH/CXG WD3 ....158 E1
Watling Lower School
  DUN/WHIP LU6 ....87 K1
Watlington & District Hospital
  WTLGN OX49 ....148 A2
Watling Vale Medical Centre
  SHEN MK5 ....42 A5
Watling Way Centre
  STSTR MK11 ....29 H9
Wavendon First School
  RMKS/WB MK17 ....44 C5
Wavendon Gate Combined
  School WTR/OFPK MK7 ....44 B6
Wavendon Golf Centre
  RMKS/WB MK17 ....44 E4
Waynflete Infant School
  BRACKY NN13 ....34 C5
Welcome Lodge
  NPAG MK16 ....30 F1
Wellismead County Middle
  School BTCHLY MK3 ....52 E1
Wellismead First School
  BTCHLY MK3 ....52 E2
Wendover Health Centre
  RAYLNE/WEN HP22 ....111 H9

Wendover House
  Special School
  RAYLNE/WEN HP22 ....123 J2
Wendover Middle School
  RAYLNE/WEN HP22 ....111 H8
Wendover Tennis &
  Squash Club
  RAYLNE/WEN HP22 ....123 H1
Wessex Primary School
  MDHD SL6 ....185 H4
Wessex Road Industrial Estate
  BNEND SL8 ....165 P7
Westacott Business Centre
  MDHD SL6 ....184 E5
Westbrook Hay Preparatory
  School HHW HP1 ....127 M5
Westbury Court Business
  Centre RBICN OX27 ....66 C5
  RBICN OX27 ....66 E6
Westcott CE Infant School
  RAYLW HP18 ....78 F9
Westcott Leisure Centre
  RAYLW HP18 ....92 F3
Westcroft Retail Park
  EMV/FZ MK4 ....51 P1
West Drayton CC
  WDR/YW UB7 ....190 C5
West Drayton Primary School
  WDR/YW UB7 ....190 E3
Western House School
  SL SL1 ....187 K1
Western International Market
  NWDGN UB2 ....191 P5
Westfield First School
  BERK HP4 ....114 B9
Westfield School
  BNEND SL8 ....165 N5
Westgate Retail Park
  SL SL1 ....187 L1
Westgate School
  SL SL1 ....187 L2
Weston Turville CE School
  RAYLNE/WEN HP22 ....110 E3
Weston Turville Golf
  & Squash Club
  RAYLNE/WEN HP22 ....110 E2
Weston Way Industrial Estate
  RAYLNE/WEN HP22 ....110 A4
West Ramp Coach Park
  WDR/YW UB7 ....190 G9
West Ruislip Elementary
  School HGDN/ICK UB10 ....171 J8
West Wycombe Caves (Hell
  Fire Caves) SKCH HP14 ....141 P9
West Wycombe Combined
  School SKCH HP14 ....141 P9
West Wycombe House &
  Park (NT) SKCH HP14 ....151 P1
West Yard Industrial Estate
  SKCH HP14 ....141 L3
Wexham Court Primary
  School SLN SL2 ....180 E8

Wexham Park Golf Club
  DTCH/LGLY SL3 ....180 E5
Wexham Park Hospital
  SLN SL2 ....180 E7
Wexham School Sports
  College SLN SL2 ....180 D8
Whaddon CE First School
  RMKS/WB MK17 ....51 K3
Whalley Drive Child Health
  Clinic BTCHLY MK3 ....52 C3
Wharf Business Centre
  BNEND SL8 ....165 N6
Whelpley Hill Park
  CSHM HP5 ....126 F8
Whipsnade Park Golf Club
  BERK HP4 ....100 G2
Whipsnade Wild Animal Park
  DUN/WHIP LU6 ....87 H9
Whitchurch Combined School
  RAYLNE/WEN HP22 ....80 G1
Whitehall Primary School
  UX/CGN UB8 ....182 C4
The White Hart Hotel
  HEN RG9 ....160 B7
Whiteheath Infant School
  RSLP HA4 ....171 H4
Whiteheath Junior School
  RSLP HA4 ....171 J4
White Hill Community Centre
  CSHM HP5 ....135 N4
Whiteleaf Golf Club
  PRRI HP27 ....121 N8
White Lion
  DUN/WHIP LU6 ....86 F9
White Spire Special School
  BTCHLY MK3 ....52 F2
White Waltham Airfield
  MDHD SL6 ....184 E6
White Waltham CE Primary
  School MDHD SL6 ....184 D7
White Waltham CC
  MDHD SL6 ....184 D8
Whittebury CE Primary
  School TOW NN12 ....26 A1
Whittlebury Hall Hotel
  TOW NN12 ....25 P3
Whittlebury Park Golf &
  Country Club TOW NN12 ....25 N3
Widewater Business Centre
  DEN/HRF UB9 ....170 C3
Widmer End Combined
  School HAZ/HG HP15 ....143 M5
Wilderness Medical Centre
  MDHD SL6 ....177 M9
Willen Combined School
  WLLN MK15 ....31 J6
William Byrd School
  HYS/HAR UB3 ....191 J7
William Harding Combined
  School AYLS HP21 ....109 P1
William Penn Leisure Centre
  RKW/CH/CXG WD3 ....157 P1

The William Penn School
  SLN SL2 ....179 P7
The Willows First School
  EAG/OLD/WT MK6 ....7 K3
Winbury School
  MDHD SL6 ....185 N3
Winchester House
  Pre-Preparatory School
  BRACKY NN13 ....34 C5
Winchester House School
  BRACKY NN13 ....35 H5
Winchmore Hill CC
  AMSS HP7 ....144 F8
Windmill Hill Golf Centre
  BTCHLY MK5 ....52 C3
Windsor Boys School
  WDSR SL4 ....187 M9
Windsor Business Centre
  WDSR SL4 ....187 M8
Windsor Castle
  WDSR SL4 ....188 A8
Windsor Cemetery
  WDSR SL4 ....193 M2
Windsor & Eton FC
  WDSR SL4 ....193 M3
Windsor Girls School
  WDSR SL4 ....193 L2
Windsor Leisure Centre
  WDSR SL4 ....187 M8
Wing Community
  Health Clinic
  LBUZ LU7 ....73 K8
Wingrave CE Combined School
  RAYLNE/WEN HP22 ....82 G5
Winslow CE Combined School
  BUCK/WIN MK18 ....60 C5
Winslow Hall
  BUCK/WIN MK18 ....60 C6
Winter Hill Golf Club
  MDHD SL6 ....165 M9
Winterhill Retail Park
  EAG/OLD/WT MK6 ....6 C7
Woburn Abbey
  RMKS/WB MK17 ....55 P5
Woburn Golf & Country Club
  RMKS/WB MK17 ....54 C4
Woburn Lower School
  RMKS/WB MK17 ....55 K4
Wolverton Health Centre &
  Day Hospital WOLV MK12 ....29 L8
Wolverton Sports Club
  WOLV MK12 ....29 M7
Wood End First School
  GTLIN MK14 ....30 C6
Wood End Park Junior School
  HYS/HAR UB3 ....191 J1
Woodham Industrial Estate
  RAYLW HP18 ....78 D6
Woodlands Business Park
  MDHD SL6 ....184 G5
Woodlands Park CP School
  MDHD SL6 ....184 G6

Woodlands School
  BUCK/WIN MK18 ....48 A7
Wood Lane Medical Centre
  RSLP HA4 ....171 L6
Woodway Farm Industrial
  Estate RAYLW HP18 ....105 M6
World Business
  Centre Heathrow
  HTHAIR TW6 ....191 J9
Wraysbury Medical Centre
  STWL/WRAY TW19 ....195 H5
Wraysbury Primary School
  STWL/WRAY TW19 ....194 G5
Wycombe Abbey School
  WYM HP11 ....5 F7
Wycombe Air Park
  SKCH HP14 ....151 P8
Wycombe General Hospital
  WYM HP11 ....5 F7
Wycombe Heights Golf Centre
  FLKWH HP10 ....154 A6
Wycombe High School
  WYM HP11 ....152 F6
Wycombe Industrial Mall
  WYM HP11 ....4 C5
Wycombe Museum
  HWYN HP13 ....5 F7
Wycombe Phoenix Harriers
  WYM HP11 ....153 K5
Wycombe Retail Park
  WYM HP11 ....153 M6
Wycombe Sports Centre
  WYM HP11 ....152 F7
Wycombe Swan Theatre
  WYM HP11 ....5 G6
Wycombe Wanderers FC
  (Causeway Stadium)
  SKCH HP14 ....152 A3
Wye Industrial Estate
  WYM HP11 ....153 L5
The Wye Valley School
  BNEND SL8 ....165 P5
Wykeham Park Day Hospital
  THAME OX9 ....118 G3
Wynne Jones Business Centre
  AYLS HP21 ....3 H5
Wyvern First School
  WOLV MK12 ....29 L7
Xscape Ski, Leisure &
  Entertainment Centre
  CMK MK9 ....7 H2
Yardley Gobion CE Primary
  School TOW NN12 ....18 A8
Yardley Hastings Primary
  School RNHPTN NN7 ....8 G1
Ye Harte & Garter Hotel
  WDSR SL4 ....187 P9
Yiewsley Health Centre
  WDR/YW UB7 ....190 E2
Youngs Industrial Estate
  LBUZ LU7 ....75 H3

Acknowledgements

The Post Office is a registered trademark of Post Office Ltd. in the UK and other countries.

Schools address data provided by Education Direct.

Petrol station information supplied by Johnsons

One-way street data provided by © Tele Atlas N.V.

Garden centre information provided by

Garden Centre Association  Britains best garden centres

Wyevale Garden Centres

The statement on the front cover of this atlas is sourced, selected and quoted from a reader comment and feedback form received in 2004

AA Street by Street QUESTIONNAIRE

Dear Atlas User
Your comments, opinions and recommendations are very important to us.
So please help us to improve our street atlases by taking a few minutes
to complete this simple questionnaire.

You do not need a stamp (unless posted outside the UK). If you do not want to remove this page from your street atlas, then photocopy it or write your answers on a plain sheet of paper.

Send to: The Editor, AA Street by Street, FREEPOST SCE 4598,
Basingstoke RG21 4GY

ABOUT THE ATLAS...

Which city/town/county did you buy?

Are there any features of the atlas or mapping that you find particularly useful?

Is there anything we could have done better?

Why did you choose an AA Street by Street atlas?

Did it meet your expectations?

Exceeded ☐   **Met all** ☐   **Met most** ☐   **Fell below** ☐

Please give your reasons

here did you buy it?

For what purpose? (please tick all applicable)

To use in your own local area ☐   **To use on business or at work** ☐

Visiting a strange place ☐   **In the car** ☐   **On foot** ☐

Other (please state)

LOCAL KNOWLEDGE...

Local knowledge is invaluable. Whilst every attempt has been made to make the information contained in this atlas as accurate as possible, should you notice any inaccuracies, please detail them below (if necessary, use a blank piece of paper) or e-mail us at *streetbystreet@theAA.com*

ABOUT YOU...

Name (Mr/Mrs/Ms)

Address

Postcode

Daytime tel no   **Mobile tel no**

E-mail address

Please only give us your e-mail address and mobile phone number if you wish to hear from us about other products and services from the AA and partners by e-mail or text or mms.

Which age group are you in?

Under 25 ☐   **25-34** ☐   **35-44** ☐   **45-54** ☐   **55-64** ☐   **65+** ☐

Are you an AA member?   YES ☐   **NO** ☐

Do you have Internet access?   YES ☐   **NO** ☐

Thank you for taking the time to complete this questionnaire. Please send it to us as soon as possible, and remember, you do not need a stamp (unless posted outside the UK).

ML92z